SIXTH EDITION

BOOK ONE

75 years CENTURY **21**

Keyboarding & Information Processing

Jerry W. Robinson, Ed.D.
Former Keyboarding Instructor
Moeller High School
Cincinnati (OH)

Jack P. Hoggatt, Ed.D.
Professor, Department of Business
Communication
University of Wisconsin
Eau Claire (WI)

Jon A. Shank, Ed.D.
Professor of Education
Robert Morris College
Coraopolis (PA)

Lee R. Beaumont, Ed.D.
Professor of Business, Emeritus
Indiana University of Pennsylvania
Indiana (PA)

T. James Crawford, Ph.D., Ll.D.
Professor of Business/Education, Emeritus
Indiana University
Bloomington (IN)

Lawrence W. Erickson, Ed.D.
Professor of Education, Emeritus
University of California
Los Angeles (CA)

contributing author:
Pat R. Graves, Ed.D.
Associate Professor
Eastern Illinois University
Charleston (Il)

Business Education
lost a dedicated friend
and teacher in 1997
with the passing of
Dr. Jerry W. Robinson.

VISIT US ON THE INTERNET
www.swep.com

South-Western Educational Publishing

an International Thomson Publishing company I(T)P®

www.thomson.com

Cincinnati • Albany, NY • Belmont, CA • Bonn • Boston • Detroit • Johannesburg • London • Madrid
Melbourne • Mexico City • New York • Paris • Singapore • Tokyo • Toronto • Washington

Team Leader:	Karen Schmohe
Development:	Penworthy, Susan Bechtel
Editor:	Kimberlee Kusnerak
Production Coordinator:	Jane Congdon
Manufacturing Coordinator:	Carol Chase
Marketing Manager:	Tim Gleim
Marketing Coordinator:	Lisa Barto
Art/Design Coordinator:	Michelle Kunkler
Designer:	Lou Ann Thesing
Production:	Cover to Cover Publishing, Inc.

Copyright © 2000
by SOUTH-WESTERN EDUCATIONAL PUBLISHING
Cincinnati, OH

ALL RIGHTS RESERVED

The text of this publication, or any part thereof, may not be reproduced or transmitted in any form or by any means, electronic or mechanical, including photocopying, recording, storage in an information retrieval system, or otherwise, without the prior written permission of the publisher.

ISBN: 0-538-69156-5

1 2 3 4 5 6 7 8 9 10 11 12 13 14 WV 09 08 07 06 05 04 03 02 01 00 99

Printed in the United States of America

Photo Credits:

Pages: 1, A13: computer: © 1999 PhotoDisc, Inc.
Pages: 10, 11, 14, 16, 18, 20-23, 25, 27, 30, 31, 33, 36-39, 41, 43, 46, 47, 49, 53, 64, 66, 68, 70, 72, 85, A14: Greg Grosse
Page A60: Courtesy of nView Corporation
Phase Opener 2: Mark Twain: Library of Congress, LC-USZ 62-28844; girl reading: Greg Grosse
Phase Opener 3: Harriet Tubman: Library of Congress, LC-USZ 62-7816
Phase Opener 4: Toyota car: Jeff Greenberg, Photographer; student at PC: Greg Grosse

Reviewers

The following teachers of keyboarding and word processing reviewed manuscripts and gave valuable feedback:

Shirley Dembo, Port Richmond High School, Staten Island, NY
Juliana Delafave, Richardson High School, Dallas, TX
Jennifer McDonald, Princeton High School, Cincinnati, OH
Nancy Purcell, Mechanicsburg (PA) High School

I(T)P®

International Thomson Publishing

South-Western Educational Publishing is a division of International Thomson Publishing Inc. The ITP logo is a registered trademark used herein under license by South-Western Educational Publishing.

Microsoft® and Windows® are registered trademarks of Microsoft Corporation.

COREL® and WordPerfect® are registered trademarks of Corel Corporation or Corel Corporation Limited.

The names of commercially available software mentioned herein are used for identification purposes only and may be trademarks or registered trademarks of their respective owners. South-Western Educational Publishing disclaims any affiliation, association, connection with, sponsorship, or endorsement by such owners.

PREFACE

You have made a wise decision to learn keyboarding skills. These skills will be extremely important to your success. For in the new millennium, keyboarding skills, Internet skills, and basic software application skills will be needed in virtually every career.

Today it is almost impossible to find a job that does not require the use of a keyboard. Most workers, including executives, managers, and administrative employees, use a computer to create, edit, analyze, and organize data. Even people who never thought they would use a computer are now banking, placing orders, balancing their checkbooks, researching, and communicating online.

The More Things Change . . .

However, over seventy-five years' worth of teaching and publishing experience packs the pages of *Century 21 Keyboarding & Information Processing*. Time has brought changes in equipment, teaching methods, and industry, and the 6th edition of *Century 21* embraces these changes with a synergy created from traditional keyboarding methodology, instructional technology, and powerful software. With the same confidence as before, the publisher offers you a textbook for the times.

For this new edition, South-Western surveyed 1,500 business teachers to determine the needs of today's keyboarding students. The following new features of *Century 21 Keyboarding & Information Processing*, 6th Edition, address those needs:

- Keyboarding is for everyone, and the cross-curricular themes throughout the text demonstrate this fact.
- The *Complete Course* contains 225 planned lessons and a semester's worth of optional activities. *Book 1* contains 150 lessons, plus the options.
- Generic word processing instructions for software features are applied in the lessons.
- Six "Your Perspective" sections provide opportunities for students to collaborate to resolve ethical, global awareness, and cultural diversity issues, thus heeding findings of the SCANS report (Department of Labor, 1992).
- Appendix material includes an entire semester's worth of extras: an overview of *Windows*; Internet basics and activities; word publishing and electronic presentations tutorials; integrated software applications; repetitive stress injury information; and an expanded Reference Guide.
- Software options are available for learning to key, building speed and accuracy, and checking documents.

- Numerous supplemental activities reinforce workplace skills, apply integrated suite applications, and increase multicultural awareness (see page iv).

. . . the More They Stay the Same

Regardless of changes in equipment and methods, instruction in *Century 21* still centers around three critical skills: keying, formatting, and information processing. The emphasis given to each facet of learning is geared to the difficulty of the learning task and the level of skill required for effective performance.

Basic keying skills. Lessons 1–37 build a strong foundation in keyboarding skills.

- To ensure master, only two alphabet or figure keys are presented in each new-key lesson. Top-row keys are not introduced until correct technique and an essential level of skill have been developed.
- Timed paragraphs are *triple-controlled* for copy difficulty (from easy to average) to ensure reliable measurement of speed and accuracy.
- Keying technique is stressed first (without timing); then, speed of manipulation (with strategic timed writings); and accuracy last (using *restricted-speed* practice). This instructional design is in harmony with skill-learning principles and research findings.

Formatting skills. Formatting involves transferring facts and ideas into meaningful, useful documents of quality. Look for these features:

- Streamlined document formats are quick and easy to produce.
- Document formats are reviewed and reinforced before new formats are introduced.
- Language skills are reviewed early on and integrated often in formatting tasks.

Information processing skills. Information processing skills are taught through a learn/practice/sustain/assess plan of skill building.

- Common errors for students to correct occur in source copy. Proofreading tips are provided throughout.
- School-to-work transition is provided with simulations occurring every half-semester after Phase 1.

FAMILY OF PRODUCTS

South-Western Educational Publishing provides everything you and your students need to have a successful keyboarding and information processing classroom.

Technology

A variety of key presentation, speed building, and accuracy development software. Each is available in either Windows or Macintosh.

 MicroType Pro: New key learning plus a word processor with timer.

MicroType Multimedia: New key learning on CD-ROM with enhanced graphics, 3-D viewer, and video clips.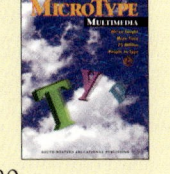

Century 21 Quick Check: Checks over 180 documents and timed writings that are created in the built-in word processor.

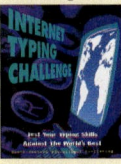 **MicroPace Pro:** Timed writing, error diagnostics, and paced skill development software.

KeyChamp: Designed to build speed. For use after keys are learned.

Skillbusters: Mystery at Wellsley Manor: Fun, interactive skillbuilding.

MLS Century 21 Multimedia: Interactive, graphical presentation of new learning, including document formats, word processing features, and language skills.

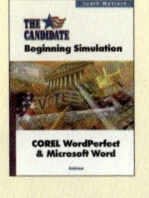 **Internet Typing Challenge:** Compete against other keyboarders nationwide. Compare rates on the Internet at itc.swep.com.

Simulations

Seven simulations apply skills ranging from entry level keyboarding to word processing and integrated applications.

The Candidate: Beginning word processing simulation. 20–25 hours.

SBI: Advanced word processing. 20–25 hours.

Line Rollering: Entry level. 15 hours.

River Oaks Mall: Intermediate level. 20 hours.

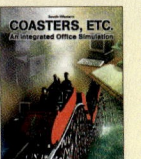 **Coasters, Etc.: An Integrated Office Simulation:** 25–30 hours.

The Word Specialists: A Collaborative Simulation: Emphasizes team building and SCANS competencies. 25–40 hours.

Sports Connection Integrated Simulation: 35–40 hours.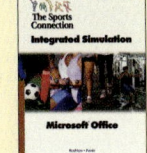

Enrichment Materials

Available in the Teacher's Resource Kit, the following materials are reproducible for classroom use.

Integrated Computer Applications: Activities apply spreadsheets, charts, database, calendar, and desktop publishing skills.

Workplace Enrichment: Projects focus on topics such as entrepreneurship, personal assessment, leadership, and ethics. Activities support or extend textbook documents. Presentation disk for teachers.

Using Technology and the Internet: Activities apply basic Internet skills presented in the textbook appendix (pages A7–A11).

Multicultural Projects: Diversity activities.

Teacher Support

Teacher's Editions: Three editions available.

Teacher's Resource Kit: Includes the following:
Certificate of Proficiency
Integrated Computer Applications
Keys; Lesson Plans
Multicultural Projects
Placement and Performance Test Packets (2)
Posters; Roll of Honor; Speed Chart
Teacher's Manual
Workplace Enrichment with presentation software
Voice Technology Basics

Transparency Masters: Includes word processing specific instruction. Available for most versions of software.

South-Western, Teaching Tools: Request these additional supplements to enrich your teaching: *Alternative Assessment, Teaching a Diverse Population and Addressing Diverse Learning Styles, Involving Parents and the Community in the Classroom, Test Preparation and Study Skills,* and *Strategies for Block Scheduling.*

CONTENTS

PHASE 3 SOCIAL STUDIES

PHASE 4 TECHNOLOGY

Contents **vi**

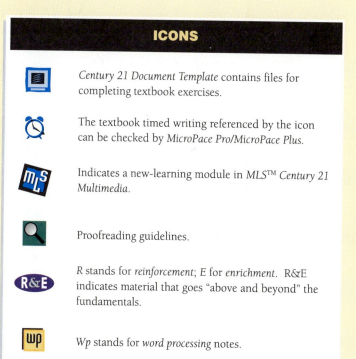

ICONS

Century 21 Document Template contains files for completing textbook exercises.

The textbook timed writing referenced by the icon can be checked by *MicroPace Pro/MicroPace Plus.*

Indicates a new-learning module in *MLS™ Century 21 Multimedia.*

Proofreading guidelines.

R stands for *reinforcement*; *E* for *enrichment.* R&E indicates material that goes "above and beyond" the fundamentals.

Wp stands for *word processing* notes.

Summary of Word Processing Functions

Generic instruction and activities are provided for the word processing functions listed below. When functions are introduced, they are applied in the lessons that follow. Also, supplemental transparency masters provide software specific instructions for these functions. Transparency masters are available for various versions of word processing software, including Word 2000 and WordPerfect 9.

GLOSSARY

Accuracy Degree of freedom from keying errors; expressed as 1 error, 2 errors, etc.; sometimes expressed as errors a minute or percent of errors.

Centering Placing text so half of the text is on each side of the center point.

Control Power to cause hands and fingers to make correct keyboarding motions; also, the ability to slow down motion to reduce keyboarding errors.

Cursor/Insertion Point Point on a display screen where the next character or space is entered.

Default Preset condition in software and electronic typewriters for margin, line spacing, and tab settings. Default settings may be changed.

Desktop Screen background area on which windows and icons are displayed.

Dialog Box In software, small window where the user can input information needed for software to perform a function.

Directory/Folder Listing of files stored on a disk.

Disk Medium used to save and store electronic files.

Document Window Area on display screen where text is keyed.

Editing Proofreading, arranging, changing, and correcting existing text.

Electronic Mail Means of sending messages from one computer to another.

Error Any misstroke of a key or variation between source copy and displayed or printed copy; departure from acceptable document format.

Facsimile (Fax) Copy of information scanned and transmitted over telephone lines.

File Information named and stored on a disk.

Font Appearance of printed text; consists of the typeface name, the style, and the size.

Format Arrangement, placement, and spacing of a document; also, to arrange a document in proper form.

Function Keys Set of keys (F1, F2, etc.) used alone or with Shift, Ctrl, and Alt keys to issue software commands.

GWAM (Gross Words a Minute) Measure of the rate of keying speed; *GWAM* = total 5-stroke words keyed divided by the time required to key those words.

Icon Picture that represents a command, program, or document.

Insert Mode Software feature that allows text to be keyed into existing text; default software mode.

Line Spacing Number of blank lines between lines of text; usually single (0 blank lines), double (1 blank line), or quadruple (3 blank lines).

Key To strike keys for printing or displaying copy.

Margins Space on a page to the left, right, top, and bottom of area that displays text, usually expressed in inches, but sometimes in line or character spaces.

Menu List of options on a display screen from which operating features are selected.

N-PRAM (Net Production Rate A Minute) Measure of document productivity; *N-PRAM* = total 5-stroke words keyed less a penalty for uncorrected errors, divided by the time used to prepare the document(s).

Prompt Message displayed on a screen to inform user that the computer is awaiting a specific response.

Proofreading Comparing keyed text to the original copy and correcting errors; one of the editing steps.

Rate Speed of doing a task; see *gross words a minute* and *net production rate a minute*.

Scroll Software feature that makes room for more lines of copy by causing the first line to "disappear" off the top of the display screen.

Software Instructions or programs that tell a computer what to do.

Status Bar (Line) Bar (or line) containing menu descriptions, prompts to action or specific information about the document on the screen.

Technique Keyboard operator's form or keying style.

Typeover Mode Software feature that allows new text to be keyed over existing text.

Formatting Abbreviations

CS	columnar spacing	**QS**	quadruple spacing
DS	double spacing	**RM**	right margin
LM	left margin	**SM**	side margins
LS	line spacing	**SS**	single spacing
PE	page end	**TM**	top margin

Know Your Electronic

The diagram above illustrates the major parts of an electronic typewriter. If you have the manufacturer's booklet, use it to identify the exact location of each major part, including special parts that may be on one machine but not on another.

1. **Left platen knob:** used to turn platen manually (not on some models).

2. **Line-of-writing (margin) scale:** indicates pitch scales (10, 12, and 15); may indicate margin positions and the printing point.

3. **Paper-bail release lever:** used to pull paper bail away from platen.

4. **Paper guide:** used to position paper for insertion.

5. **Paper support:** supports paper when it is in the machine.

6. **Print carrier:** includes ribbon cassette, correction tape, carrier adjust lever, and printing mechanism.

7. **Paper bail and rollers:** used to hold paper against platen.

8. **Platen (cylinder):** provides a hard surface against which the print mechanism strikes.

9. **Paper release lever:** used to allow paper to be removed or aligned.

10. **Backspace:** used to move printing point to left one space.

11. **Paper insert:** used to feed paper to specified loading position.

12. **Relocate (RELOC)*:** used to return printing point to previous position after corrections are made.

13. **Return:** used to return printing point to left margin and to move paper up.

14. **Right shift:** used with keys controlled by the left hand to key capitals or symbols.

15. **Correction:** used to erase a character.

16. **Space bar:** used to move printing point to the right one space at a time.

17. **Code:** used simultaneously with another key to cause that key to perform a special function.

18. **Left shift:** used with keys controlled by the right hand to key capitals or symbols.

19. **Caps Lock:** used to key text in ALL CAPS (capital letters).

20. **Tab set*:** used to set tabulator stops (tabs); tab clear may be same key on some models.

21. **Repeat:** used to repeat a previously struck key or function.

22. **Bold:** used to print boldface characters.

23. **Underline (UNDLN):** used to print underlined characters.

24. **Pitch select:** used to set type size (10-, 12-, or 15-

25. **Line-space selector:** sets machine to advance the paper 1, 1.5, 2, or 3 lines when return key is used.

26. **Centering:** used to center text automatically between the left and right margins.

27. **Auto*:** set to return the printing point automatically to the left margin, next line when it reaches the right margin.

28. **Margin release*:** used to move printing point beyond the margin settings.

29. **Left margin (L MAR):** used to set left margin.

30. **Right margin (R MAR):** used to set right margin.

31. **Tabulator (Tab)*:** used to move printing point to tab locations.

* Key that performs special functions when depressed together with the CODE key.

INTRODUCTION

Know Your Computer

The numbered parts are found on most computers, but their locations vary.

1. **CPU (Central Processing Unit):** The internal operating unit or "brain" of a computer.
2. **Disk drive:** A unit that reads and writes onto disks.

3. **Monitor:** Displays information on a screen.
4. **Mouse:** Input device.
5. **Keyboard:** An arrangement of letter, figure, symbol, control, function, and editing keys and a numeric keypad.

Keyboard Arrangement

1. **Alphanumeric keys:** Center portion of the keyboard.
2. **Numeric keypad:** A calculator-type keyboard used to enter all-number copy and perform calculations.
3. **Function keys:** Perform a software function; used by themselves or with other keys.
4. **Arrow keys:** Move the insertion point.

5. **SHIFT keys:** Make capital letters and certain symbols when used with those keys.
6. **BACKSPACE:** Deletes the character to the left of the insertion point.
7. **NUM LOCK:** Switches the numeric keypad between numeric entry and editing.
8. **CTRL (Control):** Performs a software function when depressed as another key is struck.

9. **ENTER (RETURN):** Moves the cursor to the left margin and down to the next line.
10. **ALT (Alternate):** Used with another key to execute a function.
11. **DELETE:** Erases text to the right of the insertion point.
12. **INSERT:** Switches between insert mode and typeover mode.

13. **CAPS LOCK:** Capitalizes all alphabetic characters.
14. **TAB:** Moves the cursor to a preset position.
15. **ESC (Escape):** Exits a menu or dialog box in word processing software.
16. **⌘ (Command—Mac only):** Performs a software command when depressed with another key; menu alternative.

Know How to Operate Computer Hardware and Software

Turning Computer System On and Off

Turning on:

1. Remove any disks from the disk drives.
2. Turn on the power switches on the CPU, monitor (if it has a separate switch), and printer.

Turning off:

1. Remove any disks from the disk drives.
2. In reverse order, turn off the power switch for each piece of equipment. Turn off the CPU last.

Word Processing Software Basics

More detailed information is provided in the Word Processing sections within the text and in the Windows and Word Publishing appendices. The basic functions of a word processing program are creating, opening, saving, closing, and printing documents. Word processing functions may be accessed using these tools:

Power bar/Toolbar. Buttons on the toolbar provide access to common commands. These buttons can be rearranged. Typically the buttons for starting a document appear on the left of the toolbar.

Menu bar. Functions can also be accessed through pull-down menus. Click the appropriate menu name in the menu bar; then click the desired option.

Microsoft Word 97 Opening Screen

Menu bar

Toolbar/Power bar

Keyboard commands. Specific keyboard commands, which may appear on a pull-down menu, are another way to perform word processing functions. Usually the ALT or CTRL key is used in combination with a letter key. For example, keying CTRL + S accesses the Save function.

Keyboard Commands

File Pull-Down Menu

File Edit View Insert Format Tools

New... Ctrl+N
Open... Ctrl+O
Close All
Save All
Save As...
Versions...
Page Setup...
Print Preview
Print... Ctrl+P
Create Adobe PDF...
Send To
Properties
1 reference guide.doc
2 know your typewriter.doc
3 keyboarding steps.doc
4 word processing functions.doc
Exit

Save a Document

When you save a document, you place a copy of it on a disk in one of the computer's disk drives, while leaving a copy of it on the screen. You should save a document whenever you make changes to it that you want to keep.

The first time you save a new document, use the **Save As** feature and give the document a filename. After you have saved a document once, you can resave it using the **Save** option. To save a new document, you must give it a filename.

1. Select *Save As* to name and save a new document or to save a document with a new name.
2. Name the document and specify the drive to which it is to be saved.
3. Select *Save* to save a document without renaming it.

Print a Document

1. Turn on your printer, making sure it is loaded with paper.
2. Select the print option.
3. Select new print settings or use the preset (default) print settings. The default setting usually prints on 8.5" x 11" paper in vertical (portrait) orientation.

Close a Document

Closing a document removes it from the display screen. If you have not saved the document, you will be prompted to save it before closing it.

1. Select *Close* from the File menu.
2. Elect to save or not to save the document.

Set Line Spacing

Word processing software packages offer single spacing, one-and-a-half spacing, and double spacing, with single spacing being the default setting. You can also specify other line-spacing options (1.12, 1.75, 2.5, 4, etc.).

1. Place the insertion point at the point in the document where you want the line spacing to change.
2. Select the line spacing option and specify the desired line spacing.

Computer and Disk Care

Follow the guidelines below to protect yourself, your computer, and your disks from harm.

- Place all computer components on a sturdy, flat surface out of direct sunlight, making sure ventilation openings on the equipment are unobstructed.
- Keep food and liquids away from your computer. If something does spill, unplug the computer and notify your teacher immediately.

Do not expose disks to heat, cold, or moisture.

Do not remove disks from the drive when the in-use light is on.

Keep disks away from magnets, x-ray devices, and direct sunlight.

Do not touch the exposed part of a disk.

Use a felt-tip marker, not a ballpoint pen or a pencil, to write on disk labels.

File Management in Windows

Windows Explorer

Establishing a logical and easy-to-use file management system will help you access, modify, and organize your files quickly and efficiently. Your file management program in Windows 95 and Windows 98 is called Windows Explorer. In Windows Explorer you can store files in folders and subfolders much like documents stored in folders within a filing cabinet. The Explorer window is split into two sides. The left side shows how the folders, subfolders, and files are organized in a hierarchical or "tree" view. The right side displays the contents of the selected folder or file, also arranged in a hierarchy.

Document Folder   Contents

Drill 1: Use Windows Explorer

1. Insert your data disk.
2. Click **Start.** Highlight **Programs.** Click **Windows Explorer.**
3. Maximize the Explorer window.
4. If Desktop is not the top object in the All Folders pane, click the up scroll arrow until it is displayed.
5. If a plus sign (+) displays beside the My Computer icon, click the + to extend its sublevels.
6. Click **3 1/2" Floppy (A:).**
7. From the View menu, click **List** to display the contents of drive A in numerical and alphabetical order.

Create Folders and Subfolders

The top-level folder on the disk is the main folder. On the hard drive (drive C), the main folder is Desktop. On the disk, the main folder is represented by the drive icon. This folder was created when your disk was formatted. All folders branch from the main folder.

Small boxes containing plus (+) or minus (-) symbols display to the left of some folder icons. Boxes containing a plus sign indicate folders that have sublevels not currently displayed. If a box contains a minus sign, the folder is already expanded.

In the example below, note that the Keyboarding folder has two subfolders—Classwork and Homework.

Drill 2: Create a folder and subfolder

1. From the File menu, choose *New,* then *Folder.* A new folder icon labeled "New folder" displays in the Contents pane.
2. Key the folder name and press ENTER. In this drill, enter **Documents.** A new folder named Documents has been created on your disk.
3. To create a subfolder within the new folder, double-click the folder, then click **New,** then **Folder.** Name the new subfolder. Repeat the process for as many subfolders as you need.

Select Folders and Files

Only one folder can be selected at a time in the left pane. Multiple files or folders can be selected in the right pane. To select multiple files or folders listed in consecutive order, click the first object to be selected, hold down the SHIFT key, and click the last object to be selected. To select files or folders that are scattered throughout the Contents pane, hold down the CTRL key while you click each of the desired objects.

Delete or Rename Files and Folders

To delete files or entire folders within your Windows Explorer, click the folder or file, then click **File,** and then **Delete.** Respond Yes to the inquiry, *Are you sure you want to remove the folder . . .* (or *file . . .*).

If you want to rename the file or folder, click it, then click **File,** and then **Rename.** Key the new name.

Move and Copy Files

As you create more files, you will probably need to create additional folders and then rearrange existing files by moving or copying them into the new folders. When a file is copied, the original file remains in place, and another copy of the file is placed at the destination. When a file is moved, the original file is removed from its original location and placed at the destination.

The file or folder that is to be copied is referred to as the **source copy**, and the location where the copy is to be moved is called the **destination**. Drag the object from the Contents pane to its destination. If you drag a folder to the same disk, it will be moved. If you drag a file to another disk (from A: to C:), it will be copied.

Drill 3: Move files

You will copy and move files from drive A to the **Documents** folder.

1. In Windows Explorer, click **3 1/2" Floppy (A:)** to display the contents of your disk.

2. Point to a file in the Contents pane that was created in *Word* or *WordPerfect*. Hold down the left mouse button and drag the file to your **Documents** folder.

3. Click **3 1/2" Floppy (A:)** again to display the contents of your disk.

Drill 4: Copy files

1. Click **3 1/2" Floppy (A:)**. The **Documents** folder displays in the All Folders pane under 3 1/2" Floppy (A:).

2. Hold down the CTRL key and point to another file in the Contents pane. Drag the file into the **Documents** folder.

File Naming Conventions

Selecting appropriate filenames is extremely important. Files that are named in a logical, systematic manner are easier to locate than files that are named in a haphazard way. Filenames can be 255 characters long, including spaces. The following symbols cannot be used in a filename: = [ ] : ; < > ? \ / *.

A period is used to separate the filename from the extension. Each software program has its own extension. In the filename *Lesson1.wpd* the *wpd* extension indicates that the file is a *WordPerfect* document.

Organize Files and Folders

Using a logical system of folders, subfolders, and filenames makes it easier to find files when you need them. If you need to find the first lesson that you did as classwork in your Keyboarding class, it would be logical and easy to remember to look in the Keyboarding class folder, then in the Classwork subfolder, and finally for Lesson 1. Files can be opened by clicking **File** on the menu bar, then clicking **Open**.

■ Welcome to MicroType Pro or MicroType Multimedia

MicroType Multimedia is the multimedia-enhanced version of *MicroType Pro*. With the full-featured *MicroType* or *MicroType Multimedia* software, you can use the power of your computer to learn alphabetic and numeric keyboarding and keypad operation. The Alphabetic Keyboarding and the Numeric Keyboarding modules of *MicroType* correspond to the new-key lessons in the *Century 21 Keyboarding* textbook. After you complete Lesson 19, you can use Skill Builder to boost your speed and accuracy.

Your computer should be turned on.

Start MicroType Pro/ MicroType Multimedia

Windows Users:

1. Open *MicroType Pro* or *MicroType Multimedia*.

Windows 95/98:
- ◆ Click the **Start** button.
- ◆ Point to the Programs menu; select the *South-Western Keyboarding* submenu from the program list.
- ◆ Click **MicroType** in the *Keyboarding* submenu.

Windows 3.1:
- ◆ Locate the *South-Western Keyboarding* program group, and double-click the icon to open it.
- ◆ Double-click the **MicroType** icon to start the program.

2. Click anywhere in the opening screen to remove it and bring up the Log In dialog box.

3. Select the appropriate name from the list that appears in the Log In dialog box. Then enter the correct password to continue. Click the **Guest** button only if instructed.

◆ When using the program for the first time, click the **New User** button and complete the New Student Registration dialog box (described on the next page).

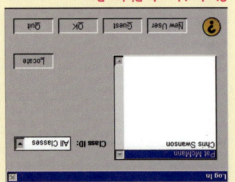

Student Log In Dialog Box

Macintosh Users:

1. Locate the *MicroType Pro//Multimedia* folder and open it.
2. Double-click the **MicroType** icon to start the program.
3. Select the appropriate name from the list that appears in the Log In dialog box. Then enter the correct password to continue. Click the **Guest** button only if instructed.

Main Menu

After you log in, the program will either display the Main menu or prompt you to continue where you left off. If the Main menu appears, choose the appropriate lesson. A check mark appears next to each lesson that you have completed unless you used the Guest option to log in. Check marks also appear on the notebook tabs to show which exercises have been completed.

New Student Registration

The first time you use *MicroType Pro*, you must enter the following information: name, class ID, and password. You must also specify where to store the data.

1. Click the **New User** button shown in the Log In dialog box. The New Student dialog box appears.
2. Enter user name (first name, last name).
3. Enter the class ID.
4. Enter a password. Write the password on a piece of paper and store it in a safe place.
5. Specify the data location if necessary. For example, for a *Windows* user, the path may already be set to **c:\mtpro\ students** (or for a Mac user, **Hard drive:South-Western Keyboarding:Students**). If you have your own subdirectory, which was created previously, you must set the path accordingly (e.g., **c:\mtpro\students\lopez** or **South-Western Keyboarding students:Mark Lopez**). You can click the **Folder** icon to browse through the directories or folders to locate the folder.
6. If necessary, click the **Preferences** button and update the required information.
7. Click **OK** to complete the registration process.

New Student Dialog Box

Main Menu

Click one of the four modules in the center of the Main menu to proceed directly to the corresponding *MicroType* module.

Alphabetic Keyboarding: These 20 lessons teach the alphabetic keys, operational keys, and the basic punctuation keys.

Numeric Keyboarding: These 12 lessons (16 lessons in *Multimedia*) teach the top-row figure keys and the more commonly used symbols. Activities focus on building skill as well as learning the top-row and symbol keys.

Keyboarding Skill Builder: After you learn the alphabetic keys, use these 20 lessons to boost your keyboarding speed and control. Each lesson can focus on either speed or accuracy, so you really have 40 lessons.

Numeric Keypad: You will learn numeric keypad operation by completing this module.

Games: Each of the keyboarding modules incorporates a game into every lesson. The games offer exciting graphics and action to help you build skill while having fun. Top-ten lists provide a way for students to compare scores.

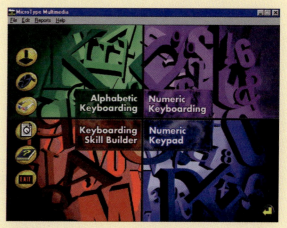

MicroType Multimedia Main Menu

Multimedia Features

3-D Viewer®: This feature demonstrates proper posture and hand positioning from all angles.

3-D Animations: This feature shows proper keystroking in action. Video clips emphasize how keyboarding is used in every profession.

Other Student Reports

In addition to the Lesson Reports, *MicroType* software provides a Summary Report, Keypad Data Sets, Top-Ten Lists, Certificate of Completion, and Performance Graphs. All of these reports, except the Lesson Report, are accessed by using the Reports menu.

Diagnostic Writing Selection

Quick Review: This feature of the Skill Builder module presents drill lines for practicing alphabetic and numeric reaches and operational keys. The Quick Review Report displays the average *gwam* for each section attempted.

Diagnostic Writings: This feature checks speed and accuracy and provides simple error diagnostics. The writings are keyed from hard copy printed from the File menu in the Diagnostic Writings screen.

New · Open · Save · Print · Spell Check · Cut · Copy · Paste · Undo · Italic · Bold · Underline · Timer

Open Screen: The Open Screen is a full-featured word processor that includes a spell checker and a built-in timer. You can practice your keyboarding skills, key letters and reports, or take a timed writing. These features can be accessed from the Menu bar, and many of them are available on the toolbar. When you take a timed writing in the Open Screen, click the **Timer** button and save each timing with its own name. For example, *16b-t1* (exercise 16b, timing 1).

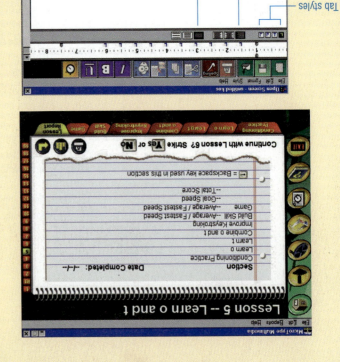

Tab styles · Justification · Line spacing

Lesson Report: The Lesson Report shows which lesson parts were completed and your speed scores and keying lines for *Build Skill* and the game. Performance graphs are accessed by clicking the **Graph** button on the Lesson Report.

Keyboarding & Language Skills

Since Samuel Clemens (Mark Twain) turned in the first typed manuscript in the mid-1870s, keyboarding has become a universal writing skill.

Reporters, short story writers, poets, and novelists today compose at computer keyboards. Likewise, many musicians now use the computer keyboard to compose and arrange music. Also, artists now use the keyboard for graphic design. In fact, a high percentage of people in all walks of life employ a computer keyboard to simplify and speed up their work.

So, too, do students from elementary school through college use their keyboarding skill to prepare school assignments, papers, and reports. In fact, many former students say that, next to language, keyboarding is the most useful skill they have ever learned.

Fortunate indeed are those who have an early opportunity to develop a skill that has so many wide-ranging uses.

GLOBAL AWARENESS

During the time you have spent in this class, in addition to learning keyboarding, you have met other students that you may have only seen in the hallway or at school activities. Some students you have met may now be your friends. Other students you may be getting to know better through conversations you have before and after class.

Friendships that have developed or are developing come about because people decided to talk (communicate) with each other. The communication may have begun by sharing how to complete a keying task. From this beginning you may have shared thoughts about a movie or feelings regarding a team's victory in the last game. From these initial conversations, you may have moved on to how your families celebrate certain holidays or to conversations that had a more personal meaning.

In good communication we begin to share our deeper thoughts and feelings. It is from this deeper level of communication that we begin to realize that though differences exist among people, important similarities exist as well. Thus we begin to understand that differences need not be a stumbling block in a relationship but rather a gift that can enrich it.

In addition to talking (face to face or by telephone), we also can communicate through the written word. Letters, e-mail, and faxes are ways that can be used to stay in touch locally, across the nation, and throughout the world.

To understand and appreciate other people and other cultures takes time, and it requires communication—both oral and written.

ACTIVITIES

Assume that you are to be the mentor for an exchange student in your school next year—"to show her/him the ropes."

You want to get to "know" the student before he/she arrives. You decide to do so by letter.

Compose/key a letter to this imaginary person from the country of your choice. Welcome the student and include comments about your school, family, town, interests, and hobbies. Include a list of questions for her/him to answer in response: goals, fears, interests, etc.

CULTURAL DIVERSITY

The foods eaten and avoided by people of different lands provide clues to the culture from which individuals come. In general, people eat foods that are native to their own country and avoid foods that are unfamiliar or perhaps are forbidden in certain cultures. For example, the eating of pork is forbidden in Arab countries and discouraged by certain groups in others. Beef is forbidden as human food in India because the cow is considered sacred. Shellfish, too, are forbidden in some cultures.

Although not forbidden, white bread, popcorn, ketchup, roast turkey, and watermelon (common American foods) are avoided by people of some cultures. Corn on the cob—one of our favorite summer foods—is considered in Europe to be food for animals and not fit for human consumption.

Often an uninformed or thoughtless host is embarrassed when certain guests are unable to eat the only entree and several of the hors d'oeuvres offered at a luncheon or dinner party.

Perhaps the statement "We are what we eat" is not farfetched, after all.

ACTIVITIES

Assume that your school has several new exchange students. At least one student is from each of the following countries: Israel, China, Mexico, Italy, Saudi Arabia, and Nigeria.

The student council is planning a picnic to welcome these students. Your job is to plan the menu for the picnic.

In groups of 3 or 4, list foods some of these students cannot eat; then list foods from which each of them could acceptably choose.

Prepare a menu of selected appetizers, entrees, salads, vegetables, and desserts that would appeal to these diverse tastes.

Learn Letter-Key Operation

LESSON 1

Home Keys (FDSA JKL;)

Objectives:

1. To learn control of home keys (**FDSA JKL;**).
2. To learn control of Space Bar and Return/Enter.

1A •
Work Area Arrangement

1. Arrange work area as shown at right.

Computers

- alphanumeric (main) keyboard directly in front of chair; front edge of keyboard even with edge of table or desk
- monitor placed for easy viewing; disk drives placed for easy access
- *Alphabetic Keyboarding* software and/or your word processing diskettes within easy reach
- book behind or at right of keyboard; top raised for easy reading

Electronics

- front frame of machine even with front edge of desk
- book at right of machine, top raised for easy reading
- paper at left of machine

2. Turn on equipment (ON/ OFF control of computer/ monitor or electronic typewriter).

3. Boot computer program (follow teacher direction).

Properly arranged work area: computer

Properly arranged work area: electronics

ETHICS: The Right Thing to Do

- *Fables, anecdotes, and stories have been used over the ages in various cultures to teach lessons in*
- *honesty and truth. One such story is the following one from Ethiopia.*

Long ago Truth, Falsehood, Fire, and Water were journeying together and came upon a herd of cattle. They discussed how to distribute the herd and decided it would be fairest to divide the herd into four parts so that each could take home an equal share. But Falsehood was greedy and schemed to get more for himself.

"Listen to my warning," he whispered, pulling Water to one side. "Fire plans to burn all the grass along your banks and drive your cattle away across the plains so he can have them for himself. If I were you, I'd extinguish him now, and then we can have his share for ourselves." Water was foolish enough to listen to Falsehood, and he dashed himself upon Fire and put him out.

Next, Falsehood crept toward Truth. "Look what Water has done," he whispered. "He has murdered Fire and taken his cattle. We should not consort with the likes of him. We should take all the cattle and go to the mountains." Truth believed Falsehood and together they drove the cattle into the mountains.

"Wait for me!" Water called, and he hurried after them; but of course he could not run uphill. So he was left all alone in the valley below.

When they reached the top of the highest mountain, Falsehood turned to Truth and laughed. "I've tricked you, stupid fool," he shrieked. "Now you must give me all the cattle and be my servant, or I'll destroy you."

"Yes, you have tricked me," Truth admitted, "but I will never be your servant." And so they fought; and when they clashed, thunder rolled back and forth across the mountaintops. Again and again they threw themselves together, but neither could destroy the other.

Finally they decided to call upon the Wind to declare a winner of the contest. So Wind came rushing up the mountain slopes, and he listened to what they had to say. "It is not for me to declare a winner in this fight," he told them. "Truth and Falsehood are destined to struggle. Sometimes Truth will win, but other times Falsehood will prevail, and then Truth must rise up and fight again. Until the end of the world, Truth must battle Falsehood and must never rest or let down his guard, or he will be finished once and for all."

And so Truth and Falsehood are fighting to this day. ✳

A C T I V I T I E S

1. Read the material at the left.

2. Discuss what it means to be honest and to tell the truth.

3. Through discussion with family and friends, try to discover any story that has been handed down through generations that demonstrates the tradition of honest behavior. Share these with the class. What ideas seem to be common in all such stories shared?

4. Compose/key a definition of honesty and describe what it means to you.

5. Compose/key a list of ways that the expectation of honesty affects your behavior at school, at home, and at work (if you have a job).

Source: Bennett, William J. (ed.). *The Book of Virtues: A Treasury of Great Moral Stories.* New York: Simon and Shuster, 1993.

1B •
Keying Position

Proper position is the same for typewriters and computers. The essential features of proper position are shown at right and listed below:

- fingers curved and upright over home keys
- wrists low, but not touching frame of machine or keyboard
- forearms parallel to slant of keyboard
- body erect, sitting back in chair
- feet on floor for balance

Proper position at computer

Proper position at electronic typewriter

1C •
Home-Key Position

1. Find the home keys on the chart: **F D S A** for left hand and **J K L ;** for right hand.

2. Locate the home keys on your keyboard. Place left-hand fingers on **F D S A** and right-hand fingers on **J K L ;** *with your fingers well curved and upright (not slanting).*

3. Remove your fingers from the keyboard; then place them in home-key position again, curving and holding them *lightly* on the keys.

1D •
Technique: Home Keys and Space Bar

1. Read the statements and study the illustrations at right.

2. Place your fingers in home-key position as directed in 1C, above.

3. Strike each letter key for the first group of letters in the line of type below the technique illustrations.

4. After striking ; (semicolon), strike the **Space Bar** once.

5. Continue to key the line; strike the **Space Bar** once at the point of each arrow.

TECHNIQUE *hints:*

Keystroking: Strike each key with a light tap with the tip of the finger, snapping the fingertip toward the palm of the hand.

Spacing: Strike the Space Bar with the right thumb; use a quick down-and-in motion (toward the palm). Avoid pauses before or after spacing.

Space once.

fdsajkl; f d s a j k l ; ff jj dd kk ss ll aa ;;

Table 1

DS; CS: 0.5"; center column headings

words	
SPEAKERS OF THE HOUSE OF REPRESENTATIVES	8

SPEAKERS OF THE HOUSE OF REPRESENTATIVES
1947–Present

Speaker	Party	State	Tenure	
				17
Joseph W. Martin Jr.	R	Massachusetts	1947-1949	27
Sam Rayburn	D	Texas	1949-1953	33
Joseph W. Martin Jr.	R	Massachusetts	1953-1955	42
Sam Rayburn	D	Texas	1955-1961	48
John W. McCormack	D	Massachusetts	1962-1971	57
Carl Albert	D	Oklahoma	1971-1977	63
Thomas P. O'Neill Jr.	D	Massachusetts	1977-1987	73
James Wright	D	Texas	1987-1989	79
Thomas S. Foley	D	Washington	1989-1995	87
Newt Gingrich	R	Georgia	1995-	93

Source: The World Almanac and Book of Facts, 1994.

(96, 107)

Table 2

1" margins; block column headings; DS

COMPUTER SUPPORT SERVICES
Support Telephone Numbers

Application	Phone	
		14
Spreadsheets	4902	27
Graphics	3067	39
Word Processing	2935	51
	2937	52
Database	6574	64
E-mail	8201	76
Network	6528	89
DOS	6723	101
Windows	4598	113
Software Installation	6573	125

(COMPUTER SUPPORT SERVICES 5; Support Telephone Numbers 10)

Table 3

1" margins; center column headings; DS between entries

COMPUTER PRODUCT DEALERS

Bold company names

June 25, ----

Indent phone nos. 0.5" (5 spaces)

DS

Name	Address & Phone	
		12
Computer Sales and Service	8210 Lakeland Dr.	21
	182-9412	23
Computer Systems	830 Robindale Dr.	30
	127-3856	32
PC Tailors	129 Pawtucket Dr.	38
	171-5674	40
Micro Solutions	1445 Antique St.	46
	127-8520	48
Office Products	920 Carolina Ave.	55
	171-8301	57
Software Specialists	8231 Algonquin Dr.	65
	171-8396	66

(COMPUTER PRODUCT DEALERS 5; June 25, ---- 8)

1E •
Technique: Hard Return at Line Endings

To return the cursor or print point to left margin and move it down to next line, strike **Return/Enter** key (hard return).

Study illustrations at right; then return 4 times (quadruple-space) below the line you completed in 1D, p. 11.

Hard Return

Striking the **Enter** (computers) or **Return** (electronics) key is called a "hard return." You will use a hard return at the end of all drill lines in this lesson and those that follow

in this unit. Reach the little finger of the right hand to the **Return** key or **Enter** key, tap the key, and return the finger quickly to home-key position.

1F •
Home-Key and Space-Bar Practice

1. Place your hands in home-key position (left-hand fingers on **F D S A** and right-hand fingers on **J K L ;**).
2. Key the lines once: single-spaced (SS) with a double space (DS) between 2-line groups. Do not key line numbers.

Fingers curved and upright

Down-and-in spacing motion

Strike Space Bar once to space.

```
1 j jj f ff k kk d dd l ll s ss ; ;; a aa jkl; fdsa
2 j jj f ff k kk d dd l ll s ss ; ;; a aa jkl; fdsa
```
Strike the Return/Enter key twice to double-space (DS).
```
3 a aa ; ;; s ss l ll d dd k kk f ff j jj fdsa jkl;
4 a aa ; ;; s ss l ll d dd k kk f ff j jj fdsa jkl;
```
DS
```
5 jf jf kd kd ls ls ;a ;a fj fj dk dk sl sl a; a; f
6 jf jf kd kd ls ls ;a ;a fj fj dk dk sl sl a; a; f
```
DS
```
7 a;fj a;sldkfj a;sldkfj a;sldkfj a;sldkfj a;sldkfj
8 a;fj a;sldkfj a;sldkfj a;sldkfj a;sldkfj a;sldkfj
```
Strike the Return/Enter key 4 times to quadruple-space (QS).

1G •
Technique: Return-Key Practice

each line twice single-spaced (SS); double-space (DS) between 2-line groups

SPACING *cue*:
When in SS mode, strike **Return/Enter** twice to insert a DS between 2-line groups.

Reach out with little finger; tap **Return/Enter** key quickly; return finger to home key.

```
1 a;sldkfj a;sldkfj
```
DS
```
2 ff jj dd kk ss ll aa ;;
```
DS
```
3 fj fj dk dk sl sl a; a; asdf ;lkj
```
DS
```
4 fj dk sl a; jf kd ls ;a fdsa jkl; a;sldkfj
```
QS

Endnotes Page

Prepare an endnotes page from the information at the right.

Document 2
Title Page

Format a title page for the report. Use your name, school name, and the current date.

Document 3
References Page

Prepare a references page from the information at the right.

3 ~~2~~. Graphics software. *that will run on the network* 245

4. A ~~micro~~ computer *capable of* to serve as the host computer. 257

5. Furniture to ~~fit~~ *accommodate* the equipment that will be pur- 269
chased. 271

DS ¶ Advantages. The ~~chief~~ *main* advantage of networking is that *share* 282
the department's 25 ~~micro~~ *computer* users will ~~use computer~~ files, 292
software packages, a scanner, and computer printers.²³ Shar- 304
ing will ~~improve~~ *increase* the quantity *and quality* of the documents and presenta- 319
tions. 320

DS ¶ Disadvantages. Most sources list network management as *one of* 333
the major problem in running a network. Installing the Ad- 345
vertising Department's network will require hiring another 357
person to coordinate the network. Even though it is not as 372
difficult as it was six years ago, finding and hiring a com- 386
petent person to maintain *and maintain* the network is not going to be *technically* 397
easy.³⁴ 399

ENDNOTES 401

¹John A. Boyer, "Networking--A Preliminary Report." 411
(Pittsburg: Office Network, Inc., 1990), p. 5, photocopied. *Consultants* 426

²Mark G. Simkin, Computer Information Systems for Business 438
(Dubuque, ~~Iowa~~ *IA*: Wm. C. Brown Publishers, 1987), p. 161. 449

³The future, According to Wang," The Office, June *1988*, p. 40. 462

⁴Barry Gerber, "1995's Hottest Networking Issues," Network 474
Computing, December 1994, p. 136. 481

LESSON 150

Assessment: Tables

Objective:
To assess table formatting skill.

150A • 5
Conditioning Practice

set 0.5" SMs
each line twice

alphabet 1 After a wild jump ball, the guards very quickly executed a zone press.

speed 2 If they do the work for us, I may go to the city and then to the lake.

figures 3 The ZIP Code for Jay's new address at 3497 Cedar Street is 87105-2628.

gwam 1' | 1 | 2 | 3 | 4 | 5 | 6 | 7 | 8 | 9 | 10 | 11 | 12 | 13 | 14 |

150B • 8
Skill Check

1. Key a 5' writing on 148C, page 354.

2. Find *gwam* and number of errors.

3. Record score.

1H •
Home-Key Mastery

1. Key the lines once (without the numbers); strike the **Return/Enter** key twice to double-space (DS).
2. Rekey the drill at a faster pace.

TECHNIQUE *cue:*

Keep fingers curved and upright over home keys, right thumb just barely touching the Space Bar.

SPACING *cue:*

Space once after ; used as punctuation.

Correct finger alignment

```
1  aa ;; ss ll dd kk ff jj a; sl dk fj jf kd ls ;a jf
                                                      DS
2  a a as as ad ad ask ask lad lad fad fad jak jak la
                                                      DS
3  all all fad fad jak jak add add ask ask ads ads as
                                                      DS
4  a lad; a jak; a lass; all ads; add all; ask a lass
                                                      DS
5  as a lad; a fall fad; ask all dads; as a fall fad;
                                                      DS
```

1I •
End-of-Lesson Routine

Computers
1. Exit the software.
2. Remove from disk drive any floppy disk you have inserted.
3. Turn off equipment if directed to do so.
4. Store materials as teacher directs.

Electronics
1. Press the **Paper Up** (or **Eject**) key to remove paper.
2. Turn machine off.

Disk removal

Paper up (or Eject)

1. Key drill once as shown to improve control of home keys.
2. Key the drill again to quicken your keystrokes.

SPACING *cue:*

To DS when in SS mode, strike **Return/Enter** twice.

```
1  ja js jd jf f; fl fk fj ka ks kd kf d; dl dk dj a;
                                                      DS
2  la ls ld lf s; sl sk sj ;a ;s ;d ;f a; al ak aj fj
                                                      DS
3  jj aa kk ss ll dd ;; ff fj dk sl a; jf kd ls ;a a;
                                                      DS
4  as as ask ask ad ad lad lad all all fall fall lass
                                                      DS
5  as a fad; as a dad; ask a lad; as a lass; all lads
                                                      DS
6  a sad dad; all lads fall; ask a lass; a jak salad;
                                                      DS
7  add a jak; a fall ad; all fall ads; ask a sad lass
```

LESSON 149

Assessment: Reports

Objective:
To assess report formatting skill.

149A • 5
Conditioning Practice

each line twice

alphabet   1   Gavin expects the banks to formalize quite a few details in July.

speed   2   The ancient maps may aid them when they do the work for the city.

figures   3   Is the charge on Order No. 5304, dated June 19, $28.67 or $28.76?

`gwam`   1' | 1 | 2 | 3 | 4 | 5 | 6 | 7 | 8 | 9 | 10 | 11 | 12 | 13 |

149B • 45
Assess Report Skills

Document 1
Report from Rough Draft

1. Format and key the report in bound style.
2. When you finish, proofread your copy.

words

STATUS REPORT   3

Advertising Department Network Project   11

The purpose of this report is to ~~inform~~ *update* you ~~of~~ *on* the *current* sta-   23

tus of the project to network the ~~micro~~computers ~~assigned to~~   33

the Advertising Department.   38

Decisions Made   42

Based on the recommendations ~~made~~ in ~~the~~ report *John Boyer's*[1] ~~(Boyer,~~   52

~~5, 1990)~~ it has been decided to install a star network: 62

One of the most popular ways of creating local area net-   73
works is with physical coaxial and a host computer. The   85
cables physically connect to the central host computer and   96
thus "hardwire" the network. This is often called a star   108
network because workstation connections (nodes) radiate   119
from the host computer like the many points of a star[2]   131

The decision has been made to net work 25 computers, 5   141
printers, *, and a scanner* to purchase a higher level graphics package; and   156
to include *an electronic-* a mail system.   164

Current Activities   168

The director of computing is ~~seeking~~ *requesting* prices *, quotes* on the   180

following items that are needed to install the network.   191

1. Network software, network cards, active and passive   203
hubs, cabling, etc.   207

2. Network versions of *existing* word processing, desktop publish-   220
ing, data base, spreadsheet, and workflow applications   231
packages. *software*   235

(continued on next page)

Home Keys (FDSA JKL;)

O b j e c t i v e s :

1. To improve control of home keys (**FDSA JKL;**).

2. To improve control of **Space Bar** and **Return/Enter**.

R1A ●
Keying Readiness

1. Arrange your work area (see p. 10).
2. Get to know your equipment (see pp. x, 1-3).
3. Use default margins and spacing (unless your teacher guides you in making format adjustments).
4. Take keying position as shown at right.

R1B ●
Home-Key Position

1. Locate the home keys on the chart: **F D S A** for left hand and **J K L ;** for right hand.
2. Locate the home keys on your keyboard. Place left-hand fingers on **F D S A** and right-hand fingers on **J K L ;** *with fingers well curved and upright (not slanting).*
3. Remove fingers from the keyboard; then place them in home-key position.

R1C ●
Technique Review

Remember to use a hard return at the end of all drill lines. To double-space (DS), use two hard returns.

Keystroke

Curve fingers over home keys. Strike each key with a quick-snap stroke; release key quickly.

Space

Strike the **Space Bar** with a quick down-and-in motion of the right thumb. Do not pause before or after spacing stroke.

Hard Return

Reach the right little finger to the **Return/Enter** key; strike the key and return the finger quickly to home key.

Letter 2

Format and key the text at the right in simplified block letter format. Address the letter to:

Ms. Annette Young, Principal
East High School
2650 Old Orchard Ln.
Montgomery, AL 36117-2341

Use **January 17,----** for the letter date. The subject line is **MULTIMEDIA COM-PUTER SYSTEM SEMINAR**. The letter is from **Jared C. Scott, Technology Consultant.**

Add an enclosure notation.

	words
	opening 29

Multimedia computer systems play a significant role in enhancing the educational environment.   If you plan to purchase a multimedia system in the near future, you won't want to miss the seminar on February 25 entitled "Selecting Your Multimedia Computer System Components."

44 / 58 / 73 / 84

The seminar will present the various components of a reasonably priced ($1,700 to $2,500) system. Included in the presentation will be a discussion of:

98 / 113 / 115

✓ operating systems	✓ memory (RAM) requirements
✓ microprocessors	✓ disk drives
✓ CD-ROM drives	✓ monitors
✓ video cards	✓ speakers
✓ sound cards	✓ telecommunication
	connection requirements

125 / 131 / 137 / 142 / 148 / 153

Time will be available for questions from the audience. Thus, issues not covered during the formal presentation can be addressed.

168 / 180

Fill out and return the enclosed card to reserve your seat at the workshop. The number of seminar participants is limited to 15 so that we can meet individual needs.

195 / 209 / 213

closing 223

148C • 8
Skill Check

1. One 5' writing.
2. Determine *gwam* and number of errors.
3. Record score.

all letters used

	gwam	1'	5'

Office productivity refers to the ratio of office input, or the cost of equipment, office space, supplies, and labor, to the output of the office work force. The ability of an organization to increase output at a faster rate than operating costs are rising is vital to its success and possibly to its survival. Most people agree that improving productivity is crucial, but the puzzle is how to go about doing so. Perhaps the first step is to dispel a myth that many people believe--that is, they must work harder to exceed their present rate of production. The better idea is that they must work smarter at their jobs, not harder.

12 2 52 / 25 5 55 / 38 8 57 / 51 10 60 / 64 13 62 / 76 15 65 / 89 18 67 / 102 20 70 / 115 23 73 / 127 25 75

To determine how to work smarter, one might first analyze the daily routine to see if some tasks that are being done manually might be performed more efficiently with the aid of technology. Through office automation, many jobs can be done more quickly and more accurately. Often, information that is complete and up to date can be provided only through automated systems, as some information becomes obsolete by the time it can be produced manually. However, care must be exercised to ensure that automation is not used to generate too much of the wrong kind of data, as has been the case sometimes.

12 28 77 / 24 30 80 / 37 33 82 / 49 35 85 / 63 38 88 / 76 41 90 / 89 43 93 / 101 46 95 / 114 48 98 / 121 50 99

gwam	1'	1	2	3	4	5	6	7	8	9	10	11	12	13
	5'		1				2				3			

Key the lines once (without the numbers), single-spaced (SS) with a double space (DS) between 2-line groups.

Technique goals
- curved, upright fingers
- quick-snap keystrokes
- down-and-in spacing
- quick return without spacing at line ending

Strike Space Bar once to space.

1 f ff j jj d dd k kk s ss l ll a aa ; ;; fdsa jkl;

2 f ff j jj d dd k kk s ss l ll a aa ; ;; fdsa jkl;

Strike the Return/Enter key twice to double-space (DS).

3 j jj f ff k kk d dd l ll s ss ; ;; a aa asdf ;lkj

4 j jj f ff k kk d dd l ll s ss ; ;; a aa asdf ;lkj

5 a;a sls dkd fjf ;a; lsl kdk jfj a;sldkfj a;sldkfj

6 a;a sls dkd fjf ;a; lsl kdk jfj a;sldkfj a;sldkfj

Strike the Return/Enter key 4 times to quadruple-space (QS).

R1D •
Home-Key Stroking

Key the lines once single-spaced (SS) with a double space (DS) between 2-line groups. Do not key the line numbers.

Goal: To improve keying and spacing techniques.

1 f f ff j j jj d d dd k k kk s s ss l l ll a a aa;

2 f f ff j j jj d d dd k k kk s s ss l l ll a a aa;

3 fj dk sl a; jf kd ls ;a ds kl df kj sd lk sa ;l j

4 fj dk sl a; jf kd ls ;a ds kl df kj sd lk sa ;l j

5 sa as ld dl af fa ls sl fl lf al la ja aj sk ks j

6 sa as ld dl af fa ls sl fl lf al la ja aj sk ks j

R1E •
Technique: Return

each line twice single-spaced (SS); double-space (DS) between 2-line groups

Technique goals
- curved, upright fingers
- quick-snap keystrokes
- down-and-in spacing
- quick return without spacing at line ending

TECHNIQUE *cue*:
Reach out with the little finger, not the hand; tap **Return/Ente**r key quickly; return finger to home key.

1 a;sldkfj a;sldkfj
DS

2 a ad ad a as as ask ask
DS

3 as as jak jak ads ads all all
DS

4 a jak; a lass; all fall; ask all dads
DS

5 as a fad; add a jak; all fall ads; a sad lass
QS

LESSON 148

Assessment: Letters

Objective:
To assess letter formatting skill.

148A • 5
Conditioning Practice
each line twice

alphabet 1 Jackson believed she might maximize profits with a quality force.

speed 2 If it is so, they may go with me to the city by the lake to work.

figures 3 In 1996, we had 287 office chairs, 143 desks, and 50 work tables.

gwam 1' | 1 | 2 | 3 | 4 | 5 | 6 | 7 | 8 | 9 | 10 | 11 | 12 | 13 |

148B • 37
Assess Letter Skill

Letter 1
Format and key the text at the right as a two-page letter in block format with mixed punctuation. Use the USPS letter address style and send the letter to:

**MS ROWANDA SMITH
MEMORIAL HIGH SCHOOL
375 BEACON ST N
BOSTON MA 02135-3882**

Use **January 14, ----** for the letter date; supply an appropriate salutation and complimentary closing. The letter is from **Ms. Janice F. Etheridge, Instructor**.

	words
	opening 22

You are right! Keeping up with today's rapidly developing technologies 36
can be a nightmare. We often struggle with these issues at the university. 52

In your letter you asked for my opinion about upgrading your computer lab 66
versus replacing as much of the old computer equipment as possible with 81
newer technologies. On a short-term basis, upgrading may be satisfactory. 96
By investing in newer technology, however, you will be able to do much more 111
than you can with your current equipment. 120

I have enclosed a copy of an article written by Odvard Egil Dyrli and Daniel 135
E. Kinnaman in the January, 1995, issue of Technology & Learning. They 150
state that only by investing in the newer technology will you and your stu- 165
dents be able to: 169

• Use complex graphical environments to control the machines. 181

• Take advantage of the newest hypertext and hypermedia software. 195

• Learn to use "photographic-quality," high-resolution graphics and video. 210

• Play and record speech, stereo music, and sound effects. 222

• Use online help features to learn about software and computer systems. 237

• Use worldwide telecommunications information services and tools with 251
help from graphical interfaces such as Mosaic. 260

• Benefit from the newest generation of high-quality educational software 275
delivered on high-density disks and CD-ROM. 284

If you are planning to use the computers only as word processors, upgrad- 299
ing to accommodate the new software you plan to purchase is sufficient. 313
However, if you want to utilize some of the newer technologies that are now 329
available and that will become available in the near future, you may wish to 344
start replacing some of your machines. There is not a simple answer to your 359
question. 361

closing 371

R1F •
Home-Key Mastery

each line twice single-spaced (SS); double-space (DS) between 2-line groups

Technique goals

- curved, upright fingers
- eyes on copy in book or on screen
- quick-snap keystrokes
- steady pace

Correct finger curvature

Correct finger alignment

Down-and-in spacing motion

1 a jak; a jak; ask dad; ask dad; as all; as all ads

Return twice to DS.

2 a fad; a fad; as a lad; as a lad; all ads; all ads

DS

3 as a fad; as a fad; a sad lass; a sad lass; a fall

DS

4 ask a lad; ask a lad; all jaks fall; all jaks fall

DS

5 a sad fall; a sad fall; all fall ads; all fall ads

DS

6 add a jak; a lad asks a lass; as a jak ad all fall

R1G •
End-of-Lesson Routine

Computers

1. Exit the software.
2. Remove from disk drive any floppy disk you have inserted.
3. Turn off equipment if directed to do so.
4. Store materials as teacher directs.

Electronics

1. Press the **Paper Up** (or **Eject**) key to remove paper.
2. Turn machine off.

R&e

1. Key each line twice SS; DS between 2-line groups.
2. Key each line again to quicken your keystrokes if time permits.

PRACTICE *cue:*
Key slowly the first time you key a line to master the required motions. As you key a line a second time, try to make each motion a bit faster.

1 ff jj dd kk ss ll aa ;; fj dk sl a; jf kd ls ;a a;

DS

2 aa ;; ss ll dd kk ff jj ja js jd jf fj fk fl f; fj

DS

3 fjf dkd sls a;a jfj kdk lsl ;a;a a;sldkfj a;sldkfj

DS

4 fdsa jkl; asdf ;lkj all all ask ask jak jak ad add

DS

5 a a as as ask ask ad ad lad lad add add fall falls

DS

6 a jak ad; a sad dad; a lad asks; a lad asks a lass

DS

7 a sad fall; all fall ads; as a lass asks a sad lad

DS

8 as a fall fad; add a jak salad; as a sad lad falls

147B • 45
Review Table Formats

Table 1
DS; CS: 1"; center column headings

WP note:
Right-align both figure columns.

Table 2
DS; CS: 1.5"; center column headings

Table 3
Format and key Document 1, 129B, p. 310.

Table 4
Arrange Table 1 in descending order by Expenditures Per Visitor. Bold the main heading and change column spacing to 0.5".

words

FOREIGN VISITORS TO THE U.S., 1990 — 7

Country of Origin	Visitors (Millions)	Expenditures Per Visitor	
			13
			20
Australia	0.5	$2,279	24
Canada	17.3	330	28
France	0.7	1,703	31
Germany	1.2	1,778	35
Italy	0.4	1,973	38
Japan	3.2	2,381	41
Mexico	6.8	592	44
Netherlands	0.3	1,422	48
New Zealand	0.2	2,181	53
United Kingdom	2.2	1,596	58
			61

Source: World Almanac, 1993. — 67

CAST FOR — 2
THE FUGITIVE — 4

Characters	Actor /Actress	
		10
Biggs	Daniel Roebuck	23
Dr. Anne Eastman	Julianne Moore	36
Samuel Gerard	Tommy Lee Jones	49
Helen Kimble	Sela Ward	63
Dr. Richard Kimble	Harrison Ford	76
Newman	Tom Wood	89
Dr. Charles Nichols	Jeroen Krabbe	102
Poole	L. Scott Caldwell	115
Cosmo Renfro	Joe Pantoliano	129
Sykes	Andreas Katsulas	142

New Keys: H and E

Objectives:

1. To learn reach technique for **H** and **E**.
2. To combine smoothly **H** and **E** with home keys.

2A •
Get Ready to Key

At the beginning of each practice session, follow the *Standard Plan* given at the right to get ready to key the lesson.

Standard Plan for Getting Ready to Key

Computers

1. Arrange work area as shown on p. 10.
2. Check to see that the computer, monitor, and printer (if any) are plugged in.
3. Boot the computer software and select the proper program as your teacher directs.
4. Align the front of the keyboard with the front edge of the desk or table.
5. Position the monitor and the textbook for easy reading.

Electronics

1. Arrange work area as shown on p. 10.
2. Adjust **Paper Guide** to line up with 0 (zero) on the **Line-of-Writing** or **Format Scale**. See p. x.
3. Insert paper (long edge against the **Paper Guide**). See p. x.
4. Set the **Line-Space Selector** to single-space (SS) your practice lines. See pp. x, RG18.
5. Use default margins unless your teacher directs you to set 1.5" margins so that your copy is more nearly centered.

2B •
Plan for Learning New Keys

All keys except the home keys (**FDSA JKL;**) require the fingers to reach in order to strike them. Follow the *Standard Plan* given at the right in learning the proper reach for each new key.

Standard Plan for Learning New Keys

1. Find the new key on the keyboard chart given on the page where the new key is introduced.
2. Look at your own keyboard and find the new key on it.
3. Study the reach-technique picture at the left of the practice lines for the new key. (See p. 18 for illustrations.) Read the statement below the illustration.
4. Identify the finger to be used to strike the new key.
5. Curve your fingers; place them in home-key position (over **FDSA JKL;**).
6. Watch your finger as you reach it to the new key and back to home position a few times (keep it curved).
7. Refer to the set of 3 drill lines at the right of the reach-technique illustration. Key each line twice SS (single-spaced).
   • once slowly, to learn new reach;
   • then faster, for a quick-snap stroke. DS (double-space) between 2-line groups.

2C •
Home-Key Review

each line twice single-spaced (SS): once slowly; again, at a faster pace; double-space (DS) between 2-line groups

All keystrokes learned

1 a;sldkfj a; sl dk fj ff jj dd kk ss ll aa ;; fj a;

2 as as ad ad all all jak jak fad fad fall fall lass

3 a jak; a fad; as a lad; ask dad; a lass; a fall ad

Return 4 times to quadruple-space (QS) between lesson parts.

of the seven wonders of the electronic world."[2] E-mail is   242

the sending, storing, and delivering of *written* messages electroni-   255

cally. ~~According to~~ Reiss *and* Donlan[3] ~~there are~~ *identify* two categories   265

of electronic mail services: 271

    1. In-house electronic mail. (E-mail *that* ~~which~~ is run on   282
a firm's computer system.)   287

2. Commercial electronic mail. (E-mail *that* ~~which~~ is supplied by   300
organizations such as General Electric Information Services   312
and MCI Communications.)   317

Summary   319

    Desktop publishing and electronic mail are but ②*sp* of the   330

changes that are shaping the future of information process-   342

ing. Each year *new* technology enhances the ability of personnel   355

to produce *quality* information. *in less time*   364

heading 2

[1] Mary Ellen Oliverio and others, *The Office Procedures*   14
and Technology (Cincinnati: South-Western Publishing Co.,   26
1993), p. 291.   29

[2] Robert Wiggins, "The Remote E-Mail Checklist,"   42
Mobile Office, August 1994, p. 32.   49

[3] Levi Reiss and Edwin G. Dolan, *Using Computers:*   59
Managing Change (Cincinnati: South-Western Publishing   70
Co., 1989), p. 529.   73

Document 2
On a separate page, prepare an endnotes page from the information at the right.

Document 3
Format a title page for the report. Use your name and school name and the current date.

LESSON 147

Prepare for Assessment: Tables

O b j e c t i v e :
To prepare for assessment of tables.

147A • 5
Conditioning Practice

each line twice

alphabet 1 Kevin justified his lowest quiz score by explaining his problems.

speed 2 She may lend the ancient map to us if the city pays for the work.

fig/sym 3 Is Check #9084 for $76.52, dated June 13, made out to Chen & Chi?

gwam 1' | 1 | 2 | 3 | 4 | 5 | 6 | 7 | 8 | 9 | 10 | 11 | 12 | 13 |

2D •
New Keys: H and E

Use the *Standard Plan for Learning New Keys* (p. 17) for each key to be learned. Study the plan now.

Relate each step of the plan to the illustrations and copy at right. Then key each line twice SS; leave a DS between 2-line groups.

h *Right index* finger

e *Left middle* finger

Do not attempt to key line numbers, the vertical lines separating word groups, or the labels (home row, h/e).

Learn h

1 j j hj hj ah ah ha ha had had has has ash ash hash

2 hj hj ha ha ah ah hah hah had had ash ash has hash

3 ah ha; had ash; has had; a hall; has a hall; ah ha

Return twice to double-space (DS) after you complete the set of lines.

Learn e

4 d d ed ed el el led led eel eel eke eke ed fed fed

5 ed ed el el lee lee fed fed eke eke led led ale ed

6 a lake; a leek; a jade; a desk; a jade eel; a deed

Combine h and e

7 he he he|she she she|shed shed|heed heed|held held

8 a lash; a shed; he held; she has jade; held a sash

9 has fled; he has ash; she had jade; she had a sale

Return 4 times to quadruple-space (QS) between lesson parts.

2E •
New-Key Mastery

1. Key the lines once SS with a DS between 2-line groups.
2. Key the lines again with quick, sharp strokes at a faster pace.

SPACING cue:
Space once after ; used as punctuation.

 note:

Once the screen is filled with keyed lines, the top line disappears when a new line is added at the bottom. This is called **scrolling**.

Fingers curved

Fingers upright

home row

1 ask ask|has has|lad lad|all all|jak jak|fall falls

2 a jak; a lad; a sash; had all; has a jak; all fall

DS

h/e

3 he he|she she|led led|held held|jell jell|she shed

4 he led; she had; she fell; a jade ad; a desk shelf

DS

all keys learned

5 elf elf|all all|ask ask|led led|jak jak|hall halls

6 ask dad; he has jell; she has jade; he sells leeks

DS

all keys learned

7 he led; she has; a jak ad; a jade eel; a sled fell

8 she asked a lad; he led all fall; she has a jak ad

Review the format guides on p. 268. Note the placement of the subject line, company name, copy notation, and postscript. Format and key:

113B, Document 3, p. 270.
114C, Letter 2, p. 272.
115C, Letter 2, p. 274.

LESSON 146

Prepare for Assessment: Reports

Objective:
To prepare for assessment of reports.

146A • 5
Conditioning Practice

each line twice

alphabet 1 Jacques planned a very sizable agenda for the meetings next week.

speed 2 Glen did the work for us, but the city officials will pay for it.

fig/sym 3 Their bill was $74.05 ($68.12 for paper and $5.93 for envelopes).

gwam 1' | 1 | 2 | 3 | 4 | 5 | 6 | 7 | 8 | 9 | 10 | 11 | 12 | 13 |

F ORMATTING

146B • 45
Review Report Formats

Document 1

1. Review the format guides for reports on pp. 211-212.

2. Format the report in unbound style; use **TODAY'S OFFICE** for the report heading.

	words
opening	3

A person returning to the office environment after a 25-year absence would have a difficult time coping with the changes that have taken place during that time. Changing technology would best describe the challenges facing today's office worker. Two "buzzwords" currently being used in the office are electronic desktop publishing and electronic mail.

Electronic Desktop Publishing (DTP)

Desktop publishing is the process of integrating text and graphics by utilizing computer software to produce a professional-looking document without using professional services.

A primary reason for using DTP is the enhanced appearance of finished documents. Almost anything that can be typeset by a professional printer can be produced using a DTP system: announcements, business cards, letterheads, newsletters, etc.[1]

Since today's firms are concerned more than ever about creating the proper image, it is expected that a greater number of firms will turn to desktop publishing to enhance their images.

Electronic Mail

The second "buzz word" used extensively in the modern office is electronic mail (e-mail). "Electronic mail is one

14
26
38
51
64
74
80
93
106
117
127
138
149
160
166
181
194
203
207
217
230

(continued on next page)

New Keys: I and R

Objectives:

1. To learn reach technique for I and R.
2. To combine smoothly I and R with all other learned keys.

3A • 3
Keying Readiness

Follow the steps on p. 17.

3B • 5
Conditioning Practice

each line twice SS; DS between 2-line groups

PRACTICE cues:

- Key each line first at a slow, steady pace, but strike and release each key quickly.

- Key each line again at a faster pace; move from key to key quickly–keep cursor or print point moving steadily.

home keys   1   `a;sldkfj a;sldkfj as jak ask fad all dad lads fall`

Return twice to DS.

h/e   2   `hj hah has had sash hash ed led fed fled sled fell`

DS

all keys learned   3   `as he fled; ask a lass; she had jade; sell all jak`

Return 4 times to quadruple-space (QS) between lesson parts.

3C • 5
Speed Building

each line once DS

SPACING cue:

To DS when in SS mode, strike **Enter** twice at end of line.

SPEED cue:

In lines 1-3, quicken the keying pace as you key each letter combination or word when it is repeated within the line.

1 `hj hj|ah ah|ha ha|had had|ash ash|has has|had hash`

2 `ed ed|el el|ed ed|led led|eke eke|lee lee|ale kale`

3 `he he|she she|led led|has has|held held|sled sleds`

4 `he fled; she led; she had jade; he had a jell sale`

5 `a jak fell; she held a leek; he has had a sad fall`

6 `he has ash; she sells jade; as he fell; has a lake`

7 `she had a fall jade sale; he leads all fall sales;`

8 `he held a fall kale sale; she sells leeks as a fad`

UNIT (32) Prepare for Assessment

LESSONS 145–147

LESSON 145

Prepare for Assessment: Letters

Objective:
To prepare for assessment of letters.

**145A • 5
Conditioning Practice**

set 0.5" SMs
each line twice

alphabet	1	The quick example Ozzie gave of adjectives and verbs was very helpful.
speed	2	He or she may work with us to make a profit for the eighty auto firms.
fig/sym	3	The cost of Model #80-93 is $425 plus 6% sales tax and 17% excise tax.

gwam 1' | 1 | 2 | 3 | 4 | 5 | 6 | 7 | 8 | 9 | 10 | 11 | 12 | 13 | 14 |

**145B • 13
Skill Check**

Key two 5' writings; calculate *gwam* and determine errors.

all letters used

gwam 3' | 5'

	3'	5'
An education is becoming more important in our society. More	4	2 42
jobs will be open to the skilled person with fewer jobs open to	8	5 45
the unskilled or less educated person. Future jobs will require	13	8 47
people who can communicate and who have basic math and reading	17	10 50
skills. It is predicted that there will be a large number of new	21	13 52
jobs available to those with the appropriate training who want to	26	15 55
work in an office. These jobs will require the skills listed	30	18 58
above and an ability to process office documents.	33	20 60
To quickly process quality office documents will take a great	37	22 62
deal of training. A person must be able to key rapidly, format a	42	25 65
variety of documents, make decisions, follow directions, recognize	46	28 67
all types of errors, and apply language skills. In addition to	50	30 70
these skills, the best office workers will be willing to put forth	55	33 73
an extra effort. You should begin to put forth an extra effort	59	36 75
today to get the training needed to become one of the skilled	63	38 78
workers in the labor force of the future.	66	40 79

gwam 3' | 1 | 2 | 3 | 4 | 5 |
5' | 1 | 2 | 3 |

3D • 18
New Keys: I and R

each line twice SS (slowly, then faster); DS between 2-line groups; if time permits, key lines 7-9 again

Technique goals
- curved, upright fingers
- finger-action keystrokes
- eyes on copy

i *Right middle* finger

r *Left index* finger

Follow the *Standard Plan for Learning New Keys* outlined on p. 17.

Learn i

1 k k ik ik is is if if did did aid aid kid kid hail
2 ik ik if if is is kid kid his his lie lie aid aide
3 a kid; a lie; if he; he did; his aide; if a kid is
DS

Learn r

4 f f rf rf jar jar her her are are ark ark jar jars
5 rf rf re re fr fr jar jar red red her her far fare
6 a jar; a rake; a lark; red jar; hear her; are dark
DS

Combine i and r

7 fir fir|rid rid|sir sir|ire ire|fire fire|air airs
8 a fir; if her; a fire; is fair; his ire; if she is
9 he is; if her; is far; red jar; his heir; her aide

Quadruple-space (QS) between lesson parts.

3E • 19
New-Key Mastery

1. Key the lines once SS with a DS between 2-line groups.
2. Key the lines again at a faster pace.

Technique goals
- fingers deeply curved
- wrists low, but not resting
- hands/arms steady
- eyes on copy as you key

reach review
1 hj ed ik rf hj de ik fr hj ed ik rf jh de ki fr hj
2 he he|if if|all all|fir fir|jar jar|rid rid|as ask
DS

h/e
3 she she|elf elf|her her|hah hah|eel eel|shed shelf
4 he has; had jak; her jar; had a shed; she has fled
DS

i/r
5 fir fir|rid rid|sir sir|kid kid|ire ire|fire fired
6 a fir; is rid; is red; his ire; her kid; has a fir
DS

all keys learned
7 if if|is is|he he|did did|fir fir|jak jak|all fall
8 a jak; he did; ask her; red jar; she fell; he fled
DS

all keys learned
9 if she is; he did ask; he led her; he is her aide;
10 she has had a jak sale; she said he had a red fir;

Timed Writings

1. A 1' writing on each ¶ for speed; find *gwam*.
2. A 1' writing on each ¶ for control; determine errors.
3. A 3' writing on ¶s 1-3 combined; find *gwam*; determine errors.

all letters used

| | gwam | 3' | 5' |

The computer is an amazing machine. It is amazing because of   4 | 2 | 39
the many things it does, the speed at which it does its opera-   8 | 5 | 41
tions, and the degree of accuracy it maintains. In short, the   12 | 7 | 44
computer is one of mankind's most important inventions and a   16 | 10 | 46
resource that seems to be everywhere and do everything.   20 | 12 | 48

Computers are used by students in many classes. They are   24 | 14 | 50
used by people who work in health, law, farming, and athletics to   28 | 17 | 53
record, keep, and process data. Rock stars use them to run   32 | 19 | 56
concerts and to write music. Computers run and work on assembly   37 | 22 | 58
lines and are used to design many consumer goods.   40 | 24 | 60

Computers have changed extensively in the short period they   44 | 26 | 62
have existed. Early ones had to be kept in special areas and run   48 | 29 | 65
by trained personnel. Today, young children use them to learn or   53 | 32 | 68
for play. The jumbo, slow computers of yesteryear have given way   57 | 34 | 70
to the small, quick computers in use today.   60 | 36 | 72

gwam 3' | 1 | 2 | 3 | 4
5' | 1 | 2 | 3

LANGUAGE SKILLS

Number Expression

Key each sentence, supplying the correct form of number expression.

1. The center is seven ft. 6 in. tall and weighs 230 lbs.
2. The technology meetings will be held in Rooms five and nine.
3. 2 of the board members will be out of town on March second.
4. He was scheduled on Flight fifty-three, which leaves at four p.m.
5. Nearly 60 members voted for Sue; that is about 3/4.
6. Problems four and five from Chapter four dealt with networks.
7. The two file servers will be connected tomorrow by nine a.m.
8. The servers were purchased at 1 State Street and 28 Lori Lane.
9. Exactly 1/2 of the computers have multimedia capabilities.
10. The play is scheduled for April third at six p.m. in Room 28.

Review

Objectives:

1. To improve reach-stroke control and keying speed.
2. To improve technique on **Space Bar** and **Enter**.

4A • 3
Keying Readiness

1. Review the steps for arranging your work area (see p. 10).
2. Review the steps required to ready your equipment.
3. Take good keying position.

- fingers curved and upright
- wrists low, but not touching frame of machine
- forearms parallel to slant of keyboard
- body erect, sitting back in chair
- feet on floor for balance

4B • 5
Conditioning Practice

each line twice SS; DS between 2-line groups

```
1 a;sldkfj fj dk sl a; jh de ki fr hj ed ik rf fj a;
2 a if is el he la as re led fir did she has jak jar
3 he has fir; she had a jak; a jade jar; a leek sale
                                                   QS
```

4C • 10
Technique: Space Bar

1. Key lines 1-6 once SS; DS between 3-line groups. Space *immediately* after each word.
2. Key the lines again at a faster pace.

Use down-and-in motion

Short, easy words

```
1 if is ha la ah el as re id did sir fir die rid lie
2 as lad lei rah jak had ask lid her led his kid has
3 hah all ire add iris hall fire keel sell jeer fall
                                                   DS
```

Short-word phrases

```
4 if he|he is|if he is|if she|she is|if she is|as is
5 as he is|if he led|if she has|if she did|had a jak
6 as if|a jar lid|all her ads|as he said|a jade fish
                                                   QS
```

4D • 10
Technique: Enter

each line twice SS; DS between 2-line groups

PRACTICE *cue*:

Keep up your pace to the end of the line, return quickly, and begin the new line without a pause or stop.

```
1 if he is;
2 as if she is;
3 he had a fir desk;
4 she has a red jell jar;
5 he has had a lead all fall;
6 she asked if he reads fall ads;
7 she said she reads all ads she sees;
8 his dad has had a sales lead as he said;
                                        QS
```

Reach out and tap **Enter**

Skill Builder

Tabulation
1. Set tabs 1", 2.5", and 4" from the left margin.
2. Key the text at the right.
3. Key three 1' writings.

Goal: Increase amount of text keyed on each writing.

				words
North Carolina Raleigh	North Dakota Bismark	Ohio Columbus	Oklahoma Oklahoma City	8 16
Oregon Salem	Pennsylvania Harrisburg	Rhode Island Providence	South Carolina Columbia	26 33
South Dakota Pierre	Tennessee Nashville	Texas Austin	Utah Salt Lake City	40 48
Vermont Montpelier	Virginia Richmond	Washington Tacoma	West Virginia Charleston	56 64
Wisconsin Madison	Wyoming Cheyenne			67 71

Keying Technique
1. Key each line once.
2. Key a 1' writing on each even-numbered line.

Alphabetic
1 zebra extra vicious dozen happen just quick forgot way limp exact
2 Everyone except Meg and Joe passed the final weekly biology quiz.

Fig/sym
3 Account #2849 | 10% down | for $6,435.70 | Lots #8 & #9 | $250 deductible
4 The fax machine (#387-291) is on sale for $364.50 until March 21.

Bottom row
5 modem zebra extinct moving backbone moon vacate exam computerized
6 Zeno's vaccine injection for smallpox can be given in six months.

Third row
7 you tip rip terror yet peer quit were pet tire terrier pepper out
8 Our two terrier puppies were too little to take to your pet show.

Double letters
9 footnote scanner less process letters office cell suppress footer
10 Jill, my office assistant, will process the four letters by noon.

Balanced hands
11 wish then turn us auto big eight down city busy end firm it goals
12 If the firm pays for the social, the eight officials may also go.

Shift keys
13 The New York Times | Gone with the Wind | Chicago Tribune | WordPerfect
14 Alan L. Martin finished writing Planning for Changing Technology.

Adjacent keys
15 were open top ask rest twenty point tree master merge option asks
16 The sort option was well received by all three new group members.

Space bar
17 it is fix and fox go key do by box men pen six so the to when big
18 Did they use the right audit form to check the city busline?

gwam	1'	1	2	3	4	5	6	7	8	9	10	11	12	13

4E • 10
Speed Building: Words

1. Key each line once SS; DS below line 3.
2. Key each line again at a faster pace; QS (4 hard returns) at end of drill.

PRACTICE *cues:*

Key the first word of each pair at an easy speed: rekey it at a faster speed. Think and say each word; key it with quick-snap strokes.

Fingers curved

Goal: to speed up the combining of letters

1 is is | if if | ah ah | he he | el el | irk irk | aid aid | aide
2 as as | ask ask | ad ad | had had | re re | ire ire | are hare
3 if if | fir fir | id id | did did | el el | eel eel | jak jaks

QS

4F • 12
Speed Building: Phrases

1. Key each line once SS.
2. Key the lines once more to improve your speed.

PRACTICE *cues:*

Speed up the second keying of each phrase: space quickly between words and phrases.

Space with right thumb

Use down-and-in motion

Goal: to speed up spacing between words

1 ah ha | ah ha | if he | if he | as if | as if | as he | as he is
2 if a | if a | a fir | a fir | a jar | a jar | irk her | irks her
3 he did | he did | if all | if all | if she led | if she fled
4 a lad | a lad | if her | if her | as his aide | as his aides

R&e

1. Key the drill once SS at an easy pace to gain control of all your reach-stroke motions. DS between 2-line groups.
2. Key the drill again to speed up your motions and build continuity (keeping the cursor or print point moving steadily across the screen or paper).

reach review

1 hj ed ik rf jh de ki fr jhj ded kik frf hj ed ik ;
2 he if fir sir she jar rid ask led kid his did risk

h/e

3 he el she elf her led had held desk dash jade fled
4 her dad led; a lad fled; he has jade; she had eel;

i/r

5 is his kid ski fir rid ire die slid kids fife dike
6 a kid led; she is fair; as her aide; he is a risk;

all keys learned

7 if he is; as she fled; risk a lead; has a red sled
8 a jade fish; ask if she slid; she has asked a kid;

all keys learned

9 as if he did; he asked a lad; his aide has a sled;
10 he has a sled; if she has a jar; see if he is here

Activity 3:

1. Read the account of the hapless job applicant as given at the right.
2. Compose/key a ¶ indicating why you believe the applicant didn't get the job.
3. Compose/key another ¶ indicating why you believe you could have had a successful interview and gotten the job.

Compose (think) as you key

I have just had my first job interview and now realize how totally unprepared I was for it. I hadn't given much thought to identifying my interests and even less to determining my competence. I didn't expect to be given a "once over" to see how I was dressed. I wanted a job. More truthfully, I wanted a paycheck; so I had to get a job to get my cash.

Before I could see the personnel manager with whom I had an appointment, I was asked to fill in an application blank. I wrote as carefully as possible, but I did a messy job. I didn't have my social security card or number. I didn't have a record of my school marks or the names and addresses of my references. I was totally unprepared.

I didn't expect the interview to be as interesting as it was. I was asked questions about my school- and church-related activities, my hobbies and personal habits, the books I have enjoyed, and the plays I have seen and concerts I have attended recently. Throughout the questioning, I felt very sure I was being "sized up" as a person rather than as a worker.

There was a test, of course. It covered some English, spelling, and math. There was also a timed writing on difficult copy. I was asked to key accurately and not to try for maximum speed. The document processing included a two-page letter with special features, a simplified memo, and a five-column table with columnar headings to be centered. All errors in documents were to be found and corrected. Who'd have thought I'd have to do all that?

It's too bad I hadn't had some work experience before going for the interview and test. It's too bad that I had not followed up on the hints my teachers had given me about what to expect in a job interview and employment test and what to do to prepare for them. It's too bad that I shrugged off as punishment my teachers' frequent directions to "proofread and correct" all work. When I go for my next interview and test, I'll be prepared; then I won't have to say "It's too bad."

Objectives:

1. To learn reach technique for **O** and **T**.

2. To combine smoothly **O** and **T** with all other learned keys.

5A • 8
Conditioning Practice

each line twice SS (slowly, then faster); DS between 2-line groups

In Lessons 5-10, the time for the *Conditioning Practice* is changed to 8'. During this time, you are to arrange your work area, prepare your equipment for keying, and practice the lines of the *Conditioning Practice* as directed.

Fingers curved

Fingers upright

home row 1 a sad fall; had a hall; a jak falls; as a fall ad;

3d row 2 if her aid; all he sees; he irks her; a jade fish;

all keys learned 3 as he fell; he sells fir desks; she had half a jar

5B • 20
New Keys: O and T

each line twice SS (slowly, then faster); DS between 2-line groups; if time permits, key lines 7-9 again

o *Right ring* finger

t *Left index* finger

Follow the *Standard Plan for Learning New Keys* outlined on p. 17.

Learn o

1 l l ol ol do do of of so so lo lo old old for fore

2 ol ol of of or or for for oak oak off off sol sole

3 do so; a doe; of old; of oak; old foe; of old oak;

Learn t

4 f f tf tf it it at at tie tie the the fit fit lift

5 tf tf ft ft it it sit sit fit fit hit hit kit kite

6 if it; a fit; it fit; tie it; the fit; at the site

Combine o and t

7 to to|too too|toe toe|dot dot|lot lot|hot hot|tort

8 a lot; to jot; too hot; odd lot; a fort; for a lot

9 of the; to rot; dot it; the lot; for the; for this

Language & Writing Skills 14

Activity 1:

1. Study the spelling/definitions of the words in the color block at the right.
2. Key the **Learn** line in the first set of sentences.
3. Key the **Apply** lines, choosing the right words to complete each sentence correctly.
4. Key the second set of lines in the same way.
5. Check work; rekey lines containing word-choice errors.

Choose the right word

cents (n) specified portion of a dollar

sense (n/vb) meaning intended or conveyed; perceive by sense organs; ability to judge

since (adv/conj) after a definite time in the past; in view of the fact; because

cite (vb) use as support; commend; summon

sight (n/vb) ability to see; something seen; a device to improve aim; observe or examine by taking a sight

site (n) the place something is, was, or will be located

Learn 1 Since you ask, I sense that this is a dollars-and-cents issue.
Apply 2 I have only a few (cents/sense/since) left out of my allowance.
Apply 3 Do you (cents/sense/since) a change (cents/sense/since) he left?
Apply 4 How long has it been (cents/sense/since) you were graduated?

Learn 5 Did you cite the article about keying by sight?
Apply 6 We visited the Olympics (cite/sight/site) on our tour.
Apply 7 Did the attorney (cite/sight/site) the case law on that issue?
Apply 8 The tournament (cite/sight/site) is now in (cite/sight/site).

Activity 2:

1. Read carefully the letter shown at the right, noting errors in capitalization, punctuation, number expression, and word choice.
2. Format/key the message as a personal-business letter, using the current date and your own return address.
   Address the letter to:
   Mr. Carlos F. Aquila
   A.G. Marshall & Sons
   2533 N. 117 Ave.
   Omaha, NE 68164-2263
   Supply an appropriate salutation and closing.
3. Correct all errors, including those you make as you key.

Proofread & correct

Your advertisement in sundays Enquirer for summer assistants in you're information processing center interests me very much. Please consider me an applicant for one of these positions.

A focus of my training during the passed 2 years were courses in Information Processing. As a result, I am skilled as a keyboard operator, are adept in the use of several software packages and have a good working knowledge of spreadsheets and databases.

Supervisors of my previous part time and summer jobs have said that I take direction positively and work well with others. In addition, they have told my teachers that I show initiative and readily step in to help others with there work.

After you review the enclosed data sheet may I please have an appointment for an interview? You can reach me at the address and telephone number shown on the data sheet.

5C • 22

New-Key Mastery

1. Key the lines once SS; DS between 2-line groups.
2. Key the lines again at a faster pace.

Technique goals

- curved, upright fingers
- wrists low, but not resting
- down-and-in spacing
- eyes on copy as you key

PRACTICE cue:
In lines of repeated words (lines 3, 5, and 7), speed up the second keying of each word.

reach review
1 hj ed ik rf ol tf jh de ki fr lo ft hj ed ol rf tf
2 is led fro hit old fit let kit rod kid dot jak sit

h/e
3 he he|she she|led led|had had|see see|has has|seek
4 he led|ask her|she held|has fled|had jade|he leads

i/t
5 it it|fit fit|tie tie|sit sit|kit kit|its its|fits
6 a kit|a fit|a tie|lit it|it fits|it sits|it is fit

o/r
7 or or|for for|ore ore|fro fro|oar oar|roe roe|rode
8 a rod|a door|a rose|or for|her or|he rode|or a rod

space bar
9 of he or it is to if do el odd off too for she the
10 it is|if it|do so|if he|to do|or the|she is|of all

all keys learned
11 if she is; ask a lad; to the lake; off the old jet
12 he or she; for a fit; if she left the; a jak salad

1. Key the drill once SS at an easy pace to gain control of all your reach-stroke motions. DS between 2-line groups.
2. Key the drill again to speed up your motions and build continuity (keeping the cursor or print point moving steadily across the screen or paper).

reach review
1 hj ed ik rf jhj ded kik frf a;sldkfj a;sldkfj fja;
2 if led ski fir she ire sir jak has did jar kid rid

o/t
3 ol ol|old old|for for|oak oak|ode ode|doe doe|does
4 tf tf|it it|to to|kit kit|the the|fit fit|sit sits

i/r
5 ik ik|if if|it it|fir fir|ski ski|did did|kid kids
6 rf rf|or or|for for|her her|fir fir|rod rod|or for

h/e
7 hj hj|he he|ah ah|ha ha|he he|she she|ash ash|hash
8 ed ed|el el|he he|her her|elk elk|jet jet|she|shed

all keys learned
9 of hot kit old sit for jet she oak jar ore lid lot
10 a ski; old oak; too hot; odd jar; for the; old jet

all keys learned
11 she is to ski; is for the lad; ask if she has jade
12 he sold leeks to her; she sells jade at their lake

Instructions from Katelynn Eastwick August 4

Please fax the attached note to Lynelle Montgomery at the Carrington Hotel.

The final counts for the meal functions are as follows:

Lunch   August 8   238
Breakfast   August 9   179
Lunch   August 9   255

I will be arriving on August 7 around 4 p.m. Would it be possible for us to meet for 20-30 minutes to go over any last-minute details? I've appreciated all the help you have given us. You have a very professional staff at the Carrington.

Instructions from Katelynn Eastwick August 14

Please send the attached thank-you letter to each of the Denver Symposium presenters at their work addresses.

<Date>

<Title> <First Name> <Last Name>
<Address>
<City,> <State> <ZIP>

Dear <Title> <Last Name>

Thank you for presenting at our symposium last week. Your topic, <Title of Presentation>, was an important part of "A Technology Vision." Many of the participants remarked that your presentation was excellent.

Professional Symposium Specialists is very fortunate to be able to provide speakers with your expertise at our symposiums. I hope that we can include your name on future programs that we sponsor dealing with technology.

You should receive a check from our main office within the next week to cover your honorarium and expenses.

Sincerely

Ms. Katelynn Eastwick
Western Branch Manager

xx

New Keys: N and G

Objectives:

1. To learn reach technique for **N** and **G**.
2. To combine smoothly **N** and **G** with all other learned keys.

6A • 8
Conditioning Practice

each line twice SS (slowly, then faster); DS between 2-line groups

home row	1	has a jak; ask a lad; a fall fad; had a jak salad;
o/t	2	to do it; as a tot; do a lot; it is hot; to dot it
e/i/r	3	is a kid; it is far; a red jar; her skis; her aide

6B • 20
New Keys: N and G

each line twice SS (slowly, then faster); DS between 2-line groups; if time permits, key lines 7-9 again

n *Right index* finger

g *Left index* finger

Follow the *Standard Plan for Learning New Keys* outlined on p. 17.

Learn n

1 j j nj nj an an and and end end ant ant land lands
2 nj nj an an en en in in on on end end and and hand
3 an en; an end; an ant; no end; on land; a fine end

Learn g

4 f f gf gf go go fog fog got got fig figs jogs jogs
5 gf gf go go got got dig dig jog jog logs logs golf
6 to go; he got; to jog; to jig; the fog; is to golf

Combine n and g

7 go go|no no|nag nag|ago ago|gin gin|gone gone|long
8 go on; a nag; sign in; no gain; long ago; into fog
9 a fine gig; log in soon; a good sign; lend a hand;

6C • 5
Technique: Return

each line twice SS; DS between 2-line groups

PRACTICE *cue*:
Keep up your pace to end of line, return quickly, and start new line without pause.

1 she is gone;
2 she got an old dog;
3 she jogs in a dense fog;
4 she and he go to golf at nine;
5 he is a hand on a rig in the north;

Reach out and tap **Enter**

Instructions from Katelynn Eastwick July 15

Format and key a references list from the following information.

Manning, George, and Kent Curtis. <u>Group Strength: Quality Circles at Work</u>. Cincinnati: South-Western Publishing Co., 1988.

Rader, M. H., and Linda A. Kurth. <u>Business Communication</u>. Cincinnati: South-Western Publishing Co., 1994.

Job 12

Instructions from Katelynn Eastwick July 20

Send the attached form letter to the work address of the speakers. The information for the Date:, Time:, Topic:, and Room: can be taken from Job 7. Merritt listed a **computer** and **Color LCD Data Projection** for **AV Equipment**. Dozier listed a **Whiteboard with Marker**. The rest of the speakers listed an **Overhead Projector**.

to the effective functioning of every facet of the operations of a business." (Rader and Kurth, 1994, p 2) ~~N~~although Numerous areas of communication could be explored, ~~E~~ffective business presentations could will be the emphasis for the first communication symposium.

Recommendations

The following recommendations are offered as a means to increase the earnings of *the Western Branch of* Professional Symposium Specialists.

1. Expand into Phoenix and Santa Fe. At least one symposium will be offered in each state in the Western Region. (Originally this was a long-term goal to be achieve*d* next year.)

2. Offer a one-day fee for those *wishing to* attending on*ly* Saturday's session.

3. Increase fee to $350 *two-day registration* ~~for each symposium~~

4. *Offer* ~~Give~~ reduced rates for organizations sending five or more individuals.

5. Offer more than one symposium per year in the more lucrative markets.

<Date>

<Title> <First Name> <Last Name>
<Company Name>
<Address>
<City,> <State> <ZIP>

Dear <Title> <Last Name>

Plans for the August symposium, "A Technology Vision," are being finalized. You are scheduled for:

> Date: <Date>
> Time: <Time>
> Topic: <Topic>
> Room: <Room>
> AV Equipment: <AV Equipment> } DS

We are pleased to have you play an important role in assisting Professional Symposium Specialists with the symposium. Call me at 503-139-4877 if you have any questions regarding the symposium.

Sincerely

6D • 17
New-Key Mastery

1. Key the lines once SS; DS between 2-line groups.
2. Key the lines again at a faster pace.

Technique goals
- curved, upright fingers
- wrists low, but not resting
- quick-snap keystrokes
- down-and-in spacing
- eyes on copy as you key

<table>
<tr><td>reach review</td><td>1</td><td>a;sldkfj ed ol rf hj tf nj gf lo de jh ft nj fr a;</td></tr>
<tr><td></td><td>2</td><td>he jogs; an old ski; do a log for; she left a jar;</td></tr>
<tr><td>n/g</td><td>3</td><td>an an|go go|in in|dig dig|and and|got got|end ends</td></tr>
<tr><td></td><td>4</td><td>go to; is an; log on; sign it; and golf; fine figs</td></tr>
<tr><td>space bar</td><td>5</td><td>if if|an an|go go|of of|or or|he he|it it|is is|do</td></tr>
<tr><td></td><td>6</td><td>if it is|is to go|he or she|to do this|of the sign</td></tr>
<tr><td>all keys learned</td><td>7</td><td>she had an old oak desk; a jell jar is at the side</td></tr>
<tr><td></td><td>8</td><td>he has left for the lake; she goes there at eight;</td></tr>
<tr><td>all keys learned</td><td>9</td><td>she said he did it for her; he is to take the oars</td></tr>
<tr><td></td><td>10</td><td>sign the list on the desk; go right to the old jet</td></tr>
</table>

R&e

each line twice SS; DS between 2-line groups; QS after each grouping

lines 1-3
curved, upright fingers; steady, easy pace

lines 4-7
space immediately after each word; down-and-in motion of thumb

lines 8-12
maintain pace to end of line; return quickly and start new line immediately

lines 13-16
speed up the second keying of each repeated word or phrase; think words

Reach review

1 nj nj gf gf ol ol tf tf ik ik rf rf hj hj ed ed fj
2 go fog an and got end jog ant dog ken fig fin find
3 go an on and lag jog flag land glad lend sign hand

Spacing

4 if an it go is of do or to as in so no off too gin
5 ah ha he or if an too for and she jog got hen then
6 he is to go|if it is so|is to do it|if he is to go
7 she is to ski on the lake; he is also at the lake;

Returning

8 he is to go;
9 she is at an inn;
10 he goes to ski at one;
11 he is also to sign the log;
12 she left the log on the old desk

Keying short words and phrases

13 do do|it it|an an|is is|of of|to to|if if|or or or
14 he he|go go|in in|so so|at at|no no|as as|ha ha ha
15 to do|to do|it is|it is|of it|of it|is to|is to do
16 she is to do so; he did the sign; ski at the lake;

revenues and expenses of the three first-time symposiums (Cheyenne, Sacramento, and ~~Eugene~~ Billings) are deleted from the figures, expenses are 46 percent of revenues.

New Topics for Next Year (Symposium

Evaluations include a section in which participants suggest topics for future symposium. The most frequently listed topics include:

1. Implementing Quality Circles at Work.
2. Organizational Communication.

Quality Circles. The quality circle concept has become more popular during the past few years. The philosophy behind quality circles is the belief that specific job-related problems can best be solved by those employees who are closest to the problem area.

George Manning and Kent Curtis have done extensive work in the area of work groups and would be excellent symposium facilitators. Part Two of there book, Group Strength, (1988, 55) ~~would~~ provide an excellent basis for a symposium. The areas explored include:

1. The management philosophy behind quality circles.
2. The social nature of people and why work groups are important.
3. How different systems of worker governance reflect a continuum of employee involvement.
4. The principles of business management and employee relations that helped Japan create a post-World War II economic success story.
5. The need for quality circles.
6. The value of quality circles.

Communication. The area of communication is always a popular seminar topic. The Chairman and Chief Executive Officer of The BFGoodrich Company, John D. Ong, states that "Communication is basic

(continued on next page)

New Keys: Left Shift and Period (.)

Objectives:

1. To learn reach technique for **Left Shift** and . (period).
2. To combine smoothly **Left Shift** and . (period) with all other learned keys.

Finger-action keystrokes

Down-and-in spacing

Quick out-and-tap return

7A • 8
Conditioning Practice

each line twice SS (slowly, then faster); DS between 2-line groups

reach review 1 ed ik rf ol gf hj tf nj de ki fr lo fg jh ft jn a;
space bar 2 or is to if an of el so it go id he do as in at on
all keys learned 3 he is; if an; or do; to go; a jak; an oak; of all;

7B • 20
New Keys: Left Shift and . (Period)

each line twice SS (slowly, then faster); DS between 2-line groups; if time permits, rekey lines 7-9

Left Shift *Left little* finger

. (period) *Right ring* finger

SPACING *cue:*

Space once after **.** following abbreviations and initials. Do not space after **.** within abbreviations. Space twice after **.** at end of a sentence except at line endings. There, return without spacing.

SHIFTING *cue:*

Shift, strike key, and release both in a quick 1-2-3 count.

Learn Left Shift key

1 a a Ja Ja Ka Ka La La Hal Hal Kal Kal Jae Jae Lana
2 Kal rode; Kae did it; Hans has jade; Jan ate a fig
3 I see that Jake is to aid Kae at the Oak Lake sale

Learn . (period)

4 l l .l .l fl. fl. ed. ed. ft. ft. rd. rd. hr. hrs.
5 .l .l fl. fl. hr. hr. e.g. e.g. i.e. i.e. in. ins.
6 fl. ft. hr. ed. rd. rt. off. fed. ord. alt. asstd.

Combine Left Shift and . (period)

7 I do. Ian is. Ola did. Jan does. Kent is gone.
8 Hal did it. I shall do it. Kate left on a train.
9 J. L. Han skis on Oak Lake; Lt. Haig also does so.

Instructions from Katelynn Eastwick July 15

Format and key the attached information as an unbound report. Please proofread again for any errors I may have missed.

WESTERN BRANCH UPDATE   > *Center*

January-June, ----   *DS*

¶ The first half of this year has been excellent. Many of the goals ~~we set~~ *established* for the Western branch have been *accomplished* ~~completed~~. Our goal of delivering a symposium every 15 days has been achieved. As of July 1, fourteen symposiums were completed in 14 cities. 11 of the symposiums were *financial* successes. The three that did not break even were first-time ventures into new markets. Based on past performance *in new markets*, we anticipated that we would likely recover around 50 percent of the expenses. Revenues generated from the *three* new markets covered 79 percent of the expenses. We was very pleased with these percentages. A complete analysis of each symposium is shown in the following table.

Location	Expenses	Revenues
San Francisco	$ 50,750	$109,400
Portland	40,690	82,500
Seattle	48,750	130,800
Boise	37,820	59,400
Salt Lake City	42,740	69,900
Las Vegas	43,690	95,700
Los Angeles	49,690	140,100
San Diego	47,280	107,400
Spokane	41,390	75,900
Denver	43,660	97,500
Cheyenne	26,590	19,800
Sacramento	34,220	28,800
Eugene	39,380	78,000
Billings	33,750	26,100
	$580,400	$1,131,300

Alphabetize · *align $*

Note that the expenses and revenues do no include meal functions. However, the expenses column does include a charge of $4,700 *or entertainment* for each symposium location to cover office salaries and office expenses. Expenses were *approximately* 51.3 percent of revenues. This is slightly higher than the 50 percent goal that had been established. However, when the

(continued on next page)

7C • 17
New-Key Mastery

1. Key the lines once SS; DS between 2-line groups.
2. Key the lines again at a faster pace.

Technique goals
- curved, upright fingers
- finger-action keystrokes
- quiet hands/arms
- out-and-down shifting

TECHNIQUE *cue:*
Eyes on copy except when you lose your place.

abbrev./ initials

1 He said ft. for feet; rd. for road; fl. for floor.
2 Lt. Hahn let L. K. take the old gong to Lake Neil.

3d row emphasis

3 Lars is to ask at the old store for a kite for Jo.
4 Ike said he is to take the old road to Lake Heidi.

key words

5 a an or he to if do it of so is go for got old led
6 go the off aid dot end jar she fit oak and had rod

key phrases

7 if so|it is|to do|if it|do so|to go|he is|to do it
8 to the|and do|is the|got it|if the|for the|ask for

all letters learned

9 Ned asked her to send the log to an old ski lodge.
10 J. L. lost one of the sleds he took off the train.

7D • 5
Technique: Space Bar and Return

1. Key each line once SS; DS at end of line 7.
2. Key the drill again at a faster pace if time permits.

SPACING *cue:*
Quickly strike **Space Bar** *immediately* after last letter in the word.

1 Jan is to sing.
2 Karl is at the lake.
3 Lena is to send the disk.
4 Lars is to jog to the old inn.
5 Hanna took the girls to a ski lake.
6 Hal is to take the old list to his desk.
7 Lana is to take the jar to the store at nine.

Return and start each new line quickly.

R&e

1. Key each line once SS; DS between 3-line groups.
2. Rekey the drill at a faster pace if time permits.

PRACTICE *cue:*
In lines 4-7, keep cursor or print point moving steadily—no stops or pauses within the line.

Spacing/Shifting

1 K. L. Jakes is to see Lt. Hahn at Oak Lake at one.
2 Janet Harkins sent the sales sheet to Joel Hansen.
3 Karla Kent is to go to London to see Laska Jolson.

Keying easy sentences

4 Kae is to go to the lake to fish off an old skiff.
5 Joel is to ask his good friend to go to the shore.
6 Lara and her dad took eight girls for a long hike.
7 Kent said his dad is to sell the oak and ash logs.

I have written in the rest of the information for the speaker list. Please make the changes and print a final copy.

"A TECHNOLOGY VISION"

Speaker List

Name	Home Address	Work Address
Jon Mathis (Dr.)	310 Buckeye St. Toledo, OH 43611-1234 419-186-8921	4290 Brooklawn Dr. Toledo, OH 43623-8102 419-132-8362
Rose LaJardin (Dr.)	8290 Quonset Ave. Warwick, RI 02889-9867 401-156-3819	2930 Lighthouse Dr. Warwick, RI 02889-5714 401-139-3865
Anne Harper (Dr.)	207 Churchill Way Hartford, CT 06111-2856 203-165-1285	P.O. Box 321 Stafford, CT 06075-8332 203-159-3825
Stan Dozier (Dr.)	3290 Craig Cir. Ogden, UT 84404-4237 801-186-1929	1320 Lorl Ln. Ogden, UT 84404-1209 801-125-7692
Ann Merritt (Ms.)	3286 Hanover Dr. Pueblo, CO 81007-8348 719-120-5656	631 Monterrey St. Pueblo, CO 81006-8460 719-121-2301
Chad Chadwick (Mr.)	4920 Hickory Dr., N. Boise, ID 83704-2839 208-130-6210	2956 Demark St. Boise, ID 83705-2243 208-160-2380
Lindon York (Dr.)	8490 Glenhill Rd. El Cajon, CA 92020-8382 714-129-4544	3847 Park Hyde St. Orange, CA 92668-8382 714-133-8767

LESSON 8 — Review

Objectives:
1. To improve use of **Space Bar, Left Shift key,** and **Enter.**
2. To improve keying speed on words, phrases, and sentences.

8A • 8
Conditioning Practice

each line twice SS (slowly, then faster); DS between 2-line groups; if time permits, practice each line again

Space once.

reach review	1	ik rf ol ed nj gf hj tf .1 ft. i.e. e.g. rt. J. L.
spacing	2	a an go is or to if he and got the for led kit lot
left shift	3	I got it. Hal has it. Jan led Nan. Kae is gone.

8B • 8
Keyboard Mastery

each line once SS; DS between 2-line groups; QS at end of drill

Technique goals
- curved, upright fingers
- low wrists, but not resting
- quick-snap keystrokes
- finger reaches; hands and arms steady

h/e	1	hj ed jhj ded ha el he she led had eke hal ale die
	2	Heidi had a good lead at the end of the first set.

DS

i/r	3	ik rf kik frf is or sir ire ore his risk fire ride
	4	Kier is taking a high risk if he rides that horse.

DS

o/t	5	ol tf lol ftf so it of too oft hot toe lot the old
	6	Ola has lost the list she took to that food store.

DS

n/g	7	nj gf jnj fgf go an got and nag gin hang gone sign
	8	Lang and she are going to sing nine songs at noon.

DS

left shift/.	9	Oak Lake; N. J. Karis; Lt. L. J. Oates; Lara Nador
	10	J. K. Larkin is going to Idaho to see Linda Jakes.

QS

8C • 4
Technique: Return

each line once SS; DS between 2-line groups

RETURN cue:
Keep up your pace to the end of the line; return *immediately;* start the new line without pausing.

1 Nan has gone to ski;
2 she took a train at nine.

3 Janet asked for the disk;
4 she is to take it to the lake.

5 Karl said he left at the lake
6 a file that has the data she needs.

7 Nadia said she felt ill as the ski
8 lift left to take the girls to the hill.

> Keep eyes on copy as you return.

Instructions from Katelynn Eastwick
July 14

Format and key the attached information in an attractive format. Use "A TECHNOLOGY VISION" for the main heading.

August 8

Presenter	Topic	Time	Room
Chadwick	Networking--An Overview	9:30-11:00	Senate A
~~Kemp~~ LaJardin	What Databases Can Do	9:30-11:00	Senate B Colorado Ballroom
Mathis	Technology "Risk Takers"	1:30-3:00	Senate A
York	Turning A Technology into Opportunity	11:30-12:30	Senate A

August 9

Presenter	Topic	Time	Room
Dozier	Boot Camp for Would-Be Internet Users	1:30-3:00	Senate B
Harper	Client-Server Architectures	1:30-3:30	Senate A
Merritt	Taking Control of Information	9:00-1:00 2	Senate A

Professional Symposium Specialists

429 Kentwood Dr.
Eugene, OR 97401-8392
503-139-4877

Purchase Order

FRIENDSHIP OFFICE SUPPLY
7830 PIEDMONT AVE NW
SALEM OR 97304-6767

PO No.: 138A
Date: July 14, - - - -
Terms: 2/10, n/30
Shipped Via: Western Freight

Quantity	Description/Stock Number	Price		Total	
10	Name badge/G240-A96 (6x)	11	50	115	00
5	Red dry erase markers/D115-001 (ea)	1	69	8	45
5	Blue dry erase markers/D115-002 (ea)	1	69	8	45
5	Green dry erase markers/D115-005 (ea)	1	69	8	45
5	Dry marker eraser (ea)	5	45	27	25
				167	60

By _____

8D • 10
Technique: Space Bar and Left Shift

each line twice SS; DS between 2-line groups

Goals

- to reduce the pause between words
- to reduce the time taken to shift/strike key/release when making capital letters

Down-and-in spacing

Out-and-down shifting

8E • 20
Speed Building

each line twice SS (slowly, then faster); DS between 2-line groups

Correct finger curvature

Correct finger alignment

Upright fingers

Space Bar (Space *immediately* after each word.)

1 if is an he go is or ah to of so it do el id la ti

2 an el|go to|if he|of it|is to|do the|for it|and so

3 if she is|it is the|all of it|go to the|for an oak

Left Shift key (Shift; strike key; release both quickly.)

4 Lt. Ho said he left the skiff at Ord Lake for her.

5 Jane or Hal is to go to Lake Head to see Kate Orr.

6 O. J. Halak is to ask for her at Jahn Hall at one.

Key words (*Think, say,* and *key* the words.)

1 an the did oak she for off tie got and led jar all

2 go end air her dog his aid rid sit and fir ask jet

3 talk side jell gold fled sign stir fork high shall

Key phrases (*Think, say,* and *key* the phrases.)

4 to do|it is|of an|if he|is to|or do|to it|if he is

5 to aid|if she|he did|of the|to all|is for|is a tie

6 is to ask|is to aid|he or she|to rig it|if she did

Key sentences (Strike keys at a brisk, steady pace.)

7 Joan is to go to the lake to get her old red skis.

8 Les asked for a list of all the old gold she sold.

9 Laska said she left the old disk list on his desk.

Format and key the attached information as a flyer to be distributed at the symposium. Consider some type of border.

Please format the attached text as a letter to the convention manager of the Carrington Hotel. List each enclosure separately.

Please fax the attached note to Lynelle Montgomery at the Carrington Hotel.

Exhibitors — DS

Telephone Specialists, Inc.
ECL Communication Systems
Computer Networking
Business Computer Connections
Computer Systems Design
HMG Computer Consultants
Mobile Communications
Telecommunications Consultants
The FAX IT Company
Teleconferencing Solutions
Freelance Computing
Micros in Action

*Resource Systems
Voice Connections*

Alphabetize

Enclosed is a copy of our symposium brochure. The schedule is printed on the inside cover.

A copy of the contract for our keynote speaker, who will present on Friday, August 8, from 1:30-3:00, is also enclosed. Approximately 250 participants will attend this session. The requirements that would pertain to the hotel setup are listed under the "Additional Terms and Considerations" section. Please let me know if you will be able to accommodate his requests.

Are you still planning for this session to be held in the Colorado Ballroom? As indicated on the contract, he would like the participants to be seated at tables.

Will July 20 fit your schedule for meeting with my assistant and me to discuss final details for the symposium? Please give me a call to confirm a meeting time.

I still have not received a copy of your audio-visual request list. Please fax me a copy ASAP.

New Keys: U and C

Objectives:

1. To learn reach technique for **U** and **C**.
2. To combine smoothly **U** and **C** with all other learned keys.

9A • 8
Conditioning Practice

each line twice SS (slowly, then faster); DS between 2-line groups

reach review 1 `nj gf ol rf ik ed .l tf hj fr ki ft jn de lo fg l.`

space bar 2 `an do in so to go fan hen log gin tan son not sign`

left shift 3 `Olga has the first slot; Jena is to skate for her.`

9B • 20
New Keys: U and C

each line twice SS (slowly, then faster); DS between 2-line groups: if time permits, repeat lines 7-9

Follow the *Standard Plan for Learning New Keys* outlined on p. 17.

u *Right index* finger

c *Left middle* finger

Learn u

1 `j j uj uj us us us jug jug jut jut due due fur fur`

2 `uj uj jug jug sue sue lug lug use use lug lug dues`

3 `a jug; due us; the fur; use it; a fur rug; is just`

Learn c

4 `d d cd cd cod cod cog cog tic tic cot cot can cans`

5 `cd cd cod cod ice ice can can code code dock docks`

6 `a cod; a cog; the ice; she can; the dock; the code`

Combine u and c

7 `cud cud cut cuts cur curs cue cues duck ducks clue`

8 `a cud; a cur; to cut; the cue; the cure; for luck;`

9 `use a clue; a fur coat; take the cue; cut the cake`

Instructions from Katelynn Eastwick June 5

Format the attached text as a two-page form letter. Eventually the letter will be sent to the Region 6 database. To check to make sure the merge will work, merge the letter with the following two addressees.

Mr. Douglas Smith
Hoyle Glass Company
308 Folsom St.
Boulder, CO 80302-0467

Ms. Kara Timms
The Printer's Company
480 Orchard Ct.
Golden, CO 80403-7512

<Date>

<Title> <First Name> <Last Name>
<Company Name>
<Address>
<City,> <State> <ZIP>

Dear <Title> <Last Name>

Plan now to attend "A Technology Vision" symposium on August 8-9 in Denver, Colorado. As today's technology continues to evolve, it becomes increasingly important for business executives to take an active leadership role in determining the role technology will play in their organizations.

Prominent technology presenters from throughout the United States will be in Denver to share their expertise with symposium participants from the Western Region. Time during the symposium will be dedicated to informal small-group discussions in which participants will be able to meet with other executives in their job-related fields to share ideas.

Dr. Jon Mathis from the Devlin Institute of Technology will be the keynote speaker. His presentation will focus on technology "Risk Takers" and the impact they have had on their organizations. The program will be completed with other prominent business and educational experts in the field of technology.

One of the suggestions from last year's symposium was to have some type of entertainment arranged for the group during the evening. On Friday night, arrangements have been made to attend a Colorado Rockies' baseball game. Saturday night's entertainment features a performance of the Denver Symphony. Of course, Denver offers a variety of other types of entertainment options for those who do not want to participate in the group functions.

Complete the enclosed form to ensure your meeting and hotel reservations at this year's symposium.

Sincerely

The newly renovated Carrington Hotel in downtown Denver is the location for the symposium. The hotel is located a block from the capitol building and is within walking distance of many fine restaurants, shopping, and entertainment. The check-in time is 7:30 a.m. in the main lobby of the hotel. A complimentary continental breakfast will be served in Conference Room 22 from 7:45 - 9:00.

9C • 17
New-Key Mastery

1. Key the lines once SS; DS between 2-line groups.
2. Key the lines again at a faster pace.

Technique goals
- reach up without moving hands away from you
- reach down without moving hands toward your body
- use quick-snap keystrokes

3d/1st rows
1 in cut nut ran cue can cot fun hen car urn den cog
2 Nan is cute; he is curt; turn a cog; he can use it

left shift and .
3 Kae had taken a lead. Jack then cut ahead of her.
4 I said to use Kan. for Kansas and Ore. for Oregon.

key words
5 and cue for jut end kit led old fit just golf coed
6 an due cut such fuss rich lack turn dock turf curl

key phrases
7 an urn|is due|to cut|for us|to use|cut off|such as
8 just in|code it|turn on|cure it|as such|is in luck

all keys learned
9 Nida is to get the ice; Jacki is to call for cola.
10 Ira is sure that he can go there in an hour or so.

9D • 5
Technique: Space Bar and Left Shift

Key the lines once SS; DS between 3-line groups. Keep hand movement to a minimum.

space bar
1 Ken said he is to sign the list and take the disk.
2 It is right for her to take the lei if it is hers.
3 Jae has gone to see an old oaken desk at the sale.

left shift
4 He said to enter Oh. for Ohio and Kan. for Kansas.
5 It is said that Lt. Li has an old jet at Lake Ida.
6 L. N. is at the King Hotel; Harl is at the Leland.

R&e

1. Key each line once SS; DS between 2-line groups.
2. If time permits, key the lines again at a faster pace.

PRACTICE *cue*:
Try to reduce hand movement and the tendency of unused fingers to fly out or follow reaching finger.

u/c
1 uj cd uc juj dcd cud cut use cog cue urn curl luck
2 Huck can use the urn for the social at the church.

n/g
3 nj gf nj gin can jog nick sign nigh snug rung clog
4 Nan can jog to the large sign at the old lake gin.

all keys learned
5 nj gf uj cd ol tf ik rf hj ed an go or is to he l.
6 Leona has gone to ski; Jack had left here at nine.

all keys learned
7 an or is to he go cue for and jak she all use curt
8 Nick sells jade rings; Jahn got one for good luck.

Instructions from Katelynn Eastwick June 5

Format and key the attached presenter information sheet; attach a copy to the Mathis letter. I have given some formatting guidelines. Let's plan on a two-page format. Use fonts and shading if available.

"A Technology Vision" Symposium

August 8-9, ----

SYMPOSIUM PRESENTER INFORMATION SHEET

Name: _____

Home Address: _____

City: _____ **State:** _____ **ZIP:** _____

Telephone Number: _____ *Social Security Number* _____

Please return this form and your biographical sketch (p. 2) by June 15, ----, to Ms. Katelynn Eastwick, Professional Symposium Specialists, 429 Kentwood Dr., Eugene, OR 97401-8392.

* * * * *

Please write a brief description of your presentation as you would like it to appear in the symposium program.

2"

Please indicate the audio visual equipment that will be required for your presentation.

_____ **Overhead Projector**
_____ **Screen**
_____ **35 MM Slide Projector**
_____ **Color LCD Data Projection**
_____ **VCR and Monitor**
_____ **Flipchart**
_____ **Laser Pointer**
_____ **Computer**
_____ **Compact Disc Player**
_____ **Easel**
_____ **Whiteboard with Marker**
_____ **Speaker Phone**
_____ **Interactive Teleconference Hookup**
_____ **Power Strip**

___ *Extension Cord*

*PRESENTER INFORMATION SHEET
Page 2
Please give a brief biographical sketch for your symposium introduction.*

Objectives:

1. To learn reach technique for **W** and **Right Shift**.

2. To combine smoothly **W** and **Right Shift** with other learned keys.

10A • 8
Conditioning Practice

each line twice SS (slowly, then faster); DS between 2-line groups

reach review 1 a;sldkfj a;sldkfj uj cd ik rf nj ed hj tf ol gf .1

u/c 2 us cod use cut sue cot jut cog nut cue con lug ice

all letters learned 3 Hugh has just taken a lead in a race for a record.

10B • 20
New Keys: W and Right Shift

each line twice SS (slowly, then faster); DS between 2-line groups; if time permits, repeat lines 7-9

w *Left ring* finger

Right Shift *Right little* finger

SHIFTING *cue:*
Shift, strike key, and release both in a quick 1-2-3 count.

Follow the *Standard Plan for Learning New Keys* outlined on p. 17.

Learn w

1 s s ws ws sow sow wow wow low low how how cow cows

2 sw sw ws ws ow ow now now row row own own tow tows

3 to sow; is how; so low; to own; too low; is to row

Learn Right Shift key

4 A; A; Al Al; Cal Cal; Ali or Flo; Di and Sol left.

5 Ali lost to Ron; Cal lost to Elsa; Di lost to Del.

6 Tina has left for Tucson; Dori can find her there.

Combine w and Right Shift

7 Dodi will ask if Willa went to Town Center at two.

8 Wilf left the show for which he won a Gower Award.

9 Walt will go to Rio on a golf tour with Wolf Lowe.

Professional Symposium Specialists

Objectives:

1. To improve your document processing skills by keying from rough draft and script.
2. To improve your ability to read and follow directions.
3. To improve your ability to detect and correct unmarked errors.

139-144A 5 (daily)
Conditioning Practice

each line twice

alphabet 1 Dr. Jurwin gave both of them excellent marks on the physics quiz.

speed 2 She may sign the form by proxy if they make an audit of the firm.

fig/sym 3 Jay & Cey wrote Check #99 for $425.76 and Check #100 for $380.75.

gwam 1' | 1 | 2 | 3 | 4 | 5 | 6 | 7 | 8 | 9 | 10 | 11 | 12 | 13 |

139-144B ● 45 (daily)
Work Assignments

Job 1

Instructions from Katelynn Eastwick June 5

Two additional speakers have agreed to present at the Denver Symposium. Please send the attached letter to them. Do NOT include the script paragraph with the letter you send to Chadwick.

Dr. Jon Mathis
310 Buckeye St.
Toledo, OH 43611-1234

Mr. Chad Chadwick
4920 Hickory Dr., N.
Boise, ID 83704-2839

<Date>

<Title> <First Name> <Last Name>
<Address>
<City,> <State> <ZIP>

Dear <Title> <Last Name>

Thank you for agreeing to be a speaker for Professional Symposium Specialists. As we discussed on the telephone, the symposium is scheduled for August 8 and 9 at the Carrington Hotel in Denver, Colorado. The theme for the symposium is "A Technology Vision."

Your presentation is scheduled for Friday, August 8, at 1:30 p.m. A presenter form is enclosed for you to complete and return to me by June 15. The information you provide will be used for the symposium program and for your introduction. A copy of one of the pages from last year's program is enclosed to give you an idea of the short descriptions that were used last year.

I am looking forward to meeting you on August 8. If you have questions before I contact you again, please call me at 503-139-4877.

I checked with the home office in Boston; they gave me permission to increase the honorarium to $2,500. Your expenses, of course, will be covered by our company.

10C • 17
New-Key Mastery

1. Key the lines once SS; DS between 2-line groups.
2. Key the lines again at a faster pace.

PRACTICE _cues:_

Key at a steady pace; space quickly after each word; keep cursor or print point moving steadily.

Goal: finger-action reaches; quiet hands and arms

w and right shift	1 Dr. Rowe is in Tulsa now; Dr. Cowan will see Rolf.
	2 Gwinn took the gown to Golda Swit on Downs Circle.
n/g	3 to go|go on|no go|an urn|dug in|and got|and a sign
	4 He is to sign for the urn to go on the high chest.
key words	5 if ow us or go he an it of own did oak the cut jug
	6 do all and for cog odd ant fig rug low cue row end
key phrases	7 we did|for a jar|she is due|cut the oak|he owns it
	8 all of us|to own the|she is to go|when he has gone
all keys learned	9 Jan and Chris are gone; Di and Nick get here soon.
	10 Doug will work for her at the new store in Newton.

10D • 5
Technique: Spacing with Punctuation

each line once DS

SPACING _cues:_

Do not space after an internal period in an abbreviation; space once after each period following initials.

No space   Space once.

1 Use i.e. for that is; cs. for case; ck. for check.

2 Dr. Wong said to use wt. for weight; in. for inch.

3 R. D. Roth has used ed. for editor; Rt. for Route.

4 Wes said Ed Rowan got an Ed.D. degree last winter.

R&e

1. Key each pair of lines once SS.
2. Key each even-numbered line again to increase speed.

Technique goals
- steady hands/arms
- finger-action keystrokes
- unused fingers curved, upright over home keys
- eyes on copy as you key

u/c	1 uj cd uc cut cut cue cue use use cod cod dock dock
	2 Jud is to cut the corn near the dock for his aunt.
w and right shift	3 Don and Willa|Dot or Wilda|R. W. Gowan|Dr. Wilford
	4 Dr. Wold will set the wrist of Sgt. Wills at noon.
left shift and .	5 Jane or Harl|Jae and Nan|L. N. Hagel|Lt. J. O. Hao
	6 Lt. Hawser said that he will see us in New London.
n/g	7 nj gf ng gun gun nag nag got got nor nor sign sign
	8 Angie hung a huge sign in front of the union hall.
o/t	9 ol tf to too dot dot not not toe toe got gild gild
	10 Todd took the tool chest to the dock for a worker.
i/r	11 ik rf or ore fir fir sir sir ire ire ice ice irons
	12 Risa fired the fir log to heat rice for the girls.
h/e	13 hj ed he the the hen hen when when then then their
	14 He was with her when she chose her new snow shoes.

Table with Clip Art

Forms with Script Font and Shading

Work Assignment

You have accepted a position with Professional Symposium Specialists (PSS) as an assistant to the branch manager. PSS sponsors professional business meetings designed to enhance the expertise of those attending the meetings. A broad range of timely topics—technology, motivation, communication, leadership, etc.— are covered at the meetings. Each symposium features short addresses from well-recognized authorities on the topic. These speakers are brought in from throughout the United States.

You will work for Katelynn Eastwick, who is the branch manager for the Western Region of PSS. As an executive assistant, you will assist Ms. Eastwick in coordinating the symposiums. Currently Ms. Eastwick is working on a technology symposium being held in the Western Region. The documents you create for this simulation all relate to the technology symposium that will be held in Denver, Colorado, on August 8 and 9.

During your training program, you were instructed to use the unbound format for all reports and the block format with open punctuation for all company letters. Ms. Eastwick likes all her letters closed as follows:

```
Sincerely

Ms. Katelynn Eastwick
Western Branch Manager
```

General processing instructions from Ms. Eastwick will be attached to each document you are given to process. Use the date included on the instructions for all documents requiring a date. You are to use your decision-making skills to arrange the documents in an attractive format. Since PSS has based its word processing manual on the Century 21 textbook, you can also use the text as a reference to assist you in making formatting decisions and learning how to enhance your documents.

Enhanced appearance. Utilize the features of your equipment/wp software to enhance the appearance of the documents. When enhancing the appearance, make sure that it is "tastefully" done, but not overdone. Consider such things as borders, font face, font size, bolding, and underlining. Use your creativity (see illustrations at left).

Notation for multiple enclosures. For documents with multiple enclosures, use the following enclosure notation format:

```
Enclosures:  Presenter Form
             Previous Program
```

Word processing features. You are expected to use the word processing features covered during your training period to decrease the amount of time required for document processing and to enhance the appearance of the documents you produce. Since time did not allow for all the features to be covered, you are expected to learn some of the features on your own. Review the Word Processing Features in the special index (p. 14) to determine which features can be used to facilitate the processing of the documents at PSS.

Business card for convention manager. When you met with the convention manager of the Carrington Hotel, she provided you with her business card.

Montgomery, Lynelle (Ms.)
Convention Manager
Carrington Hotel
310 Union Blvd.
Denver, CO 80228-8764

FAX: (303) 189-5555
Phone: (303) 189-5554
e-mail: montgolm@carringt.com

LESSON 11　New Keys:　B and Y

Objectives:

1. To learn reach technique for **B** and **Y**.
2. To combine smoothly **B** and **Y** with all other learned keys.

Fingers curved

Fingers upright

11A • 7
Conditioning Practice

each line twice SS (slowly, then faster); DS between 2-line groups

reach review　1　uj ws ik rf ol cd nj ed hj tf .l gf sw ju de lo fr

c/n　2　an can and cut end cue hen cog torn dock then sick

all letters learned　3　A kid had a jag of fruit on his cart in New Delhi.

11B • 5
Technique: Space Bar

each line once

Technique goal
Space with a down-and-in motion *immediately* after each word.

1　He will take an old urn to an art sale at the inn.

2　Ann has an old car she wants to sell at this sale.

3　Len is to work for us for a week at the lake dock.

4　Gwen is to sign for the auto we set aside for her.

5　Jan is in town for just one week to look for work.

6　Juan said he was in the auto when it hit the tree.

11C • 4
Technique: Return

1. Key each line once SS; return and start each new line quickly.
2. On line 4, see how many words you can key in 30 seconds (30").

1　Dot is to go at two.

2　He saw that it was a good law.

3　Rilla is to take the auto into the town.

4　Wilt has an old gold jug he can enter in the show.

gwam　1'　| 1 | 2 | 3 | 4 | 5 | 6 | 7 | 8 | 9 | 10 |

A **standard word** in keyboarding is 5 characters or any combination of 5 characters and spaces, as indicated by the number scale under line 4 above. The number of standard words keyed in 1' is called gross words a minute *(gwam)*.

To find 1-minute (1') *gwam*:

1. Note on the scale the figure beneath the last word you keyed. That is your 1' *gwam* if you key the line partially or only once.

2. If you completed the line once and started over, add the figure determined in Step 1 to the figure 10. The resulting figure is your 1' *gwam*.

To find 30-second (30") *gwam*:

1. Find 1' *gwam* (total words keyed).

2. Multiply 1' *gwam* by 2. The resulting figure is your 30" *gwam*.

Timed Writings: Straight Copy

1. A 5' writing on ¶s 1-3 combined; find *gwam*, determine errors.
2. Two 1' writings on each ¶; find *gwam*, determine errors.
3. Another 5' writing on ¶s 1-3 combined; find *gwam*, determine errors.

Additional Skill Building

1. Key a series of 1' guided writings on each of the 3 ¶s.
2. Key additional 5' writings to check skill increases.

all letters used

	gwam	3'	5'

New office technology continues to have a major impact on the way we exchange information. Until recently most of us shared information with other firms by using the mail service or by using the phone. Today we can still use those same media, or we can use newer electronic means to communicate with others. More and more people are using the newer electronic media because of the speed and ease with which information can be shared.

Electronic mail and fax transmission are among the most recent technologies that have had a great impact on the sending and receiving of data and text in the office. The fax machine is a machine that sends documents electronically from one place to another in a matter of a few seconds. Even though this concept is not a new one, its use in the office environment is relatively new. Even greater usage can be expected in the future.

It is hard to imagine the impact that future changes in technology will have on how we share data and text with others in the office. If changes in the next few years are as great as those we have had during the last few years, the impact will be quite amazing. Microcomputers, word processing packages, spreadsheets, and laser printers are all relatively new concepts in business. It really has not been all that long ago that most information was processed at a typewriter.

gwam	3'	1	2	3	4
	5'	1	2	3	

11D • 19
New Keys: B and Y

each line twice SS (slowly, then faster): DS between 2-line groups; QS between groupings; if time permits, rekey lines 7-9

Follow the *Standard Plan for Learning New Keys* outlined on p. 17.

b *Left index* finger

y *Right index* finger

Learn b

1 f f bf bf fib fib rob rob but but big big fib fibs
2 bf bf rob rob lob lob orb orb bid bid bud bud ribs
3 a rib; to fib; rub it; an orb; or rob; but she bid

Learn y

4 j j yj yj jay jay lay lay hay hay day day say says
5 yj yj jay jay eye eye dye dye yes yes yet yet jays
6 a jay; to say; an eye; he says; dye it; has an eye

Combine b and y

7 by by buy buy boy boy bye bye byte byte buoy buoys
8 by it; to buy; by you; a byte; the buoy; by and by
9 Jaye went by bus to the store to buy the big buoy.

11E • 15
New-Key Mastery

1. Key the lines once SS; DS between 2-line groups.
2. Key the lines again at a faster pace.

PRACTICE cues:
- reach up without moving hands away from you
- reach down without moving hands toward your body
- use quick-snap keystrokes

reach review
1 a;sldkfj bf ol ed yj ws ik rf hj cd nj tf .l gf uj
2 a kit low for jut led sow fob ask sun cud jet grow

3d/1st rows
3 no in bow any tub yen cut sub coy ran bin cow deck
4 Cody wants to buy this baby cub for the young boy.

key words
5 by and for the got all did but cut now say jut ask
6 work just such hand this goal boys held furl eight

key phrases
7 to do|can go|to bow|for all|did jet|ask her|to buy
8 if she|to work|and such|the goal|for this|held the

all letters learned
9 Becky has auburn hair and wide eyes of light jade.
10 Juan left Bobby at the dog show near our ice rink.

gwam	1'	1	2	3	4	5	6	7	8	9	10

Keying Technique
1. Key each line once.
2. Key a 1' writing on each even-numbered line.

Alphabetic

1 bug pair cute was fox hair very just zoo kite quiet long den moon
2 Jack Dover was extremely happy after completing the biology quiz.

Fig/sym

3 3/4" bolt | June 28, 1996 | check for $25.17 | 5:30 p.m. | 6.0% tax | $3.84
4 Your invoice (#392-587) for $31,286.00 was paid by check (#1544).

Bottom row

5 box can fax man van zoo came cozy main brain exact amount minimum
6 Maxine Zorn came by my vacant barn just moments ago to buy my ax.

Third row

7 out top up it tree yet pet were wet you trip quiet ripe troop pop
8 Reporter Wes Porter will take three tip top trees to the top row.

Space bar

9 say no may yet nice can day next boy up yell not box pins sin den
10 It will be a very nice day if I can get all my work done by noon.

Double letter

11 need grass cell afford better wood pebbles will dessert penniless
12 Betty and Bill will be attending the Phillies next baseball game.

Combination response

13 the bear | may exceed | their puppy | they created | and eggs | oak dresser
14 Gregg Kaufman stated the dreaded due dates of my eight tax forms.

Word response

15 men of owns firm end keys eight six wish visit so their town such
16 The firms may form a panel to handle the dismal problem downtown.

gwam 1' | 1 | 2 | 3 | 4 | 5 | 6 | 7 | 8 | 9 | 10 | 11 | 12 | 13 |

Tabulation
1. Clear tabs; set tabs 1", 2.5", and 4" from the left margin.
2. Key the text at the right.
3. Take three 1' writings.

Goal: Increase amount of text keyed in each writing.

				words
Kentucky	Louisiana	Maine	Maryland	7
Frankfort	Baton Rouge	Augusta	Annapolis	15
Massachusetts	Michigan	Minnesota	Mississippi	24
Boston	Lansing	St. Paul	Jackson	30
Missouri	Montana	Nebraska	Nevada	37
Jefferson City	Helena	Lincoln	Carson City	45
New Hampshire	New Jersey	New Mexico	New York	54
Concord	Trenton	Santa Fe	Albany	60

LESSON 12 Review

Objectives:
1. To improve spacing, shifting, and returning.
2. To increase keying control and speed.

Before you begin each practice session:

- Position your body directly in front of the keyboard; sit erect, with feet on the floor for balance.
- Curve your fingers deeply and place them in an upright position over the home keys.
- Position the textbook for easy reading (at about a 90° angle to the eyes).

Fingers properly curved

Fingers properly upright

Body properly positioned

12A • 7
Conditioning Practice

each line twice SS (slowly, then faster); DS between 2-line groups; if time permits, practice each line again

reach review 1 we ok at in be on by re no us if la do ah go C. J.

b/y 2 by rub jay fib lay rob hay big say buy boy yet but

all letters learned 3 Fran knew it was her job to guide your gold truck.

12B • 13
Technique: Space Bar and Shift Keys

1. Key lines once SS; DS between 2-line groups.
2. Key the lines again at a faster pace.

Down-and-in spacing

Out-and-down shifting

Space bar (Space *immediately* after each word.)

1 an by win buy den sly won they than flay when clay

2 in a way|on a day|buy a hen|a fine day|if they win

3 Jay can bid on the old clay urn he saw at the inn.

4 I know she is to be here soon to talk to the club.

Shift keys (Shift; strike key; release both quickly.)

5 Lt. Su; Nan and Dodi; Karl and Sol; Dr. O. C. Goya

6 Kara and Rod are in Italy; Jane and Bo go in June.

7 Sig and Bodie went to the lake with Cory and Lana.

8 Aida Rios and Jana Hardy work for us in Los Gatos.

Process Interview Follow-Up Letters

Objectives:

1. To learn/apply guides for formatting follow-up letters.

2. To compose an interview follow-up letter.

138A • 5
Conditioning Practice

each line twice

alphabet	1	Bo kept examining the size and quality of the very choice jewels.
speed	2	When the eight towns amend the maps, the visitor problem may end.
fig/sym	3	Add a tax of 5% to Sales Slip #437-92 to make a total of $182.60.

gwam 1' | 1 | 2 | 3 | 4 | 5 | 6 | 7 | 8 | 9 | 10 | 11 | 12 | 13 |

138B • 30
Follow-Up Letters

Document 1

Format and key the follow-up letter at the right to **Ms. St. John** as a personal-business letter from **Teresa A. Teasdale**. Refer to pages 324 and 325 for Ms. Teasdale's and Ms. St. John's addresses. Use **May 25, ----** for the date; supply missing letter parts. Use modified block format with mixed punctuation.

Document 2

Study the guides for interview follow-up letters on p. 323. Assume that you interviewed for the job you applied for in 135B, Document 2. Compose a follow-up letter; edit and prepare a final copy.

LANGUAGE SKILLS

138C • 15
Compose at the Keyboard

	words
opening	35

Thank you for discussing the secretarial opening at Regency Insurance [49] Company. I have a much better understanding of the position after meet- [63] ing with you and Ms. Meade. [69]

Ms. Meade was extremely helpful in explaining the specific job responsibili- [84] ties. My previous jobs and my business education classes required me to [99] complete many of the tasks that she mentioned. With minimal training, I [113] believe I could be an asset to your company. [123]

Even though I realize it will be a real challenge to replace a person like Ms. [138] Meade, it is a challenge that I will welcome. If there is further infor- [153] mation that would be helpful as you consider my application, please let me [168] know. [170]

closing [176]

1. During an interview, applicants are often asked to respond to questions similar to those shown below. Select three of the questions and compose your responses to each. Number your responses and DS between paragraphs.
2. Compose three questions that you would ask the interviewer during the interview.
3. Edit your copy, marking corrections and changes to improve sentence structure and organization.

1. What would you like to be doing five years from now?
2. Give three reasons why our firm should hire you.
3. Do your grades accurately reflect your ability?   Explain why or why not.
4. Are you considering further education?   Explain why or why not.
5. What are your greatest weaknesses?
6. What hourly wage should you be paid during the first year?
7. What are your major accomplishments in life?
8. What have you learned from previous employment?

12C • 15
Speed Building

1. Key the lines once SS; DS between 2-line groups.
2. Key the lines again at a faster pace.

Technique goals
- curved, upright fingers
- quiet hands/arms
- quick spacing—no pause between words
- finger-reach action to shift keys

Finger-action keystrokes

Down-and-in thumb motion

Key words and phrases (*Think, say,* and *key* words and phrases.)

1 by dig row off but and jet oak the cub all got rid
2 ah she own dug irk buy cog jak for yet ask led urn

3 of us | if the | all of | and do | cut it | he got | to do the
4 is to be | as it is | if we do | in all the | if we own it

All letters learned (Strike keys at a brisk, steady pace.)

5 Judy had gone for that big ice show at Lake Tahoe.
6 Jack said that all of you will find the right job.

7 Cindy has just left for work at the big ski lodge.
8 Rudy can take a good job at the lake if he wishes.

gwam 1' | 1 | 2 | 3 | 4 | 5 | 6 | 7 | 8 | 9 | 10 |

12D • 15
Speed Check

1. Key each line once DS. To DS when in SS mode, strike **Return/Enter** twice at line ends.
2. Key a 20-second (20") timed writing on each line. Your rate in gross words a minute *(gwam)* is shown word-for-word above the lines.
3. Key another 20" writing on each line. Try to increase your keying speed.

Goal: At least 15 *gwam*.

20" *gwam*

| | 3 | 6 | 9 | 12 | 15 | 18 | 21 | 24 | 27 | 30 |

1 Al is to do it.
2 Di has gone to work.
3 Jan is to go to the sale.
4 Rog is to row us to your dock.
5 Harl has an old kayak and two oars.
6 She told us to set a goal and go for it.
7 It is our job to see just how high we can go.
8 Jake will go to the city to work on the big signs.

R&e

1. Key each line twice SS (slowly, then faster); DS between 2-line groups.
2. Rekey the drill for better control of reach-strokes.

1 Rob saw the bird on the lake by the big boat dock.
2 June had left for the club just as the news ended.
3 Bro led a task force whose goal was to lower cost.
4 Lyn knew the surf was too rough for kids to enjoy.
5 Ceil hikes each day on the side roads near school.

gwam 1' | 1 | 2 | 3 | 4 | 5 | 6 | 7 | 8 | 9 | 10 |

¶ **Preparing Physically**   278

Preparing physically also plays an important part in planning   290
successful
for a ^interview. The interviewee should learn about appropri-   305
                                         prior to the interview
ate company dress and grooming standards^. The interviewer has   322
                                               _a_
to be able to picture the job applicant as ^person who would   335
                        Extreme _lc_   _image_
fit in well with current employees. ^Differences in ~~appearance~~   349

between current employees and the applicant make it difficult   361
                                              _p_
for the interviewer to picture the ap^licant as an employee of   374
his/her
~~their~~ company.   377

- -

137C • 7
Employment Test:
Timed Writing

1. A 5' writing on all ¶s.
2. Find _gwam_ and number of errors.

all letters used   gwam 3' 5'

```
            .    2    .    4    .    6    .    8    .    10   .
    Something that you can never escape is your attitude.  It    4  2 44
    12   .    14   .    16   .    18   .    20   .    22   .
will be with you forever.  However, you decide whether your     8  5 47
    24   .    26   .    28   .    30   .    32   .    34   .
attitude is an asset or a liability for you.  Your attitude    12  7 49
    36   .    38   .    40   .    42   .    44   .    46   .
reflects the way you feel about the world you abide in and     16  9 52
    48   .    50   .    52   .    54   .    56   .    58   .    60
everything that is a part of that world.  It reflects the way you  20 12 54
    .    62   .    64   .    66   .    68   .    70   .    72   .
feel about yourself, about your environment, and about other peo-  25 15 57
74   .    76   .    78   .    80   .    82   .    84   .    86
ple who are a part of your environment.  Oftentimes, people with  29 17 59
    .    88   .    90   .    92   .    94   .    96   .    98
a positive attitude are people who are extremely successful.   33 20 62

            .    2    .    4    .    6    .    8    .    10   .
    At times we all have experiences that cause us to be       36 22 64
    .    12   .    14   .    16   .    18   .    20   .    22   .
negative.  The difference between a positive and a negative per-  41 24 66
    24   .    26   .    28   .    30   .    32   .    34   .    36
son is that the positive person rebounds very quickly from a bad  45 27 69
    .    38   .    40   .    42   .    44   .    46   .    48
experience; the negative person does not.  The positive person is  49 30 72
    50   .    52   .    54   .    56   .    58   .    60   .
a person who usually looks to the bright side of things and    53 32 74
    62   .    64   .    66   .    68   .    70   .    72   .    74
recognizes the world as a place of promise, hope, joy, excite-  58 35 77
        .    76   .    78   .    80   .    82   .    84   .    86
ment, and purpose.  A negative person generally has just the   62 37 79
    .    88   .    90   .    92   .    94   .    96   .    98
opposite view of the world.  Remember, others want to be around  66 40 82
    100  .    102  .    104  .    106  .    108  .    110  .
those who are positive but tend to avoid those who are negative.  70 42 84
```

gwam 3' | 1 | 2 | 3 | 4 |
      5' | 1 | 2 | 3 |

New Keys: M and X

Objectives:

1. To learn reach technique for **M** and **X**.
2. To combine smoothly **M** and **X** with all other learned keys.

13A • 7
Conditioning Practice

each line twice SS (slowly, then faster); DS between 2-line groups

reach review 1 bf ol rf yj ed nj ws ik tf hj cd uj gf by us if ow

b/y 2 by bye boy buy yes fib dye bit yet but try bet you

all letters learned 3 Robby can win the gold if he just keys a new high.

13B • 20
New Keys: M and X

each line twice SS (slowly, then faster); DS between 2-line groups; if time permits, rekey lines 7-9

m *Right index* finger

x *Left ring* finger

Follow the *Standard Plan for Learning New Keys* outlined on p. 17.

Learn m

1 j j mj mj am am am me me ma ma jam jam ham ham yam

2 mj mj me me me may may yam yam dam dam men men jam

3 am to; if me; a man; a yam; a ham; he may; the hem

Learn x

4 s s xs xs ox ox ax ax six six fix fix fox fox axis

5 xs xs sx sx ox ox six six nix nix fix fix lax flax

6 a fox; an ox; fix it; by six; is lax; to fix an ax

Combine m and x

7 me ox am ax ma jam six ham mix fox men lax hem lox

8 to fix; am lax; mix it; may fix; six men; hex them

9 Mala can mix a ham salad for six; Max can fix tea.

Document 2
Table

DS; CS: 1"; center column headings

Document 3
Report

1. Process the copy at the right as a bound report with textual citations. Use **THE JOB INTERVIEW** for the title of the report.

2. Using the information given below, prepare a references list on a separate sheet.

Reynolds, Caroline. Dimensions in Professional Development. 4th ed. Cincinnati: South-Western Publishing Co., 1993.

Hirsch, Maurice L., Rob Anderson, and Susan Gabriel. Accounting and Communication. Cincinnati: South-Western Publishing Co., 1994.

			words
TELEPHONE PROFESSIONALS			5
Consulting Staff			8
Consultant	Specialty	Phone	14
Ken Allen	Teleconferencing	137-3897	21
Jared Austin	Specialty Training	137-3787	30
Marsha Barber	Phone Systems	137-3891	37
Grant Chi	Voice Mail	137-3792	43
Felipe Cruz	Phone Systems	137-3880	50
Tiffani Daniels	Customized Services	137-3884	59
Greg Grant	Voice Mail	137-3894	66
Sharon Norton	Intercom Systems	137-3781	74
Christian Ryan	Sound Paging	137-3888	81

heading 4

A successful letter of application and data sheet will result 16

in an invitation from a potential employer for an interview. Preparing 30

for the interview is just as important in obtaining employment 43

as developing an effective application letter and data sheet. 56

The interviewer's first impression of the applicant is 67
crucial to the success of the interview. This impression, 78
which may take as little as 60 seconds to form, determines 90
whether the interviewer is interested in learning more about 102
the potential employee. Therefore, the prospective employee 115
must make a special effort to ensure a positive first impres- 127
sion. Reynolds (1993, 57-61) suggested that to make that 138
positive first impression the applicant must be prepared men- 151
tally as well as physically. 157

Preparing Mentally 161
Preparing mentally includes learning as much as possible about the 174
company prior to the interview and anticipating questions that the employer may ask 191
during the interview. The person applying for the job should also formulate 206
questions to ask during the interview to learn as much as possible about the position and 224
the co. An interview should be considered as an interpersonal 238
conversation in which one person elicits information from 249
another. Both parties should gain some knowledge about the 261
other. (Hirsch, Anderson, and Gabriel, 1994, 164) 274

(continued on next page)

13C • 17
New-Key Mastery

1. Key each line once SS; DS between 2-line groups.
2. Key the lines again at a faster pace.

TECHNIQUE *cue:*
- reach up without moving hands away from you
- reach down without moving hands toward your body
- use quick-snap keystrokes

Goal: finger-action keystrokes; quiet hands and arms

3d/1st rows	1	by am end fix men box hem but six now cut gem ribs
	2	me ox buy den cub ran own form went oxen fine club
space bar	3	an of me do am if us or is by go ma so ah ox it ow
	4	by man buy fan jam can any tan may rob ham fun guy
key words	5	if us me do an sow the cut big jam rub oak lax boy
	6	curl work form born name flex just done many right
key phrases	7	or jam|if she|for me|is big|an end|or buy|is to be
	8	to fix|and cut|for work|and such|big firm|the call
all keys learned	9	Jacki is now at the gym; Lex is due there by four.
	10	Joni saw that she could fix my old bike for Gilda.

13D • 6
Technique: Spacing with Punctuation

each line once DS

SPACING *cue:*
Do not space after an internal period in an abbreviation, such as Ed.D.

1 Mrs. Dixon may take her Ed.D. exam early in March.
2 Lex may send a box c.o.d. to Ms. Fox in St. Croix.
3 J. D. and Max will go by boat to St. Louis in May.
4 Owen keyed ect. for etc. and lost the match to me.

1. Key each line twice SS (slowly, then faster); DS between 2-line groups.
2. Key each line once more at a faster pace.

PRACTICE *cue:*
Keep the cursor or print point moving steadily across each line (no pauses).

m/x	1	Max told them that he will next fix the main axle.
b/y	2	Byron said the boy went by bus to a bayou to hunt.
w/right shift	3	Wilf and Rona work in Tucson with Rowena and Drew.
u/c	4	Lucy cut a huge cake for just the four lucky boys.
./left shift	5	Mr. and Mrs. J. L. Nance set sail for Long Island.
n/g	6	Bing may bring a young trio to sing songs at noon.
o/t	7	Lottie will tell the two little boys a good story.
i/r	8	Ria said she will first build a large fire of fir.
h/e	9	Chet was here when the eight hikers hit the trail.

Process Employment Application Forms

Objectives:
1. To identify typical information on job application forms.
2. To complete an application form.

136A • 5
Conditioning Practice
each line twice

alphabet 1 As a freezing wave hit, the explorers quickly adjusted the beams.

speed 2 I may make the goal if I work with vigor and with the right form.

fig/sym 3 The balance due on Account #4982 after the 10% payment is $5,673.

gwam 1' | 1 | 2 | 3 | 4 | 5 | 6 | 7 | 8 | 9 | 10 | 11 | 12 | 13 |

136B • 45
Job Application Forms

Document 1
Key (or neatly print) the job application form on p. 327, using the form in stationery pack or one supplied by your teacher. Correct any errors you make as you key the copy.

Document 2
Complete an application for employment form to apply for the position you selected in Document 2, 135B. You should review the form and make a few notes before entering your personal data on the form.

Office Employment Test

Objectives:
1. To identify typical tasks in an office employment test.
2. To complete a simulated employment test.

137A • 5
Conditioning Practice
each line twice

alphabet 1 Those men were amazed by the quick, lively jumps of the gray fox.

speed 2 She may pay the men for the work and then go with us to the city.

fig/sym 3 Was Check #3657 for $98.40, dated May 21, 1996, made out to Matt?

gwam 1' | 1 | 2 | 3 | 4 | 5 | 6 | 7 | 8 | 9 | 10 | 11 | 12 | 13 |

FORMATTING

137B • 38
Employment Test

Document 1
Letter
Format the text at the right as a letter in block format with mixed punctuation. Use the current date.

	words
Ms. Carol Parker	Facilities Manager	Presido Industries	8290	12
Rockdale Dr.	Dallas, TX 75220-0396	Dear Ms. Parker:	22

You have probably heard the saying "Time is money." If you are concerned 37
about your company's time and money, you will be interested in hearing 51
how the **T**elephone **P**rofessionals can save your company both **Time** and 65
Money. 66

Improved technology continues to change the way a telephone can enhance 81
your business operations. Specialized business phone systems, call for- 95
warding, three-way calling, voice mail, and calling cards are only a few of 110
the options available today. 116

Please contact me at 137-3828 to arrange for one of our "**T**elephone **P**rofes- 131
sionals" to update you on your telephone options. 141

Sincerely, | Jason Hawthorn | New Accounts Manager | xx 151

LESSON 14 | New Keys: P and V

Objectives:

1. To learn reach technique for **P** and **V**.

2. To combine smoothly **P** and **V** with all other learned keys.

Fingers curved

Fingers upright

14A • 7
Conditioning Practice

each line twice SS (slowly, then faster); DS between 2-line groups

one-hand words	1	in we no ax my be on ad on re hi at ho cad him bet
phrases	2	is just|of work|to sign|of lace|to flex|got a form
all letters learned	3	Jo Buck won a gold medal for her sixth show entry.

14B • 20
New Keys: P and V

each line twice SS; DS between 2-line groups; if time permits, rekey lines 7-9

p *Right little* finger

v *Left index* finger

Follow the *Standard Plan for Learning New Keys* outlined on p. 17.

Learn p

1 ; ; p; p; pa pa up up apt apt pen pen lap lap kept

2 p; p; pa pa pa pan pan nap nap paw paw gap gap rap

3 a pen; a cap; apt to pay; pick it up; plan to keep

Learn v

4 f f vf vf via via vie vie have have five five live

5 vf vf vie vie vie van van view view dive dive jive

6 go via; vie for; has vim; a view; to live; or have

Combine p and v

7 up cup vie pen van cap vim rap have keep live plan

8 to vie; give up; pave it; very apt; vie for a cup;

9 Vic has a plan to have the van pick us up at five.

APPLICATION FOR EMPLOYMENT

PLEASE PRINT WITH BLACK INK OR USE TYPEWRITER

AN EQUAL OPPORTUNITY EMPLOYER

NAME (LAST, FIRST, MIDDLE INITIAL)	SOCIAL SECURITY NUMBER	CURRENT DATE
Teasdale, Teresa A.	368-56-2890	May 22, - - - -

ADDRESS (NUMBER, STREET, CITY, STATE, ZIP CODE)	HOME PHONE NO.
310 Royal Oak Ct. Daytona Beach, FL 32017-1157	(904)136-7289

REACH PHONE NO.	U.S. CITIZEN? YES X NO	DATE YOU CAN START June 8, - - - -

ARE YOU EMPLOYED NOW?	IF SO, MAY WE INQUIRE OF YOUR PRESENT EMPLOYER?
Yes	Yes

TYPE OF WORK DESIRED	REFERRED BY	SALARY DESIRED
Secretarial	Ms. Anna Cruz	$ Open

IF RELATED TO ANYONE IN OUR EMPLOY, STATE NAME AND POSITION

DO YOU HAVE ANY PHYSICAL CONDITION THAT MAY PREVENT YOU FROM PERFORMING CERTAIN KINDS OF WORK?   YES   NO X   IF YES, EXPLAIN

HAVE YOU EVER BEEN CONVICTED OF A FELONY?   YES   NO X   IF YES, EXPLAIN

EDUCATION

	EDUCATIONAL INSTITUTION	LOCATION (CITY, STATE)	DATES ATTENDED FROM MO. YR.	TO MO. YR.	DIPLOMA, DEGREE, OR CREDITS EARNED	CLASS STANDING (CHK QUARTER) 1	2	3	4	MAJOR SUBJECTS STUDIED
COLLEGE										
HIGH SCHOOL	Jefferson High School	Daytona Beach, FL	8 93	5 97	Diploma	X				Business Ed.
GRADE SCHOOL										
OTHER										

LIST BELOW THE POSITIONS THAT YOU HAVE HELD (LAST POSITION FIRST)

1. NAME AND ADDRESS OF FIRM	DESCRIBE POSITION RESPONSIBILITIES
Fischer Studio 839 Franklin Dr. Daytona Beach, FL 32019-8321	Studio Assistant. Schedule appointments, maintain customer database, respond to customer inquiries.
NAME OF SUPERVISOR Mr. Jeremiah Fischer	
EMPLOYED (MO-YR) FROM: 8/95 TO: Present	REASON FOR LEAVING

2. NAME AND ADDRESS OF FIRM	DESCRIBE POSITION RESPONSIBILITIES
The Printing Press 289 Seminole Ave. Daytona Beach, FL 32019-7585	Bookkeeper. Processed accounts receivable and reconciled bank statements.
NAME OF SUPERVISOR Ms. Ruth Stewart	
EMPLOYED (MO-YR) FROM: 5/94 TO: 7/95	REASON FOR LEAVING Started a new job.

3. NAME AND ADDRESS OF FIRM	DESCRIBE POSITION RESPONSIBILITIES
Camp Clearwater P.O. Box 382 Lake City, FL 32055-1749	Camp Assistant. Assisted Ms. Ramirez with various camp activities for 8- and 9-year-olds.
NAME OF SUPERVISOR Ms. Carmen G. Ramirez	
EMPLOYED (MO-YR) FROM: 6/93 TO: 8/93	REASON FOR LEAVING Summer employment.

I UNDERSTAND THAT I SHALL NOT BECOME AN EMPLOYEE UNTIL I HAVE SIGNED AN EMPLOYMENT AGREEMENT WITH THE FINAL APPROVAL OF THE EMPLOYER AND THAT SUCH EMPLOYMENT WILL BE SUBJECT TO VERIFICATION OF PREVIOUS EMPLOYMENT, DATA PROVIDED IN THIS APPLICATION, ANY RELATED DOCUMENTS, OR DATA SHEET. I KNOW THAT A REPORT MAY BE MADE THAT WILL INCLUDE INFORMATION CONCERNING ANY FACTOR THE EMPLOYER MIGHT FIND RELEVANT TO THE POSITION FOR WHICH I AM APPLYING, AND THAT I CAN MAKE A WRITTEN REQUEST FOR ADDITIONAL INFORMATION AS TO THE NATURE AND SCOPE OF THE REPORT IF ONE IS MADE.

Teresa A. Teasdale

SIGNATURE OF APPLICANT

14C • 17
New-Key Mastery

1. Key the lines once SS; DS between 2-line groups.
2. Key the lines again at a faster pace.

Technique goals
- reach up without moving hands away from you
- reach down without moving hands toward your body
- use quick-snap keystrokes

Goal: finger-action keystrokes; quiet hands and arms

reach review	1	vf p; xs mj ed yj ws nj rf ik tf ol cd hj gf uj bf
	2	if lap jag own may she for but van cub sod six oak
3d/1st rows	3	by vie pen vim cup six but now man nor ton may pan
	4	by six but now may cut sent me fine gems five reps
key words	5	with kept turn corn duty curl just have worn plans
	6	name burn form when jury glad vote exit came eight
key phrases	7	if they│he kept│with us│of land│burn it│to name it
	8	to plan│so sure│is glad│an exit│so much│to view it
all letters learned	9	Kevin does a top job on your flax farm with Craig.
	10	Dixon flew blue jets eight times over a city park.

14D • 6
Technique: Shift Keys and Return

Key each 2-line sentence once SS as "Return" is called every 30 seconds (30"). Leave a DS between sentences.

Goal: To reach the end of each line just as the 30" guide ("Return") is called.

The **30" *gwam* scale** shows your gross words a minute if you reach the end of each line as the 30" guide is called.

Eyes on copy as you shift and as you return

		gwam	30"	20"
1	Marv is to choose a high goal		12	18
2	and to do his best to make it.		12	18
3	Vi said she had to key from a book		14	21
4	as one test she took for a top job.		14	21
5	Lexi knows it is good to keep your goal		16	24
6	in mind as you key each line of a drill.		16	24
7	Viv can do well many of the tasks she tries;		18	27
8	she sets top goals and makes them one by one.		18	27

 R&e

1. Key each line once at a steady, easy pace to master reach-strokes.
2. Key each line again at a faster pace.

Technique goals
- keep fingers upright
- keep hands/arms steady

m/p	1	mj p; me up am pi jam apt ham pen map ape mop palm
	2	Pam may pack plums and grapes for my trip to camp.
b/x	3	bf xs be ax by xi fix box but lax buy fox bit flax
	4	Bix used the box of mix to fix bread for six boys.
y/v	5	yj vf buy vow boy vie soy vim very have your every
	6	Vinny may have you buy very heavy silk and velvet.

Check this application letter against the guidelines on p. 323. Note the kinds of information in each paragraph.

have been able to apply what I learned in these courses at Fischer Studio, where I have worked as a studio assistant for almost two years.

176
189

My work experience and school activities have given me the opportunity to work with people to achieve group goals. Participating in FBLA has given me an appreciation of the business world.

203
218
227

The opportunity to interview with you to discuss the possibility of employment will be greatly appreciated. Please call me at 136-7289 to arrange an interview.

242
257
260

Sincerely, | Ms. Teresa A. Teasdale | Enclosure

268

Document 2

Review the application letter guidelines on p. 323. Compose at the keyboard a rough-draft letter applying for one of the positions shown at the right. Edit/revise your letter; then process it in final form.

POSITIONS AVAILABLE

Office Work

Immediate opening for a dependable person to assist office manager. General office duties. Must be able to follow directions, key at least 55 wpm, and possess good telephone skills.

Should enjoy working with the public. Send data sheet and application letter to

Perry Sabato
Personnel Director
Blanchard Construction
310 Coronado St.
Anaheim, CA 92806-9276

Office Assistant

Small printing company has full-time position for an office assistant. Applicant must be able to key 45 wpm, process client orders, perform basic math operations, and project professional telephone image.

Apply to:

Jonathan Ryan
8290 Mercedes Dr.
Biloxi, MS 39531-0286

Word Processing

Rhodes Consulting Services has an opening in the Word Processing Department for a detail-oriented individual with excellent document processing skills.

Word processing training desirable. Must have keyboarding skill of 50 wpm.

Send letter of application and data sheet to

Ms. Christine Jackson
Rhodes Consulting Services
3498 Plymouth Rd.
Hartford, CT 06119-2411

Receptionist/Secretary

Small company seeks outgoing individual to do general office work. Responsibilities include answering phone, receiving clients, distributing mail, filing, and processing documents.

Interested applicants must have a minimum keyboarding skill of 55 wpm. Experience preferred, but will consider applicants with no previous experience who possess excellent keyboarding skills.

To apply, send letter of application and data sheet to
Director of Human Resources
Brooks Financial Services
482 Rosswood Ct.
Louisville, KY 40291-8329

LESSON 15

New Keys: Q and Comma (,)

Objectives:

1. To learn reach technique for **Q** and **,** (comma).
2. To combine smoothly **Q** and **,** (comma) with all other learned keys.

15A • 7
Conditioning Practice

each line twice SS (slowly, then faster); DS between 2-line groups; if time permits, rekey the lines

all letters learned   1   do fix all cut via own buy for the jam cop ask dig

p/v   2   a map; a van; apt to; vie for; her plan; have five

all letters learned   3   Beth will pack sixty pints of guava jam for David.

15B • 20
New Keys: Q and , (Comma)

each line twice SS; DS between 2-line groups; if time permits, rekey lines 7-9

Follow the *Standard Plan for Learning New Keys* outlined on p. 17.

q *Left little* finger

, (comma) *Right middle* finger

SPACING cue:
Space once after , used as punctuation.

Learn q

1 a qa qa aq aq quo quo qt. qt. quad quad quit quits

2 qa quo quo qt. qt. quay quay aqua aqua quite quite

3 a qt.; pro quo; a quad; to quit; the quay; a squad

Learn , (comma)

4 k k ,k ,k kit, kit; Rick, Ike, or I will go, also.

5 a ski, a ski; a kit, a kit; a kite, a kite; a bike

6 Ike, I see, is here; Pam, I am told, will be late.

Combine q and , (comma)

7 Enter the words quo, quote, quit, quite, and aqua.

8 I have quit the squad, Quen; Raquel has quit, too.

9 Marquis, Quent, and Quig were quite quick to quit.

LESSON 134

Process Data Sheets MLS

Objectives:
1. To learn/apply guides for formatting a data sheet.
2. To compose a personal data sheet.

134A • 5
Conditioning Practice

each line twice

alphabet 1 Wexford enjoyed checking the problems on the quiz he gave Friday.

speed 2 Sign the form for the firm to pay the men for their work with us.

figures 3 On May 20, 1997, I moved from 468 Oak Street to 5371 Glenn Drive.

gwam 1' | 1 | 2 | 3 | 4 | 5 | 6 | 7 | 8 | 9 | 10 | 11 | 12 | 13 |

134B • 45
Data Sheets

Document 1
Format and key the data sheet on page 324.

Document 2
Compose at the keyboard a rough-draft data sheet for yourself using the guidelines on p. 323 and the model on p. 324. Edit; then key a final copy.

LESSON 135

Process Application Letters MLS

Objectives:
1. To learn/apply guides for formatting an application letter.
2. To compose an application letter in response to job ads.

135A • 5
Conditioning Practice

each line twice

alphabet 1 Kevin justified his low quiz score by explaining his unusual problems.

speed 2 She and the neighbor may go downtown to sign the form for the auditor.

figures 3 Of the 830 surveyed, only 256 knew the importance of December 7, 1941.

gwam 1' | 1 | 2 | 3 | 4 | 5 | 6 | 7 | 8 | 9 | 10 | 11 | 12 | 13 | 14 |

F ORMATTING

135B • 45
Application Letters

Document 1

Format and key the application letter for Ms. Teresa A. Teasdale. Format as a personal-business letter in modified block with mixed punctuation. If necessary, refer to the illustration on p. 124. Use the data sheet on p. 324 for the return address for Ms. Teasdale.

	words
opening	10

May 10, ---- | Ms. Jenna St. John | Personnel Director | Regency Insur- | 23
ance Company | 4291 Imperial Dr. | Daytona Beach, FL 32017-3856 | | 35
Dear Ms. St. John: | 39

Ms. Anna Cruz, my information processing instructor, informed me of the | 54
secretarial position with your company that will be available June 15. She | 69
speaks very highly of your organization. After learning more about the | 83
position, I am confident that I am qualified and would like to be considered | 98
for the position. | 102

Currently I am completing my senior year at Jefferson High School. All of | 117
my elective courses have been in the information processing area. I have | 132
completed the advanced course in document formatting, the database and | 146
spreadsheet applications course, and the business procedures course. I | 161

(continued on next page)

New-Key Mastery

1. Key lines once SS; DS between 2-line groups.
2. Key the lines again at a faster pace.

Technique goals

- reach *up* without moving hands away from you
- reach *down* without moving hands toward your body
- use quick-snap keystrokes

Goal: finger-action keystrokes; quiet hands and arms

reach review
1 qa .l ws ,k ed nj rf mj tf p; xs ol cd ik vf hj bf
2 yj gf hj quo vie pay cut now buy got mix vow forms

3d/1st rows
3 six may sun coy cue mud jar win via pick turn bike
4 to go|to win|for me|a peck|a quay|by then|the vote

key words
5 pa rub sit man for own fix jam via cod oak the got
6 by quo sub lay apt mix irk pay when rope give just

key phrases
7 an ox|of all|is to go|if he is|it is due|to pay us
8 if we pay|is of age|up to you|so we own|she saw me

all letters learned
9 Jevon will fix my pool deck if the big rain quits.
10 Verna did fly quick jets to map the six big towns.

15D • 6

Technique: Spacing with Punctuation

each line once DS

SPACING *cue:*
Space once after , and ; used as punctuation.

Space once.

1 Aqua means water, Quen; also, it is a unique blue.
2 Quince, enter qt. for quart; also, sq. for square.
3 Ship the desk c.o.d. to Dr. Quig at La Quinta Inn.
4 Q. J. took squid and squash; Monique, roast quail.

R&e

each set of lines twice SS (once slowly; then again at a faster pace); DS between 6-line groups

Technique goals
lines 1-3
fingers upright
lines 4-6
hands/arms steady
lines 7-9
two quick taps of each doubled letter

Adjacent keys

1 re io as lk rt jk df op ds uy ew vc mn gf hj sa ui
2 as ore ask opt buy pew say art owe try oil gas her
3 Sandy said we ought to buy gifts at her new store.

Long direct reaches

4 ce un gr mu br ny rv ym rb my ice any mug orb grow
5 nice curb must brow much fume sync many dumb curve
6 Brian must bring the ice to the curb for my uncle.

Double letters

7 all off odd too see err boo lee add call heed good
8 door meek seen huff less will soon food leek offer
9 Lee will seek help to get all food cooked by noon.

Teresa A. Teasdale
310 Royal Oak Ct.
Daytona Beach, FL 32017-1157
(904) 136-7289

EDUCATION

    Senior at Jefferson High School
    High School Diploma, pending graduation
    Major emphasis: Administrative Services
    Grade Average: 3.70; upper 10% of class

SCHOOL ACTIVITIES

    Editor, Jefferson Telegram, senior year; reporter for two
    years.

    Vice President, Future Business Leaders of America, senior
    year; member for three years.

    National Honor Society, junior and senior years.

WORK EXPERIENCE

    Studio Assistant, Fischer Studio, Daytona Beach, FL, August
    1995 to present. Work 15 hours a week as a studio assistant;
    schedule appointments, maintain customer database, and
    respond to customer inquiries.

    Bookkeeper, The Printing Press, Daytona Beach, FL, May 1994 to
    July 1995. Processed accounts receivable and reconciled bank
    statements.

    Camp Assistant, Camp Clearwater, Lake City, FL, summer 1993.

REFERENCES (by permission)

    Ms. Ann C. Rutgers, Administrative Services Instructor,
    Jefferson High School, 8230 Riverwood Dr., Daytona Beach, FL
    32019-3827, (904) 132-8286.

    Mr. Jeremiah Fischer, Owner, Fischer Studio, 839 Franklin Dr.,
    Daytona Beach, FL 32019-8321, (904) 136-8256.

    Ms. Ruth Stewart, Manager, The Printing Press, 289 Seminole
    Ave., Daytona Beach, FL 32019-7585, (904) 132-2819.

Data Sheet

LESSON 16

Review

Objectives:
1. To learn to key block paragraphs.
2. To improve keying technique and speed.

Fingers curved

Fingers properly aligned

16A • 7
Conditioning Practice

each line twice SS (slowly, then faster); DS between 2-line groups; if time permits, practice each line again

reach review 1 Virgil plans to find that mosque by six with Jack.

shift keys 2 Pam, Van, and Quin have to be in New Hope by five.

easy 3 Vi is to aid the girl with the sign work at eight.

gwam 1' | 1 | 2 | 3 | 4 | 5 | 6 | 7 | 8 | 9 | 10 |

16B • 10
Block Paragraphs

each paragraph (¶) once SS; DS between ¶s; then key the ¶s again at a faster pace

If your equipment has **automatic return** (word-wrap), do *not* strike **Enter** at the end of each line; the equipment will return for you with what is called a "soft return." You must, however, strike **Enter** twice ("hard returns") at the end of ¶ 1 to leave a DS between ¶s.

Paragraph 1

gwam 1'

When you strike the return or enter key at the end   10
of a line to space down and start a new line, this   20
process is called a hard return.   26

Paragraph 2

If a machine returns at line ends for you, what is   10
known as a soft return or wordwrap is in use. You   20
must use a hard return, though, between paragraphs.   30

gwam 1' | 1 | 2 | 3 | 4 | 5 | 6 | 7 | 8 | 9 | 10 |

16C • 10
Speed Check

1. Key a 30-second (30") timed writing on each line. Your rate in gross words a minute (*gwam*) is shown word for word above the lines.

2. If time permits, key another 30" writing on each line. Try to increase your keying speed.

Goal: At least 18 *gwam*.

30" *gwam*

    2   4   6   8   10   12   14   16   18   20

1 I am to fix the sign for them.

2 Jaye held the key to the blue auto.

3 Todd is to go to the city dock for fish.

4 Vi paid the girl to make a big bowl of salad.

5 Kal may keep the urn he just won at the quay show.

| 2| 4| 6| 8| 10| 12| 14| 16| 18| 20

If you finish a line before time is called and start over, your *gwam* is the figure at the end of the line PLUS the figure above or below the point at which you stopped.

Format Guides:
Employment Documents

Application Letter

Job Application Documents

Extreme care should be given to the preparation of all employment documents. The data sheet, application letter, and application form are often the basis of an employer's first impression of an applicant. These documents often determine whether an applicant is invited for an interview.

Prepare application documents on a keyboard with the possible exception of the application form. You may be asked to complete the application form at the time of the interview, in which case it should be neatly prepared with a pen. Always use high-quality paper when preparing your data sheet and application letter. Make sure that each document you prepare contains accurate, appropriate information that is neat, grammatical, and well arranged.

Data sheet. In most cases, a data sheet should be limited to one page. The information presented usually covers five major areas: personal information (your name, address, and telephone number), education (courses taken, skills acquired, grades earned), school activities (organizations, positions, years involved) work experience (position, name and location of place employed, brief description of respon-sibilities), and references (reference, title, organization, address, phone number). The data sheet may also include sections listing community activities and hobbies and/or special interests.

Top, bottom, and side margins may vary depending on the amount of information presented. The specific format may also vary with personal preference. In general, the most important information is presented first, which means that a person who has been out of school for several years and has considerable work experience may place that information before educational background information.

References, however, are usually the last item on the page. (Always get permission from the individuals you plan to include as references on your data sheet before using their names.)

Application letter. An application letter should always accompany a data sheet. The letter is formatted as a personal-business letter and should be limited to one page.

The first paragraph of the application letter should indicate the position for which you are applying and how you learned of the position. It is also appropriate to include something positive that you know about the company or someone who works for the company in the opening paragraph.

The next one or two paragraphs are used to convince the reader that you understand the requirements for the position and to explain how your background experiences qualify you for the position for which you are applying. You may do this by elaborating on some of the information included on your data sheet, such as courses taken and skills achieved. End the paragraph by inviting the reader to refer to the enclosed data sheet for additional information.

The final paragraph is used to request an interview. Information is also provided to make it easy for the reader to contact you to make arrangements for the interview.

Interview follow-up letter. Appreciation for an interview is conveyed in a follow-up letter, also called a thank-you letter. In addition to thanking the interviewer for the interview, the follow-up letter may state that you are still interested in the job. The letter can provide any additional relevant information and give positive impressions of the company and/or people you met. To be effective, the letter should be written immediately following the interview. This will increase the likelihood that the interviewer will receive the letter before a hiring decision is made.

16D • 12
Technique: Space Bar and Shift Keys

each line twice SS; DS between 4-line groups

Goals

- to reduce the pause between words
- to reduce the time taken to shift/strike key/release when making capital letters

Down-and-in spacing

Out-and-down shifting

Space bar (Space *immediately* after each word.)

1 so an if us am by or ox he own jay pen yam own may
2 she is in | am to pay | if he may | by the man | in a firm

3 I am to keep the pens in a cup by a tan mail tray.
4 Fran may try to fix an old toy for the little boy.

Shift keys (Shift; strike key; release both quickly.)

5 J. V., Dr. or Mrs., Ph.D. or Ed.D., Fourth of July
6 Mrs. Maria Fuente; Dr. Mark V. Quin; Mr. T. C. Ott

7 B. J. Marx will go to St. Croix in March with Lex.
8 Mae has a Ph.D. from Miami; Dex will get his Ed.D.

16E • 11
Speed Building

each line twice SS (slowly, then faster); DS between 4-line groups

Technique goals

- quick-snap keystrokes
- quick joining of letters to form words
- quick joining of words to form phrases

Key words and phrases (*Think, say,* and *key* words and phrases.)

1 ox jam for oak for pay got own the lap via sob cut
2 make than with them such they when both then their

3 to sit | an elf | by six | an oak | did go | for air | the jam
4 to vie | he owns | pay them | cut both | the quay | for they

Key sentences (Strike keys at a brisk, steady pace.)

all letters learned

5 I may have six quick jobs to get done for low pay.
6 Vicky packed the box with quail and jam for Signe.

all letters learned

7 Max can plan to bike for just five days with Quig.
8 Jim was quick to get the next top value for Debby.

R&e

1. Key each line once at a steady, easy pace to master reach-strokes.
2. Key each line again at a faster pace.

Technique goals

- keep fingers upright
- keep hands/arms steady

q/b

1 qa bf by quo but qt. quit both quad lube quid blow
2 Bob quickly won my squad over quip by brainy quip.

x/,

3 xs ,k sxs k,k ox ox, six six, flax flax, axle axle
4 I keyed ox, six, lox, mix, fox, fix, fax, and nix.

p/m

5 p; mj p.m. map amp pep mam mop imp camp ramp clump
6 Palma and her mom made peppy caps for my pep team.

v/y

7 vf yj ivy vary envy very wavy navy have many savvy
8 Levy may have to vary the way we serve and volley.

Activity 3:

1. Read carefully the material shown at the right.
2. Make your own list of "pet peeves" or violations of good manners (etiquette).
3. Compose/key a ¶ for each item on your list, indicating why it is the wrong thing to do (why it violates good manners and shows lack of consideration and respect for others).

Compose (think) as you key

Practicing good manners (etiquette) whether you are at home or in school, with your family or your friends, will help you acquire poise and self-assurance. Being well mannered means following the recognized rules of behavior that help to make your relationships with others more pleasant, whether you are in a private or a public place. The basis of good manners is kindness, thoughtfulness, and a deep concern for others. Good manners are a reflection of your attitude toward others—whether you like people, respect them, are interested in them, and make the effort to get along with them.

Some of the things people (young and old alike) do that show disrespect or a lack of concern for others are listed below.

1. Failure to introduce a companion to an acquaintance with whom you've stopped to chat.

2. Males wearing hats or caps indoors: classrooms, theaters, and restaurants, for example.

3. Loud conversations in the vicinity of others whom you may or may not know.

4. Using off-color or vulgar language to or in the vicinity of people whom you know or may not know.

5. Boisterous behavior in places that are supposed to be relatively quiet and serene (libraries, theaters, and hospitals, for example).

6. Leaning on the car horn while in a slow lane of traffic in an attempt to get slow movers out of the way, or driving well below the speed limit in the fast lane of an expressway.

7. Congregating in a doorway, hallway, or an aisle, preventing others from passing through.

8. Attacking a sandwich or plate of food with both hands in a gluttonous manner; chewing noisily and talking while the mouth is full.

9. Opening and walking through a door first while a companion trails behind instead of holding the door for a companion (male or female).

10. Calling people unflattering or negative (pejorative) names to get their attention or to minimize their self-esteem.

New Keys: Z and Colon (:)

Objectives:

1. To learn reach techniques for **Z** and : (colon).
2. To combine smoothly **Z** and : (colon) with all other learned keys.

17A • 7
Conditioning Practice

each line twice SS; then a 1' writing on line 3; find *gwam*

all letters learned	1 Jim won the globe for six quick sky dives in Napa.
spacing	2 to own │ is busy │ if they │ to town │ by them │ to the city
easy	3 She is to go to the city with us to sign the form.

gwam 1' │ 1 │ 2 │ 3 │ 4 │ 5 │ 6 │ 7 │ 8 │ 9 │ 10 │

17B • 18
New Keys: Z and : (Colon)

each line twice SS (slowly, then faster); DS between 2-line groups; if time permits, rekey lines 7-10

z *Left little* finger

: *Left Shift* and strike **:** key

LANGUAGE SKILLS *cues:*

• Space twice after **:** used as punctuation.

• Capitalize the first word of a complete sentence following a colon.

Follow the *Standard Plan for Learning New Keys* outlined on p. 17.

Learn z

1 a a za za zap zap zap zoo zoo zip zip zag zag zany

2 za za zap zap zed zed oz. oz. zoo zoo zip zip maze

3 zap it, zip it, an adz, to zap, the zoo, eight oz.

Learn : (colon)

4 ; ; :: :: Date: Time: Name: Room: From: File:

5 :; :; To: File: Reply to: Dear Al: Shift for :

6 Two spaces follow a colon, thus: Try these steps:

Combine z and :

7 Zelda has an old micro with : where ; ought to be.

8 Zoe, use as headings: To: Zone: Date: Subject:

9 Liza, please key these words: zap, maze, and zoo.

10 Zane read: Shift to enter : and then space twice.

Activity 1:

1. Study the spelling/definitions of the words in the color block at the right.
2. Key the **Learn** line in the first set of sentences.
3. Key the **Apply** lines, choosing the right words to complete each sentence correctly.
4. Key the second set of lines in the same way.
5. Check work; rekey lines containing word-choice errors.

Choose the right word

> **affect** (vb) to influence
> **effect** (n) result; consequence
>   (vb) to cause; to accomplish
>
> **advice** (n) opinion; recommendation
> **advise** (vb) to give advice; to recommend

Learn 1 The effect of the recent change will affect our annual profit.
Apply 2 Will cutting the staff 25 percent (affect/effect) worker morale?
Apply 3 What (affect/effect) will new equipment have on productivity?

Learn 4 Since you sought my advice, I advise you to go for the new job.
Apply 5 Ms. Chin will (advice/advise) music students on Friday mornings.
Apply 6 To keep all our options open was his (advice/advise) to us.

Activity 2:

1. Read the simplified memo shown at the right, noting corrections needed in capitalization, number expression, punctuation, word choice, and subject/predicate agreement.
2. Key the simplified memo, making whatever changes are needed to make the message correct.
3. Proofread your work and correct any remaining errors you find.

Proofread & correct

May 10, ----

Pamela E. Lonewolf, counselor

ENROLLMENT IN ART 1

Because of the recent new limits on class size in art you need to no that all Sections in art one are now filled. Over 40 students have already asked to take art 1 12 more than the three planned sections will accommodate.

If the principal mr. wilson don't add another section these twelve students (as well as any others who later apply will have to be turned away. Will you please speak with him? If you wish I'll be glad to join you in the discussion.

It may be that sum students who choose Art 1 as an elective should be rescheduled into other courses. Their not likely to be as upset as students who have chosen art as a career path.

Please advice me on what you plan to do to resolve this problem.

Anna Morningstar, assistant principal

17C • 15
New-Key Mastery

1. Key the lines once SS; DS between 2-line groups.
2. Key the lines again at a faster pace.

Technique goals
- curved, upright fingers
- quiet hands and arms
- steady keystroking pace

q/z
1 zoo qt. zap quo zeal quay zone quit maze quad hazy
2 Zeno amazed us all on the quiz but quit the squad.

p/x
3 apt six rip fix pens flex open flax drop next harp
4 Lex is apt to fix apple pie for the next six days.

v/m
5 vim mam van dim have move vamp more dive time five
6 Riva drove them to the mall in my vivid lemon van.

easy
7 Glen is to aid me with the work at the dog kennel.
8 Dodi is to go with the men to audit the six firms.

alphabet
9 Nigel saw a quick red fox jump over the lazy cubs.
10 Jacky can now give six big tips from the old quiz.

17D • 10
Block Paragraphs

1. Key each paragraph (¶) once SS; DS between them; then key them again faster.
2. If your teacher directs, key a 1' writing on each ¶; find your *gwam*.

Paragraph 1

gwam 1'

The space bar is a vital tool, for every fifth or   10
sixth stroke is a space when you key. If you use   20
it with good form, it will aid you to build speed. 30

Paragraph 2

Just keep the thumb low over the space bar. Move   10
the thumb down and in quickly toward your palm to   20
get the prized stroke you need to build top skill. 30

gwam 1' | 1 | 2 | 3 | 4 | 5 | 6 | 7 | 8 | 9 | 10 |

R&e

1. Key each line once at a steady, easy pace to master reach-strokes.
2. Key each line again at a faster pace.

Technique goals
- keep fingers upright
- keep hands/arms steady

x/:
1 xs :; | fix mix | Max: Use TO: and FROM: as headings.
2 Read and key: oxen, exit, axle, sixty, and sixth.

q/,
3 qa ,k | aqa k,k | quo quo, | qt. qt., | quite quite, | squat
4 Quen, key these: quit, aqua, equal, quiet, quick.

p/z
5 p; za | ;p; zaza | zap zap | zip zip | size size | lazy lazy
6 Zip put hot pepper on his pizza at the zany plaza.

m/v
7 mj vf | jmj fvf | vim vim | vow vow | menu menu | move movie
8 Mavis vowed to move with a lot more vim and vigor.

Document 2
Save as BANK2.

A&E Bank Card Application

Last Name	First	Middle	
White	Carlos	Benito	

Street Address	City	State	ZIP	Phone
9873 Clear Crossing Ln.	Charlotte	NC	28112-8309	704-126-1580

Birth Date (Month, Day, Year)	Social Security Number	Name of Employer
06-20-59	829-23-8729	Charlotte Legal Services

Address of Employer	City	State	Annual Income	Employer's Phone
390 Dunbar St., W.	Charlotte	NC	$55,000	704-140-5554

Document 3
Save as BANK3.

A&E Bank Card Application

Last Name	First	Middle	
Castillo	Mary	J.	

Street Address	City	State	ZIP	Phone
3820 Stonegate Ct.	Greensboro	NC	27406-8631	910-156-2798

Birth Date (Month, Day, Year)	Social Security Number	Name of Employer
04-15-57	389-56-9821	Rochelle Gallery

Address of Employer	City	State	Annual Income	Employer's Phone
310 Sherman St.	Greensboro	NC	$25,500	910-190-1200

Document 4
Save as BANK4.

A&E Bank Card Application

Last Name	First	Middle	
Russell	Reed	Martin	

Street Address	City	State	ZIP	Phone
8291 Regency Dr.	Charleston	WV	25341-9938	304-129-8292

Birth Date (Month, Day, Year)	Social Security Number	Name of Employer
12-24-57	389-51-8830	Auto Glass Specialists

Address of Employer	City	State	Annual Income	Employer's Phone
8392 White Oak Dr.	Charleston	WV	$18,000	304-128-7356

LESSON 18

New Keys: CAPS LOCK and Question Mark (?)

Objectives:
1. To learn reach technique for **CAPS LOCK** and **?** (question mark).
2. To combine smoothly **CAPS LOCK** and **?** (question mark) with other learned keys.

18A • 7
Conditioning Practice

each line twice SS; then a 1' writing on line 3; find *gwam:* total words keyed

alphabet	1	Lovak won the squad prize cup for sixty big jumps.
z/:	2	To: Ms. Mazie Pelzer; From: Dr. Eliza J. Piazzo.
easy	3	He is to go with me to the dock to do work for us.

gwam 1' | 1 | 2 | 3 | 4 | 5 | 6 | 7 | 8 | 9 | 10 |

18B • 16
New Keys: CAPS LOCK and ? (Question Mark)

each line twice SS (slowly, then faster); DS between 2-line groups; if time permits, rekey lines 7-9

Depress the CAPS LOCK to key a series of capital letters. To release the CAPS LOCK to key lowercase letters: on computers, strike CAPS LOCK key again; on electronics, strike either Left or Right Shift key.

CAPS LOCK
Left little finger

? (question mark)
Left Shift; then *right little* finger

Learn CAPS LOCK

1 Hal read PENTAGON and ADVISE AND CONSENT by Drury.
2 Oki joined FBLA when her sister joined PBL at OSU.
3 Zoe now belongs to AMS and DPE as well as to NBEA.

Learn ? (question mark)

Space twice

4 ; ; ?; ?; Who? What? When? Where? Why? Is it?
5 Who is it? Is it she? Did he go? Was she there?
6 Is it up to me? When is it? Did he key the line?

Combine CAPS LOCK and ?

7 Did he join a CPA firm? I will stay on with NASA.
8 Is her dad still CEO at BSFA? Or was he made COB?
9 Did you read HOMEWARD? If so, try WHIRLWIND next.

Document 3

Send the text at the right as a fax to **Richard Curtis**. His fax no. is **715-136-4321**. The fax is from **Rebecca S. Fuller**. Use the current date and supply an appropriate subject line.

(Total words = 88)

Here are the Internet addresses that you requested for the other committee members. Our system is shut down for repairs, or I would have sent them to you via the Internet.

IN%"CHENYH/SB2@OFS.UWEC.EDU"
IN%"BARKER@RMC.NET.ROBERT-MORRIS.EDU"
IN%"TLUSTYSA@UVSC.EDU"
IN%"JCRUZ@KDC.COM"

LESSON 133   Data Entry Forms

Objective:
To learn to format and process data on forms.

133A • 5
Conditioning Practice

each line twice

alphabet   1   A critic quickly recognizes the vexing problems of judging flaws.

speed   2   They may do the work for us when the city auditor signs the form.

fig/sym   3   This model (#94-68) costs $238; the other one (#95-7) costs $150.

gwam   1' | 1 | 2 | 3 | 4 | 5 | 6 | 7 | 8 | 9 | 10 | 11 | 12 | 13 |

133B • 10
Drill: Tabulation

CS: 0.5"

1. Three 1' writings; find *gwam*.
2. Two 2' writings; find *gwam*.

					gwam 1'	2'
Hunt	Robin	3842 Inwood St.	Flagstaff	AZ	8	4
Keswick	Jane	9210 Dixon Rd.	Little Rock	AR	17	8
Langston	Bryce	8309 Pardee St.	Berkeley	CA	25	13
Ritter	Leslie	9056 Violin Rd.	Newark	DE	33	17
Lucina	Mike	4786 Ocana Ct.	Fort Myers	FL	41	21
Fairbanks	Maria	9078 Melrose Ave.	Pocatello	ID	51	25
Capri	Marge	3215 Central Ave.	Oak Park	IL	59	29

133C • 35
Data Entry

Use forms in stationery pack.

Document 1

Save as BANK1.

A&E Bank Card Application

Last Name	First	Middle	
Johnson	Beth	Anne	

Street Address	City	State	ZIP	Phone
3152 Duke St.	Fayetteville	NC	28304-4351	910-188-2111

Birth Date (Month, Day, Year)	Social Security Number	Name of Employer
04-15-49	520-66-3820	Fenton Motor, Inc.

Address of Employer	City	State	Annual Income	Employer's Phone
382 Greenbriar Dr.	Fayetteville	NC	$22,000	910-168-8399

18C • 18
New-Key Mastery

1. Key lines once SS; DS between 2-line groups.
2. Key the lines again at a faster pace.
3. Key a 1' writing on line 11 and then on line 12; find *gwam* on each writing.

TECHNIQUE *cues*:

- reach *up* without moving hands away from you
- reach *down* without moving hands toward your body
- use CAPS LOCK to make ALL CAPS

To find 1' *gwam*:

Add 10 for each line you completed to the scale figure beneath the point at which you stopped in a partial line.

Goal: finger-action keystrokes; quiet hands and arms

CAPS LOCK/? 1 Did she join OEA? Did she also join PSI and DECA?
2 Do you know the ARMA rules? Are they used by TVA?

z/v 3 Zahn, key these words: vim, zip, via, zoom, vote.
4 Veloz gave a zany party for Van and Roz in La Paz.

q/p 5 Paul put a quick quiz on top of the quaint podium.
6 Jacqi may pick a pink pique suit of a unique silk.

key words 7 they quiz pick code next just more bone wove flags
8 name jack flax plug quit zinc wore busy vine third

key phrases 9 to fix it|is to pay|to aid us|or to cut|apt to own
10 is on the|if we did|to be fit|to my pay|due at six

alphabet 11 Lock may join the squad if we have six big prizes.
easy 12 I am apt to go to the lake dock to sign the forms.

gwam 1' | 1 | 2 | 3 | 4 | 5 | 6 | 7 | 8 | 9 | 10 |

18D • 9
Block Paragraphs

1. Key each paragraph once, using wordwrap (soft returns) if available. The lines you key will be longer than the lines shown if default side margins are used.
2. If time permits, key a 1' writing on one or two of the paragraphs.

Goal: Continuity (keep the cursor or print point moving steadily across the screen or paper).

wp note:

Clearing the screen from time to time between 1' writings avoids confusion when finding *gwam*. Learn how to clear the screen on your software.

Paragraph 1

gwam 1'

When you key lines of drills, strike the return or   10
enter key at the end of each line. That is, use a   20
hard return to space down for a new line.   29

Paragraph 2

When you key copy in this form, though, you do not   10
need to strike return at the end of each line if a   20
machine has wordwrap or a soft return feature.   30

Paragraph 3

But even if your machine returns at line ends for   10
you, you have to strike the return or enter key at   20
the end of a paragraph to leave a line blank.   29

Paragraph 4

Learn now when you do not need to return at ends   10
of lines and when you must do so. Doing this now   20
will assure that your copy will be in proper form.   30

gwam 1' | 1 | 2 | 3 | 4 | 5 | 6 | 7 | 8 | 9 | 10 |

Document 1

Review the format guides for facsimilies on page 313. Format and key the fax from the model copy at the right.

MILWAUKEE STATE COLLEGE
Milwaukee, WI 53223-4004

Department of Business Education and Administration Management
(414) 136-4320
FAX: (414) 136-4959

2" TM

FAX MESSAGE TRANSMITTAL SHEET

QS

```
           TO:  Justin Baxter
      FAX NO.:  715-136-1838
         FROM:  Sandra Brown
         DATE:  January 30, ----
 NO. OF PAGES:  1
      SUBJECT:  TECHNOLOGY TASK FORCE MEETING
```
SS

DS

The next meeting of the Technology Task Force will be held at the Milwaukee Downtown Inn on Monday, February 15, at 9 a.m. The meeting should be finished before noon.

The main item of business will be the presentation of the proposals we requested from Computer Systems and Advanced Technologies. Mark Gill, Computer Systems, will present his proposal at 9:30. Sheila Beckstram will present the Advanced Technologies' proposal at 10:30.

Both representatives have been told to limit their presentations to 30 minutes. This will allow us time to ask any questions we may have regarding the proposals.

ph

Facsimile (Fax) Format

Document 2

Format and key the text at the right as a fax to **Michelle Alvarez**. Her fax no. is **718-132-9377**. The fax is from **Clayton R. Bachman**. Use the current date and supply an appropriate subject line.

	words
opening	33

Michelle, the sales reports that I received yesterday for the fourth quarter indicate a potential problem with the Southern Region. The overall sales for that region have been down appreciably during the last two quarters. For the year, they are down by almost 20 percent compared to last year.

48
62
76
90
93

The reports I receive break down sales only by region. I would like to see sales for each individual state in the region to determine if this is a problem for the entire region or only for one or two states.

107
122
135

Since I am meeting with regional representatives next Monday, I would like for you to fax me the information ASAP.

149
158

Tab Key

Objectives:

1. To learn to use the **Tab key** to indent paragraphs.
2. To improve and check keying speed.

19A • 7
Conditioning Practice

each line twice SS; then a 1' writing on line 3; find *gwam:* total words keyed

Computers

CAPS LOCK affects only the letter keys; shifted punctuation marks require the use of one of the shift keys.

Electronics

Comma and *period* as well as *colon* and *question mark* can be keyed when CAPS LOCK is on.

Fingers properly curved

alphabet	1	Zosha was quick to dive into my big pool for Jinx.
CAPS LOCK	2	Type these ZIP Codes: OR, MD, RI, NV, AL, and PA.
easy	3	Ian kept a pen and work forms handy for all of us.

gwam 1' | 1 | 2 | 3 | 4 | 5 | 6 | 7 | 8 | 9 | 10 |

19B • 12
Paragraph Indention

The **Tab key** is used to indent the first line of ¶s. Computer software and electronics use preset tabs (called default tabs). Usually, the first default tab is set 0.5" (5 spaces) to the right of the left margin and is used to indent ¶s (see copy below right).

See p. RG20 to learn to clear and set electronic tabs.

1. Locate the Tab key on your keyboard (usually at upper left of alphabetic keyboard).

2. Reach up to the Tab key with the left little finger; strike the key firmly and release it quickly. The cursor or print point will move 0.5" (5 spaces) to the right.

3. Key each ¶ once SS using wordwrap (soft returns) if available; DS between ¶s. As you key, strike the Tab key firmly to indent the first line of each ¶.

4. If you complete all ¶s before time is called, rekey them to master Tab key technique.

Tab key *Left little* finger

Tab ⟶ The tab key is used to indent blocks of copy such as these.

Tab ⟶ It should also be used for tables to arrange data quickly and neatly into columns.

Tab ⟶ Learn now to use the tab key by touch; doing so will add to your keying skill.

Tab ⟶ Strike the tab key firmly and release it very quickly. Begin the line without a pause.

Tab ⟶ If you hold the tab key down, the cursor will move from tab to tab across the line.

Document 2
Invoice

Use form in stationery pack.

Prepare an invoice using the information given at the right and listed below.

Date: **May 6, ----**
Order No.: **681B**
Terms: **2/10, n/45**
Shipped Via: **Blake Shipping**
Our Order No.: **M38-71**
Date Shipped: **May 7, ----**
Sales Tax = **5%**

(Total words = 64)

Document 3
Purchase Order

Use form in stationery pack.

Prepare a purchase order using the information given at the right and listed below.

Order No.: **632Q5**
Date: **March 15, ----**
Terms: **2/10, n/30**
Shipped Via: **Ken's Transport**

(Total words = 55)

Hilltop Orchard
839 Willow Oak Rd.
Memphis, TN 38138-3711

Quantity	Description/Stock No.	Unit Price
1	Envelopes #10/VE-38	15.75
2	Window envelopes #10/VE-58	18.95
4	Catalog envelopes 10x13/VE-79	13.50
2	Clasp envelopes 6x9/VE-80	10.95

Buckner Office Supplies
7320 Kane St.
Houston, TX 77007-8376

Quantity	Description/Stock No.	Unit Price
1	Fax machine/390-21	655.95
1	Facsimile stand/386-18	199.50
6	Facsimile paper/316-34	6.29
1	Fax message holder/306-15	7.49

LESSON 132   Facsimile (Fax)

Objective:
To learn to format and process facsimile (fax) forms.

132A • 5
Conditioning Practice

each line twice

alphabet	1	Jamison quickly realized that the beautiful gowns were expensive.
speed	2	Jane's neighbor is apt to make a big shelf for us in the cubicle.
figures	3	Of the 1,503 English majors, 879 were males and 624 were females.
gwam	1'	1 │ 2 │ 3 │ 4 │ 5 │ 6 │ 7 │ 8 │ 9 │ 10 │ 11 │ 12 │ 13 │

19C • 10
Technique: Space Bar, Shift Keys, and CAPS LOCK

each pair of lines twice SS: DS between 4-line groups

Fingers upright

space bar
1 an me so en if em by he ox go am do is no or in to
2 She may go to the city if he can fix the old auto.

shift key
3 The best dancers are: Ana and Jose; Mag and Boyd.
4 Did Ms. Paxon send us the letter from Dr. LaRonde?

CAPS LOCK
5 Masami saw the game on ESPN; Krista saw it on NBC.
6 The AMS meeting is on Tuesday; the DPE, on Friday.

19D • 14
Speed Building

1. Key the lines once SS; DS between 2-line groups.
2. Key a 1' writing on each of lines 5-8; find *gwam* on each writing (1' *gwam* = total 5-stroke words keyed).
3. If time permits, key another 1' writing on line 7 and then on line 8 for speed.

Key words and phrases (*Think, say,* and *key* words and phrases.)

1 ad my we in be on at up as no are him was you gets
2 girl quay turn rush duty down maps rich laid spend

3 an ad|to fix|an oak|to get|the zoo|via jet|in turn
4 if they|to risk|by them|the duty|and paid|she kept

Key easy sentences (Key the words at a brisk, steady pace.)

5 He is to aid the girls with the work if they wish.
6 Jan may go to the city for the bid forms for them.

7 He may go to the lake by dusk to do the dock work.
8 I did all the work for the firm for the usual pay.

gwam 1' | 1 | 2 | 3 | 4 | 5 | 6 | 7 | 8 | 9 | 10 |

19E • 7
Speed Check

1. Key each ¶ once SS using wordwrap if available; DS between ¶s.
2. Key a 1' writing on each ¶; find *gwam* on each writing (1' *gwam* = figure above the last word keyed).

Copy used to measure skill is triple-controlled for difficulty: E = easy; LA = low average; A = average.

all letters used

            .   2   .   4   .   6   .   8   .

    Be quick to excel in form and speed. If you

10   .   12   .   14   .   16   .   18

do, you can move back a word or two and watch the

20   .   22   .   24   .   26   .   28

errors fall away. Keep this in mind as you work.

        .   2   .   4   .   6   .   8

    You might be amazed how your speed will grow

10   .   12   .   14   .   16   .   18

if you first push for speed and then level off to

20   .   22   .   24   .   26   .   28

take control at just the right speed. Try it now.

LESSON 131 Purchase Orders and Invoices

Objective:
To increase proficiency at formatting purchase orders and invoices.

131A • 5
Conditioning Practice

each line twice

alphabet	1	Plans for the next management job will be finalized very quickly.
speed	2	A visit by the naughty girls may be a problem for their neighbor.
fig/sym	3	The desk (#539A28) and chair (#61B34) usually sell for over $700.

gwam 1' | 1 | 2 | 3 | 4 | 5 | 6 | 7 | 8 | 9 | 10 | 11 | 12 | 13 |

S KILL BUILDING

131B • 10
Statistical Copy Skill

Key two 3' writings; determine errors and *gwam*.

gwam 3'

all letters used

The sales report for the quarter ending September 30	4 39
indicated that sales for Easy-Korec Blue Correctable Film ribbon	8 43
(Stock #B193) were down by 40% while sales of all other ribbons	12 48
were up by an average of 15%. To boost sales of B193 ribbons, the	17 52
selling price will be reduced during the next quarter from $7.50	21 56
to $4.49 per ribbon (a 40% discount). Also, a four-color display	25 61
board emphasizing that the B193 ribbon can be used as a replace-	30 65
ment ribbon for TJK-133 and XRT-159 will be available to all	34 69
salespersons in the region.	35 71

gwam 3' | 1 | 2 | 3 | 4 |

F ORMATTING

131C • 35
Forms

Document 1
Purchase Order
Use form in stationery pack.
Prepare a purchase order using the information given at the right.

CHARLESTON JEWELERS 7645 COLUMBIA ST SEATTLE WA 98104-4289	**PO No.:** 89D39-3 2 **Date:** April 30, ---- 9 **Terms:** 2/10, n/30 14 **Shipped Via:** Vista Freight 22

Quantity	Description/Stock No.	Price	Total	
5	Anniversary bands (ea)	450.00	2,250.00	29
4	Tanzanite ring (ea)	350.99	1,403.96	35
10	Diamond earrings (ea)	299.50	2,995.00	42
3	Diamond baguette ring (ea)	1,499.00	4,497.00	51
8	14K gold earrings (ea)	44.95	359.60	58
			11,505.56	59

LESSON 20

Skills Check

Objectives:

1. To demonstrate level of technique mastery.

2. To demonstrate level of keying speed attained.

20A • 7
Conditioning Practice

each line twice SS; then a 1'
writing on line 3; find *gwam*

alphabet	1	Quig just fixed prize vases he won at my key club.
spacing	2	Marcia works for HMS, Inc.; Juanita, for XYZ Corp.
easy	3	Su did vow to rid the town of the giant male duck.

gwam 1' | 1 | 2 | 3 | 4 | 5 | 6 | 7 | 8 | 9 | 10 |

20B • 20
Technique Check

each line twice SS; DS
between 6-line groups

Fingers
curved

Fingers
upright

Finger-
action
key-
stroking

Down-and-in spacing

Ask your teacher to check your keyboarding technique as you key the following lines.

Reach review (Keep on home keys the fingers not used for reaching.)

1 old led kit six jay oft zap cod big laws five ribs

2 pro quo|is just|my firm|was then|may grow|must try

3 Olga sews aqua and red silk to make six big kites.

Space bar emphasis (*Think, say*, and *key* the words.)

4 en am an by ham fan buy jam pay may form span corn

5 I am|a man|an elm|by any|buy ham|can plan|try them

6 I am to form a plan to buy a firm in the old town.

Shift key emphasis (Reach *up* and reach *down* without moving the hands.)

7 Jan and I are to see Ms. Han. May Lana come, too?

8 Bob Epps lives in Rome; Vic Copa is in Rome, also.

9 Oates and Co. has a branch office in Boise, Idaho.

Easy sentences (*Think, say*, and *key* the words at a steady pace.)

10 Eight of the girls may go to the social with them.

11 Corla is to work with us to fix the big dock sign.

12 Keith is to pay the six men for the work they did.

gwam 1' | 1 | 2 | 3 | 4 | 5 | 6 | 7 | 8 | 9 | 10 |

130C • 30
Forms

Review the format guides for processing business forms on p. 313.

Document 1
Purchase Order

Use forms in stationery pack. Key purchase order as shown at right.

Document 2
Invoice

Use form in stationery pack. Key invoice as shown at right.

Novak Jewelers
310 Templeton Dr.
Scranton, PA 18519-8201   (717) 172-8622

Purchase Order

BEACON HILL OFFICE SUPPLIES
419 BEACON ST
BOSTON MA 02115-8321

PO No.:	B386-95	7
Date:	February 21, ----	13
Terms:	2/20, n/45	20
Shipped Via:	Penn Freight	23

Quantity	Description/Stock Number	Price		Total		
1	Desktop printer stand/DPS68-495 (ea)	34	95	34	95	32
2	CPU stands/CPUS23-129 (ea)	14	95	29	90	39
4	Printer ribbons/PR82-67 (ea)	9	95	39	80	47
5	Two-line speakerphone/TLS43-212 (ea)	115	95	579	75	57
2	Business card files/BCF20-769 (ea)	19	95	39	90	66
				724	30	67

By _____

Isham's Conference Supplies
510 Devonshire Rd.
Orlando, FL 32832-8756
(407) 128-9808

Invoice

HPJ COMMUNICATION SPECIALISTS
526 NEBRASKA ST
ORLANDO FL 32803-8721

Date:	February 6, ----	9
Customer		13
Order No.:	15 P 398	21

Terms	Shipped Via	Our Order No.	Date Shipped	
2/10, n/30	Swartz Transit	Q 230-99	2/07/--	29

Quantity	Description/Stock Number	Price		Total		
1	Transparency film/TF39-06	42	50	42	50	38
2	Mounting frames/MF27-10	35	65	71	30	46
2	Easels/EA89-03	249	00	498	00	52
1	Lectern/LN12-19	138	50	138	50	59
2	Projection screens/PS45-50	198	00	396	00	68
				1,146	30	70
	Sales tax			57	32	73
				1,203	62	75

By _____

20C • 8
Speed Check: Sentences

1. Key a 30" writing on each line. Your rate in *gwam* is shown word-for-word above the lines.
2. Key another 30" writing on each line. Try to increase your keying speed.

Goal: At least 22 *gwam*.

2   4   6   8   10   12   14   16   18   20   22

1 He bid for the rich lake land.
2 Suzy may fish off the dock with us.
3 Pay the girls for all the work they did.
4 Quen is due by six and may then fix the sign.
5 Janie is to vie with six girls for the city title.
6 Duane is to go to the lake to fix the auto for the man.

2   4   6   8   10   12   14   16   18   20   22

If you finish a line before time is called and start over, your *gwam* is the figure at the end of the line PLUS the figure above or below the point at which you stopped.

20D • 15
Speed Check: Paragraphs

1. Key a 1' writing on each paragraph (¶); find *gwam* on each writing.
2. Using your better *gwam* as a base rate, select a goal rate and key two 1' guided writings on each ¶ as directed below.

Copy used to measure skill is triple-controlled for difficulty: E = easy; LA = low average; A = average.

all letters used   gwam 2'

Tab → How you key is just as vital as the copy you   5
work from or produce. What you put on paper is a   10
direct result of the way in which you do the job.   15
Tab → If you expect to grow quickly in speed, take   19
charge of your mind. It will then tell your eyes   24
and hands how to work through the maze of letters.   29

2' | 1 | 2 | 3 | 4 | 5 |

Quarter-Minute Checkpoints

gwam	1/4'	1/2'	3/4'	Time
16	4	8	12	16
20	5	10	15	20
24	6	12	18	24
28	7	14	21	28
32	8	16	24	32
36	9	18	27	36
40	10	20	30	40

Guided (Paced) Writing Procedure

Select a practice goal

1. Key a 1' writing on ¶ 1 of a set of ¶s that contain superior figures for guided writings, as in 20D above.
2. Using the *gwam* as a base, add 4 *gwam* to determine your goal rate.
3. Choose from Column 1 of the table at the left the speed nearest your goal rate. At the right of that speed, note the 1/4' points in the copy you must reach to maintain your goal rate.
4. Determine the checkpoint for each quarter minute from the word-count dots and figures above the lines in ¶ 1. (Example: Checkpoints for 24 *gwam* are 6, 12, 18, and 24.)

Practice procedure

1. Key two 1' writings on ¶ 1 at your goal rate guided by the quarter-minute calls (1/4, 1/2, 3/4, time).

Goal: To reach each of your checkpoints just as the guide is called.

2. Key two 1' writings on ¶ 2 of a set of ¶s in the same way.
3. If time permits, key a 2' writing on the set of ¶s combined, without the guides.

Speed level of practice

When the purpose of practice is to reach out into new speed areas, use the *speed* level. Take the brakes off your fingers and experiment with new stroking patterns and new speeds. Do this by:

1. Reading 2 or 3 letters ahead of your keying to foresee stroking patterns.
2. Getting the fingers ready for the combinations of letters to be keyed.
3. Keeping your eyes on the copy in the book.

LESSON 130 Purchase Order and Invoice

Objectives:

1. To learn to format and process purchase orders and invoices.
2. To increase straight-copy keying skill.

130A • 5
Conditioning Practice

set 0.5" margins; each line twice; 1' writing on speed line

alphabet	1	Jacobson believed that he might maximize profits with quality workers.
speed	2	Their men are in good shape to box with vigor to the end of the fight.
figures	3	The total attendance for 1996 was 87,253, about a 40 percent increase.

gwam 1' | 1 | 2 | 3 | 4 | 5 | 6 | 7 | 8 | 9 | 10 | 11 | 12 | 13 | 14 |

S KILL BUILDING

130B • 15
Timed Writings

1. A 1' writing on ¶ 1; find *gwam*.
2. Add 4-8 *gwam* to the rate attained in Step 1.
3. Take two 1' guided writings on ¶ 1, trying to achieve the goal set in Step 2.
4. Practice ¶ 2 in the same way.
5. One 3' writing on ¶s 1-2 combined; find *gwam* and determine errors.

all letters used

gwam 3' 5'

Records are extremely vital for a business enterprise to   4 | 2 39
maintain. They give executives insight into the day-to-day   8 | 5 41
dealings of a firm. They also are often the sole basis for   12 | 7 43
executives to make major decisions on the future direction of a   16 | 10 46
firm. Many different types of documents are used to record data   20 | 12 48
about a firm. Three such documents that are vital to the   24 | 15 51
operation of a firm are the purchase requisition, the purchase   28 | 17 53
order, and the invoice.   30 | 18 54

A purchase requisition is a document utilized by a firm to   34 | 20 57
request the purchasing agent to order goods or services. A   38 | 23 59
purchase order is a document used by the purchasing department   42 | 25 62
of one firm to order goods or services from another firm. An in-   46 | 28 64
voice is a document used by one firm to bill another firm for   51 | 30 67
goods or services purchased from the firm that sends the invoice.   55 | 33 69
All three documents will become a record of the firm's purchas-   59 | 36 72
ing transactions.   60 | 36 72

gwam 3' | 1 | 2 | 3 | 4 |
5' | 1 | 2 | 3 |

Language & Writing Skills 1

Activity 1:

1. Study the spelling/ definitions of the words in the color block at right.
2. Key line 1 (the **Learn** line), noting the proper choice of words.
3. Key lines 2-3 (the **Apply** lines), choosing the right words to complete the lines.
4. Key the remaining lines in the same way.
5. Check your accuracy; rekey lines containing errors.

Choose the right word

do (vb) to bring about; to carry out
due (adj) owed or owing as a debt; having reached the date for payment
hear (vb) to gain knowledge of by the ear
here (adv) in or at this place; at this point; in this case; on this point

Learn 1 If you pay when it is due, the cost will be less.
Apply 2 (Do, Due) you expect the plane to arrive when it is (do, due)?
Apply 3 (Do, Due) you want me to indicate the (do, due) date of the invoice?

Learn 4 Did you hear the sirens while you were here in the cellar?
Apply 5 (Hear, Here) is the new CD you said you wanted to (hear, here).
Apply 6 To (hear, here) well, we should see if we can get seats (hear, here).

Activity 2:

1. Read Sentence 1 to decide the correct word to complete the sentence.
2. Key Sentence 1, supplying the missing word.
3. Follow Steps 1-2 to complete the other sentences.
4. Check the accuracy of your work with the teacher; correct any errors you made.

Proofread & correct

1 After a . at the end of a sentence, space _____.

2 After a ; used as punctuation, space _____.

3 After a . following an initial, space _____.

4 After a : used as punctuation, space _____.

5 After a , within a sentence, space _____.

6 After a . following an abbreviation, space _____.

Activity 3:

1. Read Sentence 1 to decide the word to supply in the blank.
2. Key Sentence 1, inserting the word that correctly completes the sentence.
3. Follow Steps 1-2 to complete the other sentences.
4. Check the accuracy of your work with the teacher; correct any errors you made.

Compose (think) as you key

1 All that glitters is not _____.

2 Do not cry over spilt _____.

3 A friend in need is a friend _____.

4 A new broom always sweeps _____.

5 A penny saved is a penny _____.

Format Guides:
Purchase Order, Invoice, and Special Forms

Fax

Purchase Order

FAX (Facsimile)

Facsimile (fax) refers to the process of transmitting an exact reproduction of information (printed messages, handwritten messages, signatures, forms, and various types of graphics, etc.) over telephone lines. Sending messages made up of electronic impulses is known as **telecommunication**, and fax has become a very common means of telecommunication.

Most fax messages involve a transmittal sheet, or cover sheet, that identifies both the sender and the receiver of the fax. If letterhead is used that contains the company name, address, telephone number, and fax number, the facsimile message transmittal sheet will look quite similar to a standard memorandum. The fax headings should be the same as those included with a standard memo (TO:, FROM:, DATE:, SUBJECT:) plus the FAX NO: and the NO. OF PAGES:. The illustration at the left shows the order of the headings. A larger font size may be used to emphasize the heading information. The message may be keyed a DS below the heading. Short messages can be keyed on a single fax transmittal page, thus reducing the cost of transmitting the document, or on pages following the transmittal sheet.

Computer users should create a file containing a template of the fax heading information that can be opened each time a fax is to be sent (see illustration). Each new fax created using the template must be saved under another filename, thus keeping the original fax template file intact while saving a copy of each fax file. Note that some software packages have templates already created that can be used for fax transmittal sheets.

Business Forms

Purchase orders, invoices, and other similar documents are prepared on printed forms or from templates. Software with templates can

be purchased, or they can be created with the Table feature on many of today's word processing software packages. Although forms vary from company to company, well-designed forms allow the keyboard operator to follow the general guidelines listed below. The best-designed forms software is programmed so that the cursor skips to the next entry point following entry in one of the columns.

1. Address. Place the address (USPS style) so that it will show through the window of a window envelope.

2. Upper right-hand area. Information in the upper right-hand area of the invoice and purchase order should be keyed 2 spaces to the right of the colon following each printed item.

3. Quantity column. Numbers should be centered in the column. Use the center justification for the column or set a tab.

4. Description column. Items keyed in the description column should start approximately 2 spaces to the right of the vertical rule.

5. Price and total columns. Items in the price and total columns should be keyed so that 1 space is left before and after the vertical rules separating the columns. Right justification of the columns for dollar amounts simplifies the aligning of figures. Typewriter users can set tabs and insert spaces to align the figures in the price and total columns. The forms software automatically calculates the amounts in the total column.

6. Spacing. SS column entries, beginning on the first or second line below the horizontal rule under the column headings.

7. Totals. Underline the last figure in the total column; then, DS before keying the total amount.

8. Tabulation. Tabulate and key across the form rather than keying all items in one column before moving to the next column.

UNIT 2

LESSONS 21–24

Master Keyboarding/ Language Skills

LESSON 21

Keying Technique/Language Skills

Objectives:

1. To learn proper response patterns to gain speed.
2. To learn to capitalize appropriate words in sentences.

21A • 5
Conditioning Practice

each line twice SS; then a 1' writing on line 3; find *gwam*

alphabet	1	Nat will vex the judge if she bucks my quiz group.
punctuation	2	Al, did you use these words: vie, zeal, and aqua?
easy	3	She owns the big dock, but they own the lake land.
gwam	1'	1 | 2 | 3 | 4 | 5 | 6 | 7 | 8 | 9 | 10 |

SKILL BUILDING

21B • 18
Technique: Response Patterns

1. Key each pair of lines twice SS; DS between 4-line groups.
2. Key a 1' writing on line 10 and then on line 12; find *gwam* (total words keyed) on each writing.
3. Key another 1' writing on the slower line to increase your speed on more difficult copy.

PRACTICE cues:

Balanced-hand lines:
Think, say, and *key* the words by word response at a fast pace.

One-hand lines:
Think, say, and *key* the words by letter response at a steady but unhurried pace.

Letter response
Many one-hand words (as in lines 3-4) are not easy to key. Such words may be keyed letter-by-letter and with continuity (steadily without pauses).

Word response
Short, balanced-hand words (as in lines 1-2) are so easy to key that they can be keyed as words, not letter-by-letter. Think and key them at your top speed.

balanced-hand words	1	ah do so go he us if is of or to it an am me by ox
	2	ha for did own the for and due pay but men may box
one-hand words	3	as up we in at on be oh ax no ex my ad was you are
	4	ad ink get ilk far him few pop set pin far imp car
balanced-hand phrases	5	of it|he is|to us|or do|am to|an ox|or by|is to do
	6	do the|and for|she did|all six|the map|for the pay
one-hand phrases	7	as on|be in|at no|as my|be up|as in|at him|saw you
	8	you are|oil tax|pop art|you get|red ink|we saw him
balanced-hand sentences	9	The man is to go to the city and do the auto work.
	10	The girl is to go by bus to the lake for the fish.
one-hand sentences	11	Jimmy saw you feed a deer on a hill up at my mill.
	12	Molly sat on a junk in oily waters at a bare reef.
gwam	1'	1 | 2 | 3 | 4 | 5 | 6 | 7 | 8 | 9 | 10 |

Timed Writings

1. Key a 1' writing on each ¶.
2. Key one 3' writing on ¶s 1-2 combined.
3. Key a 5' writing on ¶s 1-2 combined.

all letters used

gwam 3' | 5'

More time is devoted to business meetings than ever before. | 4 | 2 | 48

Today a group rather than an individual is deciding the direction | 8 | 5 | 50

of many organizations. Meetings provide the forum for decisions | 13 | 8 | 53

to be made by a group. These meetings do not succeed or fail by | 17 | 10 | 56

accident. A successful business meeting is more likely to occur | 21 | 13 | 58

when advance notice of the time, date, site, and agenda are | 25 | 15 | 61

provided. The agenda quickly informs the group members of the | 30 | 18 | 63

items of business to be conducted at the next meeting. It allows | 34 | 20 | 66

them to plan and to prepare prior to the time of the meeting. | 38 | 23 | 68

Even though the decisions are made by a group, the leader of | 42 | 25 | 71

the group is the key to the success of a meeting. The overseer | 46 | 28 | 73

determines when the meeting starts and when it will conclude, the | 51 | 30 | 76

facilities, the agenda items to be discussed, and the people to be | 55 | 33 | 78

invited to the meeting. Effective group leaders strive to start | 60 | 36 | 81

and conclude meetings on time. They provide participants with in- | 64 | 38 | 84

formation on major agenda items prior to the meeting. They make | 68 | 41 | 86

sure that the meeting site and facilities contribute to the | 72 | 43 | 89

success of a meeting rather than detract from it. | 75 | 45 | 91

gwam 3' | 1 | 2 | 3 | 4
5' | 1 | 2 | 3

L ANGUAGE SKILLS

Capitalization
Key each sentence, supplying the needed capital letters.

1. larson music and farr greenhouse donated to the united way.
2. they will see zion national park on their trip to california.
3. the company president will make a presentation on june 2.
4. mr. cole informed me that president baker will not attend.
5. the boston tea party was connected to the american revolution.
6. the new faculty member is dr. jane shoji, a ph.d. in math.
7. the sabin art gallery will display work by maija during may.
8. dr. sekiguchi will attend a seminar in new york city.
9. the hubert h. humphrey metrodome is located in minneapolis.
10. he will be in athens on monday and in atlanta on tuesday.

21C • 12
Speed Building

LS (line spacing): DS

1. Key one 1' unguided and two 1' guided writings on ¶ 1 as directed on p. 54.
2. Key ¶ 2 in the same way.
3. As time permits, key one or two 2' unguided writings on ¶s 1-2 combined; find *gwam*.

1' *gwam* goals
▽ 17 = acceptable
□ 21 = average
⊙ 25 = good
◇ 29 = excellent

gwam 2'

all letters used

Keep in home position all of the fingers not   5
being used to strike a key.   Do not let them move   10
out of position for the next letters in your copy.   15
   Prize the control you have over the fingers.   19
See how quickly speed goes up when you learn that   24
you can make them do just what you expect of them.   29

21D • 15
Capitalization

LS (line spacing): SS

Standard Plan for Mastering Language Skills

1. Read the first rule highlighted in color at right.
2. Key the Learn sentence below it, noting how the rule is applied.
3. Key the Apply sentence, supplying the needed capital letters.
4. Read and practice the other rules in the same way.
5. If time permits, key all Apply sentences again to quicken your decision-making skills.

Capitalize the first word in a sentence.

Learn 1 Mindy left her coat here. Can she stop by for it?
Apply 2 do you plan to go today? the game begins at four.

Capitalize personal titles and names of people.

Learn 3 I wrote to Mr. Katz, but Miss Dixon sent the form.
Apply 4 do you know if luci and lex bauer are with dr. tu?

Capitalize names of clubs, schools, organizations, and companies.

Learn 5 The Beau Monde Singers will perform at Music Hall.
Apply 6 lennox corp. now owns the hyde park athletic club.

Capitalize the days of the week.

Learn 7 Did you ask if the OEA contest is to be on Friday?
Apply 8 does FBLA meet on wednesday, thursday, and friday?

Capitalize the months of the year.

Learn 9 August was very hot, but September is rather cool.
Apply 10 they are to spend july and august at Myrtle Beach.

Skill Builder

Tabulation

1. Clear tabs; set tabs 1.5", 3", and 4.5" from the left margin.
2. Key the text at the right.
3. Learn the names of the state capitals.
4. Key only the names of the states.
5. Go back and insert the names of as many of the capitals as you can below the state without looking at the text.

				words
Alabama	Alaska	Arizona	Arkansas	6
Montgomery	Juneau	Phoenix	Little Rock	14
California	Colorado	Connecticut	Delaware	22
Sacramento	Denver	Hartford	Dover	29
Florida	Georgia	Hawaii	Idaho	35
Tallahassee	Atlanta	Honolulu	Boise	42
Illinois	Indiana	Iowa	Kansas	47
Springfield	Indianapolis	Des Moines	Topeka	56

Timed Writings: Script

1. Take a 1' writing.
2. Add 5 *gwam* to the rate attained in Step 1.
3. Take four 1' writings, trying to achieve rate set in Step 2.

A all letters used

	words
A basic knowledge of parliamentary procedure is an excellent	12
skill to acquire. Those who possess this skill will be able to	25
put it to use in any organization they belong to that conducts	38
meetings based on parliamentary law. A meeting that is run by	50
this procedure will be conducted in a proper and very orderly	63
fashion. Just as important, the rights of each member of the	75
group are protected at all times.	82

Reading/Keying Response Patterns

each line 3 times (slowly, faster, top speed)

Goal: To reduce time interval between keystrokes (read ahead to anticipate stroking pattern).

Emphasize curved, upright fingers; finger-action keystroking.

one-hand words

1 car no cat inn fat ink ear beg verb sea lip oil tea pull see milk
2 acre pool rest link base lily seat lion vase noun dear junk barge

Emphasize independent finger action; stationary hands.

one-hand phrases

3 at my best | in my career | best dessert | my bad debts | my exact grades
4 only rebate | in my opinion | we deserve better | minimum grade average

Emphasize continuity; finger-action with fingers close to keys.

one-hand sentences

5 Ada agreed on a minimum oil target after a decrease in oil taxes.
6 In my opinion, Edward Freeberg agreed on a greater water reserve.

gwam	1'	1	2	3	4	5	6	7	8	9	10	11	12	13

Keyboarding/Language Skills

Objectives:
1. To build skill on straight copy and script.
2. To learn to capitalize appropriate words in sentences.

22A • 5
Conditioning Practice

each line twice SS; then a 1' writing on line 3; find *gwam*

alphabet	1	Wusov amazed them by jumping quickly from the box.
spacing	2	am to | is an | by it | of us | an oak | is to pay | it is due
easy	3	It is right for the man to aid them with the sign.

gwam 1' | 1 | 2 | 3 | 4 | 5 | 6 | 7 | 8 | 9 | 10 |

S KILL BUILDING

22B • 18
Technique: Response Patterns

1. Key each set of 3 lines twice SS (slowly, then faster); DS between 6-line groups.
2. Key a 1' writing on line 10, on line 11, and on line 12; find *gwam* on each; compare rates.
3. If time permits, rekey the slowest line.

Combination response
Normal copy (as in lines 7-9) includes both word- and letter-response sequences. Use *top* speed for easy words, *lower* speed for words that are harder to key.

	1	be in as no we kin far you few pin age him get oil
letter response	2	see him | was nil | vex you | red ink | wet mop | as you saw
	3	Milo saved a dazed polo pony as we sat on a knoll.
	4	ox if am to is may end big did own but and yam wit
word response	5	do it | to cut | he got | for me | jam it | an owl | go by air
	6	He is to go to the city and to do the work for me.
	7	am at of my if on so as to be or we go up of no by
combination response	8	am in | so as | if no | is my | is up | to be | is at | is up to
	9	Di was busy at the loom as you slept in the chair.
letter	10	Jon gazed at a phony scarab we gave him in a case.
combination	11	Pam was born in a small hill town at the big lake.
word	12	Keith is off to the lake to fish off the big dock.

gwam 1' | 1 | 2 | 3 | 4 | 5 | 6 | 7 | 8 | 9 | 10 |

22C • 5
Handwritten Copy (Script)

Key the lines once DS (2 hard returns); rekey the lines if time permits.

1 Script is copy that is written with pen or pencil.
2 Copy that is written poorly is often hard to read.
3 Read script a few words ahead of the keying point.
4 Doing so will help you produce copy free of error.
5 Leave proper spacing after punctuation marks, too.
6 With practice, you will key script at a good rate.

129B • 45
Format Itineraries and Agendas

Document 1

Format and key the itinerary at the right. Refer to the model on p. 301.

Document 2

Prepare the agenda at the right. Use the following for the heading.

Agenda
for
Ruth Tennyson
May 15, ----

Use your decision-making skills to arrange in an attractive format.

Document 3

Revise Document 1 as follows:

Change the breakfast meeting with Mr. Jacobs from **April 16** to **April 17**.

Include business meeting with **Rori Votaw** on **April 17** at **4:30 p.m.** Return flight has been changed to **Flight #385** leaving at **8:15 a.m.** and arriving in Memphis at **9:57 a.m.**

Note: Additional R&E tables can be found on pp. A30 through A32.

---

		words
ITINERARY ⟩Bold ⎫DS		2
Jacinta A. Reinhart		6
HPJ Communication Specialists Symposium ⟩		14

April 15 — 16

2:30 p.m.	.8"	Depart Memphis on Coastal Airlines--Flight #714	26
	# for Boston (Logan International).		35
6:19 p.m.	Col. space	Arrive Boston. Accomodations at Ellsworth	45
	Inn, 641 Taft Hill Park.		51

April 16 — 53

7:00 a.m.	Breakfast with Harvey Jacobs at hotel.	63
8:30 a.m.	HPJ Communications Specialists Symposium,	73
	meetings until 4:30 p.m.	78
6:30 p.m.	Dinner with Sue Butler at Cambridge Club.	89

April 17 — 91

8:30 a.m.	HPJ Communications Specialists Symposium,	101
	meetings until 2:45 p.m.	106
3:30 p.m.	Meeting with Justin Browning.	115
7:30 p.m.	Performance of the Boston Symphony Orchestra at	126
	Symphony Hall.	129

April 18 — 131

7:45 a.m.	Depart Boston on Coastal Airlines--Flight #628	143
	# for Memphis.	146
9:27 a.m.	Arrive Memphis.	151

---

opening 8

Meet with	Time	Location	
Business Communications	8:30-9:30	SSS 216	21
Advisory Committee			25
Dr. Milton Sabin, Chair	9:00-10:00	SSS 401	34
Dept. of Management			38
Information Systems			42
Dr. Marie Marichal, Chair	10:00-10:30	SSS 400	51
Dept. of Accountancy			55
Dr. Joyce Sullivan, Chair	10:30-11:00	SSS 404	64
Dept. of Finance			68
Dr. Josh Kane, Chair	11:30-12:00	SSS 409	76
Department of Business			81
Communication			83
Dr. Kate McKinney--LUNCH	12:30-1:45	Oak Room	92
Dean, School of Business			97
General Meeting with School	2:00-3:15	SSS 119	107
of Business Faculty			110

22D • 10
Speed Building

LS: DS

1. Key one 1' unguided and two 1' guided writings on ¶ 1 as directed on p. 54.
2. Key ¶ 2 in the same way.
3. As time permits, key one or two 2' unguided writings on ¶s 1-2 combined; find *gwam*.

Quarter-Minute Checkpoints

gwam	1/4'	1/2'	3/4'	Time
16	4	8	12	16
20	5	10	15	20
24	6	12	18	24
28	7	14	21	28
32	8	16	24	32
36	9	18	27	36
40	10	20	30	40

all letters used | gwam 2'

```
                  .   2    .    4    .    6    .    8    .
     Are you one of the people who often look from      5
    10    .   12   .    14   .    16   .    18   .
the copy to the screen and down at your hands?  If     10
 20    .   22   .    24   .    26   .    28   .
you are, you can be sure that you will not build a     15
 30   .   32   .    34   .    36   .    38
speed to prize.   Make eyes on copy your next goal.    20
                  .   2    .    4    .    6    .    8    .
     When you move the eyes from the copy to check     24
    10    .   12   .    14   .    16   .    18   .
the screen, you may lose your place and waste time     30
 20    .   22   .    24   .    26   .    28   .
trying to find it.   Lost time can lower your speed    35
 30   .   32   .    34   .    36   .    38
quickly and in a major way, so do not look away.      39
2' |    1    |    2    |    3    |    4    |    5    |
```

22E • 12
Capitalization

Follow the *Standard Plan for Mastering Language Skills* given in 21D, p. 57.

Capitalize names of holidays.

Learn 1 Kacy and Zoe may visit their parents on Labor Day.
Apply 2 gus asked if memorial day comes at the end of may.

Capitalize the names of historic periods and events and special events.

Learn 3 The Fourth of July honors the American Revolution.
Apply 4 bastille day is in honor of the french revolution.

Capitalize names of cities, states, and other important places.

Learn 5 When you were in Nevada, did you visit Hoover Dam?
Apply 6 did he see paris from the top of the eiffel tower?

Capitalize geographic names, regions, and locations.

Learn 7 Val drove through the Black Hills in South Dakota.
Apply 8 we canoed down the missouri river near sioux city.

Capitalize names of streets, roads, avenues, and buildings.

Learn 9 Jemel lives at Bay Towers near Golden Gate Bridge.
Apply 10 our store is now in midtown plaza on kenwood road.

128C • 35
Agendas

Agenda 1

Format and key the agenda at the right; refer to the model on p. 301.

words

	words
AGENDA	1
Software Development Board Meeting	8
10:30 a.m., June 25, ----	12

1. Introductory Remarks . . . . Noriko Shoji — 25
2. New Software Proposals . . . . Ted Hubbard — 38
       Market Analyzer . . . . May Roberts — 49
       Financial Planner . . . . Ken Jetz — 60
       Visuals Unlimited . . . . Judy Kay — 71
3. Projection Reports — 76
       Production Cost Projections . . . . Brett Hill — 87
       Market Projections. . . . . Jay Griffin — 98
       Profit Projections . . . . Erika Nicole — 109
4. Discussion of Proposal. . . . . Board Members — 122
5. Adjournment — 125

Agenda 2

Format and key the agenda at the right; DS.

Agenda 3

Revise Agenda 1 to include the following as Items 5 and 6 on the agenda.

5. Summary of Discussion: Pros and Cons . . . . Tyler Parks

6. Call for Vote . . . Noriko Shoji

Renumber item that follows. Left-align the right column.

	words
AGENDA	1
Executive Meeting	5
September 15, ----	9

1. Opening Comments . . . . Kyle Lenz — 22
2. Manager's Responsibilities . . . . Sara Lloyd — 35
3. Employee Concerns . . . . Mark Scott — 48
4. Seminars — 50
       Time Management . . . . Erin Reed — 61
       Quality Control . . . . Anne Sega — 72
       Project Management . . . . Jason Graham — 83
       Employee Motivation . . . . Jan Elsner — 94
5. Committee Assignments . . . . Greg Finley — 107
6. New Seminar Proposals . . . . Eric Winget — 120
7. New Items for Discussion . . . . Kyle Lenz — 133
8. Adjournment — 136

LESSON 129

Process Itineraries and Agenda

Objective:

To format itineraries and agenda.

129A • 5
Conditioning Practice

each line twice

alphabet	1	Mom saw Rex quickly leave for his job when his dog won the prize.
speed	2	The map may aid them when they do work for the town and the city.
figures	3	Flight 8697 landed at 10:30 a.m. and left for Denver at 2:45 p.m.

gwam	1'	1	2	3	4	5	6	7	8	9	10	11	12	13

Objectives:
1. To build straight-copy speed and control.
2. To learn to capitalize appropriate words in sentences.

23A • 5
Conditioning Practice

each line twice SS; then a
1' timed writing on line 3;
find *gwam*

alphabet 1 Marjax made five quick plays to win the big prize.

CAPS LOCK 2 Did you say to send the cartons by UPS or by USPS?

easy 3 I am to pay the six men if they do the work right.

gwam 1' | 1 | 2 | 3 | 4 | 5 | 6 | 7 | 8 | 9 | 10 |

S KILL BUILDING

23B • 18
Technique: Response Patterns

1. Key each set of 3 lines twice SS; DS between 6-line groups.
2. Key a 1' writing on line 10, on line 11, and on line 12 to increase speed; find *gwam* on each.

Goal: At least 24 *gwam* on line 12.

letter response 1 kilo beef ploy were only date upon gave milk rates

2 my car|oil tax|you are|was him|raw milk|as you see

3 We ate plump plum tarts in a pink cafe on a barge.

word response 4 also form town risk fuel auto goal pens iris visit

5 apt to|go for|is also|the goal|fix them|go for the

6 Roxie is also apt to go for the goal of good form.

combination response 7 an in of at is fix pop for him ham are pen far men

8 in the|at the|and tar|for him|due you|she saw them

9 An odor of wax and tar was in the air at the mill.

letter 10 Zac gave only a few facts in a case on wage taxes.

combination 11 He set off for the sea by dusk to see a rare loon.

word 12 It is right for them to audit the work of the men.

gwam 1' | 1 | 2 | 3 | 4 | 5 | 6 | 7 | 8 | 9 | 10 |

23C • 10
Speed Building

LS: DS

1. Key one 1' unguided and two 1' guided writings on ¶ 1 and then on ¶ 2, as directed on p. 54.
2. Key two 2' unguided writings on ¶s 1-2 combined; find *gwam* on each.

1' *gwam* goals
▽ 19 = acceptable
▣ 23 = average
⊙ 27 = good
◇ 31 = excellent

all letters used   gwam 2'

     .   2   .   4   .   6   .   8   .

  The level of your skill is a major item when   5

 10   . 12   . 14   . 16   . 18   ▽

you try to get a job. Just as vital, though, may 10

 20   . 22   ▣ 24   . 26   ⊙ 28   .

be how well you can express ideas in written form. 15

    .   2   .   4   .   6   .   8

   It might amaze you to learn what it is worth 19

 10   . 12   . 14   . 16   . 18   ▽

to a company to find those who can write a letter 24

 20   . 22   ▣ 24   . 26   ⊙ 28

of quality as they key. Learn to do so in school. 29

2' | 1 | 2 | 3 | 4 | 5 |

Table 3

SMs: 1"; center column headings; right-align the date column.

Table 4

Update Table 2 to reflect the company assets at the end of the current year:

Cash	183,500
Accts. Rec.	565,600
Inv.	610,000
Prepaid Ex.	10,200
Land	270,000
Building	990,000
Depr. Bld.	(250,000)
Equip.	320,000
Depr. Equip.	(85,000)
Total Assets	2,614,300

	words
VALUE-ADDED SEMINARS	4
March 15 – April 21	8

Seminar	Date	
Advanced Presentation Skills	March 15	23
Enhancing Executive Leadership	March 19	35
Developing Assertiveness	March 24	46
Quality Control	March 29	58
Employee Evaluation	April 2	70
Stress Management	April 5	81
Effective Communication	April 9	93
Improving Customer Relations	April 12	105
You're the Consultant	April 15	117
Computer Literacy	April 17	128
Negotiating Effectively	April 21	140

(add leaders)

LESSON 128 — Process Agendas

Objectives:
1. To format agendas.
2. To increase keying skill on straight copy.

128A • 5
Conditioning Practice

each line twice

alphabet 1 Jacob purchased the exquisite gift at a zoo while moving to York.

speed 2 Sit down and aid the six girls with the ornaments for the social.

figures 3 The rate on February 29 was 10.57 percent; it was 8.46 on May 30.

gwam 1' | 1 | 2 | 3 | 4 | 5 | 6 | 7 | 8 | 9 | 10 | 11 | 12 | 13 |

S KILL BUILDING

128B • 10
Guided Writing: Speed

1. Two 1' writings; find *gwam*.
2. Add 4 words to better rate; determine 1/4' goals.
3. Two 15" writings; try to equal or exceed 1/4' goals.
4. Two 30" writings; try to equal or exceed 1/2' goal.
5. Two 1' guided writings at goal rate.

gwam 30"

Recognize that the primary element of high-speed keyboarding is to try to type or keyboard with good form and refined technique patterns. In each of the lessons of this unit, your goal should be to fix your mind on the principal keyboarding elements: finger-action keystroking, quick spacing after every word, and a fast return with a very quick start of the new line.

(line 1)	24
(line 2)	51
(line 3)	77
(line 4)	101
(line 5)	127
(line 6)	148

gwam 1' | 1 | 2 | 3 | 4 | 5 | 6 | 7 | 8 | 9 | 10 | 11 | 12 | 13 |

23D • 11
Difficult-Reach Mastery

1. Key each set of 4 lines once SS; DS between the 4-line groups.
2. Note the lines that caused you difficulty; practice them again to develop a steady pace.

Adjacent (side-by-side) keys (as in lines 1-4) can be the source of many errors unless the fingers are kept in an upright position and precise motions are used.

Long direct reaches (as in lines 5-8) reduce speed unless they are made without moving the hands forward and downward.

Reaches with the outside fingers (as in lines 9-12) are troublesome unless made without twisting the hands in and out at the wrist.

Fingers properly curved

Fingers properly aligned

Adjacent-key letter combinations

1 Rena saw her buy a red suit at a new shop in town.
2 Opal will try to stop a fast break down the court.
3 Jeremy knew that we had to pool our points to win.
4 Her posh party on their new patio was a real bash.

Long direct reaches with same finger

5 Herb is under the gun to excel in the second race.
6 My fervor for gym events was once my unique trait.
7 Music as a unique force is no myth in any country.
8 Lynda has since found many facts we must now face.

Reaches with 3d and 4th fingers

9 The poet will opt for a top spot in our port town.
10 Sam said the cash price for gas went up last week.
11 Zane played a zany tune that amazed the jazz band.
12 My squad set a quarter quota to equal our request.

LANGUAGE SKILLS

23E • 6
Capitalization

Follow the *Standard Plan for Mastering Language Skills* given in 21D, p. 57.

> Capitalize an official title when it precedes a name and elsewhere if it is a title of high distinction.

Learn 1 In what year did Juan Carlos become King of Spain?
Learn 2 Masami Chou, our class president, made the awards.
Apply 3 will the president speak to us in the rose garden?
Apply 4 mr. koch, our company president, chairs the group.

> Capitalize initials; also capitalize letters in abbreviations if the letters would be capitalized when the words are spelled out.

Learn 5 Does Dr. R. J. Anderson have an Ed.D. or a Ph.D.?
Learn 6 He said that UPS stands for United Parcel Service.
Apply 7 we have a letter from ms. anna m. bucks of boston.
Apply 8 m.d. means Doctor of Medicine, not medical doctor.

127B • 45
Process Tables

Table 1

CS: 0.7"

Center column heads; replace ---- with current year.

words

ADVISER ASSIGNMENTS — 4

Spring ---- — 6

Student	GPA	Major	Adviser	
Kruger, June	3.67	Management	Glavine	20
Burton, Kelly	2.71	*Marketing*	Brown	27
Hemls, Jason	3.34	Management	Glavine	34
Marshall, Kay	3.41	Finance	*Shoji*	41
Nicolet, Mary	2.98	Marketing	Brown	48
Gomez, Felipe	3.12	Management	Glavine	56
Downey, Aaron	2.89	Finance	*Shoji*	62
Berntsen, Wade	3.51	Finance	*Shoji*	69
Mayberry, Anne	3.87	Management	Glavine	77
Segawa, Hiroki	3.25	Marketing	Brown	84
Nagel, Jessica	3.05	Management	Glavine	92
Manzo, Matrice	3.29	Finance	*Shoji*	98

Table 2

SM: 1"

Review format guides on p. 301 and wp guides on p. 300. Replace ---- with last year.

wp note:

Space once at the end of all amounts not in parentheses in order to align with the amounts in parentheses.

ASSETS — 1

December 31, ---- — 5

		words
Cash	$ 167,300	17
Accounts Receivable	521,500	29
Inventory	620,000	40
Prepaid Expense	10,700	52
Land	250,000	63
Building	950,000	75
Accumulated Depreciation, Building	(200,000)	87
Equipment	320,000	99
Accumulated Depreciation, Equipment	(85,000)	111
Total Assets	$2,554,500	115

Keyboarding/Language Skills

Objectives:
1. To demonstrate proper keying technique.
2. To demonstrate skill on various kinds of copy.

24A • 5
Conditioning Practice

each line twice SS; then a 1' writing on line 3; find *gwam*

alphabet	1	Jack viewed unique forms by the puzzled tax agent.
?	2	Where is Elena? Did she call? Is she to go, too?
easy	3	Title to all of the lake land is held by the city.

gwam 1' | 1 | 2 | 3 | 4 | 5 | 6 | 7 | 8 | 9 | 10 |

S KILL BUILDING

24B • 10
Speed Building

1. Key the lines once SS with a DS between 2-line groups.
2. If time permits, key the lines again to improve keying ease and speed.

Technique goals
- reach *up* without moving hands away from you
- reach *down* without moving hands toward your body
- use quick-snap keystrokes

ed/de	1	ed de led ode need made used side vied slide guide
	2	Ned said the guide used a video film for her talk.
ju/ft	3	ju ft jug oft jet aft jug lift just soft jury loft
	4	Judy left fifty jugs of juice on a raft as a gift.
ol/lo	5	ol lo old lot lob lox log sold loan fold long told
	6	Lou told me that her local school loans old books.
ws/sw	7	ws sw was saw laws rows cows vows swam sways swing
	8	Swin swims at my swim club and shows no big flaws.
ik/ki	9	ik ki kit ski kin kid kip bike kick like kiwi hike
	10	The kid can hike or ride his bike to the ski lake.
za/az	11	za az zap adz haze zany lazy jazz hazy maze pizzas
	12	A zany jazz band played with pizzazz at this plaza.
alphabet	13	Olive Fenz packed my bag with six quarts of juice.
	14	Jud aims next to play a quick game with Bev Fritz.

gwam 1' | 1 | 2 | 3 | 4 | 5 | 6 | 7 | 8 | 9 | 10 |

24C • 14
Speed Check: Straight Copy

LS: DS

1. Key one 1' unguided and two 1' guided writings on ¶ 1 and then on ¶ 2, as directed on p. 54.
2. Key two 2' unguided writings on ¶s 1-2 combined; find *gwam* on each.

Goals
1': At least 22 *gwam*.
2': At least 20 *gwam*.

E all letters used

gwam 2'

. 2 . 4 . 6 . 8 .
You must realize by now that learning to key 5
10 . 12 . 14 . 16 . 18
requires work. However, you will soon be able to 10
20 . 22 . 24 . 26 . 28
key at a higher speed than you can write just now. 15
. 2 . 4 . 6 . 8
You will also learn to do neater work on the 19
10 . 12 . 14 . 16 . 18
machine than you can do by hand. Quality work at 24
20 . 22 . 24 . 26 . 28
higher speeds is a good goal for you to have next. 29

2' | 1 | 2 | 3 | 4 | 5 |

Table 2

Center column headings; replace ---- with the current year.

 note:

Right-align amount columns; left-align words.

Table 3

Arrange Table 2 alphabetically by country.

Table 4

Arrange Table 2 numerically by price in descending order.

				words
DOLLS FROM AROUND THE WORLD (DS)				6
---- Holiday Prices				10
Doll	Country	Price	Product Code	11 / 17
Elena	Russia	$ 78.99	RU107	22
Mitsutoshi	Japan	95.90	JN1073	28
Cayenana	Spain	109.99	SP235	34
Jennifer	United States	89.99	US398	41
Katerina	Germany	89.99	GY120	47
Dianna	England	84.99	EN457	52
Francois	France	85.99	FR981	58
Maria	Mexico	79.99	MX819	63
Maija	Finland	89.99	FN675	68
Ambika (1"CS)	India (1"CS)	88.99 (0.5"CS)	IN382	73

S KILL BUILDING

126C • 12
Guided Writing: Control

1. Two 1' writings; find *gwam*; determine errors.
2. Deduct 4 words from better rate; determine 1/4' goals.
3. Two 15" writings; try to reach goal with no errors.
4. Two 30" writings; try to reach goal with no errors.
5. Two 1' guided writings at goal rate. **Goal:** each writing with no more than 2 errors.

A all letters used   gwam 30"

```
      .    2    .    4    .    6    .    8    .   10   .
Every time you operate the keyboard, make the use of good      23
  12   .   14   .   16   .   18   .   20   .   22   .   24
techniques your goal.  This is the way to build your keyboarding  49
  26   .   28   .   30   .   32   .   34   .   36   .
efficiency to its highest possible level.  Keyboarding efficiency  76
38   .   40   .   42   .   44   .   46   .   48   .   50
is needed if you are to remain competitive in the world of work,  102
  52   .   54   .   56   .   58   .   60   .   62   .
and if you are to use the sophisticated equipment now in use in  127
64   .   66   .   68   .   70   .   72   .   74
the technological society in which we live and work.           148
```

gwam   1' | 1 | 2 | 3 | 4 | 5 | 6 | 7 | 8 | 9 | 10 | 11 | 12 | 13 |

LESSON 127   **Process Tables** ML S

Objectives:

1. To enhance table formatting skill.
2. To format and key tables with leaders.

127A • 5
Conditioning Practice

each line twice

alphabet 1 The expert, Judge Vincet, was amazed by the fine quality of work.

speed 2 The man with the problems may wish to see the proficient tax man.

figures 3 Dave delivered pizza to 3710 Devney, 2469 Oxford, and 580 Hudson.

gwam   1' | 1 | 2 | 3 | 4 | 5 | 6 | 7 | 8 | 9 | 10 | 11 | 12 | 13 |

24D • 8
Corrected Copy (Rough Draft)

1. Study the proofreader's marks illustrated below and in the sentences.
2. Key each sentence DS, making all handwritten changes.
3. Rekey the lines to improve your correcting speed.

∧ = insert

= add space

∽ = transpose

⟩ = delete

⌒ = close up

≡ = capitalize

1 Rough draft is ~~typed~~ work with hand written changes.   *keyed copy*

2 Special marks may be used to show changes tobe made.   *are* #

3 First, read a sentence notting changes; then ~~type~~ it.   *key*

4 Next, check to see if you made the changes correctly.   *that* *properly*

5 If not correct your copy or key that sentence again.   *work* *the*

6 Read rough draft a bit ahead of your keying piont.   *slightly* *the*

7 Doing this will help you make all the change right.   *so* *to*

8 You will key often from script and rough draft copy.   *soon*

24E • 13
Skill Transfer: Straight Copy to Script and Rough Draft

1. Key each ¶ once SS; DS between ¶s.
2. Key a 1' writing on each ¶; find *gwam* on each writing; compare the three rates.

Your highest speed should be on ¶ 1 (straight copy); next highest on ¶ 2 (script); lowest on ¶ 3 (rough draft).

3. Key one or two more 1' writings on the two slowest ¶s to improve skill transfer.

Recall

1' *gwam* = total words keyed

A standard word = 5 strokes (characters and spaces)

Straight copy   gwam 1'

No matter what form the copy takes, keep the eyes on it   11

as you key. If you look away from the copy, you lose a second 24

or two. If you look away too often, your speed will drop by 36

a word or two.   39

Script

Fix your eyes on the copy now and keep them   9
there as you key this copy. Be quick to recognize   19
that looking away from the copy drops your speed.   29

Rough draft

Read script and rough draft with ~~great~~ care to aviod a   11   *a* *real*

major error in typing. Read slightly ahead of where the fingers   23   *keying* # *a bit* *your*

are key ing; that helps too.   29

OFFICE TECHNOLOGY TERMS

For Week of February 15-20

Artificial Intelligence	the capability of the computer to perform functions normally associated with human intelligence, such as reasoning and learning; the programming of machines so that they mimic the reasoning and learning behavior of human beings
Backup	a copy of a file or disk that can be used in case the original is damaged or lost
Communication-Based Services	services including electronic mail, computerized bulletin boards, and on-line conferences
Computer Virus	self-replicating blocks of code that enter a computer via disk, telephone lines, or manually, spreading infection within the system
Desktop Publishing	designing and producing a publication using a personal computer; software programs to create newsletters, manuals, forms, proposals, and flyers
Electronic Mail (e-mail)	electronic data communication; the non-interactive communication of text, data, voice, and image messages between a sender and recipient using system links
Hard Disk	a rigid disk that has its own case or fits into the computer; can hold several million bytes of information; a storage device mounted in its own case or permanently mounted inside a computer
Random Access Memory (RAM)	temporary computer memory that erases when the power is turned off
Read-Only Memory (ROM)	type of computer memory that contains permanently stored manufacturer's instructions to start the system and read the disk operating system (DOS) instructions

Source: Susan Jaderstrom and Leonard B. Kruk, Administrative Support Systems and Procedures, Cincinnati: South-Western Publishing Co., 1992, pp. 331-336.

Complex Table

UNIT 3

Master Figure-Key Operation

LESSON 25

New Keys: 8 and 1

Objectives:
1. To learn reach technique for **8** and **1**.
2. To improve skill on straight-copy sentences and ¶s.

25A • 5
Conditioning Practice

LS: SS
SM: defaults or 1.25"
each line twice (slowly, then faster); a 1' writing on line 3; find *gwam*

alphabet 1 Max was quick to fly a big jet plane over the frozen desert.

spacing 2 Any of them can aim for a top goal and reach it if they try.

easy 3 Nan is to go to the city hall to sign the land forms for us.

gwam 1' | 1 | 2 | 3 | 4 | 5 | 6 | 7 | 8 | 9 | 10 | 11 | 12 |

25B • 16
New Keys: 8 and 1

each line twice (slowly, then faster); DS between 2-line groups; if time permits, key lines 5-7 again to build skill

8 *Right middle* finger

1 *Left little* finger

Follow the *Standard Plan for Learning New Keys* outlined on p. 17.

Learn 8

1 k k 8k 8k kk 88 k8k k8k 88k 88k Reach up for 8, 88, and 888.

2 Key the figures 8, 88, and 888. Please open Room 88 or 888.

Learn 1

3 a a 1a 1a aa 11 a1a a1a 11a 11a Reach up for 1, 11, and 111.

4 Add the figures 1, 11, and 111. Has just 1 of 111 finished?

Combine 8 and 1

5 Key 11, 18, 81, and 88. Just 11 of the 18 skiers have left.

6 Reach with the fingers to key 18 and 188 as well as 1 and 8.

7 The stock person counted 11 coats, 18 slacks, and 88 shirts.

Table 2
CS: 1"

Table 3

Alphabetize Table 1 by the last name of the managers. Add the **Data Processing** Department manager to the list. **Jay East; 482 Sunset Dr.; Golden, CO 80401-7463; 180-8356**

		words
SUGGESTED ~~RESOURCES~~ OFFICE RESOURCES		5
~~Publication~~ Publication	~~Publication Address~~ Publication Address	12
WordPerfect Magazine	Reader Service Mgt. Dept. P.O. Box 5021	22
	Pittsfield, MA 01203-9858	30
Modern Office *Technology*	A Penton Publication	
	1100 Superior Avenue	38
	Cleveland, OH 44197-8093	43
Managing Office Technology	A Penton Publication	
	1100 Superior Avenue	53
	Cleveland, OH 44197-8093	58
The Secretary	10502 N.W. Ambassador Dr.	
	P.O. Box 20404	66
	Kansas City, KS 64195-0404	69
		74
The Office	Office Publications, Inc. MO	
	P.O. Box 1682	81
	Riverton, NJ 08077-9682	84
Communications News	DS > 2504 Tamiami Trail North	89
	Nokomis, FL 34275-9987	98
MAC WORLD	Reader Service Department	103
	P.O. Box 5299	110
	Pittsfield, MA 01203-9906	113
		118

LESSON 126 — Process Tables

Objectives:

1. To enhance table formatting skill.
2. To increase keying skill on straight copy.

126A • 5
Conditioning Practice

each line twice

alphabet 1 Mary said the jacket Pam Fitzgerald bought was quite extravagant.

speed 2 Profit is no problem for the sorority social when it is downtown.

figures 3 Rooms 301, 427, 395, and 468 were cleaned and painted this month.

gwam 1' | 1 | 2 | 3 | 4 | 5 | 6 | 7 | 8 | 9 | 10 | 11 | 12 | 13 |

FORMATTING

126B • 33
Process Tables

Table 1

Use your decision-making skills to plan an attractive format.

The table on the next page can be formatted with or without lines. If the table is keyed with lines, the Table Format function presented on pp. 299-300 may be used.

New-Key Mastery

1. Key lines 1-12 once SS; DS between 2-line groups.
2. Key a 1' writing on line 13, then on line 14; find *gwam* on each writing.
3. If time permits, key a 1' writing on line 8 and then on line 12, trying to maintain your better rate in Step 2.

Technique goals

• reach *up* without moving the hand forward
• reach *down* without twisting the wrists or moving the elbows in and out

Row emphasis

figures
1 The quiz on the 18th will be on pages 11 to 18 and 81 to 88.
2 Just 11 of the 118 boys got 81 of the 88 quiz answers right.

home/1st
3 hand axe│lava gas│can mask│jazz band│lack cash│a small flask
4 Ms. Hamm can call a cab, and Max can flag a small black van.

home/3d
5 she quit│with just│that play│fair goal│will help│they did go
6 Dru said you should try for the goal of top speed this week.

Response patterns

letter response
7 as in re on we no ax up gas oil red mop fee hum are you were
8 You, in fact, saw him on a pump barge up at my mill at noon.

word response
9 if so is do id go us me am by an ox and the for men end form
10 She is to go by the zoo to sign a work form for the six men.

combination response
11 if as so in is re do on go we us no me ax am up by pi an kin
12 If she is at the inn, we may go by car to see a poppy field.

easy
13 Ty is to pay for the eight pens she laid by the audit forms.
14 Keith is to row with us to the lake to fix six of the signs.

gwam	1'	1	2	3	4	5	6	7	8	9	10	11	12

S KILL BUILDING

25D • 13

Speed Building

1. Key a 1' writing on each ¶; find *gwam* on each writing.
2. Add 2-4 *gwam* to better rate in Step 1 for a new goal.
3. Key three 1' guided writings on each ¶ at new goal rate. (See p. 54 for procedure.)

Quarter-Minute Checkpoints			
gwam	1/4'	1/2'	3/4'	Time
16	4	8	12	16
20	5	10	15	20
24	6	12	18	24
28	7	14	21	28
32	8	16	24	32
36	9	18	27	36
40	10	20	30	40

E all letters used
gwam 2'

Do you think someone is going to wait around just for a   6
chance to key your term paper? Do you believe when you get   12
out into the world of work that there will be someone to key   18
your work for you? Think again. It does not work that way.   24

Even the head of a business now uses a keyboard to send   29
and retrieve data as well as other information. Be quick to   35
realize that you will not go far in the world of work if you   42
do not learn how to key. Excel at it and move to the top.   47

2'	1	2	3	4	5	6

LESSON 125

Process Tables

Objective:
To improve table formatting skill.

125A • 5
Conditioning Practice

set 0.5" SMs;
each line twice

alphabet	1	Viki will begin to expedite the zone office's major quarterly reports.
speed	2	The haughty man may signal with a giant emblem or with the usual sign.
fig/sym	3	Ed called (505) 157-5980 before 1:15 p.m. and 113-6742 after 4:15 p.m.

gwam 1' | 1 | 2 | 3 | 4 | 5 | 6 | 7 | 8 | 9 | 10 | 11 | 12 | 13 | 14 |

125B • 8
Techniques: Return and Tab

1. Set a **right** tab 3" from left edge of paper; set a **left** tab 3.5" from left edge of paper. If you cannot set a right tab on your equipment, your teacher will give you further direction.
2. Key the lines given at the right. Concentrate on correct techniques for Enter and Tab keys.
3. Take three 1' writings; try to increase amount keyed with each writing.

words

Name:	*Jessica A. Burke*	5
Address:	*3890 Rockdale Dr.*	10
City:	*Columbus*	14
State:	*GA*	17
ZIP:	*31907-8328*	20
Phone:	*(706) 182-1296*	25

F ORMATTING

125C • 37
Process Tables

Table 1
CS: 0.5"
DS between each complete entry.

	DIRECTORY		) Bold	2
	OF			3
	DEPARTMENT MANAGERS			7

Manager	*Department*	*Address*	*Home Phone*	
Gary Musto	Accounting	310 Basswood Street	178-9215	25
		Denver, CO 80221-1342		29
Beth Alcott	Finance	839 Telluride Street	198-5657	38
		Aurora, CO 80011-8820		43
Guy Richins	Marketing	*1820 Locust St.*	*194-2102*	52
		Denver, CO 80220-8395		57
Kent Peters	Personnel	980 De Gaulle Street	183-8931	66
		Aurora, CO 80018-*5621*		71
Linda Cey	Purchasing	7665 Orchard Court	180-4132	80
		Golden, CO 80403-8338		85
Jan Wright	Word	8763 Racine Street	*161-8326*	93
	Processing	Denver, CO 80239-5438		99

LESSON 26

New Keys: 9 and 4

Objectives:

1. To learn reach technique for **9** and **4**.

2. To improve language skills and skill transfer.

26A • 5
Conditioning Practice

LS: SS

SM: defaults or 1.25"

each line twice; then a 1' writing on line 3; find *gwam*

alphabet 1 Joby quickly fixed a glass vase and amazed the proud owners.

spacing 2 She told us to add the figures 11, 88, 18, 81, 118, and 881.

easy 3 Ciel may make a bid on the ivory forks they got in the city.

gwam 1' | 1 | 2 | 3 | 4 | 5 | 6 | 7 | 8 | 9 | 10 | 11 | 12 |

26B • 18
New Keys: 9 and 4

each line twice SS (slowly, then faster); DS between 2-line groups; if time permits, key lines 5-7 again

9 *Right ring* finger

4 *Left index* finger

Follow the *Standard Plan for Learning New Keys* outlined on p. 17.

Learn 9

use the letter "l" 1 l l 9l 9l ll 99 l9l l9l 99l 99l Reach up for 9, 99, and 999.

2 Key the figures 9, 99, and 999.   Did the 9 and 99 finish it?

Learn 4

3 f f 4f 4f ff 44 f4f f4f 44f 44f Reach up for 4, 44, and 444.

4 Add the figures 4, 44, and 444.   Please study pages 4 to 44.

Combine 9 and 4

5 Key 44, 49, 94, and 99.   Only 49 of the 94 joggers are here.

6 Reach with the fingers to key 49 and 499 as well as 4 and 9.

7 My goal is to sell 44 pizzas, 99 tacos, and 9 cases of cola.

26C • 5
New-Key Mastery

1. Key each of lines 1-3 twice SS (slowly, then faster); DS between 2-line groups.

2. If time permits, key each line again for speed.

Figure sentences

1 Keep the fingers low as you key 11, 18, 19, 48, 94, and 849.

use the figure "1" 2 On March 8, 1994, 14 people took the 4 tests for the 8 jobs.

3 He based his May 1 report on pages 449 to 488 of Chapter 19.

LESSON 124 Process Tables

Objectives:
1. To improve skill in formatting tables.
2. To learn to format column headings longer than column text.

124A • 5
Conditioning Practice
each line twice

alphabet	1	Zelda gave Wayne exact requirements for taking the Ypsilanti job.
speed	2	Pam may name an official tutor to work for the widow and six men.
figures	3	We sold 26 desks, 34 chairs, and 50 tables on September 28, 1997.

gwam 1' | 1 | 2 | 3 | 4 | 5 | 6 | 7 | 8 | 9 | 10 | 11 | 12 | 13 |

124B • 7
Center Column Headings over Columns

wp users:
See Table Format function, pp. 299-300.
Electronics users see Center column headings, p. RG19.
  DS between heading and first entry; DS the entries; **CS: 1".**

Font Face	Appearance	Justification	words
			8
Courier	Bold	Left	11
Roman	Italic	Right	15
Script	Shadow	Center	19

124C • 38
Format Tables with Long Column Headings

Table 1
CS: 0.5"; DS entries; center column heads.

SELECTED STATE TIME ZONES			
			5
Eastern Standard	Central Standard	Mountain Standard	16
Florida	Arkansas	Arizona	21
Georgia	Iowa	Colorado	26
New York	Minnesota	New Mexico	31
Ohio	Missouri	Utah	35
Vermont	Oklahoma	Wyoming	40

Table 2
CS: 1"; DS entries; center column heads.

Note: Margins may need to be changed.

Table 3
Update Table 2 to include the following states:
Texas, Tex., TX
Wisconsin, Wis., WI
South Carolina, S.C., SC
Washington, Wash., WA
Virginia, Va., VA
Alphabetize by state.

STATE POSTAL ABBREVIATIONS			
			5
Name of State	Standard Abbreviation	Two-Letter Abbreviation	9 / 18
Illinois	Ill.	IL	21
Indiana	Ind.	IN	25
Alabama	Ala.	AL	28
Kentucky	Ky.	KY	31
Alaska	Alaska	AK	34
California	Calif.	CA	39
Connecticut	Conn.	CT	43
Delaware	Del.	DE	46

LS: DS
SM: defaults or 1.25"

1. Key each line once DS (2 hard returns between lines).
2. Rekey the rough-draft lines if time permits.

≡ = capitalize
∧ = insert
⌐ = delete
∿ = transpose
⌐# = delete space
= add space
/lc = lowercase
⊂ = close up

Script

1 Proofread: Compare copy word for word with the original.
2 Compare all figures digit by digit with your source copy.
3 Be sure to check for spacing and punctuation marks, also.
4 Copy in script or rough draft may not show exact spacing.
5 It is your job to insert correct spacing as you key copy.
6 Soon you will learn how to correct your errors on screen.

Rough draft

7 cap the first word an^d all proper nouns in each every sentence.

8 For example: pablo Mendez is from San juan, Puerto rico.

9 Ami Qwan and her parents will return to Taipie this fall summer.

10 our coffee comes is from Columbia Brazil; tea, from England or china.

11 How many of you have Ethnic origins in a for eign country?

12 Did Do you know which of the our states once were part of mexico?

L ANGUAGE SKILLS

26E • 10
Number Expression

Standard Plan for Mastering Language Skills

1. Read the first rule highlighted in color.
2. Key the Learn sentence below it, noting how the rule is applied.
3. Key the Apply sentence, supplying the appropriate number expression.
4. Practice the other rules in the same way.
5. If time permits, key the Apply sentences again to improve number control.

LANGUAGE SKILLS *cue:*
No space is left before or after : when used with figures to express time.

Spell a number that begins a sentence even when other numbers in the sentence are shown in figures.

Learn 1 Twelve of the new shrubs have died; 48 are doing quite well.
Apply 2 14 members have paid their dues, but 89 have not done so.

Use figures for numbers above ten, and for numbers one to ten when they are used with numbers above ten.

Learn 3 She ordered 8 word processors, 14 computers, and 4 printers.
Apply 4 Did he say they need ten or 14 sets of Z18 and Z19 diskettes?

Use figures to express dates and times (except when used with the word *o'clock*).

Learn 5 He will arrive on Paygo Flight 418 at 9:48 a.m. on March 14.
Apply 6 Candidates must be in Ivy Hall at eight forty a.m. on May one.

Format Guides

Agenda

Itinerary

In addition to the following information given to complete this unit, the Table Format Guides for Unit 22, p. 232, may be helpful. Students using the Table Format feature to process the tables in this unit should review pp. 299-300.

Column headings. Column headings can be centered in several ways, depending upon the equipment used and the length of headings in relation to column entries. In previous lessons, headings were centered along with column entries by using the keyline method (p. 157).

Sometimes column headings are shorter than any column entry. A table, of course, may have some headings that are shorter and others that are longer than the column entries. Specific procedures for centering headings in these cases appear on p. RG19. **Notes:** These procedures are recommended for electronics. The method is not recommended for use with a variable, or proportional, type font.

Another, less exact, method of centering column headings involves the operator's judgment. A blank line space is left above the columns as the entries are keyed. Then the operator estimates where to begin keying the heading in order to center it. **Notes:** This method is NOT recommended if equipment lacks an automatic correction feature. The method is appropriate when variable type is used.

On computer software, the Table Format feature allows column headings (as well as entries) to be centered automatically. **Note:** Directions in this unit include column space (CS) and line spacing (DS or SS) for students not using the Table Format feature of word processing software. Disregard these parts of the directions if you use Table Format.

Agenda. An agenda (see illustration) is an example of another business document that may use leaders (dot leader tab). A right-aligned format or left-aligned format may be used for the right column. The margins used for the agenda are: top, 2" (or centered); side, 1"; and bottom, 1". The heading of the agenda is double-spaced.

Itinerary. An itinerary (see illustration) is an outline of a person's travel activities for a specific period of time. The information on an itinerary is attractively formatted to provide the reader with information regarding the date, time, location, and activity of the person listed in the heading of the itinerary. The heading is DS. Margins are the same as for an agenda.

Leaders. Leaders, or dot leaders, are a series of periods and spaces (. . .) that are keyed between two items in tabular material to make reading easier. They "lead the reader's eye" from one columnar item to another. They are primarily used when the distance between certain items in two columns is so great that matching columnar items is difficult.

Leaders are made by alternating the period (.) and a space. The lines of leaders should be aligned in vertical rows.

To align leaders using an electronic, key all periods on either the odd or the even numbers on the line-of-writing scale guided by their position in the first line of leaders. Begin the first line of leaders on the second space after the first item in the column and end the leaders 2 or 3 spaces to the left of the beginning of the next column. Certain software packages require you to space after keying the entry in the first column and before keying the entry in the last column in order to achieve the desired spacing before and after leaders.

New Keys: 0 and 5

Objectives:

1. To learn reach technique for **0** and **5**.
2. To improve language skills and skill transfer.

27A • 5
Conditioning Practice

LS: SS

SM: defaults or 1.25"

each line twice (slowly, then faster); DS between 2-line groups; then a 1' writing on line 3

alphabet 1 Roz may put a vivid sign next to the low aqua boat for Jack.
figures 2 Please review Figure 8 on page 94 and Figure 14 on page 189.
easy 3 Tien may fix the bus panel for the city if the pay is right.
gwam 1' | 1 | 2 | 3 | 4 | 5 | 6 | 7 | 8 | 9 | 10 | 11 | 12 |

27B • 18
New Keys: 0 and 5

each line twice (slowly, then faster); DS between 2-line groups; if time permits, key lines 5-7 again

0 *Right little* finger

5 *Left index* finger

Follow the *Standard Plan for Learning New Keys* outlined on p. 17.

Learn 0 (zero)

1 ; ; 0; 0; ;; 00 ;0; ;0; 00; 00; Reach up for 0, 00, and 000.
2 Snap the finger off the 0. I used 0, 00, and 000 sandpaper.

Learn 5

3 f f 5f 5f ff 55 f5f f5f 55f 55f Reach up for 5, 55, and 555.
4 Reach up to 5 and back to f. Did he say to order 55 or 555?

Combine 0 and 5

5 Reach with the fingers to key 50 and 500 as well as 5 and 0.
6 We asked for prices on these models: 50, 55, 500, and 5500.
7 On May 5, I got 5 boxes each of 0 and 00 steel wool for her.

27C • 5
New-Key Mastery

each line once DS (2 hard returns between lines)

LANGUAGE SKILLS *cues:*

• No space is left before or after : when used with figures to express time.

• Most nouns before numbers are capitalized; exceptions include page and line.

No space

1 Flight 1049 is on time; it should be at Gate 48 at 5:50 p.m.
2 The club meeting on April 5 will be in Room 549 at 8:10 a.m.
3 Of our 108 workers in 1994, 14 had gone to new jobs by 1995.
4 I used Chapter 19, pages 449 to 458, for my March 10 report.
5 Can you meet us at 1954 Maple Avenue at 8:05 a.m. August 10?
6 Of the 590 students, 185 keyed at least 40 wam by April 18.

ACTIVITY 4:
Center Tables and Format Cells

1. Read the copy at right.
2. Learn how to format a cell, column, row, and table using your wp software.
3. Follow the directions at the right to revise the table named METRICA.
4. Save as METRICB.

Use the **Table** feature to center a table from side to side and top to bottom on a page.

Use the Table feature to align information in cells. Within a cell, information can be left-aligned (default), centered, or right-aligned. It can be centered vertically, too.

The Table feature permits you to set alignment for each cell or to set it once for a column, row, or even an entire table.

You also can choose the appearance of text (bold, italics, underline) for a cell, column, row, or table.

1. Cell A1 (main heading): centered, bold.
2. Cells A2, B2, and C2 (column headings): centered, bold.
3. Column B (the names): centered.
4. Column C (the abbreviations): right-aligned.
5. Table (content of all cells): centered vertically.
6. Table (position on page): centered.

ACTIVITY 5:
Dot Leader Tab

1. Read the copy at right.
2. Set a right dot leader tab at the right margin.
3. Key the text using the dot leader tab.

Dot leader tabs automatically place dot leaders (. . . . .) between columns of designated text. The leaders lead the eyes from the text in the first column to the text in the second column. A right dot leader tab inserts the text to the left of the tab; a left dot leader tab inserts the text to the right of the tab setting.

Hibbard	$ 2,500
Smith	1,950
Rodriguez	3,290
Sullivan	2,725
Perez	1,325
Stockton	3,250

ACTIVITY 6:
Apply What You Have Learned

1. Set a right dot leader tab at the right margin.
2. Key the text using the dot leader tab.
3. Set a left dot leader tab 1.5" from the right margin.
4. Key the text.
5. Notice how the names in the right column are aligned when a left dot leader tab is used versus when right a dot leader tab is used.

President	Kaiser
Vice President	Jasper
Secretary	Knipper
Treasurer	LaFleur
Reporter	Baylor

President	Kaiser
Vice President	Jasper
Secretary	Knipper
Treasurer	LaFleur
Reporter	Baylor

Skill Transfer: Straight Copy, Script, Rough Draft

1. Key each ¶ once SS; DS between ¶s.
2. Key a 1' writing on each ¶; find *gwam* on each writing; compare the 3 rates.
3. Key one or two more 1' writings on the two slowest ¶s to improve skill transfer.

stet = no change

∧ = insert

⤙ = delete

= add space

⊂ = close up

∿ = transpose

⊙ = insert period

Straight copy

gwam 1'

It is up to you to proofread the copy you produce to   11
find any mistakes you may have made. It is also up to you   22
to correct all the errors you find if the copy is to serve   34
a purpose other than to show that you have done the work.   46

| 1 | 2 | 3 | 4 | 5 | 6 | 7 | 8 | 9 | 10 | 11 | 12 |

Script

It is vital to check your copy word for word against   11
the source copy from which you keyed. The words should   22
be in the same order, and each word must be spelled right.   34
A space should be left after each word or punctuation mark.   46

Rough draft

Be quick to discover your errors even if you will not   11
correct them all just now. As soon as you begin to apply your   22
skill you may be taught easy ways to correct errors. For now,   35
learn to excell in marking and finding them.   44

L ANGUAGE SKILLS

27E • 10
Number Expression

Use the *Standard Plan for Mastering Language Skills,* p. 67.

Use figures for house numbers except house number *One*.

Learn 1 My home is at 8 Vernon Drive; my office, at One Weber Plaza.
Apply 2 The Nelsons moved from 4059 Pyle Avenue to 1 Maple Circle.

Use figures to express measures and weights.

Learn 3 Glenda Redford is 5 ft. 4 in. tall and weighs 118 lbs. 9 oz.
Apply 4 This carton measures one ft. by nine in. and weighs five lbs.

Use figures for numbers following nouns.

Learn 5 Review Rules 1 to 18 in Chapter 5, pages 149 and 150, today.
Apply 6 Case 1849 is reviewed in Volume five, pages nine and ten.

ACTIVITY 1:

Create and Fill in a Table

1. Read the copy at right.
2. Create and fill in the table shown in Activity 2.
3. Save the table (METRIC).

Use the **Table** feature to arrange information into rows and columns without using tab settings. Tables consist of vertical columns (named A, B, C, etc.) and horizontal rows (named 1, 2, 3, etc.). The crossing of columns and rows makes little "windows" called **cells** (named A1, A2, A3, etc.). Cell names do not appear on screen.

When text is keyed into a cell, it wraps around in that cell—instead of wrapping around to the next row. A line space is added to the cell each time the text wraps around.

To fill in cells, use the Tab key or right arrow key to move from cell to cell in a row and from row to row. (Striking Enter will simply insert a blank line space in the cell.) To move around in a filled-in table, use the arrow keys, Tab, or the mouse (click on desired cell).

ACTIVITY 2:

Insert and Delete Rows

1. Learn how to insert a row in a table.
2. Open file METRIC; insert a row above Mass; another row below Time.
3. Learn how to delete a table row in your software.
4. Delete the two blank rows.

UNITS OF METRIC MEASURE		
Units	Names	Abbreviations
Length	meter	m
Mass (weight)	kilogram	kg
Temperature	kelvin	K
Time	second	s
Electrical current	ampere	A
Luminous intensity	candela	cd
Substance	mole	mol

ACTIVITY 3:

Join Cells and Change Column Widths

1. Read the copy at right.
2. Learn how to join cells and change column widths using your wp software.
3. Follow the directions at the right to revise the table named METRIC.
4. Save as METRICA.

Use the **Table** feature to **join** cells (merge two or more cells into one cell). This feature is useful when information in the table spans more than one column or row. The main heading, for example, spans all columns.

In a newly created table, all columns are the same width. The Table feature can be used to change the width of one or more columns.

1. Join Cells A1, B1, and C1. (Result: The main heading cell spans Columns A, B, and C.)
2. Change Column B to a width of 1.25".
3. Change Column C to a width of 1.5".

New Keys: 7 and 3

Objectives:
1. To learn the reach technique for **7** and **3**.
2. To improve keying speed and language skills.

28A • 5
Conditioning Practice

LS: SS
SM: defaults or 1.25"

each line twice; DS between 2-line groups; then a 1' writing on line 3

alphabet 1 Gavin made a quick fall trip by jet to Zurich six weeks ago.

figures 2 Key 1 and 4 and 5 and 8 and 9 and 0 and 190 and 504 and 958.

easy 3 The man is to fix the big sign by the field for a city firm.

gwam 1' | 1 | 2 | 3 | 4 | 5 | 6 | 7 | 8 | 9 | 10 | 11 | 12 |

28B • 18
New Keys: 7 and 3

each line twice SS (slowly, then faster); DS between 2-line groups; if time permits, key lines 5-7 again

7 *Right index* finger

3 *Left middle* finger

Follow the *Standard Plan for Learning New Keys* outlined on p. 17.

Learn 7

1 j j 7j 7j jj 77 j7j j7j 77j 77j Reach up for 7, 77, and 777.

2 Key the figures 7, 77, and 777. She checked Rooms 7 and 77.

Learn 3

3 d d 3d 3d dd 33 d3d d3d 33d 33d Reach up for 3, 33, and 333.

4 Add the figures 3, 33, and 333. Read pages 3 to 33 tonight.

Combine 7 and 3

5 Key 33, 37, 73, and 77. Just 37 of the 77 skiers have come.

6 Please order 7 Model 337 computers and 3 Model 737 printers.

7 On August 7, the 33 bikers left on a long trip of 377 miles.

S KILL BUILDING

28C • 7
Technique:
Response Patterns

1. Key each pair of lines once SS; DS between 2-line groups.
2. Key a 1' writing on line 2 and then on line 4; find *gwam* on each writing.
3. Rekey the slower line if time permits.

letter response 1 face pump ever milk area jump vast only save upon safe union

2 As we were in a junk, we saw a rare loon feast on a crawdad.

word response 3 quay hand also body lend hang mane down envy risk corn whale

4 Tisha is to go to the lake with us if she is to do the work.

combination response 5 with only|they join|half safe|born free|firm look|goal rates

6 I sat on the airy lanai with my gaze on the sea to the east.

gwam 1' | 1 | 2 | 3 | 4 | 5 | 6 | 7 | 8 | 9 | 10 | 11 | 12 |

Reading/Keying Response Patterns

1. Key the lines as shown.
2. Key a 1' writing on each of lines 10-12; find *gwam* on each.

letter response
1 act ill bad him car mop set oil sew lip age pop tea ink fade pink
2 fast car|rare cat|red dress|car oil|best verse|brass cat|free pop
3 After I gave my opinion, you were assessed taxes on oil reserves.

word response
4 he wish them soap turns man paid risk gowns elbow girl goal giant
5 to go|eight girls|with their|to pay|lame cow|hay field|city docks
6 Pamala is apt to yell when they cut down the iris by this chapel.

combination response
7 the see for tea go lion end kill firm pull oak milk risk race she
8 for tea|the target|may stress|and my|rich estate|for free|or pink
9 Gregg and Jimmy may get the pop and milk at the cafe on the hill.

letter 10 Reese assessed a tax rate on my few acres on West Terrace Street.
combination 11 The art firm better pay the taxes on the garages and on the land.
word 12 Dick may pay the firm for the work when they sign the audit form.

gwam 1' | 1 | 2 | 3 | 4 | 5 | 6 | 7 | 8 | 9 | 10 | 11 | 12 | 13 |

Capitalization Check

Key the sentences at the right; supply capitalization as needed.

1. the sears tower is one of chicago's **tourist attractions.**
2. we will visit mount rushmore on new year's day.
3. the meeting with president Seitzer will be in los angeles.
4. jefferson city, the capital, is located on the missouri river.
5. reese morton was appointed manager for the parker playhouse.
6. weber state university was founded in 1889 in ogden, utah.
7. dr. jill s. clayton received her ph.d. from new mexico state.
8. their new home is located on fillmore, near kennedy towers.
9. the next holiday will be labor day on monday, september 5.
10. gettysburg and fredericksburg were both civil war battles.

Timed Writings: Script

Three 1' writings for speed; determine *gwam* on each timing.

A   all letters used   **gwam** 1'

The advantages of purchasing goods and services on credit   11
are numerous. Credit allows you to make purchases when you   24
do not have the extra funds available to pay cash. Most people 36
use credit to make sizable purchases such as a car or a house. 49
Credit also allows individuals to buy items on sale when they   62
don't have the money to do so. If they were intending to make   75
the purchase at some future time, using credit is a wise con-   87
sumer spending habit. Credit is also quite justifiable during   99
times of emergencies.   103

28D • 8
Speed Check

LS: DS

1. Key a 1' writing on ¶ 1 and then on ¶ 2; find *gwam* on each ¶.

2. Key two 2' writings on ¶s 1-2 combined; find *gwam* on each writing.

1' *gwam* goals

▽ 21 = acceptable

☐ 25 = average

⊙ 29 = good

◇ 33 = excellent

E all letters used

	gwam	2'	3'

Time and motion are major items in building our keying — 6 | 4

power. As we make each move through space to a letter or a — 12 | 8

figure, we use time. So we want to be sure that every move — 18 | 12

is quick and direct. We cut time and aid speed in this way. — 24 | 16

A good way to reduce motion and thus save time is just — 29 | 19

to keep the hands in home position as you make the reach to — 35 | 23

a letter or figure. Fix your gaze on the copy; then, reach — 41 | 27

to each key with a direct, low move at your very best speed. — 47 | 31

| gwam | 2' | 1 | 2 | 3 | 4 | 5 | 6 |
| 3' | | 1 | | 2 | | 3 | | 4 |

28E • 12
Capitalization and Number Expression

Use the *Standard Plan for Mastering Language Skills,* p. 67.

Capitalize nouns preceding numbers (except *page* and *line*).

Learn 1 Please see Rule 30 in Unit 3, page 45, lines 17 and 18.
Apply 2 See Volume 13, section 48, page 574, lines 78 to 90.

Spell (and initial cap) names of small-numbered streets and avenues (ten and under).

Learn 3 I walked several blocks along Third Avenue to 54th Street.
Apply 4 At 7th Street she took a taxi to his home on 43d Avenue.

Spell indefinite numbers.

Learn 5 Joe owns one acre of Parcel A; that is almost fifty percent.
Learn 6 Nearly seventy members voted; that is nearly a fourth.

Apply 7 i read 3 items from COLLECTED POEMS by robert frost.
Apply 8 he arrives on Flight 175 at 8 a.m. on friday.
Apply 9 kim is to meet us on 58th street at 5th avenue.
Apply 10 she asked over 30 students; almost a 3d of us went.
Apply 11 we attended a meeting in room 193 of columbia hall.
Apply 12 i saw the quote on Page 173b of FAMILIAR QUOTATIONS.

Tabulation

1. Clear tabs.
2. Set tabs 3" and 5.5" from the left margin.
3. Key the table.
4. Take three 1' writings; try to increase the amount keyed on each writing.

			words
3191 Birchwood	Salem, OR	97303	6
8760 Nugget Gulch	Rapid City, SD	57702	14
1917 Pine Needles	Jackson, TN	38301	21
9265 Ridgemeadow	Carrollton, TX	75006	29
4809 Cannonball Rd.	Fairfax, VA	22030	37
7623 Jasmine St.	Olympia, WA	98502	44
8361 Mohawk Rd.	Janesville, WI	53545	52
5409 Hawthorne Dr.	Casper, WY	82604	59

Timed Writings: Rough Draft

1. Two 3' writings for speed; determine *gwam* on each writing.
2. One 5' writing for speed; determine *gwam*.

A   all letters used   gwam 3' 5'

The requirements of today's secretary are changing different. The   4 3 37

ability to use a computer or a word processor is a major skill now required   9 5 40

for office support personnel by a sizeable number of   12 7 42

firms. This is a trend expected to continue with an even   16 10 44

greater emphasis on computer usage in the future. This   19 12 46

will make it more critical than ever for those pursuing a   24 14 49

position in this field to have excellent keyboarding skill   28 17 51

in order to make the best use of the costly equipment. A   31 18 53

student deciding on a career in this field will also find   35 21 56

that the role assumed by many office support staff members   39 23 58

is that of an assistant to a person at the management a higher level.   43 26 60

More and more of today's office job the titles used in offices of today   46 27 62

reflect this trend. Job titles such as administrative   49 30 64

assistant or executive assistant are quite common now. A   53 32 67

college degree for jobs positions such as these, however, may be required stipu-   58 35 69

often lated.   58 35 70

LESSON 29   New Keys: 6 and 2

MLS

Objectives:

1. To learn the reach technique for **6** and **2**.

2. To improve keying technique and speed.

29A • 5
Conditioning Practice

LS: SS

SM: defaults or 1.25"

each line twice; DS between
2-line groups; then a 1'
writing on line 3

alphabet 1 Jared helped Mazy quickly fix the big wood stove in the den.

figures 2 Bella lives at 1847 Oak Street; Jessi, at 5039 Duard Circle.

easy 3 They may make their goals if they work with the usual vigor.

gwam 1' | 1 | 2 | 3 | 4 | 5 | 6 | 7 | 8 | 9 | 10 | 11 | 12 |

29B • 18
New Keys: 6 and 2

each line twice (slowly, then
faster); DS between 2-line
groups; if time permits, key
lines 5-8 again

6 *Right index* finger

2 *Left ring* finger

Follow the *Standard Plan for Learning New Keys* outlined on p. 17.

Learn 6

1 j j 6j 6j jj 66 j6j j6j 66j 66j Reach up for 6, 66, and 666.

2 Key the figures 6, 66, and 666.   Did just 6 of 66 finish it?

Learn 2

3 s s 2s 2s ss 22 s2s s2s 22s 22s   Reach up for 2, 22, and 222.

4 Add the figures 2, 22, and 222.   Review pages 2 to 22 today.

Combine 6, 2, and other figures

5 Key 22, 26, 62, and 66.   Just 22 of the 66 scouts were here.

6 Reach with the fingers to key 26 and 262 as well as 2 and 6.

7 Key figures as units: 18, 26, 37, 49, 50, 62, 162, and 268.

8 The proxy dated April 26, 1997, was vital in Case No. 30584.

29C • 7
New-Key Mastery

each line once SS

1 Lee has sold 16 elm, 28 ash, 37 oak, 49 pine, and 50 shrubs.

2 Flights 201 and 384 will be replaced by Flights 625 and 749.

3 Key as a unit: 10, 29, 38, 47, 56; two units, 162 and 4837.

4 In 1996, 26 of our 384 workers were moved to 507 Pecos Lane.

Activity 3:

1. Read carefully the ¶s at the right.
2. Key a list of what your school does to recognize those who excel in athletics (sports).
3. Key a list of what your school does to recognize those who excel in various academic areas.
4. Compose/key a ¶ indicating whether you believe that athletics gets more recognition than academics in your school.
5. Compose/key another ¶ suggesting how your school could appropriately recognize students who excel in academic areas.

Compose (think) as you key

A high percentage of schools throughout the country have an Athletic Awards banquet annually to honor student athletes who have shown outstanding athletic performance. At these events, athletes are acclaimed by coaches, families, and friends. Often, too, they are given trophies, "letters," or other recognition.

Given the relatively low percentage of the total student body honored in this way, many students and parents believe that ways should be found to recognize students who exhibit outstanding performance in the academic or scholastic areas as well. To do otherwise, they say, suggests that the school is placing more emphasis on athletics than on academics.

Why, they ask, shouldn't there be a Scholastic Awards banquet at which students are honored who have excelled in activities other than sports? Art, business, English/ foreign language, math/science, music, social studies, student government, and so on are important subjects that should be emphasized. Surely, they insist, these are *at least* as important as football or basketball—even if they are not performed by a team.

29D • 8
Technique: Keying, Spacing, Shifting

1. Key each line once SS; DS between 2-line groups.
2. Key a 1' writing on line 7 and then on line 8 if time permits; find *gwam* on each.

quick-snap keystrokes	1	Ella may go to the soap firm for title to all the lake land.
	2	Did the bugle corps toot with the usual vigor for the queen?
down-and-in spacing	3	Coy is in the city to buy an oak chair he wants for his den.
	4	Jan may go to town by bus to sign a work form for a new job.
out-and-down shifting	5	Robb and Ty are in Madrid to spend a week with Jae and Aldo.
	6	Are you going in May or in June? Samuel is leaving in July.
easy	7	Rick paid for both the visual aid and the sign for the firm.
	8	Glena kept all the work forms on the shelf by the big chair.

gwam 1' | 1 | 2 | 3 | 4 | 5 | 6 | 7 | 8 | 9 | 10 | 11 | 12 |

29E • 12
Speed Check

LS: DS

SM: defaults or 1.25"

1. Key two 1' writings on each ¶; find *gwam* on each writing.
2. Key a 2' writing on ¶s 1-2 combined; find *gwam*.
3. Key a 3' writing on ¶s 1-2 combined; find *gwam*.

Goals

1': At least 24 *gwam*.
2': At least 23 *gwam*.
3': At least 22 *gwam*.

all letters used

gwam 2' | 3'

Success does not mean the same thing to everyone. For   6 | 4
some, it means to get to the top at all costs: in power, in   12 | 8
fame, and in income. For others, it means just to fulfill   18 | 12
their basic needs or wants with as little effort as required.   24 | 16

Most people fall within the two extremes. They work quite   30 | 20
hard to better their lives at home, at work, and in the social   36 | 24
world. They realize that success for them is not in being at   42 | 28
the top but rather in trying to improve their quality of life.   48 | 32

gwam 2' | 1 | 2 | 3 | 4 | 5 | 6 |
3' | 1 | 2 | 3 | 4 |

R&e
Proofreading

1. Print a copy of the 3' writing you keyed in 29E.
2. Note the kinds of errors marked in the ¶ at right.
3. Note how proofreader's marks above the copy are used to mark errors for correction.
4. Proofread the printout of your 3' writing; mark each error for correction, using proofreader's marks.

\# = space   ∧ = insert   ⌣ = close up   ⟋ = delete   ∿ = transpose (tr)

Sucess does not mean the same thing to every one. For some,
it means to get to the top att all costs: in power, in fame, and
in income. For others it means juts to fulfill their basic needs
or or wants wiht as little effort required.

Line 1	Line 2	Line 3	Line 4
1 Omitted letter	1 Omitted word	1 Misstroke	1 Added word
2 Failure to space	2 Added letter	2 Omitted comma	2 Transposition
3 Faulty spacing	3 Faulty spacing	3 Transposition	3 Omitted word

Language & Writing Skills 12

Activity 1:

1. Study the spelling/definitions of the words in the color block at the right.
2. Key the **Learn** line in the first set of sentences.
3. Key the **Apply** lines, choosing the right words to complete each sentence correctly.
4. Key the second set of lines in the same way.
5. Check work; rekey lines containing word-choice errors.

Choose the right word

accept (vb) to receive, to give approval, to take	**leased** (vb) to grant use or occupation of under contract in exchange for rent
except (vb) to exclude	**least** (adj) lowest in importance or rank

Learn   1   I think they will accept all my revisions except for Unit 8.

Apply   2   Juliana works every day (accept/except) Saturday and Sunday.

Apply   3   Adolpho will attend the banquet to (accept/except) the award.

Learn   4   The fact that he leased his new automobile is least important.

Apply   5   We (leased/least) the apartment at (leased/least) a year ago.

Apply   6   Last but not (leased/least), she (leased/least) the family farm.

Activity 2:

1. Read each sentence, noting needed punctuation changes, including hyphen, colon, parentheses, underline, and quotation marks.
2. Key each sentence, supplying punctuation to complete the sentence correctly.
3. Check work; then rekey any sentence that contains a punctuation error.

Proofread & correct

1 Both five room apartments will be available by August 30.

2 Dolores bought a roll of one hundred 32 cent postage stamps.

3 Village Theater is mounting a big production of Porgy and Bess.

4 Many believe The Rainmaker is one of John Grisham's best books.

5 All in the Family was a very popular TV show in the 1970s.

6 Who, she asked, is your all time favorite pop vocalist?

7 Ms. Ott said: Read Frost's poem The Housekeeper by Monday.

8 Remember the steps (1) stand up; (2) speak up; (3) shut up.

9 "A textual citation follows the quote." Roberts, 1998, 173

10 The verbs set and sit as well as lay and lie cause difficulty.

11 The space between lines of text equals one twentieth of an inch.

12 The competition is scheduled for 9 15 a.m. on April 29.

13 My goal is to develop 1 self-confidence and 2 self-esteem.

14 Twenty one of the thirty two students exceeded expectations.

15 Miss Tallchief signed a two year contract as ballet director.

16 Lana gushed as if she'd found Shangri-la, That's beautiful.

17 His article, Cyberspace, appeared in USA Weekend magazine.

18 Dr. Roe said that "30 second and 1 minute spurts build speed."

19 Check these tables 2-6, p. 39; 3-9, p. 57; 4-2, p. 73.

20 After you see the film, she said, write a two page review.

Skill Builder

Practice Procedure

1. Key each line of a group (words, phrases, and sentences) three times: first, to improve keying technique; next, to improve keying speed; then, to build precise control of finger motions. DS between 3-line groups.
2. Take several 1' writings on the two sentences at the end of each set of lines to measure your skill on each kind of copy.
3. As time permits, repeat the drills, keeping a record of your speed scores to see how your skill grows.

Each of the 120 *different* words used in the drills is among the 600 most-used words in the English language. In a study of over two million words in personal and business communications, these 120 words accounted for over 40 percent of all word occurrences. Thus, they are important to you in perfecting your keying skill. Practice them frequently for both speed and accuracy.

Balanced-hand words of 2-5 letters (Use word response.)

words
1 of is it he to by or us an so if do am go me the six and but
2 a box may did pay end man air own due big for they with when
3 make them also then such than form work both city down their
4 end they when wish hand paid name held down sign field world

phrases
5 to me|of us|and may|pay for|big box|the six|but due|own them
6 am to work|is to make|a big city|by the name|to do such work

sentences
7 He may wish to go to the city to hand the work form to them.
8 The city is to pay for the field work both men did for them.

gwam 1' | 1 | 2 | 3 | 4 | 5 | 6 | 7 | 8 | 9 | 10 | 11 | 12 |

One-hand words of 2-5 letters (Use letter response.)

words
9 a in be on we up as my at no was you are him get few see set
10 far act war tax only were best date case fact area rate free
11 you act few ever only fact card upon after state great water

phrases
12 at no|as my|on you|we are|at best|get set|you were|only date
13 get you in|act on my case|you set a date|get a rate on water

sentences
14 Get him my extra tax card only after you set up a case date.
15 As you see, you are free only after you get a case date set.

gwam 1' | 1 | 2 | 3 | 4 | 5 | 6 | 7 | 8 | 9 | 10 | 11 | 12 |

Double-letter words of 2-5 letters (Speed up double letters.)

words
16 all see too off will been well good miss feel look less call
17 too free soon week room fill keep book bill tell still small
18 off call been less free look need week soon will offer needs

phrases
19 a room|all week|too soon|see less|call off|need all|will see
20 see a need|fill a book|miss a bill|all will see|a good offer

sentences
21 It is too soon to tell if we will need that small book room.
22 They still feel a need to offer a good book to all who call.

gwam 1' | 1 | 2 | 3 | 4 | 5 | 6 | 7 | 8 | 9 | 10 | 11 | 12 |

Balanced-hand, one-hand, and double-letter words of 2-5 letters

words
23 of we to in or on is be it as by no if at us up an my he was
24 and all war six see you men too are may get off pay him well
25 such will work best then keep were good been only city needs
26 make soon ever wish tell area name bill upon paid tell great

phrases
27 is too great|they will be|box was small|their offer was good
28 if at all|may get all|off the case|to tell him|to keep after

sentences
29 If you wish to get to the rate you set, keep the hand still.
30 All of us do the work well, for only good form will pay off.

gwam 1' | 1 | 2 | 3 | 4 | 5 | 6 | 7 | 8 | 9 | 10 | 11 | 12 |

1"

adding quotation marks. A colon generally introduces a
quotation displayed in this way, though sometimes the
context may require a different mark of punctuation, or
none at all. If you quote only a single paragraph, or
part of one, do not indent the first line more than the
rest. A parenthetical reference to a prose quotation
set off from the text follows the last line of the
quotation. (73) ——— 2 spaces

DS

1/2" ——→ Continue to double-space the text following the quotation,
indenting only the first line of each paragraph one-half inch
(five spaces). An example of the "Works Cited" page is illustrated on page 3. Notice that it is also double-spaced and
arranged in alphabetical order with the second and succeeding
lines of each entry indented one-half inch.

1"

Works Cited

Gibaldi, Joseph. MLA Handbook for Writers of Research Papers.

1/2" ——→ 4th ed. New York: The Modern Language Association of

America, 1995.

Harcourt, Jules, A. C. "Buddy" Krizan, and Patricia Merrier.

Business Communication. 3d ed. Cincinnati: South-Western

Educational Publishing, 1996.

all DS

Language & Writing Skills 2

Activity 1:

1. Study the spelling/ definitions of the words in the color block.
2. Key line 1 (the **Learn** line), noting proper choice of words.
3. Key lines 2-3 (the **Apply** lines), choosing the right words to complete the sentences correctly.
4. Study/practice the other words in the same way.
5. Check your accuracy; rekey lines containing errors.

Choose the right word

> **hour** (n) the 24th part of a day; a particular time
>
> **our** (adj) of or relating to ourselves as possessors
>
> **know** (vb) to be aware of the truth of; to have understanding of
>
> **no** (adv/adj/n) in no respect or degree; not so; indicates denial or refusal

Learn 1 It is our intention to complete the work in an hour or two.
Apply 2 If I drive steadily, we should reach (hour, our) house in an (hour, our).
Apply 3 We should earn one credit (hour, our) for (hour, our) computer class.

Learn 4 Did you know that there are to be no quizzes this week?
Apply 5 If you (know, no) the chapter, you should have (know, no) fear of a quiz.
Apply 6 Did you (know, no) that they scored (know, no) touchdowns in the game?

Activity 2:

1. Key each sentence once SS, capitalizing words according to the rules you have learned.
2. Check the accuracy of your application of those rules.
3. Rekey lines containing errors.

Proofread & correct

1 this stapler is defective. please send a new one soon.
2 ask if alma and suzan took the trip with ms. diaz to zaire.
3 texas and mexico share the rio grande as a common border.
4 miss jackson is a field auditor for the irs in new mexico.
5 did alexis say that thanksgiving day is always on thursday?

6 our school year begins in late august and ends in early june.
7 is the dubois tower on sixth street or on oakland avenue?
8 marquis saw the play at lincoln center in new york city.
9 send these dental supplies to byron c. thompson, d.d.s.
10 do you know when senator metcalf asked to see the president?

Activity 3:

Key each line once SS. In place of the blank line at the end of each sentence, key the word(s) that correctly complete(s) the sentence.

Compose (think) as you key

1 A small mass of land surrounded by water is a/an _____.
2 A large mass of land surrounded by water is a/an _____.
3 The earth rotates on what is called its _____.
4 When the sun comes up over the horizon, we say it _____.

5 When the sun goes down over the horizon, we say it _____.
6 A device used to display temperature is a/an _____.
7 A device used to display atmospheric pressure is a/an _____.
8 A device used to display time is a/an _____.

Bryant 1

1/2"

1"

Jane A. Bryant

Professor Doherty

English 2140

10 February ----

DS

Standard Format for an MLA-Style Research Report

A contemporary method of documentation is appropriate for
reports that contain information from only a few sources
(Harcourt 448). The MLA-style (Modern Language Association of
America) report that is illustrated here is a method that can be
used. There are several key differences between this style and
the formats introduced in previous lessons. An MLA-style report
has one-inch side, top, and bottom margins. The entire report is
double-spaced, including quotations, documentation, and the space
below the title.

No title page is used. Information normally found on the
title page (writer's name, teacher's name, course title, and
date) is keyed on the first page beginning one inch from the top
margin starting at the left margin.

Page numbers for all pages (including the first) are keyed
at the right margin one-half inch from the top edge of the paper.
The writer's last name precedes the page number.

Another difference is the way that long quotations are keyed
in the MLA style. In the MLA Handbook for Writers of Research
Papers, Gibaldi provides these guides for keying long quotations:

If a quotation runs to more than four typed lines, set
it off . . . by beginning a new line, indenting one inch
(or ten spaces if you are using a typewriter) from the
left margin, and typing it double-spaced, without

LESSON 30

Keying Skills

Objectives:
1. To improve technique on individual letters.
2. To improve keying speed on 1', 2', and 3' writings.

30A • 5
Conditioning Practice

each line twice SS; then a 1' writing on line 3; find *gwam*

alphabet	1	Lopez knew our squad could just slip by the next five games.
figures	2	Check Numbers 267, 298, 304, and 315 were still outstanding.
easy	3	Dixie works with vigor to make the theory work for a profit.

gwam 1' | 1 | 2 | 3 | 4 | 5 | 6 | 7 | 8 | 9 | 10 | 11 | 12 |

S KILL BUILDING

30B • 30
Technique Mastery: Individual Letters

1. Key each line twice SS; DS between 2-line groups. Note the lines that were difficult for you.
2. Key those lines again.

Technique goals
- curved, upright fingers
- quick-snap keystrokes
- quiet hands and arms

A	1	Ana ate a salami sandwich and some papaya after a quick nap.
B	2	Bobby bought a beach ball and big balloons for the big bash.
C	3	Cora can serve cake and coffee to the cold campers at lunch.
D	4	David did all he could to dazzle the crowd with wild dances.
E	5	Elaine left her new sled in an old shed near the gray house.
F	6	Frank found a file folder his father had left in the office.
G	7	Gloria got the giggles when the juggler dropped his oranges.
H	8	Hugh helped his big brother haul in the fishing net for her.
I	9	Inez sings in a trio that is part of a big choir at college.
J	10	Jason just joined the jury to judge the major jazz festival.
K	11	Kurt makes kapok pillows for kayaks and ketches at the dock.
L	12	Lola left her doll collection for a village gallery to sell.
M	13	Myna asked her mom to make more malted milk for the mission.
N	14	Nadine knew her aunt made lemonade and sun tea this morning.
O	15	Owen took the book from the shelf to copy his favorite poem.
P	16	Pamela added a pinch of pepper and paprika to a pot of soup.
Q	17	Quent posed quick quiz questions to his quiet croquet squad.
R	18	Risa used a rubber raft to rescue four girls from the river.
S	19	Silas said his sister has won six medals in just four meets.
T	20	Trisha told a tall tale about three little kittens in a tub.
U	21	Ursula asked the usual questions about four issues you face.
V	22	Vinny voted for five very vital issues of value to everyone.
W	23	Wilt wants to walk in the walkathon next week and show well.
X	24	Xania next expects them to fix the extra fax machine by six.
Y	25	Yuri said your yellow yacht was the envy of every yachtsman.
Z	26	Zoella and a zany friend ate a sizzling pizza in the piazza.

LESSON 123

Report in MLA Format

Objectives:
1. To format a report in MLA style.
2. To improve language skills (quotation marks).

123A • 5
Conditioning Practice
each line twice

alphabet 1 Major Frank Valdez always sprayed extra herbicides on quackgrass.

speed 2 The small ornament on their oak mantle is an antique ivory whale.

figures 3 Robert Myer's address is 856 Moss Drive, Columbia, SC 29203-7401.

gwam 1' | 1 | 2 | 3 | 4 | 5 | 6 | 7 | 8 | 9 | 10 | 11 | 12 | 13 |

L ANGUAGE SKILLS

123B • 5
Quotation Marks

Follow the Learn/Apply procedure in 76C on p. 184.

> Use quotation marks to enclose special words or phrases used for emphasis or for coined words (words not in dictionary usage).

Learn 1. My problem is that I have "limited resources" and "unlimited wants."

Apply 2. His speech was liberally sprinkled with you knows.

Apply 3. I heard him characterized as a phony.

> Use a single quotation mark (the apostrophe) to indicate a quotation within a quotation.

Learn 4. I said, "We must take, as Frost suggests, the 'road less traveled.' "

Apply 5. I wrote, "We must have, as Tillich said, the courage to be."

Apply 6. She said, "We must be reminded to, as Kennedy said, Ask not . . . ."

123C • 10
Language Skills: Review

1. The sentences at the right may contain errors in capitalization and number expression.

2. As you key each sentence, make all necessary corrections, including any keystroking errors you may make.

3. After you key all sentences, proofread each one and correct additional errors you may find.

1. Mr. Ortiz moved to craig, colorado, from New york city in May.
2. I believe memorial day will be celebrated on sunday this year.
3. The American revolution preceded the french revolution.
4. The King climbing club will climb the Grand canyon on friday.

5. 14 of the company employees agreed to participate; 22 did not.
6. We have 12 clarinets, six flutes, and 5 trumpets in the band.
7. The 8 girls arrived on the bus at six thirty on June six.
8. The answer can be found in Chapter Five, page 389.

9. The new Baby weighed seven Pounds and was 20 inches long.
10. Our President, J. b. Sims, will meet us at the office.
11. "this car may be my first," he said, "But it won't be my last."
12. She arrived on Flight sixty-two at 4:30 p.m. on May 19.

123D • 30
MLA-Style Report

1. Read the information about formatting reports in MLA style on page 284; study the model on pp. 293-294.

2. Format and key the report on pp. 293 and 294.

R & E activities can be found on pp. A27-A30.

1. Key one 1' unguided and two 1' guided writings on ¶ 1 and then on ¶ 2.
2. Key two 2' unguided writings on ¶s 1-2 combined; find *gwam* on each.
3. Key a 3' writing on ¶s 1-2 combined; find *gwam*.

1' *gwam* goals
▽ 23 = acceptable
▣ 27 = average
◉ 31 = good
◇ 35 = excellent

all letters used   gwam 2' | 3'

When saying hello to someone is the correct thing to do,   6 | 4
make direct eye contact and greet the person with vitality 12 | 8
in your voice. Do not look down or away or speak only in a 18 | 12
whisper. Make the person feel happy for having seen you, and 24 | 16
you will feel much better about yourself as a consequence. 30 | 20

   Similarly, when you shake hands with another person, 35 | 23
look that person in the eye and offer a firm but not crushing 41 | 27
shake of the hand. Just a firm shake or two will do. Next 47 | 31
time you meet a new person, do not puzzle about whether to 53 | 35
shake hands. Quickly offer your firm hand with confidence. 59 | 39

gwam 2' | 1 | 2 | 3 | 4 | 5 | 6
3' | 1 | 2 | 3 | 4

WORD PROCESSING

1. Read the information at the right; learn to use the wp features described.
2. Key the lines given below as shown; if necessary, ALL CAP underlined words and underline or ALL CAP italicized or bold titles.
3. Using available wp features, make the following changes in your lines:

line 1
In *4,589*, change *9* to *6*; in *2,576*, change *6* to *3*.
line 2
After *My*, insert *new*.
line 3
Change *He* to *Al*.
line 4
After *has*, insert *just*; change *Madrid* to *Berlin*.
line 5
After *is*, insert *now*.
line 6
Change *up* to *in*; *desk* to *door*.

Insert Mode
To insert new text into existing text, use Insert Mode, which is automatically on when you enter a software program. Move cursor to point of insert and key new text. Existing copy will move to right.

Typeover Mode
Typeover Mode allows you to replace current text with newly keyed text.

Underline
The Underline feature underlines text as it is keyed.

Italic
The Italic feature italicizes text as it is keyed.

Bold
The Bold feature prints text darker than other copy as it is keyed.

figures
1 Of these 4,589 voters, 2,576 marked Yes and 2,013 marked No.
2 My bank card number is 274 910; your card number is 562 838.

shift-key sentences
3 He and Vi crossed the English Channel from Hove to Le Havre.
4 J. W. Parker has left Madrid for Turin for some Alps skiing.

space-bar sentences
5 If it is up to me, tell the man to pay his part of the cost.
6 He is to sign up at the desk if he wants to go to the dance.

wp features
7 <u>Effect</u> is usually a noun; whereas, <u>affect</u> is used as a verb.
8 She keys each book title in CAPS, underlined, or in italics.

wp features
9 Kendra checked out a copy of *History of Art* by H. W. Janson.
10 I have an Edward Pixley update of **Invitation to the Theatre.**

Document 2
Endnotes Page

Use the following information to create a separate endnotes page.

¹ John Grove, "New Media for Your Messages," The Secretary, March 1993, p. 6.

² Grove, p. 7.

³ Amy Gage, "Voice Mail Technology Can Be a Source of Frustration, Irritation," St. Paul Pioneer Press, August 3, 1994, p. 1C.

⁴ "Information Distribution," Modern Office Technology, January 1993, p. 36.

⁵ "Voice Mail Minds the Store While You're Out," Managing Office Technology, November 1993, p. 76.

Document 3
Title Page

Prepare a title page for the report, using your name, school name, and current date.

When voice messaging systems are used to replace a receptionist, callers may feel they have landed in Voice Mail Jail--especially if they have to deal with a complex series of choices. We believe that most businesses should use voice messaging systems as a backup for an attendant, not as a replacement.[4]

597
612
625
638
645

Voice-Mail Tips

649

Regardless of whether voice mail is used to replace an attendant or as a backup for the attendant, it must be effective. To be effective, voice mail has to be used correctly. The following tips from Pacific Bell provide a basis for effective use of voice mail.[5]

665
679
694
702

- **Provide details.** Business associates need to know specifically when you're leaving, when you'll be back in the office, and when they can expect a return call.

715
728
735

- **Be courteous and businesslike.** Maintain the same professional demeanor on your vacation greeting as your regular greeting while in the office. Keep it positive to reassure customers that it's business as usual, even though you're away.

746
761
775
783

- **Don't leave confusing or conflicting instructions.** Keep your greeting simple. If you need to leave instructions for accessing additional phone menus, make them easy to follow.

796
809
820

- **Give callers alternatives.** Let clients know who is handling their accounts in your absence, and always include the number the caller needs to press to reach your substitute.

834
846
855

- **Help callers reach a "live" person.** Callers always need the option of talking with a person. Let them know which button to push for an attendant.

868
881
886

- **Let callers know if you'll be checking your messages.** Tell callers you plan to phone in for messages from time to time while you're away--but only if you mean it.

898
912
919

- **Update your greeting as soon as you return.** Make sure callers know you've returned from vacation by updating your message with a current date and greeting. In this way, you and your associates can get back into swing right away.

933
945
957
966

By following these tips, your voice mail will give accurate, timely information. What's more, customers will not be offended and will know that their calls are valued.

979
992
1000

LESSON 31 Keying/Language Skills

O b j e c t i v e s :
1. To improve skill on sentence and paragraph writings.
2. To improve capitalization and number expression skills.

31A • 5
Conditioning Practice

each line twice SS; then a 1' writing on line 3; find *gwam*

alphabet	1	Jung quickly baked extra pizzas for the film festival crowd.
figures	2	I moved from 3748 Oak Street to 1059 Jaymar Drive on May 26.
easy	3	She paid the big man for the field work he did for the city.

gwam 1' | 1 | 2 | 3 | 4 | 5 | 6 | 7 | 8 | 9 | 10 | 11 | 12 |

S KILL BUILDING

31B • 30
Technique Emphasis

1. Key the lines once SS as shown—DS between 3-line groups.
2. Key the lines again at a faster pace.
3. If time permits, key a 1' writing on each of lines 22, 23, and 24; find *gwam*.

Technique goals
- quick down-and-in spacing
- out-and-down reaches to shift keys
- curved, upright fingers
- quiet hands and arms
- unused fingers low over home keys

figures	1	a l ; 0 g 5 us 72 or 94 am 17 is 82 do 39 by 56 go 59 up 70;
	2	On June 18, 1997, 30 of them took a bus trip of 2,465 miles.
	3	We were billed for 3,650 bulbs, 1,278 shrubs, and 495 trees.
space bar	4	When you reach a goal you have set, set one a little higher.
	5	Kevin may sign the audit form in the city when he checks it.
	6	She said to turn in our term papers by the end of next week.
shift keys & CAPS LOCK	7	Did you see LA BOHEME at the Metropolitan Opera in New York?
	8	Mary Ann saw a new production of CAROUSEL at Lincoln Center.
	9	Keiko read LINCOLN by Vidal; Kermit read MEXICO by Michener.
double letters	10	Nell took a small drill from the tool box to drill the hole.
	11	Ann took off the desk a book of odd poems to keep at school.
	12	Tommy will tell the class how a little more effort paid off.
adjacent keys	13	Kerry opted to rent a silk suit instead of buying a new one.
	14	If we buy her coffee shop, should we buy the gift shop, too?
	15	We spent a quiet week at the shore prior to the open season.
long direct reaches	16	Jenny spun on the ice, jumped the curb, and broke her thumb.
	17	We once had many mussels, but not since the recent harvests.
	18	My niece has a chance to bring the bronze trophy back to us.
alphabetic sentences	19	Mae was quickly given the bronze trophy by six fussy judges.
	20	Quinto got six big jigsaw puzzles from the very daffy clerk.
	21	Roz fixed the crisp okra, while Jane made unique beef gravy.
easy sentences	22	Alfie is to go to work for the city to fix bus sign emblems.
	23	Did he rush the rotor of the giant robot to the island firm?
	24	The busy girl works with a fury to fix the signals by eight.

gwam 1' | 1 | 2 | 3 | 4 | 5 | 6 | 7 | 8 | 9 | 10 | 11 | 12 |

Pillsbury's public relations department tries to use voice mail only at night or when staff members are in meetings, the reason being that communications employees should be readily accessible.[3]

The following lists are some of the advantages and disadvantages cited in the ongoing debate for and against voice mail.

Advantages

1. The caller makes contact with the person each time a call is placed.

2. The caller can simply leave a message. Leaving a message often takes care of the purpose of the call, as the caller's intent was not to speak directly to the person. By not having to speak directly with the person, the caller saves time and money by avoiding idle talk.

3. Unnecessary staff involvement in routine phone calls is eliminated.

4. Much paper is eliminated.

5. Company time and money can be saved.

Disadvantages

1. The caller may not like being told to "press one for . . . , press two for. . . ."

2. The caller may prefer talking to a person rather than a machine. A person provides the "personal service" better than a machine. Machines can have an adverse impact on how the company is perceived.

3. The voice-mail greeting should be changed routinely. The same old voice-mail greeting becomes tiring.

4. The messages may not be received because of an error on the part of the sender or because of malfunctioning equipment.

5. The caller may not be sure that a message is received when there is not an immediate response.

6. Some people are shy about leaving their own messages.

Should a company decide to implement voice mail, consideration should be given to how the company uses the equipment and to make sure that the equipment is used properly. According to Don Heitt, president at Voysys Corporation in San Jose:

Voice messaging is a tool that, like all tools, can be used improperly. While some voice messaging systems are easier to set up than others, it's up to the company that installs a system to make sure that the system enhances, rather than weakens, communications.

(continued on next page)

> **Note:** To enhance the appearance of enumerated items, align the second line (and succeeding lines) of each enumerated item under the first line—hanging indent style.
>
> If you prefer less space after the numbers, set a tab about 0.25" (two spaces) to the right of the period instead of using default tabs.

Speed Building: Guided Writing

1. Key one 1' unguided and two 1' guided writings on each ¶.
2. Key two 2' unguided writings on ¶s 1-2 combined; find *gwam* on each.
3. Key a 3' writing on ¶s 1-2 combined; find *gwam*.

all letters used

	gwam 2'	3'

When you need to adjust to a new situation in which new people are involved, be quick to recognize that at first it is you who must adapt. This is especially true in an office where the roles of workers have already been established. It is your job to fit into the team structure with harmony.

Learn the rules of the game and who the key players are; then play according to those rules at first. Do not expect to have the rules modified to fit your concept of what the team structure and your role in it should be. Only after you become a valuable member should you suggest major changes.

| gwam 2' | 1 | 2 | 3 | 4 | 5 | 6 |
| 3' | 1 | 2 | 3 | 4 |

gwam values 2' | 3':
6 | 4
12 | 8
18 | 12
24 | 16
30 | 20
35 | 23
41 | 27
47 | 31
53 | 36
59 | 39

R&e

Language Skills Checkup

1. Key each line given at the right, properly capitalizing words and expressing numbers.
2. Check your work and correct any lines containing errors in capitalization and number expression.

1 i know labor day is the first monday in september.

2 dr. j. d. wilkes got a d. d. s. from rutgers in may.

3 did ms. perez ask us to read THE CRADLE WILL FALL?

4 concordia bank is at mott street and laurel place.

5 was dr. eric b. roarke awarded an m.d. or ph. d.?

6 muriel getz, the club secretary, read the minutes.

7 condos 8 and 15 have 2 bedrooms; unit 9 has three.

8 the letter dated may 16 is vital in case no. 4809.

9 for the answer to problem 9, see unit 8, page 274.

10 of 63 workers, nine chose not to get the flu shot.

11 forty club members have signed up, but 8 have not.

12 did ms. ott say july 4 is always independence day?

LESSONS 121-122

Unbound Report

Objectives:
1. To format an unbound report using endnote-style documentation.
2. To improve language skills (quotation marks).

121-122A • 5
Conditioning Practice

each line twice

alphabet 1 Howie Zahn helped Joy pack four big boxes of expensive equipment.

speed 2 The box with the emblem of the duck is on the mantle by the bowl.

figures 3 Invoice No. 37A 408 was paid on May 23; No. 29A 516 was not paid.

gwam 1' | 1 | 2 | 3 | 4 | 5 | 6 | 7 | 8 | 9 | 10 | 11 | 12 | 13 |

L ANGUAGE SKILLS

121B • 10
Quotation Marks

Follow the Learn/Apply procedure in 76C on p. 184.

> Use quotation marks to enclose direct quotations. **Note**: When a question mark applies to the entire sentence, it is keyed outside the quotation marks.

Learn 1. The coach asked, "Did you practice over the summer?"

Learn 2. Was it Emerson who said, "To have a friend is to be one"?

Apply 3. The waiter asked, How was your lunch?

Apply 4. Did Shakespeare say, All the world is a stage?

> Use quotation marks to enclose titles of articles, poems, songs, television programs, and unpublished works such as dissertations and theses.

Learn 5. She had read the poem "Solitude" by Ella Wheeler Wilcox.

Apply 6. Did you watch the TV program Saved by the Bell last night?

Apply 7. My favorite poem is IF by Rudyard Kipling.

F ORMATTING

121C-122B • 35/45
Unbound Report

Document 1
Unbound Report
Format and key the text at the right as an unbound report DS with endnotes.

wp note:

This report may be opened for use later. Be sure to save it!

words

VOICE MAIL

2

"To use or not to use" voice mail is the question for business organi-   16
zations. Many businesses have already made a decision.   28

Currently two million businesses use voice mail--and use is   40
expected to grow by 40-50 percent each year. In 1988, 28 percent   53
of companies with more than 1,000 employees had voice mail; in   65
1993, 70 percent of those companies used the technology.[1]   77

Those businesses that have not yet made a decision, however, must   90
consider the advantages and the disadvantages of doing so before jump-   104
ing on the bandwagon and purchasing a voice-mail system. In spite of the   118
increased popularity of voice mail, many customer-service oriented organi-   133
zations, such as banks, have decided the disadvantages far outweigh the   147
advantages. Only six percent of the banking industry use voice   162
mail.[2] Other organizations have decided to make limited use of voice mail.   176

(continued on next page)

Language & Writing Skills 3

Activity 1:

1. Study the spelling/ definitions of the words in the color block at right.
2. Key line 1 (the **Learn** line), noting the proper choice of words.
3. Key lines 2-3 (the **Apply** lines), choosing the right words to complete the lines correctly.
4. Key the remaining lines in the same way.
5. Check your accuracy; rekey lines containing word-choice errors.

Choose the right word

lead (vb) to guide or direct; to be first	**choose** (vb) to select; to decide on
led (vb) the past tense of *lead*	**chose** (vb) the past tense of *choose*

Learn 1 Max is to lead the parade; Pam led it last year.
Apply 2 The Falcons (lead, led) now; the Friars (lead, led) at the half.
Apply 3 Marj (lead, led) at the ninth hole, but she does not (lead, led) now.

Learn 4 Jose chose a Eureka computer; I may choose a Futura.
Apply 5 After he (choose, chose) a red cap, I told him to (choose, chose) blue.
Apply 6 Mae (choose, chose) you as a partner; Janice may (choose, chose) me.

Activity 2:

1. Read the paragraph, noting errors in capitalization, number expression, and word choice.
2. As you key the paragraph, correct the errors you have noted.
3. Check your accuracy; correct any errors you may have made.

Proofread & correct

over 20 of hour students, along with 4 sponsors, chose to take a trip to south america this summer.   they are to leave hear on june fifteen and are not do back until july 11. all no that they must have valid passports and health cards as proof of required immunizations. dr. elena diaz is the led sponsor of the tour.   they will tour capital cities in brazil, chile, peru, and venezuela.

Activity 3:

Key each line once SS. At the end of each line, supply the information (noted in parentheses) needed to complete the sentence. In lines 3 and 6, also choose the correct article (*a* or *an*) to precede the information you supply.

Compose (think) as you key

1 My full name is (first/middle/last).

2 I attend (name of school).

3 I am learning to key on a/an (brand of computer/typewriter).

4 My main goal has been to develop (technique/speed/accuracy).

5 My favorite class in school is (name of subject).

6 My career goal is to be a/an (name of job).

7 My main hobby is (name of hobby).

8 I spend most of my free time (name of activity).

Note: Ellipsis marks (three periods with a space before and after each one . . .) are used to show that one or more words have been omitted from the quoted sentence.

Document 2
Endnotes Page
Use the following information to create an endnotes page on a separate sheet.

[1] James W. Davis, The American President: A New Perspective (New York: Harper & Row Publishers, 1987), p. 4.

[2] Louis W. Koenig, Chief Executive, 5th ed. (San Diego: Harcourt Brace Jovanovich, Inc., 1986), pp. 14-15.

[3] Encyclopedia Americana, Vol. 22 (Danbury, CT: Grolier Incorporated, 1993), p. 561.

Document 3
Title Page
Prepare a title page for the report, using your name, school name, and current date.

	words

to fulfill that role have increased. Koenig[2] suggested that today's President has these imposing responsibilities:

> . . . survival problems in which the very future of the human race is at stake; the threat of nuclear weapons technology; persistence of war abroad; the remorseless growth of population, production, and pollution, and their endangering of the environment; grave unemployment and inflation; blighted cities and pervasive poverty and crime; excessive violations of civil rights and liberties; grossly inadequate provisions of health services, mass transit, education and the care of the elderly.

As Koenig's description of the presidential responsibilities indicates, the President of the United States has a job with many important and varied responsibilities.

Party Affiliation

Political party backing is critical to being elected President. Even though there have been numerous political parties in the United States, only five have become powerful enough to elect a President. Three of the parties (Federalist, Democratic-Republican, and Whig) no longer exist today. Of the remaining two parties (Democrat and Republican), one or the other has occupied the White House since 1853. As can be seen from the following table,[3] the first Democrat took office in 1829, while the first Republican did not assume office until 1861.

President and Party	Term
George Washington (F)	1789-1797
John Adams (F)	1797-1801
Thomas Jefferson (D-R)	1801-1809
James Madison (D-R)	1809-1817
James Monroe (D-R)	1817-1825
John Quincy Adams (D-R)	1825-1829
Andrew Jackson (D)	1829-1837
Martin Van Buren (D)	1837-1841
William Henry Harrison (W)	1841
John Tyler (W)	1841-1845
James K. Polk (D)	1845-1849
Zachary Taylor (W)	1849-1850
Millard Fillmore (W)	1850-1853
Franklin Pierce (D)	1853-1857
James Buchanan (D)	1857-1861
Abraham Lincoln (R)	1861-1865

Party Affiliation: D = Democrat; D-R = Democratic-Republican; F = Federalist; R = Republican; W = Whig.

369, 379, 391, 403, 415, 428, 441, 453, 466, 478, 493, 507, 512, 516, 530, 544, 559, 572, 584, 598, 611, 625, 626, 632, 638, 650, 656, 661, 668, 674, 680, 689, 692, 697, 703, 709, 715, 721, 727, 730, 733, 743, 751

UNIT 5

LESSONS 32–34

Get Acquainted with Symbol Keys

LESSON 32

New Keys: /, $, %, and –

Objectives:

1. To learn reach-strokes for /, $, %, and –.
2. To combine /, $, %, and – smoothly with other keys.

32A • 5
Conditioning Practice

each line twice SS; then a 1' writing on line 3; find *gwam*

alphabet	1	Di will buy from me as prizes the six unique diving jackets.
figures	2	The January 17 quiz of 25 points will test pages 389 to 460.
easy	3	Both of us may do the audit of the work of a big title firm.

gwam 1' | 1 | 2 | 3 | 4 | 5 | 6 | 7 | 8 | 9 | 10 | 11 | 12 |

32B • 16
New Keys: / and $

each line twice SS (slowly, then faster); DS between 4-line groups; if time permits, practice the lines again

/ = diagonal
$ = dollar sign
Do not space between a figure and the / or the $ sign.

Learn / (diagonal)

1 ; ; /; /; ;; // ;/; ;/; 2/3 4/5 and/or We keyed 1/2 and 3/4.
2 Space between a whole number and a fraction: 7 2/3, 18 3/4.

Learn $ (dollar sign)

3 f f $f $f ff $$ f$f f$f $4 $4 for $4 Shift for $ and key $4.
4 A period separates dollars and cents: $4.50, $6.25, $19.50.

Combine / and $

5 I must shift for $ but not for /: Order 10 gal. at $16/gal.
6 Do not space on either side of /: 1/6, 3/10, 9 5/8, 4 7/12.
7 We sent 5 boxes of No. 6 3/4 envelopes at $11/box on June 2.
8 They can get 2 sets of disks at $49.85/set; 10 sets, $39.85.

Objectives:

1. To format a bound report with a table.

2. To format endnotes and title pages.

120A • 5
Conditioning Practice

set 0.5" SMs;
each line twice

alphabet 1 The temperature quickly plunged below zero just after Steve exercised.

speed 2 The neighbor's dog was with the girl by the big sign in the cornfield.

figures 3 He received 50 percent of the responses, 3,923 of 7,846, before May 1.

`gwam` 1' | 1 | 2 | 3 | 4 | 5 | 6 | 7 | 8 | 9 | 10 | 11 | 12 | 13 | 14 |

F ORMATTING

120B • 45
Bound Report

Document 1
Bound Report with a Table
Format and key the document shown at the right as a bound report DS.

words

THE PRESIDENT OF THE UNITED STATES   7

The highest elected office in the United States is that of President.   21
The President, who is elected by the citizens of the United States, repre-   36
sents "all the people." The President plays a major role in determining   51
the course of direction for the United States under a democratic form of   65
government.   68

Term of Office   71

Since the enactment of the twenty-second amendment to the Consti-   84
tution, the President can serve only two terms. Prior to this amendment   99
the President could serve as long as the people elected him to the office.   114
Franklin Roosevelt was the only President to serve more than two terms.   128

Qualifications   132

The qualifications required for running for the executive office of the   146
United States are outlined in the Constitution (Article II, Section 1, Para-   161
graph 5). The person must be at least 35 years of age, a natural-born citizen   177
of the United States, and a resident of the United States for at least 14 years.   194

Responsibilities   197

Also outlined in the Constitution (Article II, Sections 2 and 3) are the   212
responsibilities of the executive office. The responsibilities outlined are,   228
however, quite general and are often open to interpretation. The Constitu-   243
tion states that the President is the Commander-in-Chief of the armed   257
forces. The person holding the office is responsible for making treaties,   272
appointing ambassadors, and appointing judges of the Supreme Court.   285
Additional responsibilities of the President include giving the State of the   301
Union Address, receiving foreign dignitaries, enforcing the laws, and pro-   316
tecting the rights of the citizens of the United States.   327

The role of the President has remained about the same as when the   340
Constitution was written. However, Davis[1] stated that the responsibilities   356

(continued on next page)

32C • 16
New Keys: % and – (hyphen)

each line twice SS (slowly, then faster); DS between 4-line groups; if time permits, practice the lines again

% = percent sign
– = hyphen
Do not space between a figure and the %, nor before or after – or – – (dash) used as punctuation.

Learn % (percent sign)

1 f f %f %f ff %% f%f f%f 5% 5% Shift for the % in 5% and 15%.
2 Do not space between a number and %: 5%, 75%, 85%, and 95%.

Learn – (hyphen)

3 ; ; -; -; ;; -- ;-; ;-; 4-ply I use a 2-ply tire on my bike.
4 I gave each film a 1-star, 2-star, 3-star, or 4-star rating.

Combine % and –

5 A dash is two unspaced hyphens--no space before or after it.
6 Kyle, send the parcel by fourth-class mail--a saving of 50%.
7 The prime rate may reach 9%--but he has no interest in that.
8 You need 40 signatures--51% of the members--on the petition.

32D • 13
Skill Building

1. Key lines 1-8 once SS.
2. Key a 1' writing on line 7 and then on line 8; find *gwam* on each sentence.
3. Key a 1' and a 2' writing on the ¶; find *gwam* on each writing.

/ and $
1 Key a series of fractions as figures: 1/4, 1/3, and 1 3/10.
2 The jacket was discounted from $172.99 to $128.99 to $98.99.

% and –
3 This outlet store gives discounts of 20%, 25%, 35%, and 50%.
4 We have 1-, 2-, and 3-bath condos--he wants a separate home.

all symbols learned
5 This 10 1/2% mortgage was rewritten at 8%--a $13,496 saving.
6 These 3-part forms--minus a 10% discount--cost $75/thousand.

easy sentences
7 Shana is to key all the forms for the city auditor by eight.
8 Six of the girls do work for me; eight do work for the city.

gwam 1' | 1 | 2 | 3 | 4 | 5 | 6 | 7 | 8 | 9 | 10 | 11 | 12 |

LA   all letters used   gwam 2'

The computer came into personal use in the past decade   6
in a blaze of glory. In schools and homes all over the coun- 12
try, it has quickly expelled the standard typewriter. It is 18
used to learn, to play, to keep records, and to process all 24
sorts of information. It is being used in major ways to ar- 30
range and compose music and to design art pieces of merit. 36

gwam 2' | 1 | 2 | 3 | 4 | 5 | 6 |

and encouragement will allow their child to become the next Marino, — 140

Thomas, or Yamaguchi. *Unfortunately lc* Dreams such as these are often entirely the — 156

parents' and not the child's. Parents be come unreasonable, pushi*ng* — 170

their children to#the point of exce*s*siveness. The child ends ~~ends~~ up — 183

paying a heavy price for parental perfection *emotional* "ism.[1] — 195

The Original Purpose of Sports — 201

     Elementary children in the United States have had the — 212

opportunity to participate in compet*i*tive sports since the 1850's — 225

when the ymca was organized. The Public School athletic league — 238

was started in New York city as early as 1903. Programs such as — 251

these were designed to include di*f*ferent compet*i*tion categories for — 265

children with a variety of athletic skills, thus giving every — 277

child the opportunity to participate. 2 — 285

according to Nelson 3 The fundamental principles of these programs are still appli- — 302

cable today. "Sports participation was designed to achieve a sense — 315

of enjoyment, well-being, and competence." He cautions that "a — 328

DS{ shift away from these ideals toward intense competition, winning, — 341

and a system that rewards only excellence may have detrimental ef- — 354

fects on many children." — 360

Today's Purpose of Sports — 365

    ~~It is important for~~ parents, coaches, teachers, adminis- — 372

trators, and students participate *ing* in sports programs *need* to address — 386

the question of what is the purpose of today's sports. Is the goal — 400

to still provide a sense of enjoyment, well-being, and competence — 413

for all, or has it shifted to "win no matter what"? *the goal* *the cost* — 427

    The answer to this question may be seen at the next sporting — 439

event through observing the people associated with the ~~sporting~~ — 450

event. ~~There may not be~~ *may not be possible* a universal answer to the question ~~as~~ — 463

since attitudes vary a great deal from ~~one~~ place to place. In each place, however, — 479

DS{ the attitude toward sports programs depends a great deal on who the — 493

parents, the coaches, the teachers, the administrators, and the — 505

students are *who participate in the sports programs.* — 516

Document 2
Endnotes Page
Use the following information to create an endnotes page on a separate page.

[1] James S. Thornton, "Springing Young Athletes from the Parental Pressure Cooker," The Physician and Sports Medicine, Vol. 19, No. 7, July 1991, p. 92.

[2] Michael A. Nelson, "Developmental Skills and Children's Sports," The Physician and Sports Medicine, Vol. 19, No. 2, February 1991, p. 67.

[3] Nelson, p. 68.

Note: Endnote 3 refers to the same publication as Endnote 2. If there is more than one author named Nelson, give full name; if more than one publication by this author, give part of the title.

Document 3
Title Page
Prepare a title page for the report, using your name, school name, and current date. Refer to p. 212 (computer users) or RG20 (electronics), if necessary.

New Keys: #, &, and ( )

Objectives:
1. To learn reach-strokes for #, &, and ( ).
2. To combine #, &, and ( ) smoothly with other keys.

33A • 5
Conditioning Practice

each line twice SS; then a 1' writing on line 3; find *gwam*

alphabet 1 Racquel just put back five azure gems next to my gold watch.

figures 2 Joel used a comma in 1,203 and 2,946 but not in 583 and 750.

easy 3 The auto firm owns the big signs by the downtown civic hall.

gwam	1'	1	2	3	4	5	6	7	8	9	10	11	12

33B • 16
New Keys: # and &

each set of lines twice SS (slowly, then faster); DS between groups; if time permits, practice the lines again

= number/pounds
& = ampersand (and)
Do not space between # and a figure; space once before and after & used to join names.

Learn # (number/pounds)

1 d d #d #d dd ## d#d d#d 3# 3# Shift for # as you enter #33d.

2 Do not space between a number and #: 3# of #633 at $9.35/#.

Learn & (ampersand)

3 j j &j &j jj && j&j j&j 7& 7& Have you written to Poe & Son?

4 Do not space before or after & in initials, e.g., CG&E, B&O.

Combine # and &

5 Shift for # and &. Recall: # stands for number and pounds.

6 Names joined by & require spaces; a # sign alone does, also.

7 Letters joined by & are keyed solid: List Stock #3 as C&NW.

8 I bought 20# of #830 grass seed from Locke & Uhl on March 4.

LESSON 119 — Unbound Report with Endnotes

Objectives:
1. To format an unbound report.
2. To improve language skills (underline).

119A • 5
Conditioning Practice

each line twice SS; then two 1' writings on line 2; find *gwam*; clear screen

alphabet	1	The exquisite prize, a famous old clock, was to be given in July.
speed	2	Helen owns the six foals and the cow in the neighbor's hay field.
figures	3	Their team average went from .459 on April 17 to .286 on June 30.

gwam 1' | 1 | 2 | 3 | 4 | 5 | 6 | 7 | 8 | 9 | 10 | 11 | 12 | 13 |

L ANGUAGE SKILLS

119B • 10
Underline

Follow the Learn/Apply procedure for 76C on p. 184.

> Use an underline or italics to indicate titles of books and names of magazines and newspapers. (Titles may be keyed in ALL CAPS without the underline.)

Learn	1.	I saw the advertisement for The Client in the New York Times.
Apply	2.	He quoted the article from Business Week or the Denver Post.
Apply	3.	The story appeared in the Los Angeles Times on May 14.

> Use an underline to call attention to words or phrases (or use quotation marks). **Note**: Use a continuous underline (see preceding rule) unless each word is to be considered separately, as shown below.

Learn	4.	He did not know whether to use to, too, or two.
Apply	5.	We had to identify the correct word from our, are, and hour.
Apply	6.	She lost points because she used there instead of their.

F ORMATTING

119C • 35
Unbound Report

Document 1
Report from Rough Draft

1. Review the formatting guides for reports on pp. 211-212.
2. Format the copy at right and on the next page as a report in unbound style; use **SPORTS** for the main heading.
3. When you finish, use the spell check and proofread your copy.

words
heading 1

"When I grow up, I'm going to be just like Dan Marino and be 13

the quarterback for the Miami Dolphins." "I'm going to be just like 27

Frank Thomas and play baseball for the Chicago White Sox when I grow up." "When I 44

grow up, I'm going to be an famous ice skater, just like Kristi Yamaguchi." 59

Most children dream of becoming the next American sports hero. How- 72

ever, only a few will ever reach the apex they dreamed of as a child. 87

Children become parents, parents who had unfulfilled childhood 99

dreams. As parents they often try are ready to have those childhood dreams 112

fulfilled through by their children. They are confident that their help 126

(continued on next page)

33C • 16
New Keys: (and)

each set of lines twice SS (slowly, then faster); DS between groups; if time permits, practice the lines again

SPACING *cue:*
Do not space between ( ) and copy they enclose.

(= left parenthesis
) = right parenthesis

Learn (

use the letter "l"
1 l l (l (l ll ((l(l l(l 9(9(Shift for the (as you key (9.
2 As (is the shift of 9, use the l finger to key 9, (, or (9.

Learn)

3 ; ;);); ;;)));); 0) 0) Shift for the) as you key 0).
4 As) is the shift of 0, use the ; finger to key 0,), or 0).

Combine (and)

5 Hints: (1) depress shift; (2) strike key; (3) release both.
6 Tab steps: (1) clear tabs, (2) set stops, and (3) tabulate.
7 The new account (#594-7308) draws annual interest at 3 1/4%.

33D • 13
Skill Building

1. Key lines 1-8 once SS.
2. Key a 1' writing on line 7 and then on line 8; find *gwam* on each sentence.
3. Key a 1' and a 2' writing on the ¶; find *gwam* on each writing.

& and #
1 Rios & Cho will try Case #947-285 and Case #960-318 in June.
2 DP&L sent Invoice #67-5849-302 to Ito & Brown on October 19.

(and)
3 Waltz (the plaintiff) and Ross (the defendant) are in court.
4 The note for five hundred dollars ($500) pays 8.5% interest.

basic symbols
5 Twenty-four (31%) of the owners voted for a $250 assessment.
6 Only 1/4 picked Yes, 1/2 picked No, and 1/4 did not respond.

easy sentences
7 Did the girl row to the dock for the clams and six big fish?
8 They wish to make an issue of the work she did for the city.

gwam 1' | 1 | 2 | 3 | 4 | 5 | 6 | 7 | 8 | 9 | 10 | 11 | 12 |

LA all letters used   gwam 2'

When you key copy that contains both words and numbers,   6
it is best to key numbers using the top row. When the copy   12
consists primarily of figures, however, it may be faster to   18
use the keypad. In any event, keying figures quickly is a   24
major skill to prize. You can expect to key figures often   29
in the future, so learn to key them with very little peeking.   36

gwam 2' | 1 | 2 | 3 | 4 | 5 | 6 |

Enhance Report Formatting Skills

**Format Guides:
MLA-Style Reports**

MLA Format

MLA Works Cited Page

MLA-Style Report Guide

A variety of methods can be used to document references used in a report. Unit 13 presented the textual citation method of documentation (refer to p. 144); Unit 20 presented the endnote method of documentation (refer to pp. 211-212). The method endorsed by the Modern Language Association of America (MLA) is widely used for scholarly manuscripts and student research papers. The method, called **parenthetical reference**, is similar to the textual citation method. MLA reports involve several distinctive format features.

Margins and Page Numbers

MLA-style reports are formatted with one-inch top, side, and bottom margins. The page number for all pages (including the first) is keyed at the right margin one-half inch (0.5") from the top edge of the paper. The writer's last name precedes the page number.

Spacing

The *entire* report is double-spaced. This line spacing includes the Works Cited page as well as long quotations.

First-Page Information

The MLA-style report does not include a title page. Information normally found on a title page is keyed on the first page of the report at the left margin, beginning 1" from the top of the page. The information is double-spaced and should include the writer's name, the instructor's name, the course title, and the date.

Long Quotations

Quoted text of more than four lines is set off from the rest of the text by indenting the text 1" (10 spaces) from the left margin. It is double-spaced and no quotation marks are included. No paragraph indention is needed when quoting a single paragraph from the same source. When quoting more than one paragraph, indent each paragraph an additional 0.25" (three spaces). The parenthetical reference for the quote is placed two spaces after the quotation.

> If the writer's name introduces the quote, only the page number needs to be placed in the parenthetical reference. (18)

> If there are several works by the same author, the title or part of it should be included with the reference. (Writer's Guide 18)

> If the writer's name does not introduce the quote, it should be added to the parenthetical reference. (Miller 18)

Works Cited

The works cited in the report are listed alphabetically by author surnames at the end of the report on a separate page. The margins are the same as the rest of the report. Key the page number preceded by the report writer's name 0.5" from the top of the page, flush right. Key the heading, Works Cited, 1" from the top of the page. Each reference is DS. The first line of each reference begins at the left margin; other lines are indented 0.5".

LESSON 34 New Keys: ', ", __ , and *

Objectives:
1. To learn reach-strokes for ', ", _, and *.
2. To combine ', ", _, and * smoothly with other keys.

34A • 5
Conditioning Practice

each line twice SS; then a 1' writing on line 3; find *gwam*

alphabet	1	Bowman fixed prized clocks that seven judges say are unique.
figures	2	Only 1,453 of the 6,280 members were at the 1997 convention.
easy	3	She lent the field auditor a hand with the work of the firm.

gwam 1' | 1 | 2 | 3 | 4 | 5 | 6 | 7 | 8 | 9 | 10 | 11 | 12 |

34B • 16
New Keys: ' and "

Apostrophe: ' is to the right of ; and is controlled by the right little finger.

1. Locate new symbol on appropriate keyboard chart; read technique statement below the chart.
2. Key twice SS the appropriate pair of lines given at right; DS between pairs.
3. Repeat Steps 1 and 2 for the other new symbol.
4. Key twice SS lines 5-8.
5. Rekey the lines with which you had difficulty.

CAPITALIZATION *cue:*
Capitalize first word and all other important words in titles of publications.

Quotation mark: Depress left shift and strike " (shift of ') with the right little finger.

Note: The appearance of single (apostrophe) and double quotation marks may differ according to type style and software program. Sometimes beginning and ending quotation marks differ in direction. Whatever their differences in appearance, they serve the same purpose.

Learn ' (apostrophe)

1 ; ; '; '; ;; '' ;'; ;'; it's he's I'm I've It's hers, I see.
2 I'm not sure if it's Hal's; but if it's his, I'll return it.

Learn " (quotation mark)

3 ; ; "; "; ;; "" ;"; ;"; "Keep on," she said, but I had quit.
4 I read "Ode on a Grecian Urn," "The Last Leaf," and "Trees."

Combine ' and "

5 "If it's Jan's or Al's," she said, "I'll bring it to class."
6 "Its" is an adjective; "it's" is the contraction of "it is."
7 Miss Uhl said, "To make numbers plural, add 's: 8's, 10's."
8 O'Shea said, "Use ' (apostrophe) to shorten phrases: I'll."

Word PROCESSING 7

ACTIVITY 1:

Endnote

1. Read the copy at right.
2. Learn the Endnote feature for your software.
3. Key the information at right using the Endnote feature to format and key the endnotes on a separate page with the heading ENDNOTES.

The **Endnote** feature helps you create and format endnotes at the same time you are keying a report. The feature automatically inserts the endnote numbers in the text at specified locations and a corresponding number at the end of the document in the endnotes section. The operator is able to key the endnote immediately after specifying the location in the body of the document. A hard page break will place the endnotes on a separate page from the text of the report. The word ENDNOTES should be keyed 2" from the top of the screen, followed by a quadruple space.

DIVERSITY

Managing diversity is important to the success of today's business world. Different organizations approach diversity in a variety of ways. In many organizations, Gage wrote, "fitting the mold is no longer mandated."[1]

Diversity training programs are being utilized. The programs are based on the assumption that "the stepping stone of our relationships with others is self-consciousness."[2]

[1]Amy Gage, "More Big Firms Are Embracing Their Diversity," St. Paul Pioneer Press, June 9, 1994, p. 1E, col. 2.

[2]Pablo Casares, "Conducting Business in an Intercultural Context," Business Credit, April 1993, p. 30.

ACTIVITY 2:

Review Sort

1. Key the information at right SS in two columns leaving 2" between columns.
2. If necessary, review Sort feature on p. 267.
3. Sort by park name in ascending order.
4. Sort by state in ascending order.

Yellowstone	Wyoming
Sequoia	California
Yosemite	California
Mount Rainier	Washington
Crater Lake	Oregon
Wind Cave	South Dakota
Mesa Verde	Colorado
Glacier	Montana
Rocky Mountain	Colorado
Mount McKinley	Alaska

Underline: Depress left shift; strike _ (shift of –) with right little finger.

Asterisk: Depress left shift; strike * (shift of 8) with right middle finger.

1. Locate new symbol on appropriate keyboard chart.
2. Key twice SS the lines given at right; DS between pairs.
3. Repeat Steps 1-2 for the other new key.
4. Key twice SS lines 5-8.

wp note:
Use the Underline feature (if you have one) to underline words as you key lines 5-7.

Learn ___ (underline)

1 ; ; _; _; ;; __ ;_; ;_; I _____ go there; she _____ go also.
2 They ___ to visit _____ aunt, but _____ cousin __ at school.

Learn * (asterisk)

3 k k *k *k kk ** k*k k*k She used * for a single source note.
4 All discounted items show an *, thus: 48K*, 588*, and 618*.

Combine ___ and *

5 Use an * to mark often-confused words such as <u>then</u> and <u>than</u>.
6 *Note: Book titles (like <u>Lorna Doone</u>) are often underlined.
7 I saw a review of "La Casa Verde" in <u>Latin American Fiction</u>.
8 Did you view <u>Hornblower</u>--a 12th Century African sculpture?

LANGUAGE SKILLS

34D • 13
Capitalization

1. Read the first rule highlighted in color block.
2. Key the Learn sentences below it, noting how the rule has been applied.
3. Key the Apply sentences, supplying the appropriate capitalization.
4. Practice the other rule in the same way.
5. If time permits, key the Apply lines again at a faster pace.

Capitalize the first word of a direct quotation unless the quote is built into the structure of the sentence.

Learn 1 Yu-lan quoted the rule: "Spell the hour used with o'clock."
Learn 2 I didn't say that "making more errors makes us more human."

Apply 3 Kathleen quoted Pope: "to err is human, to forgive divine."
Apply 4 Ms. Ohms said to "Keep your eyes on the copy as you key."

Capitalize the first word of the first part of an interrupted quotation, but not the first word of the second part.

Learn 5 "To reduce errors," he said, "drop back slightly in speed."
Apply 6 "curve your fingers," she urged, "and keep them upright."

Timed Writings

1. A 1' writing on ¶ 1.
2. Add 5 *gwam* to the rate attained in Step 1.
3. Key two 1' writings on each paragraph, trying to achieve the rate determined in Step 2.
4. A 3' writing on ¶s 1-3 combined.
5. A 5' writing on ¶s 1-3 combined.

all letters used

| | gwam | 3' | 5' |

A telephone system provides us with a great deal more than   4 | 2 | 58
verbal contact between two points. Our radio and television   8 | 5 | 61
networks rely heavily on telephone service. By the use of   12 | 7 | 63
telephone wires, it is possible to send radio and television shows   16 | 10 | 66
from the point of origin to far and remote spots. If we did not   21 | 12 | 68
have this service, many people would not be able to enjoy national   25 | 15 | 71
sports contests such as the Super Bowl or important events such as   30 | 18 | 74
a special address by the President.   32 | 19 | 75

A special portable telephone, which is known as the data   36 | 21 | 77
phone, serves many useful purposes. This phone can be used by a   40 | 24 | 80
doctor to send data from the bedside of a patient to laboratories   46 | 27 | 83
or specialists for immediate analysis. This telephone can also be   49 | 29 | 85
used to obtain information from centralized data banks of all   53 | 32 | 88
types. When tied in with a computer, the telephone can be used to   58 | 34 | 91
process data and to solve many complex problems.   61 | 36 | 92

You will find a variety of telephone devices in a business   65 | 39 | 95
office. Correspondence, reports, and documents of all kinds can   69 | 41 | 97
be sent from place to place by use of a telefax machine.   73 | 44 | 100
Telephone answering sets, which record messages on tape, can be   77 | 46 | 102
used to answer the phone when no one is present. Equipment of   81 | 49 | 105
this type can also be used by out-of-town sales agents to report   86 | 51 | 107
and record sales. Similar devices are used by executives to   90 | 54 | 110
dictate material to a central word processing center.   93 | 56 | 112

gwam   3' | 1 | 2 | 3 | 4 |
        5' | 1 | 2 | 3 |

Master Keyboarding/ Language Skills

LESSON 35

Keying/Language Skills

Objectives:
1. To improve keying speed and control.
2. To identify and construct simple sentences.

35A • 5
Conditioning Practice

each line twice SS; then a 1' writing on line 3; find *gwam*

alphabet	1	Linda may have Jack rekey pages two and six of the big quiz.
6/2	2	Our house at 622 Gold Circle will be paid for June 26, 2006.
easy	3	Jena is to go to the lake towns to do the map work for them.

gwam 1' | 1 | 2 | 3 | 4 | 5 | 6 | 7 | 8 | 9 | 10 | 11 | 12 |

35B • 10
Skill Transfer

1. Key a 1' writing on each ¶; find *gwam* on each.

2. Compare rates. On which ¶ did you have highest *gwam*?

3. Key two 1' writings on each of the slower ¶s, trying to equal your highest *gwam* in Step 1.

Notes:

1. Relative speeds on different kinds of copy:
   - highest—straight copy
   - next highest—script
   - lowest—statistical copy

2. To find *gwam*, use the 1' *gwam* scale for partial lines in ¶s 1 and 2, but count the words in ¶ 3.

LA all letters/figures used   gwam 1'

You should try now to transfer to other types of copy   11
as much of your straight-copy speed as you can. Handwritten 23
copy and copy in which figures appear tend to slow you down. 35
You can increase speed on these, however, with extra effort. 48

An immediate goal for handwritten copy is at least 90%   11
of the straight-copy rate; for copy with figures, at least   23
75%. Try to speed up balanced-hand figures such as 26, 84,   35
and 163. Key harder ones such as 452 and 890 more slowly.   47

Copy that is written by hand is often not legible, and   11
the spelling of words may be puzzling. So give major attention 23
to unclear words. Question and correct the spacing used   35
with a comma or period. You can do this even as you key.   47

1' | 1 | 2 | 3 | 4 | 5 | 6 | 7 | 8 | 9 | 10 | 11 | 12 |

L ANGUAGE SKILLS

35C • 10
Number Expression

1. Read each script line, noting where spacing and number-expression changes are needed.

2. Key each line once, making needed changes.

1 *15 voted for the amendment, but 12 voted against it.*
2 *Of the twenty divers, only three advanced to the state finals.*
3 *The curtain rises at eight thirty p.m. on Saturday, October ten.*
4 *My office is at ten Park Place; my home, at 1 Key Largo.*
5 *Buy one doz. eggs, two lbs. of butter, and 8 oz. of cream.*

Skill Builder

Techniques: Figures

Set as 0.5" SM. Clear all tabs; then set tabs 2", 4", and 6" from the left margin. Key the lines slowly, tabbing from column to column. Take 3' writings. Try to key more characters on each writing.

Keep eyes on copy.

				gwam 3'
529-36-2899	12/24/80	(308) 112-2388	$ 628.00	3
358-29-1076	04/30/78	(608) 197-6655	$1,381.00	6
346-50-0190	02/28/81	(520) 130-6754	$5,672.15	9
567-82-8219	10/15/84	(715) 139-2615	$ 56.29	12
628-12-0945	03/27/82	(801) 162-2444	$3,178.87	15
820-67-1029	08/08/79	(308) 138-8567	$9,078.25	18

Reading/Keying Response Patterns

1. Lines 1-3: each word 3 times (slowly, faster, top speed).
2. Lines 4-6: each phrase 3 times (slowly, faster, top speed).
3. Lines 7-9: each sentence 3 times (slowly, faster, top speed).

Goal: Word-level keying.

Emphasize quick finger reaches, wrists low and relaxed.

balanced-hand words
1 us if he an by is jam fur hen row pay map man sit the and big may
2 dusk dock corn busy both keys firms land rock sign owns mend sick
3 docks bucks eight goals right they shame social towns vivid turns

Emphasize high-speed phrase response.

balanced-hand phrases
4 he owns it | make the signs | paid the man | go to work | if they fix the
5 go to the | they may make | to the problem | with the sign | and the maps
6 with the city | the eighth neighbor | social problem | the big ornament

Emphasize high-speed, word-level response; quick spacing.

balanced-hand sentences
7 Jaynel paid the man by the city dock for the six bushels of corn.
8 Keith may keep the food for the fish by the big antique fishbowl.
9 The haughty girls paid for their own gowns for the island social.

gwam 1' | 1 | 2 | 3 | 4 | 5 | 6 | 7 | 8 | 9 | 10 | 11 | 12 | 13 |

Number Expression Check

Key the sentences at the right; correct number expression as needed.

1. When you buy 3 cups, they will give you 1 free.

2. 12 of the 26 charter members were at the reunion.

3. If you place your order before two p.m., it will be shipped the next day.

4. Ms. King placed an order for eight copies of The Secretary and 14 copies of Modern Office Technology.

5. Approximately 2/3 of the parents attended the special meeting.

6. The package needs to be delivered to 1 Lakeshore Drive.

7. About 60 students voted for class officers on April seven.

8. The next assignment was Chapter seven, not Chapter eight.

9. Roy is 6 ft. eleven in. tall and weighs 180 lbs.

10. The final flight on July six going to Reno leaves at 8 p.m.

35D • 12
Skill Building

1. Key a 1' writing on each ¶; find *gwam*.
2. Key two 2' writings on ¶s 1-2 combined; find *gwam*.
3. Key a 3' writing on ¶s 1-2 combined; find *gwam*.

Quarter-Minute Checkpoints

gwam	1/4'	1/2'	3/4'	Time
20	5	10	15	20
24	6	12	18	24
28	7	14	21	28
32	8	16	24	32
36	9	18	27	36
40	10	20	30	40
44	11	22	33	44
48	12	24	36	48

LA all letters used

	gwam	2'	3'
Money is much harder to save than it is to earn. Some-		6	4
body is always willing to help you spend what you make. If		12	8
you confuse your needs and wants, you can quickly spend much		18	12
of it yourself. Often, friends and relations can become an		24	16
additional major drain if you allow them to assist you.		29	19
And, of course, many politicians at all levels think		34	23
that they can spend your money for you much better than you		40	27
can do it yourself. It is really amazing how ready some are		47	31
to spend the money of others. At times their motives may		52	35
be excellent; at other times, just selfish. So beware.		58	39

L ANGUAGE SKILLS

35E • 13
Simple Sentences

1. Study the guides in the color blocks and the sentences beneath them.
2. Key the Learn sentences as shown, noting the subjects and predicates.
3. Key the figure 1; opposite it key the subject and predicate of Sentence 1. Continue this procedure through line 8.

Revise sentences:

9/10

Combine the two sentences in each line into one simple sentence with two nouns as subject and one verb as predicate.

11

Combine the two sentences into one simple sentence with two nouns as subject and two verbs as predicate.

12

Combine the two sentences as in 9/10 above.

A *simple* sentence consists of one independent clause that contains a subject (noun or pronoun) and a predicate (verb).

Learn 1 Pam is president of her class.

Learn 2 Kevin walks to and from school.

Learn 3 Reading mystery novels is my favorite pastime.

Learn 4 The captain of the team is out with a badly sprained ankle.

A *simple* sentence may have as its subject more than one noun or pronoun (compound subject) and as its predicate more than one verb (compound predicate).

Learn 5 She bought a new bicycle. (single subject/single predicate)

Learn 6 Marv and I received new bicycles. (compound subject/single predicate)

Learn 7 Alice washed and waxed her car. (single subject/compound predicate)

Learn 8 He and I cleaned and cooked the fish. (compound subject and predicate)

Apply 9 Jorge read AURA by Fuentes. Rosa read it, also.

Apply 10 Hamad cooks his own meals. So does Janelle.

Apply 11 Mel chooses and buys his own training shoes. Suzy also chooses and buys hers.

Apply 12 Sara talked with Mona at the rock concert. Lee talked with her, also.

Document 1

Use the most efficient method to create letters to the individuals listed below. Format the letters in block style with mixed punctuation.

Ms. Josette Washington
861 Norled Dr.
Dayton, OH 45414-9412

Mr. Mark Jankowski
3675 Regal Hill Ct.
Dayton, OH 45430-9860

Ms. Judith Shapeero
342 Humming Bird Ln.
Dayton, OH 45459-2943

Mr. Hassan Staffords
4508 Guadalupe Ave.
Dayton, OH 45427-5419

Document 2

Use the most efficient method to send the memo at the right to the listed individuals. Each individual will receive a memo addressed to him/her.

Document 3

Using a distribution list (see page 189), prepare one memo addressed to the five individuals listed at the right.

Note: Additional R&E documents can be found on pp. A25 and A26.

	words
April 5, ----	3
<Title> <First Name> <Last Name>	7
<Street Address>	10
<City,> <State> <ZIP>	15
Dear <Title> <Last Name:>	19

Thank you for agreeing to serve on the convention planning committee for the <Current Year> National Information Management Association's convention. A listing of all committee members is enclosed. — 34 / 47 / 57

The committee will be formally introduced at NIMA's Annual Business Meeting on Friday, April 23, at 2:45 p.m. If there is time after the meeting, we will set a date for our first convention planning session. — 71 / 87 / 99

I am looking forward to working with you this next year. — 111

Sincerely, — 113

Ms. Juanita A. Pizarro — 118
Convention Chair — 121

xx — 122

Enclosure — 123

---

	words
TO: Cindy Austin, Kaye Berry, Dale Erickson, Kim Nakamoto, Mary Tietz	4
FROM: Shane Glavine, Project Coordinator	DATE: September 15, ----		17
SUBJECT: TELECOMMUNICATIONS PROJECT	25

It appears that 1:30 p.m. Monday, October 27, best fits everyone's schedule for meeting to discuss the interim progress of the telecommunications project. Please plan to give a brief update on what you have accomplished since our last meeting. — 36 / 49 / 61 / 71 / 74

The meeting has been scheduled in the conference room and should last no longer than two hours. If additional time is needed for the group to meet before our presentation to the board of directors, I will schedule another meeting. | xx — 84 / 94 / 105 / 116 / 121

LESSON 36

Keying/Language Skills

Objectives:
1. To improve keying speed and control.
2. To identify and construct compound sentences.

36A • 5
Conditioning Practice

each line twice SS; then a 1' writing on line 3; find *gwam*

alphabet	1	Jacques could win a prize for eight more dives by next week.
figures	2	In 1995, we had only 240 computers; as of 1998 we owned 376.
easy	3	The girls paid for the eight antique urns with their profit.
gwam	1'	1 | 2 | 3 | 4 | 5 | 6 | 7 | 8 | 9 | 10 | 11 | 12 |

S KILL BUILDING

36B • 20
Letter-Key Mastery

1. Key line 1 at a brisk pace. Note words that were awkward for you.
2. Key each of these words three times at increasing speeds.
3. Key line 2 at a steady, fluent rate.
4. Key each of the other pairs of lines in the same way.
5. If time permits, key again the lines in which you hesitated or stopped.

A/N	1	an and pan nap any nag ant man aunt land plan hand want sand
	2	Ann and her aunt want to buy any land they can near the inn.
B/O	3	bow lob bog rob boy mob gob fob bob body robe boat born glob
	4	Bobby bobbed in the bow of the boat as the boys came aboard.
C/P	5	cup cop cap pack copy cape cope pick pecks clips camps claps
	6	Cap can clip a copy of the poem to his cape to read at camp.
D/Q	7	did quo quid ride quit road quiz paid aqua dude squid squads
	8	The dude in an aqua shirt did quit the squad after the quiz.
E/R	9	or re ore per are her red peer here rent fore leer sore very
	10	Vera read her book report to three of her friends at school.
F/S	11	if is fish fuss soft furs self fast fans sift surf fist fees
	12	Floss said that fish on this shelf is for fast sale at half.
G/T	13	get got tag togs grit gilt gust tang right guilt fight ghost
	14	Garth had the grit to go eight rounds in that fight tonight.
H/U	15	hue hut hub hurt shut shun huge hush brush truth shrug thugs
	16	Hugh said four burly thugs hurled the man off the huge dock.
I/V	17	vie vim give view five vein dive vial vice vigor voice alive
	18	Vivian made her five great dives with visible vim and vigor.
J/W	19	jay wow jet own jab town just will jest when joke what judge
	20	Jewel jokes with your town judge about what and who is just.
K/X	21	oak fix kid fox know flax walk flex silk oxen park axle work
	22	Knox fixed an oak axle on a flax cart for a kid in the park.
L/Y	23	lay sly try ply all pry lei ally only rely reply truly fully
	24	Dolly truly felt that she could rely fully on only one ally.
M/Z	25	may zoo man zam zone make fuzz mama jazz maid jams game zoom
	26	Zoe may make her mark in a jazz band jam session at the zoo.

LESSON 118   Form Letters/Memos

Objectives:

1. To format letters/memos using the Merge feature.
2. To improve language skills (parentheses).

118A • 5
Conditioning Practice

each line twice

alphabet   1   Frank Jacobs was amazingly quiet during the extensive procedures.

speed   2   The soggy field by the dog kennels was good for a big tug of war.

figures   3   The letter dated 4/30/87 was received by the business on 6/25/91.

gwam   1' | 1 | 2 | 3 | 4 | 5 | 6 | 7 | 8 | 9 | 10 | 11 | 12 | 13 |

L ANGUAGE SKILLS

118B • 10
Parentheses

Use the standard Learn/
Apply directions in 76C,
p. 184.

> Use parentheses to enclose parenthetical or explanatory matter and added information. (Commas or dashes also may be used.)

Learn   1. Senator Simpson (Wyoming) is chair of the committee.
Learn   2. The contracts (Exhibits C and D) should be revised.
Apply   3. The salesperson with the most sales Duncan will be honored.
Apply   4. The book 1996 publication date has been ordered.

> Use parentheses to enclose identifying letters or figures of lists within a sentence.

Learn   5. Check for these errors: (1) keying, (2) spelling, and (3) grammar.
Apply   6. The three officers are 1 Sally, 2 Rebecca, and 3 Grant.
Apply   7. She emphasized two key factors: 1 speed and 2 control.

> Use parentheses to enclose a name and date used as a reference.

Learn   8. "I Have a Dream" (King, 1963) was delivered to over 200,000 people.
Apply   9. I cited "The Gettysburg Address" Lincoln, 1863 during my speech.
Apply   10. Developing Self-Esteem Palladino, 1989 was the main text for the course.

118C • 8
Speed Builder

1. Two 1' writings on each ¶ of 117B.

2. Determine best 1' *gwam* and record.

36C • 12
Skill Building

1. Key a 1' writing on each ¶; find *gwam*.
2. Key two 2' writings on ¶s 1-2 combined; find *gwam*.
3. Key a 3' writing on ¶s 1-2 combined; find *gwam*.

all letters used

gwam | 2' | 3'

.   .   2   .   4   .   6   .   8   .   10   .
It is okay to try and try again if your first efforts do | 6 | 4
12   .   14   .   16   .   18   .   20   .   22   .
not bring the correct results. If you try but fail again and | 12 | 8
24   .   26   .   28   .   30   .   32   .   34   .   36
again, however, it is foolish to plug along in the very same | 18 | 12
.   38   .   40   .   42   .   44   .   46   .   48
manner. Rather, experiment with another way to accomplish the | 24 | 16
.   50   .   52   .   54   .   56   .   58   .
task that may bring the skill or knowledge you seek. | 30 | 20

.   .   2   .   4   .   6   .   8   .   10   .
If your first attempts do not yield success, do not quit | 35 | 23
12   .   14   .   16   .   18   .   20   .   22   .
and merely let it go at that. Instead, begin again in a bet- | 41 | 28
24   .   26   .   28   .   30   .   32   .   34   .
ter way to finish the work or develop more insight into your | 47 | 32
36   .   38   .   40   .   42   .   44   .   46   .   48
difficulty. If you recognize why you must do more than just | 54 | 36
.   50   .   52   .   54   .   56   .   58   .   60
try, try again, you will work with purpose to achieve success. | 60 | 40

gwam 2' | 1 | 2 | 3 | 4 | 5 | 6 |
      3' | 1 | 2 | 3 | 4 |

LANGUAGE SKILLS

36D • 13
Compound Sentences

1. Study the guides in the color blocks and the sentences beneath them.
2. Key the Learn sentences, noting the words that make up the subjects and predicates of each sentence.
3. Key the figure 1; opposite it key the subject and predicate of each clause in Sentence 1. Continue this procedure through line 8.

Revise sentences:
In each of lines 9-12, combine the two sentences into a compound sentence. Choose carefully from the coordinating conjunctions *and, but, for, or, nor, yet,* and *so.*

A *compound* sentence contains two or more independent clauses connected by a coordinating conjunction (*and*, *but*, *for*, *or*, *nor*, *yet*, *so*).

Learn 1 Jay Sparks likes to hike, and Roy Tubbs likes to swim.
Learn 2 The computer is operative, but the printer does not work.
Learn 3 You may eat in the hotel, or you may choose a cafe nearby.
Learn 4 The sky is clear, the moon is out, and the sea is very calm.

Each clause of a compound sentence may have as its subject more than one noun/pronoun and as its predicate more than one verb.

Learn 5 Ben and I saw the game, and Bob and Marla went to a movie.
Learn 6 Nick dived and swam, but the others fished off the boat.
Learn 7 You may play solitaire, or you and Joe may play checkers.
Learn 8 Bobby huffed and puffed, but Erin scampered up the hill.

Apply 9 Karen listened to Ravel's BOLERO. Matt read FORREST GUMP.
Apply 10 You may watch STAR TREK. You and Edie may play dominoes.
Apply 11 Ken may play football or basketball. He may not play both.
Apply 12 Linda skated to CABARET music. Jon chose WEST SIDE STORY.

FORMATTING

117C • 35
Form Letters

Send the form letter at the right to the individuals listed on the computer printout below. Use block format, open punctuation and the most efficient method available with your equipment.

	Letters 1 & 2	Letters 3 & 4
March 27, ----	3	3
<Title> <First Name> <Last Name>	6	7
<Street Address>	10	11
<City,> <State> <ZIP>	15	16
Dear **<Title> <Last Name>**	18	20

As you are aware, property taxes have continued to increase each year.	33	35
Because of the state budget being proposed by the governor, another	47	49
significant tax increase is projected again this year. The local school	61	63
district has also proposed a budget with an 8 percent increase.	74	76
Our contracts for maintenance have gone up this year as well. Yard main-	89	91
tenance fees had an increase of 12 percent. We are also planning to paint	103	105
the interior of your apartment and replace the carpeting.	115	117
To cover a portion of these expenses, your rent will be increased by $25	130	132
effective with the June rent. A contract reflecting the rent increase is	145	147
enclosed. Please sign and return the contract prior to April 15.	158	160
Sincerely	160	162
Ms. Megan Sylvester	164	166
Manager	166	168
xx	167	169
Enclosure	168	170

Letter 1	Letter 2
Mr. Brent Perry	Ms. Robin Sussex
310 Parkwood Ave.	320 Parkwood Ave.
Charleston, SC 29403-7653	Charleston, SC 29403-7653
Letter 3	Letter 4
Dr. Daryl Wainwright	Ms. Danielle Warrens
314 Parkwood Ave.	318 Parkwood Ave.
Charleston, SC 29403-7653	Charleston, SC 29403-7653

LESSON 37

Keying/Language Skills

Objectives:
1. To check/improve keying speed and control.
2. To identify and construct complex sentences.

37A • 5
Conditioning Practice

each line twice SS; then a 1' writing on line 3; find *gwam*

alphabet 1 Quig was just amazed by the next five blocks of his players.

figures 2 On October 14, 1997, the 281 members met from 5 to 6:30 p.m.

easy 3 Keith may hang the sign by the antique door of the big hall.

gwam 1' | 1 | 2 | 3 | 4 | 5 | 6 | 7 | 8 | 9 | 10 | 11 | 12 |

S KILL BUILDING

37B • 19
Technique Check

1. Key each line once SS; DS between 3-line groups.
2. Key a 1' writing on each of lines 15, 18, and 21; find *gwam* on each.
3. If time permits, key another 1' writing on each of the two slower lines.

figures & symbols

1 and 163 sob 295 rid 483 fog 495 hen 637 lap 910 own 926 span

2 Case 10463 may be found in Volume 27, Section 108, page 592.

3 My note for $493 at 7.5% interest will be paid May 18, 2006.

shift keys & CAPS LOCK

4 GREAT AMERICAN SPEECHES did include King's "I Have a Dream."

5 THE ARTS by Tamplin is a history of 20th Century expression.

6 Simon & Schuster's OPERA is a quite complete reference work.

double letters

7 off odd zoo lee too door leek food hall good heel foot shall

8 Lee lost his footing and fell off a tall ladder in the mall.

9 Ella keeps a book of crossword puzzles in the school office.

adjacent keys

10 ruin part mere owes coin said true port buys flew stop point

11 Merv tried to buy a few old coins in that shop on the river.

12 Trudy said that her nephew tried out for a part in an opera.

letter response

13 dad hop few pop red you far kin gas oil vet mom get pin grew

14 As my case was set up, you saw him get only a few wage data.

15 Johnny read him rate cards on wage taxes set up at my union.

combination response

16 may few men saw pan tax ham get jam rest lend hulk bush gaze

17 A few of them ate jam tarts with the tea she served at dusk.

18 By noon they are to fix the pump at the oil rig on the hill.

word response

19 ox by got too off zoo odd lay but for fix pan with pair turn

20 Lana is to mend a map of the ancient lake town for the dorm.

21 Tish may sign a work form to aid the auditor of a soap firm.

gwam 1' | 1 | 2 | 3 | 4 | 5 | 6 | 7 | 8 | 9 | 10 | 11 | 12 |

Form Letters and Basic Skills

Objectives:

1. To learn how to format letters by the most efficient method available.
2. To increase straight-copy skill.

117A • 5
Conditioning Practice

each line twice

alphabet	1	Jack Repoz may give a few more racquetball exhibitions in Dayton.
speed	2	Their big social for their neighbor may also be held in the city.
figures	3	Case No. 3689 Z 457 will be presented on either May 19 or May 20.

gwam 1' | 1 | 2 | 3 | 4 | 5 | 6 | 7 | 8 | 9 | 10 | 11 | 12 | 13 |

S KILL BUILDING

117B • 10
Skill Check

Two 3' writings on ¶s 1-3 combined; find *gwam* and errors.

all letters used

	gwam	3'	5'

Attitude is the way people communicate their feelings or moods to others. A person is said to have a positive attitude when he or she anticipates successful experiences. A person such as this is said to be an optimist. The best possible outcomes are expected. The world is viewed as a great place. Good is found in even the worst situation.

Individuals are said to have negative attitudes when they expect failure. A pessimist is the name given to an individual with a bad view of life. Pessimists emphasize the adverse aspects of life and expect the worst possible outcome. They expect to fail even before they start the day. You can plan on them to find gloom even in the best situation.

Only you can ascertain when you are going to have a good or bad attitude. Keep in mind that people are attracted to a person with a good attitude and tend to shy away from one with a bad attitude. Your attitude quietly determines just how successful you are in all your personal relationships as well as in your professional relationships.

| 3' | 4 | 8 | 12 | 17 | 21 | 23 | 27 | 31 | 35 | 39 | 43 | 46 | 50 | 54 | 59 | 63 | 67 | 69 |

gwam 3' | 1 | 2 | 3 | 4 |
5' | 1 | 2 | 3 |

Speed Check

1. Key a 1' writing on each ¶; find *gwam*.
2. Key two 2' writings on ¶s 1-2 combined; find *gwam*.
3. Key a 3' writing on ¶s 1-2 combined; find *gwam*.

Quarter-Minute Checkpoints				
gwam	1/4'	1/2'	3/4'	1'
20	5	10	15	20
24	6	12	18	24
28	7	14	21	28
32	8	16	24	32
36	9	18	27	36
40	10	20	30	40
44	11	22	33	44
48	12	24	36	48
52	13	26	39	52
56	14	28	42	56

LA all letters used

gwam 2'

What is it that makes one person succeed and another   5 | 4
fail when the two seem to have about equal ability? Some   11 | 7
have said that the difference is in the degree of motivation   17 | 11
and effort each brings to the job. Others have said that an   23 | 16
intent to become excellent is the main difference.   28 | 19

At least four items are likely to have a major effect   34 | 22
on our success: basic ability, a desire to excel, an aim   40 | 26
to succeed, and zestful effort. If any one of these is ab-   45 | 30
sent or at a low point, our chances for success are lessened.   51 | 34
These features, however, can be developed if we wish.   57 | 38

gwam 2' | 1 | 2 | 3 | 4 | 5 | 6 |
3' | 1 | 2 | 3 | 4 |

L ANGUAGE SKILLS

Complex Sentences

Use the procedure given in 36D, p. 90.

> A *complex* sentence contains only one independent clause but one or more dependent clauses.

Learn 1 The book that you gave Juan for his birthday is lost.
Learn 2 If I were you, I would speak to Paula before I left.
Learn 3 Miss Gomez, who chairs the department, is currently on leave.
Learn 4 Students who use their time wisely usually succeed.

> The subject of a complex sentence may consist of more than one noun or pronoun; the predicate may consist of more than one verb.

Learn 5 All who were invited to the party also attended the game.
Learn 6 If you are to join, you should sign up and pay your dues.
Learn 7 After she and I left, Cliff and Pam sang and danced.
Learn 8 Although they don't know it yet, Fran and Bret were elected.

Apply 9 My PSAT and SAT scores are high. I may not get into Yale.
Apply 10 They attended the symphony. They then had a light supper.
Apply 11 Mindy is to audition for the part. She should apply now.
Apply 12 You are buying a computer. You should also get software.

116D • 27
Form Paragraphs

Create Letters 1-4 (below) using macros if equipment permits. Use block format, open punctuation. Use today's date and supply a salutation.

WP note:

Review the Macro feature (p. 188) to record each ¶ and retrieve it as needed to create a letter.

Letter 1

Ms. Sonya Cavazo
5640 Newcastle Dr.
Dallas, TX 75220-9387
Paragraphs: **B, D, F, I**
Department: **Information Processing Center**

(Total words = 170)

Letter 2

Mrs. Rebecca Broderick
446 Lake Charles Ave.
Fort Worth, TX 76103-7869
Paragraphs: **B, E, H, I**
Department: **Accounting Department**

(Total words = 151)

Letter 3

Ms. Anne Herrick
729 Richardson Dr.
Fort Worth, TX 76148-3482
Paragraphs: **A, C, F, I**
Department: **Sales Department**

(Total words = 150)

Letter 4

Mr. Bruce Sinclair
4230 Lowell St.
Dallas, TX 75214-4536
Paragraphs: **B, D, G, I**
Department: **Information Processing Center**

(Total words = 166)

A

Congratulations on your new position with Edgewater Industries! We are looking forward to having you as a member of our (Name of Department).

B

Welcome to Edgewater Industries; we are pleased that you have chosen to become part of our organization! We are looking forward to having your assistance in accomplishing our goals and objectives in the years ahead.

C

You will enjoy working with Michael Alvarado. He has been with the company for 15 years and is highly regarded by his colleagues. Since he was promoted to sales manager seven years ago, company sales have grown tremendously. The new sales strategies that he implemented have been very successful.

D

If you enjoy working with the latest technology, I am certain that you will enjoy being part of Melissa Downey's staff. Our Information Processing Center was recently featured in a national office technology magazine and is the envy of many organizations. This is due to the efforts of Ms. Downey and her talented staff.

E

You will enjoy working with Duncan Revere; he is superb! He is one of those rare individuals who possesses people skills as well as technical expertise. He has completely computerized the Accounting Department since being appointed accounting supervisor.

F

I am confident that your association with us will be rewarding. I am looking forward to visiting with you in person at the next meeting of the (Name of Department).

G

Your association with us will be rewarding. I am looking forward to meeting you the next time I visit the (Name of Department).

H

I am confident that your work in the (Name of Department) will be rewarding. I am looking forward to meeting you soon.

I

Yours very truly

Ms. Tara A. Rockford
President

xx

your PERSPECTIVE

Talk shows that deal with "how to put people down," "telling my friend what I really think," or "confronting my boss" fill the airwaves. Audiences encourage confrontation and seem disappointed when there is no pushing or shoving among a show's participants. With friends, we talk about the driver who cut us off and the person who moved ahead of us in line. We remember going to a movie where the people around us talked and laughed loudly, with no regard for those around them.

When we experience these behaviors, we ask ourselves: "Why do people behave and talk rudely to one another?" "Why don't people treat each other with more respect?"

Increasingly, it seems, people are not relating to each other with good manners, with civility. When we were young, family members taught us the behaviors we were to use in interacting with others. We were taught to say "please" when making a request and "thank you" when the request was fulfilled; "pardon me" when we bump into someone and "I'm sorry" if we offend someone.

Such expressions enable us to adapt our behavior so that we can interact smoothly and positively with others. An acceptable code of behavior increases communication and prevents problems from arising between people. The use of appropriate behavior is a glue that holds people together from varying backgrounds.

Such a system of accepted behaviors is called manners, etiquette, or civility. Whatever the term, these behaviors are everyday expressions of an ethical code—behaviors by which people interact with one another with courtesy, fairness, and justice.

Guide books on manners, such as those written by Amy Vanderbilt and Miss Manners, have become popular in the United States. People writing to Ann Landers express their pleasure when they see someone hold a chair for another person or help someone put on a coat. Interest in and reactions to such behavior patterns indicate that people are looking for ways to act in a considerate and ethical manner toward other people.

Good manners enable us to deal with others in courteous and positive ways that do not go unnoticed. Hold a door open for someone and see the look of appreciation on the person's face and hear the words "thank you." How do you think a student would respond if you helped pick up materials that perhaps you caused to be dropped? What would your reaction be if a person who offended you came to you and apologized?

Good manners are nothing more than a code of behaviors that involve treating others as you would have them treat you. Unless you follow such a code that shows respect for other people, you hardly have a right to demand respect for yourself. ✳

ACTIVITIES

1. Read the paragraphs at the left dealing with good manners and their value in human relations.

2. Key a list of good manners that you observe in your dealings with others at home, at school, and in public.

3. Key a list of poor (if not bad) manners in which you engage more often than you should.

4. Compare your lists with those of a fellow student. Have her/him tell you if you do in fact follow the good manners *and* the poor manners on your lists. Then you do the same for her/him.

5. Finally, change your lists if needed as a result of Step 4 and key two new lists: (1) Good Manners I Usually Follow; (2) Poor Manners I Need to Change.

Objectives:

1. To learn to format letters from form paragraphs.

2. To enhance language skills (colon).

116A • 5
Conditioning Practice

each line twice

alphabet 1 Jess explained why the November sales quota for Zack was so high.

speed 2 Helen and the visitor may handle the problems with the amendment.

figures 3 Your office will be 2105; your phone number, 135-4569, ext. 8572.

| gwam | 1' | 1 | 2 | 3 | 4 | 5 | 6 | 7 | 8 | 9 | 10 | 11 | 12 | 13 |

LANGUAGE SKILLS

116B • 10
Colon

Use the Learn/Apply directions given for 76C, p. 184.

| Use a colon to introduce an enumeration or a listing. |

Learn 1. Please purchase the following: tie, dress shirt, and coat.

Apply 2. Add these names to your list Jay Smith, Kay Shi, and Joe Day.

Apply 3. She brought the following cake, cookies, and pies.

| Use a colon to introduce a question or a direct quotation. |

Learn 4. Her question: "How can you make so many errors?"

Apply 5. Jay's last comment "How many times did you repeat the course?"

Apply 6. The manager's next inquiry "Will you be to work on time?"

| Use a colon between hours and minutes expressed in figures. |

Learn 7. Flight 2308 left for Dallas at 7:39 p.m.

Apply 8. You can schedule an appointment at 1015 a.m. or 330 p.m.

Apply 9. Does the play start at 730 or 830 p.m.?

116C • 8
Build Skill

1. Each line twice.
2. Try to complete each sentence on the call of 15", 12", or 10" writing, as directed.

Emphasis: one-hand words

	gwam	15"	12"	10"
In my opinion, only a few eager pupils read texts.		40	50	60
Brad saw fast deer retreat after Carter started uphill.		44	55	66
My pupil asserts that great debates are based only on facts.		48	60	72
Gregg Hill addressed my pupils on minimum state tax rates on gas.		52	65	78

| gwam | 1' | 1 | 2 | 3 | 4 | 5 | 6 | 7 | 8 | 9 | 10 | 11 | 12 | 13 |

GLOBAL AWARENESS

Many animals you see in zoos throughout the country are said to be native to (indigenous to) certain continents or geographic regions. For example, the bison (a species of buffalo) is considered to be native to western North America.

To check your global awareness, you will see how many animals in List A you can match with their native region in List B.

List A	List B
elephant	Africa
grizzly bear	Africa/Asia
ibex	Asia
iguana	Australia
koala	Central/South America
llama	India
rhesus monkey	North America
timber wolf	Northern Europe
water buffalo	South America
zebra	Southwestern North America

A C T I V I T I E S

1. Read paragraphs at left; study the two lists beneath them.

2. Key at left margin the first item of List A.

3. Tab 4 times; then key the continent(s) and/or region(s) to which the animal is considered native.

4. Key remaining items, tabbing to align the items in List B.

5. In groups of 3 or 4, compare answers and discuss reasons for choices made.

CULTURAL DIVERSITY

Language is one index of the culture from which a person comes. In the United States, many languages are spoken. Among them are Chinese, French, German, Italian, Japanese, Korean, Spanish, Vietnamese, and, of course, many dialects of English.

One of the challenges when people of differing cultures interface lies in trying to understand what different people are really saying. Can you correctly match the English expressions in List A with the same expression in another language in List B and name the language represented by the expression?

List A	List B
baby	bambino
girl	bon jour
good day	fille
good-bye	gracias
man	hai
no	hombre
plaza	nyet
please	piazza
thanks	por favor
yes	sayanara

A C T I V I T I E S

1. Read paragraphs at left; study the two lists beneath them.

2. Key at left margin the first item in List A.

3. Tab 4 times; key the expression in List B that matches the word(s) in List A; tab 4 more times and key in a third column the name of the language of the choice you made.

4. Key remaining items, tabbing to align the items in Columns 2 and 3.

5. Compare/discuss choices.

Letter 2

Format and key the text at the right as a two-page letter in modified block format with blocked ¶s and mixed punctuation to:

Ms. Othelo Weeks
Brentwood Industries, Inc.
832 Waycross Ave.
Pensacola, FL 32507-3867

Date the letter **September 28, ----.** The letter is from **Mr. Rori M. Santos, Executive Director.** Supply an appropriate salutation, complimentary closing, and closing notations.

Bold the headings in each listed item as shown. Include the following postscript:

Join before October 15 and save 20 percent off the regular membership price.

Letter 3

Reformat (or rekey) Letter 2 in block format with open punctuation. Omit the postscript.

words

	words
opening	24

Did you know that more than 3,000 companies with information management departments belong to the National Information Management Association (NIMA)? The main purpose of NIMA is to provide professional development opportunities for employees of its members. — 38, 52, 65, 77

The professional resources available to NIMA include: — 88

■ **Information Management Journal**. Your company will receive 12 issues of <u>Information Management Journal</u>. The <u>Journal</u> offers current articles relating to the latest developments in the information management field. — 101, 114, 128, 132

■ **Publications.** Your company is entitled to a 30 percent discount on publications purchased through the organization's library. In addition to a number of books relating to information management, savings are also available on a number of current periodicals. See the enclosed listing. — 146, 159, 173, 186, 190

■ **NIMA convention**. The annual NIMA convention is among the finest information management conventions in the world. Employees of your company will be entitled to reduced registration fees. — 203, 216, 229

■ **Regional workshops**. Regional workshops are sponsored quarterly in various cities throughout the United States. Employees of firms belonging to NIMA receive reduced registration fees. — 242, 255, 266

■ **Local workshops**. NIMA will make arrangements with experts in the field of information management to do in-house training for companies belonging to NIMA. — 279, 293, 298

A membership packet is enclosed to provide you with more information on the National Information Management Association. Next week I will call you to see if you have any questions about our organization. — 312, 327, 339

closing 366

L ANGUAGE SKILLS

115D • 10
Hyphen

Use the Learn/Apply directions given for 76C, p. 184.

> Use a hyphen to join compound numbers from twenty-one to ninety-nine.

Learn   1. The youngest member was twenty-six; the oldest, sixty-three.
Apply   2. She celebrated her twenty first birthday on May 6.
Apply   3. The braces were removed when she was twenty or twenty one.

> Use a hyphen to join compound adjectives preceding a noun they modify as a unit.

Learn   4. The up-to-date file always contained the latest research.
Apply   5. The door to door salesperson was here around 10:30 a.m.
Apply   6. The Over the Hill Gang meets on Wednesday evening.

Word Processing

Communication has often been called the nervous system of business and industry, sending and receiving signals to action all over world.

These signals start in the brain and move through the fingers to a keyboard that converts them into messages—memos, letters, reports, and the like. These may be transmitted as hard copy through the mail, or they may be sent electronically as e-mail or facsimile copies (faxes).

However transmitted, messages are prepared in specific arrangements (placement and spacing of messages parts) called "formats." In the lessons of Phase 2, you will learn how to process messages in the formats that are most often used. In addition, you will continue to improve your language skills.

No matter what career you choose or jobs you get along the way, a computer is likely to be the center of your communication functions. Learning now how to process messages properly and improving your language skills will give you a headstart on your future.

Objectives:
1. To format and key a two-page letter.
2. To include a postscript on a letter.
3. To improve language skills (hyphen).

115A • 5
Conditioning Practice

set 0.5" SMs;
each line twice

alphabet 1 Mr. Voldez was extremely happy after Glen quickly adjusted his brakes.

speed 2 He owns both the antique bottle and the enamel bottle on their mantle.

figures 3 Only 308 of the 967 expected participants had registered by 12:45 p.m.

gwam 1' | 1 | 2 | 3 | 4 | 5 | 6 | 7 | 8 | 9 | 10 | 11 | 12 | 13 | 14 |

115B • 7
Skill Building

1. Two 1' writings on line 1 of 115A.

Goal: Not over 2 errors in each writing.

2. Two 1' writings on line 2 of 115A.

Goal: To force speed to a new level.

115C • 28
Long Letters

Letter 1

Format and key the text at the right as a modified block letter with blocked ¶s and mixed punctuation.

words

January 2, ---- | Mr. Justin Hunter | 3451 Canyon Creek Rd. | 11
Boulder, CO 80303-8329 | Dear Mr. Hunter: | 19

When we announced our merger, we promised you expanded and 31
enhanced services. We are now ready to deliver some of those 44
services. Beginning January 15, the following services will be 56
available: 59

★ <u>Extended banking hours</u>. Banking hours will be from 7:30 71
a.m. to 5:30 p.m. Monday through Friday. This schedule 82
should provide an opportunity to bank during the week 93
before or after work. On Saturday the bank will be open 104
from 9 a.m. to 1 p.m. 109

★ <u>Automatic teller machines</u>. Automatic teller machines are 121
now available at selected locations throughout the city. 132
Use the enclosed sheet to determine the nearest location. 144

★ <u>Certified financial planning</u>. Two Certified Financial 156
Planners (CFPs) have been hired to assist you with your 167
long-term financial planning. 173

We are excited about the changes that are taking place at **Rocky Mountain** 188
Banks. *We will share additional services with you as they become avail-* 202
able. If you would like more information on any of the services that are 217
listed above, please call. 223

Sincerely, | **ROCKY MOUNTAIN BANKS** | *Lee O. Hazzard* | *Customer* 234
Services | *xx* | *Enclosure* 238

UNIT 7

LESSONS 38–40

Learn Numeric Keypad Operation

LESSON 38

New Keys: 4/5/6/0

O b j e c t i v e s :

1. To learn reach-strokes for **4**, **5**, **6**, and **0**.

2. To key these home-key numbers with speed and ease.

38A • 5
Numeric Keypad Arrangement

Figure keys 1-9 are in standard locations on numeric keypads of computers.

The zero (0 or Ø) key location may vary slightly from one keyboard to another.

The illustrations at the right show the location of the numeric keypad on selected computer keyboards.

Macintosh LCII numeric keypad

IBM PC

38B • 5
Operating Position

1. Position yourself in front of the keyboard—body erect, both feet on floor for balance.
2. Place this book for easy reading—at right of keyboard or directly behind it.
3. Curve the fingers of the right hand and place them on the keypad:
   - index finger on 4
   - middle finger on 5
   - ring finger on 6
   - thumb on 0

Note: To use the keypad, the Num (number) Lock must be turned on.

Book at right of keyboard

Proper position at keyboard

Letters 1-3

Format and key the letters shown at the right in modified block format with indented paragraphs and mixed punctuation. DS the lists in Letters 2 and 3. Date all letters **August 1, ----**.

Key the company name, **ROCKY MOUNTAIN BANKS**, in the signature lines of all three documents.

Send the letters to:

Mr. Justin Hunter
3451 Canyon Creek Rd.
Boulder, CO 80303-8329

Letters 2 and 3 are from:

Lee Q. Hazzard
Customer Services

Supply an appropriate complimentary closing; add closing notations required.

Note: If you are not able to create special characters on your equipment, you can use keyboard characters (*, −, +) or make an enumerated list of the items.

---

	words
	opening **19**

You are the first to know!!! Boulder First Bank will change its name to | **33**
Rocky Mountain Banks on September 20. This change is necessitated by | **47**
the merger of banks in Fort Collins, Laramie, and Cheyenne. | **60**

This change will have very little impact on you. The ownership, | **73**
management, and staff will remain the same. The next time you order | **86**
checks, our new name, **Rocky Mountain Banks**, will appear. You can | **100**
continue using your Boulder First Bank checks until you need additional | **114**
checks. | **116**

Our commitment to providing you with quality service will not change. This | **131**
merger will provide us with the means to expand and enhance the financial | **146**
services that will be available to you, however. We will keep you informed | **161**
of these services as they become available. If you have questions, call us. | **176**

Very truly yours, | Ms. Allison Miller-Kennedy | President | xx | **192**

---

opening **19**

We are pleased to introduce the **Monthly Summary**. The **Monthly Sum-** | **32**
mary is a special service for customers with more than one type of account. | **48**
At a glance, you will be able to locate: | **56**

✓ The balance of all accounts combined | **64**
✓ The balance of each individual account | **72**
✓ Deposits to each individual account | **80**

The primary benefit of the **Monthly Summary** is that it streamlines ac- | **93**
count information. For specific details of each account, you may still check | **109**
the familiar individual monthly statement that will accompany your | **122**
Monthly Summary. | **126**

We are providing this **Monthly Summary** to a select few of our customers | **140**
to receive feedback prior to providing it to all customers with multiple | **155**
accounts. Next month you will receive a questionnaire asking for your | **169**
input as to the value of the summary. If you have comments that you would | **184**
like to share before that time, please contact me. | **194**

closing **208**

---

opening **19**

As a preferred mortgage customer, you are preapproved for a Rocky | **32**
Mountain Banks' credit card. As long as your mortgage is serviced by | **46**
Rocky Mountain Banks, there will be no annual fee. | **56**

Your credit card comes with a variety of services at no additional cost. | **71**
Included in these services are: | **78**

■ Car rental discounts | **83**
■ Telephone calling card service | **89**
■ $500,000 travel insurance | **95**
■ Travel registration service | **101**

The enclosed brochure describes in detail all services offered through | **115**
membership with the Rocky Mountain Banks' card. To receive the card, | **129**
complete and return the enclosed authorization form; you will be able to | **144**
start taking advantage of the services as soon as you receive the card. | **158**

closing **172**

New Keys: 4/5/6/0 (Home Keys)

Complete the drills as directed below, entering the numbers in one continuous column on your wp software. The screen will fill quickly because numbers are listed vertically. Therefore, clear the screen after each drill.

1. Curve the fingers of your right hand; place them upright on the home keys:
   - index finger on 4
   - middle finger on 5
   - ring finger on 6
   - thumb on 0

2. Using the special Enter key (at right of keypad), enter data in Drill 1A as follows:

   4 Enter
   4 Enter
   4 Enter
   Strike Enter

3. Enter Columns B-F in the same way.

4. Using the special Enter key, enter data in Drill 2A as follows:

   44 Enter
   44 Enter
   44 Enter
   Strike Enter

5. Continue Drill 2 and complete Drills 3-5 in a similar way. In Drills 4 and 5, strike 0 with side of right thumb.

Note: When you can operate the keypad by touch—Lesson 40 completed—determine if your software contains a calculator accessory. If so, key each drill in Lessons 38-40 twice. (You may have to strike the + key before each number.) If the two totals of a single drill match, you have probably entered the data correctly.

TECHNIQUE _cue:_

Strike each key with a quick, sharp stroke with the _tip_ of the finger; release the key quickly. Keep the fingers curved and upright; the wrist low, relaxed, and steady.

Drill 1

A	B	C	D	E	F
4	5	6	4	5	6
4	5	6	4	5	6
4	5	6	4	5	6

Drill 2

A	B	C	D	E	F
44	55	66	44	55	66
44	55	66	44	55	66
44	55	66	44	55	66

Drill 3

A	B	C	D	E	F
44	45	54	44	55	66
55	56	46	45	54	65
66	64	65	46	56	64

Drill 4

A	B	C	D	E	F
40	50	60	400	500	600
40	50	60	400	500	600
40	50	60	400	500	600

Drill 5

A	B	C	D	E	F
40	400	404	406	450	650
50	500	505	506	540	560
60	600	606	606	405	605

Objectives:

1. To increase straight-copy keying skill.
2. To learn to key documents with special characters.

114A • 5
Conditioning Practice

each line twice

alphabet 1 Zack Plage reviewed the job requirements with fifty to sixty men.

speed 2 The haughty men did the work on the bus for my neurotic neighbor.

figures 3 My boys were born on May 2, 1964, July 3, 1975, and June 8, 1980.

gwam 1' | 1 | 2 | 3 | 4 | 5 | 6 | 7 | 8 | 9 | 10 | 11 | 12 | 13 |

S KILL BUILDING

114B • 12
Skill Check

1. A 3' writing on ¶s 1-3 combined; find *gwam* and errors.
2. A 1' writing on each ¶; find *gwam* and errors.
3. Another 3' writing on ¶s 1-3 combined; find *gwam* and errors.

all letters used

	gwam	3'	5'
People in business are concerned about what is communicated	4	2	36
by the written word. As they write memos, letters, and reports,	8	5	38
they may plan for the content but may not plan for the image of	13	8	41
the message. Experts, however, realize that neglecting the way	17	10	43
a document looks can be costly.	19	11	45
Many times a written piece of correspondence is the only	23	14	47
basis on which a person can form an impression of the writer.	27	16	49
Judgments based on a first impression that may be formed by the	31	19	52
reader about the writer should always be considered before mail-	35	21	54
ing a document.	36	22	55
The way a document looks can communicate as much as what it	40	24	57
says. Margins, spacing, and placement are all important features	45	27	60
to consider when you key a document. A quality document is one	49	29	63
that will bring the interest of the reader to the message rather	53	32	65
than to the way it appears.	55	33	66

gwam 3' | 1 | 2 | 3 | 4 |
5' | 1 | 2 | 3 |

New Keys: 7/8/9

Objectives:

1. To learn reach-strokes for **7**, **8**, and **9**.
2. To combine quickly the new keys with other keys learned.

39A • 5
Home-Key Review

Enter the columns of data listed at the right as directed in Steps 1-5 on p. 97.

A	B	C	D	E	F
4	44	400	404	440	450
5	55	500	505	550	560
6	66	600	606	660	456

39B • 45
New Keys: 7/8/9

Learn reach to 7

1. Locate 7 (above 4) on the numeric keypad.
2. Watch your index finger move up to 7 and back to 4 a few times *without striking keys*.
3. Practice striking 74 a few times as you watch the finger.
4. With eyes on copy, enter the data in Drills 1A and 1B.

Learn reach to 8

1. Learn the middle-finger reach to 8 (above 5) as directed in Steps 1-3 above.
2. With eyes on copy, enter the data in Drills 1C and 1D.

Learn reach to 9

1. Learn the ring-finger reach to 9 (above 6) as directed above.
2. With eyes on copy, enter the data in Drills 1E and 1F.

Drills 2-4

Practice entering the columns of data in Drills 2-4 until you can do so accurately and quickly.

Drill 1

A	B	C	D	E	F
474	747	585	858	696	969
747	777	858	888	969	999
777	474	888	585	999	696

Drill 2

A	B	C	D	E	F
774	885	996	745	475	754
474	585	696	854	584	846
747	858	969	965	695	956

Drill 3

A	B	C	D	E	F
470	580	690	770	707	407
740	850	960	880	808	508
704	805	906	990	909	609

Drill 4

A	B	C	D	E	F
456	407	508	609	804	905
789	408	509	704	805	906
654	409	607	705	806	907
987	507	608	706	904	908

R&e

For Calculator Accessory Users

Enter single, double, and triple digits in columns as shown, left to right.

A	B	C	D	E	F
4	90	79	4	740	860
56	87	64	56	64	70
78	68	97	78	960	900
90	54	64	60	89	67
4	6	5	98	8	80

Document 3

Format the letter in modified block format with indented paragraphs, mixed punctuation.

	words
May 10, ----	Attention Personnel Director	Beechwood Associates		13
878 Colonial Way	New Bedford, MA 02747-2511	Ladies and	24
Gentlemen :	FITNESS PROGRAMS	31

¶ More people are becoming health conscious than | 41
ever before. Because of the studies linking life expectancy | 53
to physical fitness, more people are looking for effective | 65
ways to improve their physical conditions. | 73

¶ CHADWICK FITNESS CENTER, the newest physical fitness | 84
center in New Bedford, is the most advanced fitness center | 96
in this area. Modern facilities, state-of-the-art equipment, | 108
and a well-trained staff provide the complete program. | 119

¶ Ten complimentary one-day passes are enclosed to | 129
allow your employees to become acquainted with our | 139
fitness center. They can make reservations by calling | 150
136-7509. | 153

¶ We will look forward to their visits and hope to be | 163
able to work with them to customize a fitness program | 174
to meet their needs. | 178

Sincerely, | Ms. Angela S. Dutton | Fitness Program Director | xx | 190
Enclosures : Brochure | Membership Forms | c Martin G. Vesser | 202

Document 4

Format the copy as a simplified memo.

Document 5

Reformat Document 4 as a standard memo.

	words
June 3, ----	Dwight Eastick, Office Manager	DESKTOP PUBLISHING	13
SEMINAR	14

Attached is the brochure describing the desktop publishing seminar that I | 29
spoke about with you last week.   The charge for attending the seminar is $195. | 45

Since no one in the office currently has experience with desktop publish- | 60
ing, I believe the benefits of my attending such a seminar far outweigh the | 75
costs involved.   Attending this seminar will allow me to use more produc- | 89
tively the desktop publishing package that was purchased last spring. I | 104
will be happy to share with others what I learn from the seminar. | 117

Registration forms need to be submitted by June 20 to avoid a late regis- | 132
tration fee. | 135

Sue A. Buckner, Document Processing Center | xx | Attachment | 146

New Keys: 1/2/3

Objectives:

1. To learn reach-strokes for **1**, **2**, and **3**.
2. To combine quickly the new keys with other keys learned.

40A • 5
Keypad Review

Enter the columns of data listed at the right as directed in Steps 1-5 on p. 97.

A	B	C	D	E	F	G
44	74	740	996	704	990	477
55	85	850	885	805	880	588
66	96	960	774	906	770	699

40B • 35
New Keys: 1/2/3

Learn reach to 1

1. Locate 1 (below 4) on the numeric keypad.
2. Watch your index finger move down to 1 and back to 4 a few times *without striking keys.*
3. Practice striking 14 a few times as you watch the finger.
4. Enter the data in Drills 1A and 1B.

Learn reach to 2

1. Learn the middle-finger reach to 2 (below 5) as directed in Steps 1-3 above.
2. Enter data in Drills 1C and 1D.

Learn reach to 3

1. Learn the ring-finger reach to 3 (below 6) as directed above.
2. Enter data in Drills 1E, 1F, and 1G.

Drills 2-4

Enter data in Drills 2-4 until you can do so accurately and quickly.

Drill 1

A	B	C	D	E	F	G
414	141	525	252	636	363	174
141	111	252	222	363	333	285
111	414	222	525	333	636	396

Drill 2

A	B	C	D	E	F	G
114	225	336	175	415	184	174
411	522	633	284	524	276	258
141	252	363	395	635	359	369

Drill 3

A	B	C	D	E	F	G
417	528	639	110	171	471	714
147	280	369	220	282	582	850
174	285	396	330	393	693	936

Drill 4

A	B	C	D	E	F	G
77	71	401	107	417	147	174
88	82	502	208	528	258	825
99	93	603	309	639	369	396

40C • 10
Numbers with Decimals

Enter the data in Columns A-F, placing the decimals as shown in the copy. **Note:** Use ring finger for entering the decimal.

A	B	C	D	E	F
1.40	17.10	47.17	174.11	1,477.01	10,704.50
2.50	28.20	58.28	285.22	2,588.02	17,815.70
3.60	39.30	69.39	396.33	3,996.03	20,808.75
4.70	74.70	17.10	417.14	4,174.07	26,909.65
5.80	85.80	28.20	528.25	5,285.08	30,906.25
6.90	96.90	39.30	639.36	6,396.06	34,259.90

LESSON 113

Letters/Memos Review

Objectives:
1. To review letter formatting.
2. To review memo formatting.

113A • 5
Conditioning Practice

each line twice; then 1'
writings on line 2

alphabet	1	The requirements for the dock job were truly amazing to Dave Pax.
speed	2	Diane is to make a turn to the right when the signal is in sight.
figures	3	Of the 2,387 jobs cut in 1996, over 450 were office-related jobs.

gwam 1' | 1 | 2 | 3 | 4 | 5 | 6 | 7 | 8 | 9 | 10 | 11 | 12 | 13 |

F ORMATTING

113B • 45
Review Document Formats

Document 1

Format the letter in block format, open punctuation.

words

February 5, ---- | Mr. and Mrs. Felipe Devereaux | 310 Hampshire Ln. | 13
Stamford, CT 06905-7329 | Dear Mr. and Mrs. Devereaux | CRUISE   25
INFORMATION   27

A folder with the specific information on Caribbean cruise options is being   42
mailed to you today. As I mentioned to you during our phone conversa-   56
tion, the Caribbean cruise is one of our most popular vacation packages   71
during this time of the year.   77

Information on one-week cruises to Hawaii and the Virgin Islands--two other   92
popular winter vacation spots--is included in the mailing. If you book   107
within the next week or so, I don't think you will experience any difficulties   122
in making reservations on any of the three cruises.   133

After you have had an opportunity to review these materials, call us; we will   149
be happy to handle all details of the cruise. If you have additional ques-   164
tions about any of the options, let us know.   173

Sincerely yours | Ms. Madeline St. Claire | Travel Agent | xx   184

Document 2

Format the letter in simplified block format.

March 23, ---- | MS ROCHELLE SUMMER | 429 NORTH 310 EAST | 11
LOGAN UT 84720-8987 | RECYCLING PROGRAM   18

The Logan City Council is planning to initiate a recycling program. Your   33
participation is vital to the success of the program.   44

Beginning May 1 separate containers must be used for certain products.   58
Specific information regarding this program is enclosed.   If you have ques-   73
tions about the recycling program, please contact Rita White who has been   88
hired as the recycling coordinator.   96

Your support of this program will assure a healthier environment for future   111
generations.   114

MRS. TERESA A. BREWSTER, CITY MANAGER | xx | Enclosure   124

Skill Builder

Keypad Review

Enter the columns of data listed at the right.

A	B	C	D	E	F	G
477	588	707	107	41.6	141.4	936.6
417	528	808	205	52.9	252.5	825.6
717	825	909	309	63.3	393.3	719.4

Speed/Control Building

Enter the data listed in each column of Drills 1-4.

Note: When using the calculator accessory, enter each column of data a second time (bottom to top). If you get the same total twice, you can "assume" it is correct. If you get a different total the second time, re-enter the data until you get two totals that match.

Drill 1

A	B	C	D	E	F	G
5	77	114	5,808	1,936	9,300	6,936
46	89	225	3,997	2,825	8,250	3,896
3	78	336	9,408	3,796	10,475	7,140
17	85	725	5,650	8,625	7,125	4,874
28	98	825	3,714	9,436	12,740	2,515
9	69	936	2,825	8,514	12,850	8,360
10	97	704	6,796	4,174	9,674	1,794

Drill 2

A	B	C	D	E	F	G
99	795	1,581	1,881	2,642	4,573	2,185
67	657	1,691	1,991	2,772	4,683	3,274
88	234	1,339	2,202	2,992	5,477	9,396
96	359	1,221	2,432	3,743	6,409	4,585
84	762	1,101	3,303	3,853	6,886	5,872
100	485	1,144	4,650	4,714	7,936	6,903

Drill 3

A	B	C	D	E	F
1,077	3,006	5,208	7,104	1,774	7,417
1,400	3,609	5,502	8,205	2,885	8,528
1,700	3,900	5,205	9,303	3,996	9,639
2,008	4,107	6,309	7,407	4,174	3,936
2,500	4,400	6,600	8,508	5,285	5,828
2,805	1,704	6,900	9,609	6,396	4,717

Drill 4

A	B	C	D	E	F
1.4	14.00	170.40	1,714.70	7,410.95	1,147.74
2.5	17.00	170.43	2,825.80	8,520.55	2,258.88
3.6	25.00	250.90	3,936.90	9,630.65	3,369.93
7.4	28.00	288.50	4,747.17	10,585.78	7,144.74
8.5	36.00	369.63	5,878.25	11,474.85	8,255.85
9.6	39.00	390.69	6,969.39	12,696.95	9,366.63

Format Guides:

Modified Block Letter with Special Parts

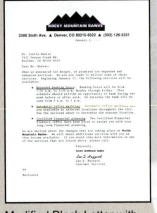

Modified Block Letter with Special Characters

Second Page of Business Letter

Occasionally, you will find several special features used in business letters and memos. In some cases, alternative formats for special parts are chosen (for example, the subject line may be placed in various positions). The simplest and most efficient formats, however, are illustrated in this unit.

Attention line. When an attention line is used in a letter addressed to a company, key it as the first line of the letter and envelope address:

```
Attention Personnel Director
Beechwood Associates
878 Colonial Way
New Bedford, MA 02747-2511
```

When a letter is addressed to a company, the correct salutation is "Ladies and Gentlemen."

Subject line. Place the subject line in ALL CAPS a double space below the salutation. If the body paragraphs are blocked, block the subject line at the left margin. If the body paragraphs are indented, indent the subject line the same number of spaces or center it.

Special characters. Special characters (✓, •, ★) can be used with text to give additional emphasis. Sometimes, special characters are used instead of numbers in listings.

Page heading. If a letter involves more than one page, key a heading at the top of each page after the first. Place the receiver's name, page number, and date on three lines at the top left margin (see illustration at left). DS below the date.

Company name. When used, place the company name a double space below the complimentary close in ALL CAPS. QS (quadruple-space) to writer's name.

Enclosure notation. Place enclosure (or attachment) notation a double space below reference initials. If multiple enclosures are referred to in the letter, follow the word "Enclosures" with a colon and two spaces and list each enclosure:

```
Enclosures: Brochure
            Membership Forms
```

Copy notation. A copy notation indicates that a copy of a letter is being sent to someone other than the addressee. Use "c" followed by the name of the person(s) to receive a copy. Place a copy notation a double space below the last line of the enclosure notation or the reference line if there is no enclosure:

```
c Robert Anderson
  Mario Sanchez
```

Postscript. A postscript is additional text that may be added after a letter has been completed. It is the last item in the letter. The postscript is used to place additional emphasis on the text or to reemphasize a part of the text included in the body. The postscript can also be used to include a personal message in a business letter.

Form letters. A standardized letter that can be sent to numerous addresses is known as a form letter or boilerplate. A form letter (or paragraphs that can be combined to create varying letters) can be stored and retrieved when needed. Through text merging, a form letter and an address list can be merged to provide an original letter to each addressee.

Language & Writing Skills 4

Activity 1:

1. Study the spelling/definitions of the words in the color block.
2. Key line 1 (the **Learn** line), noting the proper choice of words.
3. Key lines 2-3 (the **Apply** lines), choosing the right words to complete each sentence correctly.
4. Key the remaining lines in the same way.
5. Check your work; correct any errors you find.

Choose the right word

its (adj) of or relating to itself as the possessor	**than** (conj/prep) used in comparisons to show difference between items
it's (contr) it is; it has	**then** (n/adv) that time; at that time

Learn 1 It's time for the dog to have its food.
Apply 2 Before (its, it's) time to bid, check (its, it's) number.
Apply 3 If (its, it's) not yours, return it to (its, it's) shelf.

Learn 4 If she is older than you, then I am older than you.
Apply 5 We (than, then) decided that two hours were more (than, then) enough.
Apply 6 Fewer (than, then) half the workers were (than, then) put on overtime.

Activity 2:

1. Read the ¶, noting needed changes in capitalization, number expression, and word choice.
2. Key the ¶, making the needed changes. Correct any errors you make as you key.

Proofread & correct

on our trip to san francisco, 10 of us had a delicious lunch at a restaurant called china doll: pork-stuffed dumplings, shrimp fried rice, and chinese vegetables. we than shopped 'til we dropped. we bought exquisite kimonos, faux ivory chopsticks, and an assortment of gifts of cloisonne, pearl, and jade. my good friend manuel bought his mother a beautiful chinese screen. with it's friendly atmosphere and unique shops, its no wonder chinatown attracts so many locals as well as tourists.

Activity 3:

1. Key Items 1 and 2 as ¶ 1 of a short composition; at each set of parentheses, supply the information needed to complete each sentence.
2. Key Item 3 as ¶ 2, supplying the information noted in the parentheses.
3. Key Item 4 as ¶ 3, supplying the information noted in the parentheses.
4. Proofread, revise, and correct your composition. Look for misspelled words, improper capitalization, inaccurate information, and weak sentence structure.

Compose (think) as you key

1 My name, (first/last), is (African/Asian/European/Oriental, etc.) in origin.

2 My mother's ancestors originated in (name of country); my father's ancestors originated in (name of country).

3 I know the following facts about the country of my (mother's/father's) ancestors:

   1. (enter first fact here)
   2. (enter second fact here)
   3. (enter third fact here)

4 If I could visit a country of my choice, I would visit (name of country) because (give two or three reasons).

Title:	Ms.	
First name:	Halli	
Last name:	Johnson	
Address:	381 Lake Grove St.	
City:	Memphis	
State:	TN	
ZIP:	38108-7865	

Title:	Mr.
First name:	Wayne
Last name:	Walton
Address:	821 Utah Ave.
City:	Harrisburg
State:	PA
ZIP:	17109-8374

ACTIVITY 2:

Special Characters

1. Read the copy at right.
2. Learn to use special characters in your software.
3. Key the copy using a special character available in your software.
4. Replace the character with another available character.

Special characters such as ✓, ★, ❑, ●, ■, and ¶, which are not found on the keyboard, can be formed by accessing them with key and number combinations determined by your software. One of the most common uses of such characters is with listings. Instead of using numbers with the listing, special characters are used.

Please check to make sure you have included the following items:

✓ sleeping bag
✓ tent
✓ backpack
✓ hiking boots

ACTIVITY 3:

Sort

1. Read the copy at right.
2. Learn to use the Sort feature for your software.
3. Key the text at the right in two columns leaving 2" between columns.
4. Sort by last name in ascending order.
5. Sort by social security number in ascending order.
6. Sort by first name in ascending order.

The **Sort** feature arranges text in a specific order. The feature will sort alphabetic or numeric text in ascending or descending order.

Brown, Jacob	520-38-8211
Aspen, Mary	261-29-3841
Smith, Rafael	926-28-2991
Jackson, Ron	388-19-2842
Marshall, Anne	882-29-1819
Simmons, Charla	261-36-5656
Timms, Barbara	261-92-1243

ACTIVITY 4:

Review wp Features

1. Key sentences; <u>underline</u>, *italicize*, and **bold** text as you key.
2. Use the Block Delete feature to delete *who live in Germany* and the commas from line 1 and *a University of Wyoming Graduate* and the commas from line 2.
3. Delete lines 3 and 4.

1 **Mark** and **Jane**, who live in Germany, were at the **World Series**.

2 **Kari Carling**, a University of Wyoming graduate, wrote <u>Is Justice Fair?</u>

3 *Mary* would ask <u>very specific</u> questions before analyzing the **issues**.

4 Dial **9-1-1** for *EMERGENCY* service; **6-1-1** for *REPAIR* service.

5 The first test date is <u>Monday</u>, **October 17**; the second test date is <u>Monday</u>, **October 31**.

6 **Meg** bought *The Stock Buyer's Guide* to help her with investing.

7 **Aaron**, **Mays**, and **Mantle** are members of the Baseball Hall of Fame.

ACTIVITY 1:

Center

1. Read the copy at right.
2. Learn the Justification features for your wp software.
3. Key the 6 lines at the right DS so that they are centered horizontally.

Justification refers to the horizontal position of a line of text. Use the **Center** feature to center one or more lines of text between the left and right margins as the text is keyed.

Conservation Laws

Newton's Law of Gravity

Relativity and the Nuclear Age

The Solar System

Elements, Compounds, and States of Matter

The Atmosphere and Meteorology

ACTIVITY 2:

Delete

1. Read the copy at right.
2. Learn how to delete text using your wp software.
3. Key the ¶ at the right DS; underline and bold text as shown as you key.
4. Using the most efficient method, delete all text that is bolded or underlined.
5. Edit as needed to correct spacing.

The **delete** or **backspace** key may be used to correct simple keying errors. For deleting a word or phrase, however, a combination of keys and the mouse is faster. For example, in some wp packages the **Ctrl + Backspace** deletes a word and the **Ctrl + Delete** deletes a group of words.

John Homer, Naomi Kerrit, **Paul Desmond,** and Kay Ford were selected by the **five** geology faculty members to make a **short multimedia** presentation at the upcoming Delaware Valley Geological Society meeting on January 5 at the Harris Hotel in Clarks Summit. They will fly into Philadelphia from Columbus.

ACTIVITY 3:

Undelete and Undo

1. Read the copy at right.
2. Learn how to use the Undo and/or the Undelete features of your wp software.
3. Key the ¶ at the right DS using bold as shown.
4. Read the ¶ you keyed and perform the undo and undelete (if applicable to your wp software) operations as directed in it.

Use the **Undo** feature to reverse the last change you made in text. (Some wp packages undo only the most recent editing change.) Undo restores text to its original location, even if you have moved the insertion point to another position. **Undelete**, a feature available on some wp packages, restores deleted text at the insertion point. The Undelete feature usually allows you to restore any or all of the last three deletions.

After keying **this** paragraph, delete **the** bolded words and restore them at their original place. Now: If your **wp** software has an Undelete feature, delete the words Now and Next (delete : too). Next: Restore the word Now (with :) at the beginning of the paragraph and the word Next before the last sentence. Correct spacing between sentences and after colons.

ACTIVITY 1:

Merge

1. Read the copy at right.
2. Learn the Merge feature for your software.
3. Prepare form and data files from the information provided below right and on p. 267.
4. Merge the form and data files to create a personalized form letter for each person named in the data file.

The **Merge** feature is used to combine information from two sources into one document. It is often used for mail merge, which merges a form letter file (**form or primary file**) with an address file (**data or secondary file**) to create personalized letters to each person in the address file.

An address (data) file contains a **record** for each person. Each record contains **field(s)** of information about the person, such as her or his title, first name, last name, etc.

End field codes are used in the data file to separate and distinguish fields of information. **End record codes** are used in the data file to separate and distinguish each record.

The form file contains the text of the document that remains constant in each letter plus the **field codes** or **field names**. The field codes (names) are positioned in the document where the variable information from the data file is to appear.

Form (Primary) File

<Date>

<Title> <First name> <Last name>
<Address>
<City,> <State> <ZIP>

Dear <Title> <Last name>

It was a pleasure to meet with you last week to discuss your life insurance needs. As you requested, I have the costs for various options computed and would be happy to meet with you to go over the figures. I will call you next week to arrange an appointment.

Sincerely

Tom Andrews
Agent

xx

Data (Secondary) File Information

Title:	Mr.	Title:	Dr.
First name:	Angelo	First name:	Anita
Last name:	Martinez	Last name:	Burton
Address:	928 Ellsworth Dr.	Address:	298 Boswell Rd.
City:	Rapid City	City:	Raleigh
State:	SD	State:	NC
ZIP:	57706-8212	ZIP:	27610-1252

(continued on next page)

ACTIVITY 4:

Blocked Text

1. Read the copy at right.
2. Learn how to block text using your wp software.
3. Retrieve TWP1-4.
4. Use the Block feature to italicize, underline, and bold the copy as shown at the right. Use Block to center line 5 and delete the last six words of line 6.

Use the **Block** feature to select a block of text on which various operations may be performed. The block is selected by using the cursor movement keys or mouse to highlight the text. Once blocked, the block of text can be bolded, italicized, underlined, deleted, centered, copied, moved, printed, saved, etc.

1. The office of **Best & Jones** *will be* relocated soon.

2. Mary *and* Jane confused there and their in the report.

3. Twelve **computers** *and* five **printers** arrived yesterday.

4. The students just started reading A Man for All Seasons.

5. *Death of a Salesman* was written by Arthur Miller.

6. Tom and Mary saw the parade and then went to the circus.

7. Most printers can print **bold**, *italics*, or underlines.

ACTIVITY 5:

Copy and Move

1. Read the copy at right.
2. Learn how to copy and move text using your wp software.
3. Retrieve TWP1-5.
4. Make a copy of the 1st ¶ and place it as the 5th ¶.
5. Move the 2d ¶ so it is the 4th ¶; move what is now the 3d ¶ so it becomes the 2d ¶.
6. Edit so ¶s are SS with DS between, with no ¶ indention.

After you have blocked text, you can use the Move or Copy feature. The **Move** feature removes (cuts) the blocked text from one location and places (pastes) it at another location. The **Copy** feature duplicates (copies) the blocked text and places (pastes) it in another, leaving the original unchanged.

The Move feature is commonly called "cut and paste," and the Copy feature is often called "copy and paste."

The Block feature is used in the move and copy commands in the same way it is used to bold, italicize, underline, center, or delete text.

Most word processing software has button bars that can be used to cut, copy, and paste text quickly.

The text will be moved or copied to the insertion point that is selected when the "paste" command is executed.

ACTIVITY 6:

Center Page

1. Read the copy at right.
2. Learn to center copy vertically using your wp software.
3. Open a new file. Set side margins at 2".
4. Use the Center Page feature.
5. Key the ¶s at the right DS.
6. Keep this text on the screen and proceed to Activity 7.

Use the **Center Page** feature to center lines of text between the top and bottom margins of the page. This feature leaves an equal (or nearly equal) amount of white space above and below the text.

A word processor is an excellent tool that can help you demonstrate your best writing skills. When you use a word processor to write papers for school, your final draft is likely to reflect your best effort.

The ease with which you can add, delete, and cut and paste copy with word processors encourages you to write a series of drafts until you know you have done your best.

The use of the word processor's spell checker, thesaurus, and grammar checker will "help" you to identify spelling, grammar, and punctuation errors; find and use the correct word; and identify style flaws.

PHASE 4

LESSONS 113–150

Enhance Document Processing Skills

This section of the textbook gives opportunities for enhancing your information processing skills. Some lessons focus on enhancing speed and accuracy by refining keying techniques. More punctuation rules appear, along with many "checks" on rules in prior lessons.

In Phase 4 you will enhance document formatting skills, too. After reviewing correspondence, report, and table formats, you will transfer your knowledge and skill to other documents, including those used to get a job. Once again you will have a chance to apply class learning on the job.

The subject of many documents is technology. You will encounter terms, such as electronic mail and voice mail, that define the fields of communication and information processing. Remember: "No matter what career you choose . . . , a computer is likely to be the center of your communication. . . ."

In the 38 lessons of this phase, you will:

1. Refine keying techniques to enhance speed and accuracy on straight, script, and rough-draft copy.
2. Enhance document formatting skills and ability to apply language skills.
3. Prepare business forms and special-purpose documents.
4. Create employment documents.
5. Acquire (simulated) work experience in a consulting business.

ACTIVITY 7:

View

1. Read the copy at right.
2. Learn how to preview a document using your wp software.
3. Preview the document from Activity 6 to see how it will look on a printed page. Notice that the top and bottom margins are nearly equal.

It is a good practice to see how your document will appear on paper before it is printed. Most wp software has a View (or Preview) feature that lets you do so. Thus you will not waste time and paper printing a document that is not correct. The view (or preview) mode will display a miniature model of each page of your document on your monitor. In some software, a document can be edited in this mode. Typically, the model is large enough for you to judge the appropriateness of the margin settings as well as the spacing above and below document parts. If needed, the "zoom" feature can be used to enlarge specific parts of a document for closer inspection.

ACTIVITY 8:

Envelope

1. Read the copy at right.
2. Learn how to prepare envelopes using your wp software.
3. Use the envelope (delivery) and return addresses given at the right to prepare two small envelopes. Key the envelope address in ALL CAPS without punctuation, as shown. Use default settings.

An envelope may contain a return (sender's) address besides the envelope (receiver's) address. You may need to specify the envelope size; type of paper feed for your printer; and other options, including a POSTNET bar code. The bar code is a machine-readable representation of the ZIP Code + 4 and other data that speeds mail sorting at the post office.

Return address:

Envelope 1

John Desilva
7904 Waverly Rd.
San Diego, CA 92120-2436

Envelope 2

Beth Murphy
467 Bradley St.
Portsmouth, VA 23701-9823

Envelope address:

MR HENRY JOHNSON
7894 FORBES ST
DAYTON OH 45405-4174

MS LAURA ANDERSON
4234 BINGHAM DR
PORTSMOUTH VA 23703-7103

ACTIVITY 9:

Apply What You Have Learned

Key the information at the right; 2 QS (seven blank lines) between keyed lines. Center it vertically and horizontally. Use bold, italic, and underline as shown.

A Book Report

on

BLESS THE BEASTS AND CHILDREN

by

Glendon Swarthout

Completed by: <u>Kenneth Greene</u>

GLOBAL AWARENESS

The United Nations has as its main purpose the promotion of peace, understanding, and cooperation among all peoples of the world. Headquartered in the city of New York, the UN began operations on October 24, 1945. Over 180 countries are members. Writers of the UN charter realized that peace and cooperation among all nations needed to be maintained to avoid another war that likely would be worse than the one just ended—World War II.

One way the United Nations works to reduce human abuse and discrimination and to develop peace and understanding is through yearly days of remembrance. The purpose of these special days is to help us understand the issues and to encourage us to work together, nationally and internationally, to eliminate the cause of human suffering and global strife.

The following list of UN annual observances suggests major global issues.

March 8	International Women's Day	1st Monday of October	Universal Children's Day
March 21	International Day for Elimination of Racial Discrimination	October 1	International Day for the Elderly
June 4	International Day of Innocent Children Victims of Aggression	October 10	World Food Day
		October 24	United Nations Day
3d Tuesday of September	International Day of Peace	December 1	World AIDS Day
		December 10	Human Rights Day

ACTIVITIES

1. Read and discuss the material at the left.

2. In groups of 3 or 4 students, select one of the days from the list and plan a school-wide observance for that day.
   a. List the steps you need to follow in preparation.
   b. Decide on a program for the observance and who will conduct it.
   c. Decide on what you need to do to promote attendance: posters, announcements, etc.
   d. If guest speakers are to be involved, decide who they will be and compose a letter inviting them.

CULTURAL DIVERSITY

No two people are exactly alike, except for identical twins; and even they may develop slight differences. People differ biologically: hair, eyes, skin color, physique, gender, physical capability, and mental capability. We also differ by culture, including the geographical area from which we and/or our ancestors came; the economic level of our families and forebears; and the ways we make, do, and celebrate things. All these factors affect how we behave and how we appear to others.

These biological and cultural differences cause us, somewhat naturally, to develop an *us and them* attitude. We tend to think that others differ from us when it is just as true that we differ from them. Almost all of us see ourselves as the center of our universe and view others from our own perspective. To get along in a diverse society, we must learn to see others and ourselves from their perspective. To do otherwise is to encourage bias and to invite friction and disagreement.

An old sales adage summarizes this concept rather well: "To sell John Doe what John Doe buys, you must see John Doe through John Doe's eyes."

ACTIVITIES

1. Choose a fellow student you do not know very well, one who seems as different from you as possible: ethnic origin, economic background, social group, academic level, gender, and so on.

2. Discuss the outward differences each of you perceives in the other.

3. Exchange answers to these questions:
   a. How important to you are athletic achievement? scholastic achievement? being part of a certain social group? and why?
   b. What concerns you most about your life: at home? at school? in your community? and why?
   c. What do you want to be doing in five years? and why?

4. Compose/key a summary of your differences and similarities.

ACTIVITY 10:

Apply What You Have Learned

1. Key the information at the right. Use 1.5 line spacing and italicize, bold, and underline text as you key.
2. Using the most efficient means, delete all text that is bolded, underlined, or italicized.
3. Delete the last sentence.
4. Restore the last sentence.

John, Mary, **Jim**, and George are going to the show with me.

Kara read the book, *Billy Budd*, by **author** Herman Melville.

We very quietly moved ahead by completing the **seven** steps.

Matthew, Tim, Rhonda, and I completed the *science* project.

Mary *just* completed making *four quality* cards for Marilyn.

The 64 rooms in the major hotel are reserved for Thursday.

Seven **of the eight** students recited the **long** poem quickly.

ACTIVITY 11:

Apply What You Have Learned

1. Key the information directory at the right DS so that each line is centered horizontally.
2. Bold students' last names; italicize the class designation.
3. Copy "Bocktown," to the right of every name that does not have a residential area listed after it.
4. Delete each room number, including the word "Room" and the preceding comma.
5. Using Move, arrange the lines alphabetically by student's last name.
6. View the document to check formatting before printing or saving.

Scott Jewell, Bocktown, Sophomore, Room 101

Toby Jeffers, Broadhead, Junior, Room 102

Erica Johnson, Delmar, Sophomore, Room 101

Terry Jewell, Senior, Room 201

Pamela Lenhart, Sophomore, Room 101

Dino Leonetti, Delmar, Senior, Room 201

Manuel Peres, Freshman, Room 115

Kelli Means, Broadhead, Senior, Room 204

Michele Buyny, Freshman, Room 114

Mary Dutkovic, Junior, Room 102

ACTIVITY 12:

Apply What You Have Learned

Prepare a No. 10 envelope for each address at the right. Use default settings.

Return address for both envelopes:

Mary Todorczuk
453 Spring Run Rd.
Kansas City, KS 66104-2041

Mailing addresses:

Envelope 1

MS HEATHER TOLLIS
509 BOSTON AVE
TULSA OK 74103-9861

Envelope 2

MR DAVID YAJKO
722 CHESTNUT DR
ST LOUIS MO 63101-1427

your PERSPECTIVE

ETHICS: The Right Thing to Do

Television and newspapers seem to dwell on problems that confront our society. We are bombarded with stories of how people, intentionally and unintentionally, hurt others. Physical harm is an obvious way that we can hurt. Embezzlement and shoplifting are others ways in which we can be adversely affected (hurt). Shoplifting, for example, causes us to pay more for the products we buy.

While others are doing harm, we also read about people who run into a burning building to save a life, who return lost money to the owner, or who aid someone who has been in an accident. Such people impress us. We ask ourselves, "Why do some people cause harm, while others live their lives obeying the law and doing good for others?"

A possible answer is character. To most of us, character refers to the attributes people possess that make them positive, contributing members of society. Some of the attributes of character are honesty, responsibility, loyalty, and kindness.

Character is not something that just happens to us. We continually develop the traits of character throughout our lives. Many of us strive to become a better person for ourselves and for others. Character development helps each of us become a better person. Character provides the strengths each of us needs in order to make positive contributions to our school, place of work, and society.

Character development is important to all of us. USA WEEKEND (1994, 20-24) printed an article on character and its qualities. The article included a quiz to help each of us assess the levels of our honesty and responsibility. Two of the quiz questions are given below. They present situations that we could encounter in our daily lives. The answers we give to the questions can help us understand and develop character in our own lives.

ACTIVITIES

1. Read the material at the left and answer the two quiz questions. You may have more than one answer to each question, but your answers must be consistent.

2. In groups of 3 or 4 students, discuss your answers in terms of the attributes of good character.

3. Three attributes of good character are identified in the material at the left. If other attributes came out of your discussion in Step 2, add them to the others.

4. Compose/key a short report to give your definition (understanding) of good character and the attributes of which it is comprised.

Question 1. You look younger than you are. You could save $24 at an amusement park if you lie about your age. Would you do it?
a. Yes. I need the money more than they do.
b. Yes. It's unfair to make people pay more just because they're older.
c. Yes, if I couldn't afford to pay the full price.
d. No. It is unfair to the people who play by the rules.
e. No. It is dishonest.

Question 2. You are captain of your high school tennis team, one of the state's best. The coach is new and doesn't know the players well. One player has to be cut. The coach asks you, as captain, to decide which of two players should stay on the team. One is your best friend, who really wants to play; the other, a better player who could help the team more. Would you choose your friend?
a. Yes. Loyalty is very important.
b. Yes, because of the golden rule. If our roles were reversed, I would want my friend to choose me.
c. No. My duty to the team is to select the best player.
d. No. I would not like it if the coach selected players on the basis of whom he liked rather than playing skill.
e. No. It is in my own best interests to have the best players possible.
f. No. It would be unfair to the other, better player. ✳

UNIT 8
LESSONS 41–42

Learn to Center Lines/Documents

LESSON 41 Horizontal Centering

Objectives:
1. To learn to center lines horizontally (side to side).
2. To improve keying speed and control.

41A • 5
Conditioning Practice

each line twice SS; then a 1' writing on line 3; find *gwam*

alphabet 1 Jake led a big blitz which saved the next play for my squad.
fig/sym 2 Beth has ordered 26 5/8 yards of #304 linen at $7.19 a yard.
speed 3 Good form is the key if all of us wish to make the big goal.
gwam 1' | 1 | 2 | 3 | 4 | 5 | 6 | 7 | 8 | 9 | 10 | 11 | 12 |

S KILL BUILDING

41B • 10
Technique Improvement

1. Key the lines twice (slowly; then faster).
2. Key a 1' writing on each of lines 3, 6, and 9; find *gwam* on each.

letter response
1 verb milk rare pomp were jump best limp grew hump fear union
2 saw him|you are|pop art|join up|gas pump|milk cart|best hump
3 A union steward gets you a wage rate card after you join up.

word response
4 gowns their forms title ivory shall firms eight amend theory
5 six forms|the title|for their|and shall|did amend|work audit
6 An audit of the work forms may end a fight for an amendment.

combination response
7 is up to in for oil sit joy they grew work pump shall agreed
8 is up|to be|for joy|the oil|with milk|they were|the best man
9 It is up to the union man to set a rate for the rest of you.
gwam 1' | 1 | 2 | 3 | 4 | 5 | 6 | 7 | 8 | 9 | 10 | 11 | 12 |

41C • 10
Center Lines Horizontally

1. If equipment has AC (Automatic Centering) feature, learn to use it; then key Drills 1-3 DS on one page, each line centered horizontally; QS between drills.
2. If AC feature is not available, study p. RG19; then key Drills 1-3, each line centered horizontally.

1
is
they
social
problems
amendments

2
a
for
gowns
foreign
processor

3
I
when
profit
quality
quantity

Table 1
DS; CS: 1" (10 sp.); center column headings

Table 2
DS; CS: 1" (10 sp.); center column headings

Table 3
Add the information below to Table 2. Rearrange the table chronologically, with the *most recent* invention first.

1852 / Gyroscope / Jean Foucault

1896 / Radio / Guglielmo Marconi

			words
	1970-1979 NOBEL PRIZE WINNERS		6
	Literature		8
Year	Winner	Country	13
1970	Aleksandr Solzhenitsyn	Soviet Union	21
1971	Pablo Neruda	Chile	26
1972	Heinrich Boll	Germany	31
1973	Patrick White	Australia	37
1974	Eyvind Johnson	Sweden	42
	Harry Martinson	Sweden	47
1975	Eugenio Montale	Italy	52
1976	Saul Bellow	United States	59
1977	Vincente Aleixandre	Spain	65
1978	Issaac Bashevis Singer	United States	73
1979	Odysseus Elytis	Greece	79
			82
Source:	Academic American Encyclopedia, 1995.		91

			words
	INVENTIONS		2
	19th Century		5
Date	Invention	Inventor	10
1800	Gas Light	Philippe Lebon	16
		William Murdock	19
1801	Draw loom	Joseph Jacquard	26
1805	Railroad locomotive	Richard Trevithick	34
1807	Steamboat	Robert Fulton	40
1820	Calculating machine	Charles Babbage	48
1831	Reaping machine	Cyrus McCormick	56
1835	Revolver	Samuel Colt	61
1841	Vulcanized rubber	Charles Goodyear	69
1846	Sewing machine	Elias Howe	75
1867	Typewriter	Christopher Soles	82
1876	Telephone	Alexander Bell	88
1877	Phonograph	Thomas Edison	95
1880	Filament lamp	Joseph Swan	101
		Thomas Edison	104
			107
Source:	Encyclopedia Americana, 1993.		114

41D • 25
Center Lists and Announcements

TM: default (1")
LS: DS; 3 returns between problems

Problems 1-3 on 1 page
Problems 4-5 on 1 page
Problems 6-7 on 1 page

1. Read all directions before you begin.
2. Center horizontally each line of each problem.

wp note:

Before removing problems from screen, make the changes listed below.

Problem 5
Delete underline; show *Student Auditions* bold.

Problem 6
Bold the first line.

Problem 7
Change the play name to *"Fiddler on the Roof"*; raise each ticket price by $1.

∧ = insert

╱³ = delete/insert

∿ = transpose (tr)

⟨⟩ = delete and close up

≡ = capitalize

⌗ = insert a space

Problem 1

CITY NAMES

Havana

Capetown

Port-au-Prince

Rio de Janeiro

Sault Sainte Marie

Problem 2

READING LIST
Lord of the Flies
To Kill a Mockingbird
A Raisin in the Sun

Problem 3

SPELLING DEMONS

accommodate

committee

immediately

judgment

recommendation

Problem 4

ENGLISH TO SPANISH

house: casa

hotel: hostal

airport: aeropuerto

bank: banco

train station: tren estacion

Problem 5

ANNOUNCING

Student Auditions

for

Holiday Assembly Program

in

Student Activity Center

November 9

Actors at 9:00 a.m.

Vocalists at 10:30 a.m.

Instrumentalists at 1:00 p.m.

Problem 6

Health Service Center

announces

MAKE-UP FLU VACCINATIONS *SHOTS*

November 24 *3*

8:30-10:30 a.m.

Specail Events Room *Dining*

Problem 7

SCHOOL OF PERFORMING ARTS

presents

"The Mouse that Roared"

on

January 21 *and 22*

2:30 ad 8:00 p.m.

Marx Theatre

Matinee: $4.50; Evening: $5.50

(DS Body)

Christopher Columbus.   Christopher Columbus is recognized 310
as one of the earliest noteworthy explorers.   On his first voy- 322
age Columbus landed on the Bahamas, then Cuba, and Haiti (1492- 335
93).   At the time of his explorations, "No other sailor had the 348
persistence, the knowledge and the sheer guts to sail thousands 361
of miles into the unknown ocean until he found land." (Morrison, 374
1957, 80-81)   His explorations whittled away at the unknown. 386

George Rogers Clark.   George Rogers Clark was an American 398
frontiersman explorer during the last half of the eighteenth 410
century.   Like many frontiersmen who are driven to explore by 423
their need for places where fences do not exist, Clark explored 436
vast areas of wilderness.   According to Havighurst (1957, 21), 448
his name is "synonymous with the settlement of the Ohio, adven- 461
ture in the Kentucky wilderness, conquest of the frontier lands 474
of Illinois and the winning of the West for a new nation." 486
His explorations brought new options for people. 501

Delia Denning Akeley.   Delia Denning Akeley has made a 507
significant impact on the American museum visitor from her 519
explorations of Equatorial Africa.   Between 1905 and 1929 she 531
collected specimens of Africa's wild animals for American natu- 544
ral history museums.   Armed with little more than courage and 556
an empathetic understanding of the Africans, she proved that a 569
woman could travel in a dangerous country at a dangerous time. 581
(Tinling, 1989, 10)   Her explorations brought new knowledge 593
to people. 596

Everyone Explores 600

Not everyone will have the urge to explore as these noted 611
explorers did, but everyone has a little bit of an exploring na- 624
ture.   It may not be the urge to explore for glory or discov- 636
ery; it may simply be an urge to travel to a geographical area 649
that an individual has not yet visited.   The urge may be in 661
the form of exploring a museum or a book to expand one's knowl- 673
edge.   Or, it may be exploring educational and career options. 686
Regardless of the type of exploration done, all explorers are 699
changed by their explorations.   Their horizons become much 710
broader through their explorations. 717

Document 3
Title Page
Format a title page for the report. Use your name and school name and the current date.

LESSON 112

Assessment: Tables

Objective:
To assess table formatting skills.

112A • 5
Conditioning Practice

each line twice

alphabet 1 Lexi was just sure Pam would get her sizable refund very quickly.

speed 2 The heir to the endowment may work on the problems with the firm.

fig/sym 3 The shipping expenses ($27.96) were included on Invoice #435A180.

gwam 1' | 1 | 2 | 3 | 4 | 5 | 6 | 7 | 8 | 9 | 10 | 11 | 12 | 13 |

Objectives:
1. To check and improve your keying skill.
2. To center lists, announcements, and menus.

42A • 5
Conditioning Practice

each line twice SS; then key a 1' writing on line 3; find *gwam*

alphabet 1 Jacki had won first place by solving my tax quiz in an hour.

fig/sym 2 Our 1997 profit was $58,604 (up 23% from the previous year).

speed 3 Roddy may sign the six forms and work with the city auditor.

gwam 1' | 1 | 2 | 3 | 4 | 5 | 6 | 7 | 8 | 9 | 10 | 11 | 12 |

42B • 20
Skill Assessment

1. Key a 1' writing on each ¶; find *gwam* on each writing.
2. Key two 2' writings on ¶s 1-2 combined; find *gwam* on each writing.
3. Key two 3' writings on ¶s 1-3 combined; find *gwam* and circle errors on each writing.

Note: If using wordwrap, ignore hyphens at line endings. Your line endings may differ from those in the textbook.

all letters used

	gwam	2'	3'

Each of us has to make choices, and each choice has its — 6 | 4
own results. You are not an exception. You choose all your — 12 | 8
friends; you decide which career you want to pursue; and you — 18 | 12
determine how you will act or behave in every situation. — 23 | 16

If you acquire friends who set goals for a high stan- — 29 | 19
dard of behavior, you will probably do so, too. Because each — 35 | 23
friend has a major effect on what we do and how we behave, we — 41 | 27
should choose carefully and prize each excellent choice. — 47 | 31

We are often drawn to those who appear to be a lot like — 52 | 35
we are, but we should not exclude everyone who has different — 58 | 39
interests and points of view. To extend our perspective, we — 65 | 43
ought to include friends who come from various cultures. — 70 | 47

gwam 2' | 1 | 2 | 3 | 4 | 5 | 6 |
3' | 1 | 2 | 3 | 4 |

Objective:
To assess report formatting skill.

111A • 5
Conditioning Practice

each line twice; then 1'
writings on line 2

alphabet 1 Jackie will budget for the expensive zoology equipment next year.

speed 2 The man in the wheelchair may sit by the docks with their lapdog.

fig/sym 3 Invoice #4368 totalled $927.80 before deducting the 15% discount.

gwam 1' | 1 | 2 | 3 | 4 | 5 | 6 | 7 | 8 | 9 | 10 | 11 | 12 | 13 |

111B • 45
Assess Report Formatting Skills

Document 1
Report from Rough Draft

1. Format and key the report in unbound style; use **EXPLORERS** for the heading of the report.

2. When you finish, proofread your copy. Use spell check if you have it.

Document 2
References List

Use the information below to create a references list on a separate page.

Havighurst, Walter. "The Old Frontiersman--George Rogers Clark." In Helen Wright and Samuel Rapport (eds.), <u>The Great Explorers</u>. New York: Harper & Row Publishers, 1957.

Morrison, Samuel Eliot. "Christopher Columbus, Mariner." In Helen Wright and Samuel Rapport (eds.), <u>The Great Explorers</u>. New York: Harper & Row, Publishers, 1957.

Rugoff, Milton. <u>The Great Travelers</u>. New York: Simon and Schuster, 1960.

Tinling, Marion. <u>Women into the Unknown</u>. New York: Greenwood Press, 1989.

words

opening 2

What motivates an explorers? The earliest explorers ex- travelled 14

plored for the purpose of discovery. and adventure Many of the early explorers 29

mentioned stated conquest, acquisition of wealth, and territorial acqui- 42

sition as their reasons for travel. 49

Today the reasons have changed. Explorers offer the 60

following reasons for leaving the comforts of their homes and venturing into possible danger and 79

hardship. 81

1. Taking the benefits of Christianity to other lands. 93
2. Taking the benefits of modern technology to other 104
   lands. 105
3. Studying plants or wildlife. 112
4. Uncovering the remains of ancient civilizations. 123
5. Protecting the world's environmental balance. 133
6. Testing one's strength and ability to survive. 148

Backgrounds of Explorers (Tinling, 1989, xxiii) 153

Explorers come from all walks of life. Marco Polo was 164

a merchant, Robert Louis Stevenson was a novelist, and Mary 176

Kingsley was a well-born Englishwoman. Noted explorers in- 188

clude priests, conquistadors, lawyers, surgeons, naturalists, 200

etc. No station in life is immune from the "fever." 211

(Rugoff, 1960, xix)

The itch, the fever, the urge--whatever one chooses to 222
call it--is recurrent, if not constant. Once they have 233
gone off, they go again and again. . . . Often the 243
fever manifests itself in childhood . . . and sometimes 255
it stops only with death, violent death." 267

There are many examples of individuals who had the 277
"fever." Three such examples are Christopher Columbus, 289
George Rogers Clark, and Delia Denning Akeley. 298

(continued on next page)

42C • 25
Center Lists, Announcements, and Menus

TM: default (1")
LS: DS; 3 returns between problems

Problems 1-2 on 1 page
Problems 3-4 on 1 page
Problems 5-6, each on a separate page

1. Read all directions before you begin.
2. Center horizontally each line of each problem.

wp note:

Before removing problems from screen, make the changes listed below.

Problem 1
Remove underline and bold the heading.

Problem 2
Italicize the heading or underline it.

Problem 3
Change the day and date to *Friday, March 9.*

Problem 4
Change *35%* to *40%*; bold the shop name.

3. If time permits, center DS:

- your full name (ALL CAPS)
- your street address
- your city, state, ZIP Code
- your telephone number
- name of your school (ALL CAPS)
- name of your teacher
- name of your keyboarding textbook (capital and lowercase letters: C/lc) in italics or underlined

Note: See p. A15 for R & E activities for this unit.

Problem 1

National Honor Society
Joseph I. Emerik
Yuka Ito
Ricardo J. Mendoza
Billye Jean Peters
Christopher A. Thompson

Problem 2

SPANISH TO ENGLISH

por favor: please

gracias: thank you

da nada: you are welcome

hasta luego: see you later

hasta la vista: I'll see you

Problem 3

ANNUAL FUND AUCTION

Student Activity Center

Lakeshore High School

Saturday, March 10

Dinner at 6:30 p.m.

Auction at 8:00 p.m.

Admission & Dinner: $17.50 Per Person

Reservations Required: 555-4739

Problem 4

SUPER SAVER SALE

Up to 35% Off

Rings, Necklaces, Bracelets

at

THE GEM SHOP

December 1 through 15

10 a.m.-6 p.m.

Towne Shopping Center

Problem 5

RESTAURANTE LA BAMBA

Salon Buganvilea

ENTREMES

Queso Fundido con Chorizo Cantimpalo

SOPA

Crema de Elotes con Rajas

ENSALADA

Coliflor a la Vinagreta

ENTRADA

Camarones Gigantes al Mojo de Ajo

POSTRE

Rollo de Nuez con Crema

Problem 6

LA BAMBA RESTAURANT

Bougainvillea Room

APPETIZER

Grilled Cheese with Cantimpalo Sausage

SOUP

Cream of Corn with Green Chili Strips

SALAD

Cauliflower a la Vinegrette

ENTREE

Grilled Jumbo Shrimp with Garlic

DESSERT

Nut Roll in Cream Sauce

110C • 35
Assess Letter/Memo Formatting Skills

Document 1
Letter

Format and key the text at the right as a modified block letter with open punctuation and indented paragraphs.

words

December 30, ---- | Ms. Thelma White | P.O. Box 414 | Moorcroft, WY   12
82721-2342 | Dear Ms. White   18

The planning committee is thrilled to announce that the ground-breaking   32
ceremony for the **Wyoming Women's Historical Museum** will take place   46
on Friday, June 24. Many hours have been spent by our committee trying   60
to move this project forward. At times the committee was not even sure   75
there would ever be a ground-breaking ceremony.   84

As part of the celebration, we are inviting those who played an important   99
part in helping us reach this milestone to a luncheon in their honor. The   114
luncheon will be held at the Mead House at 11:30. The ground-breaking   128
ceremony will begin at 1:30.   134

The museum will be a great source of pride for Wyoming residents and will   149
give them a sense of their history. Visitors will be reminded of the part   164
Wyoming women played in the history of Wyoming as well as in the history   179
of the United States.   183

Sincerely | Mark C. Felding | Committee Chair | xx   191

Document 2
Memo

Format and key the text at the right as a standard memo to **Women's Historical Museum Committee**. The memo is from **Mark C. Felding**. Date the memo **January 5, ----**; use **CONTRIBUTION UPDATE** for the subject line.

 opening 22

The contribution figures for November and December are attached. They   36
are much higher than we anticipated.   44

The higher figures are due in large part to the $5,000 contributions. The   59
committee's idea of having a plaque at the entrance listing individuals con-   74
tributing amounts of $5,000 or more has been very successful. The bronze   89
statue of Esther Morris given to those contributing $25,000 or more has   103
also been successful. Over $700,000 has been raised by contributions in   118
this category.   121

I believe we can still reach our goal of $1.5 million in private contri-   135
butions before the ground-breaking ceremony on June 24. I'll continue to   147
send periodic updates. | xx | Attachment   157

Document 3
Letter

Format and key the text at the right in simplified block letter format. Use the USPS letter address style.

February 3, ---- | MS RACHAEL LEIGHTON | 4504 GLENWOOD   10
AVE | YOUNGSTOWN OH 44502-5371 | SOFTWARE INSTRUCTION   20
WORKSHOPS   22

Even the most user-friendly computer hardware and software will gather dust   36
unless buyers have been properly trained. When you purchased your sys-   52
tem from us, we told you that we would provide the necessary training.   66

Our workshops in word processing and spreadsheets will be offered again   81
in March. The word processing workshop is scheduled for Monday nights   95
(March 6-April 24). The spreadsheet applications class is scheduled for   109
Wednesday nights (March 8-April 26). Both classes meet from 7 to 8 p.m.   124

Registration materials are enclosed. Since the classes fill quite rapidly, you   140
should register as soon as possible.   148

TODD S. BAXTER, COMPUTER SPECIALIST | xx | Enclosure   157

Master Keyboarding/ Language Skills

LESSON 43

Keyboarding/Language Skills

Objectives:
1. To improve keying speed and control.
2. To review/improve language skills (pronoun usage).

43A • 5
Conditioning Practice

each line twice SS; then a 1' writing on line 3; find *gwam*

alphabet	1	Pete quickly coaxed eight avid fans away from the jazz band.
fig/sym	2	Of $3,482.70 taxes paid, $956.10 went to the city and state.
speed	3	Vivian is to key the forms they wish to rush to the auditor.
gwam	1'	1	2	3	4	5	6	7	8	9	10	11	12

43B • 15
Skill Building

1. Key each line twice SS; DS between 4-line groups.
2. Select lines that were awkward or caused you to slow down; key each of those lines twice more.

Note: In lines 7-8, underline the words (do not use italics).

spacing	1	us by of an to am go in is on do my elm pay she may and they
	2	Kay is to pay the man for any of the film you buy from them.
shifting	3	Shep and Mark|Jane or Ella|J. Spence & Sons|Apple & Kane Co.
	4	Dottie and Roby Park sang in the "Voice of Harmony" concert.
CAPS LOCK	5	UPS or USPS|CNN and TNT|NBC or CBS|ZIP Codes|SAN ANTONIO, TX
	6	I can use ALL CAPS for book titles; e.g., CAST OF THOUSANDS.
underline	7	its, not it's|than, not then|four, not fore|their, not there
	8	He underlines magazine titles: People and Education Digest.
apostrophe & quotation	9	you don't|he doesn't|it's his|I keyed "chose," not "choose."
	10	"To succeed," he said, "you must do your best at all times."
hyphen	11	co-op plan|two-ply tire|32-cent stamp|self-esteem|up-to-date
	12	Jay's just-in-time three-pointer gave us the half-time lead.
letter response	13	gave pink best ploy save only ever join vase edge pump facts
	14	You acted on a phony tax case only after a union gave facts.
word response	15	their field chair throw right visit risks world proxy eighty
	16	Lana may sign the form to pay for the giant map of the city.
combination response	17	paid link pair were hand only sign maps card also fast plump
	18	To get to be a pro, react with zest and care as the pros do.
gwam	1'	1	2	3	4	5	6	7	8	9	10	11	12

LESSON 110

Assessment: Letters and Memos

Objective:
To assess letter and memo formatting skills.

**110A • 5
Conditioning Practice**

set 0.5" SMs
each line twice

alphabet	1	Grandpa was quick to criticize May for purchasing six valuable jewels.
speed	2	The maid paid the men for the work they did on the shanty by the lake.
fig/sym	3	My 1997 property tax increased by 6.75% ($241); I paid $3,580 in 1996.

gwam 1' | 1 | 2 | 3 | 4 | 5 | 6 | 7 | 8 | 9 | 10 | 11 | 12 | 13 | 14 |

**110B • 10
Check Keying Skill**

Key two 3' writings on
¶s 1 and 2 combined;
calculate *gwam* and
determine errors.

all letters used

gwam 1' | 3'

	1'	3'
Quite a few of today's consumers buy on credit each day	11	4	67
without considering the consequences of the costs associated with	24	8	71
purchases made on credit. A decreased spending capacity in the	37	12	75
future is one of the main points that needs to be taken into	49	16	79
account prior to making a major credit purchase. Buyers who	62	21	83
utilize credit need to remember that earnings going toward the	74	25	87
repayment of a loan restrict funds that could be used to buy other	88	29	92
goods or services.	91	30	93
Buyers must also remember that credit can be expensive; there	12	35	97
are costs associated with it. One of those costs is interest. In-	26	39	102
terest is the sum charged for the use of money. Buyers who make	39	43	106
purchases via credit can also expect to be charged service fees or	52	48	111
finance charges. Perhaps the biggest cost of credit, however, is	65	52	115
the opportunity cost. The opportunity cost can be viewed as the	78	57	119
cost of not acquiring certain goods or services in order to ac-	91	61	124
quire other goods or services.	97	63	126

gwam 1' | 1 | 2 | 3 | 4 | 5 | 6 | 7 | 8 | 9 | 10 | 11 | 12 | 13 |
      3' | 1 | 2 | 3 | 4 |

43C • 20
Check/Improve Keying Skill

1. Key a 1' writing on each ¶; find *gwam* on each writing.
2. Key two 2' writings on ¶s 1-2 combined; find *gwam* on each writing.
3. Key two 3' writings on ¶s 1-3 combined; find *gwam* and circle errors on each writing.

all letters used

gwam	2'	3'

```
      .     2     .     4     .     6     .     8     .    10     .
A young man asked recently why he was required to take          6   4
     12    .    14    .    16    .    18    .    20    .    22
a course in keyboarding since he was sure that there would     11   8
     24    .    26    .    28    .    30    .    32    .    34
always be others to perform such tasks for him.  His false     17  12
     36    .    38    .    40    .    42    .    44    .    46
belief is common among males, particularly in high school.     23  15

      .     2     .     4     .     6     .     8     .    10
The work roles of men and women have changed quickly           28  19
     12    .    14    .    16    .    18    .    20    .    22
since the computer has become the major means of processing    34  23
     24    .    26    .    28    .    30    .    32    .    34
words and data.  As a result, all office workers are now ex-   40  27
     36    .    38    .    40    .    42    .    44
pected to bring keying and computer skills to the job.         46  31

      .     2     .     4     .     6     .     8     .    10
The old idea that in the office men think and direct           51  34
     12    .    14    .    16    .    18    .    20    .    22
while women merely type is no longer valid.  Now, everyone     57  38
     24    .    26    .    28    .    30    .    32    .    34
is expected to think, direct, and communicate through a key-   63  42
     36    .    38    .    40    .    42    .    44    .    46
board.  Learn these skills now; you will prize them highly.    69  46
```

gwam	2'	1		2		3		4		5		6	
	3'		1		2		3		4			

43D • 10
Pronoun Agreement

SM: 1" or defaults
LS: SS; DS between sets of lines

1. Read the first guide and study the applications in the Learn lines below it.
2. Key the Learn sentences, noting how the guide is applied.
3. Key the Apply sentences, using the correct pro- noun shown in paren- theses.
4. Practice the second rule in the same way.
5. If time permits, key the Apply lines again at a faster speed to quicken decision-making skill.

A personal pronoun (I, we, you, he, she, it, their, etc.) agrees in **person** (first, second, or third) with the noun or other pronoun it represents.

first person	I, we	represents the speaker or writer
second person	you	represents the person(s) spoken/written *to*
third person	he, she, it, their	represents the person(s) spoken/written *about*

Learn 1 Erica said, "I shall see the movie after I finish my project." (1st person)
Learn 2 When you finish your homework, you may watch TV. (2d person)
Learn 3 Malik said that he would drive his car to the hockey game. (3d person)
Apply 4 Students who saw the exhibit said (he/she/they) were impressed.
Apply 5 After you run for a few days, (one's/your) endurance increases.
Apply 6 Before I take the test, I want to review (our, my) class notes.

A personal pronoun agrees in **gender** (masculine, feminine, or neuter) with the noun or other pronoun it represents.

Learn 7 Ms. Wong will give her talk after the announcements. (feminine)
Learn 8 The small boat lost its way in the dense fog. (neuter)
Apply 9 Each mother will receive a corsage as she is given (her/its) award.
Apply 10 The ball circled the rim before (he/it) dropped through the hoop.

109C • 33
Reinforcement: Table Skills

Table 1

DS; CS: 1"; center column headings

TEN LARGEST BODIES OF WATER

Body of Water	Square Miles	Average Depth	words
			6
			9
			14
Pacific Ocean	64,186,300	12,925	21
Atlantic Ocean	33,420,000	11,730	27
Indian Ocean	28,350,500	12,598	34
Arctic Ocean	5,105,700	3,407	39
South China Sea	1,148,500	4,802	46
Caribbean Sea	971,400	8,448	51
Mediterranean Sea	969,100	4,926	58
Bering Sea	873,000	4,893	63
Gulf of Mexico	582,100	5,297	69
Sea of Okhotsk	537,500	3,192	74

78

Source: The World Almanac, 1996.   84

Table 2

DS; CS: 0.5"; center column headings

Table 3

Rearrange (rekey) Table 2 by the year in which the artist was born.

FAMOUS ARTISTS   3

Artist	Country	Artwork	
			8
Jacques-Louis David (1748-1826) 5	French	The Oath of the Horatii	19 / 21
Claude Monet (1840-1926)	French	Impression: Sunrise	29 / 32
Pierre Auguste Renoir (1841-1919)	French	La Loge	39 / 41
Vincent Van Gogh (1853-1890)	Dutch	The Starrey Night	50 / 52
Camille Pissarro (1830-1903)	French	Apple Harvest at Eragny	62 / 64
Michelangelo Buonarotti (1475-1564)	Italian	Last Judgment	73 / 76
Giovanni Bellini (1430-1516)	Italian	The Transfiguration	85 / 87
Edouard Manet (1832-1883)	French	Olympia	93 / 95
Auguste Rodin (1840-1917)	French	The Thinker	102 / 104
Pablo Picasso (1881-1973)	Spanish	Portrait of Vollard	113 / 115
Sir Anthony Van Dyck (1599-1641)	Flemish	Ecstasy of St. Augustine	126 / 128

132

Compiled from the Encyclopedia Americana, 1993.   141

Keyboarding/Language Skills

Objectives:
1. To check/improve keying speed and control.
2. To review/improve language skills (pronoun usage).

44A • 5
Conditioning Practice

each line twice SS; then a 1' writing on line 3; find *gwam*

alphabet	1	Spiro was amazed at just how quickly you fixed the big vans.
fig/sym	2	Of 26,374 citizens, 13,187 (50%) voted in the 1996 election.
speed	3	Diana may make a vivid sign to hang by the door of the hall.

gwam 1' | 1 | 2 | 3 | 4 | 5 | 6 | 7 | 8 | 9 | 10 | 11 | 12 |

44B • 15
Skill Building

1. Key each line once SS; DS between 5-line groups.
2. Key each line again at increased speed.
3. If time permits, rekey lines that caused you to hesitate or stop.

A	1	Andy may carry a flag of orange and black in the big parade.
B	2	Bobbie lobbed the ball to the big boy for a baseline basket.
C	3	Chuck wrote a check to cover the cost of two cruise tickets.
D	4	Dondra made a mad dash from the deli for her third delivery.
E	5	Eduardo needs to relax and let his fingers make the reaches.
F	6	Flo will take off just after four for her first solo flight.
G	7	Gig ought to get as high a grade in algebra as in geography.
H	8	Heidi hopes she can help her brother with his math homework.
I	9	Irwin is to play a violin as well as a piano in the quintet.
J	10	Judy is a just judge who seeks justice from each major jury.
K	11	Keith checks skis and quickly marks each ski by worker name.
L	12	Lolly will lead the platoon in daily field drills this week.
M	13	Matt may be the top swimmer at my new swim club this summer.
N	14	Nadia has won many gymnastic events in this city and county.
O	15	Olaf hopes to work for a good company as an account manager.
P	16	Phyllis hopes to plan a peppy party for all the top players.
Q	17	Quig quietly quit the squad and quickly quelled the quarrel.
R	18	Roxanne is ready to write a report on her recent train trip.
S	19	Stan wants a seafood salad and a single glass of spiced tea.
T	20	Tess sent a letter to her state senator to protest his vote.
U	21	Utah urged our squad to unite to upset our ubiquitous rival.
V	22	Viva visited the old village for a vivid view of the valley.
W	23	Wes was weary of waiting on the windy wharf with the welder.
X	24	Xena, fax all six x-rays if he fixes the fax machine by six.
Y	25	Yorba says that day by day his keying ability must increase.
Z	26	Zazu dazzled us and puzzled the judges with zigzag footwork.

gwam 1' | 1 | 2 | 3 | 4 | 5 | 6 | 7 | 8 | 9 | 10 | 11 | 12 |

108B • 45
Report Format Review

Review the format guides on pp. 211-212.

1. Format and key 89B, pp. 218-219, as an unbound report.
2. Format and key a separate REFERENCES page.
3. Prepare a title page. Use your name and school name and the current date.

LESSON 109

Prepare for Assessment: Tables

O b j e c t i v e :
To prepare for assessment of table formatting skills.

109A • 5
Conditioning Practice

each line twice

alphabet	1	Janet, the clerk, showed Mary the exquisite topaz before leaving.
speed	2	The girl may go to the island to visit and dismantle the bicycle.
figures	3	Our 9 a.m. meeting on May 18 will be in Room 2360, not Room 2457.

gwam 1' | 1 | 2 | 3 | 4 | 5 | 6 | 7 | 8 | 9 | 10 | 11 | 12 | 13 |

S KILL BUILDING

109B • 12
Timed Writings

1. A 1' writing on each of the three ¶s; find *gwam* and errors.
2. A 5' writing on the three ¶s combined; find *gwam* and errors.

all letters used

	gwam 1'	5'
Although the path to success is usually lengthy, you can make	12	2 45
it shorter if you will start at the beginning of your business	25	5 48
career to develop two important skills. The first is the ability	38	8 50
to see and to solve problems; the second, the ability to gather	51	10 53
facts and arrange them in logical order, from which you can draw	64	13 56
the correct conclusions.	69	14 57
Surely you can recall occasions when you devoted many hours,	12	16 59
even days, to striving unsuccessfully for a goal, and then you	25	19 62
happened to see the difficult problem from a new viewpoint.	37	21 64
Perhaps you exclaimed to a friend or yourself, "Now I see what the	50	24 67
problem is!" And once identified, the problem was easily solved.	64	26 69
As you begin work on a project, make your initial step that of	76	29 72
seeing the actual problem.	81	30 73
To solve problems, use all effectual means to get the data	12	32 75
that you will need. Books and magazine articles give facts and	25	35 78
expert opinions, and a request by mail or phone may offer added	37	38 80
aid. Enter the data on cards into logical groups, review the	50	40 83
work, and apply common sense to draw conclusions that the data	62	43 85
support.	64	43 86

gwam 1' | 1 | 2 | 3 | 4 | 5 | 6 | 7 | 8 | 9 | 10 | 11 | 12 | 13 |
5' | 1 | 2 | 3 |

44C • 20
Check/Improve
Keying Skill

1. Key a 1' writing on each ¶; find *gwam* on each writing.

2. Key two 2' writings on ¶s 1-2 combined; find *gwam* on each writing.

3. Key two 3' writings on ¶s 1-3 combined; find *gwam* and circle errors on each writing.

all letters used

| | gwam | 2' | 3' |

There is a value in work, value to the worker as well as | 6 | 4

to the employer for whom one works. In spite of the stress | 12 | 8

or pressure under which many people work, gainful work pro- | 18 | 12

vides workers with a feeling of security and self-esteem. | 23 | 16

Some people do not want to work unless they have a job | 29 | 19

of prestige; that is, a job that others admire or envy. To | 35 | 23

obtain such a position, one must be prepared to perform the | 41 | 27

tasks the job requires. Realize this now; prepare yourself. | 47 | 31

School and college courses are designed to help you to | 52 | 35

excel in the basic knowledge and skills the better jobs de- | 58 | 39

mand. Beyond all of this, special training or work experi- | 64 | 43

ence may be needed for you to move up in your chosen career. | 70 | 47

gwam 2' | 1 | 2 | 3 | 4 | 5 | 6
3' | 1 | 2 | 3 | 4

L ANGUAGE SKILLS

44D • 10
Pronoun Agreement

Follow the directions given in 43D, p. 111.

> A personal pronoun agrees in **number** (singular or plural) with the noun or other pronoun it represents.

Learn 1 Tabitha drove her new car to New Orleans last week. (singular)
Learn 2 The club officers made careful plans for their next meeting. (plural)
Apply 3 All workers must submit (his/their) vacation requests.
Apply 4 The sloop lost (its/their) headsail in the windstorm.

> A personal pronoun that represents a collective noun (team, committee, family, etc.) may be singular or plural, depending on the meaning of the collective noun.

Learn 5 Our men's soccer team played its fifth game today. (acting as a unit)
Learn 6 The vice squad took their positions in the square. (acting individually)
Apply 7 The Research Committee presented (its/their) reports at the meeting.
Apply 8 The jury will render (its/their) verdict at nine o'clock tomorrow.

107C • 25
Reinforce Letter/Memo Formatting Skills

Document 1
Memo

Format and key the text at the right as a standard memo to **Women's Historical Museum Committee**. The memo is from **Mark C. Felding**. Date the memo **February 1, ----**; use **NEXT MEETING** for the subject line.

Document 2
Letter

Format and key the text at the right in simplified block letter format. Use the USPS letter address style.

Document 3
Letter

Format and key the letter in 107B as a modified block letter with mixed punctuation and indented paragraphs.

	words
	opening 21

The next meeting of the Wyoming Women's Historical Museum Committee will be held on Monday, February 7, at 2:45 p.m. I have reserved the conference room at the city library for the meeting. — 34 / 47 / 60

Please be thinking about ideas for raising private funds for the museum. I have the information we need for national and state funding. | xx — 73 / 86 / 88

February 20, ---- | MR AND MRS JUSTIN WOODWARD | PO BOX 212 | MOORCROFT WY 82721-2342 | WYOMING WOMEN'S HISTORICAL MUSEUM — 10 / 21 / 23

Wyoming women were the first women in the United States to have the right to vote (1869). Esther Morris of South Pass City became the first woman judge in 1870. Wyoming was the first state to elect a woman to state office when Estelle Reel was elected State Superintendent of Public Instruction in 1894. Nellie Tayloe Ross became the first female governor in the United States when she was elected governor of Wyoming in 1925. — 37 / 51 / 65 / 79 / 93 / 106 / 109

It is time to honor women such as these for the role they played in shaping Wyoming and U.S. history. A Wyoming Women's Historical Museum is being planned. With your help, the museum can become a reality. — 123 / 136 / 148 / 151

Our community would benefit from the increased tourist activity. Thousands of tourists visit the nation's first national monument, Devil's Tower, each year. Since Moorcroft is only 30 miles from Devil's Tower, a museum would draw them to our city as they travel to and from the Tower. — 165 / 180 / 194 / 207 / 209

National and state funds for the project are being solicited; however, additional funding from the private sector will be required. Please look over the enclosed brochure and join the Wyoming Women's Historical Museum Foundation by making a contribution. — 223 / 238 / 251 / 260

MARK C. FELDING, COMMITTEE CHAIR | xx | Enclosure — 269

LESSON 108 — Prepare for Assessment: Reports

Objective:
To prepare for assessment of report formatting skills.

108A • 5
Conditioning Practice

each line twice

alphabet	1	The Gretzky exhibit was not quite completed when she left Jarvis.
speed	2	Diane may pay us to work for them when they dismantle the shanty.
figures	3	A truck picked up yard waste at 1047 Ash, 1258 Elm, and 3697 Oak.

gwam 1' | 1 | 2 | 3 | 4 | 5 | 6 | 7 | 8 | 9 | 10 | 11 | 12 | 13 |

Learn to Format Memos

Format Guides: Memos

Simplified Memo

Memorandums (memos) are written messages used by individuals within an organization to communicate with one another. They have often been described as "stripped down" letters because they omit certain letter parts. Memos may be formatted in two styles—simplified and standard—but both formats use the same margins.

| Top margin (TM): 2" (12 line spaces) |
| Side margins (SM): defaults or 1" |
| Page ending (PE): at least 1" |

In simplified format, begin all lines at the left margin unless some special part is to be centered. Quadruple-space (QS) between the date and the receiver's name

and between the message (body) and the writer's name. Double-space (DS) between all other parts (including ¶s) unless otherwise specified.

In standard format, begin all lines (including headings) at the left margin unless otherwise specified.

TO: Tab twice to key name.

FROM: Tab once to key name.

DATE: Tab once to key date.

SUBJECT: Tab once to key subject.

Double-space (DS) between *all* memo parts.

Compare the simplified model (p. 115) and the standard model (p. 117); note differences.

LESSON 45   Simplified Memos

Objectives:

1. To learn to format simplified memos properly.
2. To process memos from arranged and semiarranged copy.

45A • 5
Conditioning Practice

each line twice SS; then a 1' writing on line 3; find *gwam*

alphabet 1 Five kids quickly mixed the prizes, baffling one wise judge.
fig/sym 2 Joe asked, "Is the ZIP Code 45209-2748 or is it 45208-3614?"
speed 3 The firms may make a profit if they handle their work right.

gwam 1' | 1 | 2 | 3 | 4 | 5 | 6 | 7 | 8 | 9 | 10 | 11 | 12 |

45B • 45
Simplified Memos

If equipment has a default top margin, enter a sufficient number of hard returns to leave a 2" top margin (12 line spaces).

1. Study the format guides given above and the model memo illustrating simplified format on p. 115. Note the vertical and horizontal placement of memo parts and the spacing between them.

2. Format/key Memo 1 shown on p. 115; do not correct your errors as you key. Center the name as shown.

3. Proofread your copy of the memo, marking for correction any errors you find.

4. Format/key the memo again from your marked copy, errors corrected.

5. Format/key Memos 2 and 3 on p. 116 in simplified format; correct any errors you make. Save as MEM45B1 a partially completed memo to finish later.

Prepare for Assessment

LESSON 107

Prepare for Assessment: Letters and Memos

Objective:
To prepare for assessment of letter and memo formatting skills.

107A • 5
Conditioning Practice

each line twice; then 1'
writings on line 2

alphabet 1 Gary's survey helped Major Katz explain new racquetball features.

speed 2 The girls may go to the social at the giant chapel on the island.

figures 3 On June 20, 1975, I bought my first card; I now have 3,468 cards.

gwam 1' | 1 | 2 | 3 | 4 | 5 | 6 | 7 | 8 | 9 | 10 | 11 | 12 | 13 |

FORMATTING

107B • 20
Drill: Personal-Business Letter

block format; mixed punc-tuation

1. A 5' writing on the letter to determine *gwam*.
2. Key two 1' writings on opening lines through first ¶ of letter. If you finish the lines before time is called, QS and start over. Try to key more words on the second writing.
3. Key two 1' writings on ¶ 3 through last ¶ and closing lines. If you finish the lines before time is called, QS and start ¶ 3 again. Try to key more words on the second writing.
4. Key another 5' writing on the letter. Try to increase your *gwam* by 4-8 words.

words

928 Big Horn Ave. Moorcroft, WY 82721-2342   January 2, ----   12
Ms. Thelma White   P.O. Box 414   Moorcroft, WY 82721-2342   23
Dear Ms. White: 26

Are you interested in serving on a committee to discuss the merits of a   41
women's historical museum in Wyoming?   Many are not aware that   53
Wyoming's nickname (Equality State) stems from the fact that Wyoming   67
women were the first women in the United States to achieve the right to   81
vote.   They earned this right in 1869.   89

Since that time, many women have played an important part in shaping the   104
history of Wyoming.   Are you aware that the first woman governor in the   118
United States came from Wyoming?   Nellie Tayloe Ross became governor of   133
Wyoming in 1925.   136

It may be time to recognize these women by creating a museum that would   151
become a place for people to reflect on the events of the past as they con-   166
template the future.   I will call you next week to see if you are willing to   181
serve on the committee.   186

Sincerely,   Mark C. Felding   xx   192

Date   November 13, (Current year)   2" (of line 13)

QS (4 hard returns)

Addressee   Periscope Staff Members   DS

Subject   NEW WITHIN-SCHOOL MEMORANDUM FORMAT   DS

Body   You asked me to suggest a simple message format to use when you write to one another and to others within the school about school newspaper business. This message is formatted as a   DS

SIMPLIFIED MEMORANDUM   DS

All lines begin at the left margin except for centered titles. A QS (4 hard returns) separates the date and receiver's name and the last paragraph and writer's name. All other parts, including paragraphs, are separated by a DS (2 hard returns). No personal title is used before a name, but an official title or department name may follow it.   DS

If a separate document (such as an edited article) is attached to the memo, the word Attachment is keyed at the left margin a double space below the writer's name; if the document is not attached, the word Enclosure is keyed instead.   DS

The simplified memo is easy to format and key. Use it for a few days and give me your reactions. I am attaching an annotated model for your initial guidance.

QS (4 hard returns)

Keiko Sato

Writer   Keiko Sato, Sponsor   DS

Attachment

1"

Shown in 12-point (10-pitch) type, 2" top margin, 1" side margins, photoreduced.

Simplified Memorandum (Memo 1)

Job 13

Cambridge Travel Networks

Jan. 19

From the Desk of
Jason Koufax

Format a references page from the following:

"Barbados," Caribbean and the Bahamas. New York: Fodor's Modern Guides, 1991.

Solomon, Digby A. "Guide to the Caribbean." St. Paul Pioneer Press, October 16, 1994.

Job 14

Cambridge Travel Networks

Jan. 19

From the Desk of
Jason Koufax

I've computed the commission for most of the agents. Please complete the calculations and key a final table for the month of January. The commission rate is:

0.25% for sales of $0 - $50,000

0.50% for sales of $50,001 - $100,000

0.75% for sales of $100,001 - $150,000

1.00% for sales over $150,000

DS

Beach, Walter Fletcher Beach in Montego Bay, Puerto Seco at Discovery Bay, the seven-mile strip in Negril, Mallards Beach in Ocho Rios, and Boston Beach.

Cayman Islands

If you are looking for a beachfront apartment with an abundance of sunshine, quality beaches, and a view of the sea, go to the Cayman Islands. The islands are particularly enticing to those interested in scuba diving and big-game fishing.

The islands consist of Grand Cayman, Cayman Brac, and Little Cayman. The Grand Cayman's west-coast stretch of Seven Mile Beach is the island's primary vacation attraction. Even though hotels and condos have sprouted along the entire length of Seven Mile Beach, the water is still placid and clean; and the reefs just offshore still teem with life. (Solomon, 1994, 6F) Tiara Beach and Brac Reef Beach are the showpieces of Cayman Brac. Isolated beaches (Sandy Point and Owen Cay) can be found on Little Cayman.

REVENUES REPORT
January — DS

Agent	Sales for Month	Commission for month
Bass, Thelma	$125,980	$ 569.85
Chaplin, Mary	202,585	1,275.85
Donoso, Trujillo	195,875	1,208.75
Griffith, Ellen	310,865	2,358.65
Holiday, Charla	95,382	351.91
Hulett, Rebecca	275,385	2,603.85
Joazuin, Inez	195,387	1,203.87
Martin, Alexis	353,410	2,784.10
O'Brien, Kellee	340,215	2,652.15
Rinaldi, Fern	79,325	271.63
Santos, Dominic	349,295	2,742.95
Veras, Claire	245,395	
Wallace, Sheryl	287,452	
Totals		

Memo 2

1. Key in simplified format the memo shown at right.
2. Proofread your copy; correct any errors you find.

Note: Italics (rather than underlines) may be used wherever underlines appear in copy.

 note:

Change the theme name from ALL CAPS to Caps/lowercase (C/lc) italic; delete *-in-chief* in last line.

Memo 3

1. Key in simplified format the memo shown at right.
2. Color verticals indicate line endings in the opening and closing lines. Return at these points, but do not key the verticals.
3. Center the article title on a separate line; show it in C/lc enclosed in quotation marks.
4. Proofread your copy; correct all errors.

---

	words
November 14, (Current year)	4

All Class and Club Presidents | 10

MEETING TO DISCUSS MIDWINTER ISSUE OF PERISCOPE | 19

The proposed theme for "Current Focus" in the midwinter issue of the | 33
Periscope is | 36

HARMONY THROUGH INTERACTION | 41

The goal is to highlight recent activities that you believe helped to foster | 57
harmony among diverse groups in our school by getting them to interact | 71
and to work together. We would also like to report your suggestions for | 86
future activities with this focus. | 93

You are encouraged to attend a Periscope staff meeting at two o'clock on | 108
Wednesday, November 27, in Room AC 8 of the Activities Center to help in | 122
this effort. In addition to a brief Guest Editorial, we want to include three | 138
or four articles on this topic by some of you. | 148

Please come and bring your ideas and suggestions with you. | 160

Joseph Costa, Editor-in-Chief | 166

November 14, (Current year) | Sandra Alexander | PERISCOPE ARTICLE | 11

Your proposed article for the midwinter issue of the Periscope should be a | 26
winner.   I like the title INCLUSION VS. EXCLUSION | 36

The article is a few lines too long for the allocated space. I have marked | 51
some suggested cuts on the enclosed copy. Please consider these cuts | 65
along with the few other minor changes as you key your final copy. | 79

Marcella Del Rio, Associate Editor | Enclosure | 88

LESSON 46 Standard Memos

Objectives:

1. To learn to format standard memos properly.
2. To process standard memos from model and semiarranged copy.

46A • 5
Conditioning Practice

each line twice SS; then a 1' writing on line 3; find *gwam*

alphabet 1 Quincy worked six jigsaw puzzles given him for his birthday.

fig/sym 2 I deposited Hahn & Ober's $937.48 check (#1956) on March 20.

speed 3 Ellena may lend them a hand with the audit of the soap firm.

Jan. 16

From the Desk of
Jason Koufax

Attached is a rough-draft manuscript that will be included in the next issue of our newsletter. Please key a final copy so that I can give it to our newsletter editor.

THE CARIBBEAN ISLANDS

The Caribbean Islands are a renowned tourist ~~locations~~ attraction.
Known for their white sandy beaches, abundant sunshine, and pan-
oramic ocean views, the islands are a peaceful getaway ~~vacation~~ for
thousands of Caribbean tourists. Barbados, the Cayman Islands,
and ~~Barbados~~ Jamaica are featured in this month's newsletter.

Barbados

If you are looking for a picturesque island consider barbados. "Powdery beaches line the waters of the calm Caribbean Sea
on the west coast, while the waves of the Atlantic thunder in on
the eastern shore." (Fodor's, 144, 1991)

~~Barbados offers fine~~ With elegant hotels, tours, fine restaurants, and shopping options. Barbados
is one of the preferred islands in the Caribbean. Spectator
sports such as cricket, horse racing, polo, and soccer are also
available to tourists. If you are more interested in participant
sports, try windsurfing, scuba diving, and horseback riding.

Jamaica If you are looking for ~~fine hotels~~, long ~~lengthy~~ sandy beaches,
historic landmarks, and a sun-drenched climate, consider Jamaica. The
temperature ~~averages around~~ With an average of 80 degrees, it is a vacation paradise.

As can be expected, winter (December through April) brings
larger crowds and higher rates than the other seasons. The ~~best~~ finer
hotels are generally located on the north side of the island. However, for
the budget-conscious traveler, Jamaica offers several package
deals for selected resort areas. ~~With the~~ make package deals, it is
possible to stay at several resort areas during your visit.

Jamaica offers over two hundred miles of beaches. With a
few exceptions, most of the beaches are relatively quiet and
uncrowded. Some of the more popular beaches include Cornwall

TO: Tab Tab Faculty and Staff   2" (line 13)
                                DS (2 hard returns)

FROM: Tab Lenore M. Fielding, Principal
                                       DS

DATE: Tab November 15, (Current year)
                           DS

SUBJECT: Tab STANDARD MEMO FORMAT
                                 DS

At a recent meeting, department heads recommended that memos be processed on plain paper instead of preprinted forms. This recommendation is a cost-cutting measure that requires only a little more effort on the part of the keyboard operator.
                                       DS

The customary standard margins are used: 2" top margin; default (near 1") side margins; at least a 1" bottom margin.
                                       DS

⓵" Standard double spacing separates memo parts, including para-graphs, which are individually single-spaced. If someone other than the writer keys the memo, that person's initials should be keyed at the left margin a double space below the message. If an attachment or enclosure is included, <u>Attachment</u> or <u>Enclosure</u> should be keyed at the left margin a double space below the message or the keyboard operator's initials (if any). ⓵"
                                       DS

Headings begin at left margin. After TO: tab twice to key the name; after FROM: tab once to key the name; after DATE: tab once to key the date; after SUBJECT: space twice (or tab once) to enter the subject (may be keyed in ALL CAPS or C/lc--Cap and lowercase).
                 DS

Please use this format for several days; then let me know if you experienced any difficulties.
                                    DS

tbh

Standard Memorandum (Memo 1)

> Shown in 12-point (10-pitch) type, 2" top margin, 1" side margins, photoreduced.

F O R M A T T I N G

**46B • 45
Standard Memos**

If equipment has a default top margin, enter a sufficient number of hard returns to leave a 2" top margin (12 line spaces).

1. Study the format guides given on p. 114 and the model above that illustrates standard memo format. Note the vertical and horizontal placement of memo parts and the spacing between them.

2. Key in standard format the memo shown above; do not correct errors as you key.

3. Proofread your copy of the memo, marking for correction any errors you find.

4. Format/key the memo again from your own copy, errors corrected.

5. Key Memos 2 and 3 on p. 118 in standard format. Save as MEM46B# any partially completed memo to be finished later.

Job 9

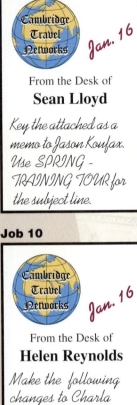

Jan. 16

From the Desk of
Sean Lloyd

Key the attached as a memo to Jason Koufax. Use SPRING-TRAINING TOUR for the subject line.

Job 10

Jan. 16

From the Desk of
Helen Reynolds

Make the following changes to Charla Holliday's appointment schedule you prepared earlier:

Cancel the appointment with Jennifer Hennesy.

Add an appointment with Mr. Jay Prye at 10:30 for Australia.

Add an appointment with Ms. Leslie Loomis at 2:30 for Disneyland.

Job 11

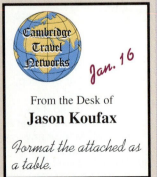

Jan. 16

From the Desk of
Jason Koufax

Format the attached as a table.

I have received a number of calls in the last few days from individuals interested in a tour of spring-training camps. Even though we do not have anything planned for this year, we may want to start making plans for next year.

Plans could include attending a Met game in Clearwater, a Yankee game in Fort Lauderdale, and a Red Sox game in Fort Myers. Perhaps we could even arrange a day for tour members to attend Epcot, Universal Studios, Magic Kingdom, Disney's MGM Studios, or Sea World. ¶We may want to consider the possibility of inviting a former Met, Yankee, or Red Sox player to lead the tour. If you think this idea is worth pursuing, let me know.

HOTELS ACCOMMODATIONS

Caribbean--Option 1

Hotel	Daily Rates	Comments
Pavillion Hotel	$ 125	Superior tourist-class hotel.
Grand Suites	275	First-class suites, newly renovated.
Grand Cayman Resort	325	First-class, all suite resort.
Santos House	150	Superior tourist-class hotel.
The Island Resort	90	Superior first-class hotel.
Little Rome Club	99	Condominium hotel.
Hotel Indies	249	First-class Mediterranean-style condominiums.
Ambassador Hotel	129	Small condominium resort.
The Grand Hotel	149	Superior first-class hotel with ocean-view rooms.
The Tatyana House	350	Condominium complex on Seven Mile Beach.

Memo 2

1. Key in standard format the memo at right. Use your initials as the keyboard operator.
2. Proofread your copy and correct all errors.

		words
TO:	Andrea Valdez, Head of Special Programs	9
FROM:	Marcus Ellerbee, Counselor	16
DATE:	November 16, (Current year)	21
SUBJECT:	ALAN WASHBURN	25

After several informal testing activities with Alan Washburn, Ms. Davilos   40
and I believe he should be sent to the Clinical Learning Center at the   54
university for special testing and observation.   64

It appears to us that Alan exhibits not only deficient reading skills but   79
also short attention span and low motivation. Any one of these factors   93
can result in poor performance. Two or three of them in combination   107
certainly do.   110

Before we can make a referral, we must meet with Alan's parents and   124
get their approval. Can you be available for such a meeting in the Guid-   138
ance Office at 4:30 next Wednesday? The Washburns are available at   152
that time. | xx   155

Memo 3

1. Key in standard format the memo shown at the right. Since you are keying the memo for Mr. Hardaway, show your initials above the enclosure notation.
2. Proofread your copy and correct all errors.

TO: Lenore M. Fielding, Principal   7
FROM: Jevon Hardaway, Business Department   16
DATE: November 16, (Current year)   21
SUBJECT: NEW MEMO PROCESSING PROCEDURE   28

I have used the plain-paper memo format for several years. I   41
have found it quite satisfactory. In fact, keying the head-   53
ings is easier than aligning copy on preprinted forms. This   65
is especially true on computers because printers do not have   77
an aligning device. Therefore, keyed copy often is slightly   89
above or slightly below the printed headings.   99

It is possible to create a computer template that when called   111
up will automatically take you to the points of copy entry.   123
You may wish to consider doing this if a sufficient number of   136
people have difficulty with the new format. I'm enclosing a   148
disk containing such a template for you to try.   158

In any case, I favor cutting cost wherever possible.   169

Enclosure   171

Job 7

Jan. 15

From the Desk of
Jason Koufax

Please send deposit confirmations to the following:

Mr. and Mrs. Devon Guidry
P.O. Box 831
Brockport, NY
14420-9271

Destination: the Caribbean Islands
Balance: $3,990
Due date: March 29
Agent: Rebecca Hulett

Ms. Danielle St. John
9640 Starwood Dr.
Rochester, NY
14625-8534

Destination: the Hawaiian Islands
Balance: $4,395
Due date: April 1
Agent: Michael Ryder

Job 8

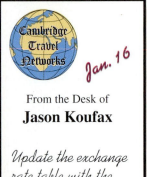

Jan. 16

From the Desk of
Jason Koufax

Update the exchange rate table with the changes indicated.

<Date>

<Title> <First Name> <Last Name>
<Address>
<City,> <State> <ZIP>

Dear <Title> <Last Name:>

Your 20 percent deposit for your cruise to <Destination> arrived today. The balance, <Amount,> is due on <Due date.>

If you have to cancel your cruise for any reason, there will be a $50 processing fee. Additional charges, ranging from 25 to 50 percent, will be assessed by the cruise line for cancellations made within 60 days of departure. Complete information regarding cancellations is enclosed.

If you have any questions about your cruise prior to departure, call me at 716-178-8376. Thank you for allowing Cambridge Travel Networks to book your reservations.

Sincerely,

<Agent's name>
Travel Agent

xx

Enclosure

FOREIGN EXCHANGE RATE

January 16, ----

Country	Unit	In $100 U.S. Equivalents	
Australia	Dollars	~~121.54~~	121.37
France	Francs	~~122.39~~	121.57
Germany	Marks	~~138.03~~	139.06
Great Britain	Pounds	~~56.90~~	57.03
Italy	lira	~~144,579.05~~	144,560.01
Japan	Yen	~~9,029.41~~	9,026.38
Mexico	Peso	~~308.00~~	307.98
Spain	Pesetas	~~11,457.60~~	11,460.01
Switzerland	francs	~~115.24~~	114.98

Simplified and Standard Memorandums

Objectives:

1. To check knowledge of simplified and standard memo formats.
2. To check the level of your memo processing skill.

47A • 5
Conditioning Practice

each line twice SS; then a
1' writing on line 3; find
gwam

alphabet 1 Rex just left my quiz show and gave back a prize he had won.

fig/sym 2 Review reaches: $40, $84, 95%, #30, 5-point, 1/6, B&O 27's.

speed 3 Di may profit by good form and a firm wish to make the goal.

gwam 1' | 1 | 2 | 3 | 4 | 5 | 6 | 7 | 8 | 9 | 10 | 11 | 12 |

47B • 5
Skill Building

1. Center lines 1-3 DS.
2. Key lines 4-6 SS.
3. If equipment has the Italic feature, change all underlines to italics in lines 4 and 5.

centering

1 FORMATTING MEMOS

2 Simplified Memos

3 Standard Memos

CAPS LOCK & underline

4 Key newspaper names: Boston Globe; Erie Sentinel; Bay News.

5 Key magazine names: Reader's Digest; TIME; Modern Maturity.

6 Key abbreviations: Atlanta, GA; NCAA title; U.S. Air Force.

F ORMATTING

47C • 40
Memo Processing

Key the memos shown at the right and on p. 120 as directed with each memo.

Memo 1

1. Key the copy at right as a simplified memo. Correct all errors.
2. Add an attachment notation.

	words
November 17, (Current year)	4
Jonathon Eagle	7
ARTICLE FOR THE PERISCOPE	12
Attached is an annotated guide sheet for the preparation of your article	26
reviewing the Native American Art Exhibit at Lakeview.	38
Because space in the Periscope is limited, we allocate that space before	52
articles are written so that you, rather than the editors, hone your copy to	68
fit the space.	71
As the guide sheet indicates, you may use two columns of 34 lines each	85
plus the equivalent of 6 lines across the two columns for the title and by-	100
line. So you have 68 lines of approximately 40 characters each for your	115
story. If you key your copy using this line length, a quick line count will	130
indicate whether cutting or expanding is needed.	140
Jacque Jordan, Associate Editor Attachment	149

Job 5

Jan. 15

From the Desk of
Helen Reynolds

Please format and key the appointment schedule for Charla Holliday. Computer template filename:
T101B5

Job 6

Jan. 15

From the Desk of
Alexis Martin

Please send the attached letter to:

Mr. Scott Shaw
3276 Keystone Dr.
Rochester, NY
14625-8328

APPOINTMENT SCHEDULE

Charla Holliday > Bold name
January 19, ----

Time	Client	Destination
9:00	Ms. Helen Woods	Hawaii
9:30	Mr. Nak Jun Yoo	Caribbean
11:00	Mr. and Mrs. Ken Reeves	Caribbean
1:00	Miss Jennifer Hennesy	San Francisco
1:30	Dr. Jana Phillip Dr. Paul Ambro	Great Britain
3:00	Mr. Roderigo Molina	Hong Kong
4:00	Mr. and Mrs. Stuart McCown	Europe

Dear Mr. Shaw:

Discussing Century Cruise options with potential first-time "cruisers" is one of the things I enjoy most about my job. I am confident that a Caribbean cruise would be an ideal anniversary gift for your wife. You can be assured that this gift would provide life-long memories. However, I must caution you. Most people can't go on just one cruise. Once they go, they want to go on another and another.

When we were discussing your plans, you wondered how you could keep the cruise a surprise if you had to have a U.S. passport. I checked to see what options may be acceptable. An original birth certificate (or certified copy) and a driver's license would meet entry requirements.

If you have additional questions regarding the information we discussed on Tuesday, please give me a call.

Memo 2

1. Key the copy at right as a standard memo. Correct all errors.
2. Add your initials as the keyboard operator.

		words
TO:	Student Council Officers	6
FROM:	Lenore M. Fielding, Principal	13
DATE:	November 18, (Current year)	18
SUBJECT:	STUDENT BEHAVIOR AT ATHLETIC EVENTS	27

Reports from a number of faculty and parents suggest that the behavior of a few of our students at two recent athletic events violated the Code of Student Conduct. 42 57 60

Only a few students were involved, and only three incidents were reported. Even so, the reported behavior does not create the image Lakeview wants to portray to members of our community or visitors from other communities. 76 90 104 105

Because you along with your fellow council officers monitor such events and participate in the evaluation of Code of Student Conduct violations, I want to meet with you and the assistant principals to review these reports and their impact on our school image. 120 135 150 158

This meeting is scheduled for 2:30 this Thursday afternoon in Conference Room B. Be prepared to tell us what you know about any such incidents and what action you think we should take. | xx 173 186 195

Memo 3

1. Key the copy at right as a standard memo. Correct all errors.
2. Add an enclosure notation.

Memo 4

If time permits, reformat or rekey Memo 3 as a simplified memo. Correct all errors.

Note: See p. A16 for R & E activities for this unit.

To: Manuel Delgado, Community Services Coordinator		10
From: Lenore M. Fielding, Principal		18
Date: November 18, (Current year)		23
Subject: Community Clean-Up Campaign		30

Congratulations to you and your junior/senior workers on a successful Community Clean-Up Campaign. 42 50

I have received many telephone calls and several letters from people in the community conveying their thanks to and admiration for these students. They freely gave their time and effort to help the elderly and others in the community who were physically unable to perform the needed work themselves. 63 75 86 98 111

Please share our compliments and gratitude with your workforce. Their attitude and conduct during this campaign have enhanced our image in the community. 122 135 142

I am enclosing an envelope containing some telephone messages and letters for you to share with the students who participated. | xx 155 166 169

Job 3

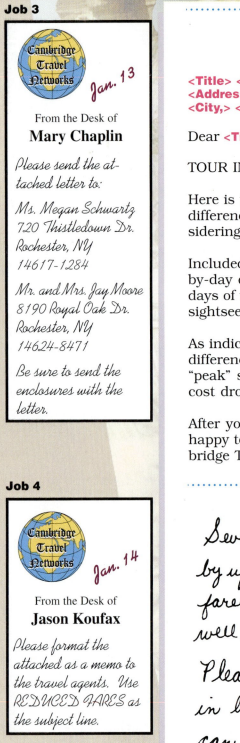

From the Desk of
Mary Chaplin

Jan. 13

Please send the attached letter to:

Ms. Megan Schwartz
720 Thistledown Dr.
Rochester, NY
14617-1284

Mr. and Mrs. Jay Moore
8190 Royal Oak Dr.
Rochester, NY
14624-8471

Be sure to send the enclosures with the letter.

Job 4

From the Desk of
Jason Koufax

Jan. 14

Please format the attached as a memo to the travel agents. Use REDUCED FARES as the subject line.

<Date>

<Title> <First Name> <Last Name>
<Address>
<City,> <State> <ZIP>

Dear <Title> <Last Name:>

TOUR INFORMATION

Here is the information you requested about the 12-day European tour. The difference between this particular tour and the 10-day tour that you were considering is that you would visit seven countries rather than five.

Included in the information is a "Tour Highlights" sheet that gives a brief day-by-day description of the tour. Although guided tours are planned for most days of the tour, you do not have to stay with the guide on days you prefer to sightsee on your own.

As indicated on the price sheet, the dates you select for your trip can make a difference in the cost. There is about a $400 difference between the cost of the "peak" summer times and the "off season" late fall months. Generally, the cost drops another $100 if you wait until December.

After you have had an opportunity to look over the information, I would be happy to answer any questions you may have. Thank you for choosing Cambridge Travel Networks as your travel agency.

Several major airlines cut their 10-day advance fares by up to 45 percent for travel before May 15. The reduced fares include travel to most major U.S. markets as well as selected Mexican and Caribbean markets.

Please contact clients who have indicated an interest in being notified of special promotions to see if we can assist them with their travel plans at the reduced fares.

X X

Skill Builder

Keyboard Review

1. Key each line twice SS; DS between 2-line groups.
2. If time permits, rekey lines that were awkward or difficult for you.

A/Z 1 Zoe had a pizza at the plaza by the zoo on a lazy, hazy day.

B/Y 2 Abby may be too busy to buy me a book for my long boat trip.

C/X 3 Zeno caught six cod to fix lunch for his six excited scouts.

D/W 4 Wilda would like to own the wild doe she found in the woods.

E/V 5 Evan will give us the van to move the five very heavy boxes.

F/U 6 All four of us bought coats with faux fur collars and cuffs.

G/T 7 Eight guys tugged the big boat into deep water to get going.

H/S 8 Marsha wishes to show us how to make charts on the computer.

I/R 9 Ira will rise above his ire to rid the firm of this problem.

J/Q 10 Quen just quietly quit the squad after a major joint injury.

K/P 11 Kip packed a backpack and put it on an oak box on the porch.

L/O 12 Lola is to wear the royal blue skirt and a gold wool blouse.

M/N 13 Many of the men met in the main hall to see the new manager.

figures 14 I worked from 8:30 to 5 at 1964 Lake Blvd. from May 7 to 26.

fig/sym 15 I quote, "ISBN #0-651-24876-3 was assigned to them in 1995."

Timed Writings

1. Key two 1' writings on each ¶; find *gwam* on each writing.
2. Key two 2' writings on ¶s 1-2 combined; find *gwam* on each writing.
3. Key two 3' writings on ¶s 1-2 combined; find *gwam* and circle errors on each writing.
4. If time permits, key 1' guided writings on each ¶ to improve speed or accuracy according to your needs.

LA all letters used

	gwam	2'	3'

As you work for higher skill, remember that how well you — 8 | 4

key fast is just as important as how fast you key. How well — 12 | 8

you key at any speed depends in major ways upon the technique — 18 | 12

or form you use. Bouncing hands and flying fingers lower the — 24 | 16

speed, while quiet hands and low finger reaches increase speed. — 31 | 20

Few of us ever reach what the experts believe is perfect — 36 | 24

technique, but all of us should try to approach it. We must — 42 | 28

realize that good form is the secret to higher speed with — 48 | 32

fewer errors. We can then focus our practice on the improve- — 54 | 36

ment of the features of good form that will bring success. — 60 | 40

gwam 2'   1   2   3   4   5   6
     3'   1   2   3   4

Skill Builder 3 · 121

Job 2

Jan. 12

From the Desk of
Jason Koufax

*Please key the attached
text with the changes.*

Tour Highlight Options

Overnight

Day 1: Transatlantic flight to London, England. *lc*

Day 2: Gala welcoming event. Tour options include: The Tower of London, Kensington's Museums, Parliament, Knightsbridge with Harrods, Westminster Abbey, St. Paul's Cathedral, Big Ben, and cruise on the River Thames.

Day 3: Free day to ~~start~~ exploring London. Consider visiting The British Museum, Madame Tussaud's, and/or the Tate Gallery.

Day 4: Depart London for the English coast. Take the North Sea crossing to Holland. Stay in Amsterdam.

Day 5: Spend the day in Amsterdam. Tour options include: Rembrandthuis, The Jewish Historical Museum, The Rijksmuseum Vincent Van Gogh, Our Lord in the Attic, The Home of Anne Frank, and the Canal Mansions. Depart for Brussels, the capital of Belgium.

Day 6: Enjoy the sights of Brussels. The Museum of Modern Art, St. Michel Cathedral, Morolles, and The Home of Erasmus are included on the tour. Depart for Bonn, *Germany.*

Day 7: Travel past the ruins of the bridge in Remagen where American soldiers attacked the West Wall of Hitler. Take a cruise on the Rhine. Arrive in Munich, Germany.

Day 8: Enjoy the morning in Munich. Tour options include: Deutsche Museum, The Alte Pinakothek, Nymphenburg Palace, and the Neuschwanstein Castle. Depart for Innsbruck, Austria. Travel the scenic mountain road by way of Lake Tegern, Achenpass, and Lake Achen.

Day 9: Travel to Lucerne by way of Liechtenstein. While in Lucerne spend the time on your own shopping for Swiss watches, taking a cable car up the mountain, or taking in a folklore party. Other sights to consider include the Lion Monument and the Wooden Bridge. *Depart for Geneva, Switzerland.*

Day 10: Morning tour options include: Jean-Gauchos Rousseau Museum, Geneva Palace, the Watch-and-Clock Museum, and Par del la Grange. Afternoon departure for Paris, France.

Day 11: Be prepared for a full day of sights on both banks of the Seine ~~during~~ day 11 tour options.

Day 12: Transatlantic flight to New York City.

Options include: the Eiffel Tower, the Louvre, Arc de Triomphe, Notre Dame, Sainte Chapelle, Invalides, and the Tomb of Napoleon.

Language & Writing Skills 5

Activity 1:

1. Study the spelling/ definitions of the words in the color block at right.

2. Key line 1 (the **Learn** line), noting the proper choice of words.

3. Key lines 2-3 (the **Apply** lines), choosing the right words to complete the lines correctly.

4. Key the remaining lines in the same way.

5. Check your work; correct or rekey lines containing word-choice errors.

Choose the right word

your (adj) of or relating to you or yourself as possessor	**for** (prep/conj) used to indicate purpose; on behalf of; because; because of
you're (contr) you are	**four** (n) the fourth in a set or series

Learn 1 When you receive your blue book, you're to write your name on it.
Apply 2 (Your, You're) to write the letter using (your, you're) best English.
Apply 3 When (your, you're) computer is warmed up, (your, you're) to begin work.

Learn 4 All four workers asked for an appointment with the manager.
Apply 5 At (for, four) o'clock the lights went off (for, four) an hour.
Apply 6 The (for, four) boys turned back, (for, four) they feared the lightning.

Activity 2:

1. Read the ¶ shown at the right, noting words that are misused or misspelled.

2. Key the ¶, correcting the errors you found.

3. Check your work to see if you have corrected all errors.

4. If your copy still contains uncorrected errors, rekey the ¶ to make the needed corrections.

Proofread & correct

Its your duty as an officer of Student Council to monitor our students' behavior during school ours. Your also expected to observe what they due at school-sponsored events after school hours, whether those events are hear or away. If you don't no what happened when misconduct is reported, how can you decide if one remedy is better then another? Hearsay evidence is not sufficient fore you to chose a remedy.

Activity 3:

1. Read carefully the two creeds (mottos) given at the right.

2. Choose one as a topic for a short composition, and make notes of what it means to you.

3. Compose/key a ¶ or two indicating what it means to you and why you believe it would be (or would not be) a good motto for your own behavior.

Compose (think) as you key

The following creeds were written by Edward Everett Hale for the

Lend-a-Hand Society

I am only one,
But still I am one.
I cannot do everything,
But still I can do something;
And because I cannot do everything,
I will not refuse to do the something
  that I can do.

Harry Wadsworth Club

To look up and not down,
To look forward and not back,
To look out and not in, and
To lend a hand.

LESSONS 101-106

Cambridge Travel Networks

Objectives:

1. To use your decision-making skills to process documents from rough-draft and script.
2. To improve your ability to read and follow directions.

101-106A • 5 (daily)
Conditioning Practice

each line twice

alphabet 1 Judge Worblitz quickly thanked them for giving excellent reports.

speed 2 They may go with us to the city to do the work for the big firms.

fig/sym 3 The #6534 item will cost Brady & Son $817.29 (less 10% for cash).

gwam 1' | 1 | 2 | 3 | 4 | 5 | 6 | 7 | 8 | 9 | 10 | 11 | 12 | 13 |

101-106B • 45 (daily)
Work Assignments

Job 1

Jan. 12

From the Desk of
Jason Koufax

Please format and key the attached text as a table.

EUROPEAN TOUR

12-Day* Excursion from New York City

Departure Date	Return Date	Tour** Price
May 6	May 17	$1,829
May 30	June 10	1,953
June 20	July 1	1,975
July 12	July 23	1,975
August 6	August 17	1,953 ~~75~~
August 30	September 10	1,975
September 26	October 7	1,829 7
October 22	November 2	1,779 5

---

* *Tour includes: Austria, Belgium, England, France, Germany, Holland, and Switzerland.*

** *Prices quoted for double occupancy; add $180 for single occupancy.*

Learn Block Letter Format

Format Guides:
Block-Style Letters

Personal-Business Letter

Business Letter

When all parts of a letter (including paragraphs) begin at the left margin (LM), as shown in the models at left, the document is arranged in block format (style). Block format is widely used for both personal and business correspondence.

Letter Margins

Side margins (SM):	defaults (1")
Top margin (TM):	2" (line 13)
Page ending (PE):	at least 1"

Note: Letters may also be vertically centered, using the Center Page feature.

Basic Parts of Letters

Basic letter parts are described below in order of their occurrence within letters.

Return address. In personal-business letters, the return address consists of a line for the street address and one for the city, state, and ZIP Code. In business letters, the letterhead (return address) includes a company name, street address, city, state, and ZIP Code (none of which must be keyed).

Date. In personal-business letters, key the month, day, and year on the line below the city, state, and ZIP Code. In business letters, key the date at the top margin.

Letter address. Key the first line of the letter address a QS below the date. A personal title (Miss, Mr., Mrs., Ms.) or a professional title (Dr., Lt., Senator) is typically used before the receiver's name.

Salutation. Key the salutation (greeting) a DS below the letter address.

Body. Begin the letter body (message) a DS below the salutation. SS and block the paragraphs (¶s) with a DS between them.

Complimentary close. Key the complimentary close (farewell) a DS below the last line of the body.

Name of writer. Key the name of the writer (originator of the message) a QS below the complimentary close. The name may be preceded by a personal title (Miss, Mrs., Ms.) to indicate how a female prefers to be addressed in a response. If a male has a name that does not clearly indicate his gender (Kim, Leslie, Pat, for example), the title Mr. may precede his name. A job title or department name may be keyed on the line with the writer's name, separated by a comma; or it may be keyed on the next line at the left margin.

Special Parts of Letters

Attention line. If a letter is addressed to a company, the address may include an attention line (the first line of the address) to call the letter to the attention of a department or a job title.

Subject line. Sometimes a subject line is used to alert the reader immediately to the content of a letter. A subject line is keyed in ALL CAPS (or Caps and lowercase) at the left margin a DS below the salutation.

Reference initials. If someone other than the originator of the letter keys it, key the keyboard operator's initials in lowercase letters at the left margin a DS below the writer's name, title, or department.

Attachment/Enclosure notation. If another document is attached to a letter, the word Attachment is keyed at the left margin a DS below the reference initials. If the document is not attached, the word Enclosure is used instead. If reference initials are not used, Attachment or Enclosure is keyed a DS below the writer's name or title.

Cambridge Travel Networks
(A School-to-Work Simulation)

Work Assignment

You have been hired by Cambridge Travel Networks to work part-time for the administrative assistant, Karin McKinley, and the receptionist, Helen Reynolds. Ms. McKinley processes documents for the travel agents. Ms. Reynolds greets telephone callers, visitors, and clients and schedules appointments for the travel agents. Ms. McKinley's immediate supervisor is Jason Koufax who is the manager of Cambridge Travel Networks.

You will be assisting both Ms. McKinley and Ms. Reynolds. You are responsible for mailing brochures requested by clients, displaying full-color posters from the cruise lines and airlines, restocking brochure racks with information about exotic places, proofreading brochure copy, updating the wall map that displays where Cambridge clients have traveled, keying weekly "welcome home" lists for agents to call, and keeping a file of newspaper ads of other agencies.

Your main responsibility, however, is to assist with processing documents for Mr. Koufax and the travel agents. Each document you receive will have written instructions from the originator. Use the date included on the instructions for all documents requiring a date. Mr. Koufax closes all of his letters with:

```
Sincerely,


Jason Koufax
Manager
```

Use the following closing lines for correspondence processed for the travel agents.

```
Sincerely,


Agent's Name
Travel Agent
```

If the instructions given with the document are not sufficiently detailed, use what you have been taught in your keyboarding course to make formatting decisions. Documents should be attractively formatted.

You are expected to produce error-free documents, so proofread and correct your work carefully before presenting it for approval.

Multiple Enclosures

When more than one enclosure is listed with the enclosure notation, format it as follows:

```
Enclosures:  Tour Highlights
             Price Sheet
```

Macros

Create macros for closing lines and other text (Cambridge Travel Networks) that you will use often.

Document Formats

Memos:	Standard
Letters:	Modified block Mixed punctuation Blocked paragraphs
Reports:	Unbound Textual citations References list on separate sheet

Return address	1049 Michigan Ave. N. Chicago, IL 60611-2273
Date	November 18, ---- (Current year)

QS (4 hard returns)

Letter address	Mr. Elden P. Carter 7257 Charles Plz. Omaha, NE 68114-3219

DS

Salutation	Dear Elden

DS

Body Your telephone call on Wednesday was a really pleasant surprise. Life for both of us since college has been exciting as well as challenging, it seems. I enjoyed the update.

DS

If you had taken keyboarding as I recommended when we were in high school, you wouldn't be asking me now for a model to use for your personal-business correspondence! But I am glad to supply this model in block format (all lines beginning at the left margin).

DS

Use the software default or 1" side margins. Begin the return address 2" (line 13) from the top of the paper. Key the date on the next line below the return address.

DS

All letter parts are separated by a double space (2 returns) with two exceptions: A quadruple space (4 returns) is left between the date and the letter address and between the complimentary close and the keyed name.

DS

I am attaching a page from a reference manual that includes an annotated model. Call again if you need more help.

DS

Complimentary close	Cordially

QS (4 hard returns)

Andrea Rialto

Writer	Andrea Rialto

DS

Attachment notation	Attachment

1" 1"

Shown in 12-point (10-pitch) type, 1" side margins, photoreduced.

Personal-Business Letter in Block Format (Letter 1)

Activity 3:

1. Read carefully the ¶s given at the right.

2. From your circle of friends and acquaintances, identify the one person you truly believe is your "best" friend, another one or two you consider to be "good" friends, and others you consider casual friends or merely acquaintances.

3. Compose/key three separate ¶s. In ¶ 1, identify and describe your "best" friend and why you consider her/him to be a "true" friend. In ¶ 2, identify your "good" friends and describe why you consider them so. In ¶ 3, identify one or two casual friends or acquaintances and describe how your relationship(s) differ from those described in ¶s 1 and 2.

Compose (think) as you key

Most of you have tossed a pebble into a pool of water and watched the ever-larger concentric circles radiate out from the point at which the pebble entered the water. The relationships we have with others are similar—concentric circles radiating out from each of us. People in the inner circles are our closest friends—pals, buddies, chums, and so on. As we move outward to larger circles, we find our casual friends or acquaintances.

***

Those who study social relationships at various levels have indicated that one is lucky to have two or three really true friends in a lifetime. Yet, we often hear people, especially young people, introducing different acquaintances at different times as "my best friend." "Best" is the superlative in the triad good/better/best. By definition, the superlative means "you can't get any better than that."

***

Ralph Waldo Emerson said, "A true friend is somebody who can make us do what we can" and "The only way to have a friend is to be one." The first quote suggests that a true friend makes us live up to our potential; the second, a true friend requires us to be one. Friendships, therefore, require us to be personally involved with others, to be interested in their well-being, in their unique identities, and in their perceptions of the world.

***

The following quote, attributed to Albert Camus, perhaps best describes the mutual acceptance and closeness that characterize real or "true" friendship:

Don't walk in front of me
I may not follow
Don't walk behind me
I may not lead
Walk beside me
And just be my friend.

Objectives:
1. To learn features of block-style letters.
2. To process personal-business letters in block format.

48A • 5
Conditioning Practice

each line twice SS; then a 1' writing on line 3; find *gwam*

alphabet	1	Zoe just may have to plan a big, unique dance for next week.
fig/sym	2	Tami asked, "Can't you touch-key 65, 73, $840, and 19 1/2%?"
speed	3	Six of the big firms may bid for the right to the lake land.

gwam 1' | 1 | 2 | 3 | 4 | 5 | 6 | 7 | 8 | 9 | 10 | 11 | 12 |

48B • 45
Personal-Business Letters in Block Format

1. Study the format guides for letters on p. 123 and the model letter illustrating block format on p. 124. Note placement of letter parts and spacing between these parts.

2. Format/key Letter 1 (the model) on p. 124.

3. Proofread your copy and correct your errors; rekey if necessary to make all needed corrections.

4. Format/key Letter 2 shown below. Correct errors as you key.

5. If time permits, rekey the model letter to increase your input speed, especially on opening and closing lines.

Letter 2

As you key from semi-arranged copy, place letter parts properly and space correctly.

 note:

Save any partially completed letter to be finished during the next class period. Suggested filename: LTR48B2, for example.

	words
2165 Granada Ave.	4
San Diego, CA 92104-3710	9
November 19, ---- (Current year)	12
Miss Maryann Figueroa	17
Human Services Director	21
Seaboard Office Products, Inc.	28
200 Academy P1.	31
Seattle, WA 98109-2239	35
Dear Miss Figueroa	39

In a recent issue of <u>Office Careers</u>, I read with high interest your article | 55
about personal characteristics needed by successful office workers. Your | 69
examples seemed to suggest that you were speaking of workers who had | 83
been on the job for a number of years. | 91

Although these personal traits are important for beginning workers as | 105
well, I am also interested in the skills firms such as yours require for | 119
entry-level employment. | 124

The topic of my term paper for a business management class here at | 138
Sooner High School is "Landing That First Office Job." In it I want to | 152
highlight the major areas of skills required for entry-level office positions | 168
in modern companies like yours. | 174

If you have written an article on this topic, would you share it with me, | 189
please. Or you may prefer to list your thoughts for me in a letter. Either | 205
way, I shall appreciate your assistance. | 213

	words
Sincerely yours	216
Miss Rikki Samuels, President	222
Business Education Club	227

Language & Writing Skills 11

Activity 1:

1. Study the spelling/ definitions of the words in the color block at the right.
2. Key the **Learn** line in the first set of sentences.
3. Key the **Apply** lines, choosing the right words to complete each sentence correctly.
4. Key the second set of lines in the same way.
5. Check work; rekey lines containing word-choice errors.

Choose the right word

die (vb) to pass from physical life
dye (n) a soluble or insoluble coloring

want (vb) need, desire; as a noun, lacking a required amount
won't (vb) will not

Learn 1 If they want additional supplies, won't they contact us?
Apply 2 Each (want/won't) was evaluated in terms of its actual cost.
Apply 3 If you (want/won't) be leaving tomorrow, you can see the play.

Learn 4 She will die when she sees the color of dye they plan to use.
Apply 5 How much (die/dye) do you estimate will be required?
Apply 6 I want to visit Africa and South America before I (die/dye).

Activity 2:

As you key the sentences shown at the right, insert semicolons, commas, exclamation points, question marks, apostrophes, and periods needed to complete each sentence correctly. Then check your work and rekey any sentence that contains a punctuation error.

Proofread & correct   Punctuation (semicolon/exclamation point/question mark/apostrophe)

1 You may not like ballet nevertheless you will go with us.
2 Mala will sing operatic arias the orchestra will accompany her.
3 She uses quick, snappy keystrokes good spacing quick returns.
4 Miss Appel said, "Insert the disk" then she showed us how.
5 "Stop," he yelled, "or you will break the window "
6 Do you know when new student government officers are elected
7 Will you please send me a copy of the report you mentioned
8 "Where," I asked, "did the deadly accident occur "
9 The new room is 16 ft. wide by 24 long and seats 20 students.
10 Doesnt she realize that daily practice is vital to success?
11 Our teacher told us to dot our is and cross our ts.
12 We keyed three 1 min. and two 3 min. writings on the paragraphs.
13 Do you know if this is Dans book, or is it Marshas?
14 What was similar about the "Gay 90s" and the "Roaring 20s"?
15 The audience is small however "the show must go on."
16 "Ready; Aim; Fire " was the order he gave the new recruits.
17 "Its maddening," he said, "when instructions arent included."
18 Rainstorms were predicted therefore, our picnic was cancelled.
19 However you divide the work, youre to finish the job today.
20 Will you please be in the auditorium by 3:15 for rehearsal

Personal-Business Letters

Objectives:
1. To improve letter processing skill.
2. To learn to format/key large and small envelopes.

49A • 5
Conditioning Practice

each line twice SS; then a
1' writing on line 3; find
gwam

alphabet	1	Wayne froze the ball, having just made the six quick points.
fig/sym	2	Flo moved from 583 Iris Lane to 836 - 42d Avenue on 10/7/97.
speed	3	Suella may row to the small island to dig for the big clams.

gwam 1' | 1 | 2 | 3 | 4 | 5 | 6 | 7 | 8 | 9 | 10 | 11 | 12 |

F ORMATTING

49B • 35
Personal-Business Letters

1. Key Letters 1 and 2 below, properly placed and spaced.

2. Proofread/correct any errors you made in arrangement or spacing.

3. If time permits, key Letter 2 again (at rough-draft speed) to increase input speed.

Letter 1	words
1764 Seminole Dr.	4
Detroit, MI 48214-2176	8
November 19, ---- (Current year)	12
Mr. Trevor L. Delong	16
1371 King George Blvd.	21
Ann Arbor, MI 48104-2657	26
Dear Trevor	28
A news item in the Detroit Free Press indicates	38
that you will be graduated from the university	47
at midyear. With honors, no less! Congratu-	56
lations!	58
When you were a student at Hillside High,	67
I worried that you might never put your poten-	76
tial to work in a serious way. But evidently	85
you have been able to continue your athletic	94
goals and at the same time pursue an aca-	102
demic major successfully. I am glad you have	111
done credit to yourself and to us at Hillside.	121
We're proud of you.	125
What are your plans after graduation? What-	134
ever they may be, your former teachers at	142
Hillside wish you well. I would enjoy a note	152
from you that I can share with others on the	161
Hillside faculty.	164
Cordially yours	168
Mrs. Barbara Snodgrass	172

Letter 2	words
4199 - 57th St.	3
Des Moines, IA 50310-4729	8
November 19, ---- (Current year)	12
Mr. Thomas E. McCarthy	17
2552 Madison Rd.	20
Cincinnati, OH 45208-3172	25
Dear Tom	27
Someone once said, "A friend in need is a	35
friend indeed," and I am in need.	42
When you were in Honors English at Hillside	51
High School, I recall your using Cliff's Notes to	61
help you through some of the more esoteric	70
reading assignments. Do you still have those	79
"Notes"?	81
Among our readings for second semester are	90
Great Expectations and Hamlet. Cliff's Notes	100
would be especially helpful for the latter, but	109
I'd appreciate having both. If you can lend me	119
these, I'll be forever grateful. Please let me	128
know if you can be of help.	134
Knowing you, I'm sure all is going well at	143
college.	145
Cordially	147
Kermit R. Dawkins	150

Applied Table Formatting

Objective:
To use decision-making skills to organize, format, and key tables from unarranged copy.

100A • 5
Conditioning Practice

set 0.5" SMs;
each line twice

alphabet 1 This bright jacket has an amazing weave and is of exceptional quality.

speed 2 When he kept the dog, it slept on the big chair in a hall of the dorm.

figures 3 The last two home games of this year drew crowds of 43,916 and 52,087.

gwam 1' | 1 | 2 | 3 | 4 | 5 | 6 | 7 | 8 | 9 | 10 | 11 | 12 | 13 | 14 |

F ORMATTING

100B • 45
Organize Information into Tables

Organize, format, and key three tables from the information given at the right. Use your decision-making skills to arrange in an attractive and meaningful format.

Table 1

In 1994 the National League was reorganized into three divisions (East, Central, and West). From the information below, prepare one table illustrating the three-division alignment.

Atlanta--East	Montreal--East
Chicago--Central	New York--East
Cincinnati--Central	Philadelphia--East
Colorado--West	Pittsburgh--Central
Florida--East	St. Louis--Central
Houston--Central	San Diego--West
Los Angeles--West	San Francisco--West

Table 2

Use the following information to prepare an interview schedule for Friday, June 27.

Raul Martinez will interview with Mr. Jackson at 8 a.m. Ms. Jasper will interview Kent Johnson at 2 p.m. Mr. Jackson will interview Marsha Sedgewick at 10 a.m. Clint Peterson will interview with Mr. Jackson at 1 p.m. Ms. Jasper will interview Anne Wilkins at 10 a.m. and Ted Thompson at 11 a.m.

Table 3

Use the following information to prepare a table. The heading for the table is **YOUR STATE'S INN**. Use **Fall, Winter, and Spring Rate Schedule** for the secondary heading. Organize the material in a way that best shows the costs for the various suites during the three seasons.

Alaska Suite	Florida Suite	Hawaii Suite
Fall ($39)	Fall ($59)	Fall ($115.50)
Winter ($63)	Winter ($83)	Winter ($145.50)
Spring ($45)	Spring ($65)	Spring ($135.50)
Colorado Suite	Texas Suite	California Suite
Fall ($49)	Fall ($69)	Fall ($89)
Winter ($73)	Winter ($93)	Winter ($113)
Spring ($55)	Spring ($75)	Spring ($95)

Note: Additional R & E tables can be found on pp. A23 and A24.

49C • 10
Envelopes

1. Study the guides at right and the illustrations below.
2. Format a small (No. 6 3/4) and a large (No. 10) envelope for each of the addresses. Use your own return address on the small envelope.

MISS ARNELLA WILSON
C/O OASIS MANOR
106 FREMONT ST
LAS VEGAS NV 89101-2277

MR PHONG HO MANAGER
ELECTRONIC PRODUCTS INC
8746 LA JOLLA PKWY
SAN DIEGO CA 92136-3927

Return address
Use block style, SS, and Caps and lowercase or ALL CAPS. *Unless equipment has an Envelope function*, begin on line 2 from top of envelope, 3 spaces from left edge.

Envelope address
Unless equipment has an Envelope function, set a tab or tab over 2.5" from left edge of small envelope and 4" from left edge of large envelope.

Space down about 2" from top edge of envelope; begin address at tab position.

USPS (postal service) style
Use block style, SS. Use ALL CAPS; omit punctuation. Place city name, 2-letter state name abbreviation, and ZIP Code + 4 on last address line. One space precedes the ZIP Code.

LESSON 50
Personal-Business Letters

Objectives:
1. To achieve mastery of personal-business letter format.
2. To develop skill in processing personal-business letters.

50A • 5
Conditioning Practice

each line twice SS; then a 1' writing on line 3; find *gwam*

alphabet 1 Vicky landed quite a major star for her next big plaza show.

fig/sym 2 Items marked * are out of stock: #139*, #476A*, and #2058*.

speed 3 Dodi is to handle all the pay forms for the small lake town.

gwam	1'	1	2	3	4	5	6	7	8	9	10	11	12

FORMATTING

50B • 45
Personal-Business Letters

1. Key Letters 1-3, p. 128, properly placed and spaced; address an envelope for each letter.

2. Proofread/correct each letter before you save it or remove it from your machine.

3. If time permits, key Letter 1 again (at rough-draft speed) to improve input speed.

Table 2

CS: 1"; SS events; DS between events

Note: This table will be used again later in this lesson.

	SELECTED UNITED STATES HISTORY DATES		7
Year		Event	10
1776	Declaration of Independence approved		18
	July 4		20
1789	George Washington chosen President by		28
	all electors voting		32
1804	Lewis and Clark expedition ordered by		41
	President Jefferson to explore what is		49
	now northwest U.S.		53
1836	Texas besieged in Alamo		58
1848	Gold discovered in California		65
1861	Seven southern states set up Confederate		75
	States of America		78
1875	Civil Rights Act		83
1903	First successful flight in heavier-than-air		92
	mechanically propelled airplane by		100
	Orville Wright		103
1908	Henry Ford introduced Model T car		110
1915	First telephone talk, New York to San		119
	Francisco, by Alexander Graham Bell and		127
	Thomas A. Watson		130
1929	Stock market crash		137
	———————		140
Source:	The World Almanac and Book of Facts, 1994.		151

99C • 10
Table Revision

Table 1

Open TAB97C2 or rekey Table 2, 97C, p. 237. Update the table to include the information at the right.

Table 2

Open (or rekey) Table 2 above. Insert the additional four dates of U.S. history in chronological order.

1991	Tom Glavine	Braves	5
1992	Greg Maddux	Cubs	9
1993	Greg Maddux	Braves	14
1994	Greg Maddux	Braves	19
1995	Greg Maddux	Braves	24

1846	Mexican War	3
1860	Abraham Lincoln elected President	11
1871	Great fire destroyed Chicago	18
1906	San Francisco earthquake	24

Letter 1

	words
2905 College Dr.	3
Columbus, GA 31096-3628	8
November 20, ---- (Current year)	12
Mr. Helmut E. Schultz	16
Bucherer Watch Company	21
730 Fifth Ave.	24
New York, NY 10019-2046	29
Dear Mr. Schultz	32

If anyone can repair a thinline Bucherer watch, you are the one. So said — 47
Hermine Wolfe, manager of jewelry repair at Loring's here in Columbus. — 61

Ms. Wolfe has repaired my watch twice before, but she believes it now — 75
needs attention that only a licensed Bucherer shop can give. In fact, she — 90
thinks the entire works may need to be replaced.   The case and band are — 105
of such value that I want to do whatever must be done to make the watch — 119
useful again. — 122

Please use the enclosed envelope to send me a rough estimate of the cost — 137
of repair and to tell me what I should do next.   The case number of the — 151
watch is 904618, in the event the number may be of use. The watch was — 165
purchased in Geneva. — 170

Sincerely yours — 173

Kyle A. Karas — 176

Enclosure — 177

Letter 2

	words

9248 Socorro Rd. | El Paso, TX 79907-2366 | — 8
November 20, ---- (Current year) — 12

Mrs. Susan L. Orr, Director | Graphic Arts — 20
Institute | 2099 Calle Lorca | Santa Fe, NM — 28
87505-3461 | Dear Mrs. Orr — 33

A graduate of your school, Ms. San-li Chou, — 42
has suggested that I write to you because of — 51
my interest in a career in graphic design. — 59

To keep my options open, I am taking a — 67
college-prep program. All my electives, though, — 77
are being chosen from courses in art, design, — 86
and graphics--including photography. I do — 95
unusually well in these courses. — 102

Can you send me a catalog that outlines the — 110
graphics programs now being offered by your — 119
school. I shall appreciate your doing so. — 128

Cordially yours | Miguel Blanco — 134

Letter 3

	words

4400 Coldwater Rd. | Fort Wayne, IN — 7
46825-3716 | November 20, ---- (Current year) — 13

Ms. Nina K. Medelin, Chair | Foreign Ex- — 20
change Committee | Rotary International | — 28
7800 S. Anthony Blvd. | Fort Wayne, IN — 35
46816-2250 | Dear Ms. Medelin — 41

Here are my completed application forms for a — 50
Rotary Foundation Scholarship to study one — 59
year in a South American country. — 66

I would especially like to study in Colombia — 75
because my mother has relatives in Bogota. — 83
Further, I visited Colombia with my family last — 93
year, and I liked the country and its people very — 103
much. — 104

As my application indicates, my minor course — 113
of study is Spanish. My career goal is to be- — 123
come a medical doctor and to serve in the His- — 132
panic community in one of our major cities. — 141

Sincerely yours | Sylvia LeClercq | Enclosures — 149

Table 2

CS: 1"; leave 1 blank line above each state; SS text pertaining to each state; see illustration on p. 232.

LEARNING cue:
For states with more than one nickname, key the first nickname; return and depress the Tab twice.

Table 3

Rearrange Table 2 alphabetically by state. Computer users should copy the table and use the Move feature to alphabetize the states.

SELECTED STATE CAPITALS

State	State Capital	State Nickname(s)	words
			5
			7
			13
California	Sacramento	Golden State	20
Wisconsin	Madison	Badger State	26
Wyoming	Cheyenne	Equality State	33
Virginia	Richmond	The Old Dominion	40
		Mother of Presidents	44
		Mother of States	47
Utah	Salt Lake City	Beehive State	54
Tennessee	Nashville	Volunteer State	61
Montana	Helena	Treasure State	67
		Mountain State	70
Michigan	Lansing	Wolverine State	77
Indiana	Indianapolis	Hoosier State	84
Florida	Tallahassee	Sunshine State	91
Colorado	Denver	Centennial State	97
		Silver State	100
Arizona	Phoenix	Grand Canyon State	110
			113

Source: Fodor's USA.   114

LESSON 99 — Tables with Multiple-Line Entries

Objective:
To format tables with multiple-line entries.

99A • 5
Conditioning Practice

each line twice

alphabet	1	Jay Beckfield took time to explain how every math quiz is graded.
speed	2	Vivian and Pam are to fix the problem with the right turn signal.
figures	3	Chapters 29 and 30, pages 187-245, will be reviewed on October 6.

gwam 1' | 1 | 2 | 3 | 4 | 5 | 6 | 7 | 8 | 9 | 10 | 11 | 12 | 13 |

FORMATTING

99B • 35
Formatting Tables

Table 1

CS: 1"; SS each evaluation item; DS between items; two spaces between column listings under Evaluator Response.

Note: If your equipment allows, define a macro for "My teacher."

wp note:
You may be asked to revise this file; save it (TAB99B1).

TEACHER EVALUATION

Evaluation Item	Evaluator Response					words
						4
						6
						11
My teacher demonstrates a clear						18
understanding of course topics.	SA	A	U	D	SD	27
My teacher has an effective						33
method of presentation.	SA	A	U	D	SD	41
My teacher is well prepared						47
for class.	SA	A	U	D	SD	52
My teacher stimulates interest in						59
course topics.	SA	A	U	D	SD	65
My teacher displays enthusiasm						71
for course topics.	SA	A	U	D	SD	78
My teacher uses many methods						84
to involve students in learning.	SA	A	U	D	SD	94
My teacher respects differing						100
points of view.	SA	A	U	D	SD	106

Business Letters

Objectives:

1. To learn features of business letters in block format.
2. To learn to format business letters in block format.

51A • 5
Conditioning Practice

each line twice SS; then a
1' writing on line 3; find
gwam

alphabet	1	Jacques worked to win the next big prize for my valiant men.
fig/sym	2	Rona's 1998 tax was $5,374, almost 2% ($106) less than 1997.
speed	3	Six of the eight girls may work for the auditor of the firm.

gwam 1' | 1 | 2 | 3 | 4 | 5 | 6 | 7 | 8 | 9 | 10 | 11 | 12 |

51B • 45
Business Letters in Block Format

Address an envelope for each letter processed in this lesson and remaining lessons in this unit.

 note:

If an Envelope function is available, use it; otherwise, follow the procedure given on p. 127.

1. Study Letter 1 (the model) on p. 130; then format/key it, errors corrected.

2. Format/key Letter 2 below; correct any errors you make as you key.

3. If time permits, key the model letter again (at rough-draft speed) to improve your input speed.

words

Letter 2

November 21, ---- (Current year) — 4

Mr. Nigel P. Byers — 7
Central High School — 11
65 Union Ave. — 14
Memphis, TN 38103-2745 — 19

Dear Mr. Byers — 22

Your question about the effect of word processing equipment on the need — 36
for keying accuracy is a good one. — 43

Accuracy of documents processed is just as important now as ever before. — 58
The ease with which keying errors can now be corrected, however, has — 72
shifted the emphasis from number of input errors made to skill in finding — 87
and correcting these errors. — 93

A major weakness of those who take employment tests is their inability — 107
to detect and correct the errors they make. Therefore, we suggest that — 121
employee training should emphasize proofreading and error correction — 135
rather than error-free input. — 141

A grading system rewarding efficient proofreading and correction skills — 156
instead of penalizing errors of initial input is worthy of your serious — 171
consideration. — 174

Sincerely yours — 177

Ms. Leslie Bancroft, Office Manager — 184

vk — 184

98B • 10
Apostrophe (continued)

Follow the Learn/Apply procedure in 76C, p. 184.

> To show possession, use an apostrophe plus *s* ('*s*) after a proper name of one syllable that ends in **s**.

Learn   1. Tim Jones's next art print will be released in July.
Apply   2. Jennifer Glass car is for sale.
Apply   3. Mary Parks grades were excellent; Paul Sims were terrible.

> To show possession, use only an apostrophe after (1) plural nouns ending in *s* and (2) a proper name of more than one syllable that ends in *s* or *z*.

Learn   4. The boys' coach will visit the Adams' home.
Apply   5. A new shipment of ladies coats should arrive this week.
Apply   6. Maria Santos plan for the officers meeting was great.

98C • 10
Drill: Multiple-Line Column Headings

Center each of the lines in the multiple-line headings over the longest entry in its column. DS between last line of heading and first entry; DS the entries.

CS: 0.6"

L EARNING *cues*:

1. When a table contains single-line column headings and column headings of two or more lines, the bottom line of the multiple-line heading is placed on the same line as the single-line heading(s).
2. Multiple-line headings are single-spaced, and the bottom line has an underline as long as the longest line in the heading.

Name of Purchaser	Date of Purchase	Seller	Selling Price
John Williams	10/30/96	McKnight	$865.50
Margaret Meade	11/08/96	Burdette	650.00
Jeremiah Stewart	11/12/96	Burdette	730.50

98D • 25
Tables with Multiple-Line Column Headings

center all headings

Table 1
CS: 0.5"; DS table

Underline longest line of heading.

				words
THE ART GALLERY				3
June Specials				6
Artist	Art Print	Regular Price	Sale Price	9 / 15
Sandager	Rocky Mountain Road	$ 1,125	$ 950	24
Richmond	Summer Home	10,230	9,250	30
Du Bois	City Lights	195	165	36
Gennrich	Brittany's Garden	489	425	43
Sinclair	Sunday Morning	1,350	1,095	50
Shoji	Christmas Morning	425	350	56
Chen	Coming Home	155	139	61
Lindquist	Dakota Country	305	280	68
Hohenstein	The Old Mill	3,525	3,325	75
Fisk-Fisher	Summer Outing	365	349	82
Debauche	Campers' Delight	199	150	89

K e n d a l ■ C o m p u t e r s

■ **738 St. Louis St.**

■ **Baton Rouge, LA 77802-3615**

OFFICE: 504-555-1278
FAX: 504- 555-1998

Dateline   November 21, ---- (Current year)   2" (or line 13)
QS (4 hard returns)

Letter address
Mr. Julio M. Basanez, Manager
La Paloma Restaurant
224 Saint Louis St.
Baton Rouge, LA 77802-3615
DS

Salutation   Dear Julio
DS

Body   Your piquant black bean soup drew me back to the La Paloma yesterday. We were taken promptly to our table, but we waited over ten
minutes before menus were presented.
DS

Several times I provided clues to the server that I was hosting the
(1") luncheon. Without noting these clues or asking who should receive (1")
the check, the server gave it to the man across from me. Had the
check been placed upside down in the middle of the table, my client
wouldn't have been "put on the spot."
DS

Several times a week someone from my company entertains clients at
La Paloma Restaurant. Will you talk with your staff about greeting
diners promptly and about handling checks properly. But please,
Julio, don't disturb the chef!
DS

Complimentary close   Cordially
QS (4 hard returns)

Mrs. Luanne Chang

Writer   Mrs. Luanne Chang, President
DS

Reference initials   mt

Shown in 12-point (10-pitch) type, 1" side
margins, photoreduced.

Business Letter in Block Format (Letter 1)

Table 3
Centered Column Headings
CS: 1"; DS table

			words
FAIR OAKS CREDIT UNION			5
Customer Phone Directory			10
Department	Department Manager	Phone	15
Business Loans	Sebastian Prado	186-1058	23
Car Loans	Forest Santori	186-4322	30
Community Service	Carol Mijatovich	186-9465	39
Customer Service	Julie Nottingwoode	168-2950	48
Financial Planning	Troy Julie Norwood	186-5227	56
Home Loans	Elizabeth Kane	186-7003	63
Human Resources Personnele	Katelynn Kingsly	186-4359	71
New Accounts	Keith Chamber	186-0095	79
Student Loans	Craig Oakmont Neal G. Williamse	186-2729e 3839	86

97D • 10
Revising Documents

wp users:
Prepare letters for both
customers.
Electronics users:
Prepare letter for Voyles
only.

Open LTR82B2, or rekey
Letter 2, 82B. Reformat the
letter in block style with open
punctuation; supply an
appropriate salutation and
complimentary closing.

Send the letter and the
customer phone directory for
Fair Oaks Credit Union to the
following customers:

MS PAULINE VOYLES
382 TWO OAKS DR
ATHENS GA 30606-8283

MR TIMOTHY BELL
1974 PEACHTREE TER
ALBANY GA 31707-8833

LESSON 98   Tables with Multiple-Line Column Headings

Objectives:
1. To learn to format multiple-line column headings.
2. To improve language skills (apostrophe).

98A • 5
Conditioning Practice

each line twice

alphabet	1	Jack Blazel reported quite extensive damage done to the freeways.
speed	2	Nancy is to make an official bid for the antique enamel fishbowl.
figures	3	By 1:30 p.m. on Tuesday, May 9, 258 of the 467 juniors had voted.
gwam	1'	1 | 2 | 3 | 4 | 5 | 6 | 7 | 8 | 9 | 10 | 11 | 12 | 13 |

Business Letters

Objectives:

1. To review features of business letters in block format.
2. To process business letters in block format.

52A • 5
Conditioning Practice

each line twice SS; then a 1' writing on line 3; find *gwam*

alphabet	1	Jarvis will take the next big prize for my old racquet club.
fig/sym	2	The Diamond Caper (Parker & Sons, #274638) sells for $19.50.
speed	3	A neighbor paid the girl to fix the turn signal of the auto.

gwam 1' | 1 | 2 | 3 | 4 | 5 | 6 | 7 | 8 | 9 | 10 | 11 | 12 |

F ORMATTING

52B • 45
Business Letters in Block Format

Letter 1

Key Letters 1-3, at right and on p. 132, in block format; proofread and correct each letter before you save it or remove it from the machine.

words

November 22, ----   4

Miss Rikki Samuels, President   10
Business Education Club   14
Sooner High School   18
2165 Granada Ave.   22
San Diego, CA 92104-3710   27

Dear Miss Samuels   30

Thank you for giving me the opportunity to tell you the main things we   45
look for in entry-level office workers.   53

First, we look for graduates who have specific skills we need: in commu-   67
nications, keyboarding, word/data processing, accounting, and records   81
management, to name a few.   A detailed personal data sheet will usually   96
provide such information.   101

Next, we seek people who show pride in themselves--those who dress   114
appropriately and are well groomed and who speak positively as well as   129
forcefully about their educational background and related experiences.   143
Usually these behavior patterns are observed in the job interview.   157

Finally, we seek people who show evidence that they can work well with   171
others.   An effective application letter and data sheet will identify group   186
activities in which the applicant has participated successfully and in what   201
roles.   203

People with these qualifications have at least the potential to develop into   218
valuable members of an office staff.   226

Sincerely yours   229

Miss Maryann Figueroa, Human Services Director   237

nt   238

97B • 10
Apostrophe (continued)
Follow the Learn/Apply procedure in 76C, p. 184.

Use an apostrophe plus s (*'s*) to form the plural of most figures, letters, and words (*6's*, *A's*, *five's*). In stock market quotations, form the plural of figures by the addition of **s** only.

Learn   1. Underline your A's and 4's. Denver Fund 99s are due in 2009.
Apply   2. You will need to reprint the memo; the ts and fs didn't print.
Apply   3. He suggested that you buy Growth Fund 99s for your portfolio.

To show possession, use an apostrophe plus **s** after (1) a singular noun and (2) a plural noun that does not end in **s**.

Learn   4. The men's department had a sale; the women's department didn't.
Apply   5. Ritas ring was found in the mens locker room.
Apply   6. The childrens play was scheduled for May 23.

97C • 25
Table Formatting

Table 1
Centered Column Headings
CS: 0.7"; DS table

			words
FILM SCHEDULE			3
Campus Theater--6:00 and 8:30 p.m.			9
Movie	Dates	Director	14
The Producers	April 1	Mel Brooks	21
To Be or Not to Be	April 8	Jim Sheridan	29
Belle Epoque	May 15	Fernando Trueba	36
Blue	May 22	Krzysztof Kieslowski	43
Short Cuts	May 29	Robert Altman	49
Guelwaar	June 6-9	Ousmane Sembene	56
The Wedding Banquet	June 13	Ang Lee	63
Betty Blue	June 17	Jean-Jacques Beineix	71
The Conformist	June 22	Bernardo Bertolucci	80
Sugar Cane Alley	June 27	Euzhan Palcy	88

Table 2
Centered Column Headings
CS: 1.5"; DS table
Save as TAB97C2 for use in a later lesson.

NATIONAL LEAGUE CY YOUNG AWARD WINNERS			8
1980 - 1990			10
Year	Player	Team	14
1980	Steve Carlton	Phillies	19
1981	Fernando Valenzuela	Dodgers	25
1982	Steve Carlton	Phillies	31
1983	John Denny	Phillies	36
1984	Rick Sutcliffe	Cubs	41
1985	Dwight Gooden	Mets	46
1986	Mike Scott	Astros	51
1987	Steve Bedrosian	Phillies	57
1988	Orel Hershiser	Dodgers	62
1989	Mark Davis	Padres	67
1990	Doug Drabek	Pirates	72

Letter 2

Note: Line endings for opening lines are indicated by color verticals. Return at these points.

wp note:

Save this letter under the filename LTR52B2. You will be asked to retrieve it in a later lesson.

November 22, ---- | Mr. Pablo J. Lobos | 733 Marquette Ave. | 11
Minneapolis, MN 55402-2736 | Dear Mr. Lobos   20

Congratulations! You are now the sole owner of the car you financed   33
through our bank. We also want to say thank you for choosing us to serve   48
your credit needs.   52

The original Certificate of Title and your Installment Loan Contract marked   67
"Paid in Full" are enclosed--evidence that you have fulfilled all the obliga-   83
tions of your automobile loan. File the papers in a safe place with your   97
other important records.   103

The promptness with which you made all monthly payments gives you a   116
preferred credit rating at our bank. Please let us know when we may be   131
of service to you again.   136

Sincerely yours | Ms. Ilya Lindgren, Auto Loan Department | hq | 148
Enclosures   150

Letter 3

Note: Do not key the diagonals; simply return at those points.

November 22, ----   4
Mrs. Glendora Ramos / 3716 Rangely Dr. /   11
Raleigh, NC 27609-4116 / Dear Mrs. Ramos   19

In these days of computers and other fancy office equipment,   31
the personal and friendly contact with people is sometimes   43
overlooked. We want you to know how much we appreciate your   55
past orders and this new opportunity to serve you.   65

The enclosed acknowledgment lists the four items you ordered   78
a few days ago. As in the past, we will carefully follow   89
your instructions for processing and shipping.   99

Although we appreciate receiving payment with an order, we   111
want to remind you that prepayment is not required. If you   123
prefer, you may simply enter your personal account number on   135
the order form, and we will send a bill later. Your account   147
number appears on your catalog address label.   156

Cordially yours / Miguel J. Maddox /   163
Mail Order Department / tm / Enclosure   170

Table 2
Centered Column Headings
and Source Note
CS: 1"; DS table

Table 3
Centered Column Headings
Update Table 1. Add the
following entries (alphabeti-
cally by author's last name)
to the table:
All for the Union
  Robert H. Rhodes
The Battle of Gettysburg
  Frank A. Haskell
Lee, Grant, and Sherman
  Alfred H. Burne

		words
CIVIL WAR		2
Eastern Theater Campaigns		7
Campaign	*Dates*	11
First Bull Run (Manassas)	July 1861	18
Peninsular Campaign	April-July 1862	25
Jackson's Valley Campaign	March-June 1862	33
Second Bull Run (Manassas)	July-September 1862	43
Antietam (Sharpsburg) Campaign	September 1862	52
Fredericksburg Campaign	October-December 1862	61
Chancellorsville Campaign	April-May 1863	69
Gettysburg Campaign	June-July 1863	76
Wilderness Campaign	May 1864	82
Spotsylvania Campaign	May 1864	88
Petersburg Campaign	May 1864-April 1865	96
Grant's Pursuit of Lee	April 3 and 9, 1865	105
Sherman's March to the Sea	November-December 1864	115
Sherman's Pursuit of Johnston	December 1864-April 1865	128
		131
Source: *Collier's Encyclopedia*, 1991.		139

LESSON 97

Three-Column Tables

Objectives:
1. To learn to format three-column tables.
2. To improve language skills (apostrophe).

97A • 5
Conditioning Practice

each line twice

alphabet	1	Gary was quite amazed by the next photo of the Jacksonville team.
speed	2	He bid on the field by the lake as the right land for the chapel.
figures	3	Pages 389, 462, and 570 were revised prior to the May 1 deadline.
gwam	1'	1 | 2 | 3 | 4 | 5 | 6 | 7 | 8 | 9 | 10 | 11 | 12 | 13 |

Block Letter Mastery

Objectives:

1. To improve skill on rough-draft copy.

2. To demonstrate mastery of correspondence formatting.

53A • 5
Conditioning Practice

each line twice SS; then a 1' writing on line 3; find *gwam*

alphabet	1	Belva had quickly won top seed for the next games in Juarez.
fig/sym	2	My income tax for 1996 was $4,870.62--up 3% over 1995's tax.
speed	3	Shana may make a bid for the antique bottle for the auditor.

gwam 1' | 1 | 2 | 3 | 4 | 5 | 6 | 7 | 8 | 9 | 10 | 11 | 12 |

53B • 10
Skill Building

1. Key two 1' writings on the ¶; find *gwam* on each.
2. Key two 2' writings on the ¶; find *gwam* on each.

gwam 1' | 2'

As you learn to type, there is a time to work for speed   11 | 5

and a time to go for accuracy. Throughout the early weeeks,   22 | 11

technique--not speed, not acuracy--is the main goal. Next,   35 | 17

spede through improved techniques be comes the primary focus   47 | 24

for a time. When you begin lerning to format documents, though,   60 | 30

acuracy of your copy (with erors corrected) is emphasized.   71 | 36

FORMATTING

53C • 35
Correspondence in Block Format

Document 1

Key the copy as a simplified memo, all errors corrected.

	words
November 18, ----	4
Adele Kliemens, Social Studies	10
STUDENT BEHAVIOR	13

Thank you for reporting the unpleasant incident you observed   25
at one of our recent athletic events.   33

This incident has been reviewed by officers of the Student   45
Council and by school administrators. The three students   57
involved have been identified and disciplined. We have also   69
set up procedures that we believe will prevent such incidents   81
from happening again.   86

The behavior of our students is of great importance to us,   98
not only for the image of our school but also as evidence   109
that our boys and girls are, through our help, growing into   121
well-behaved young men and women. Thank you for helping us   133
achieve our goal.   137

Lenore M. Fielding, Principal   142

Objectives:
1. To learn to center column headings.
2. To improve table formatting skill.

96A • 5
Conditioning Practice

each line twice; then 1'
writings on line 2

alphabet 1 Major Kowalzak thought you purchased five or six antique baskets.

speed 2 The six girls in the sorority dorm pay for the bus to go to town.

figures 3 The groups were assigned Rooms 639 and 708 for the 12:45 meeting.

gwam 1' | 1 | 2 | 3 | 4 | 5 | 6 | 7 | 8 | 9 | 10 | 11 | 12 | 13 |

LANGUAGE SKILLS

96B • 10
Apostrophe

Follow the Learn/Apply
procedure in 76C, p. 184.

> Use an apostrophe as a symbol to represent feet in billings or tabulations or as a symbol for minutes. (Quotation marks may be used to signify inches or seconds.)

Learn 1. He purchased twenty 2" x 4" x 8' studs for the new deck.

Learn 2. The relay team ran the mile in 4' 38".

Apply 3. The room measured 15 ft. 6 in. x 20 ft.

Apply 4. The trial run took 10 min. 56 sec.

> Use an apostrophe as a symbol to indicate the omission of letters or figures (as in contractions).

Learn 5. Didn't you enjoy attending the "Spirit of '76" convention?

Apply 6. She wouldnt agree to the terms; he didnt understand why.

Apply 7. They planned a reunion for the classes of 65, 75, and 85.

96C • 35
Table Formatting

Table 1
Centered Column Headings
CS: 1.5"; DS table

wp note:
Save for later use (TAB96C1).

LEARNING *cues:*
To center column headings shorter than column entries, follow these steps:
1. Determine placement of columns in usual way.
2. From column starting point, space forward once for each two strokes in longest entry. From this point, backspace once for each 2 strokes in column heading.
3. Key and underline column heading.

	words
CIVIL WAR BOOK LIST	4

Title	*Author*	words
The Blue and the Gray	Claudius M. Capps	7
Four Brothers in Blue	Robert G. Carter	15
The Price of Freedom	Calvin Coolidge	22
A Civil War Drama	Herbert P. Kakuske	30
Voices of the Civil War	Richard Wheeler	37
The Life of Johnny Reb	Bell Irvin Willey	45
The Confederate Soldier	LeGrand J. Wilson	53
		62

Document 2

Key the copy as a business letter, block format, all errors corrected.

November 23, ---- | Miss Evangeline Norcross | 666 Walnut St. | 12
Des Moines, IA 50309-2661 | Dear Miss Norcross   21

Going places?   You will go twice as far in the new Gondola 2000 Compact.   35
Yes, one gallon of gasoline will take you 40 miles or more, even in city   50
driving.   And you'll do it in "smooth as silk" comfort.   61

Going places?   You will have money to spend if you invest in the best buy   76
of all compacts--the Gondola 2000.   The price is only $11,995.   You'll   90
have more money to spend, too, because the new Gondola 2000 is really   104
a miser with gasoline on the open road.   113

Going places?   Then go right to the nearest mailbox with the enclosed   127
postal card.   Just indicate the most convenient time for your free-trial   141
demonstration.   The supply of new Gondola 2000 Compacts is going fast,   155
so you'd better hurry.   160

Sincerely yours | Han Song Ki, Sales Manager | wh | Enclosure   171

Document 3

Key the copy as a personal-business letter, all errors corrected.

Document 4

If time permits, reformat or key Document 1 as a standard memo, all errors corrected.

Note: See p. A16 for R & E activities for this unit.

7706 Circle Dr. / St. Louis, MO 63121-4583/   8
November 23, ----/   12

Dr. Yolanda M. Flores / Director of Admissions /   21
LaRhonde School of Music /1035 Bellevue   29
Ave./St. Louis, MO 63121-2758/Dear Dr. Flores   38

Please send me an application form for admission to the   49
LaRhonde School of Music. I am to be graduated in June and   61
hope to enter college in September.   68

I shall appreciate information about scholarships that are   80
available and the procedure to follow in applying for one.   92
If I am to enter college in September, as I earnestly hope   105
to do, some financial aid is needed.   112

If an audition is required, when should I plan to come to   123
campus and what records should I bring with me?   133

Sincerely yours/ Ivalee Moore   138

FORMATTING

95D • 25
Two-Column Tables

Review table format guides on pp. 157 and 232. Format the tables given at the right; block column headings; DS all lines.

Table 1
Table with Main and Column Headings
CS: 1.5"

Table 2
Table with Main and Column Headings and Source Note
CS: 2"

Table 3
Table with Main, Secondary, and Column Headings with Total Line
CS: 1.5"

LEARNING cue:
To indicate a total, underline the last entry the same width as the total amount; DS; key **Total** indented five spaces from the left margin; tab over and key total amount.

Table 4
Update Table
Update Table 2 to include World Series Champions since 1995. (Cite the current edition of *World Almanac* or *Information Please Sports Almanac*.)

INSTRUCTOR ROOM ASSIGNMENTS — 6

Instructor	Room	
		9
Jarrad Ito	4005	12
Blake Claerwater	4010	16
Lydia Johnson	4028	20
Megan Kearney	4007	24
Kelsey Kemmerer	4016	28
Michelle Estes	4013	32

1985-1995 WORLD SERIES CHAMPIONS — 7

Team	Year	DS	
			9
Kansas City (AL)	1985		13
New York (NL)	1986		17
Minnesota (AL)	1987		21
Los Angeles (NL)	1988		25
Oakland (AL)	1989		29
Cincinnati (NL)	1990		33
Minnesota (AL)	1991		37
Toronto (AL)	1992		41
Toronto (AL)	1993		44
No World Series	1994		48
Atlanta (NL)	1995		52
DS			55

Source: World Almanac, 1996. — 63

UNITED WAY — DS — 2
(May Donations) — 5

Company	Amount	
		9
West Side Auto	$2,000	13
The Bridal Shoppe	1,500	18
O'Toole Manufacturing	1,200	23
The Flooring Experts	1,000	29
Hallie Chiropractic Center	1,000	35
Five Star Computing	800	40
Kerr School of Dance	500	45
Swan Enterprises	500	50
Total	$8,500	53

LESSON 54

Keyboarding/Language Skills

From this point forward, use 1" or default side margins.

Objectives:

1. To demonstrate mastery of capitalization and number expression.
2. To demonstrate your best technique, speed, and control.

**54A • 5
Conditioning Practice**

each line twice SS; then a 1' writing on line 3; find *gwam*

alphabet	1	Jacki next placed my winning bid for the prized antique red vase.
fig/sym	2	His sales this week are $28,193.50; that's an increase of 17.64%.
speed	3	They wish their neighbor to pay for half the land for the chapel.

gwam 1' | 1 | 2 | 3 | 4 | 5 | 6 | 7 | 8 | 9 | 10 | 11 | 12 | 13 |

L ANGUAGE SKILLS

**54B • 10
Checkup**

1. Key each line, correcting errors in capitalization, number expression, and spacing.
2. Check accuracy of work.
3. Rekey each line in which you made errors.

1 the labor day parade begins at 1 elm street and ends at spruce.

2 we are inviting senator chavez to address our convention in july.

3 11 of 33 boys and nine of 27 girls scored 93 or more in english.

4 linda used the pope quote: "to err is human, to forgive divine."

5 sgt. p.t. simmons took the 911 call from merchants bank & trust.

6 myrna bought china service for 8 at the china plus gift shop.

7 kevin cruz earned his phi beta kappa key while at boston college.

8 i checked my data in volume 4, section 2, page 20, of sourcebook.

S KILL BUILDING

**54C • 15
Technique**

1. Key the drill once SS; DS between 2-line groups.
2. Key a 1' writing on each of lines 6, 8, and 10; find *gwam* on each.
3. Key the drill again.

shift keys	1	Lana and Todd will go to a New Year's party with Tonya and Spiro.
	2	R. J. Appel has been paid by the Apollo Insurance Co. of Jackson.
space bar	3	It is up to them to do their best in each try to make a new goal.
	4	Andy may use his pen to sign the work form for a job in the city.
letter response	5	Only after you set a case date were oil tax rates set in my area.
	6	You are free only after we get him set up on a gas tax rate case.
combination response	7	Polly may bid on the antique vase only if she regards it as rare.
	8	You are to sign off on all the artwork he turns in for the union.
word response	9	He is to do the sign work for both of us, and she is to pay half.
	10	The girl with the titian hair may own the title to the lake land.

gwam 1' | 1 | 2 | 3 | 4 | 5 | 6 | 7 | 8 | 9 | 10 | 11 | 12 | 13 |

LESSON 95 Two-Column Tables

Objectives:

1. To improve table formatting skill.
2. To improve language skills (exclamation point, question mark).

95A • 5
Conditioning Practice

set 0.5" SMs;
each line twice

alphabet 1 Marquis Becks enjoyed expanding his vast knowledge of Arizona history.

speed 2 The neighbor burns wood and a small bit of coal to make a giant flame.

figures 3 Test scores of 94, 83, 72, 65, and 100 gave Rhonda an average of 82.8.

gwam 1' | 1 | 2 | 3 | 4 | 5 | 6 | 7 | 8 | 9 | 10 | 11 | 12 | 13 | 14 |

L ANGUAGE SKILLS

95B • 10
Exclamation Point; Question Mark

Follow the Learn/Apply procedure in 76C, p. 184.

> Use an exclamation point after emphatic (forceful) exclamations and after phrases and sentences that are clearly exclamatory.

Learn 1. The police officer yelled, "Stop that man!"
Apply 2. The child screamed, "I want a puppy"
Apply 3. Enthusiastically the woman stated, "I want to be your governor"

> Use a question mark at the end of a sentence that is a direct question; however, use a period after a request that appears in the form of a question.

Learn 4. Did you use the graphics package to prepare the chart?
Learn 5. Will you make sure the door is locked.
Apply 6. Will you be sure to make the deposit before Friday
Apply 7. Did you enjoy the movie

95C • 10
Drill: Center Lines

1. Review horizontal and vertical centering procedures on p. 232.
2. Center text vertically and each line horizontally.

	words
TAKE ME BACK TO GETTYSBURG	5
Featuring:	8
Michaela Reynolds	11
Sebastian Fennimore	15
Clayton Mazzone	18
Trenton Hendricks	22
Victoria Green	25
February 15, ----	29
7:30 p.m.	31
McKinley Performing Arts Center	37

54D • 20
Timed Writings

1. Key a 1' writing on each ¶; find *gwam* on each.
2. Key two 1' guided writings on each ¶ for speed. (See p. 54 for procedure.)
3. Key two 2' writings on ¶s 1-2 combined; find *gwam* on each.
4. Key two 3' writings on ¶s 1-2 combined; find *gwam* and count errors.

Quarter-Minute Checkpoints

gwam	1/4'	1/2'	3/4'	1'
20	5	10	15	20
24	6	12	18	24
28	7	14	21	28
32	8	16	24	32
36	9	18	27	36
40	10	20	30	40
44	11	22	33	44
48	12	24	36	48
52	13	26	39	52
56	14	28	42	56

all letters used   gwam 2' | 3'

As you build your keying power, the number of errors you make   6 | 4
is not very important because most of the errors are accidental and   13 | 9
incidental. Realize, however, that documents are expected to be   20 | 13
without flaw. A letter, report, or table that contains flaws is   26 | 17
not usable until it is corrected.   So find and correct all errors.   33 | 22

The best time to detect and correct your errors is while the   39 | 26
copy is still on a monitor or in the machine. Therefore, just be-   45 | 30
fore you remove the copy from the screen or machine, proofread it   52 | 35
and correct any errors you have made. Learn to proofread carefully   59 | 39
and to correct all errors quickly. Up your production in this way.   65 | 44

| 2' | 1 | 2 | 3 | 4 | 5 | 6 |
| 3' | 1 | 2 | 3 | 4 |

LESSON 55

Keyboarding Check & Improvement

Objectives:

1. To check/improve keying speed on sentences.
2. To check/improve keying speed/control on paragraphs.

55A • 5
Conditioning Practice

each line twice SS; then a 1' writing on line 3; find *gwam*

alphabet 1 Frazer may have a jinx on my squad, but we kept the big gold cup.

fig/sym 2 Lizzy asked, "Wasn't R&N's check #385367-0 deposited on 1/24/97?"

speed 3 When did the field auditor sign the amendment forms for the city?

gwam 1' | 1 | 2 | 3 | 4 | 5 | 6 | 7 | 8 | 9 | 10 | 11 | 12 | 13 |

55B • 15
Sentences

1. Key a 1' writing on each line; find *gwam* on each writing.
2. Compare rates and identify the 4 slowest lines.
3. Key a 1' writing on each of the 4 slowest lines.
4. As time permits in later lessons, key this drill again to improve speed.

fig/sym 1 Leland asked, "How much is due by June 30 on Account #4829-1657?"

figures 2 By October 5 in 1997, she had planted 320 trees and 1,648 shrubs.

one hand 3 My war on waste at a union mill was based only upon minimum data.

long reach 4 June said that I must curb at once my urge to glance at my hands.

adjacent key 5 Joi hoped for a new opal ring to wear to her next violin concert.

double letter 6 Bobby will sell them the cookbook for a little less than it cost.

combination 7 They may join us for tea at the big pool if they wish to see you.

balanced hand 8 Did they make the right land title forms for the eight big firms?

gwam 1' | 1 | 2 | 3 | 4 | 5 | 6 | 7 | 8 | 9 | 10 | 11 | 12 | 13 |

Improve Table Formatting Skills

Format Guides:
Tables

Three-Column Table

Column Headings

When used, column headings may be centered over the longest line in the column. If a table has single- and multiple-line headings (see model below), the bottom line of each multiple-line heading is placed on the same line as the single-line headings. The lines of multiple-line headings are single-spaced.

Horizontal Centering

The margin and tab settings for tables may be determined by the keyline method. The keyline consists of the longest entry in each column of the table plus the space to be placed between the columns (CS). Before or after keying the keyline, use the Center feature to place half of the keyline to the left of center point and half to the right of center point. After centering, use the location of the columns in the keyline to determine the settings for the left margin and tabs in the table. See p. 157 if necessary. Delete the keyline and key the table.

Vertical Centering

Vertical centering can be done with the Center Page feature, if available with the software being used. Otherwise, vertical centering involves subtracting the number of lines of text (including blank line spaces) from the number of lines available on the sheet and dividing the remaining number of unused lines equally between the top and bottom margins.

Manual Vertical Centering

1. Count the lines to be used to key the table (include blank lines).
2. Subtract lines needed from total lines available on page (66 lines).
3. Divide the remainder by 2 to determine top margin. If the number that results ends in a fraction, drop the fraction.

Example for table at right:

Lines available	=	66
Total lines to be used for table	=	− 35
		31
31 ÷ 2 = 15 1/2		
Lines in top margin =		15
Page begins: line 16 =		16

4. Insert 16 hard returns (10 if 1" default TM).

2" or centered vertically SELECTED STATE CAPITALS **DS**

State	State Capital	State Nickname(s)
Arizona	Phoenix	Grand Canyon State **DS**
California	Sacramento	Golden State **DS**
Colorado	Denver	Centennial State Silver State
Florida	Tallahassee	Sunshine State
Indiana	Indianapolis	Hoosier State
Michigan	Lansing	Wolverine State
Montana	Helena	Treasure State Mountain State
Tennessee	Nashville	Volunteer State
Utah	Salt Lake City	Beehive State
Virginia	Richmond	The Old Dominion Mother of Presidents Mother of States
Wisconsin	Madison	Badger State
Wyoming **DS**	Cheyenne	Equality State

DS

Source: Fodor's USA.

Language & Writing Skills 6

Activity 1:

1. Study the spelling/ definitions of the words in the color block at right.
2. Key line 1 (the **Learn** line), noting the proper choice and spelling of words.
3. Key lines 2-4 (the **Apply** lines), choosing the right words to complete the lines correctly.
4. Key lines 5-8 in a similar manner.
5. Check the accuracy of your copy; rekey lines that still contain word-choice/spelling errors.

Choose the right word

> **their** (pron) belonging to them
> **there** (adv/pron) in or at that place; word used to introduce a sentence or clause
> **they're** (contr) a contracted form of *they are*
>
> **to** (prep/adj) used to indicate action, relation, distance, direction
> **too** (adv) besides; also; to excessive degree
> **two** (pron/adj) one plus one in number

Learn 1 They're to be there to present their plans for the new building.
Apply 2 Were you (their/there/they're) for the large fireworks display?
Apply 3 Do you believe (their/there/they're) going to elect her as mayor?
Apply 4 In (their/there/they're) opinion, the decision was quite unfair.

Learn 5 Is it too late for us to go to the two o'clock movie today?
Apply 6 I am (to/too/two) give everyone (to/too/two) bowls of beef soup.
Apply 7 We are going (to/too/two) the opera; Stan is going, (to/too/two).
Apply 8 She thought that (to/too/two) workers were (to/too/two) many.

Activity 2:

1. Read the ¶ shown at the right, noting errors in spelling and word choice.
2. Key the ¶, changing all words necessary to make the ¶ correct.
3. Check your copy for accuracy; correct any remaining errors you find.

Proofread & correct

That all individuals want others two respect them is not surprising. What is surprising is that some people think their do respect even when there own behavior has been unacceptable or even illegal.   Key two the issue is that we respect others because of certain behavior, rather then in spite of it.   Its vital, than, to no that what people due and say determines the level of respect their given by others.   In that regard, than, respect has to be earned; its not hour unquestioned right too demand it.

Activity 3:

1. Read the ¶ and decide whether the student's action was right or wrong (legal, ethical, or moral). Decide if stealing for any reason can be justified.
2. Compose a ¶ stating your views and giving your reasons.
3. Revise, proofread, and correct your ¶.
4. Key the ¶ at right as ¶ 1; key your corrected ¶ as ¶ 2.

Compose (think) as you key

A student sees a designer jacket hanging over the door of a locker. No one seems to be around.   The student tries it on; it looks great. He likes it and wants it.   He reasons that if the owner can afford an expensive jacket, he can afford another one.   So quickly the student puts it in his gym bag and walks away.

94C • 10
Semicolon

Follow the Learn/Apply Procedure in 76C, p. 184.

> Use a semicolon to separate a series of phrases or clauses (especially if they contain commas) that are introduced by a colon.

Learn   1. The cities are as follows: Orem, UT; Ames, IA; and Waco, TX.

Apply   2. The dates are as follows: May 1, 1996 May 5, 1996 and May 9, 1996.

Apply   3. These are the figures: 1994, $687 1995, $798 and 1996, $845.

> Place the semicolon outside the closing quotation mark; the period and comma, inside the closing quotation mark.

Learn   4. Mr. Day spoke about "winners"; Ms. Cline, about "losers."

Apply   5. She said, "Don't look at the keys" he said, "I'll try"

Apply   6. Tom said, "You can do it" Mary said, "You're kidding"

94D • 15
Script Copy

1. Two 1' writings on each ¶ for speed; find *gwam* on each writing.
2. Two 3' writings on ¶s 1-3 combined; find *gwam*; circle errors.

all letters used

	gwam	1'	3'	5'

Ethical conduct is a subject that has received a great   11   4   2
deal of attention in recent years. Many businesses have developed   24   8   5
written codes and have taken steps to ensure that employees of the   38   13   8
business and the public are aware of these codes. Making people   51   17   10
aware of the codes is a company's way of renewing its commitment   64   21   13
to ethical practice.   68   23   14

A major purpose of a code of ethics is to relay a company's   80   27   16
values and business standards to all its workers. Each worker   92   31   18
must realize that he or she is required to apply these standards   105   35   21
in all relations with co-workers, potential and current customers   119   40   24
and suppliers, and the public at large.   126   42   25

To adhere to the code, employees must be able to combine   138   46   28
personal standards with those of the business. This mixture is   151   50   30
important because each job has an ethical aspect, and each em-   163   54   33
ployee has a responsibility to carry out the functions of the job   176   59   35
in an ethical and proper manner.   183   61   37

ACTIVITY 1:

Flush Right

1. Read the copy at right.
2. Learn the Flush Right feature on your wp software.
3. Key your name so that it ends at the right margin.
4. Key the lines in each group at the right, following the directions at the beginning of each group.

Use the **Flush Right** feature when you want a line of text (or part of a line) to end even with the right margin. Flush Right can be activated before or after text is keyed. If turned on before text is keyed, the text will "back up" from the right margin as you key.

1. Use Flush Right, then key each line.

This line is keyed with flush right activated.

This line uses flush right so that it ends at the right.

2. Key each line at left margin as shown, select (highlight) the four lines, and use Flush Right to align them at the right margin.

Massey Hall

Room 315

Phone: (715) 167-8045

Fax: (715) 167-8145

3. Key each line (begin at left margin); use Flush Right to place only the ZIP + 4 at the right margin.

375 Baker Street, Jamestown, New York 14701-7598

960 Pembroke Street, New Rochelle, New York 10801-3127

ACTIVITY 2:

Learn to Use Tabs

1. Read the copy at right.
2. Learn how to clear and set tabs (left, right, and decimal tabs) with your wp software.
3. Clear the preset tabs.

Most wp software has left tabs already set at half-inch (0.5") intervals from the left margin. These preset tabs can be cleared and reset. Most wp software lets you set:

Left tabs

Left tabs align all text evenly at the left by placing the text you key to the right of the tab setting. Left tabs are commonly used to align words.

Right tabs

Right tabs align all text evenly at the right by placing the text you key to the left of the tab setting. Right tabs are commonly used to align whole numbers.

Decimal tabs

Decimal tabs align all text at the decimal point or other align character that you specify. If you key numbers in a column at a decimal tab, the decimal points will "line up," regardless of the number of places before or after the decimal point.

(continued on next page)

1. Two 5' writings for speed; find *gwam* on each writing.
2. Two 3' writings for speed; find *gwam* on each writing.
3. Two 1' writings for speed; find *gwam* on each writing.

all letters used

gwam	1'	3'	5'

Have you ever thought about becoming a teacher? Teachers | 12 | 4 | 2
are crucial to our welfare. They are put in charge of one of | 24 | 8 | 5
America's most precious resources, students. They are expected to | 37 | 12 | 7
assist in developing this resource into a well-rounded person who | 51 | 17 | 10
fits in well with other members of our culture. They are also | 63 | 21 | 13
expected to produce students who are able to contribute to society | 77 | 26 | 15
and make it a better place to live. Our culture hinges on the | 89 | 30 | 18
quality of teachers we entrust with our future. | 99 | 33 | 20

Being a teacher is quite a challenge. Teachers work with a | 111 | 37 | 22
broad range of individuals with a variety of interests, back- | 123 | 41 | 25
grounds, and abilities. Teachers try to help all students realize | 136 | 45 | 27
their potential and be able to cope with a world that is changing | 149 | 50 | 30
very rapidly every day. A teacher's job is to try to equip stu- | 162 | 54 | 32
dents with the skills necessary to be lifelong learners, to keep | 175 | 58 | 35
pace with changes, and to be productive. In order to be success- | 188 | 63 | 38
ful at teaching, a person must like working with people and enjoy | 201 | 67 | 40
learning. | 203 | 68 | 41

gwam	1'	1	2	3	4	5	6	7	8	9	10	11	12	13
	3'		1			2			3			4		
	5'			1				2				3		

LESSON 94

Keyboarding/Language Skills

Objectives:
1. To improve and assess keyboarding speed and accuracy.
2. To improve language skills.

each line twice

alphabet 1 Zac very quickly explained why most of the big projects were cut.
speed 2 She paid the men for the work they did in the shanty by the lake.
figures 3 If you call after 12:30 on Monday, you can reach her at 168-5974.

gwam	1'	1	2	3	4	5	6	7	8	9	10	11	12	13

1. Two 1' writings on each ¶ of 93D, above; find *gwam* on each writing.

2. Two 3' writings on ¶s 1-2 combined; try to equal your best 1' rate in Step 1.

3. A 5' writing on ¶s 1-2 combined; find *gwam*; find errors.

4. Set a left tab at 1.5", a right tab at 3.5", and a decimal tab at 4.5".
5. Key the first 3 lines using these tab settings.
6. Reset tabs: left tab at 2", right tab at 5", decimal tab at 6".
7. Key the last 3 lines, using the Step 6 tab settings.

Left tab at 1.5"	Right tab at 3.5"	Decimal tab at 4.5"
Mary Hale	45,789	1345.9076
Susan Huff	5,632	1.09
Jim Rust	45	23.07689

Left tab at 2"	Right tab at 5"	Decimal tab at 6"
Gwen Russell	9,010	.056
Brit Trent	143,978	243.1
John Oravetz	2,587	1.1

ACTIVITY 3:

Paragraph and Hanging Indent

1. Read the copy at right.
2. Learn how to key indented items using your wp software.
3. Key the ¶ at the right below three times SS: first without indention; then indented; finally, hanging indented.

Use the **Paragraph Indent** feature to move a complete paragraph one tab position to the right. When the Paragraph Indent feature is used, your text will wrap around to this tab position, instead of to the left margin. Use the **Hanging Indent** feature to move all but the first line of a paragraph one tab stop to the right. The first line begins at the left margin, but all other lines in the paragraph wrap around to the tab position.

Blocked (Unindented Text)
> This example shows text that is not indented from the left margin. All lines begin at the left margin.
> Xxxxxxxxxxxxxxxxxxxxxxxxxxxxxxxxxxxxxxxxxxxxx xxxxxxxxxxxxxxxxxxxxxxxxxxxxxxxxxxxx.

Indented Text (Paragraph Indent)
> This example shows text that is indented from the left margin. Notice that all lines begin at the indention point. Xxxxxxxxxxx xxxxxxxxxxxxxxxxxxxxxxxxxxxxxx.

Hanging-Indented Text
> This example shows hanging indent. Notice that the first line begins at the left margin but the remaining lines begin at the indention point. Xxxxxxxxxxxxxx xxxxxxx.

This paragraph is the one you are to key three times. The first time, key it without indenting (1" SMs and SS). The second time you key it, indent all lines so that they begin evenly at the first (default) tab setting. The third time you key the paragraph, use hanging indent so that the first line begins at the left margin and all others begin at the first (default) tab setting.

Improve Keyboarding Skills

LESSON 93

Keyboarding Techniques/Language Skills

Objectives:
1. To improve and assess keyboarding techniques.
2. To improve and assess keyboarding speed and accuracy.
3. To improve language skills.

93A • 5
Conditioning Practice

each line twice; then 1'
writings on line 2

alphabet	1	Major Peiffer realized very quickly that she had won the big box.
speed	2	A problem for the ensign was to focus on the rigor of the ritual.
figures	3	Figures 18, 27, and 35 present the data for 1986, 1990, and 1994.

gwam 1' | 1 | 2 | 3 | 4 | 5 | 6 | 7 | 8 | 9 | 10 | 11 | 12 | 13 |

L ANGUAGE SKILLS

93B • 10
Semicolon

Follow the Learn/Apply
procedure in 76C, p. 184.

> Use a semicolon to separate two or more independent clauses in a compound sentence when the conjunction is omitted.

Learn	1.	Mr. Harris is a fantastic teacher; he really enjoys his job.
Apply	2.	His dad is a professor he received his degree from Harvard.
Apply	3.	Sally is majoring in economics Mary is majoring in history.

> Use a semicolon to separate independent clauses when they are joined by a conjunctive adverb (*however*, *therefore*, *consequently*, etc.).

Learn	4.	A $500 rebate is available; consequently, they decided to buy now.
Apply	5.	I live in St. Paul however, I work in Minneapolis.
Apply	6.	Jan has to work on Friday therefore, we will change the date.

S KILL BUILDING

93C • 10
Awkward Reaches

Key each line twice SS;
DS between 2-line groups;
then 1' writings on lines 2,
4, and 6.

Adjacent keys	1	suit cure spot sale foil other prior worthy fields opened quickly
	2	Bidding on truck tires will suit the clerk's priority quite well.
Direct reaches	3	race cent fund worthy music union checks fifty zebra great length
	4	Many loans in my bright gray manual depend on large mutual funds.
One-hand words	5	upon sage yolk refer union vases zebra wages tested uphill veered
	6	Ted's greatest races in regatta races were based on a great crew.

gwam 1' | 1 | 2 | 3 | 4 | 5 | 6 | 7 | 8 | 9 | 10 | 11 | 12 | 13 |

ACTIVITY 4:

Hard Page Break

1. Read the copy at right.
2. Learn how to insert and delete a hard page break.
3. Key the ¶s at the right DS, inserting a hard page break at the end of each ¶, except the last ¶.
4. Use View to verify that you have four pages. If you do not, use Reveal Code or View to check that you inserted hard page breaks after each ¶.
5. Save the four-page document (WP2ACT4) or leave it open for use in the next activity.

Word processing software has two types of page breaks: **soft** and **hard**. Both a soft and hard page break signal the end of a page and the beginning of a new page. The software inserts a soft page break automatically when the current page is full. You insert hard page breaks manually when you want a new page to begin before the current one is full. When a hard page break is inserted, the wp software adjusts any following soft page breaks so that those pages will be full before a new one is started. Hard page breaks do not move unless you move them. If you want to change the location of a hard page break, you can either delete it and let the wp software insert soft page breaks at appropriate places, or insert a new page break(s) where you want.

Send the membership roster to each student in the sixth, seventh, and eighth grades. Direct students to return the roster with their dues within 15 days.

Collect the candy sale money from the members in Homerooms 101, 102, 105, and 203. Deposit the money in the Club's savings account.

Invite all teachers to the Club's annual open house in the main auditorium on Friday evening at 7:30 and Saturday morning at 9:30.

Send thank-you notes to the local business leaders who donated food and clothing for the Club's annual drive for needy children in the school district.

ACTIVITY 5:

Numbering Pages

1. Read the copy at right.
2. Learn how to number (and suppress page numbers) with your wp software.
3. Retrieve the document created in Activity 4.
4. Number all four pages with the page number in the upper-right corner (flush right), without the word "Page."
5. Suppress the number on page 1.
6. Use View to verify that the page numbers have been added (pages 2-4) or suppressed (page 1).

Use **Page Numbering** to select the type of page numbers you want and to place them in specific locations on the printed page. Most wp software permits the use of text with the number (such as *Page 2*) and allows you to select the kind of number or letter (Arabic numerals—1, 2, 3, etc.; lowercase Roman numerals—i, ii, iii, etc.; uppercase Roman numerals—I, II, III, etc.; uppercase letters—A, B, C, etc; or lowercase letters–a, b, c, etc.). You can usually place numbers at the top or bottom of the page aligned at the left margin, center, or right margin. Often you will need to keep a number from printing on a page (such as the first page of a school report). The feature that keeps a page number from printing (or appearing in view) is called **Suppress** or **Hide**.

Page Numbering Positions

Activity 4:

1. Read the ¶s at the right.
2. Pick an issue (one of those given or some other about which you have great concern).
3. Key a ¶ in which you identify the issue and indicate why it is of major concern to you.
4. Key another ¶ in which you indicate what, how, and by whom you believe something can and should be done to reduce or eliminate the problem.

Compose (think) as you key

A recent newspaper article reveals what is on the minds of the members of at least one high school journalism class. Their concerns and some proposed solutions were conveyed in Letters to the Editor of a national newspaper.

The letters highlighted the following concerns: teenage mischief and violence; teen motherhood and fatherhood; blame-placing instead of self-responsibility; guns, knives, and drugs in the schools and on the streets; media preoccupation with sex, violence, crime, and bizarre behavior.

In terms of teenage behavior, solutions included: more athletics; more and better part-time jobs; curfews; more money for the schools; more school- and community-sponsored free-time activities for teenagers; more stringent penalties for those who violate rules and laws; required counseling programs for parents whose sons/daughters are repeated violators.

ACTIVITY 6:

Speller

1. Read the copy at right.
2. Learn to use your wp software's Speller.
3. Open TWP2-6.
4. Use the Speller to identify words spelled incorrectly and words not in your speller's dictionary. Correct all errors detected by editing or selecting a replacement offered by the Speller.
5. Proofread after Speller is used to verify accuracy of copy. Correct any errors detected.

Use the **Speller** to check words, documents, or parts of documents for misspellings. A Speller checks a document by comparing each word in the document to words in its dictionary(ies). If the Speller finds a word in your document that is not identical to one in its dictionary(ies), the word is displayed in a dialog box. Usually the Speller lists words it "believes" are likely corrections (replacements) for the displayed word. When a word is displayed, you must make a selection:

1. Retain the spelling of the word as it is displayed in the dialog box and add it to the Speller's dictionary.
2. Replace a misspelled word that is displayed with a correctly spelled word offered by the Speller.
3. Replace a misspelled word that is displayed by editing it if the Speller does not list the correctly spelled replacement.

Spellers often use similar procedures for checking repeated words and/or irregular capitalization.

> **Note:** The copy in TWP2-6 contains 11 errors. Can the Speller find all of them? Can you?

ACTIVITY 7:

Apply What You Have Learned

Key the information at the right as shown DS.

Harvey Bubb-Clark	Associate Professor of History
Mary Deerfield	Professor of Education
Jose Emanuel	Assistant Professor of Computer Science
Maria Spanola	Professor of Quantitative Science

ACTIVITY 8:

Apply What You Have Learned

1. Set LM at 2"; clear tabs.
2. Set a left tab at 3.5", a right tab at 4.5", and a decimal tab at 6".
3. Key the text at right DS, striking **Tab** or **Enter** as shown to move to the next column.
4. Reset LM at 1"; clear tabs.
5. Set a left tab at 2.25", a right tab at 3.25", and a decimal tab at 4.75".
6. Rekey the columns.

Hydrogen	(Tab)	H	(Tab)	1	(Tab)	1.008	(Enter)
Helium	(Tab)	He	(Tab)	2	(Tab)	4.003	(Enter)
Titanium		Ti		22		47.9	
Silver		Ag		47		107.87	
Lead		Pb		82		207.2	
Radium		Ra		88		226.03	
Uranium		U		92		238.03	

Language & Writing Skills 10

Activity 1:

1. Study the spelling/ definitions of the words in the color block at the right.
2. Key the **Learn** line in the first set of sentences.
3. Key the **Apply** lines, choosing the right words to complete each sentence correctly.
4. Key the second set of lines in the same way.
5. Check work; rekey lines containing word-choice errors.

Choose the right word

> **lie** (n) an untrue or inaccurate statement; (vb) to rest or recline
> **lye** (n) a strong alkaline solution
>
> **adapt** (vb) to make fit; adjust
> **adept** (adj) thoroughly proficient; expert

Learn 1 Jeff told a lie about how the lye damaged the new carpet.
Apply 2 Sally told one (lie/lye) after another to protect herself.
Apply 3 I knew not to (lie/lye) down near the drum of (lie/lye).

Learn 4 Once he was able to adapt the form, he was adept with it.
Apply 5 Yoko will (adapt/adept) the ad to accommodate your concern.
Apply 6 Juan was quite (adapt/adept) at using integrated software.

Activity 2:

As you key the sentences shown at the right, choose the word in parentheses that correctly completes the sentence. Then, check your work and rekey any sentence that contains a noun/ verb agreement error.

Proofread & correct   Subject/Predicate agreement

1 Most of the workers (was/were) present for the presentation.
2 I (doesn't/don't) know just when I'll finish the long report.
3 If they (doesn't/don't) arrive by 8:15, begin without them.
4 The basis for their comments (elude/eludes) me.
5 It (doesn't/don't) matter to me who takes the lead role.
6 Marilyn (doesn't/don't) know whether she can attend the party.
7 Many of us (are/is) going to vote for Janet for president.
8 (Doesn't/Don't) he realize that a raise now is not possible?
9 The listed criteria (aren't/isn't) sufficient for this job.
10 (Wasn't/Weren't) you aware that the play began at 8 p.m.?

Activity 3:

As you key the sentences shown at the right, insert commas as needed to complete each sentence correctly. Then check your work and rekey any sentence that contains an error in comma usage.

Proofread & correct   Punctuation (Comma)

1 When you get to State Street make a right turn at the light.
2 She will ask Ken you and me to serve on the planning committee.
3 They moved to Las Cruces New Mexico on September 15 1997.
4 Elden be sure to turn off all equipment before you leave.
5 Ms. Rogers said "Keep the cursor moving steadily."
6 Winona who is our class treasurer couldn't attend the meeting.
7 By the middle of 1995 we had 273 employees; in 1997 318.
8 The probability is that only 1 in 280000 have the same DNA.
9 Dr. Woodburn has a pleasant strong personality.
10 The choir director Elena Spitz is planning a special program.

ACTIVITY 9:

Apply What You Have Learned

1. Using Paragraph Indent, key the text at the right. (It represents a long quotation in a report.)

2. Using Hanging Indent, key the (encyclopedia) reference.

3. Use Speller; then proofread for additional errors.

Literature has two main divisions: fiction and nonfiction. *Fiction* is writing that an author creates from imagination. The author may include facts about real persons or events, but combines these facts with imaginary situations. Most fiction is narrative writing, such as novels and short stories. Fiction also includes drama and poetry. *Nonfiction* is factual writing about real-life situations. The chief forms of nonfiction include the essay, history, biography, autobiography, and diary.

"Literature." *The World Book Encyclopedia.* Vol. 12. Chicago: Field Enterprises Educational Corporation, 1993.

ACTIVITY 10:

Apply What You Have Learned

1. Key each test essay question at the right at the top of a separate page SS.

2. Number all pages with "Page" preceding the number. Number page 1 at bottom center; all others at top right.

3. Use Speller to detect errors, then proofread.

4. Use View to verify that there are four pages.

Explain why people read literature; then explain why you do or do not enjoy reading literature.

Most every literary work includes four major elements: (1) characters; (2) plot; (3) theme, or statement; and (4) style. Briefly describe at least three of the elements.

Writers may use four kinds of discourse to tell readers what they want them to know: (1) exposition, (2) argument, (3) description, and (4) narration. Define each of the four discourses.

Essays, histories, biographies, autobiographies, and diaries are forms of nonfictional writing. Define each of the forms.

ACTIVITY 11:

Review Centering

1. Center the lines at right vertically and horizontally. Use DS.

2. Use Speller and View to check your work before proofreading.

INFORMATIONAL BOOKS/GEOGRAPHY

Where in the World Do You Live?--Al Hine and John Alcorn

The Globe for the Space Age--Carl S. Hirsch

The Ashanti of Ghana--Sonia Bleeker

My Village in Brazil--Sonia and Tim Gidal

All About the Arctic and the Antarctic--Armstrong Sperry

This Is Hong Kong--Miroslav Sasek

ACTIVITY 12:

Review Move and Copy

1. Set a right tab at 4" and 5" and a left tab at 6". Key the roster at right DS.

2. Select the words *Defensive Back*, including the space before them.

3. Copy the words on each remaining line of the roster.

4. Using Move, arrange the lines in alphabetical order by players' last names.

Brandon James	(Tab)	175	(Tab)	22	(Tab)	Defensive Back	(Enter)
Bobby Lake	(Tab)	165	(Tab)	16	(Tab)		(Enter)
Harry Schmidt		155		37			
Larry Schloat		135		25			
Jerry Packard		140		26			

countries in Asia, Latin America, and **1032**
Eastern Europe to unclog bottlenecks in **1040**
transportation and power supplies. But by **1048**
installing optical fiber, digital switches, and **1058**
the latest wireless transmission systems, **1066**
urban centers and industrial zones from **1074**
Beijing to Budapest are stepping into the **1083**
Information Age. Videoconferencing, elec- **1091**
tronic data interchange, and digital **1098**
mobile-phone services already are reaching **1107**
most of Asia and parts of Eastern Europe. **1116**

All of these developing regions see **1123**
advanced communications as a way to **1130**
leapfrog stages of economic development. **1138**

Summary **1140**

The world continues to become more glo- **1148**
balized. The trend will continue because of **1157**
three main factors: new and improved trade **1166**
agreements, rapid growth rates of developing **1175**
countries' economies, and technological ad- **1183**
vances. All of these factors foster globalization. **1193**

ENDNOTES **1195**

[1]Richard G. Harris, "Globalization, Trade, **1204**
and Income," Canadian Journal of Economics, **1213**
November 1993, p. 755. **1217**

[2]Harris, p. 763. **1221**

[3]Encyclopedia Americana, Vol. 26 **1228**
(Danbury, CT: Grolier Incorporated, 1993), **1237**
p. 915. **1238**

[4]Louis S. Richman, "Dangerous Times for **1246**
Trade Treaties," Fortune, September 20, 1993, **1256**
p. 14. **1257**

[5]"Fact Sheet: European Community," Vol. **1265**
4, No. 7, Washington, DC: U.S. Department **1274**
of State Dispatch, February 15, 1994, p. 89. **1284**

[6]Mario Bognanno and Kathryn J. Ready, **1291**
eds., North American Free Trade Agreement **1300**
(Westport, CT: Quorum Books, 1993), p. xiii. **1309**

[7]Rahul Jacob, "The Big Rise," Fortune, **1317**
May 30, 1994, pp. 74-75. **1321**

[8]Pete Engardio, "Third World Leapfrog," **1330**
Business Week, May 18, 1994, p. 47. **1338**

wp activity:
Before printing the report, use the Search to Replace feature to replace the word *agreements* with the word **accords** in the GLOBALIZATION report.

92D • 10
Topic Outline

1. Review the information at the right.
2. Format and key the outline.

Note: If you prefer less space after periods, set tabs instead of using default tabs. Use the hanging indent style for items that run longer than one line.

See pp. A21-A23 for additional R & E report activities.

SPACING TOPIC OUTLINES QS

←1st Tab ←2d Tab ←3d Tab

I. VERTICAL SPACING DS
   A. Title of Outline
      1. Two-inch top margin
      2. Followed by three blank line spaces (QS)
   B. Major Headings
      1. First major heading preceded by a QS; all others preceded by one blank line space (DS)
      2. All major headings followed by a DS
      3. All subheadings single-spaced (SS) DS

II. HORIZONTAL SPACING DS
   A. Title of Outline Centered over the Line of Writing
   B. Major Headings and Subheadings
      1. Identifying Roman numerals aligned at one-inch left margin (periods aligned), followed by a tab
      2. Identifying letters and numbers for each subsequent level of subheading aligned below the first word of the preceding heading, followed by a tab

Learn Unbound Report Format

Format Guides: Unbound Reports

Page 1

Page 2

Note: If you do *not* have an Automatic Centering feature, use the back-space-from-center (manual) method to center report headings. (See p. RG19.)

Short reports are often prepared without covers or binders. If they consist of more than one page, the pages are usually fastened together in the upper left corner by a staple or paper clip. Such reports are called **unbound reports**.

Standard Margins

Unbound reports have standard margins.

First page:	
Side margins:	defaults (or 1")
Top margin:	default + 6 hard returns (or 2"–line 13)
Bottom margin:	at least 1" (6 lines)
Page number:	often not used
Second page and subsequent pages:	
Side margins:	defaults (or 1")
Top margin:	default (or 6 hard returns–line 7)
Bottom margin:	at least 1" (6 lines)
Page number:	top right (at default top and right margins; or 1"–line 7)

Internal Spacing of Reports

QS (4 hard returns) between report title and first line of body. DS multiple-line titles.

DS between side headings and following text and between paragraphs. Key paragraphs DS unless otherwise directed.

DS between page number and text on the second and subsequent pages.

Textual (Within Text) Citations

References used to give credit for paraphrased or quoted material are cited in parentheses in the report body. The textual citation method is rapidly replacing the footnote method because it is easier and quicker to use. Textual citations include the name(s) of the author(s), the year of publication, and the page number(s) of the material cited.

Quotation marks are used for direct quotes of up to three lines within text but not for paraphrased material or a long quotation (four lines or more) set apart from text. Key such long quotations SS, block them at paragraph point, and run the lines to the right margin. Use an ellipsis (. . .) to indicate any material omitted from a quotation:

```
The ability to proofread accu-
rately is one of the most im-
portant skills for . . . daily
activities that involve working
with written communication.
(Jones and Kane, 1990, iii)
```

Reference Lists

All references cited in a report are listed alphabetically by author surnames at the end of a report (often on a separate page) under the heading REFERENCES (or BIBLIOGRAPHY or WORKS CITED). QS between the heading and the first reference.

Use the same margins as for the first page of the report, but key a page number at the default top and side margins (on line 7 at 1" right margin).

SS each reference; DS between references. Begin first line of each reference at left margin; indent other lines to paragraph point.

If the reference list appears on the last page of the report body, QS between the last line of text and REFERENCES.

regulations and tariffs were often the outcome, 263
leading to the tariff wars of the 1930s. As a 272
result: 274

Nations have found it convenient . . . to 282
agree to rules that limit their own freedom 291
of action in trade matters, and generally 299
to work toward removal of artificial and 308
often arbitrary barriers to trade.[3] 315

Many trade agreements exist in the world 323
today. Three of those agreements (General 332
Agreement on Tariffs and Trade [GATT], the 340
European Community, and the North American 349
Free Trade Agreement [NAFTA]) have had or will 358
have a significant impact on the United States. 368

GATT. The first trade agreement of major 377
significance was the General Agreement on 385
Tariffs and Trade. GATT was aimed at lower- 394
ing tariff barriers among its members. The 403
success of the organization is evidenced by its 412
membership. Originally signed by 23 countries 422
in 1947, the number of participating countries 431
continues to grow. 435

The Uruguay Round of GATT is the 442
most ambitious trade agreement ever at- 450
tempted. Some 108 nations would lower 457
tariff and other barriers on textiles and 466
agriculture goods; protect one another's 474
intellectual property; and open their bor- 482
ders to banks, insurance companies, and 490
purveyors of other services.[4] 497

The European Community. The European 504
Community is another example of how trade 513
agreements impact the production, distribu- 521
tion, and marketing of goods and services. The 531
12 member nations of the European Commu- 539
nity have dismantled the internal borders of its 549
members. 551

Dismantling the borders, however, was 558
only the first step toward an even greater pur- 568
pose--the peaceful union of European countries. 578
This first step was accomplished by the Paris 587
and Rome treaties, which established the Euro- 596
pean Community and consequently removed 604
the economic barriers. The treaties called for 614
members to establish a common market; a com- 622
mon customs tariff; and common economic, 631
agricultural, transport, and nuclear policies.[5] 640

NAFTA. A trade agreement that will have 649
a significant impact on the way business is 658

conducted in the United States is the North 666
American Free Trade Agreement. This trade 675
agreement involves Canada, the United States, 684
and Mexico. Proponents of NAFTA claim that 693
the accord will not only increase trade through- 703
out the Americas, but it will also moderate 711
product prices and create jobs in all three of 721
the countries.[6] 724

Over the years a number of trade agree- 732
ments have been enacted that promote 739
trade. The result of all of these agreements 749
has been an enhanced quality of life because of 758
the increased access to goods and services pro- 768
duced in other countries. 773

Growth in Developing Countries' Economies 782

The growth in developing countries' 789
economies is another major reason for 796
globalization. According to Jacob, the global 806
surge means more consumers who need goods 814
and services. These needs appear because of 823
the increase in per capita incomes of the de- 832
veloping countries. 836

According to the U.S. Department of 844
Commerce, the world's ten biggest emerging 852
markets include: 856

* Argentina   * Mexico 860
* Brazil   * Poland 864
* China   * South Africa 868
* India   * South Korea 873
* Indonesia   * Turkey 877

Of these emerging markets, the most dra- 885
matic increase is in the East Asian countries. 894
Estimated per capita incomes rose at an annual 904
rate of 6.5 percent from 1983 to 1993. In China 914
alone, incomes grew 8.5 percent annually.[7] 922

Changes in Technologies 927

Recent technological developments have 935
also contributed to globalization. Because of 945
these developments, the world is a smaller 953
place; communication is almost instant to 962
many parts of the world. The extent of the 970
technological developments can be sensed in 979
Engardio's comments:[8] 984

Places that until recently were incom- 991
municado are rapidly acquiring state-of- 999
the-art telecommunications that will let 1008
them foster both internal and foreign in- 1015
vestment. It may take a decade for many 1024

(continued on next page)

Title   ELECTRONIC KEYBOARDING APPLICATIONS

Report
body   Learning to key is of little value unless one applies it in
preparing a useful document--a letter, a report, and so on. Three
basic kinds of software are available to assist those with keying
skill in applying that skill electronically. DS

Side
heading   Word Processing Software DS

          Word processing software is specifically designed to assist in
the document preparation needs of individuals or businesses. Word
processing software permits the user to "create, edit, format,
Textual
citation   store, and print documents." (Fulton and Hanks, 1996, 152) The
software can be used to process a wide variety of documents such as
memos, letters, reports, and tables.

          This software has special features such as automatic center-
1" LM   ing and wordwrap that reduce time and effort. It also permits   1" RM
easy error correction, format and sequence changes, and insertion
of variables "on screen" before a copy is printed. These features
increase efficiency by eliminating document rekeying. DS

Side
heading   Database Software DS

          A database is any collection of related items stored in com-
puter memory. The data in a database may be about club members,
employee payroll, company sales, and so on. Database software
allows the user to enter data, arrange it, retrieve and change it,
or select certain data (such as an address) for use in documents.
Textual
citation   (Tilton, et al, 1996, 112-113)

At least 1"

Unbound Report with Textual Citations

(continued on next page)

92B • 10
Comma (continued)

Follow the Learn/Apply procedure in 76C on p. 184.

		Use a comma to separate the day from the year and the city from the state.
Learn	1.	On November 19, 1863, Lincoln delivered the Gettysburg Address.
Learn	2.	I attended the "Stadium of Fire" fireworks display in Provo, Utah.
Apply	3.	The next meeting was scheduled for January 3 1995 in Detroit Michigan.
Apply	4.	One of the Federal Reserve banks is located in Minneapolis Minnesota.

Use a comma to separate two or more parallel adjectives (adjectives that could be separated by the word **and** instead of a comma).

Learn	5.	The rude, discourteous fan was told to leave the game.
Learn	6.	Hank Aaron autographed the small brown bat. (no comma needed)
Apply	7.	Mary bought a small oval mirror for her room.
Apply	8.	Ms. Marichal was a dependable skilled manager for our firm.

Use a comma to separate (a) unrelated groups of figures that occur together and (b) whole numbers into groups of three digits each. (**Note**: Policy, year, page, room, telephone, and most serial numbers are keyed without commas.)

Learn	9.	By the end of 1995, 2,500 troops were stationed here.
Learn	10.	The telephone number for Room 1828 is 137-2932.
Apply	11.	The serial number on the computer in Room 1215 is 28B6389.
Apply	12.	During the summer of 1995 285670 people attended the play.

92C • 25
Bound Report

Complete the report (below and on pp. 224 and 225) begun in 91D.

Document 1
Format and key the copy as a bound report.

Document 2
Prepare an ENDNOTES page on a separate sheet. Supply page number.

Document 3
Prepare a title page; review format guides, p. 212.

GLOBALIZATION

Today, more than ever before, the term globalization is being used. According to Harris,[1] the term is being used in a variety of contexts. In a very broad context, media use it almost daily to refer to a wide variety of political, sociological, environmental, and economic trends.

The business world, however, uses this term in a much narrower context to refer to the production, distribution, and marketing of goods and services at an international level. Everyone is impacted by the continued increase of globalization in a variety of ways. The types of food we eat, the kinds of clothes we wear, the variety of technologies that we utilize, the modes of transportation that are available to us, and the types of jobs we pursue are directly linked to "globalization." Globalization is changing the world we live in.

Causes of Globalization

Harris[2] indicates that there are three main factors contributing to globalization. These factors include:

* The reduction in trade and investment barriers in the post-World War II period.

* The rapid growth and increase in the size of developing countries' economies.

* Changes in technologies.

Trade Agreements

Originally, each nation established its own rules governing foreign trade. Unfair

(continued on next page)

words:
3, 11, 20, 29, 38, 47, 57, 60, 68, 77, 86, 95, 104, 114, 124, 133, 143, 152, 161, 168, 173, 182, 191, 194, 202, 211, 220, 227, 233, 236, 244, 253

Page number · 2
DS

Side heading · · · · <u>Spreadsheet Software</u>

      A spreadsheet is an electronic worksheet made up of columns and rows of data. Spreadsheet software allows the user to "create, calculate, edit, retrieve, modify, and print graphs, charts, reports, and spreadsheets" necessary for current business operations

Textual citation · · · · and in planning for the future. (Fulton and Hanks, 1996, 156)

      Employment personnel look favorably upon job applicants who

(1" LM)   are familiar with these kinds of software and how they are used.   (1" RM)

QS (4 SS; 2 DS)

REFERENCES
QS

List of references · · · · Fulton, Patsy, J., and Joanna D. Hanks. <u>Procedures for the Office Professional</u>. 3d ed. Cincinnati: South-Western Publishing Co., 1996.
DS
Tilton, Rita S., et al. <u>The Electronic Office: Procedures & Administration</u>. 11th ed. Cincinnati: South-Western Publishing Co., 1996.

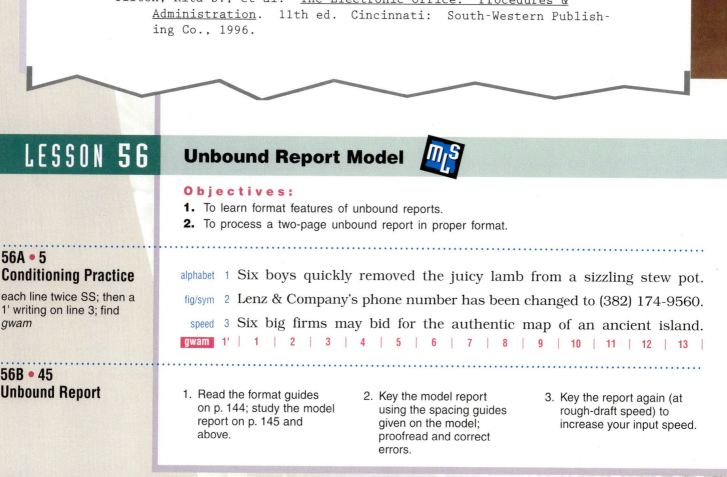

LESSON 56 — Unbound Report Model

Objectives:
1. To learn format features of unbound reports.
2. To process a two-page unbound report in proper format.

56A • 5
Conditioning Practice

each line twice SS; then a 1' writing on line 3; find *gwam*

alphabet 1 Six boys quickly removed the juicy lamb from a sizzling stew pot.

fig/sym 2 Lenz & Company's phone number has been changed to (382) 174-9560.

speed 3 Six big firms may bid for the authentic map of an ancient island.

gwam 1' | 1 | 2 | 3 | 4 | 5 | 6 | 7 | 8 | 9 | 10 | 11 | 12 | 13 |

56B • 45
Unbound Report

1. Read the format guides on p. 144; study the model report on p. 145 and above.

2. Key the model report using the spacing guides given on the model; proofread and correct errors.

3. Key the report again (at rough-draft speed) to increase your input speed.

91C • 10
Comma (continued)

Follow the Learn/Apply procedure in 76C on p. 184.

Use a comma before and after word(s) in apposition.

Learn   1. Andrea, the assistant manager, will chair the next meeting.
Apply   2. Greg Mathews a pitcher for the Braves will sign autographs.
Apply   3. The personnel director Marge Wilson will be the presenter.

Use a comma to set off words of direct address.

Learn   4. I believe, Tom, that you should fly to San Francisco.
Apply   5. Finish this assignment Mary before you start on the next one.
Apply   6. Please call me Erika if I can be of further assistance.

Use a comma to set off nonrestrictive clauses (not necessary to the meaning of the sentence); however, do not use commas to set off restrictive clauses (necessary to the meaning of the sentence).

Learn   7. The manuscript, which I prepared, needs to be revised.
Learn   8. The manuscript that presents banking alternatives is complete.
Apply   9. The movie which won top awards dealt with human rights.
Apply   10. The student who scores highest on the exam will win the award.

F ORMATTING

91D • 25
Report Formatting

Begin formatting and keying the report (92C) on pp. 223-225.

You will start keying the report for 91D and will complete it for 92C.

LESSON 92   Bound Report Project and Topic Outline

O b j e c t i v e s :
1. To format and key a bound report.
2. To improve language skills (commas).

92A • 5
Conditioning Practice

each line twice

alphabet   1 Jack said that Dr. Weiberg plans on requiring five zoology exams.

speed   2 The eight signs are downtown by the chapel by the big city docks.

figures   3 Since 1987, 352 of our guests were from Utah; 460 were from Iowa.

gwam   1' | 1 | 2 | 3 | 4 | 5 | 6 | 7 | 8 | 9 | 10 | 11 | 12 | 13 |

LESSON 57

Unbound Reports

Objectives:
1. To process a play review in unbound report format.
2. To process an unbound report with references.

alphabet 1 Dorn was quickly given a big prize for completing six high jumps.

fig/sym 2 Item #329 was sold by Zahn & Co. for $875.46 (less 10% for cash).

speed 3 A key is to name the right goals and to work for them with vigor.

gwam 1' | 1 | 2 | 3 | 4 | 5 | 6 | 7 | 8 | 9 | 10 | 11 | 12 | 13 |

57B • 45
Unbound Reports

Report 1
Play Review
Process the play review
shown at the right as a DS
unbound report. Correct
errors as you key.

	words
PLAY REVIEW	2
by	3
Denise Jackson	6

Carousel, the Rodgers and Hammerstein classic musical, has been revived in a stunning new production at Omnibus University. — 18 / 31

Students of Rodgers and Hammerstein's work will note the fresh approach from the opening curtain.   Gone is the traditional park scene. In its stead is a cleverly staged "mill" workroom complete with a gigantic loom. The scene rapidly changes to an amusement park with a modern multicolored spinning carousel. Also new in this production are nonspecific ethnic casting, streamlined musical numbers, and updated dialogue. — 44 / 58 / 72 / 85 / 99 / 112 / 116

Carousel is one of the genre's first to use a serious theme. The story recounts the life of Billy Bigelow, a "barker" for the carousel. Billy falls in love with Julie Jordan, a worker at the mill, shunning the advances of the aging carousel owner, Nellie Fowler. Billy then loses his job, marries Julie, and becomes a "worthless bum," in the opinion of Julie's friends. Julie's pregnancy, the turning point in the plot, forces Billy to evaluate his worthiness for parenthood. — 129 / 144 / 158 / 172 / 185 / 200 / 212

Billy decides to turn to thievery rather than to work to get money to support his family. An ill-fated robbery attempt ends with Billy killing himself to avoid being arrested.   The next scene finds Billy in heaven, repentant and determined to return to earth to undo some of the harm he has caused. Upon his surrealistic return, he awkwardly but effectively touches the lives of Julie and his daughter. — 226 / 240 / 254 / 267 / 282 / 294

Critics have called this musical "out of date and out of touch" because of its treatment of women. Most notable is that Billy actually strikes his wife and his daughter. Their reaction to being hit is that "it's only his way of showing affection." In spite of this apparent flaw, Carousel has found new life in this newly staged, artfully performed production. — 307 / 321 / 335 / 349 / 364 / 366

90D • 10
Comma

Follow the Learn/Apply procedure on p. 184.

Use a comma after (a) introductory phrases or clauses and (b) words in a series.

Learn	1.	When you finish keying the report, please give it to Mr. Kent.
Learn	2.	We will play the Mets, Expos, and Cubs in our next home stand.
Apply	3.	If you attend the play, take Mary Jack and Tim with you.
Apply	4.	The last exam covered memos simple tables and unbound reports.

Do not use a comma to separate two items treated as a single unit within a series.

Learn	5.	Her favorite breakfast was bacon and eggs, muffins, and juice.
Apply	6.	My choices are peaches and cream brownies or ice cream.
Apply	7.	Mary ordered ham and eggs toast and milk.

Use a comma before short direct quotations.

Learn	8.	The man asked, "When does Flight 787 depart?"
Apply	9.	Mrs. Ramirez replied "No, the report is not finished."
Apply	10.	Dr. Feit said "Please make an appointment for next week."

LESSON 91

Bound Report Project

Objectives:
1. To format and key a bound report.
2. To improve language skills (commas).

91A • 5
Conditioning Practice

each line twice

alphabet	1	The exclusive photo of a mosque by Dru Jenkins was quite amazing.
speed	2	The official goal of the spa downtown is to get my body in shape.
figures	3	Order No. 8479 was dated May 30; it was for 26 pies and 15 cakes.

gwam 1' | 1 | 2 | 3 | 4 | 5 | 6 | 7 | 8 | 9 | 10 | 11 | 12 | 13 |

91B • 10
Editing Text

Open the report keyed for 90C; make the changes outlined at the right to the first ¶ of the report. Change the endnotes and references to include the new reference (below).
Electronics: Key only the portion of the report shown at right and the endnotes and references pages.

[1]Peter D. G. Thomas, Tea Party to Independence (New York: Oxford University Press, 1991), p. 14.
Print all pages.

Americans are taxed in order to raise revenues to finance governmental activities. Taxation has never been popular. ~~Much~~ *(has devoted a great deal of time and energy)* ~~time and energy have been devoted by~~ the legislature trying to devise a system that requires everyone to pay his/her fair share.

The Boston Tea Party (a result of the 1773 Tea Act)[1] was one of the earliest indicators of just how unpopular taxes can be to Americans.

Report 2
Unbound Report

1. Process the report as a DS unbound report. Correct all errors as you key.

2. Then, make the following changes:

   a. Bold the title.

   b. Format the references as a separate page.

   c. If Italic is available, convert book titles in the references list to Italic; delete the underlines.

	words
PROOFREADING AND EDITING	5

Proofreading is the process of finding and marking for correction any mechanical and content errors in a document. Mechanical and content errors include improper capitalization, excessive or inadequate punctuation, faulty number expression, faulty agreement of subjects and verbs, misuse of personal and possessive pronouns, inaccurate facts, and misleading statements.

18
31
46
59
72
79

Editing, by contrast, is the process of checking a document for "wordiness, cliches, hackneyed expressions, logical sequence, avoidance of passive voice, improper spelling and use of words, and other things to make weak writing better." (Amsbary, 1994, 90)

94
108
123
131

Proofreading Alone

135

Usually you will proofread a document by yourself. If you are checking a paper copy, place that copy and the source copy side by side for easy comparison.   Use a card on the source copy to keep you "on line" and use one index finger on the second copy to guide your eyes word by word.   Pronounce the words as words, but read figures, symbols, punctuation marks, and capitals one by one.   Read the copy once for mechanical errors, again for meaning.

148
162
177
191
206
220
226

When you proofread copy on screen, use a card as a line-by-line guide on the source copy and use an index finger to guide the eyes along the lines on the screen.   Read the copy twice: once for mechanical errors, again for meaning. Check all format features.

240
254
268
278

Team Proofreading

282

Team proofreading involves two people: One person reads from the source copy aloud; the other person reads and marks the other copy. This method is especially effective when statistical and technical copy must be checked. (Jones and Kane, 1990, 8)

295
310
325
332

The person who reads the source copy should read each special symbol and punctuation mark individually.   Figures, however, should be read in groups: Read 3891 as thirty-eight ninety-one. Read 2,845 as two-comma-eight-forty-five.   Read the figure 0 (zero) as oh and the decimal point as point. Read .05 as point-oh-five.

345
360
373
388
397

Proofreading is an essential skill for all business workers.   Editing is an essential skill for writers and editors. The person who can do both well will be a highly prized employee.

411
427
434

REFERENCES

436

Amsbary, George S.   Proof It! Cincinnati: South-Western Publishing Co., 1994.

450
452

Jones, Ellis, and David Kane.   Proofreading & Editing Precision. Cincinnati: South-Western Publishing Co., 1990.

465
474

90C • 30
Bound Report

Save Documents 1-3 for later use.

Document 1
Bound Report with Long Quotation and Numbered List

Format and key the copy as a bound report.

Note: Quoted material of four or more lines should be SS and indented 0.5" from the left margin. The right margin for quoted material remains at 1". Double-space above and below the quoted material.

Document 2
Endnotes Page

Using the same margins as for p. 1 of the report, format and key the following endnotes on a separate page (p. 3).

[1]David J. Rachman and Michael H. Mescon, Business Today (New York: Random House, 1987), p. 529.

[2]Greg Anrig, Jr., "Making the Most of 1988's Low Tax Rate," Money, February 1988, pp. 56-57.

Document 3
References Page

Use the information from the endnotes page to key a REFERENCES page (p. 4). See examples of book and article references on p. 153. Follow these examples to change endnotes into references.

---

	words
TAXES	1

Americans are taxed in order to raise revenues to finance governmental activities. Taxation has never been popular. Much time and energy have been devoted by the legislature trying to devise a system that requires everyone to pay his/her fair share. Taxes are generally based on the benefits received and/or on the ability to pay. Two of the most common revenue-raising taxes are the personal income tax and the sales tax. — 13 25 36 49 60 72 84 87

Personal Income Tax — 91

The personal income tax is the tax individuals are required to pay on their earnings. Employers deduct this tax from employees' paychecks. When employees file their income tax returns, they will either receive a refund for any excess that has been paid or they will have to pay the balance due. — 102 114 126 139 151

Personal income taxes have been the Federal Government's largest single source of revenue and a major source of state revenues as well. On the federal level, the personal income tax is a graduated tax, which means the more you make, the higher the percentage of your income you pay in taxes.[1] — 162 173 184 195 206 210

With the Tax Reform Act of 1986, the highest tax an individual will pay is 33 percent. The amount an individual pays changes with each tax reform. In the past, the top tax rate has been as high as 70 percent.[2] — 221 233 245 253

Sales Tax — 255

The sales tax is another tax with which most people are familiar. It is a tax that is added to the retail price of goods and services. Two examples of this particular type of tax are as follows: — 266 278 290 295

1. General Sales Tax. The general sales tax is a tax levied by most states on goods and services. The amount of tax and the specific goods and services that are taxed vary by state. — 306 317 327 332

2. Excise Tax (Selective Sales Tax). The excise tax is a state tax levied against specific items. Examples of items with an excise tax include tobacco, alcoholic beverages, and gasoline. — 343 354 365 370

While the income tax is a tax based on an individual's ability to pay, the general sales tax and the excise tax are based on benefits received. For example, Taxes collected on gasoline are used for highways. Individuals purchasing gasoline are those who benefit from the construction and maintenance of highways. — 384 396 411 424 434

Objectives:

1. To key a book report in unbound report format.
2. To improve skill in keying from rough draft.

58A • 5
Conditioning Practice

each line twice SS; a
1' writing on line 3; find
gwam

alphabet	1	Zelma quickly put on a down jacket and gloves to fix her bicycle.
fig/sym	2	The rug costs $758.14 (with a 20% discount), but I had only $639.
speed	3	She may turn down the foggy lane by the shanty to their big lake.

gwam 1' | 1 | 2 | 3 | 4 | 5 | 6 | 7 | 8 | 9 | 10 | 11 | 12 | 13 |

F ORMATTING

58B • 45
Book Report

1. Review the proofreader's marks shown below.
2. Format/key the book report as a DS unbound report.
3. Key the reference list below the last line of the report body.
4. Then (wp only) make these changes:
   a. Use your own name in the byline.
   b. Italicize name of book in report body and reference list if Italic is available; delete the underlines.
5. If you finish before time is up, key the lines in 59B, p. 150.

∧ insert

— underline

⊂ close up

add space

⋏ insert comma

/ᵃ replace letter

≡ cap

∿ transpose

/ˡᶜ lowercase

∨ insert apostrophe

words

BOOK REVIEW — 2
by — 3
Colin Barker — 6

} DS

Homeland, John Jakes' formidable novel about the final explo- — 18
sive events of the *nineteenth* century, is the first in a series that — 32
will focus attention on a new "Jakes" family, the Crowns. — 43

Multiple ~~Many~~ characters and settings are the norm for Jakes; how- — 55
ever, this story *rivets* ~~focuses~~ primary attention on Paul Crown, a young — 68
german immigrant. Paul leaves behind a Germany of cholera, pov- — 81
erty, and political upheaval only to face problems of equal magni- — 94
tude in america. — 98

Undaunted by a dificult ocean crossing, Paul arrives at Ellis — 111
island penniless but naively optimistic about his future. He makes — 124
his weary way to the opulant home of his uncle, Joe Crown, a well- — 137
established brewer in Chicago. Jakes used the Chicago setting as — 151
a back grop for his "class struggle" motive which is central to — 163
the plot of his story. — 168

Paul's uncle, Joe, and cousin, Joe Jr., are foils in this — 179
class struggle that ultimately fractures the Crown family and — 192
forces Paul to leave his Uncle's home to find work on his own. — 205
The behavior and work ethic of Joe jr. who is born to wealth and — 218
pivilege in America, is juxtaposed with that of imigrant Paul. — 231
Jakes portrays ~~The author pictures~~ Joe Jr. as spoiled and without focus, espe- — 242
cially when compared to Paul's mature approach to life and work. — 255

(continued on next page)

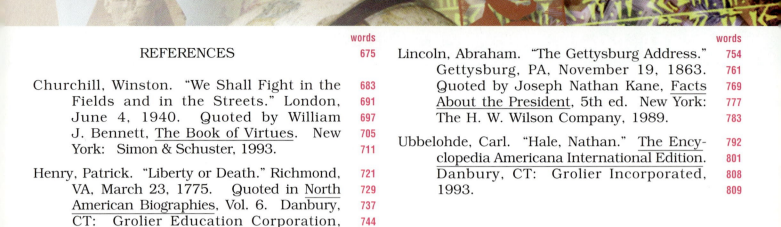

REFERENCES	words 675
Churchill, Winston. "We Shall Fight in the Fields and in the Streets." London, June 4, 1940. Quoted by William J. Bennett, <u>The Book of Virtues</u>. New York: Simon & Schuster, 1993.	683 691 697 705 711
Henry, Patrick. "Liberty or Death." Richmond, VA, March 23, 1775. Quoted in <u>North American Biographies</u>, Vol. 6. Danbury, CT: Grolier Education Corporation, 1994.	721 729 737 744 745

	words
Lincoln, Abraham. "The Gettysburg Address." Gettysburg, PA, November 19, 1863. Quoted by Joseph Nathan Kane, <u>Facts About the President</u>, 5th ed. New York: The H. W. Wilson Company, 1989.	754 761 769 777 783
Ubbelohde, Carl. "Hale, Nathan." <u>The Encyclopedia Americana International Edition</u>. Danbury, CT: Grolier Incorporated, 1993.	792 801 808 809

L ANGUAGE SKILLS

89C • 10
Number Expression

Key the sentences at the right, supplying the correct form of number expression.

1. The store was on the corner of 4th Avenue and 26th Street.
2. Almost 50 of our former students passed the CPA exam.
3. The publisher plans for Volume Two to be finished by June 7.
4. The new baby is twenty-one inches long and weighs 6 lbs. 5 oz.
5. Only 4 of the twenty applicants applying for the job will be hired.
6. Fifteen of the delegates voted for Steele; twenty voted for Myers.
7. The address of the Utah Historical Society is 1 Main Street.
8. Rules 7-10 are presented in Chapter four; Rules 11-13 in Chapter 5.
9. Of Tom's twenty-three hits, nine of them were for extra bases.
10. The office of Baker & Ortiz is located at Eight Brackett Avenue.

LESSON 90   Bound Report with Endnotes

Objectives:

1. To format and key a bound report with long quotation and numbered list.
2. To improve language skills (commas).

90A • 5
Conditioning Practice

set 0.5" SM;
each line twice

alphabet 1 Brzycki Excavating Company quit projecting when they will be finished.

speed 2 Make the panel suspend the pay of their city officials as the penalty.

figures 3 Only 6,398 of the 14,652 students scored above 70 percent on the test.

gwam 1' | 1 | 2 | 3 | 4 | 5 | 6 | 7 | 8 | 9 | 10 | 11 | 12 | 13 | 14 |

S KILL BUILDING

90B • 5
Rough Draft

Take three 1' writings on the ¶, making the marked changes. Try to increase your speed on each writing.

words

Year after year employers express there desire to hire   11
employee who have skills. those with the expertise to organize   28
and deliver ideas in writen or oral form are an asset to their   41
firm; those who do have this ability quickly become aliability.   55

If you plan on enterign the job market in the near future, you   68
want to refine skills so that you wil be an asset not a libility.   85

Jakes utilizes the character of Paul to introduce the reader   267

to the fle~d~gling business of moving pictures. Paul is fa~s~cinated   281

with this new "art form" which involves him in many adventures in-   294

cluding war, a brush with d~n~aeth, and marrying his first love.   307

This first novel of the Crown ser~ita~ei~s~ does a cred~i~ble job in   319

setting the stage for future adventures of Paul Crown and his bud-   332

ding new family.   336

REFERENCE   338

Jakes, John. Homeland. New York: Bantam Books, 1994. *(Paper-*   351

back Edition)   353

LESSON 59

Unbound Report with Listed Items

Objectives:
1. To learn how to format listed items in reports.
2. To improve skill in processing reports.

59A • 5
Conditioning Practice

each line twice SS; a
1' writing on line 3; find
gwam

alphabet	1	Quick, lively jumps of a gray fox will amaze both giddy children.
fig/sym	2	The 164 copies (priced at $18.75) may be shipped on May 29 or 30.
speed	3	Vivian may wish to make an apricot gown for the big civic social.

gwam 1' | 1 | 2 | 3 | 4 | 5 | 6 | 7 | 8 | 9 | 10 | 11 | 12 | 13 |

59B • 10
Skill Building

1. Key each line once SS; DS between 2-line groups.
2. Key a 1' writing on each of lines 2, 4, and 6 for high speed.

space bar	1	of go by at in to am so me if on man buy pan yen can tam men buoy
	2	Any of you can go by the inn for a cool swim in the pool at noon.
word response	3	both dorm they with name pens turn flap mend when girl torn their
	4	I shall make them a big name panel to hang by a door of the hall.
combination response	5	they were them pump lend gave make gear pans jump form were ivory
	6	Six of you may join my trade panel at the big union hall at noon.
double letters	7	will soon meet door took sell week book heed hall cook zoom abbey
	8	Allen said a little more effort from week to week is needed, too.
outside reaches	9	well play game next walk past spot caps toss lost next pans plaza
	10	Lowell gave his old football jersey to a happy young man at camp.
long direct reaches	11	curb must brim gyms fume much cent nice runs myth guns lace lunch
	12	Brenda was under the gun to take a bronze in the county gym meet.

gwam 1' | 1 | 2 | 3 | 4 | 5 | 6 | 7 | 8 | 9 | 10 | 11 | 12 | 13 |

Document 1
Format the copy as a bound report (review p. 211).

Document 2
Prepare a REFERENCES page on a separate sheet (p. 4).

	words
EFFECTIVE COMMUNICATORS	5

Communication is the thread that binds our society together. Effective communicators are able to use the thread (communication skills) to shape the future. To be an effective communicator, one must know how to put words together that communicate thoughts, ideas, and feelings. These thoughts, ideas, and feelings are then expressed in writing or delivered orally. Some individuals are immortalized because of their ability to put words together. A few examples of those who have been immortalized are Patrick Henry, Nathan Hale, Abraham Lincoln, and Winston Churchill. Consider the impact of their messages.

	13
	23
	32
	41
	49
	58
	67
	77
	86
	95
	104
	112
	120
	128

Patrick Henry — 131

Words will move people to action. Patrick Henry's words were a moving force behind one of the sparks that ignited the Revolutionary War in 1775. The impact of that revolution is well known to all Americans. Many Americans are familiar with his speech to the Second Virginia Convention on March 23, 1775. The most familiar part of his speech is "I know not what course others may take; but as for me, give me liberty or give me death!" (North American Biographies, 1994, 92)

	140
	149
	159
	168
	177
	187
	195
	204
	214
	223
	227

Nathan Hale — 230

Words show an individual's commitment and can be very inspirational. Nathan Hale (Ubbelohde, 1993, 710) needed only these 14 words to show his commitment to his cause: "I only regret that I have but one life to lose for my country." These words are committed to memory by many and are still inspiring.

	237
	246
	255
	264
	274
	283
	291

Abraham Lincoln — 294

One of the most famous speeches ever delivered was Lincoln's Gettysburg Address. Kane (1989, 100) refers to the speech as an immortal address. It is debatable as to whether the

	302
	312
	322
	331

opening lines "Four score and seven years ago, our fathers brought forth on this continent a new nation, conceived in liberty, and dedicated to the proposition that all men are created equal" or the closing lines " . . . and that government of the people, by the people, for the people shall not perish from the earth" are most familiar to Americans.

	340
	349
	359
	368
	378
	387
	396
	401

Winston Churchill — 405

Another speech of significant magnitude was delivered by Winston Churchill. (1940, 572) His words not only lifted the spirits of the British but also were motivational to those committed to the Allied cause.

	414
	423
	432
	442
	447

We shall go on to the end, we shall fight in France, we shall fight on the seas and oceans, we shall fight with growing confidence and growing strength in the air, we shall defend our island, whatever the cost may be, we shall fight on the beaches, we shall fight on the landing grounds, we shall fight in the fields and in the streets, we shall fight in the hills; we shall never surrender, and even if, which I do not for a moment believe, this island or a large part of it were subjugated and starving, then our Empire beyond the seas, armed and guarded by the British fleet, would carry on the struggle, until in God's good time, the New World, with all its power and might, steps forth to the rescue and the liberation of the old.

	456
	464
	473
	481
	490
	498
	507
	517
	526
	534
	544
	552
	560
	569
	577
	586
	595

Summary — 597

The power of the written and spoken word can have a significant impact on the lives of those who hear or read it. Developing a skill at using the spoken and written word is important to a person's success. Not everyone can be immortalized by their words, but everyone can have an impact on those with whom they associate by being skilled at using the written and spoken word.

	605
	614
	624
	633
	642
	651
	660
	669
	672

(continued on next page)

1. Process the report in DS unbound format, all errors corrected.

2. Block the listed items on page 2 at ¶ point; let them run to the right margin.

3. After you complete the report, proofread it and make any additional corrections.

4. Place the references on a separate sheet.

5. Then (wp only) make these changes:
   a. Bold the title.
   b. Italicize book and newspaper names in the references list; delete the underlines.

	words
THE VALUE OF WORK EXPERIENCE	6

A summer or part-time job pays more than money. Even though the money earned is important, the work experience gained has a greater long-term value when one applies for a full-time job after graduation from school. Job application documents (the application blank and the personal data sheet) ask you to list jobs you have held and to list as references the names of individuals who supervised your work. (Gieseking and Plawin, 1994, 22)

	18
	31
	46
	60
	75
	90
	94

As one young person was heard to remark, "You can't get a job without experience, and you can't get experience without a job." That dilemma can be overcome, however, by starting work early in life and by accepting simpler jobs that have no minimum age limit and do not require experience.

	108
	122
	137
	152

Jobs Teens Can Do — 156

Begin early at jobs that may not pay especially well but help to establish a working track record: delivering newspapers, babysitting, mowing lawns, assisting with gardening, and the like. Use these work experiences as springboards for such later jobs as sales clerk, gas station attendant, fast-food worker, lifeguard, playground supervisor assistant, and office staff assistant (after you have developed basic office skills). As you progress through these work exploration experiences, try increasingly to get jobs that have some relationship to your career plans. If, for example, you want a career involving frequent contact with people--as in sales--seek part-time and summer work that gives you experience in dealing with people. (Hamel, 1989, 10)

	170
	185
	200
	215
	231
	246
	261
	276
	291
	305
	308

How to Handle Yourself on the Job — 315

Whatever the job you are able to get, the following pointers will help you succeed in getting a good recommendation for the next job you seek.

	330
	344

1. Be punctual. Get to work on time and return from lunch and other breaks promptly.

	357
	362

2. Get along well with others. Do your job well and offer to assist others who may need help. Take direction with a smile instead of a frown.

	376
	390
	391

3. Speak proper English. Teenage jargon is often lost on the adults who are likely to be your supervisors.

	406
	414

4. Dress the part. Observe the unwritten dress code; dress as others on the job do. Always be neat and clean.

	427
	437

REFERENCES	439

Gieseking, Hal, and Paul Plawin. 30 Days to a Good Job. New York: Simon & Schuster, 1994.

	453
	458

Hamel, Ruth. "Making Summer Earnings Work for You." USA Weekend, 2-4 June 1989, 10-11.

	471
	475

Document 2
References Page

Review p. 212. Prepare a REFERENCES page (p. 3).

Neher, William W., and David H. Waite. The Business and Profes- 13
sional Communicator. Needham Heights, MA: Allyn and Bacon, 23
1993. 27

Nixon, Judy C., and Judy F. West. "Listening--The New Com- 38
petency." The Balance Sheet, January/February 1989,27-29. 50

88D • 10
Editing Text

Open the report keyed for 88C. Delete the text following **Ways to Improve Listening**. Replace the text with the two ¶s at the right; prepare a new references page that includes the references in Document 2 and the new reference at the right. Print page 2 and the REFERENCES page.

Ways to Improve Listening

Obstacles to listening can be overcome; However, it does take a conscientious effort on the part of the listener. A good listener will try to maintain eye contact with the speaker and work to avoid tuning the speaker out. Removing as many external distractions as possible is another means for improving listening.

Listening is also improved by directing attention to the message rather than to the speaker's appearance and mannerisms. Focusing on the main points being made by the speaker and taking notes, if appropriate, are ways of directing attention to the message. (Rader and Kurth, 1994, 510)

Rader, M. H., and Linda A. Kurth. Business Communication with Contemporary Issues and Microcomputer Applications. Cincinnati: South-Western Publishing Co., 1994.

LESSON 89

Bound Report

Objectives:
1. To format a bound report.
2. To review number expression.

89A • 5
Conditioning Practice

each line twice

alphabet 1 Judge Bezdorf quickly approved the law for the maximum penalties.

speed 2 Enrique may wish for vigor when he duels with a haughty neighbor.

figures 3 Invoices 639, 640, and 758 were paid on May 12 with Check No. 94.

gwam 1' | 1 | 2 | 3 | 4 | 5 | 6 | 7 | 8 | 9 | 10 | 11 | 12 | 13 |

Objectives:

1. To process an unbound report with listed items.

2. To format a separate references page.

60A • 5
Conditioning Practice

each line twice SS; a
1' writing on line 3; find
gwam

alphabet	1	Jane very quickly called them before swimming a dozen extra laps.
fig/sym	2	Debit her account (#73658) for $290.14 for December 10 purchases.
speed	3	Pepe may go to the shelf for the forms and then hand me the clay.
gwam	1'	1 | 2 | 3 | 4 | 5 | 6 | 7 | 8 | 9 | 10 | 11 | 12 | 13 |

F ORMATTING

60B • 45
Unbound Report with Listed Items and Separate References Page

1. DS the report, at right and on p. 153, as an unbound report, all errors corrected.
2. Block listed items at ¶ point and run them to the right margin.
3. Place the reference list on a separate sheet.

wp note:

You may, if you wish, bold the title and reference list heading. You may also italicize book and periodical titles in the reference list, instead of underlining.

words

EFFECTIVE STUDY   3

Effective learning depends upon good study skills, but "Many   15
students--both traditional and nontraditional--entering college have   29
few, if any, practical study skills." (Huber, 1994, 29) Good study skills   44
do not simply occur; they must first be learned and then applied   57
consistently. Efficient study strategies include a preset time, a desirable   73
place, and a well-designed plan for study.   81

A Time for Study   85

Many of us think we have more to do than we have time to do,   97
and studying gets shortchanged. It is important to prepare a schedule   111
of daily activities that includes time slots for doing the studying you   126
have to do. Within each study slot, write in the specific study activity;   140
for example, "Read Unit 6 in Modern Writing, answer Questions 1-10."   154
Keep the schedule flexible so that it can be modified if you meet your   169
study goals early--or late.   174

A Place to Study   178

Choose the best place to study and use the same time each day.   191
Doing so will help to put you in a study mood when you enter that   204
place. Choose a place that has the fewest distractions: people traffic,   219
conversation, telephone, TV, and outside noises. Usually study is best   233
done alone in the absence of sights and sounds that distract the eye and   248
ear. Force the mind to focus intently on the study task. (Silver, 1992, 26)   263

A Plan for Study   267

Research on the effects of specific study skills on student perfor-   280
mance suggests that the following study tactics help to improve academic   295
performance. (Dansereau, 1985, 39)   302

1. Skim a unit or a chapter, noting headings, topic sentences,   315
key words, and definitions to clue you to what you are going to study.   329

2. As you read the material, convert the headings into questions;   343
then seek answers to those questions as you read.   353

(continued on next page)

Barriers to Listening

Anything that interferes with our ability to listen ~~can be~~ *is*   128

classified as a barrier to listening. Barreirs that obstruct   141

[_____] our ability to listen can be divided into two basic   151

categories--external and internal barriers.   160

Internal Barriers *lc*. Internal barriers are those *barriers* that deal   174

with the mental or psychologcal *i* aspects of listening. The   186

perception of the importance of the message, the emotional   197

state, and the tuning in and out of the speaker by the listener   210

a few are examples of internal barriers.   219

External Barriers *lc*. External barriers are barriers other   230

than those that deal *with* the mental and psychological make up of the   244

listner *e* that tend to keep *#* the listener from devoting *full* attention to   258

what is being said. Telephone interruptions, *uninvited* visitors, noise,   273

and the physical environment are examples of external barriers.   286

Ways To Improve Listening *lc*   291

Barriers to listening can be overcome. However, it does   303
take a sincere effort on the part of the listener. Neher and   315
Waite (1993, 83-84) usggest the following: 324

1. Be aware of the barriers that are especially troublesome for   337
you. Listening difficulties are individualistic. Developing   349
awareness is an important step in overcoming such barriers.   362

2. Listen as though you will have to paraphrase what is being   374
said. Listen for ideas rather than for facts.   384

3. Expect to work at listening. Work at overcoming distrac-   396
tions, such as the speaker's delivery or nonverbal mannerisms.   409

4. Concentrate on summarizing the presentation as you listen.   422
If possible, think of additional supporting material that would   434
fit with the point that the speaker is making. Avoid trying to   447
refute the speaker. Try not to be ~~too~~ turned off by remarks you   459
disagree with.   462

(continued on next page)

wp activity:
Use the Search to Find feature to determine how many times the word *communicating* appears in the report.
   Use the Search to Replace feature to replace the word *barriers* with the word *obstacles*.

3. If you own the book, use color markers to highlight important ideas: headings, topic sentences, special terms, definitions, and supporting facts. Otherwise, make notes of these.

4. After reading the material, review the highlighted items (or your notes that contain them).

5. Using the headings stated as questions, see if you can answer those questions based on your reading.

6. Test yourself to see if you recall definitions of important terms and lists of supporting facts or ideas.

A high correlation exists between good study habits and good grades for courses taken in school.

REFERENCES

Dansereau, D. F. "Learning Strategy Research." Thinking and Learning Skills. Vol. 1. Hillsdale, NJ: Lawrence Erlbaum, 1985.

Huber, Rose. "Teaching Students How to Study." Eastside Weekend, September 1-7, 1994.

Silver, Theodore. Study Smart. New York: Villard Books, 1992.

LESSON 61 · Three-Page Unbound Report

Objectives:
1. To process a multiple-page report.
2. To improve speed/accuracy in processing reports.

61A • 5
Conditioning Practice

each line twice SS; a 1' writing on line 3; find *gwam*

alphabet 1 Buck can relax if he passed the major quiz with a very high mark.

fig/sym 2 You gave us 10% discount on Model #4736-A; 20%, on Model #8295-C.

speed 3 Roz may make a big profit if she owns the title to the lake land.

gwam 1' | 1 | 2 | 3 | 4 | 5 | 6 | 7 | 8 | 9 | 10 | 11 | 12 | 13 |

FORMATTING

61B • 45
Unbound Report

1. Process the report in DS unbound format, all errors corrected.
2. Place the reference list on a separate sheet.

wp note:

You may, if you wish, bold the title and reference list heading. You may also italicize book and periodical titles in the reference list, instead of underlining.

words

ETHICS, MORALS, AND THE LAW

6

The words "ethical," "moral," and "legal" are often misunderstood and misused. The terms are similar in that each refers to a human behavioral code. Human behavior is complex and thus no one term is sufficient to describe it. Ethical, moral, and legal issues also intertwine to create our entire understanding of behavior as it relates to our sense of right and wrong.

20
34
49
64
79
80

To further complicate matters, each civilization and culture (past and present) has its own notion of what is ethical, moral, or legal. Therefore,

94
110

(continued on next page)

LESSON 88 — Unbound Report from Rough Draft

Objectives:
1. To format and key an unbound report with a table.
2. To improve language skills (verbs).

88A • 5
Conditioning Practice

each line twice

alphabet	1	Extensive painting of the gazebo was quickly completed by Jerrod.
speed	2	The rich widow and the maid may make the usual visit to the dock.
figures	3	Train 236 left 40 minutes after the 7:45 departure of Flight 819.

gwam 1' | 1 | 2 | 3 | 4 | 5 | 6 | 7 | 8 | 9 | 10 | 11 | 12 | 13 |

LANGUAGE SKILLS

88B • 8
Verbs

1. Read the guide at the right.
2. Key the Learn sentences below it.
3. Key the Apply sentences supplying the correct verb.

If there is confusion whether a subject is singular or plural, consult a dictionary.

Learn	1.	A few alumni are planning to attend the banquet.
Learn	2.	The criteria for evaluating the projects have been identified.
Apply	3.	An analysis of that type (is, are) very time consuming.
Apply	4.	Parentheses (is, are) used to enclose the textual citation.
Apply	5.	The basis of a democratic state (is, are) liberty. --Aristotle

FORMATTING

88C • 27
Unbound Reports

Document 1
Unbound Report with a Table

Format and key the copy shown at the right as an unbound report. Correct the errors marked on the copy and any you make as you key.

Note: Use the keyline method to determine tab positions for the table.

wp note:

Students completing the **wp activity** on the next page should delay printing the document until the changes outlined in the **wp activity** are made. Save the file for later use.

	words
LISTENING	2
One of the most ~~important~~ critical skills that an individual	12
acquires is the skill of communicating. Studies indicate that	25
a person spends 70 percent to 80 percent of ~~their~~ his/her time communi-	38
cating. Nixon and West (1989, 28) give the following break down for the average individual of ~~the~~ time	58
spent communicating ~~includes (Nixon and West, 1989, 28)~~:	62
DS	
Writing 9%	64
Reading 16%	67
Speaking 30%	69
listening 45%	72
DS	
Since ~~most~~ almost half of the time spent communicating is spent listening,	86
it is important to overcome any obstacles that obstruct our	98
ability to listen and to learn new ways to improve our listening	111
ability.	113

center
Leave 1.5" between columns

(continued on next page)

REFERENCES

Elliott, Carl. "Where Ethics Comes from and What to Do About It." <u>Hastings Center Report</u>, July-August 1992.

Gifis, Steven. <u>Law Dictionary</u>. New York: Barrons, 1991.

Josephson, Michael. "Ethical Dilemmas." <u>New Age Journal</u>, July-August 1989. (Adapted from Bill Moyers' "A World of Ideas." Public Affairs Television, 1989.)

Purple, David E. <u>The Moral and Spiritual Crisis in Education</u>. New York: Bergen and Garvey, 1989.

Note: See p. A17 for R & E activities for this unit.

	words
one cannot arrive at a simple, clear definition of what each term means.	125
The "meaning" of the terms is often dependent upon who is defining	138
them.	139

Ethics
	141

Many people who write about ethics use the term when referring to the most general codes by which humankind lives; that is, those codes of behavior that, for the most part, transcend time, culture, and geography. In simple terms, ethics is the study of people's concept of right and wrong.

- 154
- 167
- 181
- 195
- 199

Therefore, we use the word "ethical" when we are speaking of that general code of right and wrong recognized by enlightened civilizations from the beginning of time. When we ask the question "Was that act or decision ethical?" we are asking if it meets the test of what is accepted as universally <u>right</u>. Writers suggest that we consider such basic concepts as honesty, fairness, and compassion as universal ethical values. (Josephson, 1989, 42)

- 213
- 227
- 241
- 257
- 272
- 285
- 290

Morals
	291

The term "moral" speaks to issues that concern a community of people rather than humankind in general. The study of morals also concerns itself with right and wrong but more directly in terms of specific groups of people. One may consider morals as specific rules of right and wrong based on universal ethical truths.

- 305
- 319
- 334
- 348
- 355

Thus, we use the word "moral" when we refer to behavior that may be acceptable for one society but not for another. Some people consider as moral issues such things as treatment of children, the aged, animals, and the environment along with questions about marriage and other human relationships. (Purple, 1989, 66)

- 368
- 383
- 398
- 411
- 419

Legal
	420

Just as <u>moral</u> can be seen as more specific than <u>ethical</u>, <u>legal</u> is seen as the most specific of the three terms. Laws are codified behaviors for members of a society enacted by a specific lawful authority. (Gifis, 1991) The law may have as its foundation moral rules and ethical truths, but it is closely allied with politics. As a result, it suffers from greater subjectivity than do ethics and morals. Laws differ not only from society to society but also from town to town. What is legal in Los Angeles, for example, may be punishable in Portland. Laws are more temporary than morals or ethics, often changed by simple majority vote or by decree.

- 435
- 449
- 464
- 477
- 493
- 507
- 522
- 535
- 550
- 553

We use the word "legal" when judging an act by the most specific set of local laws that have been codified by local authority. Issues as universal as theft and as specific as jaywalking are subject to local law. (Elliott, 1992, 28-35)

- 567
- 583
- 599
- 601

The terms "ethical," "moral," and "legal" are similar in the sense that each refers to the interpretation of right and wrong. Their differences depend upon how explicit and specific a description we use to interpret a set of behaviors.

- 616
- 630
- 645
- 649

Note: Indent the enumerated items 0.5" to the right of the left margin; let the lines run to the right margin.

Document 2

Use the following information to create a REFERENCES list on a separate page (p. 3).

Bascietto, John. "Ecotoxicity and Ecological Risk Assessment." Environmental Science & Technology. Washington, DC, January 1990.

Talbot, L. M. "Man's Role in Managing the Global Environment." Changing the Global Environment. Boston: Harcourt Brace Jovanovich Publishers, 1989.

---

	words
Since 1955	164

Since 1955, however, our interest in protecting the environment has been kindled by recognition of these environmental problems. Studies of change in the environment have led to efforts to protect it.

Environmental Changes. Changes to the environment have been significant over the past 35 years. Talbot (1989, 21-22) listed these major changes:

1. The human population has almost doubled, from fewer than three billion to more than five billion people.

2. Half the world's tropical forests have been lost.

3. The processes of overgrazing and desertification have greatly increased.

4. Chemical pollution has become pervasive and few species or lands escape its effects.

5. New hazardous wastes, not even mentioned in 1955, now represent a major problem worldwide.

6. Acid rain and carbon dioxide buildup have resulted from increased industrialization throughout the world.

Environmental Protection. As the seriousness of environmental problems has been recognized, governmental agencies and nongovernmental organizations have been established to deal with them. (Talbot, 1989, 22) In 1955 there were only a few nongovernmental environmental organizations; today there are thousands. In 1955 no government had environmental agencies; today virtually all nations have them. The purpose of the agencies is to identify, quantify, and reduce adverse impacts on the environment. (Bascietto, 1990, 14)

A clean environment is a global problem, a problem that is going to take all the inhabitants of the earth to solve. For the Earth to be habitable by future generations, today's generations must take care of it.

words
178
190
202
205
216
229
235
246
256
268
279
283
295
301
313
321
332
343
355
367
379
391
403
416
426
438
449
460
473
487
491

Skill Building

1. Key each line once SS; DS between 2-line groups.

Goal: No pauses between letters and words.

2. Key a 1' writing on each of lines 4, 6, 8, and 10; find *gwam* on each.

3. If time permits, rekey the 3 slowest lines.

space	1	am by an in ham urn buy ran dim any turn many dorm gown plan buoy
bar	2	All the men on the quay may go via bus to the lake towns to work.
shift	3	Jaime and Aida|Rosa or Pablo|Han & Fong, Inc.|the J. P. Spitz Co.
keys	4	Alma and Max left with Rob and Juana on a trip to Padua and Rome.
adjacent	5	as guy are spot were open last part rent bids walk soil suit trim
keys	6	Luis was the last guy to weigh in before stadium practice opened.
long direct	7	my any run sum ice gym nut gum tune much nice many curb vice guns
reaches	8	Wyn broke my record to receive a bronze medal at the county meet.
word	9	foam land corn lent risk town with pans when rock name than eight
response	10	Both of them may wish to make a formal bid for the big auto firm.

gwam 1' | 1 | 2 | 3 | 4 | 5 | 6 | 7 | 8 | 9 | 10 | 11 | 12 | 13 |

Timed Writings

1. Key a 1' writing on each ¶; find *gwam* on each one.

2. Key two 2' writings on ¶s 1-2 combined; find *gwam* on each writing.

3. Key two 3' writings on ¶s 1-2 combined; find *gwam* and count errors on each writing.

4. If time permits, key two 1' guided writings on each ¶: one for speed; one for control (accuracy).

all letters used

gwam 2' 3'

What is a job? In its larger sense, a job is a regular duty, 6 | 4 | 60
role, or function that one performs for pay. Therefore, when you 13 | 8 | 64
apply for and accept a job, you accept responsibility for complet- 19 | 13 | 69
ing a series of specified tasks such as data entry, recordkeeping, 26 | 17 | 73
and word processing. 28 | 19 | 74

What is a career? A career is a broad field in business, pro- 34 | 23 | 78
fession, or public life that permits one to progress in successive 41 | 27 | 83
steps up the job ladder. Whatever the tasks performed, one may 47 | 31 | 87
have a career in law, in health services, in education, or in busi- 54 | 36 | 92
ness, for example. 56 | 37 | 93

It should be very clear that a career may include many jobs, 62 | 41 | 97
each with different ability requirements. Realize, however, that 69 | 46 | 101
many of the jobs leading to increasing success in most careers are 75 | 50 | 106
better done with greater ease by people who have built a high level 82 | 55 | 110
of keying skill. 84 | 56 | 112

gwam 2' | 1 | 2 | 3 | 4 | 5 | 6 |
3' | 1 | 2 | 3 | 4 |

Quarter-Minute Checkpoints				
gwam	1/4'	1/2'	3/4'	1'
24	6	12	18	24
28	7	14	21	28
32	8	16	24	32
36	9	18	27	36
40	10	20	30	40
44	11	22	33	44
48	12	24	36	48
52	13	26	39	52
56	14	28	42	56

Objectives:
1. To format an unbound report with enumerated items.
2. To review capitalization guides.

87A • 5
Conditioning Practice

each line twice SS; then two 1' writings on line 2; find *gwam*; clear screen

alphabet	1	Jay Klugman awarded Bob sixth place for his very high quiz score.
speed	2	The auditor on the panel did not sign a key element of the audit.
fig/sym	3	The checks written on 12/4 ($57.90 and $36.80) were not recorded.

gwam 1' | 1 | 2 | 3 | 4 | 5 | 6 | 7 | 8 | 9 | 10 | 11 | 12 | 13 |

L ANGUAGE SKILLS

87B • 10
Check Capitalization

Key the sentences at the right, supplying the needed capital letters.

1. lake powell and lake mead are both located in arizona.
2. fbla is the abbreviation for future business leaders of america.
3. the largest cities in idaho are boise, pocatello, and idaho falls.
4. our next delta pi epsilon meeting will be held friday, may 2.
5. is the grand canyon national park located in arizona?
6. the green bay packers will play the dallas cowboys on sunday.
7. robert e. lee and ulysses s. grant signed the treaty at appomattox.
8. the grade school is located on tyler; the high school, on cedar.
9. this year thanksgiving will be on thursday, november 24.
10. kim told dr. dean that he had lessons 8 and 9 completed.

F ORMATTING

87C • 35
Unbound Report

Document 1
Report from Rough Draft

1. Review the format guides for reports on pp. 211-212.
2. Format the report in unbound style; use **THE ENVIRONMENT** for the heading of the report.
3. When you finish, use the spell check and proofread your copy.

	words
	heading 2

Our environment is a topic that receives a great deal of — 13

attention. The environment has been the basis of numerous televi- — 27

sion and radio commentaries as well as a multitude of newspaper — 39

and magazine articles. The environment is even the foundation for many — 54

political debates addressing issues and concerns about what — 66

is happening and what will happen to the environment over the — 78

next several years. A look at the past is helpful in — 89

understanding the present concern. — 96

Prior to 1955 — 99

Comparatively speaking, little emphasis was placed on ecology — 112

(the study of the relationship of plants and animals to their environment) — 127

prior to 1955. Air pollution, toxic — 134

waste, marine pollution, pesticides, oil spills, acid rain, etc., — 147

are relatively new problems that are taking their toll on the environment. — 162

(continued on next page)

Language & Writing Skills 7

Activity 1:

1. Study the spelling/ definitions of the words in the color block at right.
2. Key line 1 (the **Learn** line), noting the proper choice of words.
3. Key lines 2-3 (the **Apply** lines), choosing the right words to complete the lines correctly.
4. Key the remaining lines in the same way.
5. Check your work; correct or rekey lines containing word-choice errors.

Choose the right word

vary (vb) change; make different; diverge	**passed** (vb) past tense of *pass*; already occurred; gave an item to someone
very (adj/adv) real; mere; truly; to a high degree	**past** (adv/adj/prep/n) gone or elapsed; time gone by; moved by

Learn   1   Marquis said it is very important that we vary our attack.
Apply   2   The (vary/very) nature of skill is to (vary/very) the response.
Apply   3   As you (vary/very) input, you get (vary/very) different results.

Learn   4   In the past we passed the zoo before we marched past the library.
Apply   5   We filed (passed/past) the desk as we (passed/past) in our tests.
Apply   6   In the (passed/past) month, I (passed/past) up two job offers.

Activity 2:

1. **Lines 1-7:** As you key each line, select the words that correctly complete the sentence.
2. **Lines 8-14:** As you key each line, supply capitalization where needed.
3. **Lines 15-21:** As you key each line, express numbers correctly.

Proofread & correct

1   (Its/It's) up to them to (do due) the work required by the job.
2   She is (to/too/two) small (to/too/two) play on the varsity team.
3   He (passed/past) the ball as the receiver ran (passed/past) me.
4   I (know/no) that team (lead/led) by (to/too/two) touchdowns.
5   More (than/then) an (hour/our) had (passed/past) by (than/then).
6   (Choose/Chose) the right one, since (your/you're) the leader.
7   I was (hear/here) when the boys sang (their/there/they're) song.

8   ms. pardo saw the eiffel tower in paris when she was in france.
9   the senior class had its prom at the skirvin hotel last year.
10   lucia, carlos, and ana comprise this year's prom committee.
11   we had a labor day picnic in hyde park, followed by a ball game.
12   "how often," she asked, "do you watch the boston celtics on TV?"
13   did you write the check to stephen p. kendall, d.d.s.?
14   we took wilshire boulevard to the beverly wilshire hotel today.

15   12 Drama Club members attended the meeting; 4 did not.
16   I took the six thirty a.m. shuttle; he met me at Gate fifty-one.
17   Towne Center is at 1 Oak Street; Sloan Tower, at 6 Kyles Lane.
18   Her article appeared on pages three and four of the last issue.
19   Answer Questions 1-10 on page nine and Questions 1-5 on page 18.
20   Our committee met in Room ten at two p.m. on November twentieth.
21   Mai-li checked the data in Volume two, Section five, page 293.

Activity 3:

1. Study the quotations, considering the relationship between honesty and truth.
2. Compose/key a ¶ to show your understanding of honesty and truth. Describe an incident in which *honesty* and *truth* should prevail but often don't in real life.

Compose (think) as you key

Honesty's the best policy.

--Cervantes

To be honest . . . here is a task for all that a man has of fortitude.

--Robert Louis Stevenson

Piety requires us to honor truth above our friends.

--Aristotle

The dignity of truth is lost with much protesting.

--Ben Jonson

Superscripts in Report

Endnotes Page

Title Page

Headings and Subheadings

Main heading. Center the main heading in ALL CAPS over the line of writing.

Side headings. Begin side headings at the left margin. Capitalize the first letter of the first word and all other main words in each heading. Underline side headings.

Paragraph headings. Indent paragraph headings 0.5" from the left margin. Capitalize the first letter of the first word only, underline the heading, and follow the heading with a period.

Title Page

A cover or title page is prepared for many reports. To format a title page, center the title in ALL CAPS 2" from the top. Center your name in capital and lower-case letters 5" from the top. The school name is centered a DS below your name. The date should be centered 9" from the top. Electronics: see p. RG20.

Documentation

Textual citation. Documentation is used to give credit for published material that is quoted or closely paraphrased (slightly changed). One form of documentation is the textual citation method. This method includes the name(s) of the author(s), the date of the referenced publication, and the page number(s) of the material cited as part of the actual text:

(Kirkpatrick, 1996, 275)

When the author's name is used in the text introducing the quotation, only the year of publication and the page number(s) appear in parentheses:

Kirkpatrick (1996, 275) said
that . . . . .

Endnotes. Another method of documentation is the endnotes method. When using this method, a reference cited in the text is identified by a superscript number . . . .[1]

The complete documentation for the reference is placed at the end of the report in a section labeled ENDNOTES. The references listed in the ENDNOTES section are placed in the same order they appeared in the report and have the corresponding superscript number that identifies the reference in the text.

The ENDNOTES page has the same top and side margins as the first page of the report, except that it has a page number 1" from the top at the right margin. Each reference is single-spaced with a double space between references. The first line of each reference is indented 0.5" from the left margin (keyed to a superscript endnote number); all other lines begin at the left margin.

[1]Richard G. Harris, "Globalization, Trade, and Income," Canadian Journal of Economics, November 1993, p. 755.

References. Complete information about the material cited is placed in a separate section called the reference section (also referred to as the bibliography or works cited section). All references cited are listed alphabetically by author surnames under the heading REFERENCES (or BIBLIOGRAPHY or WORKS CITED). The REFERENCES page has the same top and side margins as the first page of the report, but a page number is keyed 1" from the top at the right margin. Each reference is single-spaced with a double space between references. The first line of each reference begins at the left margin; all other lines are indented 0.5" from the left margin.

Note: Both the textual citation and endnote method of documentation require a REFERENCES page. It follows an ENDNOTES page.

**Format Guides:
Tables**

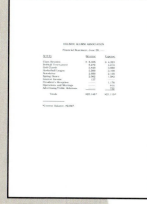

**Three-Column Table
with Source Note**

 note:

The Table format software function is introduced on p. 299.

Parts of a Simple Table

A table is a systematic arrangement of data (words/numbers) in rows and columns. Tables range in complexity from those with only two columns and a main heading to those with several columns and special features. The tables in this unit are limited to those with the following parts:

1. Main heading (title) in ALL CAPS.

2. Secondary heading in Capital and lowercase letters (C/lc).

3. Column headings (blocked).

4. Body (column entries).

5. Source note (at left margin).

6. Total line (indented 5 spaces).

The first tables in this unit consist of only a main heading and two columns of data. Later tables progress in complexity so that, finally, they include three columns and several of the parts listed above.

Format Features of Simple Tables

The following table summarizes format features of tables and their parts.

Margins	
Top:	2"
Side:	equal
Bottom:	variable
Line spacing	
Headings:	DS below
Body:	usually DS; may be SS
Totals (if any):	DS above
Divider rule (if any):	DS above/below
Source note (if any):	SS; DS above
Column spacing	0.4"–1.6" (4–16 spaces)

Centering Tables

For a table to be centered horizontally (side to side), the side margins must be about equal. Vertically (top to bottom), a table may be centered (about equal top and bottom margins), or it may begin a standard distance from the top edge of the paper. Tables in Lessons 62–67 will be formatted with a standard 2" top margin.

If Automatic Centering feature is available, use the keyline method of horizontal centering:

1. Center/key the keyline (the longest item in each column plus spaces to be left between columns).

2. Record the position of first character in each column; then delete the keyline.

3. Center main and secondary headings.

4. Reset left margin for first column at first position recorded in Step 2.

5. Clear all tabs and set needed tabs at other positions recorded in Step 2.

6. Key entries, tabbing from column to column.

Example (in 10-pitch monospace)

If Automatic Centering feature is not available, see Manual Centering Method on p. RG19.

Aligning Data in Columns

Words in columns are aligned at the left. Figures, however, are usually aligned at the right or at the decimal point.

Format Guides: Reports

Textual Citations in Report

References Page

Report Classification

Reports can be classified in a variety of ways. A few of the ways reports can be classified are by formality (formal or informal), by purpose (analytical or informative), by type (feasibility, progress, justification, periodic), by setting (internal and external), and by format (bound or unbound).

Unbound Reports

Many short reports are prepared without covers or binders. Such reports are called unbound reports (see model on pp. 145 and 146). If they consist of more than one page, the pages are fastened together in the upper-left corner by a staple or paper clip.

Bound Reports

Longer reports are generally prepared with covers or binders. Such reports are called bound reports and require a larger left margin (1.5") to accommodate the binding.

Standard Margins

With the exception of the left margin (1" for unbound and 1.5" for bound), all margin settings are the same for the unbound and bound reports. The right margin is 1". A top margin of 2" and a bottom margin of 1" are customarily used on the first page of reports. All remaining pages are keyed with 1" top and bottom margins. Since the internal spacing of report parts varies, a bottom margin of exactly 1" is often not feasible. For that reason, a bottom margin of 1" to 1.5" is acceptable. On electronics, vary the bottom margin to prevent: a side heading or first line of a paragraph from printing as the last line on a page (orphan); or the last line of a paragraph from occurring at the top of a new page (widow). The Widow/Orphan feature of word processing software may be used to prevent these problems.

Page Numbering

The first page of a report is usually not numbered. However, if a page number is used on the first page, center it at the bottom of the page. On the second and subsequent pages, place the page number 1" from the top of the page at the right margin. A DS is left between the page number and the text of the report. The page number for endnotes and reference pages should also be placed 1" from the top of the page at the right margin.

Spacing

A QS is left between the report title and the first line of the body. Multiple-line titles are DS. A DS is left above and below side headings and between paragraphs, which are usually DS but may be SS (when directions specify). The paragraphs are indented 0.5" (generally 5 spaces).

Long quotes. Quoted material of four or more lines should be SS and indented 0.5" from the left margin. The right margin for quoted material remains at 1". Double-space above and below the quoted material.

Enumerated items. Indent enumerated items 0.5" from the left margin; block the lines at that point. The right margin for enumerated items remains at 1". Single-space individual items; DS between items as well as above and below a series of items.

Keyline	Photography/Layout 2"	1.0" (10 sp.)	Malik Fredericks 4.8"

Main heading	NEW PERISCOPE STAFF		2" (or line 13) DS
	Editor		Kristi Stojko DS
	Associate Editor		Brian Poole DS
Body	Business Manager		Anita Solena DS
	Photography/Layout		Malik Fredericks DS
	Advertising/Sales		Xen Chueng DS
	Advisor		Marcella Proust

Two-Column Table Centered Horizontally (Table 1)

Shown in 10-pitch monospace, photoreduced

LESSON 62 Simple Two-Column Tables MLS

Objectives:

1. To learn placement/arrangement of basic table parts.
2. To format tables using the keyline method.

62A • 5
Conditioning Practice

each line twice SS; key a
1' writing on line 3; find
gwam

alphabet 1 Wex just received a quite sizable check from a big paper company.

fig/sym 2 Invoice #14729 was paid by Gibb & Byron's check (#6058) on May 3.

speed 3 Roz may go to the ancient island city by the lake to work for us.

gwam 1' | 1 | 2 | 3 | 4 | 5 | 6 | 7 | 8 | 9 | 10 | 11 | 12 | 13 |

62B • 45
Two-Column Tables

1. Study the format guides for tables on p. 157.
2. Learn to center horizontally, using the method appropriate for your equipment (see p. 157).
3. Study the model above: margins, column spacing, and line spacing.
4. Key the model, guided by the keyline and spacing callouts. Proofread and correct errors.
5. Key Tables 2-3 on p. 159 as directed there; correct errors.
6. If time permits, reformat the model above leaving 1.6" (16 spaces) between columns.

ACTIVITY 1:

Search

1. Read the copy at right.
2. Learn the Search to Find and Search to Replace features for your software.
3. Key the ¶ at the right.
4. Use the Search to Find feature to determine how many times the word *are* appears in the ¶.
5. Use the Search to Replace feature to replace the word *month* with **pay period**.
6. Replace the word *assessments* with the word **taxes**.

The **Search to Find** feature is used to locate a specified series of keystrokes or word(s) in a document. The **Search to Replace** feature locates a specified series of keystrokes or word(s) in a document and replaces them with another series of keystrokes or word(s).

An individual has to pay a number of assessments. FICA assessments are the assessments that support the Social Security system and are deducted from your check each month. Federal income assessments are also deducted from your check each month. Assessments that are not deducted from your check each month include property assessments and sales assessments.

ACTIVITY 2:

Orphan/Widow

1. Read the copy at right.
2. Learn the Orphan/Widow feature for your software.
3. Open RPT70C1. Turn on the feature.

The **Orphan/Widow** feature ensures that the first line of a paragraph does not appear by itself at the bottom of a page (**orphan line**) or that the last line of a paragraph does not appear by itself at the top of a page (**widow line**).

1. In RPT70C1 search to find the words . . . *greater detail*.

2. Add these sentences at the end of the paragraph: **Do not put in visuals just to pad the report or decorate the pages. Choose visuals that support and clarify the text**.
3. Search to find: *Excellent reports*. Delete the entire sentence.
4. Note how the feature reforms the text to prevent an orphan or widow line.

ACTIVITY 3:

Review wp Features

1. Key Sentences 1-5; underline, *italicize*, and **bold** text as you key.
2. Key Sentences 6-10. *Do not* bold, italicize, or underline the copy as you key. *After* keying the sentences, go back and underline, italicize, and bold existing text. In this activity, do not substitute italics for underline.
3. Use the Block Delete feature to delete lines 4, 6, and 9.

1 *Ted* saved **$25** in May, **$50** in June, and **$35** in July; *Linda* saved **$20** in May, **$40** in June, and **$60** in July.

2 Agreement **#82-789** was signed on January 18, 1997.

3 He misspelled **absence**, **calendar**, and **mortgage** on the quiz.

4 Dr. Romanski included **Chapters 8, 9,** and **11** on the exam.

5 The **Boston Symphony Orchestra** performed **Britten's** *Four Sea Interludes* and **Beethoven's** *Symphony No. 7.*

6 One of his favorite classics was **Dvorak's** *Symphony No. 9 in E Minor* from "**The New World**" Second Movement.

7 The bronze medal went to **Maria Boxmeyer**, the silver medal went to **Clinton Pizzaro**, and the gold medal went to **Charlene Biden**.

8 At **2:45 p.m.**, the team from **China** will play the **German** team.

9 The movie Major League II stars **Charlie Sheen, Tom Berenger, Corbin Bernsen,** and **Bob Uecker.**

10 The class discussed the **Indent** feature on Monday, the **Merge** feature on Wednesday, and the **Table** feature on Friday.

Table 2

Center table horizontally, 1.0" (10 sp.) between columns; DS throughout. Proofread and correct errors.

SPELLING DEMONS		words
		3
adequate	customer	7
appropriate	electrical	11
categories	eligible	15
compliance	employees	20
compliment	implemented	24
correspondence	installation	30
corporate	monitoring	34

Table 3

Center table horizontally, 1.2" (12 sp.) between columns; DS throughout. Proofread and correct errors.

Table 4

See p. 158, Step 6.

MORE SPELLING DEMONS		4
opportunity	prior	8
permanent	pursuant	12
personnel	received	15
participants	reference	20
patient	similar	23
possibility	successful	28
previously	sufficient	32

LESSON 63 · Tables with Secondary Headings

Objectives:
1. To learn to center and space secondary headings in tables.
2. To format two-column tables with secondary headings.

63A • 5
Conditioning Practice

each line twice SS; key a 1' writing on line 3; find *gwam*

alphabet	1	Cooks brought piquant flavor to exotic foods with zesty marjoram.
fig/sym	2	Orr's order (#30-967) is for 42 maps, 15 atlases, and 8 almanacs.
speed	3	The chair did signal the man to name an auditor for the big firm.

gwam 1' | 1 | 2 | 3 | 4 | 5 | 6 | 7 | 8 | 9 | 10 | 11 | 12 | 13 |

F ORMATTING

63B • 45
Tables with Secondary Headings

1. Review the procedure for centering tables horizontally (p. 157). Remember to have a 2" top margin on all tables.

2. Format/key the tables on p. 160 using the directions given with each table.

3. **Note:** Be sure to proofread and correct each table before saving it or removing it from the machine.

LESSON 86

Keying Techniques

Objectives:
1. To improve/refine technique and response patterns.
2. To increase speed on straight copy.

86A • 5
Conditioning Practice

each line twice

alphabet	1	Marie Vasquez was probably sick during the last six days of June.
speed	2	She may blame the girls for the problem with the neighbor's auto.
figures	3	Tables 8, 9, and 16 are in Chapter 12 on pages 379, 395, and 405.

gwam 1' | 1 | 2 | 3 | 4 | 5 | 6 | 7 | 8 | 9 | 10 | 11 | 12 | 13 |

86B • 18
Skill Check

1. Three 1' writings on ¶ 1 of 85E. Strive to increase rate recorded previously for 85E by 4 *gwam*.

2. Repeat Step 1 using ¶ 2.
3. Two 3' writings using both ¶s.

4. Determine better 3' *gwam* and record.

S KILL BUILDING

86C • 15
Keying Techniques

1. Key each line twice.
2. Key three 1' writings on line 3; first for accuracy, then for speed, then again for accuracy.
3. Repeat Step 2 for lines 6 and 9.

Shift keys

1 Kim, Sue, Nan, and I all live on Fenton Avenue, four blocks away.

2 We visited Texas, Colorado, New Mexico, New York, and New Jersey.

3 Janet S. Glavine, manager of Pizza Del Rio, lives on Park Avenue.

Space bar

4 Thomas will go to the city next week to buy a car for his mother.

5 Jana, Mike, and I will leave next week to see our aunt and uncle.

6 I will not be able to fix all ten of the tires by noon on Friday.

Balanced-hand sentences

7 To the right of the lake is the dismal shanty with the six ducks.

8 The maid may go with them when they go to the city for the gowns.

9 The box with a shamrock and an iris is by the door of the chapel.

gwam 1' | 1 | 2 | 3 | 4 | 5 | 6 | 7 | 8 | 9 | 10 | 11 | 12 | 13 |

86D • 12
Techniques: Figures/Tab

CS: 0.5"

1. Key copy given at the right.
2. Key two 1' writings.

			words
7820 Oakview Dr.	392 Fairland St.	390 Marsh St.	10
892 Hemlock St.	2031 Ferris Ave.	1290 Knox Rd.	19
9284 Fawn Dr.	9986 Cedar St.	982 King Ave.	28
9301 Dixie Ct.	567 Acorn Ct.	9021 Hart Ln.	36
5638 Ivy Dr.	8290 Grand Cir.	1092 Allen Ct.	45
1892 Forrest Dr.	2956 Boyd St.	8256 Butler Ln.	54

Table 1
Table with Secondary Heading
DS the table throughout, 1.0" (10 sp.) between columns

OLDEST AMERICAN UNIVERSITIES		
(Founded Before 1750)		
Harvard	1636	
Yale	1701	
Pennsylvania	1740	
Denver	1743	
Princeton	1746	
Washington and Lee	1749	

6, 10, 13, 15, 18, 21, 24, 29

Table 2
Table from Script
DS the table throughout, 1.2" (12 sp.) between columns.

FEDERAL SERVICE ACADEMIES	
(By Year Founded)	
U.S. Military Academy	1802
U.S. Naval Academy	1845
U.S. Coast Guard Academy	1876
U.S. Merchant Marine Academy	1943
U.S. Air Force Academy	1954

5, 9, 14, 19, 25, 32, 37

Table 3
Table with Source Note from Rough Draft
1. Read the table, noting changes to be made.
2. Format/key the table DS, 1.4" (14 sp.) between columns.
3. DS above and below the divider line.

Note: A divider line is a series of 15 underlines (about 1.5"); DS above and below it.

Table 4
If time permits, reformat Table 3 with 1.0" (10 sp.) between columns.

ALL-TIME GRAMMY WINNERS (TOP)	
(With Total Awards won)	
Sir George Solti	30
Quincy jones	26
Vladimir Horowitz	52
Henry Mancinni	20
Steve Wonder	17
Loenard Bernstein	16
Paul Simon	1 6
John Williams	16
DS _____	
Source: USA Today, March 3, 1994.	

6, 10, 14, 17, 22, 25, 28, 33, 35, 39, 42, 49

85D • 10
Verbs (continued)

Follow the Learn/Apply procedure in 76C, p. 184.

When used as the subject, the pronouns *I*, *we*, *you*, and *they*, as well as plural nouns, require the plural verb *do not* or the contraction *don't*.

Learn   1. I do not want to participate in the activity.
Learn   2. The painters don't want to work on Saturday.
Apply   3. They (don't doesn't) want to revise the report.
Apply   4. The actors (do not, does not) want another dress rehearsal.

When used as the subject, the pronouns *he*, *she*, and *it*, as well as singular nouns, require the singular verb *does not* or the contraction *doesn't*.

Learn   5. Judy doesn't want the design changed.
Learn   6. The quote does not include labor for installing the carpet.
Apply   7. She (don't, doesn't) like the new contract.
Apply   8. The new paint (do not, does not) match the old paint.

S KILL BUILDING

85E • 12
Straight Copy

1. A 3' writing on ¶s 1-2 combined; find *gwam* and number of errors.
2. A 1' writing on ¶ 1, then on ¶ 2; find *gwam* and number of errors on each.
3. Another 3' writing on ¶s 1-2, trying to increase your *gwam* by 2 *gwam* over first 3' writing.
4. Record your better 1' and 3' *gwam* for use in 86B.

all letters used   gwam   3' | 5'

		gwam 3'	5'

Many firms feel that their employees are their most valuable   4 | 2 | 45
resources. Excellent companies realize that people working toward   9 | 5 | 47
common goals influence the success of the business. They are also   13 | 8 | 50
aware of the need to hire qualified people and then to create a   17 | 10 | 53
work environment to allow the people to perform at their highest   22 | 13 | 55
potential. Firms that believe that the main job of managers is   26 | 16 | 58
to remove obstacles that get in the way of the output of the   30 | 18 | 60
workers are the firms that do, in fact, achieve their goals.   34 | 20 | 63

Not only do executives and managers in the most successful   38 | 23 | 65
firms admit to themselves the value of their employees, but they   42 | 25 | 68
also reveal this feeling to their workers. They know that most   46 | 28 | 70
people enjoy being given credit for their unique qualities. They   51 | 31 | 73
also know that any action on their part that aids the workers in   55 | 33 | 75
realizing their own self-worth will lead to a higher return for   59 | 36 | 78
the firm, since such people are self-motivated. When leaders do   64 | 38 | 81
not have to be occupied with employee motivation, they can devote   68 | 41 | 83
their energy to other vital tasks.   70 | 42 | 85

gwam 3' | 1 | 2 | 3 | 4
5' | 1 | 2 | 3

Objectives:

1. To learn to format tables with blocked column headings.
2. To improve skill in processing two-column tables.

64A • 5
Conditioning Practice

each line twice SS: a
1' writing on line 3; find
gwam

alphabet	1	Puma quit cutting flax when big jet clouds covered the azure sky.
fig/sym	2	I paid a $72.41 premium on a $5,000 travel policy (dated 6/3/98).
speed	3	Eighty of the city firms may form a panel to handle the problems.

gwam | 1' | 1 | 2 | 3 | 4 | 5 | 6 | 7 | 8 | 9 | 10 | 11 | 12 | 13 |

FORMATTING

64B • 45
Two-Column Tables with Multiple Features

Format/key the tables as directed.

Table 1
Table with Column Headings

1. Key the table DS, 0.8" (8 sp.) between columns.
2. Block column headings at left of columns.
3. Correct any errors you make as you key.

Table 2
Table with Multiple Features

1. Key the table DS, 1.0" (10 sp.) between columns.
2. Block column headings at left of columns.
3. Correct any errors you make as you key.

		words
SUMMER READING LIST		4
(Read at Least Three)		8
Author	Selection	12
Dante Alighieri	The Divine Comedy	20
Charles Baudelaire	Les Fleurs du Mal	26
Robert Frost	The Road Not Taken	33
Victor Hugo	Les Miserables	38
Niccolo Machiavelli	The Prince	44
William Shakespeare	Measure for Measure	52

		words
WINNERS OF MOST ACADEMY AWARDS		6
(Since 1950)		9
Actor	Years	11
Marion Brando	1954/1972	16
Sally Field	1979/1985	21
Jane Fonda	1971/1978	25
Jody Foster	1988/1991	29
Tom Hanks	1993/1994	33
Katherine Hepburn	1967/1968/1981	40
Dustin Hofman	1979/1988	45
Glenda jackson	1970/1937	50
Elizabeth Taylor	1960/1966	55
		59
DS _____		
Source: The World Almanac, 1996.		65

UNIT 19 Improve Keyboarding Skills

LESSONS 85-86

LESSON 85 — Keying Techniques/Language Skills

Objectives:
1. To improve/refine technique and response patterns.
2. To increase speed on straight copy.
3. To improve language skills (verbs).

85A • 5
Conditioning Practice

set SMs for 0.5"; each line twice

alphabet	1	Max Braatz always rejected the idea of taking over the equipment firm.
speed	2	Diana and the visitor may handle the problems of the eighth amendment.
figures	3	Sections 1, 2, and 3 of ECON 405 had 68, 67, and 69 students enrolled.

gwam | 1' | 1 | 2 | 3 | 4 | 5 | 6 | 7 | 8 | 9 | 10 | 11 | 12 | 13 | 14 |

S KILL BUILDING

85B • 15
Keying Skill: Speed

1. A 30" writing on each line; find *gwam* on each.
2. Compare rates on lines 2-6 with the rate on line 1.
3. Two 30" writings on each of the slower lines.

balanced hand	1	Orlando is apt to make the men go to the island for the coalfish.
double letters	2	Looking for food, three little rabbits were hopping between rows.
adjacent keys	3	Three of our territory reporters were told to type their reports.
long direct reaches	4	I went to a symphony concert; he decorated for a secret ceremony.
outside reaches	5	Paul Quixote won all six prizes last season for his zealous play.
one hand	6	Gregg saw a deserted cat on a battered crate in a vacated garage.

gwam | 1' | 1 | 2 | 3 | 4 | 5 | 6 | 7 | 8 | 9 | 10 | 11 | 12 | 13 |

85C • 8
Techniques: Figures/Tab

CS: 0.5"
Key the drill twice (slowly, then faster); correct errors you make as you key.

Concentrate on figure location; quick tab spacing; eyes on copy.

3296	3209	1287	6504	1389	2309	7808	134
3673	1029	3658	6145	7807	6577	2140	907
4308	1586	4584	1069	3215	8452	9961	823
4162	4545	6759	2309	4207	8211	6743	609

Table 3

Table 3

1. Format/key the table DS, 1.2" (12 sp.) between columns.
2. As you key, make indicated changes and correct any errors you make as you key.

Table 4

If time permits, reformat Table 3 with 1.4" (14 sp.) between columns.

		words
LONGEST-RUN BROADWAY PLAYS		5
Performances Through July 17, 1994		12
Play	Perf.	15
a Chorus Line	6,137	19
Oh, Calcutta (revival)	5,959	25
Cats	4,917	27
42d Street	3,486	31
Grease	3,388	33
Fiddler On The Roof	3,224	38
Life with father	3,224	43
Tobaco Road	3,182	47
Les Miserables	3,005	51
		54
DS Source: The World Almanac, 1995.		61

LESSON 65 — Three-Column Tables with Multiple Features

Objectives:

1. To learn to format three-column tables with multiple features.
2. To build skill in processing tables from rough draft.

65A • 5
Conditioning Practice

each line twice SS; a 1' writing on line 3; find *gwam*

alphabet	1	Hal just picked a bouquet of six vivid flowers growing at my zoo.
fig/sym	2	He said, "A quiz over pages 35-149 and 168-270 will be on May 5."
speed	3	Ellena is to pay the six auto firms for all the bodywork they do.

gwam 1' | 1 | 2 | 3 | 4 | 5 | 6 | 7 | 8 | 9 | 10 | 11 | 12 | 13 |

F O R M A T T I N G

65B • 45
Three-Column Tables

Table 1
Three-Column Table with Multiple Features

1. Format/key the table DS, 0.6" (6 sp.) between columns.
2. Correct all errors.

			words
PULITZER PRIZES IN POETRY			5
(Since 1990)			8
Year	Poem or Collection	Author	15
1990	The World Doesn't End	Charles Simic	23
1991	Near Changes	Mona Van Duyn	29
1992	Selected Poems	James Tate	35
1993	The Wild Iris	Louise Gluck	42
1994	Neon Vernacular	Yusef Komunyakaa	49
			53
Source: Information Please Almanac, 1995.			61

Activity 4:

1. Read the case of the 'extra change' error at the right.
2. After considering the comments and suggestions of your friends, what would you do in this situation?
3. Compose/key a paragraph to indicate your choice, how you made it, and why?
4. As a group, discuss the decision(s) reached by various members of the class in terms of *honesty*, *fair play*, and *caring* about others.

Compose (think) as you key

You are looking forward to this weekend because you and your friends have arranged to go to dinner together before separating for other activities: a ball game, a movie, and a "mixer." To pay for the dinner, you have collected money from each friend.

The restaurant is upscale, the food very good, and the service excellent. Your server has been friendly and has quickly met all your needs. Your server has not rushed you to finish, so you and your friends have enjoyed conversation and laughter long after the meal ended. It is great that all of you get along so well.

When it is time to go, you ask your server for the check and pay it. When you receive your change and are leaving a tip, you notice that your change is ten dollars more than you should have received.

A discussion takes place among the six of you regarding this error. Various comments and suggestions are made:

1. Keep the money; the server will never know to whom the extra change was given.

2. Are you lucky! This never happens to me.

3. You have to return the money. If you don't, the server will have to make up the loss of money at the end of the evening.

Several thoughts go through your mind as you listen to the comments of your friends. You know it would be great to have ten extra dollars to share with your friends. What will my friends think if I return the money, or if I keep it? The server has been very pleasant and has worked hard this evening. If I keep the money, is it right to make the server pay for the error? How would I want to be treated if I made the same mistake at my job?

Table 2
Three-Column Table from Rough Draft

1. Format/key the table DS, 0.6" (6 sp.) between columns.
2. Make all indicated changes and correct any errors you make as you key.

			words
R. JOHN WOODEN AWARD WINNERS			6
(Collegiate Basketball)			11
Year	Player	College	15
1990	Lionel Simmons	La Salle	21
1991	Larry Johnson	UNLV	26
1992	Christian Leattner	Duke	31
1993	Calvert Chaney	Indiana	37
1994	Glen Robinson	Perdue	42
1995	*Ed O'Bannon*	*UCLA*	47
			50
Sourge: The World Almanac. 1996.			57

Table 3
Three-Column Table from Rough Draft

1. Format/key the table DS, 0.4" (4 sp.) between columns.
2. Make all indicated changes and correct any errors you make as you key.

Table 4

Reformat Table 2 DS, 0.8" (8 sp.) between columns, all errors corrected.

			words
WORLD CHAMPION FIGURE SKATERS			6
1990 – 1995			8
Year	Men	Women	12
1990	Kurt Browning *(Canada)*	Jill Trenary *(U.S.)*	21
1991	Kurt Browning *(Canada)*	Kristi Yamaguchi *(U.S.)*	32
1992	Viktor Petrenko *(Unified Team)*	Kristi Yamaguchi *(U.S.)*	44
1993	Kurt Browning *(Canada)*	Oksana Baiul *(Ukraine)*	54
1994	Elvis Stojko *(Canada)*	Yuka Sato *(Japan)*	63
1995	Elvis Stojko *(Canada)*	Chen Lu *(China)*	71
			75
Source: Information Please Almanac. 1996.			83

LESSON 66

Tables with Multiple Features

O b j e c t i v e s :

1. To build skill in processing two- and three-column tables.
2. To improve skill in processing rough-draft tables.

66A • 5
Conditioning Practice

each line twice SS; a 1' writing on line 3; find *gwam*

alphabet 1 Al criticized my six workers for having quick tempers on the job.

fig/sym 2 Order #45-1073 from Wilson & Co. totals $198.56, less 2/10, n/30.

speed 3 To lend a hand to a visitor to the city is the wish of all of us.

gwam 1' | 1 | 2 | 3 | 4 | 5 | 6 | 7 | 8 | 9 | 10 | 11 | 12 | 13 |

Language & Writing Skills 9

Activity 1:

1. Study the spelling/definitions of the words in the color block at the right.
2. Key the **Learn** line in the first set of sentences.
3. Key the **Apply** lines, choosing the right word to complete each sentence correctly.
4. Key the second set of lines in the same way.
5. Check work; rekey lines containing word-choice errors.

Choose the right word

sew (vb) to fasten by stitches
so (adj/conj) in the same manner or way; in order that; with the result that
sow (vb) to plant seed; scatter; disperse

raise (vb/n) to lift up; to collect; an increase in amount, as of wages
rays (n) beams of energy or light; lines of light from a bright object
raze (vb) to tear down; to demolish

Learn   1   He can sew the bags so that we can use them to sow the grass seed.
Apply   2   I can have them (sew/so/sow) the oats if you say (sew/so/sow).
Apply   3   The design is intricate, (sew/so/sow) I can't (sew/so/sow) it now.
Apply   4   She is to (sew/so/sow) in the words "(Sew/So/Sow) seeds of kindness."

Learn   5   The sun's rays caused the flowers to raise their heads.
Learn   6   If we raise the price, will they raze the old building this month?
Apply   7   The (raise/rays/raze) of the sun will (raise/rays/raze) the fog.
Apply   8   After they (raise/rays/raze) the gym, work on a new arena can begin.

Activity 2:

As you key the lines shown at the right, select and key the proper verb shown in parentheses.

Proofread & correct   Subject/Predicate agreement

1 The debate team (has/have) won the city championship.
2 Ms. Yamaguchi and her mother (is/are) now American citizens.
3 Either the coach or an assistant (is/are) to present the award.
4 Two aides in addition to the President (was/were) to attend.
5 The planning committee (is/are) to present its proposal today.
6 The dancers as well as the orchestra (was/were) late.
7 Some of the students (has/have) chosen to do acrylic paintings.
8 The number of applicants (is are) greater this year.
9 All of the lasagna (was/were) eaten by the hungry campers.
10 A number of our workers (is/are) to receive proficiency awards.

Activity 3:

As you key the lines shown at the right, use appropriate capitalization and number expression (words or figures).

Proofread & correct   Capitalization/Number expression

1 "the jury," said the judge, "must reach a unanimous decision."
2 for what percentage of total sales is mrs. rhodes responsible?
3 i need a copy of <u>the dictionary of composers and their music</u>.
4 miss valdez told us to go to room eight of corbett hall.
5 the institute of art is at fifth avenue and irving place.
6 "don't you agree," he asked, "that honesty is the best policy?"
7 is the tony award show to be shown on tv on april seventeen?
8 dr. robin j. sousa is to address fbla members in orlando.
9 see page 473 of volume one of <u>encyclopedia americana</u>.
10 here is pbc's check #2749 for $83 (less ten percent discount).

66B • 45
Tables with Multiple Features

Table 1
Table with Column Headings

Format/key the table DS, 0.8" (8 sp.) between columns, all errors corrected.

Table 2
Table with Multiple Features

1. Fomat/key the table DS, 0.8" (8 sp.) between columns.
2. Make indicated changes and correct any errors you make as you key.

Table 3
Table with Multiple Features

Use same directions as for Table 2.

Table 4

If time permits, reformat Table 2 DS, 0.6" (6 sp.) between columns, errors corrected.

		words
WINTER LISTENING LIST		4
Selection	Composer	9
Brandenberg Concertos	Johann Sebastian Bach	17
Symphonie Fantastique	Hector Berlioz	25
Jupiter Symphony	Wolfgang Amadeus Mozart	33
Finlandia	Jean Sibelius	38
The Rite of Spring	Igor Stravinsky	45
Manfred Symphony	Piotr Ilyich Tchaikovsky	53

			words
PULITZER PRIZES IN DRAMA			5
Since 1990			7
Year	Play	Author	11
1990	The Piano Lesson	August Wilson	18
1991	Lost in Yonkers	Neil Simon	25
1992	The Kentucky Cycle	Robert Schenkkan	33
1993	Angels in America/Millennium	Tony Kushner	42
1994	Three Tall Women	Edward Albee	49
			52
Source: Information Please Almanac, 1996.			61

			words
HEISMAN TROPHY WINNERS			5
Collegiate Football			9
Year	Player	College	13
1990	Tye Detmer	Brigham Young	19
1991	Desmond Howard	Michigan	25
1992	Gino Torretto	Miami (Fla.)	31
1993	Charlie Ward	Florida State	38
1994	Marshall Faulk	San Diego State	45
1995	Rasham Salaam	Colorado	50
			54
Source: The Universal Almanac, 1996.			61

words

Ms. Charla Whitaker | Page 2 | April 15, ----   8

Finally, you need to be aware of two changes the committee members have   23
planned for the final issue of The Historical Review. The publication dead-   38
line has been changed from March 1 to April 1. The committee has decided   53
to add a new feature to each issue of the Review. It will be called "My   68
Perspective--Historically Speaking." They have invited Dr. DeWitt Danforth   83
to share his perspective for the first featured article. If either of these   98
changes does not meet with your approval, you should contact the chair of   113
the committee, Margaret Ryan, immediately.   122

I believe that I have covered all the major items of the meeting. The min-   137
utes of the meeting should be available within the next two weeks. After   152
you have had an opportunity to review them, call me if you have questions.   167

Sincerely yours | Lamar B. Santana | Executive Director | xx   178

October 15, ---- | MRS ANNA ALVAREZ | 3950 CALLE PACIFICO | 11
SANTA FE NM 87505-9321 | SATISFACTION GUARANTEED   20

We hope you and your family are enjoying the living-room furniture you   35
purchased at **Villa Furniture**. Oakwood is an excellent line of furniture   49
that should last for many years. If, however, there is any reason you are   64
not pleased with the furniture, let us know. We will take the necessary   79
steps to guarantee your satisfaction.   87

Villa Furniture has been in business for over 100 years because of satis-   101
fied customers. We are committed to keeping customer satisfaction high by   116
offering quality furniture at reasonable prices.   126

We appreciate our loyal customers and hope you will remain one of them.   141
Please let me know when we can be of further service.   152

MISS JOYCE BUTTERFIELD, FURNITURE CONSULTANT | xx   161

L ANGUAGE SKILLS

84D • 10
Plural Verbs

Follow the Learn/Apply procedure in 76C, p. 184.

Use a plural verb with a plural subject (noun or pronoun).

Learn   1. The students have completed the assignment.
Learn   2. They are ready for the examination.
Apply   3. The participants (is, are) ready to begin the race.
Apply   4. She (is, are) the first member of her family to graduate.

Use plural verbs with compound subjects joined by **and**.

Learn   5. Ms. Jensen and her daughter have purchased the play tickets.
Learn   6. The president and the secretary are reviewing the minutes.
Apply   7. Jane and Ted (is, are) going to the convention.
Apply   8. Mr. Black and Ms. Linton (has, have) been nominated.

LESSON 67

Tables with Totals and Footnotes

MLS

Objectives:

1. To learn to format tables with totals and footnotes.
2. To format tables with single-spaced entries.

67A • 5
Conditioning Practice

each line twice SS; a
1' writing on line 3; find
gwam

alphabet 1 The quick jabs and deft parries amazed several wary young boxers.

fig/sym 2 She gave him numbers and prices: #16392, $48.30; #14593, $75.95.

speed 3 To handle the problem with proficiency and vigor is a civic duty.

gwam 1' | 1 | 2 | 3 | 4 | 5 | 6 | 7 | 8 | 9 | 10 | 11 | 12 | 13 |

F ORMATTING

67B • 45
Tables with Totals and Footnotes

Table 1

1. Format/key the table SS, 0.6" (6 sp.) between columns, all errors corrected.

2. Underline the entire width of the amount columns.

3. Indent the word *Totals* 0.5" (5 sp.) from left margin.

4. Key the footnote as if it were a source note, a DS below the divider line.

Table 2

Follow the directions given for Table 1.

Table 3

If time permits, reformat Table 1 with all lines DS.

Note: See p. A18 for R & E activities.

			words
LAKEVIEW STUDENT GOVERNMENT			6
Budget for Year ----/----*			11
Item	Amount	Up/Dn.	15
Student Government Awards Night	$2,850	$150	24
Grub Day Scholarships	750	50	30
Photocopy Services	475	–25	35
Operation Youth	375	35	40
State Assn. of Student Councils	350	15	48
National Honor Society Awards	350	–50	55
Student Government Pizza Night	240	20	63
Frosh Hot Dog Night	195	15	68
Student Clubs	185	20	72
Fall Picnic	175	25	76
Executive Board Trip	165	15	83
Totals	$6,110	$270	87
			90
*Information obtained from school financial office.			100

HILLSIDE ALUMNI ASSOCIATION			6
Financial Statement, June 30, ----			13
Activity	Revenue	Expense	18
Class Reunion	$ 5,385	$ 4,323	24
Softball Tournament	5,272	4,216	31
Golf Classic	3,840	3,050*	36
Basketball League	3,500	3,100	42
Newsletter	2,950	2,135	46
Spring Dance	2,062	1,583	51
Interest Income	137	-----	57
President's Reception	-----	1,176	63
Operations and Meetings	-----	814	70
Advertising/Public Relations	-----	722	80
Totals	$23,146	$21,119	84
			88
*Some expenses still to be paid.			94

LESSON 84

Letters and Language Skills

Objectives:

1. To learn to format second-page heading for letters.
2. To increase proficiency at processing letters.
3. To improve language skills (verbs).

84A • 5
Conditioning Practice

each line twice

alphabet 1 Quite possibly Juarez will be the next city making a fuel device.

speed 2 The proficient man was kept busy with the problem with the docks.

figures 3 Of the 14,650 disks that we purchased on May 29, only 387 remain.

gwam 1' | 1 | 2 | 3 | 4 | 5 | 6 | 7 | 8 | 9 | 10 | 11 | 12 | 13 |

FORMATTING

84B • 7
Drill: Simplified Block Letter

1. Two 1' writings on opening lines (date through ¶ 1) of modified block letter on p. 193. Concentrate on letter parts. Add 2 words (10 keystrokes) on second writing.

2. Two 1' writings on closing lines (¶ 3 through copy notation) of modified block letter on p. 193. If you finish before time is called, DS and begin

again. Focus on correct placement of letter parts. Add 2 words on second writing.

84C • 28
Letter Formats

Letter 1
Personal-Business Letter

Format the text at the right as a personal-business letter in block format with open punctuation.

words

8329 Elmwood Dr. | Minot, ND 58701-4367 | August 4, ---- | 11
Ms. Tammy LaConte | Apartment #292 | 3891 West Ocotillo Rd. | 22
Glendale, AZ 85303-2883 | Dear Tammy 29

Congratulations on your new job with **Technology Specialists**! It sounds 43
very exciting. I am glad to hear that you are using all the skills you 58
gained from the Keyboarding and Computer Applications course. I am 71
particularly gratified to hear that you are using the database concepts 86
you learned in class. I remember how you struggled with this part of 100
the class and considered dropping the course. It is evident that your 114
persistence paid off! 119

Our department continues to make changes. Our new networked lab 132
is now complete. We are teaching a new desktop publishing class as 145
well as offering additional sections of the Keyboarding and Computer 159
Applications course. I am teaching full time this year. 171

I really appreciate receiving your letter. Many students leave school 185
and that is the last we hear from them. Please keep in touch and think 199
of us next winter when you see our weather reports. 210

Sincerely | Mrs. Janet Jamison 215

Skill Builder

Speed Building

1. Key each line once SS; DS between 2-line groups.
   Goal: No pauses between letters and words.
2. Key a 1' writing on each of lines 4, 6, 8, and 10; find *gwam* on each.
3. If time permits, rekey the three slowest lines.

space bar	1 2	city then they form than body them busy sign firm duty turn proxy Jan may do key work for the six men on the audit of the big firm.
shift keys	3 4	Lake Como | Hawaii or Alaska | Madrid and Bogota | Sparks & Mason, Inc. Karl left for Bora Bora in May; Nan goes to Lake Worth in August.
adjacent keys	5 6	same wire open tire sure ruin said trim went fire spot lids walks We opened a shop by the stadium to offer the best sporting goods.
long direct reaches	7 8	vice much many nice once myth lace cents under check juice center Eunice brought a recorder to the music hall to record my recital.
word response	9 10	their right field world forms visit title chair spent towns usual They wish to go with the girl to the city to make the visual aid.

gwam 1' | 1 | 2 | 3 | 4 | 5 | 6 | 7 | 8 | 9 | 10 | 11 | 12 | 13 |

Timed Writings

1. Key a 1' writing on each ¶; find *gwam* on each one.
2. Key two 2' writings on ¶s 1-2 combined; find *gwam* on each writing.
3. Key two 3' writings on ¶s 1-3 combined; find *gwam* and count errors on each writing.
4. If time permits, key two 1' guided writings on each ¶: one for speed; one for control (accuracy).

Quarter-Minute Checkpoints				
gwam	1/4'	1/2'	3/4'	1'
24	6	12	18	24
28	7	14	21	28
32	8	16	24	32
36	9	18	27	36
40	10	20	30	40
44	11	22	33	44
48	12	24	36	48
52	13	26	39	52
56	14	28	42	56

all letters used

gwam 2' | 3'

In deciding upon a career, learn as much as possible about what individuals in that career do. For each job class, there are job requirements and qualifications that must be met. Analyze these tasks very critically in terms of your personality and what you like to do.

A high percentage of jobs in major careers demand education or training after high school. The training may be very specialized, requiring intensive study or interning for two or more years. You must decide if you are willing to expend so much time and effort.

After you have decided upon a career to pursue, discuss the choice with parents, teachers, and others. Such people can help you design a plan to guide you along the series of steps required in pursuing your goal. Keep the plan flexible and change it when-ever necessary.

2'	3'
6	4	57
12	8	62
19	13	66
25	17	70
27	18	71
33	22	76
40	27	80
47	31	85
53	35	90
59	39	93
66	44	97
72	48	102
79	52	106
80	53	107

gwam 2' | 1 | 2 | 3 | 4 | 5 | 6 |
3' | 1 | 2 | 3 | 4 |

Letter 4
Business Letter

Format and key the text at the right as a business letter in modified block format with mixed punctuation. Use the USPS style for the letter address.

	words
March 28, ----	Mr. and Mrs. Jason Verde	8203 Martin Luther King	13
Blvd.	Boston, MA 02119-2698	Dear Mr. and Mrs. Verde:	24

Stearns Associates is pleased to announce that your financial planner, 38
Mr. Martin Lancaster, CFP, has qualified to join an elite group of highly 53
skilled professionals designated as **Master Planners**. Only 2 percent of all 68
financial planners are accorded this status. 77

Mr. Lancaster, as a **Master Planner**, will now have access to a wider assort- 92
ment of financial planning resources and tools. This access will allow 106
him to address your needs with a greater degree of personalization and 120
timeliness. 123

If you are interested in having Mr. Lancaster review your existing portfolio, 139
please contact him to set up an appointment. 148

Sincerely, | Jay S. Chang | Senior Vice President, Marketing | xx 160

S KILL BUILDING

83C • 12
Skill Check

1. Key a 3' writing on ¶s 1 and 2 combined; determine *gwam* and number of errors.

2. Key a 1' writing on each ¶; determine *gwam* and number of errors.

3. Key another 3' writing on ¶s 1 and 2 combined; determine *gwam* and number of errors.

wp note:

Use wordwrap instead of dividing words at the end of lines.

all letters used   gwam 3' | 5'

The quality of life is a reflection of the quality of think- 4 | 2 | 41
ing. Just contemplate what the quality of life on this earth 8 | 5 | 43
would be today without the high-quality thinking done by famous 12 | 7 | 46
inventors. Imagine what it would be like without electricity. 17 | 10 | 48
If the phone didn't exist, consider the impact on your life. Do 21 | 13 | 51
you realize how your existence would change if horses were still 25 | 15 | 53
the primary mode of transportation? Would your life be the same 30 | 18 | 56
if the computer had not been invented? 32 | 19 | 57

High-quality thinking has impacted the quality of life 36 | 22 | 60
on this earth. By the same token, the quality of an individual's 40 | 24 | 62
existence is a reflection of the quality of an individual's 44 | 27 | 65
thinking. You need to think about school and how you can be a 48 | 29 | 67
better student. You need to examine career options and plan 53 | 32 | 70
instructional training that will allow you to pursue the career 57 | 34 | 72
of your choice. You need to contemplate the future; the quality 61 | 37 | 75
of your life hinges on such thoughts. 64 | 38 | 76

gwam 3' | 1 | 2 | 3 | 4
5' | 1 | 2 | 3

Language & Writing Skills 8

Activity 1:

1. Study the spelling/definitions of the words in the color block at the right.
2. Key the **Learn** line, noting the proper choice of words.
3. Key the **Apply** lines, choosing the right words to complete each line correctly.
4. Check your accuracy; rekey lines containing errors in word choice.

Choose the right word

buy (n/vb) a bargain; to purchase; to acquire

by (prep/adv) close to; via; according to; close at hand; at/in another's home

some (n/adv) unknown or unspecified unit or thing; to a degree or extent

sum (n/vb) the whole amount; the total; to find a total; summary of points

Learn 1 She stopped by a new shop on the square to buy the new CD album.
Apply 2 We are to go (buy/by) bus to the ski lodge to (buy/by) ski togs.
Apply 3 Did you (buy/by) the new novel (buy/by) Margaret Atwood?

Learn 4 The problem was to find the sum, but some students couldn't.
Apply 5 He said, "In (some/sum), both ideas are true to (some/sum) degree."
Apply 6 I bought (some/sum) pears and apples for the (some/sum) of $4.30.

Activity 2:

1. Read the ¶ at the right, noting words that are used incorrectly or misspelled.
2. Key the ¶, correcting the errors you noted.

Proofread & correct

Sum people think that because their good at sum sport, music, or other activity, there entitled to respect and forgiveness for anything else they chose to do. Its not uncommon, than, when such people break the law or violate sum code of conduct, four them too expect such behavior two be overlooked buy those whose job it is to enforce the law or too uphold an established code of conduct. Sum parents, as well as other members of society, think that a "star's" misbehavior should be treated less harshly because of that person's "celebrity" status; but all people are the same under the law.

Activity 3:

1. Read the ¶ at the right based on a survey of people in your age group.
2. On the basis of your own experience in viewing movies and TV, compose a ¶ indicating whether you agree or disagree with the survey results, giving reasons why or why not.

Compose (think) as you key

A mid-decade poll of young people revealed that U.S. youths thought current TV and movie fare glamorizes violence and sex without portraying the negative consequences of immoral behavior. Over sixty percent of youths surveyed said that such glamorizations on the screen influenced them to engage in such behavior.

_____

Source: Armstrong Williams, <u>USA Today</u>, March 2, 1995.

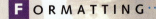
83B • 33

Letter 1
Personal-Business Letter
Format and key the letter shown at the right in modified block style with indented paragraphs and mixed punctuation. Save as LTR83B1.

	words
928 Big Horn Ave.	Moorcroft, WY 82721-8329	August 25, ----		12
Ms. Kellee Martinson	Section of Vital Statistics	2120 Capitol	24
Ave.	Cheyenne, WY 82001-8821	Dear Ms. Martinson:	34

Several weeks after the birth of our son, **Keith Mathews Anderson**, we received a letter asking for verification of Keith's name. His middle name, **Mathews**, was misspelled on that form. It was incorrectly spelled as Matthews with two "t's" instead of **Mathews** with one "t." My maiden name is **Mathews** (one "t"), and it is important to me to have it spelled correctly.

	48
	63
	77
	92
	107

We made the requested correction on the original verification form and returned it on June 17 along with a $12 check for two copies of the birth certificate. Now we have been sent a "Request for Name Change" form. We do <u>not</u> want to change his name. We just want the error corrected.

122
136
151
165

Sincerely, | Ms. Mary Mathews Anderson — 172

Letter 2
Business Letter
Format and key the text at the right as a business letter in block format with open punctuation.

August 15, ---- | Mr. Steven Swenson | 280 Westridge Dr. | Halifax, NS — 13
B3M 3K8 | CANADA | Dear Mr. Swenson — 19

The degree program plan you submitted for a Master of Science degree in business education was approved on August 14. A copy of the plan with the required signatures is enclosed. Any changes to the approved program will require submission of the **Program Change Form**, which is available in the Graduate Office.

34
48
63
77
82

In your recent letter, you mentioned that you were planning to complete your degree next summer. Please remember that you will need to register for the written comprehensive examination the first week of the semester in which you plan to take the exam. A complete listing of other important dates for you to be aware of is included on **Summer Graduation Dates Form** (enclosed).

96
111
126
141
155
157

If you have questions about any of the dates or if we can be of assistance to you as you complete your degree requirements, please stop by our office.

172
187

Sincerely | Jason R. Edwards | Assistant Dean | xx | Enclosures — 198

Letter 3
Personal-Business Letter
Open LTR83B1 (or rekey Letter 1 above). Change the format to block format with open punctuation. Include the text at the right as the last paragraph of the letter.

Please verify when this correction has been made. Let us know, also, when we will get the birth certificate copies that we paid for two months ago.

UNIT

15 Assess Keyboarding/ Application Skills

LESSONS 68–71

LESSON 68 — Assessment Preparation

Objectives:

1. To improve keying speed and control.
2. To review format features of major documents.

68A • 5
Conditioning Practice

each line twice SS; DS between 2-line groups; a 1' writing on line 3

alphabet	1	Five or six people jogged quickly along the beach in a warm haze.
fig/sym	2	This Chu & Son's May 17 check should be $45.39 instead of $62.80.
speed	3	Lana and he may cycle to the ancient city chapel by the big lake.

gwam 1' | 1 | 2 | 3 | 4 | 5 | 6 | 7 | 8 | 9 | 10 | 11 | 12 | 13 |

68B • 10
Skill Building

1. Key each line once SS; DS between 2-line groups. Do not substitute italic for underlines in lines 1 and 2.

2. If time permits, key a 1' writing on each of lines 10, 12, and 14; find *gwam* on each.

underline & CAPS LOCK	1	Ballet & Modern Dance; The Encyclopedia of Film; American Theatre
	2	Marilou has bought TEN OF THE BEST of the Reader's Digest series.
shift keys	3	The Royal Ballet; Nederlands Dans Theater; London Festival Ballet
	4	Balanchine and Kirstein founded the New York City Ballet in 1948.
apostrophe & quotes	5	Masefield's "The Dauber"; Kipling's "Gunga Din"; Bronte's "Hope";
	6	We'll read Sandburg's "Chicago" and Frost's "The Road Not Taken."
alphabet	7	hope very quit mark axle zone cord boat sign four gown such major
	8	Six able men have quietly walked off good jobs at our city plaza.
letter response	9	date upon ever only care jump sets pink fear join were milk defer
	10	As you are aware, my trade union acted upon only a few age cases.
combination response	11	fish were duty ever risk fear goal fast they safe sign hulk ivory
	12	You are to refer the big wage case to an auto union panel of six.
word response	13	then form their eight world visit title chair firms signal profit
	14	A city auditor is to sign all the work forms for the civic panel.

gwam 1' | 1 | 2 | 3 | 4 | 5 | 6 | 7 | 8 | 9 | 10 | 11 | 12 | 13 |

68C • 35
Preparation for Assessment

To prepare for assessment, key selected problems from those listed at the right. Make a list of page numbers to avoid having to return to this page as you work.

Simplified memo, p. 115
Personal-business letter, p. 124
Business letter, p. 130
Unbound report, pp. 145-146

Study the placement and spacing of document parts as a review.

words

November 10, ---- | MS MICHELE YOUNG | 491 BROOKSIDE DR | FORT   11
COLLINS CO 80526-3977 | COMMUNICATION PRESENTATION   21

After hearing you make a few comments at the Business Education   34
Advisory Council meeting, I knew you were an effective communicator and   48
would be an excellent guest speaker for my business communication   62
class. My initial assessment was confirmed by your presentation   75
yesterday.   77

The students and I appreciated your taking time to share your thoughts   91
with us. After you left, we took a few minutes to discuss some of   105
your comments. The students were in complete agreement that you   118
were an excellent role model of what we have been discussing during   131
the semester. Many of your remarks reinforced points that had previously   146
been made in class. The students are looking forward to testing some   160
of your suggestions when they give their presentations.   171

Thank you again for bringing your expertise to Lincoln High School.   185

CHAD ANDERSON, INSTRUCTOR | xx   191

82C • 8
Editing Copy

Open LTR80C1 (or rekey Letter 1, p. 194). Reformat the letter in simplified block format with the changes to the second paragraph outlined at the right. Use CONVENTION SPEAKERS for the subject line.

Should
would like additional information
~~If~~ you decide you ~~are interested in learning more~~ about any of

listed on   complete the enclosed card .
the speakers ~~after reviewing~~ the printout, ~~let us know~~ We

cassette
can provide you with a video~~tape~~ of a portion of your selected

free of charge
speaker's presentation. ~~This allows~~ you and your committee ~~to~~ can

acquainted   before making a decision
become ~~familiar~~ with a speaker's presentation and style.

LESSON 83   Letters and Basic Skill Practice

Objectives:
1. To increase skill at processing letters in various formats.
2. To increase straight-copy keying skill.

83A • 5
Conditioning Practice

each line twice

alphabet 1 Listing the exact job requirements for Eve will keep Zelda happy.

speed 2 They may visit the big chapels in the dismal towns on the island.

fig/sym 3 Warren McKinley paid me $736,000 for the 8,460 acres on 12/15/96.

gwam 1' | 1 | 2 | 3 | 4 | 5 | 6 | 7 | 8 | 9 | 10 | 11 | 12 | 13 |

Assess Keyboarding & Correspondence Skills

Objectives:
1. To build/assess keying skills.
2. To assess correspondence knowledge and skills.

69A • 5
Conditioning Practice

each line twice SS; DS between 2-line groups; a 1' writing on line 3

alphabet	1	Jack saw five prime quail and a big fox down by the old zoo lake.
fig/sym	2	The cabinet (36" x 59" x 14 1/2") is now on sale for just $78.50.
speed	3	The busy auditor may work with vigor to form the key audit panel.

gwam 1' | 1 | 2 | 3 | 4 | 5 | 6 | 7 | 8 | 9 | 10 | 11 | 12 | 13 |

69B • 10
Assessment: Keying Skill

1. Key a 1' writing on each ¶; note *gwam*.
2. Key a 2' writing on ¶s 1-3 combined; find *gwam*.
3. Key a 3' writing on ¶s 1-3 combined; find *gwam*, count errors.

all letters used

	gwam	2'	3'

For many people during a large part of the past century, stay- 6 | 4 | 57
ing in the same job with a single company or institution for their 13 | 9 | 62
entire productive lives was not uncommon.   Now it is thought that 19 | 13 | 66
many fledgling workers will switch jobs several times in their 26 | 17 | 70
working lives. 27 | 18 | 71

The pace of change in the national job arena today requires 33 | 22 | 75
that all people prepare themselves to move upward or outward in the 40 | 27 | 80
same company or from firm to firm.   Such moves demand widened ex- 46 | 31 | 84
perience and education.   Often the moves result in better pay and 53 | 35 | 88
benefits. 54 | 36 | 89

So do not envision your diploma or your initial job as the end 60 | 40 | 93
of anything. Recognize that they are merely milestones in the on- 67 | 45 | 98
going process of preparing for a richer, more responsible life. 73 | 49 | 102
Living is a process of becoming rather than a state of being. 79 | 53 | 106

gwam 2' | 1 | 2 | 3 | 4 | 5 | 6 |
3' | 1 | 2 | 3 | 4 |

Communication ⟲ Concepts Inc.

178 S. Prospect Ave. ■ San Bernardino, CA 92410-4567 ■ (714) 186-7934

Dateline   August 13, ----   2" TM or center page
            QS

Letter address   MR CARL VISQUEL
382 OLD MURFREESBORO RD
NASHVILLE TN 37217-8902   DS

Subject line   SIMPLIFIED BLOCK LETTER FORMAT   DS

Body of letter   This letter is arranged in simplified block format. Several differences distinguish this format from the block and modified block styles. DS

The **salutation** is omitted; it is replaced by a subject line. The **subject line** is keyed below the letter address in ALL CAPS. A double space is left above and below it. DS

The letter format is further streamlined by the omission of the **complimentary close**. The **writer's name** and **title** (or department) are keyed a quadruple space below the body of the letter in ALL CAPS. The name and title are separated by a comma. DS

(1")

Notice that the letter address of this letter is keyed in the style recommended by the U.S. Postal Service for OCR processing: ALL-CAP letters with <u>no</u> punctuation. As with the other letter formats, it would also be appropriate to use cap-and-lowercase letters with punctuation for the letter address. DS

Many organizations have decided to use this particular style. Their opinion is that the salutation and complimentary close serve little purpose and are obsolete. Other organizations still prefer the traditional block or modified block format. QS

Mrs. Caroline Martinez

Writer's name and title   MRS. CAROLINE MARTINEZ, WORD PROCESSING SPECIALIST DS

Reference initials   hpj

Letter in Simplified Block Format

69C • 35
Assessment: Correspondence Skills

Format/key the documents as directed below.

Document 1
Simplified Memo
SM: defaults (or 1")
Date: current year
Errors: corrected

Document 2
Personal-Business Letter
SM: defaults (or 1")
Format: block
Date: current year
Errors: corrected

Document 3
Business Letter
SM: defaults (or 1")
Format: block
Date: current year
Errors: corrected

	words
November 26, ---- | Members of Lakeview Chorale | REHEARSALS	11
FOR "SOUNDS OF LAKEVIEW"	16
On December 1, formal rehearsals for our holiday program, "Sounds	30
of Lakeview," will begin.	35
These rehearsals will be held in the auditorium at 2:30 on Monday,	48
Wednesday, and Friday afternoons. Each rehearsal is scheduled for	62
two hours. Make plans now for transportation home. If someone is	75
to pick you up, be sure he or she is here no later than 4:45 p.m.	89
We have an exciting program planned, so arrive on December 1 in good	102
voice and with your usual enthusiasm.	110
Cecilia Valdez, Choral Director | xx	117

	words
2299 Riverside Dr. | Tulsa, OK 74105-3896 | November 26, ---- |	12
Miss Amanda Monaco | Fallsington Hall for Women | 500 Ash St. |	23
Houston, TX 77044-2145 | Dear Amanda	30
How great it will be to have the "college grind" over for several days,	45
starting December 20. I look forward to seeing you during the holi-	58
days.	60
Remembering how much we enjoyed participating in the musical events	73
at Mohawk High School, I acquired two tickets for this year's holiday	87
program on December 23. I hope you will be my guest.	98
I'm sure many of our mutual friends will attend. Seeing them again	112
should be great fun for both of us. Please say you'll go.	124
Cordially | Adrian Forbes	129

	words
November 26, ---- | Mrs. Evelyn M. McNeil | 4582 Campus Dr. |	11
Fort Worth, TX 76119-1835 | Dear Mrs. McNeil	20
The new holiday season is upon us, and we invite you to beat the rush	34
and visit our exciting Gallery of Gifts. Gift-giving can be a snap this	48
year because of our vast array of gifts "for kids from one to ninety-	62
two."	64
What's more, many of our gifts are prewrapped for presentation.	77
All can be packaged and shipped from right here in the store.	89
A catalog of our hottest gift items and a schedule of holiday hours for	104
special charge-card customers are enclosed. Please stop in and let us	118
help you select that special gift, or call us if you wish to shop by	132
phone.	133
We wish you happy holidays and hope to see you soon.	144
Cordially yours | Ms. Carol J. Suess, Manager | xx | Enclosures	155

81C • 10
Singular Verbs (continued)

Follow the Learn/Apply procedure in 76C, p. 184.

Use singular verbs with the pronouns *all* and *some* (and with fractions and percentages) when used as subjects if their modifiers are singular. Use plural verbs if their modifiers are plural.

Learn   1. All of the manuscript is at the publishers.
Learn   2. Some of the girls have already left for spring break.
Apply   3. All of the materials (has, have) been purchased.
Apply   4. Some of the watermelon (is, are) left.

Use a singular verb when *number* is used as the subject and is preceded by *the*; use a plural verb if *number* is preceded by *a*.

Learn   5. A number of clients have moved to Colorado.
Learn   6. The number of men passing the CPS exam has increased.
Apply   7. The number of games on the schedule (has, have) decreased.
Apply   8. A number of individuals (is, are) going to the meeting.

LESSON 82

Simplified Block Letters

O b j e c t i v e :
To learn to format letters in simplified block style.

82A • 5
Conditioning Practice

each line twice

alphabet 1 Putting on the extravaganza was quite a big job for Lydia Camack.
speed 2 Enrique and the girls may go downtown to pay for the six emblems.
figures 3 He sold 1,307 units on Monday, 954 on Tuesday, and 862 on Friday.
gwam 1' | 1 | 2 | 3 | 4 | 5 | 6 | 7 | 8 | 9 | 10 | 11 | 12 | 13 |

82B • 37
Simplified Block Letters

Letter 1

Study the format guides for the simplified block letter on p. 189 and the model letter on p. 199. Format and key the letter on p. 199.

Letter 2

Format and key the text at the right in simplified block format.

 note:

Save this document (LTR82B2) for later use.

words

June 21, ---- | MR ANTHONY KENSINGTON | 8288 NEWCASTLE 10
LN | ALBANY GA 31701-9326 | NEW PHONE SYSTEM 18

To provide better customer service, Fair Oaks Credit Union will begin 32
using a new phone system on July 1. Although the new system requires 46
changing most Fair Oaks Credit Union phone numbers, it provides our 60
customers with direct access to all of our departments. 71

The attached listing is enclosed for your convenience. For numbers not 86
listed, dial 186-2222. We are confident that this new system will provide 101
you with better banking services. 108

MS. JULIE A. NOTTINGWOOD, CUSTOMER SERVICE | xx | Attachment 119

LESSON 70

Assess Report Skill

Objectives:
1. To build/assess keying skills.
2. To assess report knowledge and skills.

70A • 5
Conditioning Practice

each line twice

alphabet 1 Six monks in the park quietly saw a fat lizard devour juicy bugs.

fig/sym 2 Rates varied from 14.25% to 17.50% on loans from $298 to $36,500.

speed 3 Keith may make an authentic map of the ancient city for the firm.

gwam 1' | 1 | 2 | 3 | 4 | 5 | 6 | 7 | 8 | 9 | 10 | 11 | 12 | 13 |

70B • 5
Assessment: Keying Skill

1. Key a 3' writing on ¶s of 69B, p. 169; find *gwam*.

2. Proofread your 3' writing and count/record errors.

70C • 40
Assessment: Report Skills

Format/key the document shown at right and on p. 172 as a three-page unbound report, errors corrected. Place the references list on a separate sheet—as page 4. Save as RPT70C1.

words

ENHANCE YOUR REPORT IMAGE | 5

Whether in school or on the job, you must prepare and present re- | 18
ports. Written reports create an image of you--on paper. To achieve the | 33
most positive image, written reports must be prepared carefully and pre- | 47
sented forcefully. | 51

To prepare an excellent report, Clippinger (1995, 11-12) suggests five | 66
equally vital steps that must be taken in the order listed: (1) plan; | 80
(2) draft; (3) revise; (4) edit; (5) format. | 89

Plan the Report | 92

To plan, ask: What is my purpose for writing, and what is the | 105
reader's purpose for reading what I write? The answers become the core | 120
of the message. Compose and key the core idea. Then as they come to | 134
mind through listening, reading, and thinking, jot (on the computer screen) | 149
ideas and facts that are related to the core idea. Next, check the list for | 165
missing items (and add them), unneeded items (and delete them), and | 178
redundant items (and combine them). Put the items in psychological or- | 193
der (main point followed by details, usually) and arrange them logically (in | 208
chronological, geographical, or importance order, for example). Finally, | 223
check the list to see that the items are tied together and related to the core | 239
idea. When appropriate, use tables, charts, or graphs to condense data; | 253
then list only summaries of what the visuals reveal in greater detail. | 268

(continued on next page)

completion of the review. Further, the overall produc- 163
tivity of the company seems to suffer, at least for a 174
few weeks. 176

I have talked over with President Vermillion the concerns 186
that were expressed at our summer meeting. He recog- 199
nizes that improvements need to be made to our perfor- 209
mance appraisal procedures. He feels so strongly about 221
wanting to improve our review procedures that he has 231
agreed to bring in two or three outside consultants to 242
work with us for two or three days. 250

The three consultants ~~who~~ *who* I am considering bringing in 261
are Dr. Mitch Carlson, Dr. Charlayne Winger, and Mr. 271
Roul Mikva. 281

All three individuals have an extensive background in the area of employee appraisals.

Dr. Carlson is the personnel director for a California- 292
based firm, Integrated Technologies. During his eight 303
years at Integrated Technologies, the turnover rate has 314
been cut in half--we all know what that means in terms 325
of training costs. He has also given numerous workshops 337
throughout the United States and Canada. 345

Dr. Winger is a management professor at the Brickley 356
State University. She is the author of several articles 367
dealing with employee motivation and evaluation in some 379
of the leading management journals. She also has con- 389
ducted a number of seminars. 395

*Mr. Mikva has international experience in the area of 406
employee evaluation. He completed graduate work on 417
the topic at a university in England. He has done 427
consulting work in Germany, Japan, and Mexico. He 437
should be able to offer an international perspective. 448*

I believe the time that these individuals spend with us 459
will be most productive. Plans call for each of the 470
three consultants to make a short lecture-type presen- 481
tation. This will be followed by a videotape presenta- 492
tion illustrating positive and negative performance 502
appraisals. Time is also being set aside for a discus- 513
sion with the consultants on the problems encountered in 525
performance appraisals. Finally, we plan to have a 539
videotaped role-playing session that will be critiqued 547
and discussed by the consultants. 553

The consultants will be with us on November 3 and 4. 564
Please arrange to have your schedule free on both days. 575

Draft the Message

To draft or compose the message, pretend that the reader is sitting before you. Write (at the keyboard) as you would talk with that person (level of vocabulary, degree of formality, and so on). Focus on the core of your message as you follow your listed items. Ignore for now such things as grammar, spelling, and style. Complete the entire report in one work session, if possible. If that is not possible, finish at least a major section without stopping (to gain continuity).

Revise the Copy

To revise, read and study what you wrote. Try to read the text as the reader will--without knowing what you meant to say. Ask again and again: Does it do what I set out to do--to get the message from my mind into the reader's mind in a favorable way? If not, why not? Check for and eliminate cliches, faulty logic, irrelevant facts or ideas, lack of examples, or vague statements. Revise the message until it cannot be misunderstood.

Edit the Text

To edit, study the revised draft and analyze how you said what you wrote, looking at each word, phrase, and sentence. Put yourself in the reader's place again. Ask these questions: Is the text interesting? Did I use active verbs? Do sentences vary in length and structure? Do the ideas flow evenly and smoothly and support the core idea or theme? Rid the text of common defects: excess words, impressive-sounding words and technical jargon, passive verbs, indefinite words, long words, short choppy sentences or complicated ones, and ill-chosen words or lack of transitional words or phrases. For a "proof of the pudding" check, have the text read by another set of eyes and revise the text again if any part of the message is unclear or confusing. Excellent reports result from multiple revisions. (Harcourt, and others, 1996, 76)

Format the Report

To format or present the report, leave blank space around the text and between parts. Use a standard report format for placement and spacing. Use emphasis devices for items you want to stress: bold, italic, underline, and bullets. Use such devices judiciously because if you emphasize everything, you emphasize nothing.

You may choose a distinctive typeface of larger size for the report title. Generally, though, use 10- or 12-point type for the body copy and one or two emphasis devices to highlight different levels of internal headings (ALL CAPS, bold, italic, underline). Such final touches make the report appear inviting, well organized, and easy to read.

Finally, support your report with a list of references from which you paraphrased or directly quoted. Quoting or paraphrasing without giving credit is illegal; further, supporting your report with relevant references helps to authenticate what you have said.

REFERENCES

Baugh, L. Sue. How to Write Term Papers and Reports. Lincolnwood, IL: VGM Career Horizons, 1993.

Clippinger, Dorinda A. "Write This Way." The Small Business Journal, March 1995.

Harcourt, Jules, and others. Business Communication. Cincinnati: South-Western Publishing Co., 1996.

Sorrenson, Sharon. Webster's New World Student Handbook. 2d ed. New York: Prentice-Hall, Inc., 1992.

LESSON 81   Standard Memos

Objectives:

1. To format standard memos with a distribution list.

2. To format a two-page memo.

81A • 5
Conditioning Practice

each line twice

alphabet   1   Jake will become the quality supervisor for Guzzo Food next year.

speed   2   The official paid the men for the handiwork they did on the dock.

figures   3   The packages were sent to 312 Birch, 4069 Lake, and 578 Hastings.

gwam   1' | 1 | 2 | 3 | 4 | 5 | 6 | 7 | 8 | 9 | 10 | 11 | 12 | 13 |

F ORMATTING

81B • 35
Standard Memos

Memo 1

Format and key the text at the right as a standard memo.

 note:

Create a macro for standard memo headings (see p. 188).

Note: Electronic typewriter users can store the standard memo headings.

Memo 2

Format and key the text at the right as a standard memo. Review how to format memo distribution lists and two-page memo headings in the format guides on p. 189.

	words
TO: All Employees	FROM: Justin Reed, Accounting Department	DATE:	13
June 5, ----	SUBJECT: EXPENSE FORMS	21

Please start using the attached expense form when you submit your June   35
expenses. Your suggestions for improving the form were very helpful. We   50
are confident that you will find the form easier to complete.   62

We were able to accommodate those of you who requested that the form be   76
put on the computer. You can access the form on the network by retrieving   92
the EXPNFORM file. Of course, we encourage all of you to use the comput-   106
erized form, if possible; most of the delays in processing the expense forms   122
are a result of illegible writing.   129

If you encounter any problems with the form, please call Mary Nen   142
(Extension 2871). | xx | Attachment   148

```
TO:  Marsha Mastin, Accounting Manager | Kent Van Noy, Market-   12
ing Manager | Rebecca Etheridge, Finance Manager | Shelby        23
Fuller, Word Processing Manager | Kari Hefner, Personnel         34
Manager | Cori Goodwin, Graphics Manager | Christine Bennett,    45
Public Relations Manager | FROM:  Edward G. Nolta, Vice          56
President | DATE:  October 12, ---- | SUBJECT:  EMPLOYEE PERFOR-  67
MANCE REVIEWS                                                    70

It's almost time again for annual performance reviews, a pro-   83
cess that you may not anticipate eagerly.  As we discussed      94
last summer at our meeting, employees and managers often look   107
upon these conferences as a time to discuss all the things      118
employees have done wrong during the past year.  With this      130
approach to performance reviews, tension is high; and           141
neither the managers nor the employees feels good at the        152
```

(continued on next page)

LESSON 71 — Assess Keyboarding & Table Skills

Objectives:
1. To build/assess keying skill.
2. To assess table knowledge and skills.

71A • 5
Conditioning Practice

each line twice SS; DS between 2-line groups; a 1' writing on line 3

alphabet 1 Jacques asked to be given one week to reply to the tax quiz form.

fig/sym 2 The damaged carton (#29-403-567) was returned on June 18 to AF&T.

speed 3 Doris may sign the proxy form if they make an audit of the firms.

gwam 1' | 1 | 2 | 3 | 4 | 5 | 6 | 7 | 8 | 9 | 10 | 11 | 12 | 13 |

71B • 10
Assessment: Keying Skill

1. Key a 1' writing on each ¶; find *gwam* on each.
2. Key a 2' writing on ¶s 1-3 combined; find *gwam*.
3. Key a 3' writing on ¶s 1-3 combined; find *gwam*, count errors.

all letters used

gwam 2' 3'

Workers on the job have to plan their workdays and organize 6 4 72
their work so that all duties are done in a timely fashion. As a 13 8 76
result, much is being said about teaching students to prioritize 19 13 81
work. The truth is that novice office workers have only limited 26 17 85
opportunities to set their own priorities; rather, priorities are 32 21 89
often set for them. 34 23 91

For example, in a word processing center a supervisor receives 40 27 95
the work from various document writers.   He or she then assigns the 47 31 99
work to keyboard operators on the basis of their work loads and in 54 36 104
the sequence of immediacy of need. Even a private secretary is 60 40 108
often told by the "boss" which work is urgent and which may not be 67 45 112
needed immediately. 69 46 114

As workers develop on the job and are given a greater variety 75 50 118
of tasks to perform, the need to set priorities increases. By 81 54 122
then, however, they will have learned through their supervisors 88 59 126
which types of tasks take priority and which ones can be put off. 94 63 131
Realize that priorities grow out of the immediacy or timeliness 101 67 135
of need. 102 68 136

gwam 2' | 1 | 2 | 3 | 4 | 5 | 6 |
3' | 1 | 2 | 3 | 4 |

Letter 2
Business Letter
modified block; indented ¶s; mixed punctuation

wp note:
Save to open later (LTR80C2).

February 3, ---- | Mr. Rori M. Conseco | NEA President | 3890 Northcliffe 14
Manor Dr. | Houston, TX 77066-9365 | Dear Mr. Conseco: 24

As a member of the San Francisco Convention Bureau, I am pleased to 38
extend an early welcome to the National Economics Association. San 51
Francisco is a great convention city. 59

My company, **Tours Unlimited**, works with organizations such as yours to 73
customize tours of the sights of San Francisco. We provide the enclosed 88
listing of the most frequently visited sights; you select the ones your mem- 103
bership would like to see. We will take care of making sure your members 118
see everything they desire while in San Francisco. It is as simple as that. 133

I will give you a call early next week to see if you are interested in having 149
Tours Unlimited assist with your convention plans. 159

Sincerely, | Ms. Ashton Sheridan | Tour Consultant | xx | Enclosure 171

Letter 3
Personal-Business Letter
modified block format; blocked ¶s; mixed punctuation

930 Main St. | Cartersburg, IN 46114-8930 | June 6, ---- | 11
Attention Software Manager | McCarty Computer Products | 21
382 Mayhew Dr. | Indianapolis, IN 46227-8762 | Ladies 31
and Gentlemen: | USER'S MANUAL 39

Last week when I was in Indianapolis, I 47
purchased the "Fingertip Geography" software package 58
from your store. Today when I tried to use the software, 69
I found that a user's manual was not included. 79

Please send a copy of the manual as soon as 88
possible so that I will be able to install the software and 100
start using it. I've enclosed a copy of the receipt that 111
contains the identification numbers for the software. 122
Sincerely yours, | Richard LaFayette | Enclosure 131

80D • 5
Editing Text
Either open LTR80C2 or rekey Letter 2 and make the changes outlined at the right to the second paragraph.

My company Tours Unlimited works with organizations such as yours
to customize tours of the sights of San Francisco. We provide the
enclosed listing of the most frequently visited sights; you select
those
the ones your membership would like to see.

Table 1
Using standard placement, format/key the table DS with 1.0" (10 sp.) between columns; correct errors.

Table 2
Using standard placement, format/key the table DS with 1.0" (10 sp.) between columns; make indicated changes and correct any errors you make as you key.

Table 3
Format/key the table DS with 0.6" (6 sp.) between columns; correct errors.

Table 4
If time permits, format/key Table 1 again, substituting your favorite novels/authors.

		words
MY ALL-TIME FAVORITE NOVELS		6
Title	Author	9
East of Eden	Steinbeck	13
Grapes of Wrath	Steinbeck	19
The Old Man and the Sea	Hemingway	25
The Red Badge of Courage	Crane	32
The Yearling	Rawlings	36

		words
MOST VISITED CIVIL WAR SITES		6
(Managed by National Park Service)		13
Site	Mil.	15
Gettysburg, PA	1.4	19
Chickamauga-Chatanooga, GA-TN	1.0	26
Vicksburg, ~~VA~~ MS	1.50	30
Kennesaw, GA	0.9	33
Manassas, VA	0.6	36
_____		40
Source: U.S. NEWS & WORD REPORT, April 10,		49
ss 1995.		50

			words
ALL-TIME BEST-SELLING MUSIC ALBUMS			7
Title	Artist	Sold	11
Thriller	Michael Jackson	24 m.	17
Rumours	Fleetwood Mac	17 m.	23
Boston	Boston	15 m.	27
Eagles Greatest Hits	Eagles	14 m.	34
Born in the U.S.A.	Bruce Springsteen	14 m.	43
Total Sales		84 m.	46
_____			49
Source: USA Today, May 5, 1995.			56

Objectives:

1. To format letters in modified block style.
2. To increase proficiency in keying opening and closing lines of letters.

80A • 5
Conditioning Practice

set 0.5" SMs; each line twice

alphabet	1	Nan was to have completed the required textbook for the zoology major.
speed	2	She may work with the men on their problem with the city turn signals.
fig/sym	3	Blake Realty sold the houses on Lots #3 & #6 for $87,950 and $104,200.

gwam 1' | 1 | 2 | 3 | 4 | 5 | 6 | 7 | 8 | 9 | 10 | 11 | 12 | 13 | 14 |

FORMATTING

80B • 7
Drill: Modified Block Letter

1. Two 1' writings on opening lines (date through ¶ 1) of modified block letter on p. 193. Concentrate on letter parts. Add 2 words on the second writing.

2. Two 1' writings on closing lines (¶ 3 through copy notation) of modified block letter on p. 193. If you finish before time is called, DS and begin

again. Focus on correct placement of letter parts. Add about two words (10 keystrokes) on the second writing.

80C • 33
Modified Block Letters

Letter 1
Business Letter
modified block format, blocked ¶s; open punctuation

wp note:
Save to open later (LTR80C1).

words

December 12, ---- | Ms. Lindsay Magnus | NEA Convention Chair |	12
819 Country Club Dr. | Largo, FL 34641-5639 | Dear Ms. Magnus	23

Here is the printout of individuals registered with **Speakers**, **Speakers**, **Speakers** who have listed economic issues as a topic on which they give presentations. The printout provides a brief description of their presentations along with the fees charged. — 38, 51, 65, 74

If you decide you are interested in learning more about any of the speakers after reviewing the printout, let us know. We can provide you with a videotape of a portion of your selected speaker's presentation. This allows you and your committee to become familiar with a speaker's presentation and style. — 87, 101, 116, 130, 135

Given the fees being charged by speakers today, we think this preview gives you the opportunity to learn as much as possible about the speaker before making a final selection. Much of the uncertainty is eliminated. Let us know which videos you would like, and we will send them out today. — 149, 162, 176, 189, 193

Sincerely | Ms. Kim Khatib | Manager | xx | Enclosure — 202

Twin Cities Youth Camp for Fine & Performing Arts

**TWIN CITIES
YOUTH CAMP**

**(A Keyboarding
Simulation)**

Setting and Organization

This coming summer Twin Cities University (TCU) will sponsor a Twin Cities Youth Camp for Fine & Performing Arts. The camp is made possible by grants from the Carnegie Foundation and the National Endowment for the Arts. A committee of local high school teachers will assist in planning and coordinating the camp.

The purpose of the camp is to give approximately 40 qualified high school seniors in the Minneapolis-St. Paul area an opportunity to study and work with outstanding performers in the fields of art, music, theater, and dance. The camp will be limited to 8-10 students in each of those categories.

The study program will include formal classes, demonstrations, individualized coaching, and workshop-style performances of both students and teachers. Campers will also visit art galleries and museums and attend evening events in which professionals perform in recital or concert.

You have been chosen to work as a part-time office assistant to Ms. Twyla Winfrey, of Lake Como High School, who chairs the high school teacher committee. She works directly with Dr. Jorgi Franco of TCU, who chairs the university planning committee.

In addition to answering the telephone, filing correspondence and other records, and entering/retrieving information using the computer, you will process memos, letters, reports, and other documents. Even though your keyboarding teacher has verified that you know how to process documents in standard formats, Ms. Winfrey gives you the following excerpts from the *Formatting Manual* used by the Twin Cities Youth Camp office personnel.

You are to consult the excerpts if you have format questions.

Format Guides

Letters

1. Stationery: camp letterhead/envelopes.
2. Format: block style, open punctuation.
3. SM: defaults (or 1").
4. TM: 2" (or Center Page feature).
5. Spacing: QS (3 blank line spaces) between date and letter address and between complimentary close and writer's name; DS (1 blank line space) between all other parts.

Memos

1. Stationery: camp letterhead.
2. Format: standard.
3. SM: defaults (or 1").
4. TM: 2".
5. Spacing: DS (1 blank line space) between all parts; SS ¶s, DS between them.

Announcements and Tables

1. Stationery: plain paper.
2. TM: 2" (or Center Page feature).
3. Spacing: DS throughout; EXCEPTION: SS 2-line headings, source notes, and grouped items within tables.

Reports

1. Stationery: plain paper.
2. SM: defaults (or 1").
3. TM: 2", page 1 and references page, if separate; otherwise, 1".
4. PE: at least 1" bottom margin.
5. Spacing: QS (3 blank line spaces) between title and body; DS all other lines.
6. Page numbers: page 1, not numbered; other pages, at top right margin.

DOCUMENT PROCESSING SPECIALISTS
6652 Remington St.
New Haven, CT 06517-1498
(203) 555-8215

Dateline   March 27, ----   2" TM or center page
                                                             QS

Letter   Miss Anne Corless
address   Asturia Technologies
                5409 Bayview Dr.
                Miami, FL 33160-8682 DS

Salutation   Dear Miss Corless: DS

Subject line   MODIFIED BLOCK LETTER FORMAT/BLOCKED PARAGRAPHS DS

Body of   This letter is arranged in modified block format with blocked
letter   paragraphs. The only difference between this letter format and
                the block format is that the dateline and the closing lines
                (complimentary close, keyed name of the originator, and his or
                her title) begin at the horizontal center point. DS

(1")   Mixed punctuation (a colon after the salutation and a comma after   (1")
                the complimentary close) is used in this letter. If an enclosure
                is mentioned in the body of the letter, the word Enclosure is
                keyed a double space below the reference notation, flush with the
                left margin. Copy notations are placed a double space below the
                enclosure notation or below the reference initials if no enclo-
                sure has been indicated. DS

                A copy of the block format letter is enclosed so that you can
                compare the two formats. As you can see, either format presents
                an attractive appearance. DS

Complimentary   Sincerely yours, QS
close

                                            Troy Williams

Keyed name   Troy Williams
Official title   Word Processing Consultant DS

Reference   ph DS
initials

Enclosure   Enclosure DS
notation

Copy   c Ms. Kimberlee Rodriguez
notation

Letter in Modified Block Format (Letter 1)

A Keyboarding Simulation

Objectives:

1. To apply keying skills in a work setting.
2. To work under direction but with few *specific* directions.

72A-75A • 5
Daily Warmup

alphabet	1	The judge quizzed my expert witness before making the vital call.
fig/sym	2	Both started today (6/7): Tina at $421.89/wk.; Vic at $10.53/hr.
speed	3	A city panel may work with the six big firms to fix the problems.

gwam 1' | 1 | 2 | 3 | 4 | 5 | 6 | 7 | 8 | 9 | 10 | 11 | 12 | 13 |

FORMATTING

72B-75B • 45
Simulation

Document 1
Standard Memo

From the desk of:
Ms. Winfrey

TO: Members of Youth Camp Planning Committee
FROM: Twyla Winfrey, Chair, H.S.
DATE: January 5, ----
SUBJECT: Youth Camp Participant Selection Process

Document 2
Summary Report in Unbound Format

From the desk of:
Ms. Winfrey

Format: Unbound DS report; bold the title; italicize side headings (if Italic is available)
Purpose: To promote summer youth camp

Here is a first draft of a summary of the selection process to be used in choosing students for the Twin Cities Youth Camp for Fine & Performing Arts to be held at Twin Cities University this summer.

I believe the decisions reached at our last joint meeting are accurately reflected in the summary. To be sure, please read the summary carefully and note any changes you think should be made.

After I receive your feedback, I'll prepare a revised summary to be included in a packet of material to be given to prospective participants and their parents.

xx | Enclosure

TWIN CITIES YOUTH CAMP FOR FINE & PERFORMING ARTS

July 9-22, ----

The Twin Cities Youth Camp for Fine & Performing Arts on the Twin Cities University campus is scheduled for two weeks, from Sunday afternoon, July 9, to Saturday night, July 22. Made possible by grants from the Carnegie Foundation and the National Endowment for the Arts, the camp will give approximately forty students a rare opportunity to study and work with outstanding specialists in the fields of art, music, theater, and dance. The camp can accommodate up to ten students in each of these fields.

Art Camp

Up to ten art students will be chosen on the basis of their entries in a competitive art exhibit to be held at Roseville High School on Saturday, May 13. Entries will be judged by an art professor from TCU, an art teacher from a local high school, and an art critic from the Minneapolis Institute of Art. Each student must enter at least three but not more than five pieces--at least one in oils, one in watercolor, and one in charcoal. Other categories include sculpture and computer graphics.

Music Camp

As many as ten music students will be chosen based on their performance at competitive auditions to be held at Hiawatha High School on Saturday, May 13.

(continued on next page)

Modified Block Letters

Objectives:

1. To format business letters in modified block style.
2. To use word processing features to edit documents.

79A • 5
Conditioning Practice

each line twice

alphabet 1 Zac Jurkovic was quite eager for the next two games to be played.

speed 2 The girl and man may signal the proficient maid with a big flame.

fig/sym 3 The 11% tax on Order #624 is $13.80; for Order #209 it is $37.50.

gwam 1' | 1 | 2 | 3 | 4 | 5 | 6 | 7 | 8 | 9 | 10 | 11 | 12 | 13 |

79B • 35
Modified Block Letters

1. Study the modified block letter format guides on p. 189 and the model letter illustrating modified block on p. 193. Note the differences between the block letter and the modified block letter format.

2. **Letter 1**: Format and key the letter on p. 193. Correct your errors as you key. Proofread the document. On screen use the View feature to check the format of the letter before saving the letter under the filename CORLESS.

3. **Letter 2**: Retrieve (or rekey) the letter and format it as a modified block letter with the following changes:

a. Address the letter to:

**MR BRANDON SMOLTZ
HOILAND PLASTICS
876 KENILWORTH AVE
PONTIAC MI 48058-8723**

b. Delete the subject line.

c. Include the following sentence at the end of the first paragraph: **The paragraphs of a modified block letter may or may not be indented**.

d. Use SMOLTZ for the filename.

79C • 10
Editing Text

Either key copy or open MEM78B3 (or rekey Document 3, p. 191) and make the changes outlined at the right to the first two paragraphs of the memo.

Last week President Simonson ^and I attended a seminar on managing conflict. ^We were She was so impressed with the seminar that ^we she would like ^to have all department managers to take part in a future seminar ^attend the seminar next month. ^"You Can Manage Conflict,"

The one-day seminar ^is geared to help you deal constructively with conflicts that arise in the ^day-to-day normal operations of your department. Ms. Simonson ^and I believes that each department manager who participates in a seminar will ^become be more effective in dealing with conflicts. ^We She thinks that you will be able to build and maintain stronger departmental ^and interdepartmental relationships will exist if all managers attend.

The judges will include two professors of music from TCU, two music teachers from local high schools, and two music critics (one from the Star Tribune, the other from the Pioneer Press). Both vocalists and instrumentalists may enter the competition. For the first time, a computerized synthesizer may be used for accompaniment.

Theater Camp

Eight to ten theater students will be chosen on the basis of their performance at competitive auditions to be held at Richfield High School on Saturday, May 20. Judges will include two professors of drama and theater from TCU, two class play directors from local high schools, and one drama/theater critic from each of our local newspapers. Musical theater students may enter as actors, vocalists, or both.

Dance Camp

Up to ten dance students will be selected on the basis of their performance at a dance competition to be held at Falcon Heights High School on Saturday, May 13. Judges will be specialists in ballet and modern dance from TCU, a dance theater critic from the Star Tribune, and the director of Twin Cities Dance Company. Entrants may dance solo, in pairs, or in groups.

Living Accommodations

All students will live in campus dormitories. Each group will be mentored by a TCU faculty member and a high school teacher. Meals will be provided for all youth campers in the Student Center cafeteria. Student living costs are covered by the grants.

Document 3
Youth camp faculty list

From the desk of: Ms. Winfrey

Format: 3-column table; SS body, but DS between departmental groups— *open File TCAMP3*
TM: 2" (or Center Page feature)
CS: 0.6" (6 sp.)
Purpose: To include in promotion packet for students/parents

YOUR CAMP FOR FINE & PERFORMING ARTS

Participating TCU Faculty & Staff

Name	Function	Department
Dr. John M. Lenz	Coordinator	Art
Ms. Lucia del Rio	Instructor	Art
Mr. Frederick Marx	Instructor	Art
Miss Bella Spear	Coach	Art
Mr. Paul Mehta	coach	Dance
Miss Ana de Avila	Coordinator	Dance
Mr. Ari Baccus	Instructor	Dance
Ms. Tamara Jones	Instructor	Dance
Mr. Darius Brown	Cordinator	Music
Mr. Felix Ardello	Instructor	Music
Ms. Anita Fry Carr	Instructor	"
Miss Susan Parish	Coach	"
Dr. Olivia Habjan	Coordinator	Theatre
Ms. Serena Conte	Instructor	"
Mr. Henri DeLong	Instructor	"
Mr. Cyril Pierce	Coach	"

Document 2
Business Letter

Format and key the text at the right as a business letter in block format with open punctuation (see p. 130 to review).

words

May 18, ---- | Miss Jessica A. Kelley | 910 Longbrook Ave. | Bridgeport, 13
CT 06497-2325 | Dear Miss Kelley 20

Speaking to your FBLA chapter was my pleasure. I particularly en- 33
joyed responding to the questions of your members after the pre- 46
sentation. 48

I have enclosed copies of the articles in The Wall Street Journal and 62
Business Week about which you inquired. Perhaps the article that appeared 77
in last week's Time magazine, "Let's Talk Trade," will also assist you 92
in preparing your report. 97

Representatives from our bank always enjoy speaking to student groups. 112
If you need presenters in the future, please let me know. 123

Sincerely | Yorick Kelsey | Customer Relations | xx | Enclosures 135

Document 3
Standard Memo

Format and key the text at the right as a standard memo (see p. 117 to review). Save to open later. Filename: MEM78B3.

TO: Department Managers | FROM: Rhett Canton, Human Resources | 12
DATE: June 15, ---- | SUBJECT: MANAGING CONFLICT SEMINAR 23

Last week President Simonson attended a seminar on managing conflict. 37
She was so impressed with the seminar that she would like all department 52
managers to take part in a future seminar. 61

The one-day seminar is geared to help you deal constructively with 74
conflicts that arise in the normal operations of your department. 87
Ms. Simonson believes that each department manager who participates 101
in a seminar will be more effective in dealing with conflicts. She thinks 116
that you will be able to build and maintain stronger departmental 129
relationships. 132

Two seminars are scheduled for next month. The first is scheduled 146
for July 12 in Milwaukee. The second is scheduled for July 23 and will 160
be held in Madison. Please let me know which seminar you would like 174
to attend, and I will make the necessary arrangements. | xx 185

Document 4
Simplified Memo

Format and key the text at the right as a simplified memo (see p. 115 to review).

February 2, ---- | Word Processing Department | SELECTION OF NEW 12
WORD PROCESSING DEPARTMENT MANAGER 19

As you may have heard by now, Diane Chi announced her plans to retire at 33
the end of March. The position will be advertised both internally and exter- 48
nally. 51

For those interested in applying for the position, a resume and letter 65
of application should be sent to Director Rhett Canton, Human Resources 79
Department, by February 16. Interviews will be conducted the following 93
week so that the new manager can be hired by March 1. This schedule 107
will allow the new manager to work with Ms. Chi for a month prior to 121
her retirement. 124

Ms. Kathy Lind | Human Resources | xx 131

Document 4
Announcement

From the desk of:
Ms. Winfrey

Format: 2" TM; DS; center each line, bold the main heading

Purpose: To place on high school bulletin boards

Document 5
Final Event Program

From the desk of:
Ms. Winfrey

Format: 2-column table; DS body

TM: 2" (or Center Page feature)

CS: 0.8" (8 sp.)

Purpose: To include with letter inviting parents to final event

Document 6
Proposed Letter to Parents

From the desk of:
Ms. Winfrey

Format: Block style, open punctuation

TM: 2" (or Center Page feature)

Date: January 6, ----

Address: Mr./Mrs. John C. Dunn, 178 Royal Oak Blvd., Brooklyn Center, MN 55430-4322

Salutation: Dear Mr./Mrs. Dunn

Complimentary close: Cordially

Signature: Miss Adele Chiodi, Chair Invitation Committee

Purpose: To invite parents of participating students to final event

TWIN CITIES UNIVERSITY, *AND* MINNEAPOLIS/ST. PAUL

an~ounce

Twin Cities Youth ~~Cared~~ *Camp* for Fine & Performing Arts

TCU Campus, *July 9-22*

for

High School *Student* Artists, Musicians, Actors, and Dancers

Participants Determined by Competitive Auditions *Exhibits*/

Admission ~~Attendance~~: # Free

Courtesy Carnegie Foundation and National Endowment for the Arts

Further Information to be Available Soon!

VOICES OF HARMONY
Youth Camp ~~Main~~ *Final* Event

Theme	Focus
Voices of Freedom	Gospel music/drama
Voices of Expression	Hispanic music/~~drama~~ *dance*
Voices of the Spirit	Native American poetry/~~cadence~~ *rhythm*
Voices of Jazz	African-American jazz/dance
Voices of Movement	Orient~~ia~~*al* music/~~drama~~ *dance*
Voices of Tradition	Classical/folk music
Voices of the American Stage	Tribute to american musicals
Voices of ~~Youth~~ *Hope*	Youth looks toward the future

You are invited to attend the Final Event of the Twin Cities Youth Camp for Fine & Performing Arts. This exciting event, "Voices of Harmony," will be held in Nokomis Auditorium on the TCU campus at 7:30 p.m., July 22. Admission for parents is free.

A copy of the preliminary program is enclosed. You will note the multicultural focus of the program, which reflects the theme of the two-week camp in which the student participants will be engaged. The youth campers are highlighted, but some TCU faculty and students are included when necessary to supplement the cast.

In addition to the variety of music, drama, and dance that comprise the program, you will enjoy viewing the artwork of the Art Campers that will be exhibited in the foyer of the auditorium.

The Final Event is designed to delight you, to surprise you, and to expand your perspective. Please come and bring other members of your family (if any) to support these happy campers. | xx

Objectives:

1. To review letter and memo formatting.
2. To increase proficiency in keying opening and closing lines of letters.

78A • 5
Conditioning Practice

each line twice SS; then two 1' writings on line 2: find *gwam*; clear screen

alphabet	1	Jasper Markowitz, the tax manager, believed he could not qualify.
speed	2	A formal social for the girl is to be held in the ancient chapel.
figures	3	Pat quickly found the total of 8.25, 9.16, and 10.43 to be 27.84.

gwam	1'	1	2	3	4	5	6	7	8	9	10	11	12	13

FORMATTING

78B • 45
Letters and Memos

Document 1
Personal-Business Letter
Review the model personal-business letter on p. 124. Format and key in block style the letter shown at the right. Italicize or underline *The Wall Street Journal* and *Business Week;* bold **International Partnerships**.

wp note:

Wherever you see underlined words, you may use italic if you prefer. Do NOT use both underline and italic, though.

words

910 Longerook Ave. | Bridgeport, CT 06497-2325 | May 17, ---- | Mr. Yorick — 14

Kelsey | First National Bank | 2995 Mt. Pleasant Dr. | Bridgeport, CT — 27

06611-2301 | Dear Mr. Kelsey — 32

¶ Thank you for taking time to speak to our FBLA chapter. — 43
Your comments were most appropriate for our members. — 54

¶ During your presentation you referred to articles appearing — 66
in The Wall Street Journal and Business Week. Do you remember — 79
in which issues those articles appeared? I'm preparing a — 91
report for my social studies class on trade barriers; I believe — 104
the articles you referred to would be excellent sources of — 115
information for the report. Are you aware of other sources — 127
that would be appropriate for the topic? — 136

¶ Thank you again for sharing your expertise. Your — 146
talk on International Partnerships made us realize the — 157
importance of American business abroad. — 165
Sincerely | Miss Jessica A. Kelley | FBLA Member — 174

Document 7
Table of Art Museum
Tour Highlights

From the desk of:
Ms. Winfrey

Format: 3-column table; SS body of table, but DS below data for each gallery
TM: 2" (or Center Page feature)
CS: 0.4" (4 sp.)
Purpose: To include in promotion packet for students/parents

Document 8
Letter to Judge of
the Dance Contest

From the desk of:
Ms. Winfrey

Format: Block style, open punctuation
TM: 2" (or Center Page feature)
SM: defaults (or 1")

Documents 9–11
Letters to Judges of Other
Competitions

From the desk of:
Ms. Winfrey

Process the message of Document 8 to each addressee listed at the right. Change the salutation as appropriate; make needed changes in ¶ 1 as indicated below the addresses. Use your initials as the keyboard operator.

HIGHLIGHTS OF ART MUSEUM TOUR

New Perspectives

Gallery	Artist	Subject
African-American Gallery	A Collection	Prints
	Robert Scott Duncanson	Murals
Hispanic Gallery	Julio Larraz	Sketches
	Rafael Ortiz	Abstracts
Main Gallery	Thomas Sierak	Sketches
	Camille Pissaro	Landscapes
Oriental Gallery	Tat Shinno	Florals
	Sherrie McGraw	Still Life

January 7, ----

Mr. Alexi Kosov
Star Tribune
800 N. First St.
Minneapolis, MN 55401-3627

Dear Mr. Kosov

How fortunate we are to have you join the panel of judges who will select the winners of the dance contest to be held at Falcon Heights High School at 2 p.m. on May 13.

You will be joined on the panel by selected faculty members from Twin Cities University and local high schools.   It is especially fitting, though, to have a professional critic on the panel.

Your insistence on serving without honorarium is most commendable. Please know how grateful we are.

As the contest date nears, I'll send a friendly reminder.

Cordially yours

Ms. Twyla Winfrey, Chair
Planning Committee, H.S.

xx

Ms. LuAnn Chang
Pioneer Press
345 Cedar St.
St. Paul, MN 55101-2266

¶ 1, line 2: *art contest;*
Roseville High School

Mr. Anton Navarro
Star Tribune
800 N. First St.
Minneapolis, MN 55401-3627

¶ 1, line 2: *music contest;*
Hiawatha High School

Mrs. Nadia Horowitz
Pioneer Press
345 Cedar St.
St. Paul, MN 55101-2266

¶ 1, line 2: *drama contest;*
Richfield High School

¶ 1, line 3: *May 20*

Format Guides

Modified Block with Indented ¶s and USPS Letter Address

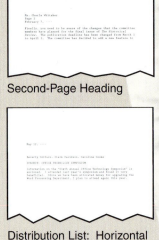

Second-Page Heading

Distribution List: Horizontal

Distribution List: Vertical

Two variations of the block letter format presented in Unit 11 are the modified block and the simplified block formats. The following guidelines present the changes required for formatting these two styles of letters.

Modified Block Letter Format

"Modified block" (illustrated on p. 193) simply means that the block format has been modified. The date and the closing lines (complimentary close, writer's name, and writer's job title or department) start near the horizontal center of the paper instead of at the left margin. Use the default tab at 4" position.

Paragraphs. The paragraphs of a letter formatted in the modified block style may be indented, or they may be blocked at the left margin.

Open and mixed punctuation. The modified block letter may be formatted with open or mixed punctuation. A letter formatted with mixed punctuation has a colon following the salutation and a comma following the complimentary close. A letter formatted with open punctuation has no punctuation following the salutation or the complimentary close.

Simplified Block Letter Format

The simplified block letter format (illustrated on p. 199) is another variation of the block letter format. The salutation (Dear Mr. Visquel:) and the complimentary closing (Sincerely yours,) are omitted. A subject line is always included. The writer's name and title are keyed in ALL CAPS a QS below the final paragraph of the letter.

Second-Page Headings

Leave a 1" top margin above the second-page heading of a letter or memo. Key the heading SS in block format at the left margin. Include the name of the addressee, the page number, and the date. DS between the heading and the body. (See illustration at left.) If the document is going to multiple individuals, use a name that describes the group of individuals collectively; for example, *Managers, Executive Board, or Planning Committee.*

Memo Distribution Lists

When a memo is sent to several individuals, a distribution list is used. The simplified memo uses the horizontal listing; the standard format uses the vertical listing. (See illustrations at bottom left.)

Special Letter Parts

Subject line. The subject line specifies the topic discussed in the letter or memo. Key the subject line in ALL CAPS, a DS below the salutation (or letter address for simplified letter format).

Attention line. When an attention line, such as *Attention Human Resources Manager,* is used in a letter addressed to a company, key it as the first line of the letter and envelope address. When an attention line is used, the correct salutation is "Ladies and Gentlemen." (An attention line is used ONLY when the person's name is unknown to the letter writer.)

USPS Letter Address Style

The letter address for any letter format may be keyed with uppercase and lowercase letters, or it may be keyed in ALL CAPS with no punctuation (USPS Style). See illustration at top left.

your PERSPECTIVE

ETHICS: The Right Thing to Do

Robert Frost once said, "Good fences make good neighbors." This statement reflects the common practice of erecting fences, walls, and other barriers to human interaction. Walls and fences are often erected to keep people *out*, but sometimes they are erected to keep people *in*.

A fence can be erected around a yard to keep pets in and to provide a safe place for children to play. On the other hand, a fence may be erected to keep out the neighbors' children and pets as well as other invaders of privacy. Walls and fences surround prisons to keep inmates in and to control who on the outside can have direct contact with those on the inside.

We see walls and fences used to protect the privacy and property of those inside; at other times, we see them used to protect the lives and property of those on the outside. In other situations, we see them used merely to keep out or to keep in the unwanted.

Walls and fences can be *invisible* as well as *physical*. Invisible walls and fences may take the form of qualifications for membership in a club or other organization, as expressed in bylaws. They may be unwritten or outwardly unspoken preferences or attitudes of one group of people toward another group.

Thus, we see that walls or fences erected to protect one group may seem positive to those included, but to those in the excluded group may seem restrictive and negative. This is often especially evident in the behavior of rival gangs, but it is at least subtly apparent in the attitudes and behaviors of various factions in clubs, schools, churches, and communities.

Richard Lovelace, in *"To Althea, from Prison,"* said: "Stone walls do not a prison make, nor iron bars a cage." He added that so long as his mind was innocent and free, he enjoyed liberty even though in prison.

Edwin Markham, speaking of invisible fences used to shut out others, wrote in "Outwitted":

> He drew a circle that shut me out—
> Heretic, rebel, a thing to flout.
> But love and I had the wit to win;
> We drew a circle that took him in. ✴

ACTIVITIES

1. Read carefully the comments at the left about physical and invisible walls and fences people use to include or exclude others.

2. Key a list of the kinds of walls and fences used to include and protect in a positive way those within.

3. Key a list of the kinds of walls and fences (or circles) used to exclude people in a negative way.

4. Using your lists as background, compose a short theme on the positive (good) and negative (bad) effects of walls and fences (physical and invisible) and how you deal with them.

Zoom and Save As

1. Read the copy at right.
2. Learn to use the Zoom and Save As features of your software.
3. Open the letter keyed in Lesson 52 (LTR52B2).
4. Use the Zoom feature to increase and decrease the amount and size of text on the screen.
5. Make the changes outlined at the right; save the document as WHITMAN.

The **Zoom** feature allows you to manipulate the amount and size of text appearing on the screen. The feature can be used to view the entire page by decreasing the print size or can be used to view a portion of the page more clearly by enlarging the print size.

The **Save As** feature is used to save an existing file under another filename, thus keeping the original document intact. This feature is frequently used when a document is opened and changes are made. To be able to open the original document as well as the revised document, the revised document should be saved under another filename using the Save As feature.

Address the letter to:

Ms. Jessica Whitman
561 Woodcliff Dr.
Atlanta, GA 30350-8821

Change salutation to:

Dear Ms. Whitman

ACTIVITY 6:

Macro

1. Read the copy at right.
2. Learn to define macros using your software.
3. Define a macro for **Thompson Floral & Greenhouse.**
4. Key the text at the right using the macro key each time *Thompson Floral & Greenhouse* appears in the text.

The **Macro** feature of a software package allows the operator to save (record) keystrokes and retrieve (playback) them at a later time. For example, if the headings for a standard memo (TO:, FROM:, DATE:, and SUBJECT:) were saved as a macro, the operator could depress the defined macro keys instead of keying the headings each time a standard memorandum was created.

Thompson Floral & Greenhouse sells fresh cut bouquets.

Thompson Floral & Greenhouse delivers balloon bouquets.

Thompson Floral & Greenhouse sells green plants.

Thompson Floral & Greenhouse delivers fruit baskets.

Thompson Floral & Greenhouse has silk and dry arrangements.

Thompson Floral & Greenhouse has beautiful wedding flowers.

Thompson Floral & Greenhouse has flowers for all occasions.

Thompson Floral & Greenhouse is your full flower center.

GLOBAL AWARENESS

Climate, in addition to other factors, causes different countries to produce or manufacture certain products by which those countries are often identified. Although the United States produces many of these same products, it is not especially noted for doing so. In fact, the United States often imports the products in List B from the countries in List A.

To check your global awareness, you will see how many countries/products you can match correctly.

List A	List B
Australia	coffee/cocoa
Brazil	corn/wheat products
China	cotton/textiles
Cuba	electric/electronic products
Ecuador	diamonds/gold
Egypt	oil products
Japan	rice/silk
Mexico	sugar products
Saudi Arabia	tropical fruits
South Africa	wheat/wool

A C T I V I T I E S

1. Read paragraphs at left; study lists below them.

2. Key at left margin the first country in List A.

3. Tab 4 times and key the item(s) in List B with which that country is most closely associated.

4. Key remaining items in the same way, tabbing to align items in List B.

5. Compare/discuss answers and reasons for choices.

CULTURAL DIVERSITY

Many countries have national holidays of celebration to honor or remember special people or events in their history. One of those in the United States is Independence Day, or the Fourth of July, which commemorates the breakaway of the original thirteen Colonies from British rule.

How many of the national holidays in List A can you match with the country of their observance as given in List B?

List A	List B
Bastille Day	Canada
Buddha's Birthday	France
Confucius' Birthday	Great Britain
Commonwealth Day	Kenya
Constitution Day	Korea/Japan
Guy Fawke's Day	Mexico
Jamburi Day	Japan
Joan of Arc's Day	Taiwan
National Foundation Day	
Victoria Day	

A C T I V I T I E S

1. Read paragraphs at left; study lists below them.

2. Key at left margin the first item in List A.

3. Tab 4 times; key name of country you believe celebrates that holiday.

4. Key remaining items in the same way, tabbing to align items in List B.

5. Compare/discuss answers and reasons for choices.

ACTIVITY 1:

Date Text and Date Code

1. Read the copy at right.
2. Learn the Date Text and Date Code features for your wp software.
3. Key the information at the right using the Date Text and Date Code features as indicated.

The current date can be inserted into a document by using the **Date Text** feature. The **Date Code** feature also inserts the current date into the document. However, the Date Code feature replaces the previous date with the current date each time the document is opened or printed. The date and time on your computer must be current in order for the date to be correct.

<Date Text>

Mr. Jason Winchell
428 North 500 West
Salt Lake City, UT 84103-8321

<Date Code>

Ms. Rochelle Wilson
351 Parkwood Cir.
Anderson, SC 29621-8256

ACTIVITY 2:

Automatic Hyphenation

1. Read the copy at right.
2. Learn to activate the Hyphenation feature.
3. Key the text at the right with hyphenation off.
4. Key the text again with hyphenation on.

The **Automatic Hyphenation** feature divides (hyphenates) words that would normally wrap to the next line. This gives the right margin of the document a more attractive appearance.

A very useful feature in most of today's best word processing software packages is the feature that automatically hyphenates long words at the right margin. This feature will automatically divide such words rather than wrap them to the next line. By dividing these words automatically, the hyphenation feature makes the right margin less "ragged."

ACTIVITY 3:

Cursor Move

1. Read the copy at right.
2. Learn to move the cursor using **Home**, **End**, **PgUp**, **PgDn**, and **Home (Ctrl)** + arrow key *or* + arrow key combinations.
3. Key Sentence 1; edit as instructed in Sentences 2, 3, and 4 using the cursor move keys.

The **Home**, **End**, **PgUp**, and **PgDn** keys can be used to move the cursor quickly from one location to another location in a document.

The **Home** or **Ctrl** key in combination with the arrow keys can also be used to move the cursor to various locations.

1. Key the following.

   Ellen will be in New York on Monday.

2. Make the following changes, using the cursor move keys.

   Ellen will be in New York on Monday. [*Castino* *Albany,* *, June 25*]

3. Make these additional changes, utilizing the cursor move keys.

   Ellen Castino will be in Albany, New York, on Monday, June 25. [*ms.* *, the manager,* *Tuesday* *6*]

4. Make these changes.

   Ms. Ellen Castino, the manager, will be in Albany, New York, [*g.* *new*]
   on Tuesday, June 26 [*, from 11 a.m. to 3 p.m.*]

PHASE 3

Improve Keyboarding, Formatting, and Language Skills

This part of the textbook will enable you to improve present skills. Some activities will help you improve keying techniques, which can lead to higher speed and greater accuracy. Language skills can be improved, too, by familiar Read/Learn/Apply activities.

The thrust of Phase 3 is on improving your ability to format documents. After reviewing the formats for memos, letters, reports, and tables, you will apply your skill to longer, slightly harder forms of these documents. Then you will "go to work" again, applying your learning to work place situations.

Many documents involve topics you might find in a social studies course; for example, economics, geography, government, and history. Preparing these documents should remind you that ". . . people in all walks of life employ a computer keyboard. . . ."

In the 37 lessons of this phase, you will:

1. Refine keying techniques.
2. Improve language skills.
3. Improve keying skill on rough-draft and script copy.
4. Improve formatting skills on memos, letters, reports, and tables.
5. Gain work experience in a (simulated) travel agency.
6. Assess keying and formatting skills.

77D • 10
Singular Verbs (continued)

Follow the Learn/Apply procedure in 76C, p. 184.

> Use a singular verb with singular subjects linked by **or** or **nor**. *Exception*: If one subject is singular and the other is plural, the verb agrees with the closer subject.

Learn 1. Neither Jan nor Alice was invited to the banquet.
Learn 2. Either the council members or the chair has the agenda.
Apply 3. Neither Bill nor Jim (is, are) going to the game.
Apply 4. Either the cabinet members or the President (has, have) the gift.

> Use a singular verb with a singular subject that is separated from the verb by phrases beginning with **as well as** and **in addition to**.

Learn 5. The teacher as well as the students is going to attend.
Apply 6. The shirt as well as the dresses (has, have) to be ironed.

> Use singular verbs with collective nouns (**committee, team, class, jury,** etc.) if the collective noun acts as a unit.

Learn 7. The social committee has made the necessary arrangements.
Apply 8. The team (has, have) a game on Friday.
Apply 9. The jury (has, have) been sequestered.

S KILL BUILDING

77E • 15
Skill Check

1. A 1' writing on ¶ 1; determine *gwam*.
2. Add 2-4 *gwam* to the rate attained in Step 1, and note quarter-minute checkpoints from the table below.
3. Take three 1' guided writings on ¶ 1 to increase speed.
4. Practice ¶ 2 in the same way.
5. One 3' writing on ¶s 1 and 2 combined; determine *gwam* and find errors.

		Quarter-Minute Checkpoints			
gwam	1/4'	1/2'	3/4'	1'
28	7	14	21	28
32	8	16	24	32
36	9	18	27	36
40	10	20	30	40
44	11	22	33	44
48	12	24	36	48
52	13	26	39	52
56	14	28	42	56
60	15	30	45	60

all letters used

	gwam	3'	5'
The value of an education has been a topic discussed many		4	2	36
times with a great deal of zest. The value is often measured in		8	5	39
terms of costs and benefits to the taxpayer. It is also judged in		13	8	42
terms of changes in the individuals taking part in the educational		17	10	44
process. Gains in the level of knowledge, the development and		21	13	47
refinement of attitudes, and the acquiring of skills are believed		26	15	49
to be crucial parts of an education.		28	17	51
Education is a never-ending process. A person is exposed to for-		32	19	53
mal and informal education throughout his or her life. Formal learning		37	22	56
takes place in a structured situation such as a school or		41	25	59
a college. Informal learning occurs from the experience gained		45	27	61
from daily living. We are constantly educated from all the types		50	30	64
of media with which we come in contact each day as well as by each		54	32	66
person with whom we exchange ideas.		57	34	68

3' | 1 | 2 | 3 | 4 |
5' | 1 | 2 | 3 |

LESSON 76

Keying Technique/Language Skills

Objectives:
1. To improve and assess keying techniques.
2. To improve and assess keying speed and control.

76A • 5
Conditioning Practice

each line twice SS; then two 1' writings on line 2; find *gwam;* clear screen

alphabet	1	Jack Gomez will be our equipment manager for the next seven days.
speed	2	Their neighbor on the island is the chair of the sorority social.
fig/sym	3	She paid Invoice #382 ($6.79 with a 5% discount) with Check #104.

gwam 1' | 1 | 2 | 3 | 4 | 5 | 6 | 7 | 8 | 9 | 10 | 11 | 12 | 13 |

S KILL BUILDING

76B • 15
Technique:
Letter Keys

each line twice; rekey the lines that are most difficult for you

Goal: To keep keystroking action limited to the fingers.

Emphasize continuity and rhythm with curved, upright fingers.

A After Diana Aaron ate the pancake, she had an apple and a banana.

B Barbi Babbitt became a better batter by batting big rubber balls.

C Chi Chang from Creekcrest Circle can catch a raccoon for Chelcia.

D Did Dave and Don decide to delay the date of departure for a day?

E Ed and Eileen were elected to chaperone every late evening event.

F Fred figured fifty fast rafts floated from Fairfax to Ford Falls.

G Gary and Gregg glanced at the gaggle of geese on the green grass.

H His haphazard shots helped them through half of the hockey match.

I I think Ike insisted on living in Illinois, Indiana, or Missouri.

J Jackie just objected to taking Jay's jeans and jersey on the jet.

K Ken kept Kay's knickknack in a knapsack in the back of the kayak.

L Large and small holes in the lane by her dwelling will be filled.

M Mike meets my mom most mornings at the mall in the summer months.

gwam 1' | 1 | 2 | 3 | 4 | 5 | 6 | 7 | 8 | 9 | 10 | 11 | 12 | 13 |

Keying Technique/Language Skills

Objectives:
1. To improve and assess keying techniques.
2. To improve and assess keying speed and control.

77A • 5
Conditioning Practice

each line twice

alphabet 1 Jay Zuvella had two questions to complete before taking the exam.
speed 2 Their neighbor may dismantle the ancient shanty in the big field.
figures 3 Jim's score was 86 percent; he missed Numbers 17, 29, 35, and 40.
gwam 1' | 1 | 2 | 3 | 4 | 5 | 6 | 7 | 8 | 9 | 10 | 11 | 12 | 13 |

S KILL BUILDING

77B • 15
Technique: Letter Keys

each line twice; rekey the lines that are most difficult for you

Goal: To keep keystroking action limited to the fingers.

Emphasize continuity and rhythm with curved, upright fingers.

n Norman's niece and nephew can be tended by a new nanny on Monday.
o One of our boys opposed opening more offshore moorings for boats.
p Peter's playful puppies pulled the paper wrapping off the apples.
q Quinten quit questioning the quantity of bouquets at the banquet.
r Robert and Rae arrived after a carriage ride over the rural road.
s Sue sat still as soon as Sam served his sushi and sashimi dishes.
t Ty took title to two tiny cottages the last time he went to town.
u Uko usually rushes uptown to see us unload the four sugar trucks.
v Val voted to review the vivid videos when she visits the village.
w Will was waving wildly when a swimmer went wading into the water.
x Six tax experts explained that he was exempt from the excise tax.
y Your younger boy yearns to see the Yankees play in New York City.
z Zeno puzzled over a zealot who seized a bronze kazoo at a bazaar.
gwam 1' | 1 | 2 | 3 | 4 | 5 | 6 | 7 | 8 | 9 | 10 | 11 | 12 | 13 |

77C • 5
Speed Forcing Drill

Each line once at top speed; then, try to complete each sentence on the call of 15", 12", or 10" writing as directed. Force speed to higher levels as you move from line to line.

Emphasis: high-frequency balanced-hand words

	gwam	15"	12"	10"
Sue owns the chair in the shanty by the big field.		40	50	60
The girl will hand the sorority emblem to the visitors.		44	55	66
The handyman is to go to the field to cut ivy for the bowls.		48	60	72
Their goal is to surprise the four city officials during a visit.		52	65	78

gwam 1' | 1 | 2 | 3 | 4 | 5 | 6 | 7 | 8 | 9 | 10 | 11 | 12 | 13 |

76C • 10
Singular Verbs

1. Read the first rule.
2. Key the Learn sentences below it (with number and period), noting how the rule has been applied.
3. Key the Apply sentences using the correct verb shown in parentheses.
4. Read and practice the other rules in the same way.

> Use a singular verb with a singular subject.

Learn   1. The administrative assistant has left for lunch.
Learn   2. Marshall has already finished the assignment.
Apply   3. The author (has, have) already finished the manuscript.
Apply   4. She (is, are) leaving for college next Friday.

> Use singular verbs with indefinite pronouns (*each, every, any, either, neither, one,* etc.) used as subjects.

Learn   5. One of the members is expected to vote.
Learn   6. Each of the girls has been given an assignment.
Apply   7. Either of the two candidates (is, are) a good choice.
Apply   8. Neither of the artists (is, are) very good.

S KILL BUILDING

76D • 20
Skill Check

1. A 1' writing on ¶ 1; determine *gwam*.
2. Add 2-4 *gwam* to the rate attained in Step 1, and note quarter-minute checkpoints from table below.
3. Take three 1' guided writings on ¶ 1 to increase speed.
4. Practice ¶ 2 in the same way.
5. Two 3' writings on ¶s 1 and 2 combined; determine *gwam* and find errors.

Quarter-Minute Checkpoints

gwam	1/4'	1/2'	3/4'	1'
28	7	14	21	28
32	8	16	24	32
36	9	18	27	36
40	10	20	30	40
44	11	22	33	44
48	12	24	36	48
52	13	26	39	52
56	14	28	42	56
60	15	30	45	60

all letters used

gwam   3'   5'

Many options are available for people to ponder as they   4   2 39
invest their money. Real estate, savings accounts, money market   8   5 41
accounts, bonds, and stocks are but a few of the options that   12   7 44
are open to those who wish to invest their extra money. Several 17 10 46
factors will determine which type of investment a person will   21 12 49
choose. These factors pertain to the expected rate of return, the 25 15 52
degree of liquidity desired, and the amount of risk a person is   29 18 54
willing to take.   30 18 55

An investor who seeks a high rate of return and who is   34 20 57
willing to take a high degree of risk often considers the stock 38 23 59
market. Stock markets or stock exchanges are organizations that 43 26 62
bring investors together to buy and sell shares of stock. Stock 47 28 65
represents a share in the ownership of a company. Since more   51 31 67
risk is associated with an investment that has a high rate of   55 33 70
return, judgment must be exercised by those thinking about the   60 35 72
purchase of stock.   61 36 72

gwam   3' | 1 | 2 | 3 | 4
       5' | 1 | 2 | 3

APPENDICES

WINDOWS 95/98 AND WORD PROCESSING TUTORIAL

Explore Windows

Windows 95 and *Windows 98* are operating system software programs that control the operation of the computer and the peripherals such as the mouse and printer. Software applications that run under *Windows* have many common features. They all use similar icons and consistent menus. A typical *Windows* desktop is shown below. The icons represent some of the features common to either *Windows 95* or *Windows 98*.

Windows 95/98

The opening screen of *Windows 95/98* simulates a *desktop* working environment. The icons shown represent some of the features contained on your system.

 My Computer displays the disk drives, CD-ROM, and printers attached to the computer.

 Network Neighborhood allows you to view the available resources if you are connected to a network environment.

 Recycle Bin stores documents that have been deleted from the hard drive. Documents deleted in error can be retrieved and returned to their folders.

 Start displays the Start menu. From the Start menu, you can open a program, open Help, change system settings, close and exit *Windows 95/98*, and more.

The Start button is located on the *taskbar* at the bottom of the desktop. It is always visible when *Windows* is running. When you click Start, a menu displays with the commands for using *Windows*. Each time you open a program, a button with the name of the program displays on the taskbar. The taskbar below shows that *Microsoft Word* is open.

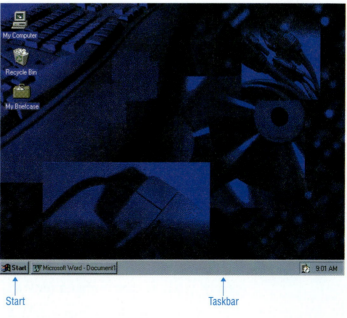

Start   Taskbar

Windows 95 Opening Screen

Skill Builder

Words/Sentences

1. Key each line once SS; DS between 2-line groups.
2. Key two 1' writings on each of lines 6 and 8; find *gwam* on each writing.

Goal: Variable rhythm—speed up easy words; steady pace on harder words

Paragraphs

1. Key two 3' writings on ¶s 1-3 combined; find *gwam* and count errors on each writing.
2. Key two 5' writings on ¶s 1-3 combined. If you finish ¶ 3 before time is up, rekey ¶ 1. Find *gwam* and count errors on each writing.

alphabet 1 maze five next jabs deft lazy quiet found close power light known
2 Xyros amazed seven young people with quick jabs and deft parries.

adjacent keys 3 cover opted point ropes hands smart tries walks toils leads azure
4 Keri was smart when she opted to try for a position as a trainer.

combination response 5 busy pink half join body limp world great throw eager handy extra
6 Signe may join the trade union to work in the nylon firm in town.

word response 7 sight angle shape corps risks turns theme world dials turns chair
8 Rodney may handle six social problems for the chair of the panel.

gwam 1' | 1 | 2 | 3 | 4 | 5 | 6 | 7 | 8 | 9 | 10 | 11 | 12 | 13 |

all letters used

gwam 3' | 5'

	3'	5'
In almost any position you might seek in the world of work,	4	2	51
you may discover a number of tedious aspects that are an integral	8	5	54
part of the job. You can anticipate a certain amount of routine,	13	8	57
also; so you must learn to accept it when you begin working full	17	10	59
time. Moreover, all jobs include events that will occupy vital	21	13	62
hours of the work week. Expect them; accept them; endeavor to	26	15	64
do them efficiently.	27	16	65
If you learn to organize your work carefully, you should be	31	19	68
able to handle details of a routine nature without undue stress or	35	21	70
irritation. As a result, you will have more time and energy to	40	24	73
concentrate on the crucial activities. When you have varied jobs	44	26	75
to do, size up the entire situation first. Then decide in what	48	29	78
sequence the various jobs should be handled. With that done, begin	53	32	81
to work.	54	32	81
You can learn quickly to move smoothly from one type of pro-	57	34	83
duction problem to another. Your ability to do this will reveal,	62	37	86
to a considerable extent, how well you can handle routine details.	66	40	89
Many keyboarding students do not take time to analyze the next task	71	43	92
in the light of the one just finished. As a consequence, they	75	45	94
merely rush to the subsequent task and begin from scratch as if	79	48	97
none of the problems were related.	82	49	98

gwam 3' | 1 | 2 | 3 | 4 | 5 |
5' | 1 | 2 | 3 |

Windows software requires the use of a mouse or other pointing device. The mouse is used to select items, to find and move files, to execute or cancel commands, to move and size items, and to draw images. The mouse pointer changes in appearance depending on its location on the screen and the task that it is doing.

I   The I-beam indicates that the mouse is located in the text area. When you pause, it blinks. As you use your software, most of the time you will see the I-beam.

    The arrow selects items. It displays when the mouse is located outside the text area.

    The hourglass indicates that *Windows* is processing your command. You must wait until *Windows* finishes its task before you key text or enter another command.

Using the Mouse

Move the mouse on a padded, flat surface. The mouse performs the following actions:

- *Point:* Move the mouse so that the pointer touches the icon or text.
- *Click:* Point to the desired item, the press and release the left mouse button once.
- *Double-click:* Point to the item and quickly press and release the left mouse button twice.

- *Click with the right mouse button:* Press and release the right mouse button once. A shortcut menu appears (*Windows 95/98*).
- *Drag:* Point to the desired item; hold down the mouse button; drag the item to a new location; then release the button.

Open Windows 95/98

Activity 1
Open Windows

1. Turn on the computer and monitor.
2. Click the **Start** button to display the Start menu. (Your Start menu may not look exactly like the illustration.)

3. Point to the *Programs* menu; a submenu displays to the right listing all the programs.

Start Your Word Processing Software

WP **note:**

This tutorial shows two popular word processing packages, *Microsoft Word* and *WordPerfect*, as examples. The points apply to other "for *Windows*" programs.

To open your word processing software, you may double-click on the word processing icon on your desktop or you may access the program through the Start menu under *Programs*. (*Corel WordPerfect* is located at the top of the Start menu.)

Skill Builder

Words/Sentences

1. Key each line once SS; DS between 2-line groups.
2. Key two 1' writings on each of lines 8 and 10; find *gwam* on each writing.

Goal: Fewer pauses between letters and words

alphabet
1 zinc work sold paid jell post flex lock move boat gone they quota
2 Jeremy paid for moving my quaint old zinc workbox to a warehouse.

outside reaches
3 slaw polo wash stop laps rope pony squad lapse quash sport splash
4 Paula saw the woman lead two sorrel polo ponies down to the quay.

double letters
5 seek cool loss roof meek zoom marry offer issue dizzy foggy happy
6 Lonnie will soon choose a college to attend at the end of summer.

combination response
7 maps card with gets pair join rich tear pale seek gush loin tight
8 Holly may go with him to get the maps at the address on the card.

word response
9 goal widow visit bugle blame civic bland panel flame shale dismal
10 The goal of the bland widow is to visit an ancient island chapel.

gwam 1' | 1 | 2 | 3 | 4 | 5 | 6 | 7 | 8 | 9 | 10 | 11 | 12 | 13 |

Paragraphs

1. Key two 3' writings on ¶s 1-3 combined; find *gwam* and count errors on each writing.
2. Key a 5' writing on ¶s 1-3 combined. If you finish ¶ 3 before time is up, rekey ¶ 1. Find *gwam*; count errors.

all letters used

	gwam	3'	5'

A job description is a formal statement of the duties performed by a worker. It may include both quality and quantity factors. The job description is used to select new workers and place them in jobs that best fit their abilities. A brief summary of the job description may be given to people who show interest in working for a company.

4	2	43
8	5	46
12	7	48
17	10	51
21	13	54
23	14	55

A performance appraisal form is a formal method of assessing the performance of workers. It defines each level of excellence a person may reach. It then lists in major groups the duties workers in a job class perform. The supervisor rates the person on each duty, using a scale of one to five, with a rating of three representing the standard.

27	16	57
31	19	60
36	21	62
40	24	65
44	27	68
46	29	68

A job description and an appraisal form may have a section on work habits: attitude on the job, working well with others, proper use of time, skill in writing and speaking, and initiative. When a job is done equally well by two workers, the one who shows better work habits and attitudes will usually get the prized promotion or pay increase.

50	30	71
54	33	74
59	35	76
63	38	79
68	40	81
69	41	82

gwam 3' | 1 | 2 | 3 | 4 | 5 |
5' | 1 | 2 | 3 |

Opening Screen

The opening screens of word processing programs for *Windows* include many of the same features.

- **Title bar.** Shows the name of the application software and the document.

- **Menu bar.** Click to display a pull-down menu. Select an option by moving the mouse pointer on top of the item and clicking the left mouse button. To close a pull-down menu, click the name again.

- **Toolbar/Power bar.** Provides a quick way to access frequently used features.

- **Formatting toolbar/button.** Provides a quick way to access commands.

- **Insertion point (cursor).** Indicates where text will appear next on the screen.

- **Status bar.** Indicates the position of the cursor and shows information about the document.

- **Scroll bar.** The vertical bar on the right of the screen contains a button that shows the approximate position of the window in the documents. You may scroll through the document by clicking and dragging the center button or by clicking the up/down arrow buttons.

Microsoft Word 97 **Opening Screen**

Create a Document

To create a document, simply begin to key on a clear screen. Text is entered to the left of the insertion point (cursor). Copy will wrap to the next line when the line is filled. To move the insertion point with your mouse, move the mouse pointer (↖) to the desired position and click the left mouse button. The pointer changes to a blinking vertical line (I).

Print a Document

1. Click on the File menu; choose *Print*.
2. The Print dialog box displays. Click **Print** (*WordPerfect*) or **OK** (*Microsoft Word*).
3. **Option:** Click the Print button on your Power bar/toolbar to print your document in one step.

Skill Builder

Words/Sentences

1. Key each line once SS; DS between 2-line groups.
2. Key two 1' writings on each of lines 8 and 10; find *gwam* on each writing.

Goal: Less wasted motion

alphabet	1 mend size then jerk flax sign buoy wave turn quit span luck quiet
	2 Thurman quickly fixed big holes in jibs pounded by sizable waves.
long, direct reaches	3 once myth brig hump numb much orbit bring curve dance nylon cents
	4 Marv may bring a large number of bright nylon flags for my dance.
adjacent keys	5 riot open acre sale here suit peer sort mere port flew walk juice
	6 Viola said we will offer for open sale twelve acres for building.
combination response	7 dish bear fuel lion corn read lake hill city drag town pill right
	8 They are to fix a gear on a big fuel pump at the city nylon mill.
word response	9 fight blend field eight shelf ivory proxy audit usual works vigor
	10 The eight girls work with right form and vigor to make the goals.

gwam 1' | 1 | 2 | 3 | 4 | 5 | 6 | 7 | 8 | 9 | 10 | 11 | 12 | 13 |

Paragraphs

1. Key a 1' writing on each ¶; find *gwam* on each one.
2. Key two 2' writings on ¶s 1-2 combined; find *gwam* on each writing.
3. Key two 3' writings on ¶s 1-2 combined; find *gwam* and count errors on each writing.

Quarter-Minute Checkpoints

gwam	1/4'	1/2'	3/4'	1'
64	16	32	48	64
60	15	30	45	60
56	14	28	42	56
52	13	26	39	52
48	12	24	36	48
44	11	22	33	44
40	10	20	30	40
36	9	18	27	36
32	8	16	24	32
28	7	14	21	28
24	6	12	18	24
20	5	10	15	20

all letters used

gwam 2' | 3'

A career is vastly more divergent than a job. If you talk 6 | 4 | 60
about landing a job when you finish school, you are saying that 12 | 8 | 65
all you are interested in is some kind of work with regular wages. 19 | 13 | 69
A career, however, has larger implications. It implies a life's 25 | 17 | 73
work in which you have interest and in which you have received 32 | 21 | 78
some training and education. But within any one career field, 38 | 25 | 82
there may be numerous and distinct choices. 42 | 28 | 85

In almost any of the careers you may choose, two basic items 49 | 32 | 89
are required for the career to grow—flexibility and an openness 55 | 37 | 93
for learning. Nowhere is this more true than in the world of busi- 62 | 41 | 97
ness. There are millions of workers in business today, and their 68 | 45 | 102
jobs range from accountants to zoologists. Regardless of your de- 75 | 50 | 106
sires, a career in business is open to just about all men and women 81 | 54 | 111
of nearly every field of interest. 85 | 56 | 113

gwam 2' | 1 | 2 | 3 | 4 | 5 | 6 |
3' | 1 | 2 | 3 | 4 |

Dialog Boxes

A dialog box displays when your software needs more information to carry out a task. Selecting a menu item that is followed by an ellipsis (...) will open a dialog box. The illustration below shows the parts of a dialog box and how to use them.

Option buttons: Turn an option on or off. You can only select one option in each group.

Check boxes: More than one box can be selected when available.

Spin buttons: Up arrow increases the value; down arrow decreases the value.

The arrow on some boxes indicates that a drop-down list is available for that option.

Command buttons: Execute a command or display another dialog box.

***Print* Dialog Box**

Activity 2
Create and print a document

1. Open your word processing program.
2. Identify the screen parts: title bar, menu bar, toolbar, status bar, Start button. (Refer to p. A4.)
3. Move your pointer around the screen. Notice how the pointer changes to an I-beam as it moves over the document work area.
4. Key your name. Strike ENTER 4 times. Notice the change on the status line.
5. Key the paragraph below using word wrap.
6. Choose *Print* from the File menu. Study the parts of the dialog box.
7. Print the page.
8. Keep the document open to use in Activity 3.

Keep in home position all of the fingers not being used to strike a key. Do not let them move out of position for the next letters in your copy.

Save a File

Activity 3
Name and save a file

Your computer has a hard drive (drive C) for storing files. The word processing software will automatically save your files to a special folder on your hard drive, unless you specify a different disk drive. For this exercise, save your document to drive A. Follow these steps:

1. Insert your storage disk into drive A.
2. From the File menu, choose *Save As*. The Save As dialog box displays.
3. In the Save in box, click the down arrow. Click **3 1/2" Floppy (A:)**.
4. Key this filename in the File name box: **Act3save**. Click **OK** or **Save**.

Click the drop-down arrow in the Drives box, then click A:.

Filename appears in List box after it is saved.

Key filename

***Save As* Dialog Box**

Skill Builder

Words/Sentences

1. Key each line once SS; DS between 2-line groups.
2. Key two 1' writings on each of lines 8 and 10; find *gwam* on each writing.

Goal: Finger-action keystrokes

alphabet	1	doze quit pack just exit have land them with clay gold risk bluff
	2	Jack may dazzle our awards banquet after his very exciting trips.
outside reaches	3	zoo apt spa opt laps aqua open says owes soap axle spot play slow
	4	Asa has opted to open a spa near our town hall as soon as he can.
double letters	5	add too odd err ill seen poor full food mall door hall wood shall
	6	Donna will get a glass door at the mall for her small front hall.
combination response	7	they pool lend wear then jump rich fear pale milk dorm cart their
	8	Edward may pump the treated water into the big dorm pool by noon.
word response	9	amend their ivory eight sorry spent dorms firms worry shall spend
	10	The chair may amend the form for the eight girls to do the audit.

gwam 1' | 1 | 2 | 3 | 4 | 5 | 6 | 7 | 8 | 9 | 10 | 11 | 12 | 13 |

Paragraphs

1. Key a 1' writing on each ¶; find *gwam* on each one.
2. Key two 2' writings on ¶s 1-2 combined; find *gwam* on each writing.
3. Key two 3' writings on ¶s 1-2 combined; find *gwam* and count errors on each writing.

all letters used   **gwam** 2' 3'

We live in a society of numbers. From the number of a birth   6 4 59
certificate to the number of a death certificate, numbers play a 13 8 63
very vital role in the daily life of each of us. Virtually all 19 13 68
typed personal and business papers contain figures. Quite often 25 17 72
these documents contain some commonly used symbols, also. There- 32 21 76
fore, skill in keying on the top row is critical to your future 38 26 81
use of the keyboard.   40 27 82

Data arranged in table form shows a common use of figures and 47 31 86
symbols. Although some tables include no figures, a very high per- 53 35 91
centage of them do. Just as top skill on a letter keyboard may pay 60 40 95
well, expert skill on figure copy may land you a prized job as a 66 44 99
technical operator that will pay even better. Workers in account- 73 49 104
ing and data processing offices must know how to operate the top 80 53 108
row and keypad with efficiency.   83 55 110

gwam 2' | 1 | 2 | 3 | 4 | 5 | 6 |
3' | 1 | 2 | 3 | 4 |

Quarter-Minute Checkpoints

gwam	1/4'	1/2'	3/4'	1'
64	16	32	48	64
60	15	30	45	60
56	14	28	42	56
52	13	26	39	52
48	12	24	36	48
44	11	22	33	44
40	10	20	30	40
36	9	18	27	36
32	8	16	24	32
28	7	14	21	28
24	6	12	18	24
20	5	10	15	20

Close a Document

When you are finished working with a file, close it to clear the work area. If you have made any changes to the document since saving it, you will be prompted to save the document before closing.

Activity 4
Close a document

1. Click the File menu and then click **Close**.

2. If you are prompted to save the file before closing it, click **Yes** in the dialog box.

Open a File

When you need to work with a file that has been closed, open the file to display it in the work area.

Activity 5
Open a file

1. Click **File** in the Menu bar.
2. Choose *Open.* **Option:** Click the **Open** button on the toolbar. The Open File dialog box displays.

3. Click the down arrow in the Look in box. Select drive A (or the drive where your data is located).
4. Click the filename and then click **Open.** The file displays.

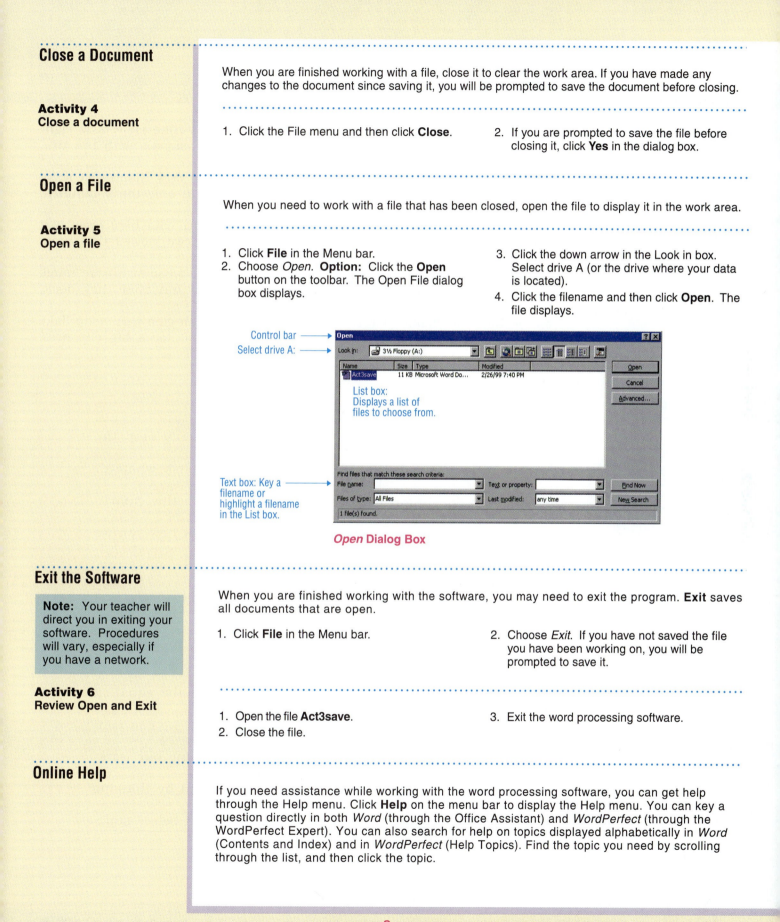

Control bar
Select drive A:

List box:
Displays a list of files to choose from.

Text box: Key a filename or highlight a filename in the List box.

Open **Dialog Box**

Exit the Software

Note: Your teacher will direct you in exiting your software. Procedures will vary, especially if you have a network.

When you are finished working with the software, you may need to exit the program. **Exit** saves all documents that are open.

1. Click **File** in the Menu bar.

2. Choose *Exit.* If you have not saved the file you have been working on, you will be prompted to save it.

Activity 6
Review Open and Exit

1. Open the file **Act3save**.
2. Close the file.

3. Exit the word processing software.

Online Help

If you need assistance while working with the word processing software, you can get help through the Help menu. Click **Help** on the menu bar to display the Help menu. You can key a question directly in both *Word* (through the Office Assistant) and *WordPerfect* (through the WordPerfect Expert). You can also search for help on topics displayed alphabetically in *Word* (Contents and Index) and in *WordPerfect* (Help Topics). Find the topic you need by scrolling through the list, and then click the topic.

J BASIC SKILL BUILDING

Words/Sentences

1. Key each line once SS; DS between 2-line groups.
2. Key two 1' writings on each of lines 8 and 10; find gwam on each writing.

Goal: Quiet (steady) hands/arms

alphabet 1 joke play boss quay dive coat muff gone arms zone show axle eight
2 Kozac piqued their defenses by mixing major signals with bravura.

long, direct 3 many peck tune cent must curb sums bran myth deck numb sync serve
reaches 4 Cecil must serve lunch to many hungry men in only thirty minutes.

adjacent 5 we ire few over stop rest owes ruin same part coin here open last
keys 6 Vera knew that this was the last stop before we viewed the ruins.

combination 7 the are pen gag cut pop did you sit jump form wear torn were name
reaches 8 A few of their crew are to be at the ancient inn after they dock.

word 9 they worn make dish when roam dorm than fish glen turn soap flake
response 10 The field work may aid them to make a profit for a big city firm.

gwam 1' | 1 | 2 | 3 | 4 | 5 | 6 | 7 | 8 | 9 | 10 | 11 | 12 | 13 |

Paragraphs

1. Key a 1' writing on each ¶; find gwam on each one.
2. Key two 2' writings on ¶ 1-2 combined; find gwam on each writing.
3. Key two 3' writings on ¶s 1-2 combined; find gwam and count errors on each writing.

all letters used

gwam 2' 3'

A great many people alibi that if they could only stop the 6 4 58
clock or hold the hands of time, they could accomplish whatever 12 8 62
they desire to do. Unfortunately, time marches on whether human 19 12 66
beings do or not. The question therefore becomes not how can we 25 17 70
acquire more time for ourselves, but how can we utilize more pro- 32 21 75
ductively the time allotted us. Learning to use time wisely is a 38 25 79
major step toward success. 41 27 81

Time is a constant, for everyone has an equal amount of it. 47 31 85
How we use time, however, is a critical variable in the equation 53 36 89
of excellence. Thinking requires time, of course; but we can con- 60 40 94
serve our time by taking time to plan before beginning our work. 66 44 98
The likelihood of having to do work over is decreased by thinking 73 48 102
through all related problems and planning the project before start- 80 53 107
ing work. 81 54 108

Quarter-Minute Checkpoints

gwam	1/4'	1/2'	3/4'	1'
64	16	32	48	64
60	15	30	45	60
56	14	28	42	56
52	13	26	39	52
48	12	24	36	48
44	11	22	33	44
40	10	20	30	40
36	9	18	27	36
32	8	16	24	32
28	7	14	21	28
24	6	12	18	24
20	5	10	15	20

gwam 2' | 1 | 2 | 3 | 4 | 5 | 6 |
3' | 1 | 2 | 3 | 4 |

INTERNET ACTIVITIES

Open Internet Browser

Word 97 users can quickly access the Internet while in *Word* by using the Web Toolbar. Display the Web Toolbar by clicking the Web Toolbar icon on the Standard toolbar.

Open the Internet browser by clicking the Start Page icon on the Web Toolbar. The web page you have designated as Home or Start Page displays.

Start Page

Corel WordPerfect 8 users can access the Internet while in *WordPerfect*. Select *Internet Publisher* from the File menu, then select *Browse the Web*.

Activity 1
Open Internet browser (*Word*)

1. Begin a new *Word* document.
2. Display the Web Toolbar.
3. Click the **Start Page** icon to open the Internet browser.

Note: You may also open the Internet browser from the **Windows** desktop or from any web toolbar located in a Microsoft Office application.

Activity 1
Open Internet browser (*WordPerfect*)

1. Begin a new *WordPerfect* document.
2. Display the Internet Publisher dialog box.
3. Choose *Browse the Web* to launch the Internet browser.

Web Addresses

A web address—commonly called the URL or Uniform Resource Locator—is composed of one or more domains separated by periods; e.g., http://www.house.gov or http://www.li.suu.edu. A domain name is the name given to a network or site that is connected to the Internet. As you move from left to right in the address, each domain is larger than the previous one. For example, in the web address http://www.house.gov, *gov* (United States government) is larger than *house* (House of Representatives). The table below identifies types of high-level domains.

.gov	Non-military government sites
.com	Commercial organizations
.edu	Educational institutions
.org	Other organizations
.mil	Military sites

A web address may also include a directory path and filenames separated by a slash; e.g., http://msstate.edu/athletics/. The web document named *athletics* resides at this site.

Activity 2
Understand web address names

1. Identify the high-level domain for the following web sites:
   a. http://www.senate.gov
   b. http://www.fbla-pbl.org
   c. http://www.army.mil
   d. http://www.ibm.com

2. Identify the filenames for the following web sites:
   a. http://www.reebok.com/soccer/
   b. http://www.espn.sportszone.com/soccer
   c. http://www.cnn.com/QUICKNEWS/
   d. http://nike.com/girls/

Prepare the text at the right as p. 5 of a report. Import the map graphic from a graphics package. Import the sales data for Colorado from the spreadsheet prepared in Activity 6.

Proofreading alert:

Assume that *any* copy you key may contain errors.

Illustration 1 depicts Region 6 territory as well as the number of sales reps in each state of the territory. All states except Colorado have 3 reps; Colorado has 5 reps.

Illustration 1

Number of Sales Reps

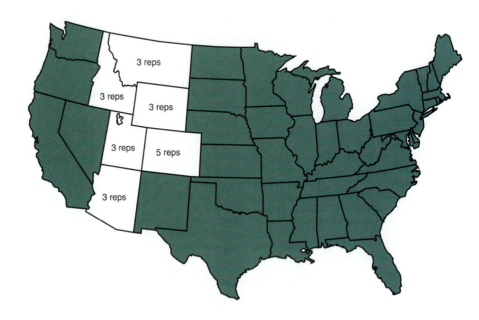

The sales figures for the first quarter reflect the munber of sales reps in each state. As could be expected, Clorado has the highest total sales for the first quarter (insert from spreadsheet) and the highest monthly average (insert from spreadsheet). Table 3 gives the complete sales figures for the Colorado reps.

Table 3

First Quarter Sales

Colorado

Name	January	February	March	Total Sales First Quarter	Monthly Average
Hundley, Ann	25,730	12,830	45,769	84,329	28,110
Johnson, Marge	38,654	38,020	36,908	113,582	37,861
Kent, Kellee	38,310	28,095	34,789	101,194	33,731
Martinez, Justin	33,810	23,789	28,210	85,809	28,603
Phillips, Josh	27,690	33,760	28,809	90,259	30,086
	164,194	136,494	174,485	475,173	158,391

Activity 8

Using the information in the spreadsheet, prepare a pie chart showing the percent of total sales for each state for the first quarter. Supply appropriate heading and size the chart to fit on a half page.

Open a Web Site

To open a web site from your Internet browser, click **Open Page** from the File menu (or click the Open icon if available on your browser toolbar). Key the URL **http://www.weather.com** as shown below and click **Open**. The home page for The Weather Channel displays.

Shortcut: Click inside the netsite entry box, key the URL, and press ENTER.

Activity 3
Open web sites

1. http://weather.com
2. http://www.abc.com
3. http://www.cnn.com/QUICKNEWS/
4. http://www.espn.sportszone.com/soccer
5. http://www.usps.gov/ctc/welcome.htm

Explore the Browser Toolbar

The browser toolbar is a helpful means for exploring ("surfing") the Internet. Become familiar with your browser toolbar by studying the items shown below. Browsers may vary slightly.

Netsite or Address Entry Box: Displays the active URL or web site address.

Back: Moves back to web sites previously visited since opening the browser.

Forward: Moves forward to sites visited prior to using Back icon. (The Forward icon is ghosted if the Back icon has not been used.)

Print: Prints a web page.

Home: Returns to the web page designated as Home or Start Page.

Stop: Stops computer's search for a web site.

Search: Opens one of the Internet search engines.

Bookmarks or Favorites: Moves to a list of web sites marked for easy access.

Activity 4
Practice using browser tools

1. Open each of the following web sites:
   a. http://www.nike.com
   b. http://www.adidas.com
   c. http://www.reebok.com
   d. a site of your choice
2. Click the **Back** icon twice. The _____ web site displays.
3. Click the **Forward** icon once. The _____ web site displays.
4. Print the active web page.
5. Keying in the netsite entry or address box, open **http://www.msstate.edu**. Stop the search before the web site is located.

Activity 6

Create a spreadsheet by importing the information in the table (Activity 5) into a spreadsheet program. When you finish Activity 6, your spreadsheet will look like the one on the right. The shaded areas will contain the computed total figures.

Do the following:

1. Insert the spreadsheet heading.

   SALES REPORT
   First Quarter

2. Group the sales reps alphabetically by state.

3. Insert 3 blank rows below each state group.

4. Compute the total sales for each month for each state. Include the appropriate labels (i.e., Arizona Totals, Colorado Totals, etc.).

5. Include a column heading for **Total Sales First Quarter**. Compute the total sales for the first quarter for each rep. Figures should appear in bold.

6. Include a column heading for **Monthly Average**. Compute the average monthly sales for each rep. Figures should appear in bold.

7. Compute the total first quarter sales for each state and the monthly average for each state.

8. Compute the Total First Quarter Sales and Monthly Average Sales for all states combined.

SALES REPORT

First Quarter

Sales Rep	Territory	January	February	March	Total Sales First Quarter	Monthly Average
Martin, Jerry	Arizona	50,790	32,370	19,239		
Walker, Sue	Arizona	18,180	18,832	28,389		
Walton, Don	Arizona	33,676	25,801	22,731		
Arizona Totals						
Hundley, Ann	Colorado	25,730	12,830	45,769		
Johnson, Marge	Colorado	38,654	38,020	36,908		
Kent, Kellee	Colorado	38,310	28,095	34,789		
Martinez, Justin	Colorado	33,810	23,789	28,210		
Phillips, Josh	Colorado	27,690	33,760	28,809		
Colorado Totals						
Cooper, Devlin	Idaho	15,790	40,308	32,798		
O'Neill, Mark	Idaho	44,215	28,905	20,200		
Vizquel, Mario	Idaho	18,890	18,705	29,389		
Idaho Totals						
Burks, Ellen	Montana	40,400	15,790	21,589		
Duncan, Trevor	Montana	19,796	28,209	31,292		
Mathews, Erika	Montana	23,902	31,801	53,389		
Montana Totals						
Anderson, Mike	Utah	34,790	23,870	54,389		
Gonzalez, Maria	Utah	18,763	24,808	28,109		
Reed, Scott	Utah	38,790	9,715	21,389		
Utah Totals						
Finley, Jessica	Wyoming	18,140	38,761	30,189		
Gomez, David	Wyoming	28,760	32,120	52,675		
Guerin, Mary	Wyoming	33,860	33,790	23,390		
Wyoming Totals						
Total Sales		**602,936**	**540,279**	**643,642**		

Use Bookmarks

When readers put a book aside, they insert a bookmark to mark the place. Internet users also add bookmarks to save the addresses of their favorite web sites for later browsing. Often bookmarks are added to and accessed from folders called "favorites."

To add a bookmark:

1. Open the desired web site.
2. Click **Bookmarks** (or **Favorites**), then click **Add Bookmark** (or **Add to Favorites**). (Browsers may vary on location of Bookmark icon.)

To use a bookmark:

1. Click **Bookmarks** (or **Favorites**).
2. Select the desired bookmark. Click or double-click, depending on your browser. The desired web site displays.

Activity 5
Practice using bookmarks

1. Open these favorite web sites and bookmark them on your browser.
   a. http://www.weather.com
   b. http://www.cnn.com
   c. http://www.usps.gov
   d. Add a web site of your choice.

2. Use the bookmark to go to the following web sites:
   a. The Weather Channel
   b. CNN
   c. The United States Postal Service
   d. web site you bookmarked

Hyperlinks

A **hyperlink** is text or a graphic image that links one web document to another web document. The hyperlink inserted in the web site may be a link to another page in that web site or to another web site. For example, the web page for a university may include hyperlinks to the various academic departments within the university (pages within the web site) and a hyperlink to the local visitors' and convention center (another web site).

Hyperlinked text displays in a different font color and is underlined. When the mouse is pointed at hyperlinked text or images, the mouse pointer changes to a pointing hand. Click the hyperlink and the new web document displays. Remember to click the Back icon to return to the original web site.

Activity 6
Explore hyperlinks

1. Go to the web site at http://www.army.mil and click the following hyperlinked text:
   a. Installations
   b. database

   Click the **Back** icon twice to return to the original web page.
2. At http://www.yahoo.com, click the following hyperlinked text and images:
   a. Email
   b. People Search
   c. Image for What's New

3. Open a web site for a university or college of your choice.
   a. List two hyperlinked images.
   b. List two text hyperlinks.
   c. Which text or image is linked to another web document within the web site?
   d. Which text or image is linked to another web site?

Activity 5

Prepare the table shown at the right. Compute the total sales for each month. Total sales figures should appear in bold.

(Do not include $ and other format features because data from the table will be imported into a spreadsheet.)

Sales Rep	Territory	January	February	March
Guerin, Mary	Wyoming	33,860	33,790	23,390
Phillips, Josh	Colorado	27,690	33,760	28,809
Gonzalez, Maria	Utah	18,763	24,808	28,109
Anderson, Mike	Utah	34,790	23,870	54,389
O'Neill, Mark	Idaho	44,215	28,905	20,200
Burks, Ellen	Montana	40,400	15,790	21,589
Finley, Jessica	Wyoming	18,140	38,761	30,189
Duncan, Trevor	Montana	19,796	28,209	31,292
Cooper, Devlin	Idaho	15,790	40,308	32,798
Kent, Kellee	Colorado	38,310	28,095	34,789
Hundley, Ann	Colorado	25,730	12,830	45,769
Reed, Scott	Utah	38,790	9,715	21,389
Gomez, David	Wyoming	28,760	32,120	52,675
Martinez, Justin	Colorado	33,810	23,789	28,210
Vizquel, Mario	Idaho	18,890	18,705	29,389
Mathews, Erika	Montana	23,902	31,801	53,389
Walton, Don	Arizona	33,676	25,801	22,731
Martin, Jerry	Arizona	50,790	32,370	19,239
Walker, Sue	Arizona	18,180	18,832	28,389
Johnson, Marge	Colorado	38,654	38,020	36,908

Set Up E-Mail

Electronic mail or **e-mail** refers to electronic messages sent by one computer user to another computer user. To be able to send or receive e-mail, you must have an e-mail address, an e-mail program, and access to the Internet.

Many search engines such as Yahoo, Excite, Lycos, AltaVista, and others now provide free e-mail via their web sites. These e-mail programs allow users to set up an e-mail address and then send and retrieve e-mail messages. To set up an account and obtain an e-mail address, the user must (1) agree to the terms of agreement, (2) complete an online registration form, and (3) compose an e-mail name and password. To set up your e-mail, access the search engine of your choice and closely follow the directions for setting up e-mail. Be certain that you understand the terms of agreement and choose an e-mail name and password that are easy to remember.

Send E-Mail

To send an e-mail message, you must have the address of the computer user you wish to write to. Business cards, letterheads, directories, etc. now include e-mail addresses. Sometimes you may need to call the person by telephone and ask for his or her e-mail address. An e-mail address includes the user's login name followed by @ and the domain name(s); e.g., sthomas@yahoo.com or sdt3@jn.ndu.edu.

Creating an e-mail message is quite similar to preparing a memo. The e-mail header includes TO, FROM, and SUBJECT. Key the e-mail address of the recipient on the TO line and compose a subject line that concisely describes your message. Your e-mail address will automatically display on the FROM line.

Activity 7
Send e-mail

1. Open the search engine used to set up your e-mail account. Click **E-mail** or **Free E-mail**.
2. Enter your e-mail name and password when prompted.
3. Enter the e-mail address of your instructor or another student.
4. Compose a brief message. Be sure to include a descriptive subject line.
5. Send the message.

Read E-Mail

Reading one's e-mail messages and responding promptly are considered important rules of netiquette (etiquette for the Internet). However, avoid responding too quickly to sensitive situations—once sent, e-mail cannot be retrieved before it is read by the recipient.

Activity 8
Read e-mail

1. Open your e-mail account.
2. Read your messages and respond immediately. Click **Reply** to answer the message. (E-mail programs may vary.)

Attach Files to E-Mail

Electronic files can be attached to an e-mail message and sent to another computer electronically. Recipients of attached documents can transfer these documents to their computers and then open the files for use.

Activity 9
Create an attachment

1. Open your e-mail account if necessary.
2. Create an e-mail message to your teacher that states that your homework is attached. The subject line should include the specific homework assignment (for example, 44b-d1).
3. Attach the file by clicking **Attach**. Use the browser to locate the homework file. (E-mail programs may vary.)
4. Send the e-mail.

Activity 1

Open the title page created for 111B, p. 261. Insert an appropriate graphic figure between the title and your name. Center the graphic horizontally.

Activity 2

Open the title page created for 91D-92C, p. 223. Do the following.

1. Change the font face to **Courier New** and the type size to 17 for the title.
2. Change the font face to **Courier New** and the type size to 15 for the remaining information on the page.

3. Insert an appropriate figure between the title and your name. Center the graphic horizontally.

Activity 3

Format the text at the right as a personal-business letter in block format with open punctuation to:

**Ms. Mary Renault
1818 Fairfield Ave.
Santa Ana, CA 92714-1828**

Date the letter **June 24, ----**.

Supply an appropriate salutation and complimentary closing.

The letter is from Grant L. Lemaster, 1922 Jovan Blvd., Santa Ana, CA 92728-0919.

I've finished my assignment! All ten of the firms that were assigned to me have been contacted. Only one of the ten refused to contribute; eight contributed; and I'm still waiting to hear from the last one.

Meeting with them in person rather than talking with them on the phone does make a difference. Last year the phone calls resulted in only three of the businesses making contributions for a total of $1,500. This year the total amount increased to $8,500. A complete summary of the contributions is shown below.

Open Table 3 from p. 234 and copy it here. Delete the main and secondary headings. SS the table.

I will be on vacation when you meet on June 15. If you need any additional information that I can provide for the meeting, please call me.

Activity 4

Using the table in Job 14, p. 253, prepare a bar graph showing all sales representatives with sales over $200,000 for the month of January.

The graph should be created as follows:

1. Use landscape (11" wide x 8.5" long) orientation.
2. Label the X-axis **Thousands**.
3. Label the Y-axis **Agent**.
4. Use **JANUARY SALES** for the title of the graph.
5. Use **Letter Landscape** for the paper size.
6. Make the size of the graph 10" x 7.5".

Explore Search Engines

The World Wide Web contains millions of pages of information and is growing rapidly. Search engines locate specific information. Just a few examples of search engines are AltaVista, Excite, Infoseek, Dogpile, Metacrawler, LookSmart, Lycos, and Yahoo. To go to a search engine, click the Search or Net Search icon on your web browser. (Note: Web browsers will vary.)

Search

Activity 10
Search with multiple engines

1. Go to search engines on your browser. Click the first search engine. Browse the hyperlinks available, i.e., Maps, People Finder, News, Weather, Stock Quotes, Sports, Games, etc.
2. Click each search engine and explore the hyperlinks.

3. Conduct the following search using Dogpile, a multi-threaded search engine that searches multiple databases:
   a. Open the web site for Dogpile (http://www.dogpile.com).
   b. In the Search entry box, key the key-words **American Psychological Association publications**; click **Fetch**.

Yellow Pages

Searching the Yellow Pages for information on businesses and services is a common, every-day task. Several search engines provide convenient hyperlinks to the online Yellow Pages.

Activity 11
Search Yellow Pages

1. Browse the search engines on your browser to locate the hyperlink for the Yellow Pages; click to open this valuable site.
2. Determine a city that you would like to visit. Use the Yellow Pages to find a listing of hotels in this city.

3. Your best friend lives in (provide the city); you want to send him or her flowers. Find a listing of florists in this city.
4. Write a third scenario and find the appropriate listing.

Comprehensive Search Engines

Using a comprehensive search engine can be very helpful in locating various information quickly. The All-in-One web site (http://www.albany.net/allinone/) is a compilation of various search tools found on the Internet. Search tools include various categories, such as People, News/Weather, Desk Reference, and Other Interesting Searches/Services.

Activity 12
Comprehensive search engine

1. Access http://www.albany.net/allinone/. Browse the categories and search tools within the categories.
2. From the People category: Find at BigFoot the e-mail address for (provide a name).
3. Find at Ahoy! the home page for (provide a name).

4. From the News/Weather category: Find at Pathfinder, Weather and then your current weather.
5. Find at one of the news searches, news articles about (provide current event).
6. Choose a category and determine a search. List category, question, and answer.

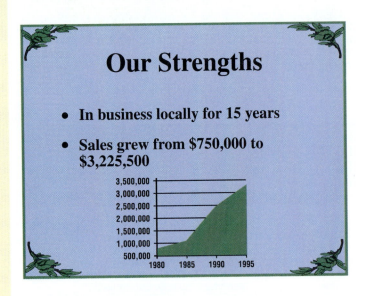

Our Strengths

- In business locally for 15 years
- Sales grew from $750,000 to $3,225,500

	1980	1985	1990	1995
3,500,000				
3,000,000				
2,500,000				
2,000,000				
1,500,000				
1,000,000				
500,000				

Our Strengths

- Outstanding selection of superior trees, shrubs, perennials, and annuals
- Guaranteed installation
- Consistent record of customer satisfaction

What Should You Do?

- Don't let winter get you down!
- Stop by for a catalog of our product line.
- Make a list of what you want.
- Plan now for planting in the spring!

We Appreciate You and Your Business!

Call Green Gardens, Inc., at 555-127-9932 to set up a free consultation

---

10-11B • 90
Screenshow Development Project

1. Create a similar presentation on a topic of your choice, for example:
   - a class paper
   - personal background
   - family vacation
2. Select an appropriate background, font sizes, and font colors.
3. Use graphic enhancements such as arrows, starbursts, lines, boxes, or clipart as appropriate.
4. Create at least one diagram.
5. Include graphs if appropriate for your topic.
6. Be sure to include a title chart, presentation objective chart, bulleted list for important points, and a conclusion visual.
7. Arrange all charts in a screenshow.
8. Use two transition effects.

Repetitive stress injury (RSI) is a result of repeated movement of a particular part of the body. A familiar example is "tennis elbow." Of more concern to keyboard users is the form of RSI called carpal tunnel syndrome (CTS).

CTS is an inflammatory disease that develops gradually and affects the wrist, hands, and forearms. Blood vessels, tendons, and nerves pass into the hand through the carpal tunnel (see illustration below). If any of these structures enlarge, or the walls of the tunnel narrow, the median nerve is pinched and CTS symptoms may result.

Palm view of left hand.

Symptoms of RSI/CTS

CTS symptoms include numbness in the hand; tingling or burning in the hand, wrist, or elbow; severe pain in the forearm, elbow, or shoulder; and difficulty in gripping objects. Symptoms usually appear during sleeping hours, probably because many people sleep with their wrists flexed.

If not properly treated, the pressure on the median nerve, which controls the thumb, forefinger, middle finger, and half the ring finger, causes severe pain. The pain can radiate into the forearm, elbow, or shoulder and can require surgery or result in permanent damage or paralysis.

Causes of RSI/CTS

RSI/CTS often develops in workers whose physical routine is unvaried.

Common occupational factors include: (1) using awkward posture, (2) using poor techniques, (3) performing tasks with wrists bent (see below), (4) using improper equipment, (5) working at a rapid pace, (6) not taking rest breaks, and (7) not doing exercises that promote graceful motion and good techniques.

Improper wrist positions for keystroking.

Reducing the Risk of RSI/CTS

CTS is frequently a health concern for workers who use a computer keyboard or mouse. The risk of developing CTS is less for keyboard operators who use proper furniture or equipment, keyboarding techniques, posture, and/or muscle-stretching exercises than for those who do not.

Keyboard users can reduce the risk of developing RSI/CTS by taking these precautions:

1. Arrange the work station correctly:

   a. Position the keyboard directly in front of the chair.

   b. Keep the front edge of the keyboard even with the edge of the desk so that wrist movement will not be restricted.

   c. Position the keyboard at elbow height.

   d. Position the monitor about 18 to 24 inches from your eyes with the top edge of the screen at eye level.

   e. Position the mouse next to and at the same height as the keyboard and as close to the body as possible.

Preparing Screenshows

Objectives:
1. To identify the purposes of screenshows.
2. To learn to organize visuals in a screenshow for audience viewing.

**10-11A • 90
Screenshow
Development**

1. Review the information on p. A60 about the purposes of screenshows.

2. Determine how to create a screenshow using your software.

3. Create a screenshow using the examples shown below.

4. Select a similar template.

5. Insert appropriate clipart as shown.

6. Add transition effects.

A **screenshow** (or slide show) is a series of presentation visuals presented in a preplanned sequence. A screenshow can be projected from a computer screen for a small audience. For a larger audience, projection equipment is necessary to display the visuals on a large screen.

(continued on next page)

2. Use a proper chair and sit correctly:

   a. Use a straight-backed chair that will not yield when you lean back.

   b. Use a seat that allows you to keep your feet flat on the floor or use a footrest.

   c. Sit erect and as far back in the seat as possible.

3. Use correct arm and wrist positions and movement:

   a. Keep your forearms parallel to the floor and level with the keyboard so that your wrists will be in a flat, neutral position rather than flexed upward or downward.

   b. Keep arms near the side of your body in a relaxed position.

4. Use proper keyboarding techniques:

   a. Keep your fingers curved and upright over the home keys.

   b. Keep wrists and forearms from touching or resting on any surface.

   c. Strike each key lightly using the fingertip.

5. When using a keyboard or mouse, take short breaks. A rest of one to two minutes every hour is appropriate.

6. Exercise the neck, shoulder, arm, wrist, and fingers before beginning to key each day and often during the workday.

Ergonomic Keyboards

Ergonomic keyboards are designed to improve hand posture and make keying more comfortable. Generally they have a split design with left and right banks of keys and the ability to tilt or rotate the keyboard for comfort. More research is needed to determine just how effective ergonomic keyboards are in preventing RSI injuries and carpal tunnel syndrome.

Trackball

Like the mouse, a trackball is a pointing device that moves the insertion point. A trackball enables the user to control the pointer without hand or wrist movement. The thumb or finger moves the ball directly. The ergonomic design of the trackball generally features buttons contoured to the shape of the hand.

Line graph data:

1985	30
1987	33
1989	37
1991	38
1993	40
1995	45

Pie chart data:

Southern 45
Midwest 40
Eastern 30
Mountain Plains 25
Western 20

Show values as percents.

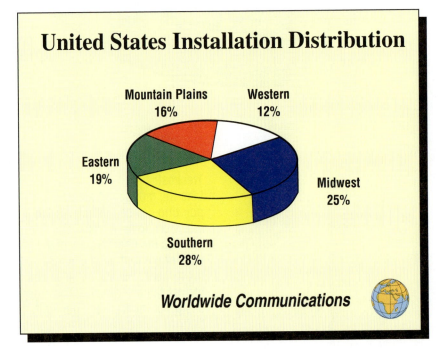

United States Revenue 1986-1995

Sales in Millions

Worldwide Communications

United States Installation Distribution

Mountain Plains 16%
Western 12%
Eastern 19%
Midwest 25%
Southern 28%

Worldwide Communications

FINGER GYMNASTICS

Brief daily practice of finger gymnastics will strengthen your finger muscles and increase the ease with which you key. Begin each keying period with this conditioning exercise. Choose two or more drills for this practice.

DRILL 1. Hands open, fingers wide, muscles tense. Close the fingers into a tight "fist," with thumb on top. Relax the fingers as you straighten them; repeat 10 times.

DRILL 2. Clench the fingers as shown. Hold the fingers in this position for a brief time; then extend the fingers, relaxing the muscles of fingers and hand. Repeat the movements slowly several times. Exercise both hands at the same time.

DRILL 3. Place the fingers and the thumb of one hand between two fingers of the other hand, and spread the fingers as much as possible. Spread all fingers of both hands.

DRILL 4. Interlace the fingers of the two hands and wring the hands, rubbing the heel of the palms vigorously.

DRILL 5. Spread the fingers as much as possible, holding the position for a moment or two; then relax the fingers and lightly fold them into the palm of the hand. Repeat the movements slowly several times. Exercise both hands at the same time.

DRILL 7. Hold both hands in front of you, fingers together. Hold the last three fingers still and move the first finger as far to the side as possible. Return the first finger; then move the first and second fingers together; finally move the little finger as far to the side as possible.

DRILL 6. Rub the hands vigorously. Let the thumb rub the palm of the hand. Rub the fingers, the back of the hand, and the wrist.

Pie Chart 3

1. Read the copy at the right.
2. Emphasize one pie slice (Chart 2) by exploding it.
3. Remove the legend.
4. Display labels and % values with each slice.

A single pie slice can be emphasized by exploding (pulling one slice away from the other slices) and using a high-contrast color for that slice.

Pie charts are probably easiest to interpret when both the identifying labels and slice values are positioned beside or on the pie slices. If space on the pie is limited, then arrange the labels in a list or use a legend to identify the content of the slices.

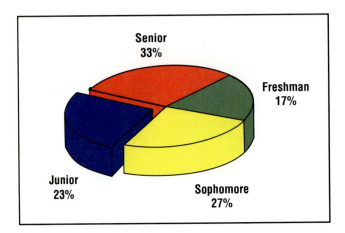

7-9F • 35
Graph Screenshow

1. Read the copy at the right about designing effective graphs.
2. Create three graphs in coordinating colors. (Assume these three graphs are used in a larger presentation.)
3. Select a similar template.
4. If possible, add the company name and clipart image of the globe to the master slide.

Bar graph data:

	United States	Europe
January	145	120
February	130	135
March	160	155

If actual numeric values are needed in a bar graph, these values can be displayed with each bar; values also can be displayed beside or below the graph image.

• Be sure of visual integrity on the graphs so that relationships accurately reflect data.
• Adjust colors for maximum legibility and to highlight key information.

• Avoid showing too many details in one graph.
• When needed for clarity, display both the graph image and the data from which it is derived.
• Be sure the design of these charts blends with other visuals being used.

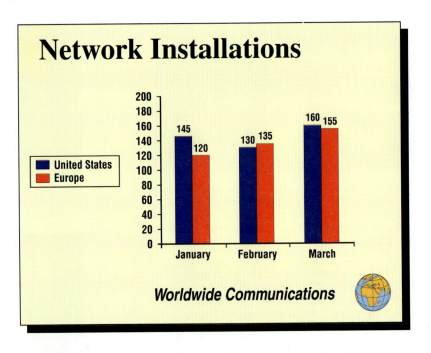

R&e ## Centering

Document 1
Centered Lines

1. Center horizontally by the longest line in the poem.
2. Vertical placement: standard top margin.

	words
THE MAN I MEANT TO BE	4
I look back over my shoulder	10
And there I see	13
The boy I once was	17
And the man he meant to be.	23
And I wonder how it happened	29
That the boy I see	33
Became the man I now am--	38
Not the man he meant to be.	44
I remember him well--the boy I once was;	52
I remember the man he dreamed I would be.	60
Now the dreams are forgotten by the boy and me--	70
For I'm not the man he dreamed I would be.	79
--D. D. Lessenberry	83

Document 2
Centered Lines

1. Center each line horizontally.
2. Vertical placement: standard top margin.

AFRICA IN MOTION PICTURES	5
Academy Auditorium	9
LIFE IN HOT WET LANDS	13
Typical Day of a Family in the Congo Basin	22
Wednesday, November 2, at 2:30 p.m.	29
AFRICAN BIG GAME	32
African Animals in Their Native Habitat	40
Friday, November 4, at 8:30 p.m.	47
A GIANT PEOPLE (The Mangbetu)	53
Primitive People of Relatively Advanced Culture	63
Monday, November 6, at 11:10 a.m.	70
LION COUNTRY	72
A 2200-Mile Safari into African Lion Country	81
Tuesday, November 7, at 3:15 p.m.	88

7-9E • 30
Pie Chart

Pie Chart 1

1. Read the copy at the right.
2. Create the pie chart shown.

Chart data:

Freshman   **25**
Sophomore   **40**
Junior   **35**
Senior   **50**

3. Display the legend on the right.

Pie Chart 2

1. Read the copy at the right.
2. Using the same chart data, change Pie Chart 1 to give it a 3D appearance.
3. Add the slice values beside each slice.

Pie charts (or graphs) are best used to display parts of a whole. They show clearly the proportional relationship of only one set of values. Without any numbers displayed, the chart shows only general relationships. In the first example shown below, the different colors used for the pie slices are identified in a legend. Colors used on the pie should provide adequate contrast between the slices. Consider, also, the color scheme of your entire presentation so that the pie chart will coordinate with other visuals.

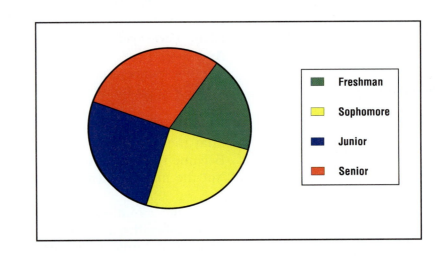

Usually pie charts look attractive with a 3D appearance, as long as the circle does not look distorted. The pie slice values (shown as actual numbers or percentages) can be displayed beside each of the slices to show relationships exactly.

(continued on next page)

Memo & Letter

Document 3
Memo

1. Format/key as a simplified memo the message given at the right.
2. Use current date; address to **Shirlie L. Beerman, Chair**.
3. As a subject, use **LANDSCAPE COMMITTEE MEETING**.
4. Use hanging-indent style for the listed items.
5. The writer of the memo is **Jolene Golden, Member**.

Document 4
Letter

1. Format/key in block style with open punctuation the letter given at right.
2. Indent the quotation 0.5" (5 sp.) from left margin as shown.

Note: The book title may be in italic instead of underlined.

	words
	heading 14

The most recent issue of <u>Tollgate News & Notes</u> indicates that we are 29
to begin landscape renovation this coming spring. Because of the 41
limited money budgeted this year for this purpose, I propose that the 56
following topics be discussed at our next meeting: 66

1. Which section of the community (north or south) is in greater need 80
    of immediate renovation? 85

2. What kinds of trees, shrubs, and perennials will in the long term 99
    best serve our goals? 104

It seems better to work on one section at a time than to dabble a bit in 118
both sections at once. Further, we need to avoid plantings that will in 133
a few years overgrow walkways and porches. 142

closing 146

(Current date) | Mr. Thomas A. Raleigh | Department of Public Instruction | 13
Juneau, AK 99801-9999 | Dear Mr. Raleigh 22

In response to your recent letter requesting some ideas for "brain- 36
storming" sessions, perhaps the following ones will help. 47

<u>First, judging of proffered ideas must be delayed</u>. Criticism of any 61
suggestion must be withheld until a later time. As Osborn said in 76
<u>Applied Imagination</u>: 80

> If you try to get hot and cold water out of the same faucet at the 93
> same time, you will get only tepid water. And if you try to criticize 107
> and create at the same time, you can't turn on either cold enough 121
> criticism or hot enough ideas. 127

<u>Second, "free wheeling" is welcomed</u>. The wilder the idea, the better. It 142
is easier to tame down than to think up. 151

<u>Third, quantity is wanted</u>. The greater the number of ideas, the more 165
likelihood of winners. 170

<u>Fourth, combination and improvement are sought</u>. In addition to 182
contributing ideas of their own, participants should suggest how ideas 198
of others can be turned into better ideas; or how two or more ideas can 212
be joined into still another idea. 219

These four basic principles are the guides we follow in conducting "brain- 233
storming" workshops for teachers and administrators in schools and col- 248
leges and for workers and executives in firms throughout the country. 262

Sincerely yours | Ms. Nelda S. Gibson, Director | xx 271

7-9D • 30
Line and Area Graphs

Line Graph

1. Read the copy at the right.
2. Create a line graph showing one data set.

Graph data:

1970	20
1975	43
1980	30
1985	50
1990	45
1995	60

3. Include a grid.

Area Graph

1. Modify the line graph to make it an area graph.
2. Consider the difference in appearance to determine which graph is easier to interpret.

Line graphs are best suited for displaying changing quantities over time. Usually the X-axis is used to show the particular period of time; the Y-axis shows the measurements of quantity at different times. The baseline of the Y-axis should be zero because this provides a consistent reference point when several graphs are used in a presentation or report. When the numbers for the X-axis are entered, a line will be formed to reflect these changing amounts. A grid on the graph will help the viewer interpret quantities.

Several different sets of data could be displayed by using lines in different colors or patterns.

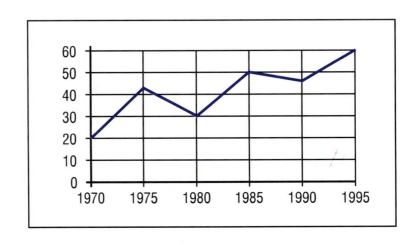

If the line needs more emphasis, then an *area* graph would be a better choice. The area below the line is filled in with a contrasting color.

If exact data are required, however, a vertical bar graph would be a better graph choice than an area graph because each bar can be labeled with the appropriate measurement.

Book Report

words

Document 5
Unbound Report

1. Format/key the book report in unbound report style, DS.
2. Number the second page.
3. Place the reference below the body on page 2.
4. Proofread and correct all errors you make as you key.

THE OLD MAN AND THE SEA · · · · · · · · · · · · · · 5

He was an old man, thin and gaunt, with deep wrinkles in the back · · · 18
of his neck and brown blotches on his cheeks. His hands had deep- · · · 31
creased scars from handling heavy fish on the cords. Everything about · · · 45
him was old except his eyes, and they were the color of the sea and · · · 59
were cheerful and undefeated. He fished alone in a skiff in the Gulf · · · 74
Stream, and this was the eighty-fourth day he had gone without taking · · · 88
a fish. · · · 89

Every day is a new day, the old man knew; and long before it was · · · 102
light the next morning, he had his baits out and was drifting with the · · · 116
current. Hours later, watching his lines, he saw one of the projecting · · · 130
green sticks dip sharply. He reached out for the line, unleashed it from · · · 145
the stick, and let it run gently through his fingers without the fish · · · 159
feeling any tension. A marlin, one hundred fathoms down, was eating · · · 174
the sardines that covered the point and the shank of the hand-forged · · · 187
hook. · · · 188

So began a three-day battle between the old man and the big fish. · · · 202
The old man had to battle thirst and hunger; the loss of sleep; and the · · · 215
pain of cut and bleeding hands and cramped fingers. Pain did not · · · 229
matter--a man could endure; but defeat he could never admit. "Man is · · · 245
not made for defeat," he said. "A man can be destroyed but not defeated." · · · 259

The Old Man and the Sea is simple, compelling, magnificent. · · · 271
Every word is right. The old man embodies the essential nobility in · · · 285
human striving. The giant fish is the embodiment of what is noble in · · · 299
animate nature. And the sea--la mar, which is what the people call her · · · 314
in Spanish when they love her--was the home of the great fish and the · · · 328
love of the old man. · · · 332

This is a work of great power. The strong, crisp words tell a mov- · · · 346
ing story and express the basic attitudes the author held toward all life. · · · 361
What one gets from him is not so much a fragment of his art as the · · · 374
totality of his being. He was the best and most natural craftsman of · · · 388
our time. Reading this book is a profound experience. It is like living · · · 403
a tragedy, which, at the last, emerges without grief into beauty. · · · 416

REFERENCE · · · 418

Hemingway, Ernest. The Old Man and the Sea. New York: Charles · · · 432
    Scribner's Sons, 1952. · · · 436

Bar Graphs

Bar Graph 1

1. Read the copy at the right.
2. Create the graph shown with the presentation software you are using.

Graph data:

	Shirt Sales	Bag Sales
October	87	60
November	80	75
December	45	90

3. Select similar colors for the bars.
4. Display data values above the bars.
5. Display labels below the bars.
6. Display a legend at the bottom of the graph.

Bar Graph 2

Modify the first bar graph as follows:

1. Remove the data values above the bars.
2. Add a dimensional effect as shown.

Bar graphs (or charts) display a single set or multiple sets of data that are plotted on the horizontal X-axis and the vertical Y-axis. The X-axis usually contains category information (such as years or months); the Y-axis usually contains measured quantity values.

Vertical bars (also called columns) are easy to interpret; the baseline on the Y-axis should begin at zero for consistent comparisons when several graphs are used in a presentation. Many special effects can be added, but a simple graph is effective for showing relationships.

Multiple data sets can be shown by using a cluster of bars on each point on the X-axis. When multiple data sets are used, the colors must provide an adequate contrast and yet blend with the other colors used in a presentation.

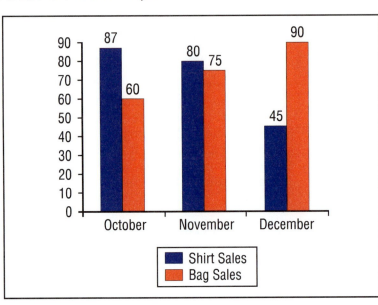

The first graph you prepared was displayed in two dimensions—height and width. When a third dimension (3D) is added, the bars are shaded to create an illusion of depth. A 3D appearance can be used on bar, pie, and line/area graphs. Notice, however, that, while this illusion might make the graph more interesting, the illusion of depth can make the bar values more difficult to interpret.

Document 6
Table
TM: standard
LS: SS entries
CS: 0.4" (4 sp.)

			words
	FEDERAL HOLIDAYS		3
Event	1998	1999	7
New Year's Day	Jan. 1	Jan. 1	13
Martin Luther King Jr. Day	Jan. 19	Jan. 18	22
Presidents' Day	Feb. 16	Feb. 15	28
Memorial Day	May 25	May 31	34
Independence Day	July 4	July 4	40
Labor Day	Sept. 7	Sept. 6	45
Columbus Day	Oct. 12	Oct. 11	51
Veterans' Day	Nov. 11	Nov. 11	57
Thanksgiving Day	Nov. 26	Nov. 25	64
Christmas Day	Dec. 25	Dec. 25	70
			73
Source: The Universal Almanac, 1995.			80

Document 7
Table
TM: standard
LS: DS
CS: 0.8" (8 sp.)

			words
COMPARATIVE TEACHING TIME BY COUNTRY			7
(Average Hours per Year, Secondary School)			16
Country	J.H.S.	S.H.S.	21
Turkey	1,080	1,080	25
United states	1,042	1,091	30
Netherlands	954	954	34
Spain	930	930	37
New zealand	897	813	41
Finland	798	760	44
Ireland	729	792	47
Germany	761	673	50
			54
Source: USA Today, april 12, 1995.			61

Displaying Numeric Information

O b j e c t i v e s :

1. To learn the graph to use for particular situations.
2. To learn various graph elements.
3. To create graphs.

7-9A • 10
Graph Purposes

Study the copy at the right about types of graphs and the uses of each type.

The meaning of numeric information can be easier to understand when portrayed as a graph, instead of as a table of figures. The relationships between data sets or trends can be compared with *bar, line/area*, or *pie* graphs (also called charts). Even combinations of these graphs can be used for some applications. Each type of graph is best suited for a particular situation:

- **bar**—comparison of item quantities
- **line/area**—quantity changes over time
- **pie**—parts of a whole

7-9B • 15
Graph Elements

1. Study the copy at the right.
2. Locate the various graph elements in the software you are using.

Elements common to most graphs are identified on the bar graph shown below. They include:

- **X-axis**—the horizontal axis; usually for categories
- **Y-axis**—the vertical axis; usually for values
- **scales**—numbers on the Y- or X-axis representing quantities

- **tick marks**—coordinate marks on the graph to help guide the reader
- **grids**—lines that extend from tick marks to make it easier to see data values
- **labels**—names used to identify parts of the graph
- **legends**—the key that identifies the shading or coloring used for the parts of the graph

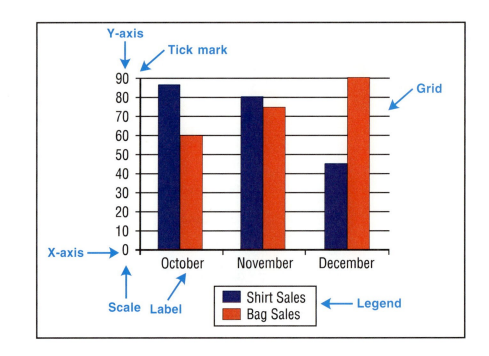

R&e Memo and Letters

Document 1
Standard Memo
Key the memo at right in standard format. Use the following information.
TO: All Employees
FROM: Marjorie Clemens, Personnel
DATE: November 4, ----
SUBJECT: PROFESSIONAL DEVELOPMENT SEMINARS

Document 2
Personal-Business Letter
Key the letter at right in block format, open punctuation.

Document 3
Business Letter
Key the letter at right in block format, open punctuation.

words

heading 24

The company is implementing a new program for professional development 39
this year. Every employee will be given one day off to attend one of the 53
company-sponsored professional development seminars. 64

Tentative topics for this year's seminars are the value of leadership, improving 81
oral communication skills, integrated software applications, and stress man- 96
agement.   Indicate your preference for each of the seminars on the attached 111
form by placing #1 by your first choice, #2 by your second choice, and so 126
forth. 127

We will try to accommodate everyone's first or second choice. The more 142
popular programs will be offered twice during the year in an effort to control 158
the number of participants at each seminar. | xx | Enclosure 169

3716 Rangely Dr. | Raleigh, NC 27609-4115 | October 14, ---- | 12
Mr. Robert C. Johnson | Wayler Insurance Company | 206 Polk St. | 24
Raleigh, NC 27604-4120 | Dear Mr. Johnson | INFORMATION ON 35
CAREER OPPORTUNITIES 40

Please send information on career opportunities available with Wayler Insur- 55
ance Company in the administrative services area. As part of a class 69
assignment, I will be giving an oral report on a company for which I would 84
like to work. Wayler Insurance is an impressive company, and I would like 98
to do the report on career opportunities with your firm. 110

The report needs to address job titles, job requirements, educational require- 126
ments, salary, and opportunities for advancement. Any information that 140
you are able to provide on these areas will be greatly appreciated. 154

Sincerely | Richard B. Lyons | xx 160

October 20, ---- | Mr. Richard B. Lyons | 3716 Rangely Dr. | Raleigh, NC 14
27609-4115 | Dear Mr. Lyons 19

Wayler Insurance Company is always interested in potential employees. 34
We hope that you will consider us once you are graduated. 45

As you will see from reading the information that is enclosed, we have 59
different levels of administrative support positions in our company. Job 74
titles, job requirements, educational requirements, and starting salaries are 90
included for each level. Our company philosophy is to reward loyal employ- 105
ees; therefore, we like to promote from within when qualified employees are 120
available. We also reimburse employees for additional job-related schooling 135
completed during their employment. 142

If you need further information or would like one of our administrative 157
support supervisors to talk with your class, please call us. 169

Sincerely yours | Robert C. Johnson | Customer Relations Director | xx | 182
Enclosure 184

Cluster

1. Create a cluster diagram.
2. Position an oval for the "Main Topic" text as shown; add the text for this oval.
3. Duplicate both the oval and text and position in the place for Item 1. Edit this oval to make it smaller and change the text to "Item 1."
4. Duplicate the "Item 1" oval and text—repeat this process for each item.
5. Retrieve an arrow; adjust size and color as necessary. Duplicate and position an arrow for each oval.
6. Enter the bulleted list text above the diagram:

♦ **Shows concepts related to central topic.**

♦ **Can be displayed one at a time.**

Cluster. This cluster diagram begins with an oval at the center containing the text for the main topic being explained. Additional ovals with text are positioned around the main topic. For a screenshow, these items could be made to appear one at a time as the discussion progresses.

Document 4
Business Letter

Key the letter at right in modified block format with blocked paragraphs and open punctuation.

Date: **March 1, ----**

Address:

Mr. Morris E. Young
904 Beatrice St.
Titusville, FL 32780-8192

Salutation: **Dear Mr. Young**

Document 5
Business Letter

Key the letter at right in modified block format with indented paragraphs and mixed punctuation.

Note: To place a table within the body of a letter:
1. DS above and below the table; SS the body of the table.
2. Clear all tabs.
3. Decide how much space you will place between columns. (The table must fit within the margins of the letter.)
4. Determine and set a tab for each column of the table, including the first column.
5. After keying the table, clear the tabs and restore default tabs.

	words
	opening 18
¶ Walstram Industries has informed us that you have	28
accepted a position in their Accounting Department and	39
soon will be moving to Rockville. Congratulations	49
and best wishes.	52
¶ Our bank has designed a packet of information to	62
help new citizens in the community become acquainted with	74
the local area. The packet includes a map of the city,	85
housing and rental guides, and a brochure that	94
highlights upcoming cultural and civic events. This material	107
will provide you with information that will make relocating	119
a little easier.	122
¶ Once you arrive in Rockville, we would appreciate hav-	133
ing the opportunity to discuss ways that the First National	145
Bank of Rockville can accommodate your banking needs.	156
Sincerely / Ms. Marge L. Bowman / Customer Service / xx / Enclosures	168

March 1, ---- | Mr. Cody G. Sykes | 625 Pacific Ave. | Rockville, MD 20853-3107 | Dear Mr. Sykes: — 13 / 18

How quickly time passes! It seems like only yesterday that you renewed your 24-month certificate of deposit (B-2987) with our bank. On March 15 it will again mature. — 32 / 46 / 52

For your convenience, we processed the certificate so that it would be renewed automatically for the same time period at the current market rate. If we do not hear from you prior to the maturity date, your certificate will be renewed at 5.5 percent for the next two years. The value of your certificate as of March 15 will be $1,323.08. — 66 / 81 / 97 / 111 / 120

Should you wish to have the certificate renewed for a longer period at a higher interest rate, we can also do that. The time periods and current interest rates are as follows: — 134 / 149 / 156

36-month certificate	5.75 percent	163
48-month certificate	6.00 percent	169
60-month certificate	6.25 percent	176

Call or stop in if you decide to go with a longer period for your certificate. We appreciate your patronage and look forward to assisting with your banking needs in the future. — 190 / 205 / 212

Sincerely, | Mrs. Eiko R. Kimura | Investments | xx — 221

Stair Steps

1. Create a stair steps diagram using the same template you used for the choice diagram.
2. Position the first box at the bottom.
3. Enter the text in a suitable size for the box.
4. Duplicate both the box and the text three times and position the new images as shown.
5. Edit the text in the second, third, and fourth boxes as shown.
6. Add the following bulleted list at the left:

♦ **Shows discussion points building like stair steps.**

♦ **Begin at the bottom.**

Stair steps. This stair steps diagram begins with a box at the bottom containing the text for the first idea being explained. Additional boxes with text are positioned to look like stairs going up. For a screenshow, you could prepare four separate slides so that the stair steps appear one at a time as the discussion progresses.

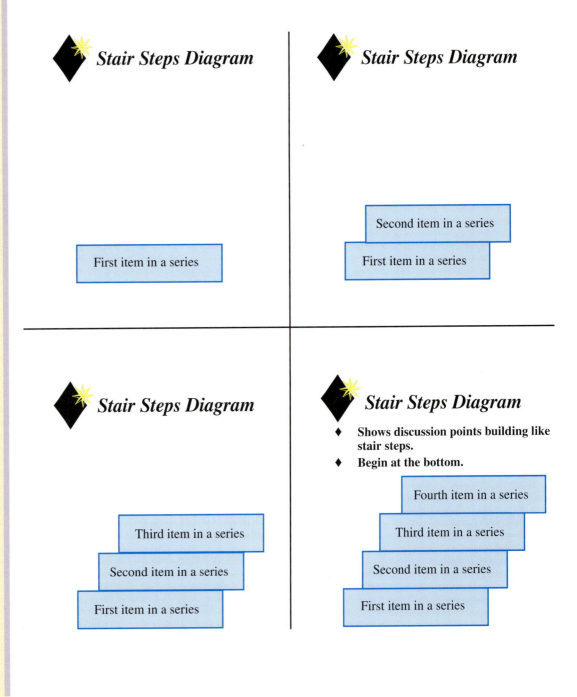

**Documents 6-9
Bound Report with
Endnotes**

Key the copy at right and on
p. A22 as a report to be
bound at the left. Prepare an
Endnotes page; then create
a References page, adapting
the endnotes information.
Finally, create a title page for
the report.

wp note:

If your software has an
Endnotes feature, use it.

words

COMPUTERS — QS | 2

Computers have become a way of life. Almost every area | 13

of of business and many aspects of our personnel lives have | 24

felt their impact. Some refer to this period of time as the | 36

Computer Revolution. | 41

Computer Revolution is a widely used term these days. | 52
It implies that society is undergoing a radical trans- | 62
formation. . . . In his book, The Micro Millenium, | 74
Evans argued that the societal impacts of computers in | 85
general, and pesonal computers in particular, would rival | 96
the effects of the Industrial Revolution.[1] | 105

Who will use computers? | 110

Although computers have personal and business disadvan- | 121

tages as well as advantages, there is little doubt that these | 133

devices will have an increasing impact on our daily lives in | 145

the years to come. Computers are essentail tools of todays | 158

society. . . . Today, everyone needs to understand them.[2] | 170

Learning to use a computer is nearly as important as learning | 182

to read. | 184

What Will Computers be Used For? | 191

Recent technological advances have produced supercomputers and | 204

improved microcomputers with increased speed for processing information. | 219

These computers are being used by government agencies, banks, | 231

retailers, schools, homes, and individuals for a variety of | 242

purposes. A few example include the following: | 252

1. after-hour electronic banking | 258
2. automatic scoring | 263
3. electronic controls in home appliances | 271
4. electronic check-out devices in supermarkets | 281
5. electronic information displays in cars | 290
6. electronic patient records in hospitals | 299
7. employee performance monitoring |
7. 8. business applications | 304

(continued on next page)

Developing Diagram Charts

O b j e c t i v e s :

1. To observe how diagrams can portray processes and add variety to a presentation.
2. To create diagrams with boxes and connecting arrows or lines.
3. To create diagrams showing various processes.

5-6A • 40
Process Information

1. Read the copy at the right.
2. Learn how to use the drawing tools in the software you are using.
3. Create diagrams using text on boxes and connecting lines and arrows.

Diagrams. The shapes in a diagram can help an audience understand relationships or a sequence of events. Text can be arranged in boxes that are connected with lines or arrows to help the audience visualize a process. Diagrams may simply add variety to a display of text—however, the shape of some diagrams also conveys meaning. While diagrams can become quite complex, the best ones are quite simple. When creating diagrams, be sure to:

- Arrange text information in boxes or other appropriate shapes.
- Show connections with lines and specific directions with arrows.
- Blend fonts and all colors used with other visuals in a presentation.

5-6B • 60
Diagrams

1. Notice the "message" in the diagrams at the right and the two diagrams on pp. A69-A70.
2. Select a similar template or slide master.
3. Create each diagram, following the directions for each.

Choice

1. Create a box in a similar color; position it at the left. Make it large enough to hold the "Option One" text; enter the text.
2. Duplicate the box and text and position the duplicate at the right side, allowing enough room for the arrows; change "Option One" to "Option Two."
3. Retrieve and position a similar arrow pointing in one direction.
4. Duplicate the arrow and rotate it. Position it as shown.
5. Insert the bulleted list at the bottom of the screen.

Choice. This diagram indicates that a choice between two options must be made. The arrows pointing in opposite directions indicate an either/or situation. This same technique can be used to represent conflict.

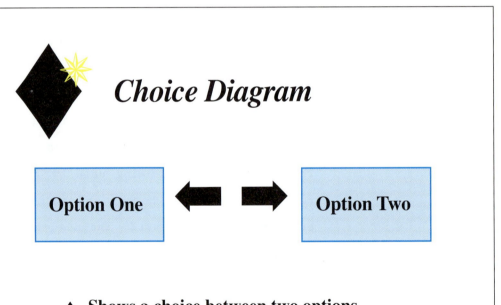

Choice Diagram

Option One ← → **Option Two**

- **Shows a choice between two options.**
- **Can portray a decision point or a conflict.**

words

Why Are Computers Used in Business? — 311

DS Computers fulfill three major needs ~for~ in business ~and industry~. These — 325
needs are as follows: — 330

* Correspondence — 333
* Budgeting, planning, and decision making — 342
* Decentralized processing[3] — 348

Correspondence. The word processing capabilities of — 358
computers provide a means for creating written communication. — 371
Information documented via written communication is important — 383
to the existence of business organizations. — 390

DS Budgeting, Planning, and Decision Making. Information ~in~ — 401
generated by spreadsheets supports management with budgeting, — 413
planning, and decision making. Electronic spreadsheets cre- — 425
ated on computers allow management to manipulate the data — 437
more easily and with much greater speed than when the calcu- — 449
lations were done manually. — 455

Decentralized processing. Because today's computers are — 466
small and inexpensive, they provide a means for decentralized — 479
processing. More ~and more~ workers are creating and processing their — 492
own information rather than relying entirely on word process- — 505
ing ~and data processing~ centers as they once did. This decentralized processing — 521
gives shorter turnaround time for the person needing the — 532
information. — 535

heading 2

[1] Kathryn Schellenberg, ed., Computers in Society, 3d — 13
ed. (Guilford, CT: The Dushkin Publishing Group, — 23
Inc., 1990), p. 2. — 27

[2] David R. Adams and Gerald E. Wagner, — 36
Computer Information Systems: An Introduction, 2d ed., — 45
(Cincinnati: South-Western Publishing Co., 1986), p. 26. — 56

[3] Randolph Johnston, Microcomputers: Concepts and — 67
Applications (Santa Cruz, CA: Mitchell Publishing, — 76
Inc., 1987), p. 1. — 81

3-4D • 30
Lists with Clipart

1. Create these two text charts using the same template as your title and bulleted list charts.

2. Position the bulleted lists on the left of the screen to allow room for the clipart images on the right.

3. Retrieve similar images and position them as shown.

4. For the "Humor" chart, add text at the lower right in a different color in the same, but smaller, typeface. Add a line in a different color to emphasize the last word.

Humor

- Use humorous clipart on visuals–if appropriate for the presentation topic.

- Be sure no images could be offensive to the audience.

Remember to . . .

poofread

proofreed

proofread!

Speaker Tips

- Dress professionally.
- Be enthusiastic.
- Speak clearly and distinctly.
- Maintain eye contact.
- Use natural gestures.

Document 10
Topic Outline

Key the copy at right as a topic outline. Refer to 92D on p. 225 if necessary.

[wp] **note:**

If your software has an Outline feature, use it.

words

EMPLOYMENT COMMUNICATIONS 5

QS

I. PERSONAL DATA SHEET 10

   A. Personal Information 15
      1. Name, address, and Telephone number 23
      2. Social Security number (work permit number) *if needed* 35
      3. Personal interests: hobbies/recreational interests 46
   B. Educational Information 51
      1. Schools attended *and dates of attendance* 60
      2. Special areas of study; activities; awards *received* 72
   C. Work Experience 76
      DS 1. Jobs held; what you experienced; commendations 86
      2. Volunteer work 90
   D. References (Teachers, Work Supervisors) 98

II. LETTER OF APPLICATION 104

   A. Source of Information about Job *Opening* 113
   B. Expression of Interest in Being Interviewed for the Job 125
   C. Brief Summary of Work Skills and How They Fit the Job 136
      1. Special courses that are applicable to the job 146
      2. Work experiences *that* make you qualified for the job 158
   D. Request for Interview 163

III. THANK-YOU LETTER FOLLOWING INTERVIEW 172
   DS A. Appreciation for Courtesies Shown During Company Visit 183
   B. Positive Impressions of Company and Employees 193
   C. Expression of Continued Interest in the Job 203

Document 11
Table with Note

Prepare the information at right as a three-column table, centered vertically and horizontally. DS; **CS:** 0.5". In secondary heading, replace ---- with current year.

Note: Refer to p. 157 to review how to create a keyline using the Center feature/key for horizontal centering. See p. RG19 if Center feature/key is not available. Refer to p. 232 to review procedure for vertical centering, if Center Page feature is not available.

HAMBURG SCHOOL OF BALLET ITINERARY 7

---- Summer Tour* 11

Sponsor	City	Date	
Boston Ballet	Boston	June 4	15
Ballet Academy of Miami	Miami	June 11	20
Dallas Ballet Academy	Dallas	June 18	28
Ruth Page Foundation	Chicago	June 25	35
Northwest Ballet	Minneapolis	July 1	43
Colorado Ballet Center	Denver	July 8	50
Dancers' Stage Company	San Francisco	July 15	57
Pacific Northwest Ballet	Seattle	July 22	66
			75
			78

*Leave for Boston on June 1; return to Hamburg on July 27. 89

3-4C • 25
Text on Boxes

1. Create the text chart at the right using the same template as your title and bulleted list charts.

2. Create a box in the color of your choice, and position it at the left as shown; duplicate this box and position the second box on the lower right.

3. Enter text in each box; choose the size and color. You may need to adjust the box sizes to frame the text nicely.

4. Retrieve a star and change its color to yellow. Size and position the star on the first box. Duplicate the star for the second box and position it as shown.

5. Retrieve an arrow, change its color and size, then position it as shown to indicate order.

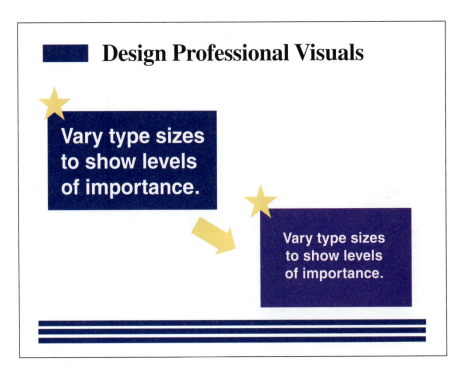

words

COMMON U.S./METRIC EQUIVALENTS

Approximate Values

		words
	COMMON U.S./METRIC EQUIVALENTS	6
	Approximate Values	10
1 inch	25.4 millimeters (mm)	16
1 inch	2.54 centimeters (cm)	22
1 foot	0.305 meter (m)	26
1 yard	0.91 meter (m)	31
1 mile	1.61 kilometers (km)	36
1 pint	0.47 liter (1 or L)	42
1 quart	0.95 liter (1 or L)	47
1 gallon	3.785 liters (1 or L)	53
1 ounce	28.35 grams (g)	58
1 pound	0.45 kilogram (kg)	63

MARCH SALES

Sales Manager	Territory	Sales	words
	MARCH SALES		2
Sales Manager	Territory	Sales	9
Diane Aldredge	Connecticut	$204,500	16
Marcia Kelly	Maine	135,200	22
Ruth Peterson	Massachusetts	125,000	29
Rebecca Johnston	New Hampshire	135,800	37
Orlando Martinez	New York	172,900	43
Jonathan Akervik	Rhode Island	88,200	51
Roger McDonald	Vermont	115,200	57
Total Sales		$976,800	61

---- SPRING RECRUITMENT SCHEDULE

Martin Bartlett

University	Date	Area of Specialization	words
---- SPRING RECRUITMENT SCHEDULE			7
Martin Bartlett			10
University / State	Date	Area of Specialization	18
San Diego State University	March 3	Marketing	27
Arizona State University	March 10	Management Information	39
University of Colorado	March 17	Management Information	50
University of Kentucky	March 24	Management	58
Tennessee State University	March 31	Accounting	68
Florida A & M	April 7	Marketign	74
Duke University	April 14	Accounting	81

Document 12
Table with Decimal Numbers

Prepare the copy at right as a two-column table, centered vertically and horizontally. DS; **CS:** 1". Align numbers at the decimal point.

Note: If a Decimal Tab feature is available, use it to align decimal numbers.

Document 13
Table with Amount Column and Total

Key the copy at right as a three-column table SS. TM: 2"; SM: 1.25". Left-align column headings.

Note: The underline preceding the total should be the same length as the longest item in column (including the $).

Document 14
Table with Centered Column Headings

Key the copy at right as a three-column table centered vertically and horizontally. DS; **CS:** 0.25". Center column headings. In main heading, replace ---- with current year.

Refer

Create keyline using Center feature/key — p. 157.

Horizontal centering without Center feature — p. RG19.

Vertical centering (manual) — p. 232.

Centering short column headings — 96C, p. 235.

Centering multiple-line column headings — 98C, p. 239.

Adding Graphic Enhancements

Objectives:

1. To observe the importance of using appropriate graphic images, lines, and boxes.

2. To retrieve and position graphic images, lines, and boxes.

3. To create charts with graphic enhancements.

3-4A • 25
Graphic Images

1. Read the copy at the right.

2. Learn how to use the drawing tools in your software to create, size, and position graphic images.

3. Retrieve images similar to the ones shown at the right.

4. Position the images in different locations on the screen.

5. Duplicate an image to create more of the same image; resize the duplicated images.

6. Change colors on the arrow and star images.

Graphic images. Symbols and art (clipart or original) can enhance a message and help to convey ideas. Symbols such as arrows or starbursts can focus an audience's attention. Art might include photo images or even original artwork scanned and converted to a digitized image. Clipart can often be used to add humor or to contribute to the text-based message. Be creative, but use images in good taste. An image isn't necessary on every chart shown in a presentation.

3-4B • 25
Graphic Lines/Boxes

1. Learn how to create and position lines/rules as shown on p. A66.

2. Change the length and thickness of the lines.

3. Create boxes in various sizes and colors.

4. Create boxes with fancy borders.

Graphic lines/boxes. Lines, or rules, can be used to separate sections of a visual, to emphasize key words, or to connect elements. Boxes, too, can separate elements and provide a distinctive background for text. Boxes will appear to stand above the background when shading is applied on two sides. Fancy borders can call attention to the contents of a box.

(continued on next page)

R&e Letters and Memos

Document 1
Personal-Business Letter with Special Characters

Format the letter at right in block format with open punctuation. Use the special character shown for the listed items in ¶ 3.

Document 2

Rekey Document 1 in modified block format with indented paragraphs, mixed punctuation. Use a different character than in Document 1 for the listed items.

	words
1231 Woodlawn Dr. | Toledo, OH 43612-1712 | April 5, ---- | Mr. Jeffrey	13
A. York | Lakeview Condominium Association | 599 Miller Rd. | Knox-	27
ville, TN 37920-4119 | Dear Mr. York	32

Thank you for sending the lease so quickly. My check for the $450 secu- — 48
rity deposit is enclosed along with the signed lease. I will pay the first — 63
month's rent when I arrive in Knoxville. — 70

I do have a few questions that you can answer for me regarding the condo- — 85
minium complex. — 88

- Do you arrange to have the electricity transferred to my name, or do I — 102
  need to contact the electric company? — 111
- To what address will my mail be delivered? — 120
- Is garbage disposal included with the rent? — 129
- Is storage space available outside the condominium? — 140

I am looking forward to receiving the information so that I can take care of — 156
these arrangements before arriving in Knoxville on July 1. — 168

Sincerely \| Jennifer A. Rose \| Enclosure — 175

Document 3
Simplified Memo with Distribution List

Prepare the copy at right as a simplified memo. Create a horizontal distribution list (see p. 189).

Document 4
Standard Memo with Distribution List

Reformat or rekey Document 3 as a standard memo on plain paper. Use the vertical style distribution list (see p. 189).

December 27, ---- \| Charlie Meade, Annette Nye, Greg Anderson, Emma — 13
Sims, Chi Sen \| NEW BROCHURES — 19

Here are the new brochures that I talked about at the last staff meeting. — 34
The printing company did an excellent job in designing them. I believe they — 49
should help us provide the public with information about the various — 63
services our bank offers. — 68

Since you are the first contact the public has with our bank, it is extremely — 84
important for you to be aware of what is included in each brochure so that — 99
you can provide our customers with the appropriate brochure to answer — 113
their questions. If you have questions about any of the information — 127
included in the brochures, please check with the person in charge of the — 141
particular program you have questions about. — 151

Remember to mark your calendars for our next staff meeting, which is sched- — 166
uled for January 28. — 170

Linda G. Gomez \| Administrative Assistant to the Vice President \| xx \| — 183
Attachments — 185

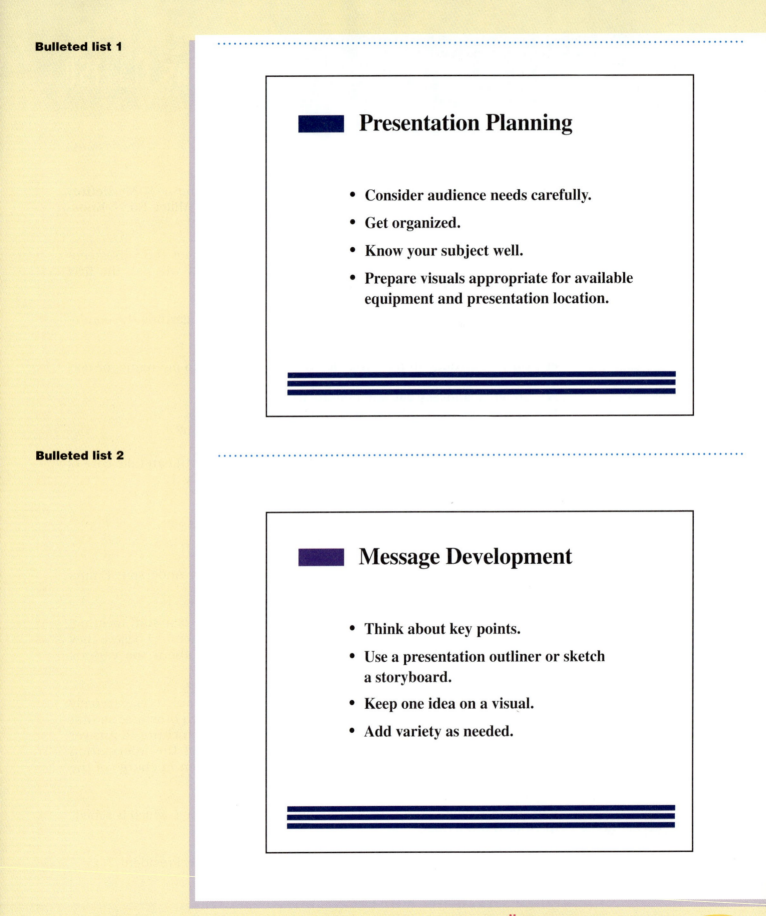

words

Document 5
Simplified Block Letter

Prepare the letter at right in simplified block format with open punctuation.

Note: Omit those letter parts shown that should not be included in simplified block format. Add any missing letter parts.

Letters with Variable Information, Special Features

Document 6

Prepare the letter below in modified block format with blocked ¶s; mixed punctuation. Insert the following information for the numbers in parentheses:

(1) **May** (2) **Houston** (3) **managing human resources** (4) **May 13** (5) **Milwaukee** (6) **Marc Plaza**

Special features: Company name in closing lines: **BANKING INSTITUTE**
c Natasha J. Bartlett
Mark L. Kostner
Postscript: **Will I see you at next week's convention in Hawaii? I'm looking forward to some warmer weather.**

Document 7

Prepare Document 6 in block format; open punctuation with the following changes:

Ms. Renae A. Santiago
Suwannee National Bank
5507 Ranchero Rd.
Tallahassee, FL 32304-9340

(1) **June** (2) **Pittsburgh** (3) **customer advertising** (4) **October 1** (5) **Houston** (6) **Hyatt Regency**

Special features: same as Document 6; no postscript

(Total words = 167)

---

	words
(Current date) | Miss Roberta J. Payson | 310 Ledgewood Rd. | Portland, ME	13
04108-6482 | Dear Miss Payson	21

Here are the two tables that show the cost of a $50,000 home loan. The — 36
first table displays various interest rates for a 15-year loan, while the — 50
second one gives the rates for a 30-year loan. As you can see from the — 65
tables, you would decrease your monthly payment by approximately $120 — 79
per month by assuming a 30-year loan. The total amount repaid, how- — 92
ever, would be considerably more. — 99

The tables can also be used to determine the difference between the monthly — 114
payments for a fixed mortgage versus the adjustable rate mortgage. — 128
Currently our adjustable mortgage rate is 8 percent. As I mentioned — 142
yesterday, this type of loan is based on the index tied to the U.S. Treasury — 157
securities. The initial rate is guaranteed for two years. At the end of two — 173
years the rate can be increased or decreased by two percentage points each — 188
year up to a maximum rate of 12 percent. — 196

If you have any additional questions about the loans we discussed yester- — 211
day, please call me. — 215

Sincerely \| Mark R. Nelson \| Loan Officer \| xx \| Enclosures \| c Marshall — 226
S. Gagne — 227

- -

November 15, ---- \| Mr. Lewis G. Mackenzie \| Human Resources Man- — 12
ager \| Bank of Nottingham \| 1295 Kensington Ave. \| Detroit, MI 48230- — 25
5286 \| Dear Mr. Mackenzie: — 30

The seminar you presented last (1) in (2) for the Banking Institute on — 45
(3) was very well received. Several institute members have requested that — 64
the seminar be offered again this coming year. — 74

The seminar is scheduled for (4) in (5) at the (6). Are you available — 91
on this date to present the seminar? The honorarium for conducting the — 105
seminar has been increased to $1,800. Of course, all your expenses — 119
would be paid by the institute. — 126

Please let me know by December 1 whether you will be able to work with — 140
us on this year's seminar. — 145

Sincerely, \| Ryan S. Woodward \| Institute Director \| xx — 155
closing 186

Displaying Text Charts

Objectives:

1. To learn to vary text to show levels of importance.
2. To learn to create a title chart.
3. To learn to create bulleted list charts.

2A • 30
Title Chart

1. Read the copy at the right.
2. Select a similar template or master slide from those available in your software. It will give a consistent "look" to the series of charts you will create in this lesson.
3. Create the title chart using a similar typeface.
4. Select appropriate font sizes to emphasize the presentation title and presenter title.

Title chart. A presentation should begin with a title chart. Include the presentation title, presenter name, and other needed information. The text for this chart should be larger than for other charts, yet should blend with the other visuals in the series.

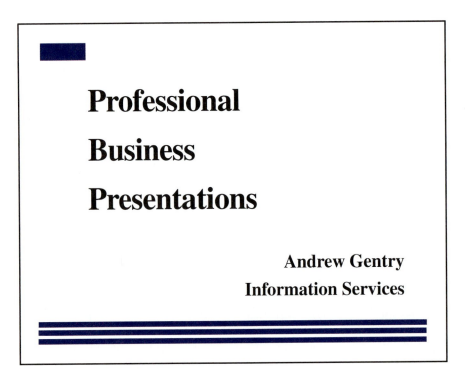

2B • 30
Bulleted Lists

1. Read the copy at the right.
2. Create the two bulleted lists displayed on the next page.
3. Use the same template to match your title chart. To the extent possible, follow the design shown.

Bulleted lists. Use lists to guide discussion and to help the audience follow a speaker's ideas. If too much information is placed on a single chart, the text becomes difficult to read. Therefore, keep the information on the visual concise—do not write complete sentences.

When using lists, be sure to

- Write phrases, not sentences.
- Use parallel structure.
- Limit the number of items on one list to about six.
- Limit long wraparound lines of text.
- Be concise.

(continued on next page)

words

STUDENT ORGANIZATIONS — 4

Student organizations plays a vital role in the educational process — 18
of students. Students who participate in such organizations are given — 32
opportunities to test the concepts they were taught in the formal — 45
classrooom environment. Two such organizations that are widely rec- — 59
ognized in the business education field are Future Business Leaders of — 73
America and Business Professionals of America (formerly called Office — 87
Education Association. — 92

Future Business Leaders of America — 99

Future Business Leaders of America is a vocational association — 112
that helps studdnts bridge the gap between the classroom and the business — 126
world. Two of the major goals outlined in the Future Business Leaders — 141
of America Handbook are as follows:[1] — 148

1. Develop competent, aggressive business leadership. — 159

2. Create more interest in and understanding of American business — 173
enterprise. — 175

Business leadership. Students have the opportunity to develop — 188
leadership skills by serving as officers, attending conferences, working — 203
with businessmen and businesswomen in the community, and partici- — 216
pating in competitive events sponsored by the organization. the — 229
organization's strong emphasis on community service provides another — 242
avenue for the development of leadership skills. — 252

Business enterprise. A greater understanding of business enter- — 265
prise is gained by students as they participate in chapter projects — 279
dealing with this important subject. These projects give students ex- — 293
periences in learning more about the operation ofbusiness enterprise in — 308
America. — 310

Business Professionals of America — 317

Business Professionals of America is another vocational business — 330
and office education program for students interested in developing per- — 344
sonal, leadership, and office skills. — 352

Accoridng to Goodman, the executive director of the organization — 365
for 1987-88, the goal of the organization has been to promote — 377
leadership and professionalism among students in order to pre- — 389
pare them for satisfying and successful careers in the business — 402
world.[2] — 404

(continued on next page)

1D • 15
Makeover Example

Example 1
Visual

1. Examine the visual at the right. Its design does not follow visual design guidelines for font treatments. It is not easy to read.

2. Identify what is wrong with this visual.

Example 2
Visual

1. Examine the visual at the right. This visual presents the same information, yet it is much easier to read than Example 1. Its design follows visual design guidelines for font treatments.

2. Identify what makes this design more effective than Example 1.

Poor visual example

PRESENTATION SOFTWARE

PRESENTATION SOFTWARE CAN HELP YOU TO COMMUNICATE MORE EFFECTIVELY. THE FEATURES OF PRESENTATION SOFTWARE INCLUDE OUTLINERS TO HELP YOU GET ORGANIZED, TEMPLATES TO HELP YOU MATCH COLORS, CLIPART TO HELP YOU VISUALIZE IDEAS, AND SCREENSHOWS TO SHOW YOUR VISUALS ONE AT A TIME.

OVERHEAD TRANSPARENCIES, 35-mm SLIDES, AND COMPUTER-PROJECTED PRESENTATIONS CAN BE CREATED WITH PRESENTATION SOFTWARE.

WHEN YOU CREATE VISUALS TO AID IN YOUR PRESENTATION, YOUR PREPARATION WILL HELP TO GIVE YOU CONFIDENCE.

Good visual example

Presentation Software

- • Presentation effectiveness improved

- • Key features include:
  - • Outliners and templates
  - • Clipart selections and screenshows

- • Output includes:
  - • Overhead transparencies and 35-mm slides
  - • Computer-projected presentations

Document 10
Title Page

Create a title page for the report you prepared in Document 9.

Document 11
Report

Prepare the text at right and on p. A29 as a report in bound format. SS and indent paragraphs. The material is to become part of an office manual numbered pp. 24-27.

Bold the main and secondary headings and the heading on the separate ENDNOTES page. Number p. 24 at the bottom center; number remaining pages at the upper right. Use the secondary heading as a bold header on each page after p. 24.

Replace underlines with italic (except side headings) if available. Use hanging-indent style for the enumerated list. Set a tab to reduce the space between numbers and beginning of first word.

words

The two goals, developing business leadership and understanding business enterprise, emphasized by FBLA are also emphasized by Business Professionals of America. They, too, have programs designed to provide studetns with the opportunity to develop their leadership skills and to foster a greater understanding of the role of the entrepreneur in the free enterprise system. 416 430 444 458 473 479

ENDNOTES 481

[1]Future Business Leaders of America Handbook (Reston, VA: FBLA-PBL Incorporated, 1985), p. 5. 493 500

[2]Goodman, Dorothy M., "A New Image for Our Organization," 1987-88 Chapter Handbook (Columbus, OH: Office Education Association, 1987), p. 11. 512 525 529

ADDRESSING THE SITUATION 5

Guides for Processing First-Class Mail 13

The cost of an average business letter is roughly $16 to $17.[1] The U.S. Postal Service (USPS) continually strives to increase the speed and lower the per-unit cost of mail delivery. In 30 years of effort, USPS has transformed mail service through the use of optical character recognition (OCR) scanners, authorized (2-letter) state[2] abbreviations, expanded ZIP Codes (ZIP+4), barcoding, and high-speed sorting devices. 25 40 55 70 85 97

USPS Standards 101

Businesses such as this one have improved internal operations in line with changing practices of USPS. Obvious changes include faster equipment and better trained personnel in the mail room. Other important changes include the use of specific addressing guidelines by the document specialists who prepare first-class mail.[3] 114 128 142 157 166

These guidelines are updated regularly on the basis of USPS bulletins. Publication 28[4] is the current reference. Addressing guides are also updated with information from office management journals, secretarial conferences and workshops, word processing user's guides, and computing magazines. 178 194 209 223 226

Company Standards 229

At a cost of $16 to $17 apiece, first-class mail in this organization is viewed as serious business. Nearly four hundred first-class items leave this company's mail room each week. The goals for each piece are the same: 243 259 274

- Go to the right place. 279
- Go in the shortest possible time. 287
- Grab and hold receivers' attention.[5] 295

(continued on next page)

Getting Started

O b j e c t i v e s :

1. To learn basic presentation terms.

2. To apply presentation templates.

3. To learn to select fonts for readability and consistency.

1A • 10
Orientation

1. Read the copy and study the illustrations at the right.

2. Learn to select portrait and landscape orientations on your software.

3. With your software set for landscape orientation, key your name, course name, and current date centered on the visual.

4. Change the orientation for this visual to portrait and notice the difference in appearance.

The **landscape orientation** for presentation visuals provides a work space wider than it is tall. More horizontal space is available to arrange text information and illustrations. This size fits better on a computer screen during development and better on the viewing screen when visuals are projected as transparencies, slides, or electronic presentations.

The **portrait orientation** provides a work space taller than it is wide. If a visual for projection is displayed in portrait orientation, often the bottom of the viewing screen is not visible to the entire audience. Portrait orientation, however, is appropriate for many paper-based applications.

Landscape Orientation

xxxxxxxxxxxxxxx
xxxxxxxxxxxxxxxxxxxxxx
xxxxxxxxxxxxx

Portrait Orientation

xxxxxxxxxxxxxxx
xxxxxxxxxxxxxxxxxxxxxx
xxxxxxxxxxxxx

1B • 10
Templates

1. Read the copy at the right.

2. Examine the various templates available with your software.

Presentation software provides *templates* that contain background designs and a *palette* of coordinated colors for text. An appropriate display template should be selected first in preparing a presentation.

Several different templates will be used for the visuals shown in this unit. Suggestions will indicate what makes a template appropriate in a given instance.

1C • 15
Font Selection and Treatment

1. Read the copy at the right.

2. Determine the fonts available with your software and learn how to select them.

3. Learn how to change font color and sizes.

Readability of text is very important; therefore, carefully select fonts and font treatments for easy reading and consistency throughout a presentation.

- Establish a heading/text hierarchy with font sizes and colors—make the most important items show up more.

- Limit use of words in all capital letters—lowercase text is easier to read.

- Be careful when combining different fonts to avoid confusing the audience.

- Strive for consistency in font size, color, and use throughout a presentation.

- Be sure text on all visuals is large and bold enough to be seen from the back of the presentation room when projected.

words

First-Class Mail Guidelines

301

The following first-class mail guidelines were designed to reach these goals. Guidelines for handling other classes of mail and using special services begin on p. 28. A postal rate chart appears in Appendix D (blue pages).

314
326
341
346

1. Key envelope addresses in block style, using uppercase letters and omitting punctuation (except hyphens).

359
368

2. Place the address block about four inches from the left edge and two inches from the top edge of a No. 10 envelope, or use the default setting of the Envelope feature on the word processing software.

382
394
407
409

3. Use an attention line ONLY when attempts to determine a person's name have failed. Place the attention line (when used) on the first line of the address block. Example: ATTENTION MARKETING COORDINATOR.

421
435
448
451

4. Key the street address or box number on the line below the addresses' name, followed by applicable apartment or suite numbers.

465
478

5. Key only the city, state abbreviation, and ZIP+4 Code on the last line. Space once before the ZIP Code. Do NOT place the postal codes of other countries on the last address line of international mail. Show only the country name (no abbreviation) on the last address line.

490
503
517
530
534

6. Use USPS authorized abbreviations for directions and street suffixes; for example, N for North, ST for Street, BLVD for Boulevard, and STE for Suite. Never abbreviate the city name. Extremely long company names may be abbreviated if USPS standards are used. Example: ACCENT ON EXEC SVCS for ACCENT ON EXECUTIVE SERVICES.

548
561
575
587
598
600

7. When using the Envelope software feature, print a postnet bar code above the envelope address.

614
621

8. Use a personal (MISS, MR, or MS) or professional (DR, PROF, REV, etc.) title in envelope and letter addresses, with few exceptions as noted in the following paragraph. (MR/MRS is an acceptable form of Mr. and Mrs.)

634
648
662
665

If a woman's marital status is unknown, use MS. If a person's first name does not indicate gender or if only initials are shown, call the person's office and ask the switchboard operator if MR or MS is correct. If the information cannot be obtained by calling, omit a personal title from

678
692
707
723

(continued on next page)

Screenshow Presentation Purposes

A **screenshow** is a basic feature of presentation software. Different programs may use other names for this feature, but any true presentation program will have this capability. A screenshow has two purposes: to keep related files organized and to project the visuals in a preplanned sequence for audience viewing. Presentation software can be used with a computer and projection equipment to create "electronic" presentations. Even portable computers can be used for this purpose.

Once the necessary projection equipment is purchased, screenshow production is low in cost because files can be saved to the computer hard drive or to a removable disk. The charts are all saved in advance and arranged in a particular sequence; if necessary, last-minute changes can be made. This flexibility is not possible when slides or transparencies are used for a presentation. Plus, the vivid colors of well-designed visuals make watching them much more interesting than slides or transparencies.

The computer used for projection must be connected to a large-screen projection device such as a/an

- LCD (liquid crystal display) panel—a notebook-sized panel that is easily portable. (It requires, however, an overhead projector with a high-intensity [very bright] light to project through the panel.)

- LCD data/video projector—a portable unit containing its own light source that is easily portable.

- CRT data/video projector—a unit that is usually ceiling mounted because of its size (portable units are available).

- Video monitor—a large-sized video monitor is effective for smaller groups; the need for a projection screen is eliminated.

Animation. Interesting transition effects are one form of animation used to control how visuals go on and off display. Also, objects on the visuals can be animated in such a way as to have a person walk across a scene on the visual or to have a title drop into place one letter at a time. Animation provides significant benefits for capturing and retaining the audience's attention.

Video and sound. Some presentation software allows the user to incorporate multimedia elements of video and sound. Additional needs for hardware make presenting with video and sound a little more complicated.

Design and delivery tips. Use more visuals than you would for a transparency-based presentation—and put less on each visual. Show a visual just as you are ready to discuss its content.

- Arrange lists as *builds* to present listed concepts one at a time as discussion progresses.

- Use a building technique to create process diagrams or models by adding parts as discussion progresses.

- To maintain eye contact with the audience, position the computer where its screen can easily be seen instead of turning around to face the projection screen while talking.

words

the envelope and use simplified block format (no salutation) for the let-   737
ter, OR use the first and last names in the salutation of a block format   752
letter. Examples: Dear J. P. Russell, Dear Kim Bunzel. (The use of M to   767
represent MR or MS is NOT recommended.)   775

ENDNOTES   777

[1]This estimate is derived from an early-90s Target Study conducted   790
by the Dartnell Institute of Business Research in Chicago. Postage repre-   805
sents only about 2 percent of the costs, based on the 1995 rate of $.32 for   820
the first ounce. Most of the cost involves salary and wages of individuals   835
who originate and process business letters.   844

[2]Authorized in 1963 as part of the conversion from postal zones to   858
ZIP Code areas, the 2-CAP abbreviations include District of Columbia (DC),   873
Guam (GU), Puerto Rico (PR), and the Virgin Islands (VI).   884

[3]Each document specialist is to have a copy of "Addressing the Situ-   898
ation" at her or his work station.   905

[4]Postal Addressing Standards. Washington, DC: U. S. Postal Service,   919
1992. Additional copies may be obtained by asking for USPS Form 7380   933
from the mail room.   937

[5]A former company president set a 3 percent maximum return rate   950
on company mail in 1965, a challenge unmet for the next 6 years. The   964
return rate last year: 0.47 percent.   972

	Date of Publication
Willey	1962
Capps	1969
Coolidge	1924
Wilson	1973
Wheeler	1976
Carter	1978
Kakuske	1970

Change	To
teacher	instructor
SA	2
A	1
U	0
D	-1
SD	-2

Document 12
Expand Existing Table
Open TAB96C1 and add a column for publication dates. CS: 0.5"; arrange in ascending order by date.

Note: The original table appears on p. 235 (96C, Table 1).

Document 13
Revising a Table
Open TAB99B1 and make the changes shown at right throughout the document.

Note: The original table appears on p. 240 (99B, Table 1). Use the Search to Replace feature if available.

Presentation Software Features

Presentations are an important part of communication in business. Their purpose is often to **inform** (deliver facts) or **persuade** (change behavior, attitudes, or beliefs). In both cases, the presenter has information to share and hopes the audience will react favorably to it. Typical business situations involving presentations include product introductions, award presentations, sales promotions, training sessions, and other meetings.

To help an audience understand the presentation message, visuals such as transparencies or slides are frequently used. With the necessary equipment, a series of visuals can be projected directly from a computer system for audience viewing. Today's presentation software provides many possibilities for using color and other design techniques to make presentations more dynamic.

The key features of presentation software are

- word processing capabilities
- drawing features
- graphing abilities
- importing capabilities for clipart, photographs, or data from other programs
- exporting capabilities for transferring images to other programs
- screenshow development and display using text and diagram builds and, possibly, animation and digital video import
- presentation design and management
- printing capabilities

Design

The condition of the final output, of course, will depend on the available equipment and the skill of the presenter who creates the presentation. Many of the design concepts appropriate for word and desktop publishing are also important to the design of visuals for presentations—and yet many differences exist, also.

Presentation visuals can spur interest and illustrate major points. They should help the speaker explain and help the audience understand the speaker's message. **Visuals** (also called *charts* or *slides*) should be well designed to serve this purpose.

Templates (Slide Masters)

The series of visuals prepared for a presentation should have a consistent and uncluttered look achieved through color, graphics, and type. An attractive appearance is often the result of a simple design. Presentation programs provide background **templates** (also called *slide masters*) for this purpose. These templates provide a design and color scheme for the background and text information for a consistent look for all visuals in a presentation. Even when printing with black and white, a similar appearance can be achieved so that all visuals look like they belong together.

words

Document 14
Three-Column Table

Format table at right. **CS:** 1" between Columns 1 and 2; 0.5" between Columns 2 and 3.

SS data; center all headings.

SALES DEPT BUDGET PERFORMANCE — 7

Month Ended July 31, ---- — 12

Expense item	Budget Allocation	Amount Spent	
			15
			22
Salaries	$ 18,600	$ 18,450	27
Benefits	4,985	4,857	31
Suppiles	1,125	1,250	35
Telephone	650	595	48
Postage	475	575 515	42
Travel	3,275	3,075	46
Totals	$29,110	$28,802 742	51

Document 15
Table

Format table at right. Arrange the entries in descending order by selling price. DS data.

Add column headings:

Col. 1: **Cellular Telephone**

Col. 2: **Regular Selling Price**

Col. 3: **Clearance Price**

CELLULAR TELEPHONES — 4

End-of-Month Clearance Sale — 10

TEC P-9100	$1,699.99	$888.88	27
TEC P-9110	1,999.99	999.99	33
Rawlins CP-1000	1,549.99	825.88	39
Rawlins CP-2000	1,749.99	925.88	46
Cellatel 380	1,224.99	749.99	51
Cellatel 480	1,924.99	974.99	57
Carfone XT	1,399.99	649.99	63
Carfone ST	1,599.99	848.88	68
Carfone ZT	1,799.99	949.88	73

Document 16
Table

Format table at right. **CS:** 6 sp. between longest headings; SS data; center all headings.

ACCOUNTING DEPARTMENT — 4

Proposed Salary Increases for ---- — 11

Employee	Cost of Living Increase	Merit Increase	New Salary	
				16
				24
Sandra Morris	$1,500	$ 900	$ 32,400	31
Jane Raleigh	1,140	1,140	25,080	38
William Bossey	990	792	21,582	44
Rita Perez	945	850	20,695	49
Hiro Hito	930	1,116	20,646	54
Harry Kaskie	500	450	12,950	61
Totals	$6,005	$5,248	$133,353	66

Flyer

1. Key the text in the flyer at the right.

2. Change margins all around to 1".

3. Retrieve a similar image to represent the sun (a starburst would be suitable, too) and position it at the top right.

4. Begin the text about 2.5" down from the top of the page.

5. Use a large, bold typeface for the attention-getting text.

6. Retrieve a similar image for the suitcase; duplicate the image and position four as shown. (If you cannot find a similar image to suggest travel, a solid black line could be used here to separate the page.)

7. Create a coupon to be returned to the travel agency for information. Use a border for this section. If available, use a border that resembles the one shown with scissors to suggest cutting along the line. (A solid-line border could be used instead.)

8. Use a smaller text size for the coupon text.

9. Add white space as appropriate.

This flyer uses a large, bold typeface to emphasize the text and clipart images to suggest travel to a sunny location. The border is used to create a coupon to return for additional information. The border shown suggests cutting the coupon out of the paper.

For FUN in the SUN . . . call Lee Travel at 217-152-2230

Return this coupon with your name and address for information on our summer vacation packages!

Name _____

Address _____

_____

Phone _____

Lee Travel
719 W. Marketview
Champaign, IL 61801-2223

Document 17
Table

Format table at right. DS data; **CS:** 8 sp. between longest items in columns; center all headings.

MONEY MARKET FUNDS

Percents for Week Ending May 30, ----

Fund	Average Annual Yield	Change from Last Week
AAPMny	8.35	-.02
ActAsMny	7.64	.01
AlexGrn	7.52	---
CDAMny	8.44	.01
Lndpt	8.23	.06
MPS Life	7.90	-.03
NassCash	8.31	.16
VenPe	6.86	-.12
WllngHS	7.89	.06
XtrMny	6.98	-.04

(word counts: 4, 11, 15, 22, 25, 29, 32, 35, 38, 42, 46, 49, 52, 55)

Document 18
Table

Format table at right on plain full sheet; short edge at top. DS data; **CS:** 8 sp. between longest items in columns; block column headings.

Tall Buildings in New York City
Listed by Height in Feet and Meters

Building	Feet	Meters
World Trade Center	1,350	411.750
Empire State (without TV tower)	1,250	381.250
Chrysler	1,046	319.030
American International	950	289.750
40 Wall Tower	927	282.735
Citicorp Center	914	278.770

Source: The World Almanac, 1996.

(word counts: 6, 14, 18, 25, 34, 39, 46, 51, 57, 60, 66)

1. Prepare the flyer at the right.
2. Change all margins to 0.5".
3. Set center justification.
4. Create a double line border and stretch it to fill the page.
5. For the word *Circus*, use a serif typeface; make the first and last letters larger than the middle of the word. (The example shows 66 and 44 points.)
6. For all other text, use a sans serif typeface and vary the sizes used.
7. Adjust the line height for the title lines so that the word *Mario* fits tightly above the word *Circus*.
8. Use reverse type for the word *Featuring*.
9. Insert iconic symbols as shown for the diamond shapes and pointing hands.
10. Add white space as appropriate.

This flyer would be suitable for posting or for a newspaper advertisement. To gain attention, a double border is placed close to the edge of the page. Words are emphasized by changing the sizes and adding decorative iconic symbols.

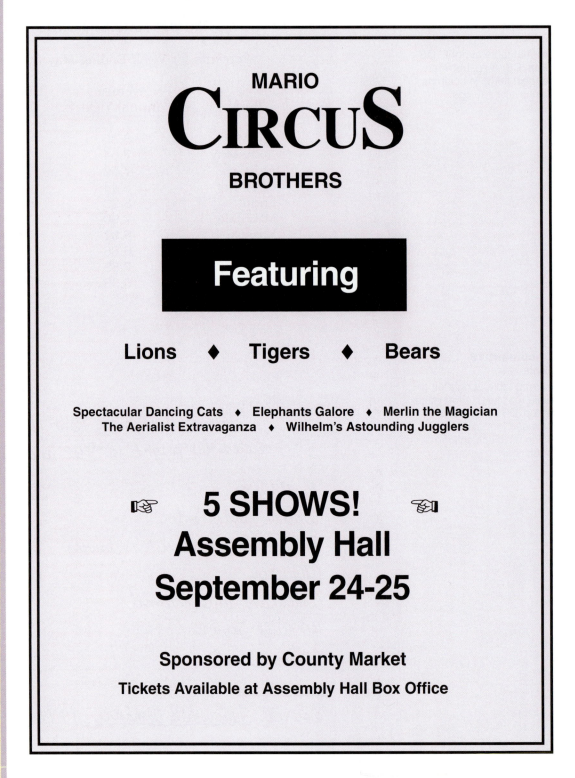

Publishing Techniques

Many people use word publishing techniques to produce professional quality documents. Today's word processing software has many capabilities for combining text and graphics to create documents that are visually appealing. The design and graphic treatments help strengthen the message a document contains.

Complex designs, such as for magazines or brochures with photographs, are created using page layout software that has even more advanced features. These programs are known as desktop publishing software. (The term *desktop publishing* is often applied to the document-design features of word processing. In this textbook, however, the latter will be called **word publishing**.)

While it is possible to practice many publishing techniques using a dot matrix printer, better results can be achieved with an ink jet or laser printer.

Publishing techniques include

- using proportional fonts
- adding emphasis, such as shadows, to some text
- using lines or boxes to separate page elements
- including original artwork or clipart to illustrate the message
- opening up pages with white space

Document Planning

With any document design, the first consideration should be the *purpose* of the document. A flyer designed to advertise a circus, for example, would have quite a different appearance than one designed to announce a formal banquet.

The second consideration is the *audience* (either one person or a group of people) who will receive the document. Audience backgrounds and interests should be considered, along with the document appearance, in the design of a document.

Document Design

Document appearance and the image a document creates are influenced in several ways. Because many documents consist mostly of text, an understanding of *type* is necessary in selecting a typeface appropriate to the purpose. A **typeface** is a trade name for a collection of characters from a-z in uppercase and lowercase with all related symbols. A *font* is a particular typeface in a certain size and style.

Thousands of typefaces are available. Some might be selected for their readability; others might be selected for a look of elegance or a strong, bold appearance.

The typeface *size* and *style* affect the emphasis text receives. Words printed in a large, bold typeface stand out and will be noticed when a reader quickly scans a page to learn what a document is about.

Lines (rules) and/or *boxes* can help to divide groups of text and to emphasize information on a page.

Artwork, consisting of *clipart* images or originally created drawings, can add impact and focus readers' attention on the message.

The *white space* (empty space) on a page is an important design element for grouping related information and making a document more inviting to read.

Effective use of these publishing techniques requires practice to develop a sense of "design."

12-14C • 35
Certificate

1. Change paper to landscape orientation (11" wide x 8.5" long).
2. Use 1" margins all around.
3. Retrieve a border image and stretch it to fill the page.
4. Using center alignment, key the text of the certificate.
5. Insert white space as needed.

Notes:

- The example shows the typeface Times in three sizes—the title is the largest text line; names under the signature lines are the smallest.
- The name of the person receiving the certificate is shown in the typeface Syntax UltraBlack.

This certificate has a decorative border to give it an elegant look suitable for framing.

A bold typeface is used to emphasize the name of the person receiving the award.

Certificate of Achievement

is awarded to

Nathan Jefferson

for outstanding civic contributions to the
Marshall High School Boosters Club

_____   _____
Angela Mason, President   Greg Hall, Adviser

Understanding Type

Objectives:

Objectives:
1. To learn about parts of a character.
2. To learn about fonts and typefaces.
3. To key text using different typefaces.

1A • 10
Character Parts

1. Read the copy at the right.
2. Identify parts of a character of type.

The type chosen for a document affects its image or the impression it makes. To begin understanding differences in type, learn the parts of type, as shown and defined below.

Parts of a character of type

baseline: the imaginary line on which all characters of type are placed.

x-height: the height of characters such as *x*, *e*, *m*, or *a*.

ascender: the part of characters that extends above the x-height.

descender: the part of characters that extends below the baseline.

serif: the small lines or "feet" that appear at the ends of some characters.

1B • 15
Fonts and Typefaces

1. Read the copy at the right.
2. Learn how to change typefaces on the software you are using.
3. Compose two short paragraphs using a different typeface for each one. Compare the appearance of each paragraph.

A **font** is a single *typeface*, *type style*, and *type size*. You will learn about type style and type size in another lesson. A **typeface** is a collection of characters and symbols that have a related design. All typefaces are identified by unique names. For example, some are named after the person who created them; others, by the place where they were created.

Typefaces are divided into two main categories: *serif* and *sans serif*. Serifs are the small finishing strokes that appear on the ends of some characters. Serif typefaces are often used for the body text in documents because the serifs make text easier to read. Sans serif typefaces do not have serifs; often they are used for headlines and larger print.

Serif typefaces

Bookman
Garamond MT
Goudy Old Style
Palatino
Times New Roman

Sans serif typefaces

Arial
AvantGarde
Futura
Helvetica
Univers

1. Create a report title page with the title framed in a simple border.
2. Insert white space as appropriate.

Notes:

- The title in the example is shown in a serif typeface set at 24 points in bold.
- The title and border begin about 2.5" from the top of the page.
- Other text information is in the same typeface as the title set at 15 points in bold.

On this title page, the title words are emphasized by framing them in a simple border. The border is a single, thick line.

The title and border are positioned on the top half of the page; other information is positioned on the bottom half of the page.

A Comparison of

Publishing Features

in Two

Word Processing Programs

Your Name

Business Computer Applications

Current date

1. Study the examples of special-purpose typefaces.
2. Select a special-purpose typeface and key the paragraphs above right.
3. Block and copy the paragraphs two times; change the typefaces used for the new paragraphs and compare their appearance with the first version.

Differences between typefaces may be subtle or they may be dramatic. Certain typeface designs are excellent for readability, while others are meant for special purposes only and should be used sparingly.

The choice of typefaces, however, is often up to the document designer; for example, some people prefer to use sans serif typefaces for body text because sans serif typefaces tend to have a more contemporary appearance than serif typefaces.

Some typefaces are very bold and dramatic and would be suitable for attention-getting announcements. Other typefaces resemble script writing and are suitable for formal invitations.

Special-purpose typefaces

Brush Script

Kaufmann

Playbill

STENCIL

Syntax UltraBlack

This is the typeface Syntax UltraBlack. Notice how the characters are dark and bold. This appearance would create a dramatic effect for eye-catching announcements and would be suitable for headings in reports or in memorandums.

This is the typeface Kaufmann. Notice how the characters are slender and resemble handwriting. This typeface would create an elegant image for formal announcements and invitations. This text seems much smaller even though it is printed in the same size as the example of Syntax UltraBlack typeface.

Using Borders

Objectives:

1. To learn to frame an entire document with a border.
2. To observe how borders emphasize parts of a document.
3. To prepare documents with various border treatments.

12-14A • 15
Borders as Frames

1. Read the copy at the right and examine the illustrations.
2. Determine the types of borders available with your software.
3. Practice creating borders in different sizes.

Borders give a page a distinctive appearance and separate elements on the page. Borders can be simple boxes with lines that match on all four sides, or the line thicknesses can be varied for a shadow effect or other illusions. Many programs have selections of decorative borders. Illustrated below are simple borders and decorative borders.

Spacing around and within borders is always important. When borders are used in a document to divide elements of the page, the white space outside the border must be large enough to keep other page elements away from the border. The white space within the border also must involve a margin to prevent a crowded or cramped appearance.

Understanding Type Styles and Type Sizes

O b j e c t i v e s :

1. To learn about type styles.

2. To consider proportional and monospaced typefaces.

3. To arrange text in different type styles and sizes.

2A • 10
Type Styles

1. Read the copy at the right.
2. Study the type style examples.
3. Compare the two paragraphs in the box below. Which typeface is easier to read?

People experienced in design can use more than one typeface in a document, but doing so requires knowledge of which typefaces work well together. A less experienced designer should select one typeface and then emphasize certain text with variations such as bold, italic, outline, or shadow. These variations are called **type styles**. In the illustration below, CG Times is the name of the typeface and the other words represent various styles of that typeface.

Typeface styles

CG Times

CG Times Bold

CG Times Italic

CG Times Outline

Proportional typefaces have the appearance of professional printing, while monospaced typefaces resemble typewriter output. With monospaced typefaces, such as Courier, all characters occupy *the same amount* of space regardless of the character width. This spacing makes wide characters such as *m* or *w* appear close together and thin characters such as *l i f t j* appear spread apart. Proportional spacing, on the other hand, allows characters to fit together evenly and contributes to easier reading.

Proportional

This text is an example of the typeface Times New Roman set at 12 points. It has a professional appearance because the characters fit together evenly. Text printed with this proportional spacing is easier to read than text printed with monospacing.

Monospaced

```
This text is an example of the typeface Courier set at 10 cpi.
This print resembles typewriter output.  Notice how the charac-
ters occupy the same space so that narrow letters seem to be
spread out.  This text is not as easy to read as proportional
spacing.  Can you feel your eyes jumping from word to word?
```

Retrieve the file you created for Report 1 in Lesson 4. Modify this document by making the following changes.

1. Change the top/bottom margins to 0.5" so that the shaded line will almost fill the page vertically.

2. Change the left/right margins to 0.7".

3. Create a shaded vertical line at the left margin, 0.5" wide and 10" long. (The shading shown is 20%.)

4. Change the font size for the title to 30 points.

5. Add a horizontal line below the title for emphasis.

6. Set a tab at about 1.25" then paragraph indent the text to provide white space between the shaded line and the text.

7. Set a line height slightly larger than the default line height of 11 points (the example shows 0.194").

8. To call attention to the beginning of each paragraph, use an initial cap. Make this single letter large (20 points) and bold.

9. Set the body text at 11 points; headings, at 18 points in bold.

10. Insert rules below the headings for emphasis.

11. Insert white space as appropriate.

This report uses a wide, shaded line at the left to serve as a decorative element on the page and the title and side headings overlap this shaded area. Horizontal lines add still more emphasis. The line below the title is thicker than the lines below the side headings. *Initial caps* (large, bold letters) begin the text following a side heading to help highlight the beginning of each section.

The Evolution of Publishing

Publishing is a very old industry dating back to the mid-1400s when Guttenberg invented the first printing press in Germany. Individual letters were carved out of little blocks of wood; lead eventually replaced wood because of its increased durability.

The Printing Process

To create pages of text, letters were arranged one letter at a time to form words and sentences. The letters were arranged in rows on big trays called plates. This process was called *setting type*. Strips of lead were used between the rows to spread them apart for easier reading. The printer would place the finished plate in the printing press, apply ink to the plate, position a sheet of paper on the plate, then press down on the paper to make an impression. The process was repeated for multiple copies of the same page and the whole cycle completed for different pages.

All aspects of publishing have evolved in five hundred years, and yet some of the same terminology is still used. For example, strips of lead are no longer placed between lines, but the term *leading* is used to indicate the spacing between lines. Historically, typesetters stored their supply of letters in little boxes arranged in cases; the capital letters were kept in the upper case and the little letters were kept in the lower case. Thus, capital letters are called *uppercase* letters; small letters are called *lowercase* letters.

Printing Today

Today's publishing industry is extremely sophisticated, with electronic typesetting and high-speed presses to produce books, magazines, and an array of printed products such as brochures and sales publications. Professional designers arrange layout based on certain publishing conventions and artistic compositions.

The term *desktop* became important in the mid-1980s with the introduction of equipment and software that could produce professional publications and yet fit on the top of a desk. This combination of computer, laser printer, and page layout software gave everyone the tools once reserved for skilled graphic artists and professional publishers. Since then, hardware and software have improved dramatically and many more people are aware of this computer application. Today, word processing and other programs have evolved to include many capabilities of desktop publishing. Learning how to use the software and equipment is not adequate, however, unless an individual also learns the techniques for arranging information effectively on a page.

2B • 10
Type Sizes

1. Read the copy at the right.
2. Study the illustration of type sizes.
3. Learn how to change type sizes in the software and printer you are using.

Another important difference between monospaced and proportional text relates to type sizes. For example, titles and headings can be larger than paragraph text when proportional type is used.

Dot matrix printers usually measure type size in characters per inch (cpi)—the most common settings include 10 or 12 characters per inch (also called 10 or 12 pitch). Laser or ink jet printers allow a typeface to be *scaled* to make it larger or smaller. *Type sizes* are measured in *points;* one inch contains 72 points.

Text sample at 10 points.
Text sample at 11 points.
Text sample at 12 points.
Text sample at 16 points.
Text sample at 24 points.
Text sample at 36 points.
Text at 72.

2C • 30
Announcements

Document 1
Sale Announcement

This announcement uses a large, bold, attention-getting font. All text lines are centered.

1. Select a sans serif typeface.
2. For the first text line, change the font size to 36 points in bold; use 20 points in bold for all other text lines.
3. Center vertically.

Even when the same point size is used, some typefaces will appear larger than others because of the thickness of characters and the difference in x-height.

SALE   SALE   SALE

Inventory Clearance
All Items Must Go!

Furniture Warehouse
200 E. Main

1. Key the text in the data sheet/resume shown at the right.

2. Set the top margin at 1" and change the bottom margin to 0.5" to provide space for the horizontal rules.

3. Insert horizontal lines to draw attention to the page, using thicker ones at the top and bottom.

4. Use a serif typeface. (The body text is set at 12 points, headings at 15 points in bold, and the name at 24 points in bold.)

5. Set tabs for indents appropriately sized for the bullets (about 0.25").

6. Insert bullets for listed information. Be sure listed text wordwraps as shown.

7. Insert em dashes as shown.

8. Add white space as needed.

Notes: The last line of text, *References Available upon Request*, is an alternative to listing three or more names. Before using this line, you, as a job applicant, should know whose names you will supply if requested *and* obtain the permission of those individuals.

You may apply similar word publishing techniques to the data sheet/resume you prepared in Lesson 134 or Lesson 215.

This data sheet/resume uses various text treatments to emphasize the divisions of information; for instance, headings are larger than the body text and horizontal graphic lines add visual appeal. For information arranged in lists, bullets (special characters) mark the beginning of each item. The tab spacing is adjusted to an appropriate size for the font size used.

Ashley Ellen Miller

345 Reynolds Dr.
Charleston, IL 61920-2836
217-145-9331

Job Objective
Technical assistant trainee for a medical company.

Education
Central High School—Charleston, Illinois, graduated May 1995
- Recognized on Honor Roll 1993–94 and 1994–95.
- Obtained 3.4 grade point average.
- Completed the following business courses: Information Processing, Desktop Publishing, Accounting, Office Procedures, and Business Law.

Work Experience
Support Staff in Management Development, Lincoln Hospital—Charleston, Illinois
June 1994–Present (full-time during summer; part-time during school year)
- Demonstrated proficiency in advanced word processing through the production of correspondence, reports, and other related documents.
- Gained practical experience in developing document layouts.
- Performed data entry tasks using the hospital mainframe computer system.
- Distributed and filed medical records.

Sales Clerk, Computer World—Charleston, Illinois
June–August 1993
- Stocked shelves as new inventory was received.
- Gained experience in customer service.

Activities
National Honor Society
Future Business Leaders of America
- Treasurer, 1994–95
- Publicity chair, 1993–94

References Available upon Request

Document 2
Invitation

This invitation uses a soft, delicate font for a formal appearance. The information is arranged with all text lines centered in a uniform type size.

1. Select a similar script typeface.
2. Change the font size to 14 points for all text lines.
3. Center vertically.

You are invited to attend the

Central High School All Sports Banquet

to be held in Robinson Gymnasium

at 6:30 p.m. on April 20, ----

Special entertainment provided by the Chamber Singers

R.S.V.P. Athletic Office

Aligning Text

Objectives:
1. To learn about alignment options.
2. To arrange text with different alignments and line heights.

3A • 25
Text Alignment

1. Read the copy at the right and the text in each example.
2. Practice each kind of alignment by making appropriate settings and keying the text as shown in the examples.

The *alignment* of text—left, right, centered, or full—affects a document's readability and image. Some software uses the term *justification* to mean how the text is aligned. Often the choices are indicated by icons on the screen representing each effect.

Left alignment is appropriate for paragraph text because reading is easier when all lines begin at the same position and uniform spacing appears between words. Left-aligned paragraphs produce a ragged (uneven) right edge; this effect creates a less formal appearance. Appropriately used hyphenation will make line endings less uneven on the right. Headings may be left-aligned or centered depending on a document's overall design.

> **Left alignment**
>
> appropriate for paragraph text and may be used for headings
> easy to read and appears less formal
> hyphenation usage desirable

Full alignment is achieved by expanding or contracting the spacing between words so that all paragraph lines begin and end evenly at the left and right margins. This alignment creates a more formal appearance. Hyphenation should be used to make word spacing as uniform as possible for easier reading. Full alignment is not appropriate for headings.

> **Full alignment** is appropriate for paragraph text when a formal appearance is desired. Full alignment can cause gaps in text as extra space is added between words to make the text lines end evenly at the right margin. Hyphenation usually is needed.

Center alignment is appropriate for titles and headings. It can be used to center all text lines such as in a wedding invitation. This technique seems more formal and is more difficult to read because of the ragged line beginnings. Hyphenation is not appropriate.

(continued on next page)

Title Page 1

1. Use 1" bottom and side margins. Begin the left-aligned title 2" from the top of the page.

2. Use a serif typeface set at 30 points in bold for the title. Increase the line height slightly for this text.

3. Insert a rule longer than the title below the title. (The line shown is 6.5" long.)

4. Insert a line above the text area at the bottom. This line is 3.5" long.

5. Right-align text at the bottom using the same serif typeface set at 15 points in bold.

6. Insert white space as needed.

Title Page 2

Modify Title Page 1 as follows (shown at right).

1. At the TM, create a 0.25" thick horizontal line with 20% shading extending from left margin to right margin. Copy this line and position a second line at the bottom margin.

2. Begin the title about 3" from the top edge of the page. For the centered title, use a serif typeface set at 24 points in bold.

3. Insert horizontal lines above and below the title; keep the space even between the text and the rules. Line length should be equal to the length of the longest text line.

4. Center the remaining text set at 12 points in bold. Add white space as needed.

This report title page uses an informal arrangement (called *asymmetrical balance*) where one page element is offset by another page element—a concept similar to the way a teeter-totter works on an elementary school playground. The title is left-aligned using three text lines and emphasized using larger text. Horizontal lines provide interest.

A Comparison of Publishing Features in Two Word Processing Programs

Your Name

Business Computer Applications

Current date

The second title page uses a formal arrangement (called **symmetrical balance**) in which all elements of the page are centered. The title is set off by two horizontal lines and large text.

A Comparison of Publishing Features in Two Word Processing Programs

Your Name

Business Computer Applications
Current date

> **Center alignment**
> appropriate for titles and headings
> appears formal
> hyphenation is not appropriate

Right alignment can be used for special purposes such as headings. Several lines of right-aligned text can be difficult to read because of the ragged line beginnings, so use this alignment sparingly. Hyphenation would not be appropriate.

> **Right alignment**
> appropriate for titles and headings in certain designs
> more difficult to read because of uneven line beginnings
> hyphenation is not appropriate

3B • 15
Leading/Line Height

1. Read the copy at the right.
2. Key the first paragraph in the box at right, using automatic line height.
3. Copy the paragraph; increase the line height as described in the second paragraph.
4. Print and compare the spacing between the lines of each paragraph.

Leading (rhymes with *wedding*) is the amount of space between printed text lines. By default, word processing and desktop publishing programs generally add 20 percent of the size of the font so that ascenders and descenders do not overlap. As font sizes change, the leading automatically changes, also.

For some software, the leading can be adjusted by changing the *line height*. Line height is measured from baseline to baseline. For typewriter-like output, the line height for 10- or 12-pitch, single-spaced printing results in 6 lines printing in a vertical inch (66 lines on a page and 0.167" for each line). If a larger font is selected, however, the line height automatically increases to an appropriate amount; and far fewer lines can be entered on a page.

> This text is an example of a serif typeface set at 10 points with the default setting for automatic line height. Note the spacing between the lines of text.
>
> This text is an example of a serif typeface set at 10 points with the default setting increased from the automatic line height of 0.167" to 0.20". Note the spacing between the lines of text.

3C • 10
Line-Height Adjustments

1. Read the copy at the right.
2. Type the two-line title set at 15 points in bold.
3. Change the line height to make the lines print closer together as shown in the second example.

Sometimes the automatic line height should be changed. For example:

- If a small font size (10 points) is used to conserve space, the line height could be increased slightly from the automatic setting to make the text easier to read.
- When headings within a document are larger than body text, a line height larger than the body text size may produce better-looking copy. This is especially true when columns are involved because the baseline should be even across the columns.
- When a large font size is used for multiline titles, the text may look better if the line height is decreased, bringing the lines closer together.

> **New Careers in Computer**
>
> **Training and Support**
>
> **New Careers in Computer**
> **Training and Support**

Letterhead 2

Modify Letterhead 1 to fit the following description and illustration at the right.

1. Change the top/bottom margins to 0.5".

2. All text lines are centered. The business name is set at 25 points in bold italic; the address remains at 11 points in bold italic.

3. The graphic line is thinner than the line in Letterhead 1. Its length is equal to the length of the company name and centered below the name. (The example shown is 3.75" long.)

4. The same graphic image is placed on both sides of the company information. The image on the right is a mirror image of the one on the left. No borders are used.

The second letterhead version uses the same typeface, but in a smaller size, for the business name. It includes a small graphic image on both sides of the centered text.

Letterhead 3

Modify Letterhead 2 to fit the following description and illustration at the right.

1. Change the top/bottom margins to 0.7".

2. The business name is set at 30 points in bold italic; the address remains at 11 points in bold italic.

3. The graphic line is thicker than the line in Letterhead 2. (The example is shown as 5.5" long.)

4. The graphic image is placed on the right side of the page parallel with the company information. No borders are used.

The third letterhead version uses the same typeface. All text is aligned on the left, and a graphic image is positioned on the right.

Organizing Text with Headings

Objectives:
1. To name the purposes of headings.
2. To prepare text with different heading treatments.

4A • 10
Headings/White Space

1. Read the copy at the right.
2. Compare the report on this page to the two versions on pp. A41 and A42.

When designing single- or multiple-page documents, *headings* should be used to guide the reader. Headings introduce sections of related information and provide hints about the document's contents when a reader is quickly scanning the text.

Word processing and desktop publishing software provide flexibility for adding emphasis to headings. When the heading font is bold and larger than the font used for the body of the report, the headings will be more noticeable.

Shown below is a two-page document in unbound report format. It is prepared with left justification, monospaced 10 cpi font, 0.5" paragraph indents, and double spacing. Selected words within the document are underlined for emphasis.

This report has what desktop and word publishers call a "gray" appearance. Nothing is distinctive to catch a reader's eye—all text is the same darkness and spaced the same on both pages.

THE EVOLUTION OF PUBLISHING

Publishing is a very old industry dating back to the mid-1400s when Guttenberg invented the first printing press in Germany. Individual letters were carved out of little blocks of wood; lead eventually replaced wood because of its increased durability.

The Printing Process

To create pages of text, letters were arranged one letter at a time to form words and sentences. The letters were arranged in rows on big trays called plates. This process was called <u>setting type</u>. Strips of lead were used between the rows to spread them apart for easier reading. The printer would place the finished plate in the printing press, apply ink to the plate, position a sheet of paper on the plate, then press down on the paper to make an impression. The process was repeated for multiple copies of the same page and the whole cycle completed for different pages.

All aspects of publishing have evolved in five hundred years, and yet some of the same terminology is still used. For example, strips of lead are no longer placed between lines, but the term <u>leading</u> is used to indicate the spacing between lines. Historically, typesetters stored their supply of letters in little boxes arranged in cases; the capital letters were kept in the upper case and the little letters were kept in the lower case. Thus, capital letters are called <u>uppercase</u> letters; small letters are called <u>lowercase</u> letters.

2

Printing Today

Today's publishing industry is extremely sophisticated, with electronic typesetting and high-speed presses to produce books, magazines, and an array of printed products such as brochures and sales publications. Professional designers arrange layout based on certain publishing conventions and artistic compositions.

The term <u>desktop</u> became important in the mid-1980s with the introduction of equipment and software that could produce professional publications and yet fit on top of a desk. This combination of computer, laser printer, and page layout software gave everyone the tools once reserved for skilled graphic artists and professional publishers. Since then, hardware and software have improved dramatically and many more people are aware of this computer application. Today, word processing and other programs have evolved to include many capabilities of desktop publishing. Learning to use the software and equipment is not adequate, however, unless an individual also learns the techniques for arranging information effectively on a page.

Business reports are often single-spaced. The *white space* (empty space) on the page, necessary for easy reading, is achieved by inserting blank lines between paragraphs and adding space around the headings.

More space may be provided before a heading than after a heading. This spacing technique serves to connect the heading to the text it introduces and to separate the text from previous text.

Using Lines (Rules)

O b j e c t i v e s :

1. To recognize how rules can add emphasis to text.

2. To create vertical and horizontal lines (rules).

3. To develop documents using lines (rules).

9-11A • 15
Lines

1. Read the copy at the right.

2. Study the different line treatments illustrated.

3. Create both horizontal and vertical lines with your software. Make the lines in varying lengths and widths.

9-11B • 45
Letterheads

Letterhead 1

1. Change all margins to 0.7".

2. Create a vertical line at the left margin 1.25" wide and 10" long. Shade the line at 40%.

3. For the business name, use a sans serif bold, italic typeface. (The example is shown in Helvetica Bold Italic set at 36 points.)

4. The graphic line below the company name is right-aligned and extends partially into the shaded area. The example shows the line as 6.6" long and 0.03" thick.

5. Use the same typeface for the address, but change the size to 11 points.

Horizontal lines (also called rules) can extend from margin to margin or be printed in specific line lengths. The width (thickness) of horizontal lines can range from very thin to very thick. The shading ranges from 100 percent to any lower percentage.

These same characteristics apply to *vertical lines.*

Some software measures the thickness of lines in inches; other software measures thickness in points.

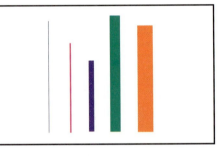

This letterhead has a wide, shaded vertical line extending down the left side and a black horizontal line used to emphasize the business name. To print a letter on this letterhead, the letter margins should fit the open area on the page—the letter would not be centered horizontally.

The Sports Connection

202 Morton St.
Springfield, IL 62702-2826
708-154-5512

Report Production

Report 1

1. Key the report at the right SS.

2. Select a similar typeface and follow these settings as much as possible:

Margins: 1"; full justification

Title: on line 1.33"

Title font: CG Times Bold (serif typeface) set at 25 points

Body text font: CG Times set at 12 points

Side heading font: CG Times Bold set at 15 points (delete underlines)

3. Double-space between paragraphs and above/below side headings.

The report (p. A40) that required two pages when set in a monospaced font is now arranged on one page. The font selection and treatment shown below is space efficient—and yet the text is not crowded on the page.

The larger, bold headings stand out, highlighting the topics in the report. Words that were underlined are now shown in italics. Full justification makes the report look more formal.

The Evolution of Publishing

Publishing is a very old industry dating back to the mid-1400s when Guttenberg invented the first printing press in Germany. Individual letters were carved out of little blocks of wood; lead eventually replaced wood because of its increased durability.

The Printing Process

To create pages of text, letters were arranged one letter at a time to form words and sentences. The letters were arranged in rows on big trays called plates. This process was called *setting type*. Strips of lead were used between the rows to spread them apart for easier reading. The printer would place the finished plate in the printing press, apply ink to the plate, position a sheet of paper on the plate, then press down on the paper to make an impression. The process was repeated for multiple copies of the same page and the whole cycle completed for different pages.

All aspects of publishing have evolved in five hundred years, and yet some of the same terminology is still used. For example, strips of lead are no longer placed between lines, but the term *leading* is used to indicate the spacing between lines. Historically, typesetters stored their supply of letters in little boxes arranged in cases; the capital letters were kept in the upper case and the little letters were kept in the lower case. Thus, capital letters are called *uppercase* letters; small letters are called *lowercase* letters.

Printing Today

Today's publishing industry is extremely sophisticated, with electronic typesetting and high-speed presses to produce books, magazines, and an array of printed products such as brochures and sales publications. Professional designers arrange layout based on certain publishing conventions and artistic compositions.

The term *desktop* became important in the mid-1980s with the introduction of equipment and software that could produce professional publications and yet fit on the top of a desk. This combination of computer, laser printer, and page layout software gave everyone the tools once reserved for skilled graphic artists and professional publishers. Since then, hardware and software have improved dramatically and many more people are aware of this computer application. Today, word processing and other programs have evolved to include many capabilities of desktop publishing. Learning how to use the software and equipment is not adequate, however, unless an individual also learns the techniques for arranging information effectively on a page.

Flyer

Follow directions below to create an advertising flyer for a florist shop.

1. Use reverse text to create the box with the business name. The box has a black fill with white print in a large sans serif typeface.

2. This document could be completed in several ways. You could use two columns, or you could place the text in a box at the right with no borders.

3. The hearts are typographic symbols in a very large size. To condense the vertical space between the hearts, the line height was changed from the automatic height of 2.81" to 2.5" as a fixed line height. These heights will vary depending on the typeface used.

4. Adjust the white space between the lines of text so that the three blocks of text are parallel with the three hearts.

Notes:

- The reverse type is shown in Helvetica bold set at 30 points.

- The text is in bold using different sizes: 25, 20, 15, and 12 points.

- The heart symbols are 200 points.

Vicki's Creations

For your loved one on Valentine's Day

- Roses, roses, roses
- Friendship arrangements
- Balloon bouquets
- Candy assortments

Free delivery
Call (217) 153-4900

600 S. Sale St.
Open Monday-Saturday 9-5

Report 2

1. Modify the settings from your first version layout to produce the second layout.
2. Use the same typeface and sizes that you used in Report 1.
3. Change to left justification.
4. Set parallel columns for two columns with column margins: left, 1" and 2"; right, 2" and 7.5".
5. Be sure the side heading lines are arranged as shown.
6. Double-space between paragraphs and insert extra space above the side headings as space permits.

This arrangement uses left alignment for the title. The side headings are set in the same point size as Report 1; however, the document is arranged in two columns. The left column is just wide enough for the words in the side headings and about 0.25" for the white space between the side headings in the first column and the report text in the second column. Left justification makes the report look less formal.

The Evolution of Publishing

Publishing is a very old industry dating back to the mid-1400s when Guttenberg invented the first printing press in Germany. Individual letters were carved out of little blocks of wood; lead eventually replaced wood because of its increased durability.

The Printing Process

To create pages of text, letters were arranged one letter at a time to form words and sentences. The letters were arranged in rows on big trays called plates. This process was called *setting type*. Strips of lead were used between the rows to spread them apart for easier reading. The printer would place the finished plate in the printing press, apply ink to the plate, position a sheet of paper on the plate, then press down on the paper to make an impression. The process was repeated for multiple copies of the same page and the whole cycle completed for different pages.

All aspects of publishing have evolved in five hundred years, and yet some of the same terminology is still used. For example, strips of lead are no longer placed between lines, but the term *leading* is used to indicate the spacing between lines. Historically, typesetters stored their supply of letters in little boxes arranged in cases; the capital letters were kept in the upper case and the little letters were kept in the lower case. Thus, capital letters are called *uppercase* letters; small letters are called *lowercase* letters.

Printing Today

Today's publishing industry is extremely sophisticated, with electronic typesetting and high-speed presses to produce books, magazines, and an array of printed products such as brochures and sales publications. Professional designers arrange layout based on certain publishing conventions and artistic compositions.

The term *desktop* became important in the mid-1980s with the introduction of equipment and software that could produce professional publications and yet fit on the top of a desk. This combination of computer, laser printer, and page layout software gave everyone the tools once reserved for skilled graphic artists and professional publishers. Since then, hardware and software have improved dramatically and many more people are aware of this computer application. Today, word processing and other programs have evolved to include many capabilities of desktop publishing. Learning how to use the software and equipment is not adequate, however, unless an individual also learns the techniques for arranging information effectively on a page.

Follow the directions below to create an advertising flyer for a computer company.

1. Use two open starburst clipart images and position them as shown.

2. Select a serif typeface and make it bold.

3. Use a square bullet for the list of software features. Set a tab for appropriate space after the bullet.

4. Increase the line height slightly for the bulleted text. The example was changed from .22" to 0.25" for this text only.

5. Use right alignment for the business name and location.

6. The street address is the same size as the text in the list.

Notes:

- The text used for the price, product name, and business name is shown in Times bold at 25 points.

- The text used in the list is set in bold at 14 points.

- The text in the second starburst is set at 12 points in bold.

$2,898

Multimedia Computer

- ■ **Pentium/100MHz processor**
- ■ **1.6G hard drive**
- ■ **16 MB memory**
- ■ **15" SVGA noninterlaced color monitor**
- ■ **1 MB video memory**
- ■ **Quad-speed CD-ROM drive**
- ■ **16-bit stereo sound card and speakers**
- ■ **14.4 internal fax/modem**
- ■ **Preloaded and CD-ROM software**
- ■ **3-year computer warranty**

**0% Financing!
No payments!
No interest
for 6 months!**

Computer Headquarters

606 W. Anthony Dr.

Using Bullets and Typographic Conventions

Objectives:

1. To learn the purpose of bullets and how to use them.

2. To learn about professional typographic symbols.

3. To prepare lists with bullets and to create typographic symbols.

5A • 15
Bullets

1. Read the copy at the right.

2. Determine the bullets available in your software and practice using them in different sizes.

Typographic symbols can be used to enhance the appearance of a document. The symbols can call attention to listed information or be used as a major design element on a page.

Probably the most common typographic symbol is a **bullet**. This symbol, a small black dot, gets its name from the fact that it looks like a bullet hole. Bullets are frequently used with listed information because the bullet draws attention to the beginning of each item in the list. Many other symbols can be created;

however, the name "bullet" is used for any symbol used for this purpose.

Iconic symbols—such as a check mark, heart, or pointing hand—can be used for bullets or as design elements when created in larger sizes. Some software programs call these symbols **dingbats**.

The size of these symbols is controlled by the size of the typeface currently in use. Therefore, to use an iconic symbol as a design element on a page, the font size should be increased.

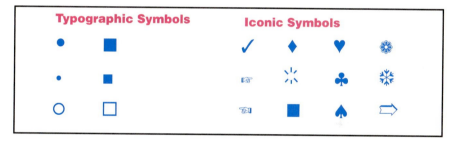

5B • 15
Bulleted List

1. Key the information at the right using a serif typeface.

2. Make the title large and bold.

3. Use a small black square for the first-level bullet; use a small black dot for the second-level bullet.

Note: The first-level bullet should always stand out more than the second-level bullet.

Listing Information with Bullets

Organizing information in a vertical list makes the text more noticeable than when information is written as a series of paragraphs. Each item in a list should begin with a *bullet*, a symbol used to call attention to the beginning of each item.

- Use different bullets for various levels of detail.

- Use a tab about 0.25" after the bullet (depending on the font size being used). The default tab of 0.5" on most software creates too much space after the bullet when it is used in the body of a document, as in this example.

- Make the text hang under the first letter (not under the bullet) when the information is too long for one text line. This technique will make the beginning of each item stand out more.

- Write the information so that it is parallel in grammatical form:

  • Begin each item with a verb (as in this list).

  • Begin each item with a noun.

  • Begin each item with a gerund (verb ending in *ing*).

Combining Clipart and Text

Objectives:

1. To emphasize document text with clipart images.
2. To observe the need for adequate spacing for legibility.
3. To develop announcements combining clipart and text.

7-8A • 20
Clipart and Text Combined

1. Read the copy at the right.
2. Prepare the examples combining clipart and text as shown.

Starburst

1. Select a star image from those available with your software.
2. Make the star approximately 4" wide and center it on the page.
3. Use a large, bold font for the text.

Box

1. Select a border like the one at the far right.
2. Make the border approximately 4" wide and 3" high.
3. Use a large, bold font for the text.

7-8B • 10
Reverse Type

1. Read the copy at the right; then create a text box that is 4" wide and about 1" high (or use automatic line height). Make the box fill color black.
2. Select a sans serif typeface and make it bold. (The illustration is shown in Helvetica bold set at 36 points.) Change the font color to print in white.
3. If time permits, create additional reverse type boxes.

Some clipart images appear open in the middle for the purpose of placing text inside the image. For example, the image might be a banner, starburst, trophy, or a fancy border. The techniques for inserting text in an image will vary depending on the software used.

Be sure that text inside an image is legible and uncrowded. Plan for the text alignment that looks best with the image. Usually, the text will be centered both up and down and left and right; however, sometimes right alignment or left alignment may look better.

Reverse type is a dramatic way to emphasize text. When creating a black box for the text background (that is, a **text box**), be sure the box is large enough to hold the text with enough black space around the text on all sides so that the text is easy to read.

Another important consideration is the typeface used. Because serif typefaces often have slim areas in the curves of letters, they might not show up well. Sans serif typefaces, especially when printed in bold, are a better choice for reverse type.

5C • 5
Additional Typographic Symbols

1. Study the examples of typographic symbols at right.
2. Determine how to create these symbols with your software and practice making them.

Today's word processing and desktop publishing software can create many of the symbols formerly used only by professional typesetters when they created publications, such as books and magazines. Correct use of these symbols will make documents appear more sophisticated.

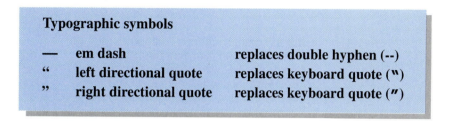

Typographic symbols

—	em dash	replaces double hyphen (--)
"	left directional quote	replaces keyboard quote (")
"	right directional quote	replaces keyboard quote (")

5D • 15
Typographic Conventions

1. Key the information at the right.
2. Insert em dashes as shown.
3. Note the changes described in the list. These changes will be used in later assignments in this unit.

Conventions are rules governing the treatment of text and punctuation spacing.

Typesetting conventions differ from typewriting conventions as listed below.

Using Typographic Conventions

Changing from typewriting to typographic conventions adds to the appearance of any document. These changes are easy to make.

- Avoid all caps—Instead of using capital (uppercase) letters to emphasize text, use lowercase letters in bold and a larger size. Lowercase letters are easier to read than all-capital letters.

- Avoid underlining—The underline appears so close to the baseline of text that it often cuts through the descenders. Instead, use italics for emphasis. A graphic line placed below text is appropriate for some headings.

- Use an em dash— In typewriting conventions, a break in the thought pattern of a sentence is shown like this--with a double hyphen. Instead, use an em dash—a long, single-line dash.

- Insert directional quotes—When quoting someone, insert a left quotation mark (") at the beginning of the quote and a right quotation mark (") at the end of it.

Using Clipart

Objectives:

1. To observe the effect that clipart images have on appearance.
2. To position images and text with adequate white space.
3. To develop an announcement using good design techniques.

6A • 20
Clipart

1. Read copy at the right.
2. Determine the images available in your software.
3. Practice positioning images in different sizes and places on a page.

Clipart (graphic images or figures) can add visual interest to a document. Images should be carefully chosen to ensure they are appropriate to the audience and the purpose of the message. For example, a flyer designed to advertise a product might display a large image of the product, or an image of a person using it.

Word processing and desktop publishing software contain files of images suitable for many different purposes. Additional images can be purchased. If the software you are using has drawing tools, you may be able to create your own images by ungrouping (taking apart) existing images, changing them in some way, then grouping them again.

When clipart images are imported into a document, they can be positioned with or without a border around the image. Also, fancy borders may surround an entire page or a portion of a page.

Images should be kept in correct proportion. With some software, the image is positioned on the page by entering the image location in inches. With other software, the image is positioned by selecting it with a mouse pointer and dragging it to the desired location. When using this method, be sure not to stretch an image out of proportion when trying to position it or to adjust its size.

6B • 30
Flyer

1. Key the flyer at the right.
2. Use a standard-sized sheet turned sideways. (This 11" wide x 8.5" long orientation is called **landscape**, in contrast to the regular page orientation [8.5" wide x 11" long], which is called **portrait**.)
3. Set 1" margins all around.
4. Select a similar image from those available with your software. Position the image on the left.
5. Allow room on the right for the text.

Note: Vary the font sizes to emphasize some words more than others. (The typeface shown is Syntax UltraBlack with right alignment.)

Our Gift to You!

A 30% discount on any one item at our regular price

Bring this gift certificate to

Rogards Jewelers
513 S. Scott St.

(217) 555-3566
UPS Shipping Available

REFERENCE GUIDE

CAPITALIZATION GUIDES

Capitalize

1. The first word of every sentence and the first word of every complete direct quotation. Do not capitalize (a) fragments of quotations or (b) a quotation resumed within a sentence.

   She said, "Hard work is necessary for success."
   He stressed the importance of "a sense of values."
   "When all else fails," he said, "follow directions."

2. The first word after a colon if that word begins a complete sentence.

   Remember this: Work with good techniques.
   We carry these sizes: small, medium, and large.

3. First, last, and all other words in titles of books, articles, periodicals, headings, and plays, except words of four or fewer letters used as articles, conjunctions, or prepositions.

   Century 21 Keyboarding   "How to Buy a House"
   Saturday Review   "The Sound of Music"

4. An official title when it precedes a name or when used elsewhere if it is a title of distinction.

   President Lincoln   She is the Prime Minister.
   The doctor is in.   He is the class treasurer.

5. Personal titles and names of people and places.

   Miss Franks   Dr. Jose F. Ortez   San Diego

6. All proper nouns and their derivatives.

   Canada   Canadian Festival   France   French food

7. Days of the week, months of the year, holidays, periods of history, and historic events.

   Sunday   Labor Day   New Year's Day
   June   Middle Ages   Civil War

8. Geographic regions, localities, and names.

   the North   Upstate New York   Mississippi River

9. Street, avenue, company, etc., when used with a proper noun.

   Fifth Avenue   Avenue of the Stars   Armour & Co.

10. Names of organizations, clubs, and buildings.

    Girl Scouts   4-H Club   Carew Tower

11. A noun preceding a figure except for common nouns such as *line, page,* and *sentence,* which may be keyed with or without a capital.

    Style 143   Catalog 6   page 247   line 10

12. Seasons of the year *only* when they are personified.

    icy fingers of Winter   the soft kiss of Spring

NUMBER EXPRESSION GUIDES

Use words for

1. Numbers from one to ten except when used with numbers above ten, which are keyed as figures. Note: Common business practice is to use figures for all numbers except those which begin a sentence.

   Was the order for four or eight books?
   Order 8 shorthand books and 15 English books.

2. A number beginning a sentence.

   Fifteen persons are here; 12 are at home sick.

3. The shorter of two numbers used together.

   ten 50-gallon drums   350 five-gallon drums

4. Isolated fractions or indefinite amounts in a sentence.

   Nearly two-thirds of the students are here.
   About twenty-five people came to the meeting.

5. Names of small-numbered streets and avenues (ten and under).

   1020 Sixth Street   Tenth Avenue

Use figures for

1. Dates and time, except in very formal writing.

   May 9, 2002   10:15 a.m.
   ninth of   four o'clock

2. A series of fractions.

   Key 1/2, 1/4, 5/6, and 7 3/4.

3. Numbers following nouns.

   Rule 12   page 179   Room 1208   Chapter 15

4. Measures, weights, and dimensions.

   6 ft. 9 in. tall   5 lbs. 4 oz.   8 1/2" x 11"

5. Definite numbers used with the percent sign (%); but spell out approximate amounts. Spell out *percent* with approximations in formal writing.

   The rate is 15 1/2%.
   About fifty percent of the work is done.

6. House numbers except house number One.

   1915 - 42d Street   One Jefferson Avenue

7. Sums of money except when spelled for extra emphasis. Even sums may be keyed without the decimal.

   $10.75   25 cents $300
   seven hundred dollars ($700)

PUNCTUATION GUIDES

Use an apostrophe

1. As a symbol for *feet* in billings or tabulations or as a symbol for *minutes*. (The quotation mark may be used as a symbol for *seconds* and *inches*.)

   12' x 16'   3' 54"   8' 6" x 10' 8"

2. As a symbol to indicate the omission of letters or figures (as in contractions).

   can't   wouldn't   Spirit of '76

3. To form the plural of most figures, letters, and words used as words rather than for their meaning: Add the *apostrophe and s*. In market quotations, form the plural of figures by the addition of *s* only.

   6's   five's   ABC's   Century Fund 4s

4. To show possession: Add the *apostrophe* and *s* to (a) a singular noun and (b) a plural noun which does not end in *s*.

   a man's watch   women's shoes   boy's bicycle

   Add the *apostrophe* and *s* to a proper name of one syllable which ends in s.

   Bess's Cafeteria   James's hat   Jones's bill

   Add the *apostrophe only* after (a) plural nouns ending in *s* and (b) a proper name of more than one syllable which ends in *s* or *z*.

   boys' camp   Adams' home   Melendez' report

   Add the *apostrophe* after the last noun in a series to indicate joint or common possession by two or more persons; however, add the possessive to each of the nouns to show separate possession by two or more persons.

   Lewis and Clark's expedition
   the manager's and the treasurer's reports

Use a colon

1. To introduce an enumeration or a listing.
   These are my favorite poets: Shelley, Keats, and Frost.
2. To introduce a question or a long direct quotation.
   This is the question: Did you study for the test?
3. Between hours and minutes expressed in figures.
   10:15 a.m.   12:00   4:30 p.m.

Use a comma (or commas)

1. After (a) introductory phrases or clauses and (b) words in a series.
   If you plan to be here for the week, try to visit Chicago, St. Louis, and Dallas.
2. To set off short direct quotations.
   She said, "If you try, you can reach your goal."
3. Before and after (a) words which come together and refer to the same person, thing, or idea and (b) words of direct address.
   Clarissa, our class president, will give the report.
   I was glad to see you, Terrence, at the meeting.
4. To set off nonrestrictive clauses (not necessary to the meaning of the sentence), but not restrictive clauses (necessary to the meaning).
   Your report, which deals with the issue, is great.
   The girl who just left is my sister.
5. To separate the day from the year and the city from the state.
   July 4, 2000   New Haven, Connecticut
6. To separate two or more parallel adjectives (adjectives that could be separated by the word "and" instead of the comma).
   a group of young, old, and middle-aged persons
   Do not use commas to separate adjectives so closely related that they appear to form a single element with the noun they modify.
   a dozen large red roses   a small square box
7. To separate (a) unrelated groups of figures which come together and (b) whole numbers into groups of three digits each (however, policy, year, page, room, telephone, and most serial numbers are shown without commas).
   During 1997, 1,750 cars were insured under Policy 806423.
   page 1042   Room 1184   (213)125-2626

Use a dash

1. For emphasis.
   The icy road--slippery as a fish--was a hazard.
2. To indicate a change of thought.
   We may tour the Orient--but I'm getting ahead of my story.
3. To introduce the name of an author when it follows a direct quotation.
   "Hitting the wrong key is like hitting me."--Armour
4. For certain special purposes.
   "Well--er--ah," he stammered.
   "Jay, don't get too close to the--" It was too late.

PUNCTUATION GUIDES [continued]

Use an exclamation mark

1. After emphatic interjections.

   Wow!   Hey there!   What a day!

2. After sentences that are clearly exclamatory.

   "I won't go!" she said with determination.

   How good it was to see you in New Orleans last week!

Use a hyphen

1. To join compound numbers from twenty-one to ninety-nine that are keyed as words.

   forty-six   fifty-eight   over seventy-six

2. To join compound adjectives before a noun that they modify as a unit.

   well-laid plans   six-year period   two-thirds majority

3. After each word or figure in a series of words or figures that modify the same noun (suspended hyphenation).

   first-, second-, and third-class reservations

4. To spell out a word or name.

   s-e-p-a-r-a-t-e   S-u-s-a-n   G-a-e-l-i-c

5. To form certain compound nouns.

   WLW-TV   teacher-counselor   AFL-CIO

Use parentheses

1. To enclose parenthetical or explanatory matter and added information.

   The amendments (Exhibit A) are enclosed.

2. To enclose identifying letters or figures in lists.

   Check these factors: (1) period of time, (2) rate of pay, and (3) nature of duties.

3. To enclose figures that follow spelled-out amounts to give added clarity or emphasis.

   The total award is five hundred dollars ($500).

Use a question mark

At the end of a sentence that is a direct question; however, use a period after a request in the form of a question.

What day do you plan to leave for Honolulu?

Will you mail this letter for me, please.

Use quotation marks

1. To enclose direct quotations.

   He said, "I'll be there at eight o'clock."

2. To enclose titles of articles and other parts of complete publications, short poems, song titles, television programs, and unpublished works like theses and dissertations.

   "Sesame Street"   "Chicago" by Sandburg
   "Lara's Theme"   "Murder She Wrote"

3. To enclose special words or phrases, or coined words.

   "power up" procedure   "Murphy's Law"

Use a semicolon

1. To separate two or more independent clauses in a compound sentence when the conjunction is omitted.

   Being critical is easy; being constructive is not so easy.

2. To separate independent clauses when they are joined by a conjunctive adverb (however, consequently, etc.).

   I can go; however, I must get excused.

3. To separate a series of phrases or clauses (especially if they contain commas) that are introduced by a colon.

   These officers were elected: Lu Ming, President; Lisa Stein, vice president; Juan Ramos, secretary.

4. To precede an abbreviation or word that introduces an explanatory statement.

   She organized her work; for example, putting work to be done in folders of different colors to indicate degrees of urgency.

Use an underline

1. With titles of complete works such as books, magazines, and newspapers. (Such titles may also be keyed in ALL CAPS or italic without the underline.)

   Superwrite   The New York Times   TV Guide

2. To call attention to special words or phrases (or you may use quotation marks). **Note:** Use a continuous underline unless each word is to be considered separately.

   Stop keying when time is called.

   Spell these words: steel, occur, separate.

BASIC GRAMMAR GUIDES

Use a singular verb

1. **With a singular subject.**
   The weather is clear but cold.
2. **With an indefinite pronoun used as a subject (*each, any, either, neither, one,* etc.).**
   Each of you is to bring a pen and paper.
   Neither of us is likely to be picked.
3. **With singular subjects linked by *or* or *nor.*** If, however, one subject is singular and the other is plural, the verb should agree with the *closer* subject.
   Either Jan or Fred is to make the presentation.
   Neither the principal nor the teachers are here.
4. **With a collective noun (*committee, team, class, jury,* etc.) if the collective noun acts as a unit.**
   The jury has returned to the courtroom.
   The committee has filed its report.
5. **With the pronouns *all* and *some* (as well as fractions and percentages) when used as subjects if their modifiers are singular.** Use a plural verb if their modifiers are plural.
   All of the books have been classified.
   Some of the gas is being pumped into the tank.
6. **When *number* is used as the subject and is preceded by *the;*** however, use a plural verb if *number* is preceded by *a.*
   The number of voters has increased this year.
   A number of workers are on vacation.

Use a plural verb

1. **With a plural subject.**
   The blossoms are losing their petals.
2. **With a compound subject joined by *and.***
   My mother and my father are the same age.

Negative forms of verbs

1. **Use the plural verb *do not* (or the contraction *don't*) when the pronoun *I, we, you,* or *they,* as well as a plural noun, is used as the subject.**
   You don't have a leg to stand on in this case.
   The scissors do not cut properly.
   I don't believe that answer is correct.
2. **Use the singular verb *does not* (or the contraction *doesn't*) when the pronoun *he, she,* or *it,* as well as a singular noun, is used as the subject.**
   She doesn't want to attend the meeting.
   It does not seem possible that winter's here.

Pronoun agreement with antecedents

1. **Pronouns (*I, we, you, he, she, it, their,* etc.) agree with their antecedents *in person*—person speaking, first person; person spoken to, second person; person spoken about, third person.**
   We said we would go when we complete our work.
   When you enter, present your invitation.
   All who saw the show found that they were moved.
2. **Pronouns agree with their antecedents *in gender* (feminine, masculine, and neuter).**
   Each of the women has her favorite hobby.
   Adam will wear his favorite sweater.
   The tree lost its leaves early this fall.
3. **Pronouns agree with their antecedents *in number* (singular or plural).**
   A verb must agree with its subject.
   Pronouns must agree with their antecedents.
   Brian is to give his recital at 2 p.m.
   Joan and Carla have lost their homework.
4. **When a pronoun's antecedent is a collective noun, the pronoun may be either singular or plural depending on whether the noun acts individually or as a unit.**
   The committee met to cast their ballots.
   The class planned its graduation program.

Commonly confused pronoun sound-alikes

it's (contraction): it is; it has
its (possessive adjective): possessive form of *it*
   It's good to see you; it's been a long time.
   The puppy wagged its tail in welcome.
their (pronoun): possessive form of *they*
there (adverb/pronoun): at or in that place/used to introduce a clause
they're (contraction): they are
   The hikers all wore their parkas.
   Will he be there during our presentation?
   They're likely to be late because of the snow.
who's (contraction): who is; who has
whose (pronoun): possessive form of *who*
   Who's been to the movie? Who's going now?
   I chose the one whose skills are best.

NOTE: See pp. RG5 and RG6 for other sound-alike words that are often confused.

CONFUSING WORDS

accept (vb) to receive; to approve; to take
except (prep, vb) with the exclusion of; leave out

adapt (vb) to make fit; to adjust
adept (adj) skilled; thoroughly proficient

affect (vb) to produce a change in or have an effect on
effect (n) result; something produced by an agent or a cause

bases (n) plural of base or basis
basis (n) the fundamental ingredient of a thing or an idea

beat (vb) to strike repeatedly; to defeat
beet (n) a food plant with a dark red root

board (n/vb) a piece of thin sawed wood; daily meals offered for pay; group of managers; to get onto a bus, airplane, or ship
bored (vb/adj) pierced with a twisting or turning movement of a tool; weary and restless

buy (n/vb) to purchase; to acquire; a bargain
by (prep/adv) close to; via; according to; close at hand; at/in another's home or work place

cease (vb) come to an end; discontinue; stop
seize (vb) to take hold of suddenly; to take by force; to take possession of

cents (n) specified portion of a dollar
sense (n/vb) meaning intended or conveyed; to perceive; ability to judge
since (adv/conj) after a definite time in the past; in view of the fact; because

choose (vb) to select; to decide
chose (vb) past tense of choose

cite (vb) use as support; commend; summon
sight (n/vb) ability to see; something seen; a device to improve aim
site (n) location

complement (n) something that fills, completes, or makes perfect
compliment (n/vb) a formal expression of respect or admiration; to pay respect or admiration

cooperation (n) working together willingly and harmoniously
corporation (n) a business entity that acts as an individual; a company; a firm

do (vb) to bring about; to carry out
due (adj) owed or owing as a debt; having reached the date for payment

done (adj) brought to an end; through; finished
dun (vb/n) to make demand for payment; a bill

fair (adj/n) just, equitable, beautiful or visually admirable; a competitive exhibition
fare (n) a charge for personal transportation

farther (adv) greater distance
further (adv) additional; in greater depth or extent

feat (n) an act or deed notable for its courage, skill, ingenuity, or endurance
feet (n) plural of foot, terminal part of legs; unit of measure equaling 12 inches; bottom

flew (vb) moved through the air
flue (n) a channel in a chimney

for (prep/conj) used to indicate purpose on behalf of; because of
four (n) two plus two in number; the fourth in a set of series

hear (vb) to gain knowledge of by the ear
here (adv) in or at this place; at or on this point; in this case

heard (vb) past tense of hear; perceived by the ear; listened attentively
herd (n/v) group of animals of one type; to guide into a group

hole (n) an opening in or through something
whole (adj/n) having all its proper parts; a complete amount or sum

hour (n) the 24th part of a day; a particular time
our (adj) of or relating to us as possessors

knew (vb) past tense of know; understood; recognized truth or nature of
new (adj) novel; fresh; having existed for a short time; created in recent past

know (vb) to be aware of the truth or nature of; to have an understanding of
no (adv/adj/n) in no respect or degree; not so; indicates denial or refusal

lead (vb/n) to guide or direct; to be first; a heavy soft metal
led (vb) past tense of lead

leased (vb/adj) granted use or occupancy or under contract in exchange for rent; something so used or occupied
least (adj) lowest in rank, size, or importance

lessen (vb) to cause to decrease; to make less
lesson (n) something to be learned; a period of instruction; a class period

lie (n/vb) an untrue or inaccurate statement; to tell an untrue story; to rest or recline
lye (n) a strong alkaline substance or solution

loan (n/vb) a sum of money lent at interest; to lend something of value
lone (adj) solitary; single; companionless

might (vb) used to express possibility, probability, or permission
mite (n) tiny insect; very little; a bit

miner (n) one who removes minerals/ore from the earth; machine used for that purpose

minor (adj/n) lesser/smaller in amount, extent, or size; one under legal age

once (adj/conj) one time and no more; at any one time; at the moment when

ones (n) two or more things or people of loosely defined similarity

one (adj/pron) a single unit or thing

won (vb) past tense of win; gained a victory as in a game or contest; got by effort or work

passed (vb) past tense of pass; already occurred; moved by; gave an item to someone

past (adv/adj/prep/n) gone or elapsed; time gone by

peace (n) state of tranquility or quiet; a state of agreement within or between

piece (n/vb) a part of a whole; a fragment; artistic composition; to join

personal (adj) of, relating to, or affecting a person; done in person

personnel (n) a staff of persons making up a workforce in an organization

plain (adj/n) with little decoration; a large flat area of land

plane (n) an airplane or hydroplane

pole (n) a long, slender rounded piece of wood or other material

poll (n) a survey of people to analyze public opinion; a politician

poor (adj) having little wealth or value

pore (vb/n) to study carefully; a tiny opening in a surface

pour (vb) to make flow or stream; to rain hard

principal (n/adj) a chief or leader; capital (money) amount placed at interest; of or relating to the most important thing or matter

principle (n) a central rule, law, or doctrine

raise (vb/n) to lift up; to collect; an increase in amount, as of wages or salary

raze (vb) to tear down; to demolish

real (adj/n) genuine; not artificial

reel (n/vb) revolving device on which to wind lines; to turn round and round

right (adj) factual; true; correct

rite (n) customary form of ceremony; ritual

write (v) to form letters or symbols; to compose and set down in words, numbers, or symbols

rote (n/adj) use of memory with little thought; mechanical repetition

wrote (vb) past tense of write; composed and set down in words, numbers, or symbols

seam (n) the joining of two pieces

seem (vb) to give the impression of being

sew (vb) to fasten by stitches

so (adj/conj) in the same manner or way; in order that; with the result that

sow (vb) to plant seed; scatter; disperse

some (n/adv) unknown or unspecified unit or thing; to a degree or extent

sum (n/vb) the whole amount; the total; to find a total; summary of points

stationary (adj) fixed in a position, course, or mode; unchanging in condition

stationery (n) paper and envelopes used for processing personal and business documents

than (conj/prep) used in comparisons to show differences between items

then (n/adv) that time; at that time; next

threw (vb) past tense of throw; flung; tossed

through (prep) passage from one end to another; indicates a period of time or a range of space

to (prep/adj) used to indicate action, relation, distance, direction

too (adv) besides; also; to excessive degree

two (pro/adj) one plus one in number

vary (vb) to change; make different; diverge

very (adv/adj) real; mere; truly; to high degree

waist (n) narrowed part of the body between chest and hips; middle of something

waste (n/vb/adj) useless things; rubbish; spend or use carelessly; nonproductive

wait (vb/n) to stay in place or pause; to serve as a waiter; act of waiting

weight (n/vb) amount something weighs; give relative importance to something

want (vb/n) to need or desire; lacking a required amount

won't (vb) will not

weak (adj) lacking strength, skill, or proficiency

week (n) a series of 7 days; a series of regular days within a 7-day period

wear (vb/n) to bear or have on the person; diminish by use; clothing

where (adv/conj/n) at, in, or to what degree; what place, source, or cause

whose (adj/pron) of or to whom something belongs

who's (contraction) who is

your (adj) of or relating to you as possessor

you're (contraction) you are

WORD DIVISION

Word-division guides

1. Divide words between syllables only; therefore, do not divide one-syllable words. **Note:** When in doubt, consult a dictionary or a word-division manual.

through-out	pref-er-ence	em-ploy-ees
reached	toward	thought

2. Do not divide words of five or fewer letters even if they have two or more syllables.

into	also	about	union	radio	ideas

3. Do not separate a one-letter syllable at the beginning of a word or a one- or two-letter syllable at the end of a word.

across	enough	steady	highly	ended

4. Usually, you may divide a word between double consonants; but, when adding a syllable to a word that ends in double letters, divide after the double letters of the root word.

writ-ten	sum-mer	expres-sion	excel-lence
will-ing	win-ner	process-ing	fulfill-ment

5. When the final consonant is doubled in adding a suffix, divide between the double letters.

run-ning	begin-ning	fit-ting	submit-ted

6. Divide after a one-letter syllable within a word; but when two single-letter syllables occur together, divide between them.

sepa-rate	regu-late	gradu-ation	evalu-ation

7. When the single-letter syllable *a, i,* or *u* is followed by the ending *ly, ble, bly, cle,* or *cal,* divide before the single-letter syllable.

stead-ily	siz-able	vis-ible	mir-acle
cler-ical	trop-ical	lov-able	
but	musi-cal	practi-cal	techni-cal

8. Divide only between the two words that make up a hyphenated word.

self-contained	long-range	well-developed

9. Do not divide a contraction or a single group of figures.

doesn't	$350,000	Policy F238975

10. Try to avoid dividing proper names and dates. If necessary, divide as follows.

Mary J./Pembroke	*not*	Mary J. Pem-/broke
November 15,/2001	*not*	November/15, 2001

CORRECTION SYMBOLS

Proofreader's marks

Sometimes keyed or printed copy may be corrected with proofreader's marks. The keyboard operator must be able to interpret these marks correctly in rekeying the corrected copy or *rough draft* as it may be called. The most commonly used proofreader's marks are shown below.

Cap or ≡	Capitalize
⊂	Close up
ℒ	Delete
∧	Insert
⩘	Insert comma
# or */	Insert space
⌄	Insert apostrophe
⌄ ⌄	Insert quotation marks
⊐	Move right
⊏	Move left
⌐⌐	Move down; lower
⌐⌐	Move up; raise
lc or /	Lowercase
¶	Paragraph
no new ¶	No new paragraph
‖	Align copy
⊙	Spell out
stet	Let it stand; ignore correction
∩ or *tr*	Transpose
___	Underline or italics

BASIC FORMAT GUIDES*
for
Memos, Letters, & Reports

Document	Guides
Simplified Memo (117)**	TM: 2" (line 13). SM: 1" or defaults. PE: at least 1". LS: SS. Other: QS between date/receiver's name, body/sender's name. DS between other parts.
Standard Memo (115)	TM: 2" (line 13). SM: 1" or defaults. PE: at least 1". LS: SS. Other: DS between lines of heading, other parts. After headings, align fill-ins 1" from LM.
Personal-Business Letter (124)	TM: 2" (line 13). SM: 1" or defaults. PE: at least 1". LS: SS. Other: Key return address above date. May be block or modified block format letter.
Envelopes (127)	TM: 2" (line 13). SM: L = 2.5" (small) L = 4" (large). LS: SS. Other: Use USPS style, standard abbreviations, 2-letter state abbreviations, and ZIP + 4.
Block Format Letter (130)	TM: 2" (line 13). SM: 1" or defaults. PE: at least 1". LS: SS. Other: All lines at LM. QS between date/letter address, complimentary close/writer's name. DS between other parts. Key reference initials (lowercase) below writer's name.
Modified Block Format Letter (193)	TM: 2" or centered. SM: 1" or defaults. PE: at least 1". LS: SS. Other: Key at center: date, complimentary close, keyed name, and official title. May indent ¶s 0.5". All other lines at LM. QS between date/letter address, complimentary close/writer's name. DS between other parts.
Simplified Block Format Letter (199)	TM: 2" or centered. SM: 1" or defaults. PE: at least 1". LS: SS. Other: Omit salutation, complimentary close. Key writer's name and title in ALL CAPS on one line. All lines at LM. QS between date/letter address, body/writer's name. DS between other parts.
Unbound Report (145)	TM: 2" (page 1); 1" other pages. SM: 1" or defaults. PE: at least 1". LS: DS (may be SS). Other: Underline (or bold) side headings. Key page number at top RM (except page 1). To document, use textual citations, endnotes, or footnotes. Key references/bibliography on last page or on separate page in hanging-indent style.
Bound Report (RG12)	TM: 2" (page 1); 1" other pages. SM: LM = 1.5"; RM = 1". PE: at least 1". LS: DS (may be SS). Other: Underline (or bold) side headings. Key page number at top RM (except page 1). To document, use textual citations, endnotes, or footnotes. Key references/bibliography on last page or on separate page in hanging-indent style.
Endnotes Page (RG13) & Footnotes (RG14)	Endnotes page: TM: 2". SM: at least 1". PE: at least 1". LS: SS; DS between items. Other: Use superscript numbers to relate endnotes/footnotes to text. List endnotes in order of occurrence; list footnote on page with related text. Indent entries 0.5".
Report in MLA Style (293)	TM: 0.5". SM: 1". PE: 1". LS: DS (all parts). Other: Key writer's last name and page number at top RM (all pages). Key title page text 1" from top at LM. Center main heading in c/lc. To document, use parenthetical references and Works Cited page.

*Use Index to find more detailed format guides.

**Indicates page number where model can be found.

2"

November 13, ... **QS**

Periscope Staff Members **DS**
NEW WITHIN-SCHOOL MEMORANDUM FORMAT **DS**

You asked me to suggest a simple message format to use when you write to one another and to others within the school about school newspaper business. This message is formatted as a

SIMPLIFIED MEMORANDUM

All lines begin at the left margin except for centered titles. A QS (4 hard returns) separates the date and receiver's name and the last paragraph and writer's name. All other parts, including paragraphs, are separated by a DS (2 hard returns). No personal title is used before a name, but an official title or department name may follow it.

1"   If a separate document (such as an edited article) is attached to the memo, the word Attachment is keyed at the left margin a double space below the writer's name; if the document is not attached, the word Enclosure is keyed instead.   **1"**

The simplified memo is easy to format and key. Use it for a few days and give me your reactions. I am attaching an annotated model for your initial guidance. **QS**

Keiko Sato

Keiko Sato, Sponsor

Attachment **DS**

Simplified Memo

2"

TO: Faculty and Staff **DS**

FROM: Lenore M. Fielding, Principal

DATE: November 15, ----

SUBJECT: STANDARD MEMO FORMAT **DS**

At a recent meeting, department heads recommended that memos be processed on plain paper instead of preprinted forms. This recommendation is a cost-cutting measure that requires only a little more effort on the part of the keyboard operator.

The customary standard margins are used: 2" top margin; default (near 1") side margins; at least a 1" bottom margin.

Standard double spacing separates memo parts, including paragraphs, which are individually single-spaced. If someone other **1"** than the writer keys the memo, that person's initials should be keyed at the left margin a double space below the message. If an attachment or enclosure is included, Attachment or Enclosure should be keyed at the left margin a double space below the message or the keyboard operator's initials (if any). **1"**

Headings begin at left margin. After TO: tab twice to key the name; after FROM: tab once to key the name; after DATE: tab once to key the date; after SUBJECT: space twice (or tab once) to enter the subject (may be keyed in ALL CAPS or C/lc--Cap and lowercase).

Please use this format for several days; then let me know if you experienced any difficulties.

tbh **DS**

Standard Memo

2"

1049 Michigan Ave. N.
Chicago, IL 60611-2273
November 18, ---- **QS**

Mr. Elden P. Carter
7257 Charles Plz.
Omaha, NE 68114-3219 **DS**

Dear Elden **DS**

Your telephone call on Wednesday was a really pleasant surprise. Life for both of us since college has been exciting as well as challenging, it seems. I enjoyed the update.

If you had taken keyboarding as I recommended when we were in high school, you wouldn't be asking me now for a model to use for your personal-business correspondence! But I am glad to supply this model in block format (all lines beginning at the left margin).

1"   Use the software default or 1" side margins. Begin the return address 2" (line 13) from the top of the paper. Key the date on the next line below the return address.   **1"**

All letter parts are separated by a double space (2 returns) with two exceptions: A quadruple space (4 returns) is left between the date and the letter address and between the complimentary close and the keyed name.

I am attaching a page from a reference manual that includes an annotated model. Call again if you need more help.

Cordially **QS**

Andrea Rialto

Andrea Rialto **DS**

Attachment

Personal-Business Letter in Block Format

K e n d a l ■ C o m p u t e r s

■ 738 St. Louis St.
   ■ Baton Rouge, LA 77802-3615

OFFICE: 504-555-1276
FAX: 504-555-1998

2"

November 21, ---- **QS**

Mr. Julio M. Basanez, Manager
La Paloma Restaurant
224 Saint Louis St.
Baton Rouge, LA 77802-3615 **DS**

Dear Julio **DS**

Your piquant black bean soup drew me back to the La Paloma yesterday. We were taken promptly to our table, but we waited over ten minutes before menus were presented.

Several times I provided clues to the server that I was hosting the luncheon. Without noting these clues or asking who should receive the check, the server gave it to the man across from me. Had the check been placed upside down in the middle of the table, my client wouldn't have been "put on the spot."

1"   Several times a week someone from my company entertains clients at La Paloma Restaurant. Will you talk with your staff about greeting diners promptly and about handling checks properly. But please, Julio, don't disturb the chef!   **1"**

Cordially **QS**

Luanne Chang

Mrs. Luanne Chang, President

mt **DS**

Business Letter in Block Format

Second-Page Heading Enumerated Items (Hanging Indent Format)

Mr. Jason Arris
Page 2
April 9, ----
DS
You will need to perform the following steps:
DS
1. Review the sample projects and proposed guidelines.

2. Determine the specific responsibilities of the project manager and put these in writing.

Thank you, Mr. Arris, for your cooperation. It is always a pleasure working with you.

Very truly yours

Postscript

Sincerely
QS
Ms. Rae Mathias, President
DS
pr
DS
The cashmere sweaters will be shipped by air to you just as soon as our stock is replenished. You will find them well worth the wait.

Envelope with Mailing Notation

Turner Roofing Co.
10318 Rearview Ave.
Dayton, OH 54309-1927

CERTIFIED MAIL

MR JACK BROWN
QUALITY TRAINING ASSOCIATES
28 REVINA DR
ATLANTA GA 30346-9105

Attention Line/Subject Line

Samantha's Fashions
422 Main St.
Wichita KS 67202-1304 • (316) 125-3342

March 15, ----

Attention Fashion Buyer
Amason Fashion Mart
4385 Felten Dr.
Hays, KS 67601-2863

Ladies and Gentlemen
DS
FALL FASHION CAMPAIGN
DS
The demand for two of the items that were sent last week was much greater than originally expected; there-

Company Name

Your order should be shipped via Pony Express within the next two weeks.

Thank you for your order; we appreciate your business.
DS
Sincerely
DS
STYLES BY REX
DS
Ms. Ellen Turnquist
General Manager
DS
rt

Mailing Notation

MUSIC BY MAIL
3716 Rangely Dr
New Haven, CT 06513-2357
(203) 146-8873

March 15, ----
DS
CERTIFIED MAIL
DS
Mr. John West Buyer
Tarnal Music Center
4385 Dove Ave.
Rigby, ID 83442-1244
DS
Dear Mr. West
DS
The items that you ordered last week were sent by overnight delivery so that you could have these items by

Business Letter in Modified Block Format

DOCUMENT PROCESSING SPECIALISTS
6652 Remington St.
New Haven, CT 06517-1498
(203) 555-8215

March 27, ----
QS
Miss Anne Cortess
Asturia Technologies
5409 Bayview Dr.
Miami, FL 33160-8682
DS
Dear Miss Cortess
DS
MODIFIED BLOCK LETTER FORMAT/BLOCKED PARAGRAPHS
DS
This letter is arranged in modified block format with blocked paragraphs. The only difference between this letter format and the block format is that the dateline and the closing lines (complimentary close, keyed name of the originator, and his or her title) begin at the horizontal center point.

Mixed punctuation (a colon after the salutation and a comma after the complimentary close) is used in this letter. If an enclosure is mentioned in the body of the letter, the word Enclosure is keyed a double space below the reference notation, flush with the left margin. Copy notations are placed a double space below the enclosure notation or below the reference initials if no enclosure has been indicated.

A copy of the block format letter is enclosed so that you can compare the two formats. As you can see, either format presents an attractive appearance.
DS
Sincerely yours,
QS
Troy Williams
Troy Williams
Word Processing Consultant
DS
ph
DS
Enclosure
DS
c Ms. Kimberlee Rodríguez

Business Letter in Simplified Block Format

Communication Concepts Inc.
178 S. Prospect Ave. ■ San Bernardino, CA 92410-4567 ■ (714) 186-7934

August 13, ----
QS
MR CARL VISQUEL
382 OLD MURFREESBORO RD
NASHVILLE TN 37217-8902
DS
SIMPLIFIED BLOCK LETTER FORMAT
DS
This letter is arranged in simplified block format. Several differences distinguish this format from the block and modified block styles.

The **salutation** is omitted; it is replaced by a subject line. The **subject line** is keyed below the letter address in ALL CAPS. A double space is left above and below it.

The letter format is further streamlined by the omission of the **complimentary close**. The **writer's name** and **title** (or department) are keyed a quadruple space below the body of the letter in ALL CAPS. The name and title are separated by a comma.

Notice that the letter address of this letter is keyed in the style recommended by the U.S. Postal Service for OCR processing; ALL-CAP letters with no punctuation. As with the other letter formats, it would also be appropriate to use cap-and-lowercase letters with punctuation for the letter address.

Many organizations have decided to use this particular style. Their opinion is that the salutation and complimentary close serve little purpose and are obsolete. Other organizations still prefer the traditional block or modified block format.
QS
Caroline Martinez
DS
MRS. CAROLINE MARTINEZ, WORD PROCESSING SPECIALIST
DS
hpj

Envelope Guides

Return Address

Use block style, SS, and Caps/lowercase or ALL CAPS. Unless equipment has an Envelope feature, begin on line 2 from top of envelope, 3 spaces from left edge.

Envelope Address

Unless equipment has an Envelope feature, set a tab 2.5" from left edge of small envelope and 4" from left edge of large envelope.

Space down about 2" from top edge of envelope; begin address at tab position.

USPS (Postal Service) Style

Use block style, SS. Use ALL CAPS; omit punctuation. Place city name, 2-letter state abbreviation, and ZIP Code + 4 on last address line. One space precedes the ZIP Code.

Mailing Notations

Key mailing and addressee notations in ALL CAPS.

Key mailing notations, such as SPECIAL DELIVERY and REGISTERED, below the stamp and at least 3 lines above the envelope address.

Key addressee notations, such as HOLD FOR ARRIVAL or PERSONAL, a DS below the return address and about 3 spaces from the left edge of the envelope.

If an *attention line* is used, key it as the first line of the envelope address.

International Addresses

Omit postal (ZIP) codes from the last line of addresses outside the U.S. Show *only* the name of the country on the last line. Examples:

```
MS INGE D FISCHER
HARTMANNSTRASSE 7
4209 BONN 5
FEDERAL REPUBLIC OF GERMANY

MR HIRAM SANDERS
2121 CLEARWATER ST
OTTAWA ONK1A OB1
CANADA
```

Standard Abbreviations

Use USPS standard abbreviations for states (see list below) and street suffix names, such as AVE and BLVD. Never abbreviate the name of a city or country.

Folding Procedures

Small Envelopes (Nos. 6 3/4, 6 1/4)

1. With page face up, fold bottom up to 0.5" from top.
2. Fold right third to left.
3. Fold left third to 0.5" from last crease.
4. Insert last creased edge first.

Large Envelopes (Nos. 10, 9, 7 3/4)

1. With page face up, fold slightly less than one-third of sheet up toward top.
2. Fold down top of sheet to within 0.5" of bottom fold.
3. Insert last creased edge first.

Window Envelopes (Letter)

1. With page face down, top toward you, fold upper third down.
2. Fold lower third up so address is showing.
3. Insert sheet into envelope with last crease at bottom.
4. Check that address shows through window.

2-Letter State Abbreviations

State	Abbr.	State	Abbr.	State	Abbr.	State	Abbr.	State	Abbr.
Alabama	AL	Guam	GU	Massachusetts	MA	New York	NY	Tennessee	TN
Alaska	AK	Hawaii	HI	Michigan	MI	North Carolina	NC	Texas	TX
Arizona	AZ	Idaho	ID	Minnesota	MN	North Dakota	ND	Utah	UT
Arkansas	AR	Illinois	IL	Mississippi	MS	Ohio	OH	Vermont	VT
California	CA	Indiana	IN	Missouri	MO	Oklahoma	OK	Virgin Islands	VI
Colorado	CO	Iowa	IA	Montana	MT	Oregon	OR	Virginia	VA
Connecticut	CT	Kansas	KS	Nebraska	NE	Pennsylvania	PA	Washington	WA
Delaware	DE	Kentucky	KY	Nevada	NV	Puerto Rico	PR	West Virginia	WV
District of Columbia	DC	Louisiana	LA	New Hampshire	NH	Rhode Island	RI	Wisconsin	WI
Florida	FL	Maine	ME	New Jersey	NJ	South Carolina	SC	Wyoming	WY
Georgia	GA	Maryland	MD	New Mexico	NM	South Dakota	SD		

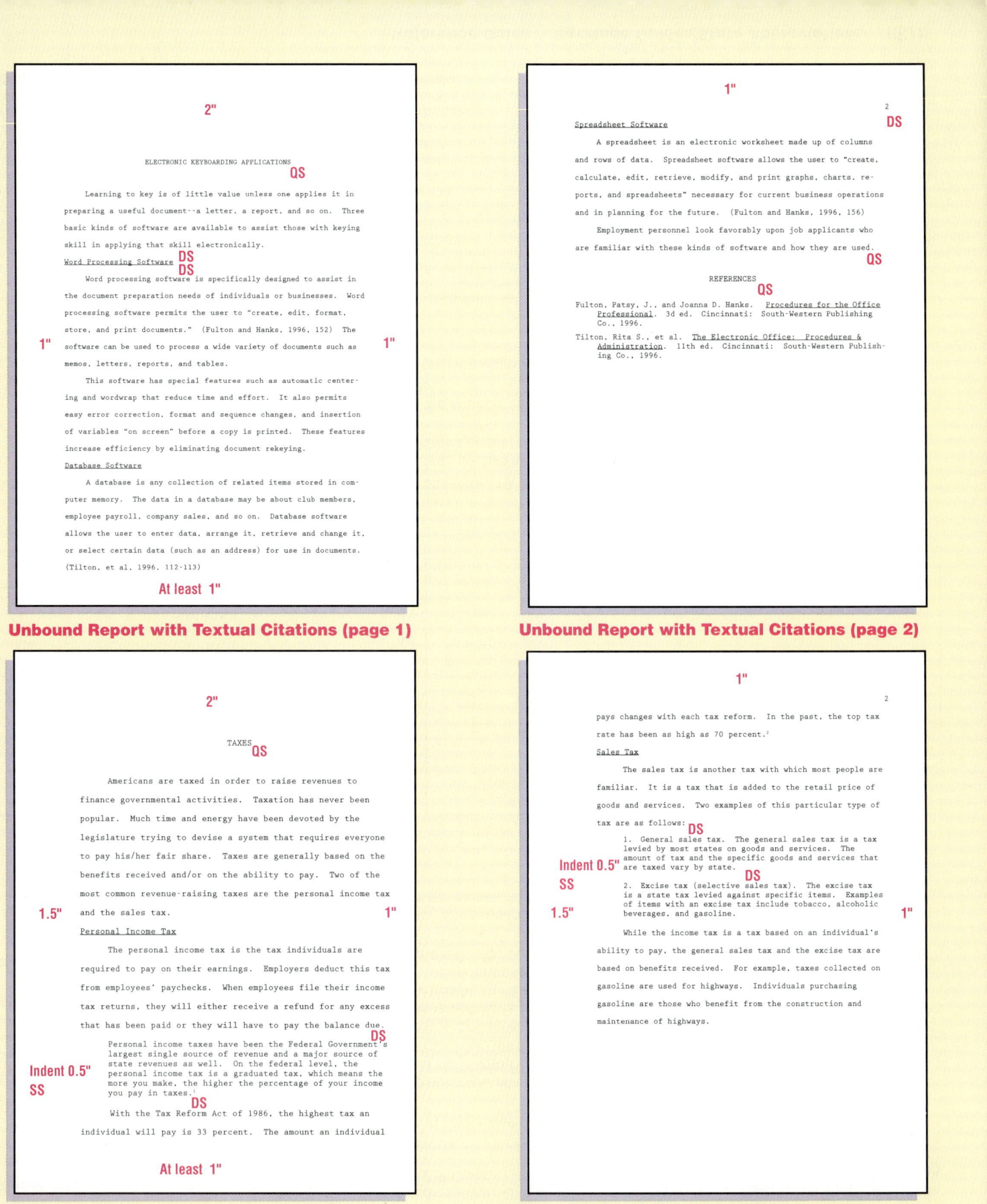

Unbound Report with Textual Citations (page 1)

2"

ELECTRONIC KEYBOARDING APPLICATIONS

QS

Learning to key is of little value unless one applies it in preparing a useful document--a letter, a report, and so on. Three basic kinds of software are available to assist those with keying skill in applying that skill electronically.

Word Processing Software

DS
DS

Word processing software is specifically designed to assist in the document preparation needs of individuals or businesses. Word processing software permits the user to "create, edit, format, store, and print documents." (Fulton and Hanks, 1996, 152) The software can be used to process a wide variety of documents such as memos, letters, reports, and tables.

1"   1"

This software has special features such as automatic centering and wordwrap that reduce time and effort. It also permits easy error correction, format and sequence changes, and insertion of variables "on screen" before a copy is printed. These features increase efficiency by eliminating document rekeying.

Database Software

A database is any collection of related items stored in computer memory. The data in a database may be about club members, employee payroll, company sales, and so on. Database software allows the user to enter data, arrange it, retrieve and change it, or select certain data (such as an address) for use in documents. (Tilton, et al, 1996, 112-113)

At least 1"

Unbound Report with Textual Citations (page 2)

1"   2
                     DS

Spreadsheet Software

A spreadsheet is an electronic worksheet made up of columns and rows of data. Spreadsheet software allows the user to "create, calculate, edit, retrieve, modify, and print graphs, charts, reports, and spreadsheets" necessary for current business operations and in planning for the future. (Fulton and Hanks, 1996, 156)

Employment personnel look favorably upon job applicants who are familiar with these kinds of software and how they are used.

QS

REFERENCES

QS

Fulton, Patsy, J., and Joanna D. Hanks. Procedures for the Office Professional. 3d ed. Cincinnati: South-Western Publishing Co., 1996.

Tilton, Rita S., et al. The Electronic Office: Procedures & Administration. 11th ed. Cincinnati: South-Western Publishing Co., 1996.

Bound Report with Long Quotation (page 1)

2"

TAXES QS

Americans are taxed in order to raise revenues to finance governmental activities. Taxation has never been popular. Much time and energy have been devoted by the legislature trying to devise a system that requires everyone to pay his/her fair share. Taxes are generally based on the benefits received and/or on the ability to pay. Two of the most common revenue-raising taxes are the personal income tax

1.5"   1"

and the sales tax.

Personal Income Tax

The personal income tax is the tax individuals are required to pay on their earnings. Employers deduct this tax from employees' paychecks. When employees file their income tax returns, they will either receive a refund for any excess that has been paid or they will have to pay the balance due.

DS

Personal income taxes have been the Federal Government's largest single source of revenue and a major source of state revenues as well. On the federal level, the personal income tax is a graduated tax, which means the more you make, the higher the percentage of your income you pay in taxes.[1]

Indent 0.5"
SS

DS

With the Tax Reform Act of 1986, the highest tax an individual will pay is 33 percent. The amount an individual

At least 1"

Bound Report with Numbered Paragraphs

1"   2

pays changes with each tax reform. In the past, the top tax rate has been as high as 70 percent.[2]

Sales Tax

The sales tax is another tax with which most people are familiar. It is a tax that is added to the retail price of goods and services. Two examples of this particular type of tax are as follows:

DS

1. General sales tax. The general sales tax is a tax levied by most states on goods and services. The amount of tax and the specific goods and services that are taxed vary by state.

Indent 0.5"
SS

DS

2. Excise tax (selective sales tax). The excise tax is a state tax levied against specific items. Examples of items with an excise tax include tobacco, alcoholic beverages, and gasoline.

1.5"   1"

While the income tax is a tax based on an individual's ability to pay, the general sales tax and the excise tax are based on benefits received. For example, taxes collected on gasoline are used for highways. Individuals purchasing gasoline are those who benefit from the construction and maintenance of highways.

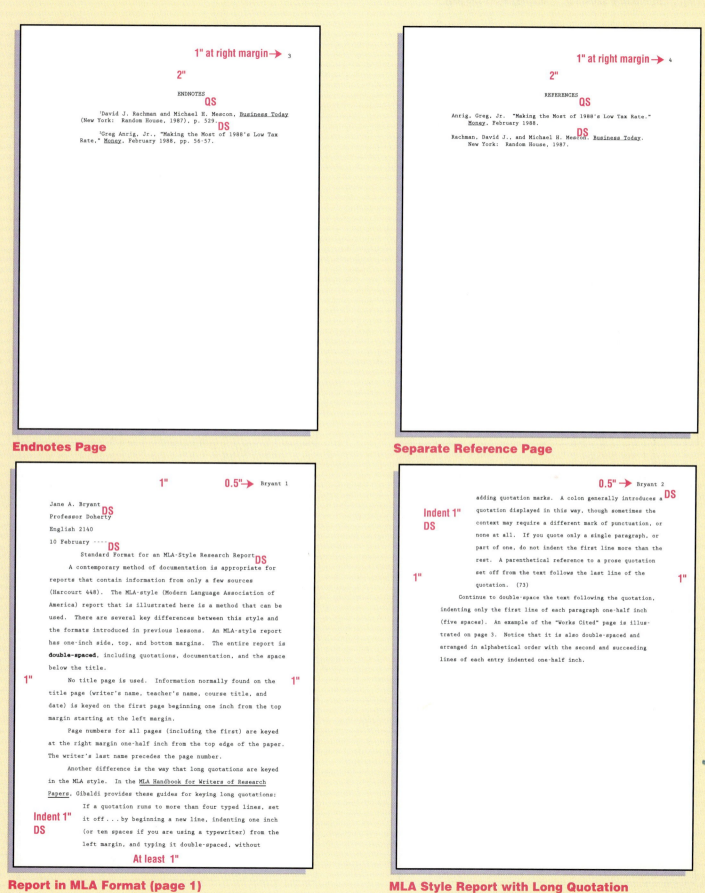

Endnotes Page

1" at right margin → 3

2"

ENDNOTES

QS

¹David J. Rachman and Michael H. Mescon, <u>Business Today</u> (New York: Random House, 1987), p. 529.

DS

²Greg Anrig, Jr., "Making the Most of 1988's Low Tax Rate," <u>Money</u>, February 1988, pp. 56-57.

Separate Reference Page

1" at right margin → 4

2"

REFERENCES

QS

Anrig, Greg, Jr. "Making the Most of 1988's Low Tax Rate." <u>Money</u>, February 1988.

DS

Rachman, David J., and Michael H. Mescon. <u>Business Today</u>. New York: Random House, 1987.

Report in MLA Format (page 1)

1"   0.5" → Bryant 1

Jane A. Bryant
DS
Professor Doherty

English 2140

10 February ----
DS
Standard Format for an MLA-Style Research Report
DS
A contemporary method of documentation is appropriate for reports that contain information from only a few sources (Harcourt 448). The MLA-style (Modern Language Association of America) report that is illustrated here is a method that can be used. There are several key differences between this style and the formats introduced in previous lessons. An MLA-style report has one-inch side, top, and bottom margins. The entire report is **double-spaced**, including quotations, documentation, and the space below the title.

1"   No title page is used. Information normally found on the   1"
title page (writer's name, teacher's name, course title, and date) is keyed on the first page beginning one inch from the top margin starting at the left margin.

Page numbers for all pages (including the first) are keyed at the right margin one-half inch from the top edge of the paper. The writer's last name precedes the page number.

Another difference is the way that long quotations are keyed in the MLA style. In the <u>MLA Handbook for Writers of Research Papers</u>, Gibaldi provides these guides for keying long quotations:

Indent 1"   If a quotation runs to more than four typed lines, set
DS   it off...by beginning a new line, indenting one inch (or ten spaces if you are using a typewriter) from the left margin, and typing it double-spaced, without

At least 1"

MLA Style Report with Long Quotation

0.5" → Bryant 2
DS
adding quotation marks. A colon generally introduces a
Indent 1"   quotation displayed in this way, though sometimes the
DS   context may require a different mark of punctuation, or none at all. If you quote only a single paragraph, or part of one, do not indent the first line more than the rest. A parenthetical reference to a prose quotation

1"   set off from the text follows the last line of the   1"
quotation. (73)

Continue to double-space the text following the quotation, indenting only the first line of each paragraph one-half inch (five spaces). An example of the "Works Cited" page is illustrated on page 3. Notice that it is also double-spaced and arranged in alphabetical order with the second and succeeding lines of each entry indented one-half inch.

Works Cited Page (MLA)

1" 0.5"→ Bryant 3

Works Cited **DS**

Gibaldi, Joseph. <u>MLA Handbook for Writers of Research Papers.</u> **DS**
    4th ed. New York: The Modern Language Association of
    America, 1995.

1" Harcourt, Jules, A. C. "Buddy" Krizan, and Patricia Merrier. 1"
    <u>Business Communication.</u> 3d ed. Cincinnati: South-Western
    Educational Publishing, 1996.

Works Cited Page (MLA)

Bound Report with Footnotes (page 2)

1"   2

    <u>Reason</u>. One reason for selecting Derme & Associates is
that they will develop the content of the seminars around
Keeling and Kallaus' definition of leadership,[1] which we
want to emphasize with employees.

<u>Seminar Development</u>

    We have had two meetings with partners of Derme &
Associates since the signing of the agreement two weeks ago.

    <u>Meeting #1</u>. The first meeting was held so that we
1.5" could learn about the content of leadership seminars that 1"
Derme & Associates, Inc., has presented for other clients.

    <u>Meeting #2</u>. The specific content of the four seminars
was identified at the second meeting. Also, we decided to
use the prepared content for each seminar except for the
changes we suggest. These suggestions will be based on the
feedback we get from the participants at the end of each
seminar.

<u>Seminar Dates</u>

    The first seminar will be on October 15 at the
Logansport Plant; the second will be at the Muncie Plant on
October 22; the third meets at the Fort Wayne Plant on
October 29; and the fourth will be at the Evansville Plant
_____ **DS**

SS [1]B. Lewis Keeling and Norman F. Kallaus,
<u>Administrative Office Management</u>, 11th ed. (Cincinnati:
South-Western Educational Publishing Co., 1996), p. 46.

Bound Report with Footnotes (page 2)

Table of Contents

2"

TABLE OF CONTENTS **QS**

Table of Contents

Topic Outline

2"

LEADERSHIP SEMINAR PROGRESS REPORT **QS**

  I. INTRODUCTION **DS**

 II. SEMINAR PRESENTER **DS**
      A. Selection--Derme & Associates Selected
      B. Reason--Derme & Associates' Definition of Leadership

1" III. SEMINAR DEVELOPMENT 1"
      A. Meeting #1--Learned About Content of Previous Derme
          Seminars
      B. Meeting #2--Decided the Content of the Four Scheduled
          Seminars

 IV. SEMINAR DATES AND LOCATIONS
      A. October 15--Logansport
      B. October 22--Muncie
      C. October 29--Fort Wayne
      D. November 5--Evansville

  V. SEMINAR CONTENT
      A. Leadership Characteristics--Social and Environmental
          Responsibility, International Awareness, Honesty, and
          Consistency
      B. Leadership Styles--Autocratic to Democratic

Topic Outline

Agenda

2" or centered

```
                          AGENDA   DS
              Software Development Board Meeting
                   10:30 a.m., June 25, ----
1.  Introductory Remarks . . . . . . . . . . . . . . . Noriko Shoji
2.  New Software Proposals . . . . . . . . . . . . . . Ted Hubbard
        Market Analyzer . . . . . . . . . . . . . . . May Roberts
        Financial Planner . . . . . . . . . . . . . . Ken Jetz
        Visuals Unlimited . . . . . . . . . . . . . . Judy Kay
3.  Projection Reports
        Production Cost Projections . . . . . . . . . Brett Hill
        Market Projections . . . . . . . . . . . . . Jay Griffin
        Profit Projections . . . . . . . . . . . . . Erika Nicole
4.  Discussion of Proposal . . . . . . . . . . . . . Board Members
5.  Adjournment
```
1" ... 1"

Agenda

Itinerary

2"

```
                          ITINERARY   DS
                      Jacinta A. Reinhart
              HPJ Communication Specialists Symposium   DS

April 15   DS
2:30 p.m.              Depart Memphis on Coastal Airlines--Flight #714 for
                       Boston (Logan International).

6:19 p.m.              Arrive Boston.  Accommodations at Ellsworth Inn,
                       641 Taft Hill Park.

April 16

7:00 a.m.              Breakfast with Harvey Jacobs at hotel.

8:30 a.m.              HPJ Communication Specialists Symposium, meetings
                       until 4:30 p.m.

6:30 p.m.              Dinner with Sue Butler at Cambridge Club.

April 17

8:30 a.m.              HPJ Communication Specialists Symposium, meetings
                       until 2:45 p.m.

3:30 p.m.              Meeting with Justin Browning.

7:30 p.m.              Performance of the Boston Symphony Orchestra at
                       Symphony Hall.

April 18

7:45 a.m.              Depart Boston on Coastal Airlines--Flight #628
                       for Memphis.

9:27 a.m.              Arrive Memphis.
```
1" ... 1"

Itinerary

Summary Minutes

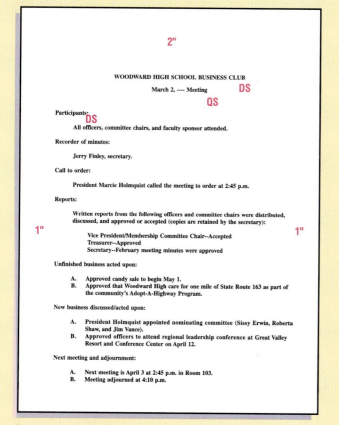

2"

WOODWARD HIGH SCHOOL BUSINESS CLUB

March 2, ---- Meeting   DS

QS

Participants: DS
All officers, committee chairs, and faculty sponsor attended.

Recorder of minutes:
Jerry Finley, secretary.

Call to order:
President Marcie Holmquist called the meeting to order at 2:45 p.m.

Reports:
Written reports from the following officers and committee chairs were distributed, discussed, and approved or accepted (copies are retained by the secretary):

Vice President/Membership Committee Chair--Accepted
Treasurer--Approved
Secretary--February meeting minutes were approved

Unfinished business acted upon:

A. Approved candy sale to begin May 1.
B. Approved that Woodward High care for one mile of State Route 163 as part of the community's Adopt-A-Highway Program.

New business discussed/acted upon:

A. President Holmquist appointed nominating committee (Sissy Erwin, Roberta Shaw, and Jim Vance).
B. Approved officers to attend regional leadership conference at Great Valley Resort and Conference Center on April 12.

Next meeting and adjournment:

A. Next meeting is April 3 at 2:45 p.m. in Room 103.
B. Meeting adjourned at 4:10 p.m.

1" ... 1"

Summary Minutes

News Release

LAKELAND AMPHITHEATER

12348 Hwy. 155 N. & I-20
Tyler, TX 75702-5503

Telephone: 903-177-9236
Fax: 903-177-9237

News Release   2" For Release: Immediately
                       Contact: Johnny Williams

```
     TYLER, TX, March 18, ----.  Prepare for lift off with New
Space Spectacular, a new show that is destined to delight
science fiction fans of all ages.
     The show will land at Lakeland Amphitheater in Tyler at
8:15 p.m. on June 24 featuring the world renowned Dallas Symphony
in a multimedia symphonic concert using laser beams.  Music
featured includes both classical and movie soundtrack selections
of a celestial nature.
     Tickets are $24.75 for gold circle seats, $18.75 for re-
served seats, and $10.25 for lawn seats.  They go on sale April 1
at all Ticketpoint locations.  The charge-by-phone number is
123-5349.

                           ###
```
1" ... 1"

News Release

Interview Follow-Up Letter

310 Royal Oak Ct.
Daytona Beach, FL 32017-1157
May 25, ----

Ms. Jenna St. John
Personnel Director
Regency Insurance Company
4291 Imperial Dr.
Daytona Beach, FL 32017-3856

Dear Ms. St. John:

Thank you for discussing the secretarial opening at Regency Insurance Company. I have a much better understanding of the position after meeting with you and Ms. Meade.

Ms. Meade was extremely helpful in explaining the specific job responsibilities. My previous jobs and my business education classes required me to complete many of the tasks that she mentioned. With minimal training, I believe I could be an asset to your company.

Even though I realize it would be a real challenge to replace a person like Ms. Meade, it is a challenge that I would welcome. If there is further information that would be helpful as you consider my application, please let me know.

Sincerely,

Teresa A. Teasdale

Ms. Teresa A. Teasdale

"2"

Job Application Form

APPLICATION FOR EMPLOYMENT

AN EQUAL OPPORTUNITY EMPLOYER

PLEASE PRINT WITH BLACK INK OR USE TYPEWRITER

NAME (LAST, FIRST, MIDDLE INITIAL): Teasdale, Teresa A.
CURRENT DATE: May 22, ----
SOCIAL SECURITY NUMBER: 368-56-2890

ADDRESS (NUMBER, STREET, CITY, STATE, ZIP CODE): 310 Royal Oak Ct., Daytona Beach, FL 32017-1157
HOME PHONE NO: (904)136-7289
REACH PHONE NO:
DATE YOU CAN START: June 5, ----
U.S. CITIZEN? YES X NO

ARE YOU EMPLOYED NOW? Yes
IF SO, MAY WE INQUIRE OF YOUR PRESENT EMPLOYER? Yes

TYPE OF WORK DESIRED: Secretarial
REFERRED BY: Ms. Anna Cruz
SALARY DESIRED: $ Open

IF RELATED TO ANYONE IN OUR EMPLOY, STATE NAME AND POSITION

DO YOU HAVE ANY PHYSICAL CONDITION THAT MAY PREVENT YOU FROM PERFORMING CERTAIN KINDS OF WORK? YES NO X IF YES, EXPLAIN

HAVE YOU EVER BEEN CONVICTED OF A FELONY? YES NO X IF YES, EXPLAIN

EDUCATION	EDUCATIONAL INSTITUTION	LOCATION (CITY, STATE)	DATES ATTENDED FROM MO-YR	TO MO-YR	CLASS STANDING (CHK QUARTER) 1 2 3 4	DIPLOMA, DEGREE OR CREDITS EARNED	MAJOR SUBJECTS STUDIED
HIGH SCHOOL	Jefferson High School	Daytona Beach, FL	9 93	5 97	X	Diploma	Business Ed.
COLLEGE							
OTHER							

LIST BELOW THE POSITIONS THAT YOU HAVE HELD (LAST POSITION FIRST)

1 NAME AND ADDRESS OF FIRM: Fischer Studio, 839 Franklin Dr., Daytona Beach, FL 32019-8321
DESCRIBE POSITION RESPONSIBILITIES: Studio Assistant. Schedule appointments, maintain customer database, respond to customer inquiries.
NAME OF SUPERVISOR: Mr. Jeremiah Fischer
REASON FOR LEAVING:
EMPLOYED MO-YR: FROM 8/93 TO Present

2 NAME AND ADDRESS OF FIRM: The Printing Press, 289 Seminole Ave., Daytona Beach, FL 32019-7585
DESCRIBE POSITION RESPONSIBILITIES: Bookkeeper. Processed accounts receivable and reconciled bank statements.
NAME OF SUPERVISOR: Ms. Ruth Stewart
REASON FOR LEAVING: Started a new job.
EMPLOYED MO-YR: FROM 5/94 TO 7/95

3 NAME AND ADDRESS OF FIRM: Camp Clearwater, P.O. Box 382, Lake City, FL 32055-1749
DESCRIBE POSITION RESPONSIBILITIES: Camp assistant. Assisted Ms. Ramirez with various camp activities for 8- and 9-year-olds.
NAME OF SUPERVISOR: Ms. Carmen G. Ramirez
REASON FOR LEAVING: Summer employment.
EMPLOYED MO-YR: FROM 6/93 TO 8/93

I UNDERSTAND THAT I WILL NOT BECOME AN EMPLOYEE UNTIL I HAVE SIGNED AN EMPLOY-MENT AGREEMENT THAT I SHALL NOT BE IN VIOLATION OF ANY PRIOR EMPLOYMENT AGREEMENT, AND THAT I CAN MAKE A WRITTEN RE-QUEST FOR ADDITIONAL INFORMATION AS TO THE NATURE AND SCOPE OF THE REPORT IF ONE IS MADE.

SIGNATURE OF APPLICANT: *Teresa A. Teasdale*

Data Sheet

Teresa A. Teasdale
310 Royal Oak Ct.
Daytona Beach, FL 32017-1157
(904) 136-7289

EDUCATION

Senior at Jefferson High School
High School Diploma, pending graduation
Major emphasis: Administrative Services
Grade Average: 3.70; upper 10% of class

SCHOOL ACTIVITIES

Editor, Jefferson Telegram, senior year; reporter for two years.

Vice President, Future Business Leaders of America, senior year; member for three years.

National Honor Society, junior and senior years.

WORK EXPERIENCE

Studio Assistant, Fischer Studio, Daytona Beach, FL, August 1993 to present. Work 15 hours a week as a studio assistant: schedule appointments, maintain customer database, and respond to customer inquiries.

Bookkeeper, The Printing Press, Daytona Beach, FL, May 1994 to July 1995. Processed accounts receivable and reconciled bank statements.

Camp Assistant, Camp Clearwater, Lake City, FL, summer 1993.

REFERENCES (by permission)

Ms. Ann C. Rutgers, Administrative Services Instructor, Jefferson High School, 8230 Riverwood Dr., Daytona Beach, FL 32019-3627, (904) 132-8286.

Mr. Jeremiah Fischer, Owner, Fischer Studio, 839 Franklin Dr., Daytona Beach, FL 32019-8321, (904) 136-8256.

Ms. Ruth Stewart, Manager, The Printing Press, 289 Seminole Ave., Daytona Beach, FL 32019-7585, (904) 132-2819.

"1"

Letter of Application

310 Royal Oak Ct.
Daytona Beach, FL 32017-1157
May 10, ----

Ms. Jenna St. John
Personnel Director
Regency Insurance Company
4291 Imperial Dr.
Daytona Beach, FL 32017-3856

Dear Ms. St. John:

Ms. Anna Cruz, my information processing instructor, informed me of the secretarial position with your company that will be available June 15. She speaks very highly of your organization. After learning more about the position, I am confident that I am qualified and would like to be considered for the position.

Currently I am completing my senior year at Jefferson High School. All of my elective courses have been in the information processing area. I have completed the advanced course in document formatting, the database and spreadsheet applications courses, and the business procedures course. I have been able to apply what I learned in these courses at Fischer Studio, where I have worked as a studio assistant for almost two years.

My work experience and school activities have given me the opportunity to work with people to achieve group goals. Participating in FBLA has given me an appreciation of the business world.

The opportunity to interview with you to discuss the possibility of employment will be greatly appreciated. Please call me at 136-7289 to arrange an interview.

Sincerely,

Teresa A. Teasdale

Ms. Teresa A. Teasdale

Enclosure

"2"

REPORT DOCUMENTATION

In a good report the writer gives proof, called references, that the statements are sound. The process is called *documenting*.

Most school reports are documented: **(1)** in the body and **(2)** in a list. A reference in the body shows the source of a *quotation* (someone else's actual words) or *paraphrase* (someone else's idea stated in writer's words). A list shows all references alphabetically.

In the report body, references may be noted: **(1)** in parentheses in the copy (*textual citations* or *parenthetical notes*); **(2)** by a superscript in the copy, listed on a separate page (*endnotes*); or **(3)** by a superscript in the copy, listed at the bottom of the text page (*footnotes*). A list may contain only the sources noted in the body (REFERENCES or Works Cited) or include related materials (BIBLIOGRAPHY).

Rules for documenting reports are set down in style manuals, of which there are dozens. Two popular styles are shown: *Century 21* and *MLA Handbook* (Modern Language Association).

CENTURY 21

Note: Examples listed in the following order: Textual citation, Endnote/Footnote, and REFERENCES/BIBLIOGRAPHY page.

Book, One Author

(Amsbary, 1994, 90)

[1]George S. Amsbary, Proof It! (Cincinnati: South-Western Publishing Co., 1994), p. 90.

Amsbary, George S. Proof It! Cincinnati: South-Western Publishing Co., 1994.

Book, Two or Three Authors

(Jones and Kane, 1990, 8)

[2]Ellis Jones and David Kane, Proofreading & Editing Precision (Cincinnati: South-Western Publishing Co., 1990), p. 8.

Jones, Ellis, and David Kane. Proofreading & Editing Precision. Cincinnati: South-Western Publishing Co., 1990.

Book, Four or More Authors

(Tilton, et al., 1996, 112-113)

The Latin phrase *et al* may be translated: *and others*.

[3]Rita S. Tilton, et al., The Electronic Office (Cincinnati: South-Western Publishing Co., 1996), pp. 112-113.

Tilton, Rita S., et al. The Electronic Office. Cincinnati: South-Western Publishing Co., 1996.

Encyclopedia or Reference Book

Page number may be omitted; subjects in alphabetical order.

(Encyclopedia Americana, 1993, p. 915)

[4]Encyclopedia Americana, Vol. 26 (Danbury, CT: Grolier Incorporated, 1993), p. 915.

Encyclopedia Americana, Vol. 26. Danbury, CT: Grolier Incorporated, 1993.

Magazine Article

(Clippinger, 1995, 11-12)

[5]Dorinda Clippinger, "Write This Way," The Small Business Journal (March 1995), pp. 11-12.

Clippinger, Dorinda. "Write This Way." The Small Business Journal, March 1995, 11-15.

World Wide Web (WWW)

(Mannix, 1995)

[7]Mannix, Margaret, "The Home-Page Help Wanteds," U.S. News & World Report (October 30, 1995).

Show full http address and date of online visit.

Mannix, Margaret. "The Home-Page Help Wanteds." U.S. News & World Report. HTTP://WWW.OCC.COM (30 October 1995).

MODERN LANGUAGE ASSOCIATION (MLA)

Note: Examples include reference in parenthetical note and on Works Cited page.

Book, One Author

(Amsbary 90)

Amsbary, George S. Proof It! Cincinnati: South-Western Publishing Co., 1994.

Book, Two or Three Authors

(Jones and Kane 8)

Jones, Ellis, and David Kane. Proofreading & Editing Precision. Cincinnati: South-Western Publishing, 1990.

Book, Four or More Authors or Editors

(Tilton et al. 112-113)

Tilton, Rita S., et al. The Electronic Office. Cincinnati: South-Western Publishing Co., 1996.

Encyclopedia or Reference Book

(Gifis)

Gifis, Steven. "Laws." Law Dictionary. New York: Barrons, 1991.

Magazine Article

(Clippinger 11-12)

Clippinger, Dorinda. "Write This Way," The Small Business Journal. Mar. 1995: 11+.

World Wide Web (WWW)

(Mannix, 1995)

Show full http address and date of online visit.

Mannix, Margaret. "The Home-Page Help Wanteds," U.S. News & World Report. HTTP://WWW.OCC.COM (30 Oct. 1995).

TYPEWRITER USER'S GUIDE

Prepare your Typewriter

Inserting Paper

Numbers in parentheses correspond to typewriter part numbers on the illustration on p. x.

1. Align paper guide (4) with zero on the paper guide scale. Place paper against paper guide (4), behind the platen (8).

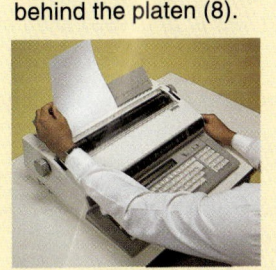

2. Strike **Paper Insert** key (11) repeatedly to feed paper into machine. If paper is not straight, pull paper release lever (9) forward; straighten paper; push back paper release lever.

3. Check position of paper bail rollers (7). Slide them so that they divide paper into fourths.

Setting Line-Space Selector

To set line spacing, use the following line-space selector (25) settings: 1 for single spacing, 1.5 for one-and-a-half spacing, or 2 for double spacing.

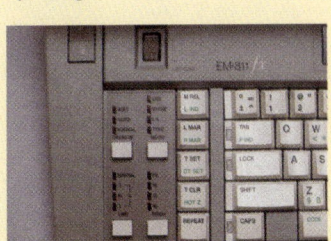

Plan and Set Margins

Refer to your typewriter's User's Guide for the specific procedure for setting margins on your machine.

Electronic Set

Using the space bar (16), move the print carrier (6) to the desired left margin on the line-of-writing scale (2). Depress the **Left Margin** key (29) and strike the **Code** key (17). Set the right margin using the Right Margin key (30) in the same manner.

Plan Margin Settings

A typewriter may have 10-pitch (pica) type (10 spaces to a horizontal inch) or 12-pitch (elite) type (12 spaces to a horizontal inch).

Machines have at least one line-of-writing scale (2) that reads as follows: from 0 to at least 90 for machines with 10-pitch type; from 0 to at least 110 for machines with 12-pitch type.

When 8.5" x 11" paper is inserted into the machine with the left edge of the paper at 0 on the line-of-writing scale, the exact center point is 42.5 for 10-pitch machines and 51 for elite machines. Use 42 and 51, respectively, for center. Illustrations below show margin settings for equal LM and RM (1") and for LM 1.5", RM 1". Subtract 3 or 4 from the RM when using the warning bell.

10-pitch (Pica)

Left edge	Center Point	Right edge
0	42	85
10 (1" LM)		(1" RM) 75
15 (1.5" LM)		(1" RM) 75

12-pitch (Elite)

Left edge	Center Point	Right edge
0	51	102
12 (1" LM)		(1" RM) 90
18 (1.5" LM)		(1" RM) 90

Manual Method of Horizontal Centering

Note: Use this method only if your machine does *not* have an Automatic Centering (AC) feature. If you have an AC feature, follow procedures given in the lesson.

Get Ready to Center

1. Set LM and paper guide at 0; set RM at 85 (10-pitch) or 102 (12-pitch).
2. Clear all tab stops.
3. Set a tab stop at center point: 42 (10-pitch) or 51 (12-pitch).

Center a Line of Text

1. Tab to the center point.
2. From center, backspace *once* for each 2 characters or spaces in the line. Do not backspace for an odd or leftover character at the end of the line.
3. Begin keying the text where backspacing ends.

Example:
● center point
backspace ▶ 1 1 1 1 1 1 1 1 1
LEARNING TO CENTER

Center Columns of a Table

1. Follow the steps listed in the *Get Ready to Center* section.
2. If column spacing (CS) is not specified, decide how many spaces to leave between columns.
3. Set the left margin.
   a. From the center point, backspace once for each 2 characters and spaces in the longest entry of each column and once for each 2 spaces to be left between columns. If the longest entry in one column has an odd number of characters, combine the extra keystroke with the first character in the next column, as in **Photography/Layouts####Denise Richardson**.

```
                    YEARBOOK STAFF
Main                                DS
heading  Editor-in-Chief       Susan Druhan
                                        DS
Body     Assistant Editor      Elizabeth Poole

         Business Manager      Robert Banks

         Photography/Layouts   Denise Richardson

         Advertising/Sales     Diane Blust

         Advisor               Anthony Diaz
         |        19      |  4 |      17     |
```

If you have one character left over after backspacing for all columns, disregard the extra keystroke.
   b. Set LM at point where all backspacing ends.
4. Set tab stop(s).
   a. From LM, space forward once for each character and space in the longest entry of first column and once for each space to be left between first and second columns.
   b. Set a tab stop at this point for the second column.
   c. For each additional column, space forward in the same way to set a tab stop for it.

Center Column Headings

When a heading is shorter than column entries, center the heading over the longest entry:

1. Identify the longest entry in column.
2. Find center point of longest entry by spacing forward once for every two characters and spaces. Drop a leftover character.
3. From the center point of the longest column entry, backspace once for every two characters and spaces in the column heading. Begin the heading where the backspacing ends.

When heading is longer than column entries, center entries under the heading:

1. Set the left margin and tabs for columns.
2. Key the column headings; DS.
3. Find center point of first column heading by spacing forward once for every two characters and spaces. Drop a leftover character.
4. Identify the longest line in the column entries.
5. From the center point of the heading, backspace once for every two characters and spaces in the longest entry (drop leftover or extra stroke). Set new tab where backspace stops.
6. Repeat Steps 2 through 5 for each remaining column.

```
                 MAIN HEADING

              Secondary Heading

   These        Are       Column       Heads

  xxxxxx      longest      xxxx        xxxxx
  xxxx         item       longest       xxx
  xxxxx       xxxxx        item        longest
  longest     xxxxxx      xxxxx         item
  item         xxxx        xxx          xxx

  longest 1234longest 1234longest 1234longest
```

Clear and Set Tabs

Numbers in parentheses refer to machine parts identified on p. x.

To clear one tab stop:
1. Strike the **Tab** key (31) to move the print point to the stop you want to clear.
2. Press the **Tab Clear** key (20) to delete the stop.

To clear all tab stops:
Press the **Tab Clear** key; then press the **Repeat** key (21).

To set tab stops:
Note: Electronics generally have preset tabs at 0.5" intervals. If you clear a preset tab and want to use it again during the session, you must reset it. When the machine is turned off, however, it will reset the original (default) tabs. Some electronics allow the operator to save tabs so that the machine will not default to the initial settings when turned off.

1. Move the print point to the desired tab position by striking the **Space Bar** (16) or **Backspace** key (10).
2. Press the **Tab Set** key (20). Repeat these steps for each tab stop needed.

Center Column Headings, Mathematical Method

1. To the number on the line-of-writing scale immediately under the first character of the longest entry, add the number shown under the space following the last character of the item.
2. Divide this sum by 2. The result is the center point of the column.
3. From the center point of the column, backspace once for every two characters and spaces (1 for 2).
4. From the number of spaces in the longest item, subtract the number of spaces in the heading.
5. Divide this number by 2; ignore fractions.
6. Space forward this number from the tab or margin and key the column heading.

Flush right

1. Set the desired RM.
2. From the RM, backspace once for every character and space in the text to be aligned at the RM.
3. Begin keying the text where backspacing ends.

Rules, Horizontal

To make horizontal rules in a table, depress **Shift Lock** and strike the **Underline** key. Single-space above and double-space below horizontal rules.

Rules, Vertical

Operate the automatic line finder. Place a pencil point through the cardholder or other guide around the print point. Roll the paper up until you have a line of the desired length. Remove the pencil and reset the line finder.

Title page (Format)

1. Center title in ALL CAPS on line 16.
2. Center your name in capital and lowercase letters on the 16th line below the title.
3. Center the school name a DS below your name.
4. Center the current date on the 16th line below the school name.

Title Page

GLOBALIZATION — Line 16

Student's Name / Name of School — Line 32

Current date — Line 50

Footnotes

In the body of a report, indicate a footnote by keying a reference number a half space *above* the line of text (superscript) immediately after quoted or closely paraphrased material. A matching numbered footnote must be keyed at the bottom of the page, separated from the last line of text by a 1.5" underline (DS above and below the underline). Plan the vertical spacing so that the footnote will fit before keying more of the report.

In planning footnote placement, allow at least a 1" bottom margin below footnotes on all pages except the last. On the last page, the dividing line and footnote(s) may begin a DS below the last line of text *or* be placed at the bottom of the page, leaving at least a 1" bottom margin.

These guides will help you place footnotes properly:

1. Make a light pencil mark at the right edge of the paper 1" from the bottom. The mark shows where the last line of the last footnote should be keyed.
2. As you key each footnote reference number in the body of the report, make another pencil mark 0.5" *above* the previous one. These marks will help you reserve about three line spaces for each footnote (two line spaces for the note and one blank line space between notes).
3. Key the last line of the report body about three line spaces above the top pencil mark. Insert the dividing line as described. Then key the footnote(s).

INDEX